THE LOGIC OF DESIRE

THE LOGIC OF DESIRE

An Introduction to
Hegel's *Phenomenology of Spirit*

PETER KALKAVAGE

PAUL DRY BOOKS
Philadelphia 2007

First Paul Dry Books Edition, 2007

Paul Dry Books, Inc.
Philadelphia, Pennsylvania
www.pauldrybooks.com

Text type: Minion
Display type: Ellington
Designed and composed by P. M. Gordon Associates

The cover image shows Hector fighting Achilles. From a red-figured volute-krater attributed to the Berlin Painter, Greece, circa 500–480 B.C.

Printed in the United States of America

Library of Congress Cataloging-in-Publication Data

Kalkavage, Peter.
The logic of desire : an introduction to Hegel's Phenomenology of Spirit / Peter Kalkavage. — 1st Paul Dry books ed.
p. cm.
Includes bibliographical references and index.
ISBN 978-1-58988-037-5 (alk. paper)
1. Hegel, Georg Wilhelm Friedrich, 1770–1831. Phänomenologie des Geistes. 2. Spirit. 3. Consciousness. 4. Truth. I. Title.
B2929.K29 2007
193—dc22

2007041089

FOR STANLEY ROSEN

ACKNOWLEDGMENTS

I WISH TO THANK MY FORMER TEACHER, STANLEY ROSEN, TO WHOM this book is gratefully dedicated, for inspiring my life-long interest in Hegel. His lectures on the *Science of Logic* at Penn State University continue to play an important role in my philosophic efforts. I am also indebted to Joseph Flay, another of my teachers at Penn State, with whom I first studied the *Phenomenology of Spirit.*

This introduction to the *Phenomenology* began with a lecture entitled "Hegel's Logic of Desire," which I delivered at St. John's College in Annapolis in the spring of 1996. The lecture was published in the *St. John's Review,* and was the product of a National Endowment for the Humanities grant I received through St. John's. I am grateful to the College for awarding me this grant, and for giving me release time from teaching in order to study Hegel and write the lecture.

Friends and colleagues were a constant source of encouragement and wise counsel. Eva Brann, who supported my project from the start, read drafts of all my chapters and made many valuable suggestions regarding form and content. My friend and former philosophy teacher, Donald Lindenmuth, was very helpful in the final stages of the book's composition. Erica Freeman, my former student, read drafts of the chapters on Reason and offered astute comments and suggestions based on her own recent study of the *Phenomenology.* During the writing of this book, I had many conversations about Hegel with colleagues and students. Their enthusiasm for my project was a consolation and a joy.

I owe a special debt of thanks to my friend and colleague, Eric Salem, who served as editor. His attention to detail, knowledge of the history of philosophy, insight into Hegel, sound judgment, wit, and personal encouragement are very much a part of this book. More than an editor, he was a co-worker and midwife.

I am also grateful to my publisher, Paul Dry, who read my chapters with great interest and imagination, posed tough questions, and helped me get a sense of the whole.

Finally, I wish to thank my wife, Christine, who first encouraged me to write this book. She has been my strong and patient ally throughout the whole journey of my Hegel consciousness. She too read drafts of chapters and offered many insightful suggestions. I could not have completed this daunting project without her support, admiration for Hegel, and unwavering belief in the worth of what I was trying to do.

CONTENTS

AN ITINERARY TO THE JOURNEY OF CONSCIOUSNESS

Religion

Absolute Knowing

Prologue

The Ladder and the Labyrinth

THERE IS MUCH TO COMMEND THE STUDY OF HEGEL: HIS ATTENTIVENESS to the deepest, most fundamental questions of philosophy, his uncompromising pursuit of truth, his amazing gift for characterization and critique, his appreciation for the grand sweep of things and the large view, his profound admiration for all that is heroic, especially for the ancient Greeks, those heroes of thought in whom the philosophic spirit first dawned, his penetrating gaze into modernity in all its forms, his enormous breadth of interests, and his audacious claim to have captured absolute knowing in a thoroughly rational account. There is no genuine philosophic education that does not include more than passing acquaintance with this modern giant, who absorbed all the worlds of spiritual vitality that came before him and tried to organize them into a coherent whole.

The *Phenomenology of Spirit*, the great philosophic epic of modernity, appeared in 1807. Hegel finished writing it (minus the Preface) on October 14, 1806. On that day, Napoleon, the hero of the Revolution, defeated the Prussian army and marched into Jena, where Hegel was living at the time. Conceived as the prelude to philosophic Science, the *Phenomenology* offers the reader what Hegel calls a *ladder* to the absolute [26].*

But oh, how difficult it is to climb this ladder! Hegel's epic often seems more labyrinth than ladder. In the words of one commentator, "no book is less suited to a beginner."[1] The Minotaur of these regions, the Demon of Difficulty, haunts every chamber. The monstrous difficulty of Hegel is both legend and cliché. It is so great and persistent, so much a part of how Hegel thinks and speaks, that we risk losing our way at every turn. Add to this that

*The numbers in brackets refer to paragraphs in A. V. Miller's edition of the *Phenomenology*. I have occasionally adjusted Miller's translation to a more faithful rendering of Hegel's German.

the *Phenomenology* is not only conceptually demanding but also allusive in ways that baffle the most experienced reader. "Who, or what, is Hegel talking about here?" is a question that often comes to mind as we struggle to connect the logical exposition with a concrete experience, historical event, philosopher, or character in a novel or play.

This book is an introduction to the *Phenomenology of Spirit*. It is not for Hegel scholars, although I hope they will find it useful. It is for the courageous non-specialist, who is just starting to read the *Phenomenology* and would like some help understanding it as a whole. I have tried to provide a thread through Hegel's labyrinth: to help the reader see and appreciate what it has to teach us. Commentaries on the *Phenomenology* tend to give the reader a summary of its conclusions and teachings, often brilliantly, without necessarily helping him become a better reader of Hegel's book. They speak from a position above the text. My approach is to take the reader with me into the thick of the argument and to try to make sense of things from the inside, as they unfold.

My plan is to go through the whole of Hegel's text, starting with the Introduction. The Preface, which precedes the Introduction, was written soon after the *Phenomenology*. Although it contains some of Hegel's most memorable pronouncements, and has a grandeur all its own, it is not an integral part of the *Phenomenology* itself. Rather than treat the Preface in a separate chapter, I simply refer to crucial statements that Hegel makes there, as they become relevant.

My introduction presupposes some familiarity with the history of philosophy. I also assume that my readers are currently reading the *Phenomenology* and are attempting to make sense of it on their own. They will need patience and fortitude. First-time readers in particular must bear in mind that even the most strenuous effort at clarity on the part of a would-be guide is bound to have its shortcomings, and will not remove, or appreciably soften, Hegel's hardness. Nor should it. As Hegel reminds us in his Preface, philosophy is hard work. It requires "the seriousness, the suffering, the patience, and the labor" of real thinking [19].

We do not have to agree with Hegel's ultimate claims in order to learn important things from him. We learn from his dialectical way of thinking, which challenges our most basic assumptions about what it means to think, his trenchant character studies, and the many powerful insights that appear throughout the *Phenomenology*. Above all, we learn about the complex spirit of modernity, and so come to know ourselves, and our origins, more deeply.

As my title indicates, I will treat the *Phenomenology* as Hegel's logic of desire. Desire, as we shall see, has a specific meaning in Hegel's book. I use the term more broadly to refer to the passionate striving by which consciousness "presses forward to true knowledge" [77] and climbs the ladder to absolute knowing. I do so to suggest an analogy between the "education of consciousness" in the *Phenomenology* [78] and the account of philosophy as erotic striving in Plato's *Symposium.* In that dialogue, Diotima, Socrates' mentor in love-matters, also uses the image of a ladder to depict the soul's ascent to the divine (211C). The *Phenomenology* is a *logic* of desire because it attempts to give a rational account, a *logos,* of the mortal striving for immortal truth. It is the account of thought *on its way* to Science.

Desire and its completion are closely connected with another central theme of this introduction: *selfhood.* The self is the point around which the *Phenomenology* turns. It is the central concern of the so-called German idealists: Fichte, Schelling, and Hegel. Truth, as Hegel says in the Preface, must be grasped "not as *substance* but just as much as *subject*" or self [17]. The task of the *Phenomenology* is to demonstrate how truth and subject, being and thought, God and man, are ultimately one. *Geist,* which means both *spirit* and *mind,* is the condition of fully developed selfhood. This is selfhood that exists as the living interrelation and community of human individuals. Hegel's book tells us how this condition has been produced in the course of history. More importantly, it reveals the precise way in which our communal or social being is essential to the history and perfection of *knowledge.* For Hegel, the history of our sociality is most deeply and properly understood as the history of *reason.*

Alexandre Kojève begins his famous commentary on the *Phenomenology* with the following definition: "Man is self-consciousness." My efforts take their cue from Kojève's gloss. They are devoted to an exploration of *what self is* for Hegel, what follows from the identification of human nature with selfhood understood as self-consciousness, and why, as Hegel says at one point, "self-consciousness is desire" [174]. One implication of identifying man and self-consciousness is that man, for Hegel, does not just come to know the truth: he comes to know that he *is* the truth. The meaning of this extraordinary claim will become clearer as we proceed.

The identity of man and truth is closely connected with a question central to this introduction: Why is so much of the *Phenomenology* devoted to the *practical* realm, to man as a *social* being? The question points to the double goal of Hegel's book. The *Phenomenology* chronicles the path to Science. Hegel's goal is to transform philosophy as the *love* of knowing into *actual knowing* [5]. But the book also shows the path by which man as self-consciousness comes to be self-actualized and *free* in the context of human community. In the *Phenomenology* these two paths converge and become one path: human self-actualization and absolute knowing, the practical and the theoretical aspects of spirit, are ultimately identical. Or, as I mentioned above, the history of our sociality is the history of reason. In the course of our journey, we will explore the meaning of this identity between the practical and the theoretical.

Several commentators are especially helpful to one's journey through Hegel's labyrinth. The provocative commentary by Alexandre Kojève, although I disagree with some of its conclusions, is useful for its treatment of self-consciousness, and its discussion of Hegel's Wise Man or Sage (*Introduction to the Reading of Hegel,* Nichols translation, 1969). Stanley Rosen's *G. W. F. Hegel: An Introduction to the Science of Wisdom* (1974) offers an insightful overview of Hegel's *Science of Logic* and *Phenomenology.* Rosen spells out Hegel's relation to Plato, Aristotle, and Fichte. He argues that the *Science of Logic* is Hegel's most fundamental work, and that a proper understanding of the *Phenomenology* presupposes a study of the *Logic.* The definitive scholarly commentary in English on the *Phenomenology* is the two-volume *Hegel's Ladder* by H. S. Harris (1997). Harris is indispensable for his painstaking treatment of Hegel's topical references and his grasp of the overall argument. His dogged attempt to identify the historical *Gestalten* or human "shapes" that Hegel sets out to analyze reminds us that the *Phenomenology,* in spite of its abstract language, is about concrete human experiences. Harris saved me from many mistakes and prompted many new ideas. My debt to him will be evident in the endnotes to my chapters.

The book on the *Phenomenology* that I find most congenial is *Genesis and Structure of Hegel's Phenomenology of Spirit* by Jean Hyppolite (1946). Hyppolite makes Hegel's book come alive. His account is spirited and generally faithful to Hegel's text and argument. Hyppolite is especially good on the connection between logic and human existence, and on the controversial role of religion in Hegel's thought.

The clearest, most concise summary of Hegel's philosophy as a whole is that of Richard Kroner. It is entitled "Hegel's Philosophical Development," and appears as the Introduction to Hegel's *Early Theological Writings,* translated by T. M. Knox. Kroner's engaging essay is well suited to the first-time reader.

The *Phenomenology of Spirit* is the first fruit of Hegel's youthful enthusiasm for the absolute. Here Hegel is still on his way to the more mature elaboration of his System that will appear in the *Science of Logic* (first edition, 1812–13) and the *Encyclopaedia of the Philosophical Sciences* (1830). Like these two later masterworks, the *Phenomenology* is conceptually daunting. But unlike them, it is also exuberantly imaginative, rhetorically charged, and often, it seems, deliberately cryptic. Hegel strikes the note of inspired revelation: of shocking reversals, secrets brought to light, and pretensions unmasked. The tone of high drama and sudden disclosure befits a book that puts us in the thick of spirit's "immediate existence" [35]. It is a wild, sprawling work that gives credence to Hegel's claim that truth is "a bacchanalian frenzy in which no one is not drunk" [47].

The *Phenomenology* fascinates and instructs largely because of its thematic prodigality, bacchic exuberance, and wealth of images. Difficult to grasp as a whole, it tends to reveal its riches in its individual parts, more so than any of Hegel's other works. In attempting to bring some clarity to the *Phenomenology,* I have tried to preserve the colorfulness, vitality, and high drama of this astonishing book.

The intention and the structure of the 1807 *Phenomenology* have long been the subject of scholarly debate. It has been argued that the book is essentially incoherent, the product of Hegel's conflicting goals and changes in attitude. Some have argued that Hegel abandoned the work as a necessary introduction to Science. Most scholars agree, however, that the *Phenomenology* continued to be essential to Hegel's philosophic project, even if its precise function is difficult to grasp and inherently problematic. I have steered clear of these issues. I have tried to get into the spirit of what Hegel is doing as much as possible, and take his argument at its best. My goal has been, above all, to make my reader *want* to read Hegel. Like Plato's dialogues, the *Phenomenology* ought to surprise us with each new reading. To be critically open to what it has to teach us, we must follow the saying of Heraclitus: "If you do not expect the unexpected, you will not find it out."

First-time readers of the *Phenomenology* experience two major problems: grasping the shape of the whole book, and understanding terms like "in itself" and "for itself." I address the first problem in Chapter 16, entitled *Interlude,* by providing some diagrams of the whole "journey of consciousness." Readers may want to consult these diagrams at an early stage of their journey. As for Hegel's baffling terminology, I have not provided a glossary but will instead define important terms as they come up. My reason for doing so is that the meaning of Hegel's terms is somewhat fluid and depends on the context in which they are used. My first attempt at defining "in itself" and "for itself" appears early in Chapter 3, *Of Mere Being.*

In writing this introduction to the *Phenomenology,* I used the English translation by A. V. Miller (Oxford: Clarendon Press, 1977). I also consulted the older version by J. B. Baillie (New York: Humanities Press, 1910, latest reprint 1977), and the two-volume French translation by Jean Hyppolite (Aubier: Paris, 1941, 1946). My German text was the one edited by Johannes Hoffmeister (Hamburg: Felix Meiner, 1952).

There is an excellent translation of Chapter Six of the *Phenomenology* ("Spirit") by Daniel E. Shannon (Indianapolis: Hackett, 2001), and a good translation of Hegel's Preface, with a running commentary, by Yirmiyahu Yovel (*Hegel's Preface to the Phenomenology of Spirit* [Princeton: Princeton University Press, 2005]).

I offer this book in celebration of the bicentennial of Hegel's *Phenomenology of Spirit.*

Peter Kalkavage
1 November 2007

PREPARING THE JOURNEY

Each of us suffers his own shade.
Virgil, *Aeneid,* Book 6

1

A World of Knowing

The *Phenomenology* belongs to the quartet of greatest works on education. The others are Plato's *Republic,* Dante's *Divine Comedy,* and Rousseau's *Emile.*

Despite their profound differences, these works have important similarities. One is that each reflects on education through some overarching story. In the *Republic,* this is the myth of founding the best city in speech, a large part of which is devoted to the education of the city's guardians; in the *Divine Comedy,* it is Dante's journey to God with the aid of Virgil and Beatrice; in *Emile,* it is Rousseau's fiction of playing governor to a child not his own by nature. So too, in the *Phenomenology*—which, according to some commentators, is patterned after the *Bildungsroman* or "novel of education" that was popular in Hegel's day—education is not simply talked about but presented as a drama or story.[1] It is the turbulent tale of how spirit or mind, *Geist,* struggles to achieve self-knowledge in the form of philosophic Science.

Another similarity is that all four are tales of liberation. Each tells of how man is freed from bondage: from the cave of deceptive opinions (Plato), or the dark wood of spiritual self-forgetting (Dante), or the corrupting influence of society (Rousseau). In the *Phenomenology,* the role of cave, dark wood, and corrupting influence is played by what Hegel calls *natural consciousness* [26, 77, 78]. Natural here means uneducated, unformed, or undeveloped, in a word, naïve. Natural consciousness is the familiar. In the *Phenomenology,* the human spirit finds itself *within* natural consciousness, like Ariel within the cloven pine, and struggles to be free.[2] But natural consciousness is not merely our prison. It is also a manifestation of spirit: the mode in which our human essence is immediately *there.* In overcoming natural consciousness, in becoming free, spirit therefore overcomes the most elementary condition of its own existence.

Finally, each work in the quartet explores the bond between reason on the one hand, and action and passion on the other: between man as thinker, and man as the being who acts and feels. We are reminded of what Socrates says in the *Republic* about philosophic conversion: that the *whole soul*, not the intellect alone, must be compelled to turn from the dark of error to the light of truth (7.518C). Genuine education must be complete and radical. It must change our lives, not just our minds.

Hegel educates his reader by initiating him into the minds of others. He reveals the education of consciousness that has already occurred in history.[3] The *Phenomenology*, he says, is a picture gallery [808]: a colorful array of human types or "shapes [*Gestalten*] of consciousness" [89]. These are the *phenomena* of which the *Phenomenology* is the *logos* or reasoned account.[4] In the course of the book, we meet all sorts of characters, just as we do when we read Plato's dialogues, or when we journey with Dante through his threefold cosmos. We meet the Scientist and the Warrior, the Stoic and the Skeptic, the God-haunted Unhappy Consciousness and the self-deifying Beautiful Soul. Sometimes we meet characters lifted from the pages of fiction: Antigone, Faust, or Rameau's crazy nephew. All have their place in Hegel's philosophic picture gallery. All are stages on the way to the fully developed selfhood that is spirit.

Each of these shapes embodies a specific *claim to know* that has appeared on the stage of world-history. These claims are necessary to the flowering of philosophy as Science. The shapes do not ask questions: they assert. To use a word that appears often in the works of Hegel and his philosophic contemporaries, they *posit* [*setzen*, to put or place].[5] Positing combines understanding and will.[6] To posit something is not merely to report that it is true, or to say what one sees. It is to *affirm* a truth, to invest oneself in that truth, to take a stand or position. In the act of positing, the I *risks itself.*

Spirit comes to know itself, not through calm methodical inquiry but through passionate self-assertion. Spirit is spirited. As we see repeatedly in Hegel's examination of spirit's claims to know, this spirited self-risking is spirit's folly: all the claims fall to the ground. They do so because they are finite or partial, because they fail to capture the *whole* of truth. But the act of positing is also spirit's bravery. Spirit cannot make progress, or even make a beginning, without self-assertion and positing. It cannot become wise without making a fool of itself. An extremist at heart, spirit, our human essence, is fated by the demands of its nature to learn through suffering.

The shapes of consciousness we are about to examine are not mental faculties but universal stances that have come on the scene in history. They are instances of knowledge as it exists or *is there.* (One of Hegel's words for existence is *Dasein*, being *there*, *da.*) Prior to the culminating stage of absolute knowing, spirit's claims to know constitute pseudo-knowledge. They are all in the realm of *Schein,* illusion. But it is not illusory that these claims to know have *come on the scene* in history as objective manifestations of spirit's effort to know itself.[7] In that sense, they are not *Schein,* illusion, but *Erscheinung,* appearance as a shining forth and a presence [76].

Sense-certainty, for example, the very first shape of consciousness, is not a psychological state but an objectively manifest claim to know, a burst of spiritual energy upon the world stage. It is mind incarnate at the lowest stage of its development. Sometimes Hegel speaks as if a shape of consciousness had a life of its own. He presents sense-certainty as a character that asserts its claim, reverses its position, and undergoes experience [101, 103]. The human individuals who posit sense-certainty as absolute are incarnations of its spirit. They are the hosts of sense-certainty, which is the soul of their claim to know.

Hegel's shapes of consciousness are human types: the most significant types that history has produced. But they are also determinate manifestations of what Hegel calls the "universal individual" [28]. This is "self-conscious spirit," the universal self that undergoes the historical process and dies in one age in order to be reborn in the next. Here, we have the most important respect in which the *Phenomenology of Spirit* differs from the other three greatest works on education. The *Phenomenology* is not only the path by which man comes to know himself and God. It is also the path by which God, as divine Mind, comes to know himself *in and through man.*[8] This is the goal of Hegel's *Phenomenology:* to demonstrate the presence of divine Mind within human history, eternity within time, God within the human community [671].

In the Introduction, Hegel uses the Stations of the Cross to suggest a bond between the journey of consciousness and the Passion of Christ [77]. At the very end of the final chapter, he refers to history as the "inwardizing and Place of Skulls [or Calvary] of absolute spirit" [808]. These unorthodox appropriations of Christian imagery emphasize that Hegel's book is no mere epistemology, psychology, or anthropology. At its deepest level, it is the unfolding of God's suffering in time—his coming to full self-consciousness in the course of human history.[9]

The theological dimension of Hegel's thought derives from both pagan and Christian sources. The pagan influence is Aristotle, whom Hegel deeply admired.[10] From Aristotle, Hegel derives the teaching that Mind, *nous,* is divine, and that, contrary to what the poets tell us, we should strive to *be* divine, to transcend our finitude, in the act of thinking.[11] In philosophizing, we un-deathify ourselves.[12] But Aristotle's Mind—the thinking of thinking (*Metaphysics* 12.7)—is completely removed from time and has no connection with human individuality. Christianity makes up for this lack by assimilating mortality into the nature of God. It posits a God who "empties himself" into time, *deathifies* himself, and thus becomes present both to mankind and to himself: God *suffers* in the form of human history. This human-divine suffering is necessary in order for God to know himself and to become actual. Christianity also gives birth to the idea that God manifests himself in *community.* Both together—the divine as pure thinking, and the divine as the suffering God who is present in history and in human community—go together to produce *spirit.* Nevertheless, it is Christianity that produces the definitive representation of the absolute, since it alone unites the divine with complete human individuality (and therefore death). In his Preface, Hegel calls spirit "the most sublime concept and the one that belongs to the modern age and its religion" [25].

In Christianity, the absolute truth is "revealed" [*offenbar*], not because books of inspired revelation do what reason cannot, but because Christianity alone teaches that God, in his Incarnation and Passion, became fully manifest or "open" [*offen*].[13] Christianity is the penultimate stage of the *Phenomenology.* Only absolute knowing, philosophy in the form of Science, surpasses it. Christianity contains spirit's self-knowledge in the form of images or symbols. Science comes on the scene when these absolute symbols are conceptually grasped. To this extent, we may say that philosophy, for Hegel, *is* the rational understanding of the Christian religion.

Everything, for Hegel, is defined by its history. But the *Phenomenology* is neither the history of philosophy nor the history of the world simply.[14] As we see from its chapter headings alone, the book does not highlight the teachings of philosophers. Often the realm of *praxis* rather than that of *theory* occupies center stage. In its "upper" regions, the *Phenomenology* examines historical *phainomena* like the ancient Greek *polis,* modern culture, and the French Revolution. The social realm in which human beings live, act, interact, and speak is the soil from which knowledge springs, and the medium in which it lives. The *Phenomenology* is thus Hegel's attempt to show how the realm of praxis (which is principled, self-conscious action) transcends itself and *becomes* the realm of theoretical knowing—how life *becomes* knowledge. But it is no less an account of how knowledge, or rather self-knowledge, *comes to life* in the context of human interaction and community.

The history of philosophy, for Hegel, is the interconnected series of efforts to reach truth in a purely conceptual way. Wisdom emerges as a process of becoming, and all the great philosophic systems of the past contribute to the full flowering of wisdom. Strictly speaking, therefore, no philosophic theory is false. The history of philosophy shares in the risks of positing. Plato's Forms are not derived but risked and "put forth." In the

Phaedo, Socrates calls them a hypothesis (107B). Descartes asserts rather than demonstrates his mind-body dichotomy. And Kant denies rather than disproves our access to intellectual intuition. All these positings and risks are in the context of a conscious effort to reach the truth by means of rational inquiry. In the *Phenomenology,* however, we witness something more basic, and visceral. Spirit risks itself, "wakes up," not by soberly thinking things through, but by entering the unpredictable realm of life. Spirit is not the divine puppet-master who plans everything out in advance and moves history toward a providential end. Time is not a cloak that spirit wears but the outpouring of what spirit *is.* History is spirit wandering in its self-created labyrinth, searching for its self-knowledge and its freedom.[15]

It is important to stress that although spirit is the universal, communal self that transcends our singular mortal selves, it is not a transcendent being that exists outside of time, or apart from these finite mortal selves, whose interrelation constitutes spirit. It is not like a Platonic Form, or a Kantian thing-in-itself. Aristotle's God, we recall, is not a being that acts but *activity itself:* the thinking of thinking. This activity or *energeia,* however, is *beyond* the world of finite things and finite human self-consciousness. Hegel preserves the Aristotelian idea of God as pure self-relating activity, the thinking of thinking. But he brings this act of self-relating down into time and humanity. H. S. Harris puts this very well: "But Hegel's God is Aristotle's God only after he has undergone his Incarnation in his human family" (1:60).

In his Preface, Hegel tells us that the *Phenomenology* is about *experience, Erfahrung:* "The *element of immediate experience* is . . . what distinguishes this part of Science from the others" [35]. Immediate experience, here, means something much more fundamental and primitive than the philosopher's conscious effort to reach the truth through rational inquiry. Experience is the historical, spontaneous emergence of spirit's effort to know itself *in relation to the world in which it appears.* The *Phenomenology,* as the "Science of experience" [88], attempts to lay bare the logical structure of a process that is more down-in-the-depths or primordial than the history of philosophy. By the time a philosopher comes on the scene, there is already an objectively existing world out of which the philosopher grows, in which he finds his context, and whose communal spirit he expresses. In a later writing, Hegel says that the philosopher cannot leap over the Rhodes of his time, that philosophy is "its time grasped in thoughts," and that "every one is in any case a son of his time."[16]

This social world, no less than the inquiry of the philosopher, is the work of spirit. Spirit, the universal or communal self that both transcends and dwells among finite individuals, struggles in time in order to know itself. Before it can know itself in the philosopher's effort to make knowing conceptual, there must be a world that embodies knowing in a pre-conceptual or immediate form—a lived knowing. Spirit learns by making itself present to itself. It does this by generating a *world of knowing.* It must first generate this world, or rather series of worlds, before it can know itself in and through that which it has generated, before it can "wake up" to itself.[17] Antigone is not a philosopher. But she embodies a world of knowing. This is the world of the ancient Greek *polis,* in which Antigone knows and articulates her position with respect to family, gods, and city. This world, together with all the other realms of social life in the *Phenomenology,* is essential to the emergence of philosophy in the form of Science, and the completion of philosophic desire or *erōs.*

Strictly speaking, the idea of a *world* does not emerge until Hegel's chapter on spirit [438–39]. I use the term "world of knowing" more broadly to suggest that even in its "lower," more abstract stages, before human community has come on the scene, spirit or mind is making a universal claim to truth that applies to everything in human experience. Perception is a good example of what I mean here. It is not only the perception of sensuous things but also the general *attitude* or mode of "healthy common sense" [131].

History includes the play of contingency or chance. In revealing itself in time, spirit abandons itself to this play and therefore can neither reconstruct its past (until the final stage) nor predict its future. Spirit does not know where it is going until it gets there; it emerges rather than guides. The task of the phenomenologist is to take the archetypal shapes of knowing that spirit has assumed and grasp them in a purely conceptual way: not as merely successive but as logically interconnected. This is to regard them, in Spinoza's famous phrase, "under a certain look of eternity."[18] What makes this knowledge possible is that the individual shapes of knowing are modes of universality, thought-structures, in historical garb. The shape qua shape is contingent, but the logical structure the shape embodies is not. The *Antigone* of Sophocles does not exist necessarily. But the universal form of knowing that Antigone embodies (together with her adversary Creon) does. To borrow Plato's language, the *Phenomenology* compels us to think the *idea* within the *image,* the eternal within time.

We see the logical necessity within the play of chance by looking back. The phenomenologist must first identify the shapes of knowing that are spread out in time, and then reorganize them to bring out their logically necessary connections. As Hegel tells us in the final chapter, spirit in the *Phenomenology* is engaged in *recollection, Erinnerung,* a word that also means inwardizing [808]. This recollection of history, which is itself the product of history, is the philosopher's act of revealing the logically necessary within the contingent. To accomplish this goal, the philosopher must occasionally reorganize the temporal sequence. This is why the order in which shapes appear in the *Phenomenology* is often confusing, why it is anything but straightforwardly chronological. The modern theory of force, for example, comes before the medieval idea of the Christian God, and modern Reason comes before the Greek *polis.*

Ordinary experience helps us see what it means to grasp the logic of time. Suppose I am looking back at the events of my life, not merely to remember those events but to make logical sense of them. In composing my philosophic memoir, I do not just record things in chronological order. Instead, I search for the deep connection—Heraclitus' "hidden joining"—between events that are perhaps chronologically remote. Temporal sequence may occasionally even be inverted in this search for meaning.

Another example of finding order within the contingent comes from the experience of having serious conversations with a group of people. In the course of a conversation, say, about Hegel's *Phenomenology,* all sorts of opinions and arguments arise. The talk may be chaotic. It may consist of digressions, misfires, half-formed ideas, blind alleys, as well as brilliant insights. After the conversation, I may want to make sense of it. To do so, I go back over everything that was said, bring the various opinions and arguments into focus, and try to make connections, find the "hidden joinings" or harmonies, between things said by the same person and by different people at different times. The result is not a fiction but a shining forth of what was *there.* This is what Hegel must do in order to be spirit's faithful interpreter. He must take what spirit has brought to light in the realm of time and find the logical thread that runs through the labyrinth.

The *Phenomenology* is a series of spirited exposés or unmaskings. Hegel's book is the logical revelation of the apparent as such. A given shape of consciousness *undercuts itself* in the very effort to make good on its claim to know: it turns into its opposite. This is the tragic dimension of spirit's journey and the more precise sense in which, for Hegel, learning is suffering. No gadfly Socrates, no god of refutation, is needed to bring about this undercutting. On the contrary, refutation is generated *from within consciousness itself.* As Hegel colorfully puts it: "Consciousness suffers this violence at its own hands: it spoils its own limited satisfaction" [80]. But within this tragic motion of self-defeating claims, there is also resurgence. The death of one shape is the birth of another, higher shape. Spirit is like the legendary Phoenix, always rising up again out of the ashes of its past life—or like the Son of Man, who breaks the bonds of the merely natural and rises from the dead. The series of shapes is finite. Eventually, the long arduous road, which Hegel calls a Way of Despair [78]), reaches its destination, as the drama of unmasking gives rise, in the final chapter, to spirit's self-knowing. At this point, all the finite claims to know, the mortal shapes of consciousness, are preserved as *eternal moments* in the philosopher's non-temporal grasp of the temporal whole.

Let us sum up what we have seen so far.

The *Phenomenology* is a picture gallery in which shapes of consciousness are "on exhibit" for the individual reader. This exhibit is the individual's education, his *ladder* to absolute knowing [26]. The various shapes or stages are the archetypal claims to know that have "come on the scene" in the course of history, and whose ordered series constitutes the education of consciousness in general: the education of *man*. By no means limited to the reflective teachings of philosophers, they highlight the unreflective risks of action, social life, and culture: a *world of knowing*. These claims are posited as unquestioned and unqualified, in other words, as absolute.

Absolute knowing is not confined to the final chapter but permeates the whole of the *Phenomenology*. It is present in all the preceding chapters as the illusory claim to know absolutely. Hegel's word for this passionate claim to an immediate absolute knowing is *certainty*. Consciousness strives repeatedly to transform its certainty into *truth*, that is, into a certainty that has *proved* itself. The movement of consciousness is tragic: learning is suffering. The more a shape struggles to transform mere certainty into truth, the more it suffers the consequences of its finitude, and generates the exact opposite of what it posited. In Hegel's own dramatic terms, the more a shape of certainty gives birth to itself through speech the more it undercuts itself, *kills itself*, before being reborn as a new and higher shape. In the end, there is Hegel's version of a "divine comedy," as all these tragic conflicts are resolved, and preserved, in *genuine* absolute knowing.

Finally, the shapes of knowing that embody man's effort to know the divine are also the shapes in which the divine, which is incarnate in man, comes to know itself. Spirit, for Hegel, is not the human or the divine simply but the dialectical identity of the human and the divine. This identity comes on the scene in the man-God of Christianity. In the *Phenomenology*, Hegel attempts to spell out the logical structure, and true meaning, of the suffering of God in time.

The six main stages of the journey of consciousness, the rungs of the ladder to the absolute, are Consciousness, Self-Consciousness, Reason, Spirit, Religion, and Absolute Knowing. (There are *eight* numbered chapters in the *Phenomenology* because Hegel lists the three stages of Consciousness as separate chapters.) A figurative, and therefore inadequate, rendering of the story in terms of the wayfaring Self might go as follows.

As **Consciousness**, the Self (Man) is fascinated by the external world, by *nature* and by nature's promise of being the source and standard of truth. The Self at this stage is not interested in doing, making, or desiring anything. Its obsession with objectivity makes it a purely theoretical bystander.

As **Self-Consciousness**, the Self goes to the other extreme. Obsessed with itself and its individuality, and overwhelmed by a desire for self-assertiveness and freedom, it enters the realm of *action*. But its violent desire dissolves into a yearning for a pure Self it can never reach. Its pride is humbled before this higher Self.

As **Reason**, the Self asserts its individuality. It rises up and makes a heaven of its former hell, glories in its sheer humanity, and seeks to master the world through its own resources, to experience itself *as* the external world. But Reason's "certainty of being all reality" is shown to be abstract, a mere dream. For all its exertions, the Self fails to generate a world and remains trapped inside its individuality.

At the level of **Spirit**, this external thing that has always opposed the Self acquires selfhood or soul. It becomes a social *world* or concrete community: universality that is actual and alive. The Self is now fully conscious of itself as embodied and substantial. World acquires selfhood or inwardness, and selfhood has been made concrete and real, as the Greek nation (Hellas), the Roman Empire, modern culture, and Kantian morality. Man is now aware of himself as the self and substance of the world, although he is not yet aware of *history* as the revelation of his human-divine nature.

At the stage of **Religion**, Spirit as the communal Self manifests itself in concrete teachings, institutions, stories, poetry, and art—all modes of divine self-contemplation. These modes capture absolute truth, *but only in the guise of images and picture thinking.*

Absolute Knowing takes the pictorial content of Religion in its highest phase, the Manifest Religion of Christianity, and gives it a purely conceptual form. It transforms image into logic. Selfhood (as divine inwardness) is now completely transparent to itself, knows itself, as philosophic Science. To use a Christian term that is central to Hegel's book, the Self now experiences *reconciliation* [*Versöhnung*] with the external world. Spirit *is* the reconciliation of self and world, subject and object, thought and action. In the condition of absolute knowing, Man grasps himself *as spirit.* He knows that externality is essential to his inwardness, and that spirit, in order to be spirit, must be *self-opposed.* As Hegel says in his definition of spirit: "spirit is the knowing of its own self in its externalization; the essence that is the movement of retaining the sameness with itself in its being other" [759].

I have presented these stages as chapters in a coherent story. But as we make our way through Hegel's labyrinth, the transitions from one stage to the next often seem obscure, even after we have struggled mightily to make sense of them. The *Phenomenology* is the philosophic history of consciousness. In this history, stages are supposed to *grow out of* each other. But some transitions are more perplexing than others. The unfolding of consciousness at times seems not to be as logical as Hegel wants us to believe.[19] My goal in this introduction to the *Phenomenology* has been not to wrestle with Hegel on these points but simply to follow the journey of consciousness. The reader must nevertheless be on his guard. At every transition point, in spite of my attempt to make the transition persuasive, the reader must ask: But *was* that persuasive? Did Hegel offer a convincing argument for the "move" from this stage to the next, or is there a gap?

In any case, discontinuity is a crucial part of spirit's dialectical unfolding. By discontinuity I mean that one stage gives rise to a genuinely *new* stage that has its own character, development, and problems. In dramatic terms, a new *character* comes on stage. We appreciate this newness when, having seen that the previous character's claim to know contradicted itself, we ask ourselves whether we would have been able to *predict* who would now step forth from behind the curtain. The extreme difficulty of doing such a thing highlights Hegel's problem in writing the *Phenomenology.* Hegel must first select the peak moments of universal human experience and then figure out which ones come after which, making sure that stages do not merely succeed each other but logically evolve. Whether Hegel has accomplished this, whether the *Phenomenology* is both complete in the sense of covering all the peak moments of past experience *and* logically coherent, I leave for my reader to decide.

The *Phenomenology* is not only the philosophic history of consciousness. It also embodies what Hegel called his personal "voyage of discovery."[20] The *Phenomenology of Spirit* is the book in which Hegel became Hegel, just as the *Divine Comedy* was the poem in which Dante became Dante. It is the result of Hegel's struggle to unify, in the words of one commentator, the conflicting influences of his intellectual life: "Apollo, Jesus, and Kant."[21] In reading the *Phenomenology,* we are invited to share that personal journey—and to ask in what sense it is our journey as well.

I cannot keep my subject still. It goes along befuddled and staggering, with a natural drunkenness. I take it in this condition, just as it is at the moment I give my attention to it. I do not portray being: I portray passing.
MONTAIGNE, "Of Repentance"

 2

What Is Experience?

(HEGEL'S INTRODUCTION)

WE NOW TURN TO HEGEL'S INTRODUCTION. OUR QUESTIONS WILL be the following. What do these terms mean: consciousness [*Bewußtsein*] and experience [*Erfahrung*]? Why does consciousness suffer the violence of refutation at its own hands? How can this recurring pattern of violence lead to anything positive? What is the logical method that will unmask the shapes of consciousness and bind them together in a continuous whole? And what makes consciousness tense or desirous—impelled from within to "press forward to true knowledge" [77]?

The Introduction is hard going. Like the Preface, it expresses universal truths that can be adequately understood only after reading the main body of Hegel's text. In this chapter, I will attempt to guide the reader through this rocky terrain. The sections that follow correspond to the main stages of the Introduction.

Natural Consciousness Builds a Fence [73–75]

Let us begin with the commonly accepted notion that if we could analyze things thoroughly, then we would know them. Error, we think, comes from fuzzy thinking, from the failure to make proper distinctions and clearly identify all the elements of a complex whole. To know is to be unconfused. As Hegel will show, there are serious limits to this simple identification of truth with "clarity and distinctness."

Distinction making plays a central role in Hegel's conception of Science. It is the work of understanding, *Verstand.*[1] In his Preface, Hegel praises the understanding. He calls it "the most astonishing and mightiest of powers, or rather the absolute power," and links it with negativity and *death* [32]. The divisiveness of the understanding keeps philosophy from degenerating into edification, an evil Hegel warns against in the strongest terms [9]. "Bereft of force, beauty," Hegel asserts, "hates the understanding for asking of her what she cannot do" [32], that is, analyze and therefore *kill* that which beauty has lovingly produced. Understanding, as the analytic moment of thought, is necessary to the dialectical process by which something loses its identity, becomes its opposite, and is then reconstituted as a higher, more concrete unity. This process is summed up in Hegel's word Concept or *Begriff*, which is the dialectical form of all truth and intelligibility.[2]

In the opening of the Introduction, Hegel presents the preoccupation with distinctions and boundaries as the source of error. I shall call this error the *epistemological attitude.* According to this attitude, philosophy must make a beginning by first examining human cognition as either instrument or medium, either that *by which* or that *in which* truth is grasped. This assumption Hegel calls a "natural representation [*Vorstellung*]" [73]. The target of his polemic is Kant. The epistemological attitude, grandly exhibited in Kant's *Critique of Pure Reason,* draws a distinction between things as they are "in themselves" and things as they appear "for us." Kant builds a fence between the thinking subject and the coveted object of knowledge—a "boundary [*Grenze*] between cognition and the absolute" [73]. He then proceeds to examine what is on one side of this fence—namely, the thinking subject or cognition—in order to determine the *mode* of knowledge and the *kind* of object that suit the human subject. The epistemological attitude seems to stem from wisdom, moderation, and a concern for what is just or legitimate. But the true origin, Hegel claims, is distrust and fear.

Although Kant is clearly the target of Hegel's opening salvo, the deeper object of his critique is *natural consciousness.* The journey depicted in the *Phenomenology* is "the path of the natural consciousness as it presses forward to true knowledge" [77]. As I noted in Chapter 1, natural consciousness is consciousness in its philosophically uneducated, undeveloped condition, its state of nature. It is the realm of the familiar, which, as Hegel pointedly says in the Preface, is not cognitively understood precisely because it is familiar [31]. Natural consciousness is "healthy human understanding," or common sense [131]. It is *natural* for consciousness to build a fence between subject and object, and to distinguish that which is "in itself" (or objective) from that which is only "for us" (or subjective).

Hegel's critique of Kant shows that natural, uneducated thought is not limited to the man on the street. Kant's project in the *Critique of Pure Reason* is the systematic inquiry into the radical conditions of human knowing. In spite of its impressive goal, Kant's system is governed by the natural: by something *given to* rather than *generated from* the thinking self.[3] This given is the manifold of sense data, which the understanding (in Kant's use of the term) unifies by means of concepts or categories.

Natural consciousness makes a necessary distinction but fails to go beyond it. It fails to think it through or, to use one of Hegel's favorite words, to *mediate* the distinction between subject and object.[4] The failure is due largely to the influence of representation generally—*Vorstellung*, which is the result of my *placing* something [*stellen*] *before* myself [*vor*]. Natural consciousness builds a fence because all its ideas are, or ultimately derive from, pictures in an imagined space. Uneducated consciousness, consciousness that has not yet risen to genuine thoughts, represents or pictures the thinking subject as "over here" and the intended object "over there." To bring in another crucial term in the *Phenomenology* that is influenced by spatial thinking, the object is made into a *Jenseits*, which in German refers to something *on the other side* of me—a Beyond [80].

The fence of consciousness leads to the natural representation of cognition as a tool or a medium one "uses" to "get" the truth. This way of regarding cognition is closely related to the view that thinking, in order to reach the truth, must have recourse to a formal, artificially constructed *method.* The method of Descartes comes to mind as a prime example. Method-driven thinking is an example of the formalism Hegel criticizes at length in his Preface [15, 48–51, 56].[5]

What is wrong with this way of thinking? For one thing, it implies the absurdity of even trying to grasp what is true in itself. If cognition were a tool, then, in order to get at the object itself, we would have to undo whatever the tool did to transform that object. But then we would also have undone the tool's use and advantage. It would be like averting our eyes from visible objects in order to see what those objects *really* look like. Something similar happens in the case of the medium. A medium, though passive, has a certain power that allows it to function as a medium. Without that, it is not a medium. A medium would therefore not be capable of receiving an object without doing something to the object. Hegel puts it in terms of the modern theory of light. The cognitive medium has its "law of refraction," according to which the medium "bends" what it receives. Subtract this and you subtract the ray of truth that enters the medium. Tool thinking and medium thinking lead to the same result: the impossibility of knowing the truth. If to know means to use a tool, and to use a tool means to impose a structure, then the means by which we know is tragically at odds with knowledge.[6]

The problem of knowledge is that of bridging the gap between subject and object, of mediating. It is the problem of getting the objective in-itself to be subjective or *for us* without its ceasing to be objective or true. Tool thinking and medium thinking fail in their appointed task as mediators. Instead of bringing subject and object together, they perpetuate the chasm they were designed to bridge.

This way of proceeding, based on the familiar ways in which we represent things or "place" them "before" ourselves [*vor-stellen*], is wrong in every conceivable way. It leads to the absurdity of tool and medium mentioned above. Also, as we saw above, in spite of the apparent sensibleness, even modesty, of building a fence between subject and object, the real motivators, for Hegel, are the passions of fear and distrust. This false modesty absolves us from engaging in "the hard work of Science" [76]. It leads to self-deception and sophistry. In light of the supposed impossibility of reaching the absolute truth, the object as it is in itself, consciousness conveniently fabricates a non-absolute or relative truth in the form of an object that is not *in itself* but only *for consciousness.* This is the object Kant calls appearance, as opposed to the unknowable thing-in-itself.

The invention of a relative truth only obscures the meaning of the terms truth and knowledge. How can truth be only "for me" or "for us" and still deserve the name of truth? Will I say that I know *absolutely* that this sort of truth is only relative? How do I *know* that it is only relative? Perhaps it is really the absolute revealing itself to me and I am mistaken in calling it relative. Can I know that this truth is only relative without having some access to the truth that is not relative? How can I know that X is not Y unless I know both X and Y? Besides, where did this distinction, this fence, between cognition and the absolute come from in the first place? Was it not posited by consciousness itself?

Apparent Knowing [76–78]

Hegel has a blunt answer to the evasions of the epistemological attitude: the evasions *vanish* as soon as genuine knowledge or Science comes on the scene [76]. But precisely because Science "comes on the scene," it is itself no more than the mere appearance of knowing. It is "not yet Science in its developed and unfolded truth" [76]. Science must liberate itself from this mere appearance or doubt and prove that it is Science. This task falls to the *Phenomenology of Spirit.*[7]

For Hegel, natural consciousness is dynamic, or inwardly tense. It is more than a cave or dark wood, a passive state from which some external agent must deliver us (either a Socrates or a Beatrice). Natural consciousness has a drive to prove itself, a desire to *know absolutely.* It is, one might say, pregnant with its history. Desire propels consciousness to go beyond its state of nature. The *Phenomenology* traces "the path *of the natural consciousness* [my emphasis] that presses forward to true knowledge" [77].

Hegel stresses the radical negativity of this path. His discussion here should be compared with what he says in the Preface, where natural consciousness feels that Science is asking it to do violence to itself and its familiar ways of looking at the world and to "walk on its head" [26]. The path by which natural consciousness is educated is no mere path of Cartesian doubt but a Way of Despair [78]. And the shapes that consciousness takes on in the course of its journey are, as we have seen, like the Stations of the Cross [77]. It is no use following the Polonius-like advice of the Enlightenment: "Think for yourself, and have the courage of your convictions—to thine own self be true!" Why should my ideas, just because they are mine, be any less faulty than those that come to me from other people? Hegel leaves no room for such self-serving authenticity and calls it conceit [78]. All natural ideas, all the undeveloped, taken-for-granted notions that spring from what is familiar and "homey," must be refuted, regardless of whose ideas they are. If consciousness is to achieve its goal of absolute knowing, it must come to experience the sheer nothingness of everything that is familiar and natural. It must become a stranger in its own land in order to dwell, at last, in the kingdom of truth.

The Nothing That Is Something [79–80]

It is one thing to become aware of falsehood, another to grasp the truth. Disenchantment or skepticism is not knowledge. The negativity of experience that Hegel has described so far would not lead anywhere, certainly not to Science, unless something positive came out of it. There must be some way *out of* despair.

Here, we touch on Hegel's most original idea. It is the idea that negation is positive because it *has content,* or preserves what it negates. As Hegel puts it, negation is "specifically the nothingness of that *from which it results*" [79]. The term for this idea, which Hegel first mentions in the Preface, is *determinate negation* [59].[8] Determinate negation is why spirit is Phoenix-like, why the death of one shape of knowing is the birth of another. The resurgence of spirit is beautifully summed up in the passage from the Gospel of John: "Verily, verily, I say unto you, except a corn of wheat fall into the ground and die, it abideth alone: but if it die, it bringeth forth much fruit" (12:24).

Determinate negation is at the root of Hegel's most important term: *Aufhebung.* Translations of this term include sublation (from Latin *sublatio,* a lifting up) and supersession (from Latin *supersedere,* to sit above or refrain from). *Aufhebung* comes from the verb *aufheben,* which has the exactly opposite meanings of *preserve* and *abolish* or *cancel out.*[9] It also means *lift up.* It is roughly what we mean in English when we "set something aside," where that which is set aside is lifted up in the sense of being given special treatment.[10] Hegel's view of negation contains these three meanings of the term. A thing is sublated, *aufgehoben,* when it is cancelled, preserved, and lifted up. Hegel will call these three phases *moments.* Sublation is the full expression of what it means for something to be determinately, and therefore completely, negated.[11]

It is difficult to find instances of determinate negation in ordinary experience. We come close to it in the phenomenon of "protesting too much," that is, when our insistence that something is not so reinforces the fact that it is; or when our hatred for an enemy preserves the enemy as a force in our lives and gives him a place of honor; or when bitter life experience leads to positive learning. Forbidden fruit is a determinate negation, since singling it out as a Not *That* draws attention to the *That* and even heightens its charm, lifts it up. Determinate negation and *Aufhebung* are prominent in the mysteries of the New Testament. There is the passage from John I quoted earlier. There is also the hard-to-grasp relation that Jesus has to the law as something fulfilled but also canceled and transcended (Matthew 5:17). And ordinary language, whose waywardness Hegel loves, seems to capture sublation in nay-saying moments like the following: "Last night's music was beautiful —*no,* it was sublime!" The "no" here both cancels the previous statement and lifts it to a higher level.

Hegel's brief discussion of determinate negation occurs within his account of the radical negativity required for true education. This negativity is familiar to us from the refutations that occur in Plato's dialogues. The path of natural consciousness is one negation or "death" after another. This negation, however, is not Socrates-induced but self-induced. The series of self-refutations has a logical order. A shape does not merely follow its predecessor but is generated out of it. The reason lies in the logical structure of negation: "this nothingness [the demonstrated nothingness of a given shape of consciousness] is specifically the nothingness of that from which it results" [79]. Logical order, in other words, comes from negation, which generates a new specific *something.* Negation is not an explosion that annihilates what was once a stable structure (which is how natural consciousness represents negation). On the contrary, it is like organic growth, in which a flower's blossom may be said to refute and supplant the bud [2].

Determinate negation is not only at work in the process of transition. It is also the guarantor of completeness: "The necessary progression and interconnection of the forms [*Formen*] of unreal consciousness will of itself [*selbst*] bring about the *completion* of the series" [79]. Because of the nothing that is something—the logical engine of the whole *Phenomenology*— there is not only a rising up of successive shapes but also a *culminating shape* that completes the series as its goal. This is what Hegel calls absolute knowing. To sum up, natural consciousness, thanks to the work of determinate negation, does the following. It generates various shapes or claims to know; it generates them in a given order; and it is destined, through an inner necessitation, to reach an end, where "the *goal* is as necessarily fixed for knowledge as the serial progression" [80]. This last reminds us of Hegel's definition of *reason, Vernunft,* as "goal-directed activity" [22].

Paradoxically, the thought of inevitable completion leads Hegel to his most lurid depiction of suffering in the whole Introduction. The tone seems inappropriate, since Hegel has just emphasized the positive character of negation. Then again, perhaps the tone is not that odd. Having drawn attention to the necessity of self-completion, Hegel must explain why consciousness is impelled, driven to its goal. We would not search for gratification if we did not experience *desire.* For Hegel, desire is a profound unhappiness or anxiety. Hegel's task is to explain how this anxiety impels consciousness to its destined goal: how absolute knowing comes from the unhappiness of desire. His depiction of unhappiness provides the context for a question I raised at the beginning of this chapter: why does consciousness suffer the violence of refutation at its own hands?

To follow Hegel's meaning, we must distinguish consciousness generally from the finite shapes of consciousness. The various shapes and stages of consciousness—the various "characters" of the *Phenomenology*—must be seen in light of the overall dialectic of consciousness that animates these shapes. Consciousness is not confined to a single shape. The finite shapes, like ordinary natural entities, are mortal because they cannot transcend themselves. But consciousness in general, the consciousness of which the shapes are shapes, *goes beyond itself* [80]. In order to dramatize what this means, Hegel ranges over the whole extent of spirit's journey.

Consciousness "is explicitly or for itself [*für sich*] the concept of itself." In other words, it thinks its own thinking. It is both aware of its object and aware of itself as a mode of knowing that object. *Consciousness implies self-consciousness.* In being aware of an apple, I am also aware that I am aware. Consciousness is always outside itself looking at itself looking. It cannot be otherwise, since consciousness is *my* consciousness. Consciousness, then, "is something that immediately goes out of the limited, and since the limited belongs to it, it is something that goes out of itself" [80].[12] What Hegel is describing here is the dynamic of unrest. It is his first formulation of a *logic of desire.* Consciousness is aware of its instability and of the inadequacy of its claims, aware that it is on the move. It feels the constraint of its finite shapes and the remoteness of its posited objects. To use a term that will be crucial at a later point, consciousness knows itself as overreaching all its finite objects. This overreaching or infinity *is* self-consciousness [166].

At this point, Hegel launches into the tale of passion that spells out the love-hate relation consciousness has with the absolute, and with itself.

Consciousness spoils its satisfaction because it cannot be aware of anything without being aware of its desire for *more*, for the absolute. It feels the finitude or self-negativity of the finite—a sort of death. And so it grows anxious and fearful of positing anything. It tries not to think, but its trying is a thinking, and so anxiety is perpetuated. Then it tries to console itself with the bromide that everything is "good in its kind," but reason comes along and exposes this view as an attempt to glorify the vulgar and cheap. Another ruse is that, in its unhappiness and fear of truth, consciousness assumes the posture of the Ardent Lover of Truth, who prides himself on knowing that all is vanity and that it is impossible to know the truth. Upon this self-proclaimed lover of truth who knows how to "belittle every truth" in a frenzy of conceit, Hegel lavishes his most searing rhetoric [80]. His resolve to leave this "barren ego" to itself, because it "flees from the universal," reminds us of what Virgil tells Dante when they behold the Indifferent or Non-Committal outside the gates of Hell: *Guarda e passa,* "Look—and move on!"

This tale of passion and evasion springs from the fear that consciousness has of its limitation or finitude. Consciousness does not experience its self-transcendence, its necessary "going beyond itself," as a determinate negation. In existential terms, man, for Hegel, fears the truth because he fears the mortality of all finite perspectives on the truth. *He fears death.* The *Phenomenology of Spirit* is largely devoted to analyzing, and eventually overcoming, this fear. In absolute knowing, the philosopher grasps the connection between eternal truth and death. He is reconciled to time. Viewed in this way, the *Phenomenology* is a response to the problems taken up in Plato's *Phaedo.* It is Hegel's version of why philosophy, as Socrates says, is "the care of death" (81A).[13]

Experience as the Testing of Consciousness [81–89]

To a great extent, consciousness has revealed itself in what we have already said about natural consciousness. Hegel now turns to the most important part of his Introduction, "the method of carrying on the inquiry" [81]. He tells us more precisely what consciousness is, and what it means for consciousness to become educated through a process of self-testing.

For Plato and Aristotle, the problem of knowledge is that of uniting thinking and being. Hegel puts the problem in terms of *concept* [*Begriff*] and *object* [*Gegenstand*]. Concept is that which is intellectually grasped [*gegriffen*], and object is that which stands [*steht*] over and against [*gegen*] consciousness. The goal of consciousness is "the point where knowledge no longer needs to go beyond itself, where knowledge finds itself, where concept corresponds to object and object to concept" [80]. To reach this goal, consciousness inflicts disillusionment on itself by confronting the nothingness of its natural shapes. It must test itself, and fail the test over and over again. But how is consciousness to do this before it has genuine knowledge? Every test has a criterion by which something is determined as either right or wrong. How can consciousness use a criterion without presupposing the knowledge that consciousness does not yet have, the knowledge that is precisely the result of the test?

To answer this question, Hegel reveals the structure of consciousness: "Consciousness simultaneously *distinguishes* itself from something, and at the same time *relates* itself to it, or, as it is said, this something exists *for* consciousness; and the determinate aspect of this *relating,* or of the *being* of something for a consciousness, is *knowing*" [82].

This is the key sentence in the Introduction. From it, Hegel draws a number of important conclusions. The definition of consciousness transforms the fence that divides subject and object into a *relating* of subject to object. Consciousness does not simply await the arrival of objects. It does something, namely, the work of relating. Strictly speaking, the subject does not "have" a relation with the object but actively relates itself to the object. In a sense, it goes beyond itself to meet the object, all the while staying within itself. The relating here has two aspects. On the one hand, consciousness distinguishes itself from the object; on the other, it "directs itself" to this object. Let us say that I am conscious of this apple that is before me. Being aware of it is to confront it as object. To confront it as object means that I preserve my distinctness from it, even as I direct my gaze, vector-like, toward it. Because consciousness is this relation to object, awareness is always the awareness *of* something. It is never without content. It is this determinate aspect of the relation of subject to object that allows me to say that in being aware of an object, I *know* it.

The structure of consciousness obliges the object to take on a double life. The object is both "in itself" (other than consciousness) and "for consciousness." The apple is *for me* something *other than me.* The double life of the object is signaled by Hegel's emphasis on the word *being* [*des Seins*] in the definition of consciousness quoted above. Hegel goes on to say: "whatever is related to knowledge or knowing is also distinguished from it, and posited as also *being* [*seiend*] outside of this relation; this aspect of the in-itself is called *truth*" [82]. Simply put, I am aware of the external world as something real or genuinely other than me.

At this point, a skeptic might object by saying that what Hegel is calling an object "in itself" is only an object *for us* (the world is only "in our heads"). But this imposes a theory on the object and raises the problems noted earlier, especially the problem of how we can *know* that the object is only for us without having some access to the object as it is in itself. Hegel takes the object more seriously. He does so because *consciousness* does. His strategy is to enter into the structure of consciousness itself, not impose a theory on it but faithfully report what consciousness intends as object. This intended object is *other than consciousness,* an object that is *both* something in itself *and* something for us. Strange to say, Hegel's convoluted language comes from his effort to be simple and unobtrusive.

Philosophic simplicity, however, tends to be complicated. Phenomenology is the critical examination of apparent knowing. Apparent, here, means both illusory and historically manifest. In the *Phenomenology,* knowledge is our object. Ultimately, we want to know what knowledge is in truth or in itself. But knowledge, in addition to being our *object,* is also *our* object. It is "*for us*" [83]. For the phenomenologist, consciousness thus participates in the double life of all objects of consciousness. If knowledge is *our* object, if it is "for us," then the criterion for testing consciousness must, it seems, come from us. But then it would not be the criterion of the knowledge we are investigating, the criterion it sets for itself. How are to overcome this difficulty?

Earlier in this chapter, I asked where the fence of consciousness, the distinction between subject and object, came from. Hegel's answer is, from consciousness itself: "Consciousness provides its own criterion from within itself, so that the investigation becomes a comparison of consciousness with itself; for the distinction made above falls within it" [84]. The distinction between consciousness and its object, and between what is "for us" and what is "in itself," is *posited* by consciousness and therefore *within* consciousness. To use Fichte's terms, it is the I that distinguishes between the I and the non-I, between subject and object. That is, the distinction between the for-us and the in-itself derives from consciousness as the general awareness of objects. Consciousness is a relation with two sides or aspects—the conscious subject and the object.

Relation, here, is not a "third something" stuck between the poles of subject and object, but the relation itself, or rather the subject's *act of relating.* Picture thinking cannot help us grasp this, since we would have to picture a part that was also the whole. We must instead make an effort (as we will repeatedly in following Hegel's argument) to *think relation.* This effort will become even more important, and more difficult, when we take up the logical structure of *self*-consciousness.

The upshot of Hegel's analysis is that consciousness itself provides the criterion by which consciousness is to be tested: "in what consciousness affirms from within itself as the in-itself or the true we have the criterion that consciousness itself sets up by which to measure what it knows" [84]. The testing of consciousness and its claims to know is unlike the testing or measuring of anything else. The reason is that consciousness has its own unique structure: the relating and distinguishing of subject and object. As that which posits specific claims to know, consciousness contains its own measuring-stick, its own mark of success or failure.

Hegel emphasizes that the two moments—concept and object, being-for-another and being-in-itself—"both fall within that knowledge which we are investigating" [84], and that the comparison between the two, the comparison that will determine whether object and concept correspond to one another, is undertaken by consciousness itself. Indeed, "this consciousness is itself their comparison" [85]. From this, Hegel draws an important conclusion: the phenomenologist is only an observer. It is not his job to judge whether consciousness (as a determinate claim to know) measures up to his criteria or "bright ideas." He must instead limit himself to "pure on-looking" [*reine Zusehen*] [85]. The phenomenological observer "looks on," as a determinate shape of consciousness compares its mode of knowing with what it regards as the object in itself: "Something is *for it* the in-itself; and knowledge, or the being of the object for consciousness, is *for it*, another moment" [85].

We can now answer the question that is the title of this chapter: What is experience? Experience, *Erfahrung*, is the process of self-examination by which consciousness learns, through suffering contradiction, that a determinate claim to know is finite and illusory.[14] The traditional definition of truth is the adequation or correspondence between subject and object, thought and thing. Consciousness suffers the lack of this correspondence, and consequently the lack of truth, as a disharmony between concept (the mode of knowing) and object (that which is *for it* the in-itself). It suffers this lack—or violence, as Hegel says—at its own hands [80]. It is driven to establish the correspondence because that is what consciousness implicitly is: the correspondence of object and concept.

Once consciousness discovers the lack of correspondence between concept and object at any particular stage of its development, it finds fault with its mode of knowing and "alters its knowledge to conform to the object" [85]. But the object, too, undergoes a transformation. This recalls the structure of consciousness, which is a determinate relating of subject to object. Consequently, "as the knowledge changes, so too does the object, for it essentially belonged to this knowledge" [85]. In this process, consciousness, which posits an in-itself or truth distinct from itself, comes to learn that this in-itself is not a genuine in-itself at all, that it is "only an in-itself *for consciousness*" [85].

This can be stated more simply: consciousness discovers that its claim to absolute knowing is false, that its "knowing" was only perspectival or relative. But it also realizes that its finite *object* is only relative—relative, that is, to its finite, deficient mode of knowing. The objectivity of the object dissolves into mere subjectivity, or, as Hegel puts it, the object "sinks for consciousness to the level of its way of knowing it" [87]. The object, in other words, becomes a *mere* concept or thought of an object. To use our own picture thinking here, consciousness tries to get outside itself and reach the object but in the course of experience falls right back inside itself again.

We first witness this origination [*Entstehung*] of the new object in the transition from sense-certainty to perception. For sense-certainty, the truth is the sheer immediate presence of reality as an infinite set of particulars or thises. The This is not yet a thing, since, for sense-certainty, there is no order whatsoever in the infinite sea of thises (everything and anything counts as a This). As sense-certainty tries to sustain the pure particular, the atomic particular broadens into a band of particulars—a *universal.* (How this happens we shall see in the next chapter.) It becomes its opposite. But there is a name for a sensuous particular that also shares in universality: "thing." The thing with its many properties is the new object that *arises out of* the experience of sense-certainty. The thing, the object of perception, is a mediated This. It preserves the sensuous particularity of the preceding This but incorporates universals into its structure in the form of universal or shared properties (color, shape, etc.).

What we have seen so far is summed up in Hegel's definition of experience: "*Inasmuch as the new true object springs from it,* this *dialectical* movement which consciousness exercises on itself and which affects both its knowledge and its object, is precisely what is called *experience*" [86]. The object, along with the subject, has been altered in the course of this process: "This new object contains the nothingness of the first, it is what experience has made of it." Experience, in other words, as determinate negation, is a form of *work.*

Dialectical experience differs from ordinary experience. In the latter, mis-identifying an object does not automatically give rise to a new object. To recall the sort of mis-identifying discussed in Plato's *Theaetetus,* let's say that I see from a distance a man I think is Socrates. But as I approach to get a better look, I realize that it is not Socrates after all but Theaetetus, who happens to resemble Socrates. The discovery of my error does not result in the sudden metamorphosis of Theaetetus into Socrates, or in the sudden arrival of Socrates, who, if he showed up as my new object, would do so "by chance and externally" [87]. The ordinary experience of mis-taking, unlike the dialectical experience of consciousness, is non-generative: I learn only that I mis-took. The contrast brings out what is most remarkable in experience as Hegel defines it: "the new object shows itself to have come about through a *reversal of consciousness itself*" [87].

The most fundamental distinction in Hegel's book, after that between subject and object, is the distinction between the perspective of consciousness and that of the phenomenological observer. What does consciousness "see"? And what do we alone "see," we who are engaged in pure on-looking? To address this question, I return to the theme of education in Chapter 1.

Experience, for Hegel, is ultimately not passive but productive. It generates a new mode of knowing and a new object—a whole new shape of consciousness that results from the *reversal* of a cognitive stance. Sense-certainty, for example, generates perception. Hegel sometimes calls this reversal a *Verkehrung* or inversion. He observes: "This way of looking at the matter is something contributed by *us*, by means of which the succession of experiences through which consciousness passes is raised into a scientific progression, but it is not known to the consciousness that we are observing" [87]. The phenomenological observer sees what is going on "behind the back of consciousness." He sees what consciousness does not: the logical necessity in the *movement* [*Bewegung*] and the *becoming* [*Werden*], that is, in the process by which the reversal of consciousness gives rise to a new object. It is this vision of necessity that transforms the Way of Despair into "the Science of the *experience of consciousness*" [88].

As we have seen, Hegel distinguishes experience in his sense of the term from ordinary experiences like discovering Theaetetus when we were looking for Socrates. The former is a determinate negation. But the dialectic of consciousness has this in common with ordinary experience: consciousness is not aware that its suffering is the work by which a new object is produced. For it, experience is simply the ordinary experience of mis-taking, except that it is more painful (its whole world of knowing crumbles in its hands), and there is no Socrates, no second object, anywhere to be found.

I have referred several times to the passage in which Hegel speaks of natural consciousness as "pressing forward" to true knowledge. We are now in a position to say more precisely what this means, and in what sense consciousness itself, not just the individual reader of the *Phenomenology*, is educated.

A perplexity arises when we consider the limited perspective of consciousness. How can consciousness learn or "press forward" if it does not see what is going on behind its back—if it does not grasp "the *origination* [*Entstehung*] of the new object" [87]? Is this not tantamount to saying that it cannot make sense of its own experience and therefore cannot learn? How can consciousness, under these conditions, be on a path at all?

We must observe here that consciousness in its universal meaning must not be confused with its individual finite shapes. It is the former that undergoes the transition from one shape to the next. As we saw in our discussion of negation, consciousness, as the concept of itself, is not confined to its finite shapes. It is restless because it constantly senses, or divines, the finitude of these shapes. But an individual shape is not aware of the transition from one shape to another. It cannot leap outside itself. It is true that experience generates a new object, but consciousness is not aware that this has happened. The positive result of suffering (the determinate negation) is implicit for it and explicit only for the phenomenological observer. That is why learning, for consciousness, is a Way of Despair. For it, the result of its experience of every one of its natural shapes is nothing but contradiction and failure—a purely negative dialectic.

Consciousness learns, in other words, by exhausting itself, by experiencing the finitude of its natural shapes and thereby coming to despair of all things natural. Consciousness does not "take its pulse" along the way. Sense-certainty, for example, does not have an epiphany and turn into perception. Nor does perception say to itself: "Well, I may not be at the end, but at least I'm farther along than sense-certainty!" It does not remember where it has been, and so does not experience itself as being *on a path.* The path as such is evident only from the perspective of the philosophic observer—*only from the standpoint of absolute knowing.* If perception knew that it was only a stage on the way to true knowing, it would not be perception, since perception claims, erroneously, to be absolute knowing. Differently stated, spirit as consciousness puts its whole heart and soul into each finite shape of knowing. At each stage, it affirms its partial knowledge as the whole. This is why spirit's learning is a series of painful disenchantments. If spirit, as consciousness, knew that its shapes were stages along the way, its journey would not be a Way of Despair but rather a nice, consoling gradualism, a glide to greater perfection. It would be most people's idea of progress.

Spirit, as consciousness or the opposition between subject and object, spills out into time, all in a rage to know itself. The result is a colorful array of finite shapes of consciousness, spread out all over history in different times and places. Like Leibniz' monads, each contains the whole from a particular, and specifically confused, point of view. There is an implicit order in this dappled robe of time, a figure in the carpet: some shapes are more reflective, higher, and more complex, than others. But spirit does not see this figure, not yet. First, the spill: then the gathering. First, the going forth: then the turn within. The spill of positings (which Hegel calls a kenosis or emptying [808]) is driven by spirit's desire to know itself in the act of revealing itself, making itself present to itself in history. Consciousness presses forward to true knowledge. But only at the end can the manifold shapes of knowing be unified to form a path. To know absolutely is to know how to look back or "recollect." It is to know, not only the result (philosophy in the form of Science), and all the previous stages that led to this result, but also the logical *process* that made all the stages cohere with one another and with their end. Spirit cannot know itself until it is capable of thinking the logic of determinate negation that is at work within its own historical unfolding.

As we have seen, consciousness is the opposition of subject and object. It is always a two or dyad. To be aware is to be aware of an *other:* the object as the other of my thinking. This otherness haunts the entire journey of spirit. At every stage, there is something external to the self and to thinking—a something "out there"—that sets a limit to the self's claim to absoluteness (the claim that truth is subject [17]). Out-there-ness is not limited to spatial relations. A thing is "out there" if it remains undigested by the work of dialectic, if it is not thought through or mediated. The apple is an "out there." But so are innate ideas, first principles, the categorical imperative, and a transcendent God.

The first large stage of spirit is called Consciousness (sense-certainty, perception, understanding) because spirit at this stage is preoccupied with non-thinking objects. *Self*-consciousness has not yet come on the scene. But throughout its entire journey, spirit is "burdened" with the otherness inherent in consciousness, the subject-object opposition. That is why the journey of spirit in the *Phenomenology* is, more properly, the journey of *consciousness.* The adjective "natural" reminds us that consciousness, the cave-like attitude of pre-philosophic thought, must be purged of its limited vision and its tendency to identify the truth with what is familiar, self-evident, and therefore dialectically undeveloped—in a word, the given.

At the culminating stage of absolute knowing, the subject-object opposition is obliterated. It is replaced by the unity of *pure thinking,* which communes only with itself and at the same time expresses all that *is.* It is *subject* that knows itself as the enduring *substance* of all things [17]. Absolute knowing, to recall the saying of Parmenides, is the stage at which being and thinking are the same. The flowering of this thinking is the *Science of Logic,* the Olympian peak to which the *Phenomenology* provides a ladder.

We now embark on the journey of consciousness, as it moves through its various shapes. At each level, consciousness will begin with *certainty* and end with *truth.* Experience will be the thread that connects them.

CONSCIOUSNESS

The leaves cry. It is not a cry of divine attention,
Nor the smoke-drift of puffed-out heroes, nor human cry.
It is the cry of leaves that do not transcend themselves . . .
WALLACE STEVENS, "The Course of a Particular"

 3

Of Mere Being

(SENSE-CERTAINTY)

THE JOURNEY OF CONSCIOUSNESS BEGINS WITH THE MOST BASIC mode of knowing: sense-certainty. What does "begin" mean here? It means that Hegel, who already sees things from the divine perspective of absolute knowing and knows how the journey ends, has surveyed all the modes of knowing that have appeared in time, and finds that *this* one, logically, must come first.[1]

As I noted in the previous chapter, sense-certainty is not a psychological event but a claim to know. A personified mode of universality, it claims that the knowledge of absolute truth is the immediate intuition of the sensuous This, the Here-and-Now. In this "world" of knowing, there are no things with properties, only radical particulars—details without a whole to which they belong.[2] Since sense-certainty uses language (up to a point), names for things will enter the discussion. But they refer only to instances of the un-nameable This. For sense-certainty, there is no kind-character, no coming-to-be, no causes or effects, no relations, no hierarchies, no ordered whole, no things with properties. Nor is the particular an *appearance* of some deeper *essence*. There is only the world as an endless repository of instances. In Kant's terms, it is the spatiotemporal manifold without the unifying function of a concept. Sense-certainty's claim is *that* things are, not what, why, or how they are. For sense-certainty, the absolute is simple *presence:* "only the *being* [*das Sein*] of the thing" [91].[3]

What is attractive about this claim to know? We should ask this question at every stage of the journey, since in order to know a shape of consciousness we must "get inside its character" and perform a sort of philosophic mimesis—*imagine* what it would mean to be this shape. Sense-certainty appears to be the richest kind of knowledge, for which the world is unbounded and infinitely detailed [91]. It also seems to be the truest knowledge because it lets the world in all its unprocessed glory simply *be*, without the trammels of theory and thinking.

It might seem that the sort of person who finds this view attractive is limited or naïve, and cannot think of anything more intelligent to claim about reality. But we can also imagine a cultured human being, who is disenchanted with reason and seeks refuge in the anti-universal, anti-discursive realm of pure Thises. Such a human being is an example of the misology or hatred of reason Socrates decries in the *Phaedo* (89D). In any case, whether as the Man on the Street or the Disenchanted Thinker, sense-certainty must think away the world as it is ordinarily experienced. It must deny that apples are not just Thises but fruits of a certain kind endowed with certain properties—and good to eat.

Sense-certainty is first because it is the most immediate, most unthought-through, of all cognitive stances. For sense-certainty, the world is an infinitely diverse *given.* At the beginning of the chapter, Hegel warns us not to impose our bright ideas on sense-certainty. In taking hold of sense-certainty, we must refrain from conceptually grasping [*das Begreifen*], which would falsify the very phenomenon we want to observe [90]. In the course of Hegel's chapter, sense-certainty will undergo mediation: it will be thought through and logically developed. Immediacy will start to "leak" and give rise to process. The dialectic at work here is not a phenomenological method that we apply to sense-certainty, but rather the logical structure that *is* sense-certainty.[4]

It cannot be emphasized enough that dialectic, here, is not one of the cognitive tools Hegel criticized in his Introduction but the rational *soul* of things as they are. In spite of the static, architectural associations of the word, structure, for Hegel, is fluid. It is the spontaneous process of logical unfolding through an ordered series of interconnected negations (like organic growth). Form is a self-forming movement. The truth of sense-certainty cannot be summed up in a proposition. It reveals itself only in the entire process of logical evolution.[5] Hegel makes this all-important point later in the chapter by referring to *history:* "It is clear that the dialectic of sense-certainty is nothing else but the simple history [*Geschichte*] of its movement or of its experience, and sense-certainty is nothing else but just this history" [109].

What is true of sense-certainty holds for all the shapes of consciousness. Their nature is not a static Platonic Form that transcends speech and is accessible only to intellectual intuition, but a logical motion fully manifested in speech. The *logos* or logic of a mode of knowing *is* that mode's being or nature, and being manifests itself as movement, *Bewegung. Logos* (or intelligibility), being, and motion are all the same. *Logos* is not *about* being but rather is the *self-manifestation* of being as it relates itself to itself, as it makes itself other than itself in order to be fully itself. This unity of *logos*, being, and motion is what makes Hegel, Hegel.[6]

We turn now to the dialectic of sense-certainty.

A claim to know is just that—a mere claim. This constitutes *certainty* [*Gewißheit*]. A given shape of consciousness seeks to transform this certainty into *truth*, to make its subjective "yes" objective or manifest to itself. In the course of entering into its own position (the process of experience), sense-certainty will undercut itself. The more it affirms its cognitive stance the more the radical particular—the singular This—will change into its opposite, the universal. The magical transformation of the particular into the universal can be summed up in the innocuous-seeming word "this." The word is intended to reach the non-linguistic particular, *this* as opposed to everything else in the world, but in fact refers to any particular whatsoever.

There is also an immediacy of *subject* involved in this claim to know. Just as the *It*, for sense-certainty, is a radical particular, so too is the *I*. The I, like the It, has no properties as such. It contains no separate faculties, no "manifold imagining or thinking." This consciousness "is 'I,' nothing more, a pure 'This'" [91].

The dialectic of sense-certainty has three stages. These correspond to the three ways in which the I interprets its relation to the object. Sense-certainty, in spite of its immediacy, draws a distinction (in the first two stages) between what is essential and what is non-essential in this relation. In the first stage, the object is essential: it *is* and is true, whether there is a subject there or not. When this fails, sense-certainty shifts its ground and makes the subject essential: the I abides and *is*, as various Thises come and go. This second stage also fails. Finally, at the third stage, sense-certainty glues the subject and object together in a singular act of intuiting, an always immediate and self-contained S-O module, such that the sensing subject never compares a past with a present This, or a past with a present I, but lives in an infinitely repeatable Here-and-Now.

These three stages correspond, respectively, to three logical relations: **in itself** [*an sich*], **for itself** [*für sich*], and **in and for itself** [*an und für sich*].[7] This sequence of relations will recur throughout the journey of consciousness. The **in-itself** stage is objective, that is, oriented toward an object taken as absolute. It comes first because it expresses a potential or immediacy that has not yet been mediated or *thought through*. The object is simply *there*. It is not posited as the result of a positing. It is not yet explicitly related to the subject. The **for-itself** stage is subjective. Here, the self posits the object, puts it forth, as the result of the self's positing. The object is explicitly an object *for* consciousness.[8] The **in-and-for-itself** stage expresses the unity of subject and object. It is the stage at which something is logically complete.

At each of its stages, sense-certainty suffers contradiction: the particular shows itself to be in truth universal, and the immediate shows itself to be *mediated,* that is, a process. By the end, sense-certainty is logically exhausted, thoroughly thought through, and its claim to know is unmasked as illusory. We enter into the experience of sense-certainty and share the negativity of that experience. But we see what sense-certainty does not: the transition to the next shape of consciousness, and to the second object Hegel talked about in the Introduction. The chapter ends with an I: not the I of sense-certainty, but the I of the phenomenological observer [110]. It is for this I that *perception* emerges as mediated sense-certainty, and the *thing with many properties* as the mediated sensuous This.

We now proceed to the "history" of sense-certainty, that is, to the dialectical process of being sensuously certain of an object. Sense-certainty claims to be immediate: a Here-and-Now is immediately present to an I-right-now. But in every act of sense-certainty, the immediacy of the act "splits up" into *two Thises*—a subject and an object. In other words, the immediacy here is not so immediate that the subject simply disappears into the object. The subject persists as the being that says, "I am certain of This." The subject does not say to itself, "Ah, certainty!" This would express a subjective state, not a claim to truth. It says rather, "I am certain of This because it is immediately present to me." At this first stage of experience, the object is essential and the subject non-essential, where essential means, "where the truth is coming from." The subject is *mediated:* it has certainty only *through* the immediate object, to which it is directed [93]. The test focuses, at this stage, on the object. Does this object measure up to what sense-certainty claims? Is it really immediate? Experience will decide.

First Stage: The Object Is Essential [95–99]

The This has two aspects, a Here and a Now. Hegel examines them separately. First, he takes up the Now. The Now is the existential *right now,* right at this very moment. We enter the stance of sense-certainty, look at the Now through its eyes, and ask ourselves, "What is the Now?" We answer, "The Now is Night."[9] Hegel then exhorts us to write down this truth, impishly adding, "a truth cannot lose anything by being written down" [95]. The next day, when noon comes around, yesterday's question, "What is the Now?", gets a different answer: "Now is Day." The reason is that Now means only the particular Now, the Moment. Only the Moment can be true because it alone counts as presence or being. The written truth of yesterday has thus become "stale" or, as we say, passé. Day has supplanted Night. It has done so *within the structure of the Now.*

The problem here is that the particular Now is empty and refers, indifferently, to both Night and Day. The whole point of sense-certainty is to "live," cognitively speaking, in the moment. Sense-certainty is a cognitive romantic.[10] But how am I to "live" in the moment when one particular moment is no different from another? The second Now, Day, does not just replace the first Now, Night: the *same* Now is first Night, then Day. This Now that is both Hegel calls a "self-preserving Now." It is neither Night nor Day but that which can be both. But something that remains what it is as it ranges over its instances is what we call a *universal.* "Triangle" is not that triangle on the blackboard or this one on the page of my geometry book. Triangle as a universal remains itself, and is fully present, in both instances. And yet, it *is not* either of them: it is, indifferently, this one or that. Hegel calls the Now a not-This to signal that a universal cannot be pinned down in a particular instance. It is, he says, "a *negative* in general" [96].

Few of us would define universality as negation. But Hegel has a point. I cannot think a universal without thinking it as something that transcends and therefore negates its particular instances. A universal is a not-This, where This is a particular. In this very first section of the *Phenomenology,* Hegel shows us the birth of the universal out of the particular: universality *is* the self-negation of the particular. To cite Kant's terminology again, it is as though we were watching the spatiotemporal manifold spontaneously unify itself and give rise, if not yet to concepts, then at least to sensuous universals that are on their way to concepts. We are witnessing sensuousness *on its way to thought.*

Night cannot sustain itself as an enduring Now, nor can Day. The Now that sense-certainty means to get at cannot sustain itself as something immediate but is subject to a process. The Now that *can* sustain itself as always Now is the *mediated* Now, Now that is a universal or a not-This. And so, the truth of sense-certainty, in one aspect of the This (the Now), is shown, through experience, to be the opposite of the initial certainty.

Hegel reminds us, as he does repeatedly in the *Phenomenology,* that language is on the side of dialectic. We *mean* the radical particular, but we *say* the universal. Language, here, "is the more truthful" [97]. The dialectic of the Now required that we compare one act of sensuous intuiting with another. That was the point of writing down the first truth. Without the act of comparing, universality would not arise in consciousness. Language is more truthful because, unlike sense-certainty, it lets universality, fluidity, and negation *be.* Language turns the tables on sense-certainty by revealing that the purported letting be of sense-certainty is in fact a *not* letting be.

The truth of the Now is that it negates itself. To grasp the *Here,* we enter sense-certainty once more and follow its experience of the This. The Here is a tree. But then I turn around and, lo, the Here, which was supposed to be immediately true, turns into a house! It does so because the intended Here is indifferent to content. The Here does not vanish when a particular content vanishes. It *abides* and can indifferently accommodate a tree and a house because it is neither of them. The true Here is thus not the one sense-certainty means but "a *mediated simplicity*, or a *universality*" [98]. Experience shows that the truth of the Here, like that of Now, is *process:* I cannot experience a Here without experiencing it as becoming a There, or a Now without experiencing it as becoming a Then. It is not immediacy that abides, but process and transition.

Second Stage: The Subject Is Essential [100–102]

The result of the foregoing is that the objective This cannot be immediate, as sense-certainty had claimed. Its concept and object fail to correspond. Since the object has been experienced as non-immediate and self-negating, the certainty must lie at the other pole of consciousness, the subject. At this second stage, the subject-object relation is reversed and the *knowing* is made essential. The truth now comes from the object's being *my* object: objective Thises come and go, but my sensing is always there to greet them.

It is important at this second stage to keep in mind that the I is meant to be a radical particular, a singular I that lives only in the immediacy of a moment. I means, I-right-here-and-now. Sense-certainty wants nothing to do with a universal I (a We), or with an I that has a personal history (or process of becoming). Its positing of immediacy precludes continuity.[11] That is why sense-certainty, at this second stage, will fail.

Now is Night because I see it. Now is Day because I see it. Here is a tree because I see it. Here a house because I see it. I carry with me my very own personal Here-and-Now-ifier, and so am no longer bothered by Night becoming Day, or Tree becoming House. Let them vanish—I abide! Now is the Now of my seeing. Here is the Here to which I direct my attention. But who is the I in the shift from Night to Day, and from Tree to House? It cannot be the same I for both these seeings, since I must be the radically particular I, the I-right-now. It must be *one I* that sees Night and Tree, and *another I* that sees Day and House. Sense-certainty, through experience, thus generates an infinite series of I's, one for each moment of particular seeing.

But there is unmistakably an I that endures in this self-othering, since the I *compares* one seeing with another and realizes that what it has is a constantly vanishing "truth." The I is not an amnesiac. Like the objective This, the I or sensing subject has become a *universal* through this comparison [102]. The word "this" refers to anything and everything. So too, the word "I" refers to any and every I. Hegel is not playing a language game here. He is observing that language *seconds* what the dialectic of experience has revealed all on its own, that radical particularity is self-negating, or becomes its opposite.

Third Stage: The Dialectic of Pointing [103–9]

The third and final stage of sense-certainty is the most complex of its attempts to prove itself in the arena of experience. Before taking up this stage, let us note the sequence of the first two stages. First, the object is made essential, then the subject. It makes sense that the first candidate for essentialness is the object. The reason is that sense-certainty, as a shape of consciousness, is always directed toward something other than itself. The positing of an essential subject arises in response to the failure of the essential object, only when sense-certainty has been "expelled from the object" and "driven back into the 'I'" [100]. Subjectivity is a reflex action. I turn toward myself by turning away from external objects.[12]

We who have entered sense-certainty's labyrinth now "posit the *whole* relation of sense-certainty as its *essence*" [103]. By so doing, we seek to avoid the previous two undercuttings, in which I and It turned into universals. I and It are now glued together in an immediate *relation* of intuiting, in which "I do not compare Here and Now themselves with one another, but stick firmly to *one* immediate relation: the Now is day" [104]. Having been recently burned by my experience with comparisons, I will have no more to do with them. I refuse to step outside the immediate singularity of my relation-to-object. The relation is that of a radically particular I-right-now that is always and only immediately related to a This-Now-Here. "At last," our cognitive romantic consoles himself, "I can 'live' in the moment!"

The goal here is to avoid process (that is, mediation) and language once and for all. It is to transform the shifts of time and place into a constantly reiterated self-sameness, while avoiding the transformation of either subject or object into a universal. That transformation, we recall, was the result of the act of comparing. But now I forswear all comparisons. As a sensuously certain subject, I enter time, but I claim to experience time as a Now always repeating itself. I live each incomparable moment fully *by denying time as process.* Each Now is a unique moment of intuiting in which subject and object are united in a Here-and-Now that is never other than itself. I no longer say "Now" and "Then," or "Here" and "There." I say only (or rather *point,* for my claim prohibits speech), "Now," "Now," "Now," and "Here," "Here," "Here." In this way, through a sort of enforced amnesia, I am always the particular I, and the object is always a particular Here-and-Now that never becomes a There-and-Then. By confining myself to the S-O module, I hope to experience pure immediate *presence,* which is the soul of my claim that sense-certainty is absolute truth.

This is the most difficult part of Hegel's account. The logic of the third stage will, in effect, uncover the dialectical structure of *time,* time as pure process. The third stage will show how process and transition into an opposite arise, not in the comparison of one Now and Here with another but *within* what sense-certainty takes to be an immediate relating of I and It. Immediate presence will become passage. Once again, the very effort to hold on to the particular as such will transform it into a universal: dialectic is also irony.

The universal arises here from the act of pointing, *Zeigen.* Pointing to a Here-and-Now seems simple enough. It is an especially good idea if I want to avoid language, which oozes universality. The whole refutation of sense-certainty at this third stage consists in experiencing pointing as a process—more precisely, a process of *determinate negation* and *sublation.*

It does not take much to bring about this result. In the subject's very act of pointing, the Now "has already ceased to be" [106]. "Now!"—there it goes, it has just slipped through my fingers. To be sure, Nows keep sprouting up like daisies, but the Now I pointed to, the Now I thought I could stick with in the immediacy of my S-O module, is gone, gone precisely *because* I pointed to it![13] I lose what I am pointing to in the act of pointing to it. Just when the Now is pointed to, it is not. It is like Proteus, Homer's old man of the sea, who takes on various forms when anyone grabs hold of him.[14] The Now that is pointed to by sense-certainty in its pure intuiting is not a being at all but a has-been, or rather a having-been (in German, a *Gewesenes* [106]). It is consequently not the *being as presence* sense-certainty intended.

Pointing is not the immediate act I thought it was. It is rather a movement or process with three phases or moments. These moments (which bear a logical rather than a temporal sense) are Hegel's first spelling out of determinate negation and sublation or *Aufhebung.* Throughout this dense passage [106–7], Hegel uses forms of the verb *aufheben,* whose meaning we discussed in Chapter 2. If the reader succeeds in grasping this dialectic of pointing, he will then grasp the paradigm for all dialectical movement in the *Phenomenology.*

In the first logical moment, I point out the Now as the truth. Realizing that it has vanished in the act of pointing to it, I sublate this truth in the sense of canceling it. This is the first negation. Then I posit another truth: that the first Now *has been* (which I have just experienced), something that has been sublated [*Aufgehobenes*]. But a having-been cannot be the truth: the truth must *be.* And so, in the third moment, I negate the first negation (since what has been *is not*) and return to the first assertion: that the Now *is.*[15] This logical movement is something that *we* see [107]. But logic is not a "method" that we have "applied" to the Now. It is the *truth* of the Now, which fully manifests itself in language.

The last, positive phase of the dialectic of the Now captures what is true to the experience of pointing: the Now cannot disappear without immediately re-appearing as another Now, without transcending itself to beget a continuum of Nows. I cannot "live" exclusively in my S-O module. The truth that is revealed here is that time both is and is experienced as an evanescence that abides.[16] In spite of what sense-certainty claims, time is process and mediation. It is the dialectical identity of appearing and disappearing. The Now that *is* in the third moment of the dialectic of pointing is a newly constituted, expanded Now, a Now that has stepped outside itself in order to be related to itself. It is a universal Now, a Now of Nows, that accommodates all the Nows that appear and disappear within it. This new, genuine Now is a Day-of-hours, an Hour-of-minutes, a Minute-of-seconds. In sum, the experience of pointing reveals that the Now, in truth, is a universal [107]. Needless to say, this truth contradicts the certainty that the Now is an immediate radical particular—a This.

Something similar happens when I try to point to an immediate Here. Point to the figure below with your mind's eye, and let it be your Here:

H

What *exactly* is the Here you are attending to? Can you point to the letter without sensing any motion at all, any navigation within or around the Here, any straying into the Forbidden Zone of the not-Here? The figure to which I point is a *mix* of interrelated Heres. The crossbar of the **H** is a Here, and so is each vertical post. But the point at which the crossbar meets the left vertical post is also a Here, as is the point where it meets the right post. Also, the top of the left post is a Here, as is the bottom. Even "top" is ambiguous and is composed of Heres, as is "bottom." This process can be repeated indefinitely for any part of the letter, no matter how small.[17]

I cannot isolate an atomic Here. There is no Here I can point to that is not a Here of Heres: a *set of relations* like "to the left of" or "above" or "between."[18] But if this is true, then the Here is not immediate. And it shows itself to be non-immediate in my act of trying to point to it as immediate. Pointing is the *motion* by which I navigate through a Here of Heres. As I point to what I *mean* to be an atomic, immediate Here, I really supplant that Here, cancel it, jump outside it into another Here, and then jump back inside a Here, which, like the Now, has expanded and become a universal. I cannot determine the position of a Here without relating it to other Heres. In the very moment that pointing becomes relating, otherness and mediation enter the picture and the immediacy I *meant* is gone.

Sense-certainty posited the immediate Here-and-Now as absolute truth. In the act of pointing, it generated the universal Here-and-Now. In one sense, something new comes on the scene: the Here of Heres and the Now of Nows. But in another sense, the dialectic has uncovered the universality that was present all along. Logically, it takes us *back* as well as moves us forward. It discloses the universal as something *pre-posited,* that is, logically prior to what I posited. We will see this same circular, back-bending motion throughout the *Phenomenology.* Absolute knowing, the culminating stage of the whole journey of consciousness, will also be the true *archē* or beginning of all the stages that came before it. As the whole of all the shapes, absolute knowing is alone the shape that has no logical presupposition: it does not pre-posit anything but knows the whole truth of its content.

This completes the dialectical suffering of sense-certainty. The claim of sense-certainty has been thoroughly thought through, *mediated,* and just as thoroughly refuted—not by us, but by sense-certainty itself in its attempt to transform its certainty into truth through the experiential process. In the wake of sense-certainty, Hegel tells us that the dialectic of sense-certainty is the history of its experience, and, moreover, that sense-certainty *is* its history [109]. He adds that natural consciousness, too, the ordinary empirical consciousness of the individual, keeps experiencing the dialectic we just went through. But it remains entrenched in its familiar certitude, unable to store the result of its experience as a determinate negation.

Later in his account, Hegel will call the journey of consciousness a "forgotten path" [233]. At each stage, consciousness forgets what it has learned and posits another immediate truth. Only at the very end, with absolute knowing, does the self experience what Hegel (following Plato) calls *recollection* [808]. At that end-point, now so far away, consciousness preserves rather than flees the process that is consciousness itself. Only then does it grasp its *truth* as its *history.*

The Pretensions of Sense-Certainty [109–10]

Hegel ends the chapter with an attack on the self-styled skeptics. These skeptics pander to natural consciousness by affirming that the truth of sense data is a universal experience [109]. As the preceding dialectic has shown, universal experience is, on the contrary, experience of the universal. Sense-certainty is necessary to the self-knowing of spirit. But this logical necessity does not stop Hegel from attacking the sense-data theorists, who would have us believe that sense-certainty is self-evidently true.

The attack on the skeptics like Hume leads to the praise of *animals,* who seem to have an uncanny intimation of divine truth. The skeptics, Hegel says, should go back to the ancient mysteries of Bread and Wine (Ceres and Bacchus), the wisdom from which even the animals are not excluded [109].[19] Animals know the truth about sensuous particulars. They know that these sensuous givens exist to be *given up* to eating and drinking. They *despair* of the reality of such things and, "completely assured of their nothingness," gobble them up. The animals, in other words, can teach Hume a thing or two about what it really means to be a skeptic. In their practical skepticism, the animals foreshadow the "turn" in the *Phenomenology* from consciousness to *self-consciousness.* This is the moment when consciousness discovers that the world exists for the sake of the self and its desire [167].

Hegel ends, fittingly, with an ode to language. The skeptics fail to learn from language. They *mean* to get at the radical particular in the belief that this is real and concrete, and that language is abstract. But their speech betrays them: they cannot help uttering the universal. As a sense-data advocate, I could try to cling to the particular by refusing to write it down or to express what I mean in language. But there would still be the dialectic of non-verbal *pointing*, the experience in which the particular becomes a universal through self-negation. Not only that, but if I remained locked within my non-verbal certitude, I would be unable to make a claim to truth, both to myself and to another. My publishing career would be over. What good is a claim that cannot be stated?

Sense-certainty, as a finite shape of consciousness, keeps going around in its dialectic like a gerbil in its wheel. It suffers negation but does not grasp its experience as a *determinate* negation, an advance. It is like someone who has been refuted by the Platonic Socrates and says, "But I *still* think justice is the advantage of the stronger." We see what sense-certainty does not: that a new *concept* and a new *object* have arisen. The new concept or mode of knowing—perception—*lets universality be* within the realm of the sensed. It lets Thises be *things* with universal properties. Playing on the German word for perception [*Wahrnehmung*], Hegel tells us that consciousness will now *take* the This [*nehme*] in a way that is *true* [*wahr*].

Here, at the end of the first stage of experience, Hegel speaks in the first person. He takes on the role of the I that experiences the dialectic of pointing and sees the determinate negation it contains. This is also the I of the reader, who, with Hegel, experiences the transition to perception from *within* sense-certainty.

Sense-certainty tried, and failed, to make the temporal moment or Now absolute. But that moment grew beyond itself into a larger Now that preserved what was negated and lifted it up. So too, sense-certainty, as a shape of consciousness essential to absolute knowing, *for us* grows beyond itself and is preserved as a *logical, eternal* moment within the greater whole. The remainder of the *Phenomenology* pays tribute to this humble beginning, this stingy claim to know that refuses to do any work of mediation. The whole journey yet to come will be the continued mediation of sense-certainty and its immediate Here-and-Now.

The uninitiated are those who think nothing else is, other than what they are able to grasp tightly with both hands, and who will not accept that actions and processes and anything invisible has a share in being.

PLATO, *Theaetetus* (155E)

 4

The Crisis of Thinghood

(PERCEPTION)

PERCEPTION IS BOTH AN ADVANCE AND A NEW BEGINNING. IT IS AN advance because it emerged necessarily from the previous stage. Perception takes the universal that was generated by sense-certainty and embraces it as its object. It is a new beginning because it takes this object not as the result of mediation but immediately. For perception [*Wahrnehmung*], universality is not a thought or a process but a property of the thing, something true [*wahr*] that one simply "takes" [*nimmt*] in the act of perceiving.[1] Perception is higher than sense-certainty because its object is more logically complex. But as a mode of knowing, it is just as static, just as resistant to mediation.

It is not hard to see the appeal of this world of knowing. Unlike sense-certainty, perception lets things *as things* be. It lets them be manifold unities that gather properties to themselves like different kinds of flowers assembled in a vase. The world is teeming with things, *Dinge,* not just high organic beings like the individual horse, ox, or man, but also this lowly individual bit of salt or that individual piece of wood, all testimonies to reality as the realm of *rēs,* things. In addition to being friendly to ordinary experience, perception, unlike sense-certainty, is friendly to language. It lets me say things like: "This bit of salt is white, cubical, and sharp-tasting." Perception, we must note, makes assumptions about reality that extend beyond sensuous things. There is a perceptual *attitude* that colors our thinking. When philosophers discourse about the soul and try to determine whether it is simple or complex, mortal or immortal, or when theologians study God as a person with various attributes, they are treating soul and God as a thing with properties.[2] What would it take to de-stabilize this familiar world of knowing, to bring death into the seemingly safe garden of things and their properties?

Perception, like sense-certainty, is not a faculty but a claim to know. It does not say, "There are things in the world, and I experience them as stable units," but rather, "This thing that I experience as a stable sensuous unit is, all by itself, absolute truth." Absolute here means that things, taken individually, are ultimate, non-derivative, and irrefutable. They are not part of some greater truth but the truth itself. The thing, for perception, is radically independent, a world unto itself. The law of perception is thus self-identity, "a thing is the same as itself," A=A [116]. In the last chapter, I noted some important omissions from sense-certainty's world of knowing. Perception, in spite of its greater wealth, is similarly ungenerous. It excludes cause and effect, motion, and a community or interaction of things. The radical individuality and independence of things recalls the radical human individuality posited in the social-political theories of Hobbes and Locke, for whom community is artificial and contractual. This view of the individual as real and the community as abstract constitutes modern liberalism. If sense-certainty is a cognitive romantic that wants to live in the moment, then perception, it seems, is an *ontic liberal.*

In doing geometric demonstrations like the ones we find in Euclid, we are wise to keep in view the truth we seek to prove. This truth is stated in the enunciation that appears at the head of each proposition. In the *Phenomenology,* we do well to follow a similar procedure: we should, as Solon tells Croesus in Herodotus, "look to the end." Formally, the end of every chapter (with exceptions we will meet later) is the same: the death of one cognitive shape and the birth of another. A claim to know is refuted, and a new one comes on the scene. With respect to each claim we must ask: What would it take to generate a contradiction in it? If we can answer this question, then we know what is essential to the claim itself and also have a sense for where the dialectic is fated to go. This looking to the end guides our reading of Hegel's book. It also helps keep up our spirits when we feel lost in Hegel's labyrinth and encounter terms, sentences, and parts of the argument we do not understand.

Following this advice, we can make a few predictions. Essential to perception is the logical stability of the thing with many properties: this one thing all by itself. The thing must "hold up" in speech, be free of contradiction. But the thing is a unity of opposites: a One and, because of its properties, also a Many. Perception must make sure that these opposed aspects of the thing do not contradict each other. The thing must be One *in one sense* and Many *in another.* If these two senses themselves became identical—if the thing was a One insofar as it was Many, and Many insofar as it was One—then the thing with many properties, the presumed absolute of perception, would be refuted. Likewise, the thing with its many properties, *this thing,* must be utterly independent of other things and essentially self-related. It must be a fortress of self-containment. If this self-relating turned into a relation to other things, then the walls of the fortress would become porous and thinghood would fall.

The negative conclusions listed here all arise in the course of perception's effort to prove itself. This world of knowing will collapse, and a new object and mode of knowing will arise, as consciousness moves from *sense* to *thought* [132]. This new object that emerges from the contradiction of One and Many will be force [*Kraft*]. And the new mode of knowing will be what Hegel calls understanding [*Verstand*].

The Secret Life of the Thing [111–17]

The chapter on perception is harder than the one on sense-certainty. This greater complexity is evident in Hegel's opening paragraph. The *principle* of perception (unlike that of sense-certainty) is universality. And its *essential moment* of the subject-object opposition is the object perceived [111]. For sense-certainty, universality was the *process* by which particularity negated itself [96, 107]. Perception starts where sense-certainty left off. It takes the universal as a given: something statically represented in the perceived object as a property [*Eigenschaft*]. It thinks universality simply or without negation. This is characteristic of consciousness generally, which represents process as something congealed, out there, and other than consciousness itself. Consciousness *reifies* motion.

Hegel's order of presentation within a single chapter is often confusing. It is sometimes hard to tell whether what he is saying embodies the for-us perspective or that of the consciousness under investigation. Another source of confusion is that, at the beginning of a chapter, Hegel often presents the truth that consciousness has not yet experienced and gives a hard-to-follow précis of the dialectic to come. He does this in the present chapter when he reveals the logic of the thing before taking us through perception's dialectical experience of the thing. As phenomenological observers, we see what is going on "behind the back of consciousness."

Hegel does not want the thing to come on the scene immediately, as though it suddenly appeared before us. He emphasizes that the thing is derived from the previous shape of knowing and from the universality that was dialectically generated. The thing *is* this universality taken by perception as a simple given, a new immediacy. Sense-certainty revealed universality as negation, a This that was also a not-This. The expanded Now (the hour-of-minutes) resulted from a particular Now jumping outside itself. As the determinate negation of sense-certainty, perception retains this multiplicity and negation in its object. It does so through the thing's many properties, each of which expresses universality. The manyness of these properties *suppresses* the negativity of the universal by presenting it as a non-dialectical sum of simple differences. In the experiential process, this suppressed negativity will exact its revenge.

Perception does not know how interesting its object really is. It does not know that the thing has a secret inner life. This life resides in the play of logical relations that define the thing and manifest themselves, not to perceiving but to thinking.[3] What is immediate and static to perception is mediated and fluid to us. When we think the thing, enter into its distinctions and structure, we find that the thing, like the This of sense-certainty, contains three logical moments. Hegel proceeds to take us through them. Echoing the discussion of determinate negation in the Introduction, he reminds us that sublation [*Aufheben*] is a double process of negating and preserving [113]. He does so to explain how the sensed element in perception is different from what it was in sense-certainty. The world is no longer a kaleidoscope of radical Thises. It is now the realm of *sensed universals,* properties, gathered in the unity of the thing. In the move from sense-certainty to perception, the meaning of the word "this" changes. It refers no longer to a "this whatever, which is here and now" but to "this One that is also a Many." The thing, the refurbished This, is a little world unto itself.

In its first stage, the thing exhibits universality only positively, according to the law of identity, A = A. Each property is only self-related (color is color: shape is shape). In the second, negative stage, the various properties are negatively related to each other: they exclude each other as they would their opposites (color is *not* shape: shape *is not* color). The third stage combines the previous two to complete the thing. The three stages spell out the mediation or logic implicit in the immediacy of the thing with many properties.

In the first logical moment, the properties have no relation to one another. They are *indifferent* to one another and exclusively self-related. To personify this indifference or non-relation, we could say that color does not care what shape the object is. The social equivalent would be the random commingling of human individuals with different "values" and "lifestyles." Each individual property of the thing is only the same as itself. This simple self-identity is reflected in the thing that has the properties. The thing is only self-related and has no *essential* relation to other things. It is a passive *medium* in which the properties "interpenetrate, but without *coming into contact* with one another" [113].[4] In this logical moment, the thing is no more than an indifferent Here-and-Now of indifferent properties, a blank receiver that Hegel calls an Also. It is precisely not a *whole* but an *all.* In the example of the cube of salt, the white color has no relation to the sharp taste or to the cubical shape.[5] Each property is radically on its own, and the medium or Also is radically on its own. This is in keeping with perception's law of identity, according to which the true is that which is absolutely the same as itself, with no necessary relation to other.

This emphasis on self-identity sounds trivial, but it is not. Sense-certainty posited *mere being* in its object, not self-identity but only presence.

It is one thing to say, "It is," another to say, "It is itself." For perception, "It is" is not enough. The object (A) must not only be, or be present: it must also be related to itself as self-same (A = A).[6] At this first logical stage, both the thing as passive medium and the properties express the simple, self-identical universal that is the principle of perception.

The Also, however, is only the first layer of thinghood, what first strikes us about the thing. Delving more deeply into the thing's secret life, we realize that negation must be at work for a thing to be a thing: that self-sameness implies, or pre-posits, otherness. Mere self-identity, as positively conceived in the first logical moment, is not sufficient to account for the thing's being *this* thing with *these* properties. Because the thing has many properties, there must be some principle at work that makes each property *not* another property. In order for the distinguished properties, taken individually, to be self-same, they must also be *other* than their others. Different properties must exclude each other as their *opposites* [114]. This shape must exclude that color, and this color that shape. If the thing were only an indifferent passive medium, it would contain but not distinguish. In the Spinoza formula that Hegel is fond of quoting, "every determination is a negation." In addition, therefore, to being an indifferent Also that gathers and contains, the medium must also be a *One that excludes.* Hegel calls this One "the moment of negation" within the inner life of the thing. Thanks to the active power of this negative One, each property holds its own, and so, the thing as a whole also holds its own.

The third stage is the result of applying the second stage to the first. It is the negative One at work in the field of the indifferent medium [115]. The many properties within the thing are contained as "matters" within their passive Also, and actively distinguished from each other by the negative One. To express this union of moments, Hegel uses the image of *emanation.* The thing, in its complete truth, is "the point of singular individuality in the medium of subsistence radiating forth [*ausstrahlend*] into plurality" [115].[7] This reference to emanation foreshadows the expressivity of *force,* which we meet in the next chapter.

In this third and final moment, the thing's properties themselves are concretized, made into the substantial means by which the thing manifests itself. The thing does not merely *have* properties: it expresses its thinghood in and through them. The thing distinguishes itself from other things, wins its independence or this-ness, by gathering a host of materialized properties into an indifferent Here, at the same time distinguishing these properties from each other as a negative One.

Sense-certainty and perception, we must note, have a pictorial model of reality. This model will change—process will enter the picture—when we get to the concept of force and the intelligible realm of the understanding. Perception cannot think the third stage of its object as a movement from

One to Many (which is why it cannot think force). This third stage, in which the thing is "completed," will be the thing's undoing. The unity of the thing will evaporate in the manyness of concretized properties. The very means by which the thing expresses its thinghood will undermine the thing as radically independent or absolute. The thing will show itself to be nothing more than "the many properties themselves" [115].

The first two stages of thinghood correspond to the distinction between content and form. As an Also, the thing passively makes room for different kinds of "stuff" or matters. These matters provide the material ground of sensed properties: colored matter, heat matter, odorific or "smelly" matter, etc. In its capacity as a One, the thing acts as a formal principle that keeps the different properties distinct. This opposition of passive matter and active form will become explicit with the emergence of force.

We now proceed to how consciousness actually experiences the thing. Hegel reminds us that the dialectic of experience is already contained in the dialectic of the object. Our examination of consciousness, therefore, consists in "developing the contradictions" implicit in the three-fold logic of the thing [117]. Throughout all the complexities of this section, we must not lose sight of perception's fundamental task: to maintain the thing as a noncontradictory union of One and Many. Perception here wrestles with the common-sense notion that a thing is a *whole* made out of *parts* (the properties). The problem is how to prevent the whole, which must be a One, from suffering division by its parts, thereby becoming a Many.[8]

Experiencing the Thing [118–29]

The title of Hegel's chapter is "Perception: Or the Thing and Deception." Deception [*Täuschung*] is present because I can be mistaken about the thing perceived. Sense-certainty rejected deception. Its concern was immediate presence. Perception is more self-reflective. Since I perceive what a thing is only through its properties, I might, in "taking" the object, take it wrongly. I might see from afar properties that tell me that the man up ahead is Socrates but on closer inspection discover that it is really Theaetetus.[9] What looks like salt sometimes turns out to be sugar. If, therefore, in the course of perception's experience of its object, the concept (my notion of the object) fails to correspond with the actual object, then the problem must lie with me, the perceiving subject. This is how consciousness will try to save the object of perception as the true. It will guard objective self-identity, try to avoid contradiction, by assuming responsibility for any apparent discrepancies within the not-to-be-compromised *thing*.

There will be three such attempts, by analogy with the three attempts of sense-certainty. In the first, perception finds contradictions in the object and absorbs them into itself as perceiving subject: the unity of the thing vanishes in the multiplicity of the properties [117–18]. This stage represents the *in itself* or objective moment of consciousness because the object is initially posited as both One and Many.

In the second attempt, perceiver and perceived, subject and object, share responsibility for the One and the Many. Perception alternates between making the subject responsible for the unity of the thing and the object responsible for the many properties, and making the subject responsible for the many properties and the object responsible for the unity [119–22]. This is the *for-itself* or subjective moment of perception in which the subject assumes an active role as perceiver.

Finally, perception posits the object as both a One and a Many in relation to the perceiver, who engages in the comparison of objects. It tries to avoid contradiction by consciously using the relations, for-itself (that is, independent of other things) and for-another (that is, dependent on other things) [123–28].[10] This third stage is perception that is *in and for itself* because the object now has a thoroughly mediated relation both to the perceiving subject and to other objects. All the logical relations of One and Many, in-itself and for-another, subject and object, are explicitly present and interrelated.

First Stage: The Object as One and Many [117–18]

In its first attempt, perception recapitulates the dialectic of the object. The moments are in a different order because we are now following the stages of how we experience the object. The argument is a quick succession of shifts and reversals, as we attend to how the thing gradually reveals itself to consciousness. These twists and turns of the perceptual labyrinth are the direct result of our not imposing a theory on perception (so Hegel claims). We simply let unfold the logical relations that perception hides within its immediacy. If contradictions arise, as they will, then we *let* them.

Upon entering the actual perceptual process, I notice that the thing—say, this book on my desk—is a One. It is *this* thing. But I also perceive that it has a property, the blue of its cover. This property is a universal, which "transcends the singularity [of the thing]" [117]. Simply stated, blue refers to many things other than the cover of my book. The universality of the property *contradicts* the singularity or this-ness of the thing. The property "spills over" into other blue things. In light of this discovery, I cancel my first position (since the thing itself cannot be untrue) and shift the "objective essence" from the property by itself to a *community* or being-together of properties within one and the same thing. All the properties taken together in a seamless continuity are necessary if the thing is to be *this* thing. But then I perceive a discontinuity: the color is different from, and opposed to, the shape. So my commonality thesis must be an untruth that resides in me: the thing cannot be a simple continuity of properties, since each property is determinate or specific and therefore excludes the others. The properties do not merge but *stand out.* My object, the thing, remains a *This.* But now, as I have learned through experience, it is a One that is the ground of mutual exclusion among the properties.

The thing is now a "broken up One," a patchwork of properties. There are many determinate individual properties in the thing, each of which excludes the others. The thing, if it is to be *this* thing, must hold them all together as their "universal common medium" [117]. But this medium (which is not itself a property) is so vague, so *not* a One, that it lets the properties float freely and usurp the thing's own substantiality. The properties are more real than the thing itself! If we actually perceive a thing and let ourselves dialectically shift our perspective on it (as experience requires), then at this point we would perceive that what is real in the thing is nothing *but* its properties. That is, I am back to the individual property, blue, which, through its determinateness—and the indeterminateness of the medium—is a sensed universal all on its own.

Having gone back and forth between the first two logical moments of thinghood (the Also and the One), perception arrives at the third. Here, the properties take on a life of their own apart from their medium. With the medium demoted to a mere Also, the *property* becomes what is truly substantial in the object of perception. But blue qua blue is not a property *of* anything. There is no One to which it belongs. Thinghood has vanished, and I am left with the mere being or sensuous presence of blue. Perception has fallen back into *sense-certainty* [117]. It has lost its distinctive object, the thing, in attempting to grasp it through the act of perceiving.

Second Stage: One and Many Shared between Subject and Object [119–22]

When sense-certainty experienced the fall of its objective This, it was "driven back" into itself and made itself the essence of its knowledge [100]. At the second stage of perception, something similar happens. Here, however, the subject accuses itself of being the source of the object's apparent vanishing. Whereas sense-certainty at its second stage placed the *truth* in the subject, perception in its corresponding phase places *untruth* there [118]. Perception posits the thing as absolute. It cannot secure this absoluteness unless the thing is a stable One. So if dissolution comes from the multiplicity of properties, then the multiplicity must have its ground in me, the perceiving subject.[11] I make the thing a Many in my act of perceiving it. This is perception's way of correcting the untruth it has just experienced. The salt "is white only to *our eyes, also* tart only to *our* tongue, *also* cubical to *our* touch" [119]. *We* are the universal medium for the many properties, and the thing in itself is One. This, perception hopes, will be the way to keep the Many and the One from undercutting each other.

This second attempt proves to be very mortal indeed. For how can this thing that I perceive be *this* One and differentiate itself (as it must) from other things, if it has no inherent properties? Hegel here invokes Leibniz' Identity of Indiscernibles: if there is no *real* determinate difference in quality between two things, then they are one and the same thing.[12] The property [*Eigenschaft*] must belong to the thing: it must be the thing's *own* [*eigene*]. Once again, perception has failed to "take what is true," this time because it tried to posit unity without real determinateness. If the thing is a One distinct from other Ones, then it must *in itself* be the Also or medium of many properties. The properties do not vanish, nor are they there only *for me* to distinguish one thing from another: they abide and are "in the thing itself" [120].

In the course of this experience, the thing has changed from a One into an Also. But consciousness has also experienced a change. Since the thing *itself* is now an Also, and since the One necessarily plays a role in perception, the *perceiver* must be responsible for the perceived unity in the thing: I must be the One. Unity is not the work of an objective One. It is rather my work of *positing* the many properties *as one* [*das Ineinssetzen*]. The thing itself is a Many, and it is a One only *insofar as* it is *for me.* The thing itself thus becomes a mere collection of different matters—colored matter, odorific matter, heat matter, etc.—all bounded off in a spatial compartment or "enclosing surface."[13]

The result of the second stage of perceiving is a double oscillation: a shift within subject and within object, perceiver and perceived, with respect to One and Many. What we see, and what consciousness learns, is that the opposite stances consciousness has adopted necessarily imply each other. Consciousness has experienced logical movement. More especially, it has experienced movement *in the thing itself.* Hegel calls this movement in both subject and object "reflection into self." The contradiction generated by the second stage is captured in the following sentence: "The thing is a One, reflected into itself; it is *for itself,* but it is also *for another;* and, moreover, it is an *other* on its own account, just *because* it is for an other" [123]. Consciousness will now try to think this union of for-itself and for-another, independence and dependence, in a static non-dialectical way. It will try to neutralize the dialectical movement it has just experienced.

Third Stage: The Thing in Itself and Its Relation to Other Things [123–28]

Reflection, for Hegel, is a logical term. Generally, it refers to the relations of same and other, identity and difference, especially when these two relations go together to convey the logical act of returning to identity out of difference or otherness, thus re-flecting or bending back from otherness to establish self-identity. At the third stage of sense-certainty, for example, when the Now becomes a Now-of-Nows, this new Now "is something that has been reflected into itself, or a simple entity which, in its otherness, remains what it is" [107]. This reflection, or withdrawal from otherness and return to self, is precisely the logical event that takes place at the corresponding stage of perception.[14] The thing is now reflected into itself because, although a One, it has difference or manyness *within* it.[15] Clearly, consciousness will not be happy with this dialectical result, since the thing can be posited as absolute only if difference or manyness falls *outside* the One, only if the unity of the thing remains uncompromised.

I repeat the crucial sentence that captures the contradiction at Stage Two: "The thing is a One, reflected into itself; it is *for itself*, but it is also *for another;* and, moreover, it is an *other* on its own account, just *because* it is for an other." The object here has a double life: it is on its own or for itself, and it is for me (as the object of my consciousness). It is also in itself One and Many. As Hegel asserts, the thing is "*doubly* differentiated but *also* a One" [123]. Something must be done to avoid this contradiction within the object. The solution consciousness posits is to take the relation of for-another, which so far has meant "for consciousness" and to re-interpret it as *for, or in relation to, other things.* Through this appeal to other things, "the unity of the thing is preserved and at the same time the otherness is preserved outside of the thing as well as outside of consciousness" [123].

And so, at Stage Three of its experience, perception invents a new, objective form of relativism: the *vis-à-vis.* The thing is a One. But its reflection is not with respect to itself (for then it would be other than itself) but vis-à-vis or with respect to other things. The properties no longer divide the One. They are not parts of a whole but rather the multiple *relations* the thing has to other things. My copy of the *Phenomenology* is one thing. It is bulky, blue-covered, worn, and shaped like a rectangular box. But these do not divide the book. The book is bulky vis-à-vis objects that are smaller, blue vis-à-vis objects green or purple, worn vis-à-vis things new, rectangular vis-à-vis things rounded or cubical.[16] These many relations are like different clothes the thing wears for different occasions. They in no way affect what the thing is as itself. If other things were not around, the thing (my book) would be just itself—a naked One: "In and for itself, the thing is self-identical, but this unity with itself is disturbed [*gestört*] by other things" [123]. Properties are mysteriously "evoked" by the presence of other things. In the language of force, which will concern us in the next chapter, properties somehow "solicit" each other. Through this attempt to make properties non-essential and merely occasional, consciousness hopes to keep otherness *outside* the fortress of thinghood.[17]

How, we might ask, is this an advance over the previous stage, in which consciousness tried to save the thing by distinguishing the contributions of subject and object? The answer seems to be that at the previous stage, consciousness experienced the oscillation *within the thing itself* between the poles of in-itself and for-another. At its third stage, perception will attempt to explain the apparent oscillation within the object through the phenomenon of the subject's perceptual *comparisons*. It will seek refuge in the higher category of *relation* as the cause of qualitative difference. Through this category, perception will try to explain why the in-itself and the for-another aspects of the thing seem to, but do not really, become each other.

Stage Three is fascinating and deeply instructive. Here Hegel shows how tangled up we get in the very distinctions we think will keep our ideas from getting tangled up. He mounts a metaphysical refutation of perception's ontic liberalism, according to which individuality is inherent and absolute, and relation-to-other external. This is the first step toward the conclusion that community is more real than individuality, and that there is no true individuality except through relation-to-other and community. These reflections will take on staggering proportions once consciousness enters the realm of human life.

The refutation begins with our noticing that each separate thing is other *in and of its own self.* This observation echoes what happened at the previous stage, where the thing needed an intrinsic property to distinguish itself from other things. To prevent a contradiction from arising, consciousness posits otherness as in the thing but *not essentially* in the thing [124]. The thing is essentially for itself or independent and only superficially, externally related to other things or dependent.

The problem with this strategy is that the thing cannot establish itself as independent or absolute without being opposed to other things, that is, inherently opposed to them. It is a One that excludes. If I took away the other things, the thing that remained would no longer be independent: it would have nothing to "push against" and distinguish itself from, and would thereby *fail* to be for itself or on its own. When the thing (personified) proclaims, "I am myself, not those others," it defines itself vis-à-vis those others, thus making the vis-à-vis essential. To be essentially itself, it must essentially *be* other with respect to those other things. *It must be their other.* The strenuous, emphatic being-on-its-own is precisely what makes the opposition to other things, and therefore the dependence on other things, essential.

As Hegel dramatically puts it, "It is just through the absolute character of the thing and its opposition that it relates itself to others, and is essentially only this relating. The relation, however, is the negation of its self-subsistence, and it is really the essential property of the thing that is its undoing" [125]. Perception would like to keep relation-to-other, the vis-à-vis, in the non-essential category, but this, as Hegel says, is only nominal, purely a matter of terminology [127]. The attempt is refuted by the experience of actually taking the thing by perceiving it.

I can perceive the thing, "take it truly," only by going outside it and appealing to other things. The thing, in short, is *not* a world unto itself. The dialectic of perception here recapitulates the dialectic of the Here and the Now in sense-certainty. Trying to stay "inside" an individual thing, taking it as something essentially for itself or on its own, as absolute, pushes me outside the bounds of the thing. The problem is like that of trying to stay inside the figure **H** in order to hold onto it as an absolute Here. The thing thus ceases to be an absolute and becomes relative—a relating of thing to thing. It is a *being-between* rather than a being. This same result can be stated as a logical necessity: the relation of strict being-for-self is self-canceling because, as the negation of *all* otherness, it negates its own otherness from other things, its own radical independence [126].

In this last phase of experience, the fence that consciousness built between the two aspects, being-for-self and being-for-another, is destroyed. This destruction is summed up in Hegel's ultimate statement of the contradiction: "the object is *in one and the same respect the opposite of itself: it is for itself, insofar as it is for another,* and *it is for another, insofar as it is for itself*" [128]. The relations of "insofar as" are no longer side-by-side. They grow together in a single act or process of self-differentiation or self-othering. To anticipate a word that will be crucial in the next chapter, the world of perception has been *inverted.* Being-for-self has become unessential, and being-for-another essential. Differently stated, the posited independence of the individual thing is a mere moment in the more encompassing *relation* of thing to thing. The substance of individual things has become a relation-to-other. The vis-à-vis has become essential. With this third phase of its dialectical experience, perception, like sense-certainty, has been thoroughly thought through. It has been mediated and refuted. A certainty has indeed been transformed into a truth. But the truth, ironically, contradicts the certainty.

We should note that consciousness has become increasingly intellectual in the course of its experience. At first, with sense-certainty, it had nothing universal at all, nothing to *think.* Perception then posits universality. But a property is not purely thinkable (it is not a concept), since it is still subordinate to, and anchored in, sensuous things. Playing on the German word, Hegel calls this sensed universal "conditioned," *bedingt,* literally "bethinged."

At its third stage of experience, perception seems to be on the threshold of thinking. It posits *relationality.* But it does so only as a means of saving the sensuous thing as absolute: relation is posited as non-essential. The next shape of consciousness, understanding [*Verstand*], will be more knowing. It will give relation a more privileged place by identifying the substance of a thing with its *essential* relation to other things. Understanding will posit a genuine universal that will not be "afflicted" with the oppositions that plagued perception [129]. This new universal will have the remarkable feature of being purely thinkable while still "connecting" with the world of sense. It will be universality that is *unbedingt:* unconditioned or "unbethinged." The object that embodies this new universality is *force.* In the concept of force—the glory of modern science—understanding will think in one unity the opposite relations, which, for perception, formed an unresolved contradiction or intellectual dissonance. Force will be the synthetic unity of One and Many, being-for-self and being-for-another.

The Sophistry of Perception [130–31]

The story of sense-certainty ended with that shape going around in its wheel of self-negation, constantly forgetting what it has learned. Hegel attacked modern skeptics, whose sense-data theories are at odds with language. At the end of the chapter on perception, Hegel does something similar. Having just alerted the reader to the positive result of perception's experience (the unconditioned universal), he launches into an attack on what he calls "the sophistry of perception" [130]. Perception here takes us beyond the mere sensuous taking of things and their properties to *aspectual thinking.* Here, natural consciousness—the cave of spirit—appears in the guise of "perceptual, often so-called healthy human understanding" [131]. Like sense-certainty, perception keeps wheeling around. But the wheel here is far more complex, and more insidious.

Most striking about the chapter's end is Hegel's move from perception in the strict sense to perceptual *understanding.* This broadening of the term reveals that perception is closer than sense-certainty to our everyday habits of thought. The turn to perception as a kind of understanding was prepared by what we saw earlier, when perception, in order to save the thing with many properties, appealed to the logical category of *relation.*[18] Hegel's emphasis on understanding, *Verstand,* takes us back to understanding as the general power of analyzing and making distinctions (Chapter 1). Here, the distinctions are different aspects or perspectives [*Rücksichten*], different ways of considering one and the same thing. Such aspects include the Also, the insofar as, the essential, the unessential. Hegel calls them empty abstractions, with which common sense tries to avoid contradiction and deception [131]. The dialectical transition of these abstractions into their opposites goes on all the time, right under the nose of consciousness. But instead of grasping the unity of these opposites, perceptual understanding, everyday common sense, keeps shifting its ground and pretending not to have affirmed what it said a moment ago.

"Sophistry of perception" is an awfully strong term for what Hegel is describing, namely, the process in which consciousness is the victim of these wayward and fleeting abstract relations. Hegel is thinking not so much of the victims as of the perpetrators of the shiftiness that keeps common sense safe and truth at a distance. We witnessed this shiftiness in the very experience of perception. He is also thinking of the complacency and arrogance of the non-philosopher, who thinks that common sense is absolute truth, and that philosophy is abstract and unreal [131]. Philosophy, Hegel asserts, does deal in abstractions. But it focuses on them, sees their true nature, and "is master over them," whereas perceptual understanding, proud in its bondage to abstractions, is led by the nose from one error to another.

The irony of perceptual understanding, or common sense, is that it thinks it has accounted for deception, *Täuschung*, with respect to things, whereas in fact it is self-deceived. The self-deception arises from the attempt to distinguish between what a thing is *essentially* or in itself and the various *necessary but inessential* relations to the perceiving self, or what the thing is for consciousness [131]. As we have seen, this distinction cannot be maintained.

The positive insight that emerges from Hegel's diatribe against "healthy human understanding" is that thoughts, like words, have a life of their own. So-called common sense keeps spinning in its wheel. This happens, not just because it is confused, but because the "pure essences" that common sense uses all the time and thinks it understands—the relational creatures of the understanding, such as "like," "unlike," "same, "other," "in itself," and "for itself"—themselves spin in the bacchanalian whirl of genuine intelligibility, the circle of self-negation in which truth is revealed [131]. In his Preface, Hegel called these relational essences "pure self-movements" [58]. A similar phenomenon occurs in the Platonic dialogues, where the *logos* takes on a life of its own. Socrates does seem to be a master of these so-called abstractions and logical relations, and those with whom he speaks are often the victims of this motion.

Hegel's chapter provokes our wonder at the complexity of perception and thing. Our wonder here is greater than it was at the end of the previous chapter, since perception embodies our everyday experience of the world, with all its beguiling things, *rēs.* These ever seek to persuade us that they are unimpeachably real. The perceptual world is the cave of common sense, which offers convenient support for the teachings of perception. Hegel's chapter is the *pharmakon* or drug that acts as antidote to the spell and suasion of thinghood. Things still *are* at the end of the chapter on perception: negation for Hegel always preserves what it cancels. But they can no longer be regarded as absolute. They have become passé, or rather *aufgehoben.* Perception points beyond itself to a new world of knowing. This new world, the world of *thought,* will be more encompassing than what we have seen thus far. And its dialectic will be vastly more difficult.

Force is among those things which are reached, not by the imagination, but by the intellect.
LEIBNIZ, "On Nature Itself"

 5

The Dynamics of Self-Expression

(UNDERSTANDING)

CONSCIOUSNESS, AS WE KNOW, HAS TWO MEANINGS IN THE *Phenomenology.* In its broad sense, it is the opposition of subject and object. This is the consciousness that undergoes the educational process in the course of Hegel's book. In its restricted sense, consciousness is the affirmation of object rather than subject as absolute truth. Its three stages are Sense-Certainty, Perception, and Understanding.

The stages of consciousness plot the course of universality—thinkableness—as it emerges dialectically from the sensuous particular. Sense-certainty denied universals altogether. It posited the sensuous This as absolute. But the This, in its very this-ness, negated itself and turned into the universal, the Here of Heres and the Now of Nows. In negating itself, sense-certainty generated a new object: the sensed universal, or property of a thing. But the thing too was logically unstable. In perception's "last stand," the thing's being-for-self or individuality turned into a being-for-another, a relation (or rather set of relations) to other things. For perception, this was a contradiction and a dead end. For us, this unity of opposites is the birth of a new universal. Hegel calls it the *unconditioned universal.* It is universality that has been liberated from the limits of sensuous this-ness. Consciousness, as understanding, interprets this new universal as an object. Its name is force.[1]

With understanding, *Verstand,* the world springs into action. It becomes a world of *happening.* For sense-certainty and perception, the world was a kaleidoscope of Thises and a list of things. The thing was a mere tableau, a One *and also* its properties. As force, the One is no longer a mere presence, as it was in sense-certainty, or a One that excludes, as it was in perception. It is now a vibrant center that expresses itself, and sensuous properties are now the result of this self-expression. Thing becomes action. Moreover, the now-active One enters into relations with other Ones, which are also expressing themselves: *action implies interaction.* The force-world of understanding makes the two previous worlds of knowing seem dead by comparison.

Hegel's account of understanding draws heavily on the mathematical physics of Galileo, Descartes, Newton, and Leibniz. Newton and Leibniz are especially important here as the co-founders of the modern science of force (dynamics), and of the higher mathematics that the analysis of force requires (the calculus). Armed with the concept of force, the modern physicist attempts to save the perceptual world from disunity and randomness. He raises questions like: What is the source and beginning of motion? Why do bodies cohere? Why does a stone fall to earth and the moon orbit around it? Why does the stone keep moving after I have thrown it? What happens at the moment of impact between two colliding bodies? Why does a magnet attract metal filings? Why do like electrical charges repel each other, and opposite charges attract?

The hypothesis of forces (gravitational, electrical, magnetic, elastic, etc.) is the attempt to answer these questions, and many others like them.[2] For this reason, it may seem at first that force is the same as cause. As we will soon see, however, force and cause are not the same. In an early formulation of his System, Hegel says that the modern concept of force "rises above" the more limited concept of cause.[3] Whereas cause is distinct from its effect, force is cause *and* effect, source *and* manifestation, the act of expressing *and* what is expressed.

In addition to the hypothesis of force, the modern theoretical physicist also posits *laws* of force. By means of these laws, he *explains* the perceptual world. Newton's three Laws of Motion, stated at the beginning of the *Principia,* provide the universal basis for explanation.[4] Laws of nature generally take mathematical form. In Galileo's famous metaphor, nature is a book "written in the language of mathematics."[5] We are used to thinking of force, law, and explanation as three non-dialectical aspects of the praxis of modern theoretical physics. For Hegel, however, truth is revealed as logical motion: sense-certainty, for example, *is* its history [109]. In the present context, Hegel will reveal the understanding as a history or process. Force, law, and explanation will be, not static aspects or elements, but logical moments of this process.

This is the first time a shape of consciousness posits phenomena, *appearances.* We now go beneath the perceptual surface of things to their intelligible core or *essence.*[6] Indeed, the subtitle of Hegel's chapter is "Appearance and the Supersensible World." To use one of Leibniz' terms, the perceptual qualities of things (especially their extension and motion) are, to understanding, *phenomena bene fundata,* well-grounded appearances. They are appearances rooted in the purely intelligible workings of force.[7] The distinction between appearance and essence, outer and inner, expressed and expressing finds its most provocative formulation in Spinoza, who distinguishes between *natura naturata* and *natura naturans.* The former term refers to nature as the finite things that have been "natured forth." The latter is nature as ground—nature continually at work "naturing" as the infinite source of finite appearances.[8]

Since phenomena or appearances first come on the scene in this chapter, we may expect Hegel's analysis of force to have a special importance for the *Phenomenology* as the *logos* of the *phainomena* of spirit. Force is self-manifestation, a One that becomes a Many, an invisible inner that shows itself in the perceptual, outer world. But Hegel's book does not end with force. Force is not the absolute. Why is this the case? Why is force not sufficient to explaining how an inner makes itself outer? In pursuing this question, we will come to see why consciousness must move beyond the pseudo-depth of nature to the genuine depth of spirit—why nature points beyond itself to *man* and his history.

The previous two shapes of consciousness had their charm and their privations. The force-world is vastly more interesting than the static picture-world of Thises and things. But it is not the whole of experience. What, then, is missing from the world of force?

To begin with, this world contains motion and vibrant emergence but no organic *life.* This in spite of Leibniz' *vis viva,* living force, which operates in inanimate things like colliding bodies.[9] Also absent is the diversity of beings according to *kind,* which was absent at the previous two stages as well. Kind or genus will come on the scene with organic life.[10] Another privation is *purpose.* Force is not fully spontaneous. It is not self-initiating and self-directing, as we shall see, but must be "solicited" by something outside it. As Hegel notes in the *Encyclopaedia Logic,* force "works blindly" (193). Understanding thinks in terms of law rather than purpose.[11] It is not yet *reason,* which, as Hegel says in the Preface, is "purposive or goal-directed activity" [22]. To sum up, what is missing in the world of force is nature in Aristotle's sense of the term: nature (*physis*) as living, speciated, and directed to an end.[12]

The preceding shapes of consciousness manifested three stages of dialectical experience: *in-itself, for-itself,* and *in-and-for-itself.* In the first, truth was in the object; in the second, it was in the conscious subject; and in the third, truth was in the relation of subject and object. Understanding will undergo a similar tripartite experience in force, law, and explanation. **Force** is understanding's effort to locate the truth in an external object. **Law** is the truth as an inner, purely thinkable essence. And **explanation** is the attempt to mediate and connect the outward looks of sensed things with their inner, invisible essence.

In the present chapter, I take up the dialectic of force: in the next, the dialectic of law and explanation. Below is a brief summary of Hegel's entire account of understanding.

In the first phase of the dialectic [132–42], we are introduced to our new object, force, and follow its *logos* to the eventual collapse of force as an independent, substantial being. Force ultimately becomes something non-essential, an insubstantial "play" of vanishing moments that Hegel calls appearance, *Erscheinung.*

In the second phase [143–53], Hegel develops a powerful critique of "incomplete idealism." I use this term to suggest that understanding *almost sees* that thought itself, the I, is the substance of things or the absolute: that thinking and being, to quote Parmenides, are the same. In its incomplete idealism, the understanding posits a supersensible world or Beyond [*Jenseits*] as the objectified interior of things. This interior is the understanding's unwitting projection of *itself.* Hegel calls it the "restful kingdom of law." This "other world" is somehow above, beneath, within, and beyond the world of appearance. It is what the world "really" is, its invisible core or essence.

In the third phase [154–65], the process of explaining [*Erklären*], the characteristic act of the scientific understanding, mediates between essence and appearance, inner and outer, sober law and playful force. But the kingdom of law is ultimately infected by the very instability and flux it was intended to ground. The relation of ground to grounded becomes reflexive, or reversed. Like the thing of perception, law becomes logically porous. The otherness of appearance invades its kingdom and makes law other than itself. Sobriety becomes drunkenness—the bacchanalian frenzy of Hegel's Preface [47].

The perversion of law is embodied in a second supersensible world. This is the famous *inverted world,* which continues to puzzle commentators. The inverted world transforms the finite determinations of the first supersensible world into their opposites. In this topsy-turvy world, the stable principles the understanding posited in order to stabilize motion and appearance are de-stabilized. They are shown to be nothing other than flux itself.

The transition from perception to understanding is more dramatic than the previous shift from sense-certainty to perception, as consciousness now moves from the realm of sense to the realm of thought. This corresponds to the transition on Plato's divided line from the lower regions of imagination (*eikasia*) and trust (*pistis*) to the region of *dianoia* or mathematical intelligence (*Republic* 6.509D ff.). The transition at the end of Hegel's chapter on understanding will also be more dramatic than any we have witnessed so far. It is in fact the most momentous transition in the whole *Phenomenology:* the turn from *consciousness* (in its restricted sense) to *self-consciousness.* As self-consciousness, consciousness (in its broad sense) ceases to look for truth in objects and posits *itself* as absolute. At this crucial point in spirit's journey, the most dynamic, expressive being of all—man—first comes on the scene.

With this sketch of things to come, let us now enter the labyrinth of force. Here, we will witness the ironic spectacle of thought running away from its destiny as the universal soul and essence of things. Universality is the offspring of thought, the very act and movement of thinking. But thought *as understanding* does not yet recognize itself in its object: force. Renouncing its paternity, it keeps trying to make universality into something other than thought itself—something static, objectified, and "out there."

The Concept of Force [132–36]

Hegel's for-us prelude, here, is more complex than those of previous chapters.[13] The opening paragraph is especially difficult. The word force occurs only later [136]. Hegel wants to make sure that we do not treat this new object merely as the next topic. He stresses, as he did in the chapter on perception, that this object is the logical result of the previous stage. "In the dialectic of sense-certainty, seeing and hearing," Hegel tells us, "have been lost to consciousness," and in the dialectic of perception "consciousness has arrived at thoughts" [132]. What arises now is truth as *Concept* [*Begriff*]. This is the intelligible as such. But just as perception had a new object that it did not know was the result of the previous dialectical process, so too, understanding fails to grasp the true nature of what it now posits. In its blindness, it takes the Concept, not as the dialectical motion that it is, but as a thinkable, static, thing-like *object.*

Thinghood failed because perception could not sustain its fundamental distinction between the thing's being-for-self or independence and its being-for-another or dependence. The distinction vanished and, in vanishing, gave rise to a new universal: the *unity* of being-for-self and being-for-another. This unity, the result of determinate negation, is what Hegel called "unconditioned absolute universality" at the end of the chapter on perception [129]. As the thing dissolved into its relations, relation itself became true and real. That is what force logically is, as Hegel explicitly states in an early version of his System. It is the category of *relation* made real in the world of things, their properties, and their behavior.[14] Force is the former One of perception now re-conceived as a One that "reaches out" to connect with other Ones like itself. In positing force, understanding embraces as essential what for perception was unessential.

A good example of force is *hardness.* For perception, hardness is a static property lodged in a body (along with other properties like shape and color). It was a *conditioned* or be-thinged [*bedingt*] universal. But for the scientific understanding, hardness is the force of resistance inherent in all matter. It is the counter-striving I feel when I hit my fist against a wall. The action of my fist arouses—or, to use the term Hegel borrows from Leibniz, *solicits*—an equal and opposite reaction by the wall. This is Newton's famous Third Law, which states the equality of action and reaction. For perception, the arousal of properties by the presence of other things was non-essential—a fluke of perceptual comparisons. For the understanding, it is essential. That is to say, *interaction* or being-for-other is now essential to what a thing is. In opposing the force of my fist, in being hard, the wall asserts itself: it expresses its being as a being-for-self. When we get to self-consciousness, there will be a collision of human egos in a fight to the death [187]. There, hardness will be the unyielding being-for-self of egotism.

For us, the *unconditioned* universal that has come on the scene is thought itself, or the Concept. Thought and force ultimately *are* each other. This identity the understanding does not know. Thought, like force, is essentially the power or force of *relation.* It does not list attributes, like perception, but tries to establish logical connections. It wants necessity. Thought binds and connects even as it distinguishes and separates. Whereas a thing is a One *and* a Many, thought maintains its unity and self-sameness, becomes concrete, in the context of expansion, interconnectedness, and self-difference. In Platonic terms, the Form or Idea of justice, for example, is not less itself, less of an identifiable One, for having relations with the Forms or Ideas of moderation and courage. On the contrary, in these relations it is more itself, more fulfilled as the Form that it is. This is to say that there is an intelligible cosmos or whole.[15] To think is to relate, to grasp unity within difference and difference within unity. In the transition from perception to understanding, Hegel shows us that thought, as relation, is precisely the transcendence or sublation of *things.* As things logically dissolve in a network of relations, thought as relation logically appears. Thought is the vanishing of things.

The unconditioned universal, the Concept or thought itself, is now "the true object of consciousness" [132]. *We see* that consciousness has in fact generated this new universal out of its own experience and that the universality is consciousness itself. But consciousness does not: "the true object of consciousness is still just an *object* for it; consciousness has not yet grasped the Concept of the unconditioned [the absolute] as Concept." The object is a thinkable thing but not yet thought itself. This limited vision of the understanding is the incomplete idealism I mentioned earlier. Echoing the recurrent theme of *fear of the truth,* Hegel tells us that consciousness steps back or shrinks from what it has generated, as though on the brink of an abyss, from thought as the substance of things. Understanding has a curious relation to thought at this point. It hovers between perceiving and thinking, between things and thoughts. It wants to render motion thinkable, but it does not want to think motion as such. Although understanding posits intelligible objects, it still clings to a perceptual, thingly view of them. This view prevents consciousness as understanding from recognizing itself in its object.

Hegel draws an important conclusion from the understanding's incomplete idealism. Since consciousness does not recognize itself in its object, it has a merely passive relation to that object. The object, force, is hypothesized as simply *there.* Its work and effects are apprehended, perceived, but there is no process that connects this object to the understanding. Understanding does not regard itself as a process at all. It merely "looks on" (or is objective in the ordinary sense of the term) and takes its object immediately [133]. We, therefore, must do what it does not. We must, Hegel says, *be the Concept* (that is, think dialectically) and lift consciousness above the mere spectacle of forces at work in nature (and from the general hypothesis of force) to the logical development of what force is in truth.

The crucial word concept, *Begriff,* has two different meanings, here and elsewhere in the *Phenomenology.* The high sense is the one we have been discussing: the Concept as pure intellectual transparency, thought itself or intelligibility. But in its other, "lower" sense, concept refers to the mere thought of something *as opposed to* what that thing is in reality, a *mere* concept or an abstraction. This more ordinary meaning of concept springs from the finite, thingly habits of the understanding. We hear this usage in phrases like "the concept of force" or "the concept of anxiety." If force is to be absolute, it must be real or objective. It must be the substance of things.[16] That is why Hegel says: "In order, then, that force may in truth *be,* it must be completely set free from thought" [136]. Force, in other words, must not be a mere idea in the mind. It must be substantial or real—something actual or *at work* in the perceptual world.

Things as objects of perception, though they are no longer absolute, are still very much with us in the force-world. This is another way of saying that the refutation of perception was a *determinate* negation, which preserved sensed properties by absorbing them into a higher unity. Force is the effort to save sensuous apparency by re-interpreting the thing's properties as the expression of force. Force is posited as the substance *of* things. For understanding, perceptual properties are present in the world, but they are no longer passively lodged in things. Instead, they radiate from an absolutely self-identical dynamic center. Although the thing is no longer absolute, there is still present the fundamental distinction that characterized thinghood: the distinction between the various matters (sensed properties) gathered in a Medium and the One that is "reflected into itself" [135]. What is new is that these two sides of the thing—One and Medium—are now unified by the new object (force).

In perception, this unity proved contradictory because the two sides (the logical relations of being-for-self or independence and being-for-other or dependence) were kept strictly apart. Now they grow together or coalesce in a single process. They "are no longer separate from one another at all but are in themselves essentially [*wesentlich*] self-superseding or self-canceling aspects, and what is posited is only their going-over [*Übergehen*] into one another" [135]. Once force is named as the new object, these two sides will also acquire their names. They will be *force proper* (being-for-self) and *force expressed* (being-for-other). The former will be force as a One contracted into itself, the latter force that has expanded into a Many or perceptual spread-out-ness. We may call them, respectively, *intensive* and *extensive* force.

The account of force as a process of self-negating moments, we must note, embodies *our* perspective. Understanding, like perception, has forgotten its logical past. It does not think its object as the dialectical unity of for-itself and for-another, independence and dependence. From its perspective, force is simply a means of saving the perceptual world from incoherence and instability. The expression of force, the emanation of perceptual qualities from a vibrant center, is, for understanding, direct and positive. It is the simple, non-dialectical translation of inner to outer. As we shall see, this portrayal of expression as purely positive or non-dialectical is why force-manifestation, the self-manifestation in which *natura naturans* presents itself as *natura naturata,* lacks both depth and truth. Truth, for Hegel, requires negation and self-sundering. It is not enough for the One of Plotinus or the *deus sive natura* ("God or nature") of Spinoza simply to radiate world and intelligence.[17] A true One must *sacrifice* its unity, tear itself in two, and suffer being an other to its own self. In short, *it must become self-conscious.*[18] This extraordinary idea of a One that sacrifices its own unity in order to be fully itself comes on the scene historically with Christianity and God's Incarnation. We will return to this search for a genuine, self-differentiating One in our next chapter.

Having established the purely logical character of the new object, Hegel finally names it: force, *Kraft*. Force is a movement or *Bewegung* [136]. The being of force consists wholly in its act. Force is the movement in which the many matters present in the thing of perception are posited as independent and simultaneously canceled as independent. These materialized properties radiate from a center that both sustains them in their existence (by giving them a medium) and cancels that independent existence (in order to draw them to itself). This was unthinkable for perception, which had a One-and-Many but not a One-expanding-into-Many and a Many-contracting-into-One. As a center of force, the One lets the properties out only to pull them back toward itself. Force is the movement in which "the 'matters' posited as independent directly pass over into their unity, and their unity directly unfolds its diversity, and this once again reduces itself to unity" [136]. The moment of expansion is expression or "utterance" [*Äußerung*]; and the moment of contraction to center (the vanishing point of properties) is force proper [*eigentliche Kraft*]. These moments are not successive but simultaneous.[19]

Hegel makes the crucial point that force proper *must* express itself. A force without an expression makes no sense. It would be like the force of heat that did not make things hot, or the force of motion that did not make a body move. Also, when force does express itself or comes out, it still remains "within itself." This must be true if the expression is the expression *of* force proper. Here we see most clearly why force is not identical with cause. Force is self-contained, like one of Leibniz' monads. It is a totality or relation that *contains,* or rather *is,* both cause and effect.[20] Force is not inner as opposed to outer but is rather the whole dynamic relation between inner core and outer appearance. Hyppolite puts it succinctly when he says that force, for Hegel, "is the unity of itself and its externalization" (121).

An analogy based on ordinary experience may help us see this identity of inner and outer. When I express myself, say, by uttering (that is, "outering") a strong opinion, I do not become other than myself. The utterance is not an ironic deception that masks and displaces a hidden interior, nor is it a change or transition into something other than what I was before. It is rather a direct coming out or unfolding of what is within. I am still "inside myself" during this process, since the strong opinion that I express or utter is an exact translation of what I hold within myself. Moreover, such expressions of opinion are addressed to others capable of receiving and understanding them. That is, human expression occurs in the context of human interaction. Also, my verbal expressions tend to be provoked or solicited by someone else's opinion, just as my saying what I think is likely to provoke my listener to say what he thinks, to express himself. Force is like the strong opinion that comes out in the context of human interaction. It is the naked exposure of an interior, for another and in response to another.

Just as force proper must express itself, and cancel its pure inwardness, so too, the expressed properties or matters must both "come out of" and *vanish back into* the unity whence they came. That is how force unifies the appearances. If the matters "came out" and existed, but did not at the same time go back in or return to the center, then we would be back in the thing of perception, where the properties took on a life of their own apart from their sustaining medium. Force would spend itself in its expression, squander its being-for-self, and be *only* a being-for-another. Lacking unity, it would not be force as the substance of things.[21] Force proper must be that which does the expressing *and* that into which the expressed matters return or disappear as their vanishing point. As force expresses itself, it cancels its mere inwardness. But at the same time, expressed force too is canceled as something other than, and independent from, the expressive unity. As the identity of inner and outer, force must express itself. But it must also *stay within itself.* It must remain an inner unity or monad in the midst of its outward expression [136]. What understanding considers as the direct, unproblematic move from inner to outer, we will experience as the dialectical process by which force undermines itself.

Hegel concludes his for-us discussion by reminding us that this double movement from intensive One to extensive Many, and from Many to One, is in fact nothing but the movement that defined *perception.* This is a timely reminder of what Hegel had said in his Introduction: that in the dialectic of experience, the new object is generated by the subjective experience of the old object [85]. As perception, consciousness went back and forth between ascribing unity to the object and manyness to itself, and ascribing manyness to the object and unity to itself. This oscillation of consciousness between One and Many "here has objective form and is the movement of force" [136]. In the course of this movement, force will *lose* its objective form. It will give rise to the unconditioned universal as "the *inner* of things qua *inner* [142]." This inner is *law.*

The Work of Force [136–41]

After this complex setting out of force as it is "for us," the experience of force gets underway. Force will suffer a fate similar to that of the sensuous This and the thing of perception. Just as the This "jumped outside itself" and became other Thises, and the thing dissolved in its relations to other things, so too the single force will "jump outside itself" and ultimately dissolve in a relation or "play of forces." This self-negation takes place in two stages. Initially, the single force will split into two opposed forces: active and passive. These two forces will become identical. They will lose the determinateness that makes them independent. The truth of force is that force is not substantial or real at all. It is rather a passing moment in the more encompassing process called *appearance* [*Erscheinung*]. The scientist posits force in order to explain and ground motion. In the end, force turns out to *be* motion.

The logical spelling out of how force is actual, or at work, in the perceptual world relies heavily on the phenomenon of *solicitation.* This term, which Hegel takes from Leibniz, refers to the process by which a potential releases its expressive power and becomes actual.[22] Solicitation suggests prompting, and even sexual enticement. Logically, it represents the attempt to explain how force can be independent or for itself while still depending on another for the occasion and "arousal" of its independence.

Hegel begins, as I mentioned above, with a single force as an intensive *point* of expressivity. He compels us to focus, momentarily, on a pure potency or striving, apart from its expression. This is force proper: what Newton calls a "center of force." Force here is a One "reflected into itself," that is, withdrawn from all difference and dispersion. It is force implicit or un-manifested. This potency is the very substance of force as force, the point of emergence that transcends mere thinghood, grounds properties in a dynamic unity, and at the same time prevents them from taking on a life of their own. We must note that the opposition we saw in the thing—that between the One and the Medium—is still operative here. Understanding quite logically first identifies force with the One and then *discovers* that force must also be the other as well, the Medium.

In using the word potency, we must be careful not to confuse force with Aristotelian potency or *dynamis*. For Aristotle, a *dynamis* may or may not express itself as an actuality (*energeia* or being-at-work). It is like a beast in the jungle. The beast can stay hidden and not pounce for as long it wants. Not so for force, which must express itself [136]. Force, dynamism, is force-at-work, a potency always in act, a beast always pouncing.[23] Force is no more potency, *as opposed to* actualization, than it is cause *as opposed to* effect. The modern concept of force as a form of inner necessitation is close to the Megarian doctrine Aristotle criticizes in the *Metaphysics.* According to this doctrine, "a thing is potent only when it is at work" (10.3.1046B29–30). Force proper is not, strictly speaking, an about-to-express-itself but an already-having-expressed-itself. It does not exist apart from its expression.

The argument by which Hegel derives two forces from one is frustratingly difficult. The following is my attempt to make some sense of it.

When we take force as an isolated One, then the unfolded matters (the former properties of the thing), by virtue of their belonging to the external realm of sensuous actuality, are *outside* of force, and force is *outside* of them. That is, the One and the Medium are first regarded as outside each other. By isolating force in its pure potency, we see that something *other than this force* must prompt force to express itself and "come outside," to get beyond its potency. Why can't force proper ignite its own expression? Because when it is taken with logical strictness, the isolated center of emergence, force prior to its actualization, cannot be more than itself, more than pure potency. The inciting influence, therefore, can only be "matters" that already exist *actually* in the external world. Hegel here recapitulates, within a modern context, an important teaching from Aristotle's *Metaphysics:* that actuality must be prior to potentiality (Book 9.8). But, as Hegel goes on to say, the "other" that approaches force and solicits it to act is really force itself in its expressed aspect. Where else could actual "matters" or properties come from in the force-world of understanding except expressed force?

Force is therefore not only the compressed, intensive One. It is also force that has expanded or expressed itself. This is the subsisting Medium of the unfolded matters [137]. So what was formerly thought of as other than force is really force itself. At first, it seemed as though the One and the Medium of matters were outside each other, and that the matters qua "other of force" were responsible for soliciting unexpressed force to express itself, and for soliciting expressed force to turn within. Solicitation at first seemed to be the action on force of matters external to force. But this proves not to be the case, for these matters are themselves *force that has expressed itself.* Solicitation must therefore be the direct action of force on force.[24]

At this decisive juncture, force splits into "two wholly independent forces" [138]. Their interaction recalls Newton's Third Law. The splitting or *Entzweiung* of force prefigures the doubling of self-consciousness in Hegel's next chapter. Just as force is independent only in the context of another, opposing force, so too a human One will seek its independence in the forceful confrontation with an opposing human One [175 ff.].[25] As we proceed through the *Phenomenology,* we will witness many reappearances of this self-splitting, which first comes on the scene with force.

We now have two interacting forces, one soliciting or active, the other solicited or passive. A force is prompted to express itself, and to withdraw from its expression, by another force. This distinction between action and reaction, which is affirmed in Newton's Third Law, is the rock on which the logical stability of force is founded. If it dissolves, then force falls as the substance of things and their properties. This, of course, is precisely what happens.

In this phase of the dialectic, Hegel reminds us that for consciousness *two* distinctions are at work simultaneously. There is a difference regarding content: force held within versus force expressed. And there is a difference of form or function: active or soliciting force versus passive or solicited force. Both distinctions, through their mutual relations, will prove problematic for understanding's effort to make force real.

We have two forces, each with a designated, exclusive function or determinateness. One solicits: the other is solicited. Furthermore, to bring in the difference in content, the soliciting force solicits by virtue of its *having expressed itself* or revealed its content. It therefore plays the role of the medium or unfolded matters with respect to the first force. But it could not have expressed itself, had its effect, unless it too had been solicited to unfold and then to withdraw back into unity by the very force that it was soliciting. This chicken-and-egg relation is the reciprocity that is necessary to force: what the soliciting force does to the other force, the other force does to it. But this means that the two opposite forces have *exchanged* their determinatenesses or *have become each other:* "each *is* solely through the other, and what each thus is it immediately no longer is, since it *is* the other" [141]. Hegel refers to this exchange, which constitutes the logical breakdown of force, as a play, *Spiel* [138].

The play of force, which is the dissolution of force's being-for-self, is beautifully illustrated in Leibniz' account of the collision of two bodies. Let moving body **A** hit resting body **B**, both metal spheres of equal mass. When **A** hits **B**, **B** responds. At the moment of impact, **A** and **B** act on each other equally and in opposite directions. This is in accord with Newton's Third Law. Both bodies suffer compression as they approach each other, then expansion as they recede. **A** awakens the force of resistance in **B**, *but* **B** *just as much awakens the force of resistance in* **A**. The resistance in both is the cause of the resultant motion in the system of two bodies. Each force is solicited and soliciting, passive and active. Each is active *insofar as* it is passive, and passive *insofar as* it is active: the action is a response or passivity, and the passivity is an action. The two opposed forces are not merely complementary but identical: they exchange their logical determinateness. To anticipate a phenomenon we meet in the next chapter, the opposite poles of force *contain each other.* Leibniz presents this reciprocity as a beautiful dance of forces, a harmonious solution to the problem of impact.[26] For Hegel, however, it spells the logical breakdown of force, the violation of the distinction on which force depends: active and passive, soliciting and solicited.

The identity of active and passive can be seen in our earlier example of the interaction between my fist and the wall. According to Newton's Third Law, when I hit the wall, the wall hits back with equal force. At first, it seems that my fist was active, and the wall passive or merely reactive. But I could not hit the wall unless, at the moment of impact, it acted on me and solicited the hardness of my fist. This hardness is just as much solicited by the hardness of the wall, as the hardness of the wall is by my fist. Fist and wall have exchanged logical determinations, and it is impossible to call one the agent and the other the patient. Each is both. Newton's Third Law thus expresses the *nullity* of force. The vanishing of the determinations of force into each other foreshadows the more dramatic identity of opposites that arises later in the context of Hegel's "inverted world."

The self-defeating truth of force is brought about through a conspiracy of the distinction with respect to content and the distinction with respect to form. On the side of content, force was either a self-withdrawn One or the Medium of unfolded matters (perceptible qualities). On the side of form, it was either active or passive, soliciting or solicited. Both distinctions collapse in the dialectic of force. Consciousness as understanding witnesses a double collapse. We, however, witness it as a single collapse, as the collapse of the very distinction of form and content. The reason is that we see *across* the distinctions of form and content. We see that the active, soliciting, and independent side of form is really the same as the intensive One on the side of content; and that the passive, solicited, dependent side of form is really the same as the medium of expressed, unfolded matters [140].

The task of the understanding was to liberate its concept of force from mere ideality, from being a *mere* thought [136]. Thus did understanding hope to transform its certainty into truth. That attempt resulted in the splitting of force into two opposed forces, which subsequently *became* each other. In light of this "identity loss," the distinction between the two forces dissolves and the duality melts into "an undifferentiated unity" [141]. This unity is not the original *objective* unity we started with—force proper—for this was shown to be only a passing moment in the dialectic of force. It is rather force's "concept qua concept." Thanks to the dialectic of experience, we now have the *truth* and *actuality* of force, which turn out to be the *thought* of force! That is what Hegel means by saying, "The *concept* of force preserves itself as the *essence* in its very actuality" [141]. In Hegel's striking formulation, "The realization of force is at the same time a loss of reality."

Another World [142–44]

This loss of reality, however, is also a gain. Force as substance has vanished in a play of forces. But since negation is determinate, the collapse of force generates yet another universal: "the inner of things qua inner" [142].

What understanding has uncovered in this generation of an inner qua inner is *idealism*. This is the doctrine that thought itself is the substance and truth of the world. (Idealism will emerge fully at the level of reason [232].) But consciousness recoils from this conclusion. It clings to the notion that truth must be objective and therefore grounded in something other than thought itself. Understanding takes its own experience of force, its own process of reflection, and projects it as a static entity *outside* the world of things. The result is a weird objectified non-object [136]. Hegel calls this unwitting self-projection a *Jenseits* or Beyond [144], Another World, as opposed to the *Diesseits* or This World. *We* see that this other world is thought itself. But understanding, which finitizes and objectifies everything it touches, and which "does not yet know the nature of the Concept" [143], regards this newly generated universal as a purely intelligible world *over and above* the vanishing world of sense. Forces are no longer posited as independent substances or Ones. They are now only vanishing moments that playfully exchange identities. This play is what we call appearance, *Erscheinung*.[27]

With the emergence of the opposition between appearance and the supersensible world, the chapter enters its most fascinating territory. Here, Hegel mounts a critique of what may be called the understanding's *ontological legalism*, the identification of being with law. In this second part of his chapter, he takes us through the process by which the laws of nature, put forth by physicists like Newton, prove to be logically incoherent. But in its broader sweep, the critique applies to all instances of otherworldliness as examples of incomplete idealism. These include Plato's Forms, Kant's thing-in-itself, and the Christian Kingdom of Heaven.

Oh, judge for yourselves: I have been concealing it all the time, but now I will tell you the whole truth. The fact is, I—corrupted them all!
DOSTOEVSKY, "The Dream of a Ridiculous Man"

 6

Principles of Motion and the Motion of Principles

(UNDERSTANDING, CONTINUED)

IN EACH OF ITS THREE PHASES, CONSCIOUSNESS POSITED AN ABSOLUTELY self-same One. For sense-certainty, this was the spatiotemporal atom or This, for perception the thing, and for understanding force. In the dialectic of experience, each of these Ones became a process of self-othering or self-differentiation. The Here and the Now became self-different as a series of Here's and Now's, the thing a relating of the thing to other things, and force the identity of active and passive forces.

In all these phases, consciousness posited difference or otherness outside its One. The One was kept self-same and uncompromised. But in the course of experience, difference invades the One, becomes internal to it, thus revealing the One (the This, the thing, force) as self-different and self-contradictory. As we saw at the beginning of the last chapter, each moment of self-differentiation or inner difference gave birth to a new universal. *We* see this new universal for what it is: the process of mediation [20–21]. But consciousness always takes it as a simple, non-dialectical *object*. It has not yet arrived at the stage at which truth is grasped as *subject* [17]. Consciousness, in other words, is not yet able to think the Concept.

The culmination of the dialectic of understanding is the metamorphosis of consciousness into self-consciousness. This transition signals the emergence of self-differentiation or inner difference within the One. Self-differentiation is the work of self-consciousness. As self-consciousness, I distinguish myself from myself in order to identify myself with myself. I generate an inner difference or "gap" between myself and myself. Self-consciousness is self-identity through self-differentiation. It is the human experience of the dialectical structure of identity. It is also the source of the movement that undermined all the attempts consciousness has made so far to posit an absolutely self-same, restful One. This movement is the negativity that Hegel identifies with subject or self in the Preface [37].

Internal difference or self-differentiation helps us see what is at work in the *Phenomenology* as a whole, and why self-consciousness is crucial to the full revelation of the Concept as dialectical knowledge or Science. Hegel's chapter begins with Concept and ends with self-consciousness. These endpoints are ultimately identical. Concept and self-consciousness have the same logical structure: the self-differentiation of the self-same. In his Preface, Hegel calls this process mediation, *Vermittlung*, or "self-moving self-sameness" [21]. Genuine thought is conceptual self-development. It is the dialectical motion in which a logical structure or category spontaneously unfolds by revealing its inner tensions and differences. This is the key point: that in the genuine, dialectical thinking that is the Concept, thought *generates its own content* by producing differences from within itself. It is like the organic processes of cell division and embryonic development. This is why Concept and self-consciousness, as generators of inner difference, are identical.[1]

The whole journey of consciousness is the search for a self-differentiating One that *knows itself* as a self-differentiating One. This is truth in the form of subject or self [17]. This One is philosophy in the form of Science. It is thought that is no longer dependent on immediate givens, contents, and differences that come from the outside, but is free to develop content and difference spontaneously or from itself. Science, for Hegel, is the autonomy of thought. And the Concept, in its precise designation, is autonomy as self-differentiation. As Hegel says in the *Science of Logic:* "with the Concept, therefore, we have entered the realm of *freedom*" (582). When self-consciousness steps forth as the truth of understanding, and of consciousness in general, it is the Concept itself finally making its appearance. This is perhaps Hegel's most remarkable idea: that as self-conscious beings, we bear within us the prefigurement of philosophy in the form of Science, absolute knowing. In the final chapter of the *Phenomenology*, consciousness or subject will experience its identity with objective, divine truth.

The dramatic conclusions here indicated begin to emerge in the dialectic of law. Law, *Gesetz*, will give rise to explanation, and explanation will be revealed as tautological or circular, as the process in which differences are posited only to be canceled. The cancellation of difference then becomes internal to law itself. This in turn gives rise to the inverted world, and to the internal differentiation that *is* self-consciousness.

The First Supersensible World [143–55]

In our last chapter, the collapse of force produced a new universal: "the *inner* of things qua *inner*" [142]. This will soon be "the law of force" [148]. In this supersensible or inner world, consciousness posits the opposite of what it had put forth in sense-certainty. Sense-certainty wanted to make the sensuous This the absolute. As I noted at the end of Chapter 3, the *Phenomenology* is the continued mediation of the sensuous This. By now, the This has been so thoroughly mediated that the sensuous world has lost all claim to being independent or for itself, something on its own. It is now only a flux and play of ever-shifting relations, sheer otherness. Sensuous objects have become appearance.

We saw in our last chapter that universality, for Hegel, emerges from, and is, a dialectical process. Consciousness will interpret this process as a non-dialectical object or *Gegenstand.* The "old" universal was force proper, intensive force that was "driven back into itself" [142]. The "new" universal is the result of what consciousness has just experienced: force's loss of reality and the identification of the *being* of force with the *thought* of force. Understanding, still attempting to save the perceptual world from dissolution, takes this being that is also a thought and makes it into a more rarefied, purer universal—"the *inner* of things *qua* inner" [142]. If force is the interior of perceptual things, then this new universal is "the interior of the interior" (Rosen, 148).

From the perspective of understanding, the inner world has opened up *beyond* the realm of appearances. Consciousness looks toward this world but only indirectly "sees" it. The seeing must be indirect because all Thises have vanished in the play of force. Consciousness "has a mediated relation to the inner being and, as the understanding, *looks through this mediating play of forces into the true background* [*Hintergrund*] *of things*" [143]. Understanding does not look *away* from appearance to see being. Rather it looks through appearance as through a veil. It sees appearance pointing to a stable being beyond appearance, not realizing that this projected being is itself. Hegel points out that appearance [*Erscheinung*] is not mere illusion or show [*Schein*] but a "*totality* of show." What he seems to mean is that appearance must be seen in light of the inner world to which it points. The inner world contains and grounds appearance, thus making it into a gathered, unified realm—a theatrical display of universality. This is what the ancient Greeks called a beautifully ordered whole or *kosmos.*

This is the first time consciousness posits a system of mediation. As understanding, it posits a structure composed of three terms: the understanding itself, the supersensible world, and appearance. To the watchful eye of the philosophic observer, this structure is the *syllogism* [145].

The syllogism is not a formal method but the truth and substance of things. As we hear in the *Science of Logic,* "Everything is a syllogism" [669].[2] The syllogism is mediation, *rationality,* made explicit. Ordinarily, the syllogism is understood as a formal, linear mode of inference in which two propositions called premises yield a third, the conclusion:

All men are mortal.
Socrates is a man.
Therefore, Socrates is mortal.

For Hegel, however, the syllogism properly understood is not an argument composed of three propositions, but a dialectical interrelation of three terms: two extremes and a mean. In the syllogism above, the extreme term "Socrates" refers to something *individual* (**I**). The mean term "man" is one of Socrates' *particulars* (**P**) or properties. And the other extreme term, "mortal," is a *universal* (**U**) that contains the particular. In schematic form, the syllogism is **I – P – U**, which indicates that the individual, *Socrates,* unites with its logical extreme, *mortality,* through the particular property, *humanity.* My silver pen is a syllogism, although it is hardly a series of three propositions. It is an individual thing (**I**) that experiences a unity with the universal "color" (**U**) through its determinate property "silver" (**P**).

In both these examples, the determinate property, as middle term, mediates between the extremes of individuality and universality. It is not a tertium quid or "third something" inserted "between" the two extremes. These extremes are not separate from each other. In the genuine syllogism, the syllogism of terms rather than propositions, the middle term is the unity of opposites. It is the logical moment in which universal and individual *pass into each other.* Sometimes Hegel describes the all-important middle term as suffering a *dichotomy* or *splitting* [*Entzweiung*] into its extremes. Force, for example, was portrayed as a middle term that split into the extremes of active and passive [136]. Hegel will use similar language to describe self-consciousness, which splits into two opposed, mutually antagonistic self-conscious individuals [184].

In the present context, the extreme terms are the understanding and the supersensible world. The mediating or mean term is appearance as the play of force.[3] The individual here (**I**) is the individual consciousness that seeks knowledge. The ultimate object of that knowledge is the supersensible realm of pure universality (**U**)—the stable essence that the individual knower longs to "see." Appearance is the rich, if unstable, realm of endless particulars (**P**) like "hot" and "cold," which are instances of the pure universals or Forms, Hot and Cold. Understanding posits these three terms but does not grasp their fluid interrelation. Playing on the German word for syllogism, *Schluß* (literally, closure or conclusion), Hegel says that understanding will come to experience the "being-bound-together" [*Zusammengeschlossensein*] of its three terms. In particular, it will experience the *vanishing* of the middle term, appearance, as a separately existing realm. With this disappearance of the "curtain" separating the individual from the supersensible world, the two extremes will become identical, and understanding, in peering into the Beyond, will gaze into *itself* [165].

Hegel likes catching the bird just as it is about to take flight. He did this with force when he isolated force proper. Here Hegel catches the bird of false transcendence. He pauses to consider the sheer emptiness of the Beyond that understanding has unwittingly projected. He reflects at some length on how this Beyond, which is "merely the nothingness of appearance," has taken hold of the human imagination and speculative thought. The projection of a Beyond, we must note, applies to both hard-core rationalists and orthodox Christians. Both are victims of the superstition of the Beyond. The prime example of rationalist projection is Kant, whose things-in-themselves (the *noumena* or pure thinkables) represent the Unknowable with respect to human cognition. For Hegel, the reason why the Beyond is unknowable is that there is nothing there to know! He observes that, divining the emptiness of the Beyond, we proceed to call it "the holy" and to fill it with *dreams* [146]. The passage is not mere rhetoric. Hegel is indicating the danger involved in positing a supersensible world. As we shall see in his account of self-consciousness, the self's projection of a Beyond, though necessary to the education of consciousness, is the source of man's unhappiness, self-estrangement, and un-freedom.

Before identifying the inner world as law, Hegel first dwells on the logical structure of this new object. He shows us appearance for what it is. In one of the most revealing passages in the *Phenomenology,* Hegel reminds us that the inner world is not a given, but rather something that has *originated from* appearance [147]. Although this inner world is posited as the pure transcendent essence of appearances, appearance is in fact the essence and "filling" of the inner world.[4] This fact foreshadows the upcoming phenomenon of inversion. Essence is, in fact, not transcendent but immanent. It is *within* the actual world of appearance. Essence is nothing other than the mediation or self-cancellation that constitutes appearance as the play of force. This is the meaning of Hegel's crucial sentence: "The supersensible [the realm of intelligible essence] is therefore *appearance qua appearance.*"[5]

Let us examine the meaning of this pronouncement.

For Hegel, as for Plato, appearance is becoming or flux [148–49]. It is the sensed world conceived, not as thises or things but as a thoroughly unstable and fascinating play, in which all sorts of finite determinations (hot, cold, wet, dry, bitter, sweet) are always turning into each other and have no being of their own. We see this play in the receptacle of Plato's *Timaeus.*[6] Like time, appearance as flux is always negatively transcending itself. It continually cancels and *goes beyond* whatever appears.[7] As appearance, the world is experienced as inherently dialectical: as ceasing to be what it is and coming to be what it is not. In its natural or uneducated condition, consciousness as understanding turns away from this flux as the truth of things. It takes the immanent "beyond-ing" or self-cancellation that appearance *is* and objectifies this essence as a transcendent Beyond.

The dialectic of the inner world begins with *difference* [148]. Difference, or self-otherness, defines the flux of appearance. As we recall, the attempt to maintain force as the absolute substance of things required several distinctions or oppositions: form versus content, proper versus expressed force, the One versus the Medium of materialized properties. All these opposites vanished in the course of experience. They were reduced to passing moments. Hegel calls what is left "absolute exchange or flux" [*Wechsel*] [148]. This is difference as such, universal difference or otherness. It is difference without regard for the *things* that are different: strictly speaking, things as things have vanished. Understanding recoils from a dialectical grasp of this difference and expresses it as "*the simple in the play of force itself* and what is true in it." This "simple" now defines the supersensible world. It is the "*law of force*" [148].

It seems strange to define law in terms of difference. We tend to think of law as abiding and self-same. But the eternal self-sameness of law is unthinkable without difference. Law governs things that are constantly shifting: matter in motion. It expresses the eternal self-sameness *of* the perpetually self-different.

Galileo's law of free fall is a case in point [152]. According to this law, a falling body traverses spaces that vary as the square of the times. This is expressed mathematically as $s \propto t^2$ ("s varies as the square of the time"), where $\propto$ is the symbol for variation or mathematical *difference*. Its equation-form is $s = \frac{1}{2}gt^2$, where g is the constant force of gravitational attraction. Bodies fall. They exhibit difference with respect to location and time. But when they fall, regardless of the circumstances, Galileo's law, with its constant ratio, is there to "catch" them, that is, to universalize them and gather the fallings into its restful unity. The law is the eternal self-sameness of spatiotemporal differences. It is universality at work within the appearances. Law is itself a negative "force." It cancels or negates particulars as such (this particular rock, planet, or magnet). It thinks away all their irregularities and qualitative differences in order to "lift" them into universal differences mathematically expressed—into the ether of *pure theory.*

Law makes no more sense without flux than does force without its expression, or a governor without a country to govern. Like a Platonic Form, law is the stabilizer of unstable appearances.[8] But in order to govern, law must also be kept strictly separate from that which it governs. Self-sameness and self-difference must be kept apart. Law must paradoxically touch, pervade, and even contain the realm of appearance without being corrupted by the otherness that realm exhibits. The problem of law is the same as that of *separateness* and *participation* in the *Parmenides.* Plato's dialogue poses the following question: How can a purely intelligible One, the separate *eidos* or Form, manifest itself in its sensuous instances without being infinitely divided or infinitely duplicated and thus made other than itself? If the Forms are radically separate and constitute a pure realm as opposed to the impure realm of sense, how can these absolutely separate spheres have anything to do with each other?[9] How is appearance possible at all? And if the Forms are radically separate from one another, as well as from sensuous participants, then, to use an image from Plato's *Sophist,* how is speech itself possible as an "interweaving of Forms" (259E)?

The connection with Plato is made even stronger by the language Hegel uses in describing the supersensible world as the "restful kingdom of laws" [149]. This kingdom is "the *constant* image or picture [*Bild*] of unstable appearance." Image, in this context, recalls Plato's designation of the perceptual world as a place of images. This designation is memorably captured in the allegory of the cave in the *Republic* and elaborated in the cosmology of the *Timaeus.* Even more striking is Hegel's inversion of the relation of image to original. The fact that the kingdom of law was dialectically derived from the play of force means that this kingdom is the *image,* and appearance the *original.* This is a re-play of the inversion of essence and appearance we saw earlier. The inversion reminds us that what the understanding takes as immediately "there" is for us the result of mediation, and that what it takes as original is in fact the unwitting projection of itself.

As we now grapple with Hegel's brilliant exposé of law, let us recall how experience works in the *Phenomenology.* Consciousness posits an absolute, and then tries to transform this mere concept or certainty into truth. Law is the new prospective absolute. Understanding must now put it to work as an actual governor of appearances.

The problem is that law, as universal, is purely formal or empty. All content is in the realm of unstable appearance. As we saw earlier, understanding appeals to law, not in order to fly off mystically into a billowy Beyond, but to ground the appearances. Law must apply to its instances. In order to be true, it must "fill out appearance" [150]. Law must regulate and therefore pervade the ever-shifting appearances. This will not happen unless appearances have every vestige of independence or being-for-self taken away from them. There must be nothing in the appearances that remains uncovered by law. Casting ahead to Hegel's next chapter, law, in order to be master, must make appearance its slave.

The instances law must "cover" are particulars within the ever-shifting realm of appearance. No one law is sufficient to this task for the simple reason that law, though stable, is general or empty, while appearance, though shifty, is full or differentiated. Since any one law is always an idealization or abstraction, there must be many laws to accommodate ever-changing circumstances or cases. An account of free fall, for example, that did justice to the appearances would have to include a law governing air resistance. This effort to give law content and inner difference poses a problem. Law, as a One, must unify. It cannot unify the appearances if it fails to unify itself. The understanding therefore posits a universal law of force—the law of attraction—as the mega-law into which all other laws of force "collapse" [150]. This refers to Newton's famous law, according to which the force of attraction (F) between two masses varies inversely as the square of the distance (r) between them: $F \propto 1/r^2$. Other laws, such as Galileo's law for free fall, or Kepler's laws of planetary motion, are special cases of the mega-law.[10]

If understanding were willing to rest content with mental constructs, mere notions, then this intellectual bread and water (formalism) would be enough for it. But it does not want abstractions. It wants the meaty truth of experience. And so, the dialectic goes on, as understanding struggles to connect the abstract formalism of law with the concrete content of appearance. What this means is that the inner, supersensible world of law, in order to reveal itself for what it is, must, as I noted above, absorb all aspects of appearance into itself. This absorption will be completed, as we shall see, only with the emergence of the inverted world [161].

The purported solution to the understanding's problem of "participation" is *necessity* [*Notwendigkeit*]. Necessity is how law, which is otherwise formally detached from appearances, becomes actual, how it goes to work *within* the appearances.[11] Necessity is necessitation, or the determinism of cause and effect. Hegel here gives his version of the problem of "necessary connection," first propounded by Hume (Hyppolite, 129). The understanding has the *idea* of necessary connection or causality. The question is whether it can make the idea actual. Hegel demonstrates that, notwithstanding Kant's effort to refute Hume, it cannot.[12] What understanding posits as inner necessity is, to quote Hume, no more than *constant conjunction.* As Hume had rightly stated, "necessity [as natural causality] is something that exists in the mind, not in objects."[13]

The non-necessity of necessity comes out in understanding's act of positing of differences that are not real differences in the thing. Understanding makes all sorts of distinctions in order to give law content, to make it "fit" and "cover" the wealth of appearances. These distinctions are various ways in which the essence of law is revealed as simple difference. Electricity, for example, is a simple force. But according to its law, electricity necessarily manifests itself as positive and negative. Hegel grants that once one kind of electricity is given, then its opposite is also given. There is a constant conjunction. But he denies that electricity as a simple force necessarily divides itself or, conversely, that the difference derives from electrical force as such. Hegel reaches a striking conclusion: "Electricity, as *simple force,* is indifferent to its law—*to be* positive and negative; and if we call the former its concept but the latter its being, then its concept is indifferent to its being" [152]. In other words, the two kinds of electricity might just as well be different properties, like white and cubical, constantly conjoined or lodged in an indifferent Also. What understanding posits as "inner necessity" is no more than two things that always appear together. Necessity in this case, says Hegel, is "an empty word" [152], fact masquerading as a cause or ground.

This logical indifference that masquerades as necessity gives Hegel an opportunity to revisit a theme from his Preface: the critique of mathematics. For Hegel, mathematical thinking, thinking in terms of quantity, lacks the self-development and inner necessity of the Concept [42–46]. Its cognitive model is that of a sequence of externally related steps rather than a dialectical, genetic unfolding of inner difference. In the present chapter, the example of mathematical thinking applied to nature is Galileo's formula for free fall: $s = ½gt^2$. Hegel's point is that although this law is verifiable by experiment, and mathematically demonstrable from more basic properties of motion, the terms combined in the law have no *inner* logical relation to one another. They are indifferent to one another and lack the genuine necessity of dialectical self-development. This logical indifference can be seen, Hegel claims, when we trace the mathematical demonstration of the law of free fall to its simplest elements. The mathematical physicist treats speed, distance, time (v, s, t) as magnitudes and for that reason as external to each other—as merely combined without being thought through. The mathematical formulation $v = s/t$, for example, simply states that these three elements "always go together." It does not explain the conceptual interrelation of speed, space, and time. Mathematical physics thus fails to express precisely what it is intended to express: the necessary connection among physical concepts.[14]

In stressing the deficiencies of mathematical laws of nature, we must not conclude that such laws are false or insignificant. On the contrary, Hegel says that Newton's law of universal attraction "has great importance" in that it wards off the thoughtless portrayal of nature as merely contingent and a collection of sensuous Thises [150]. The mathematical physicist is right to look for necessary order—that is, intelligibility—in nature. In the *Encyclopaedia* account of nature, he says that modern laws of motion are "immortal discoveries which constitute the highest honor of the analysis of the understanding" (remark to paragraph 267), and that the law of attraction in particular is "a profound thought" (remark to paragraph 269). What understanding fails to grasp is the dialectical, inner necessity, the work of the Concept, which makes these laws true, deeply true. Shrinking from philosophic truth, understanding transforms inner, conceptual relations into external quantitative ones. It substitutes mathematical empiricism for philosophy, and prides itself on doing so.[15]

With the breakdown of objective or natural necessity, understanding has failed to put law to work in the appearances. The differences posited within the law fail to be differences within the force itself that law is supposed to govern. The reason lies in the law's formality, made explicit as mathematical formalism (equations). Law cannot be filled, made to apply, without prejudice to its lawfulness; and it cannot be guarded as an absolute One without keeping it empty. This problem of formalism will recur throughout the *Phenomenology.*

Understanding has learned through experience that necessity is not in the actual forces that law governs, that law and force "are indifferent to one another" [153]. It concludes that difference as necessary self-unfolding must therefore be *within itself:* "It is, therefore, only its *own* necessity that is asserted by the understanding; the difference, then, is posited by the understanding in such a way that, at the same time, it is expressly stated that the difference is not a *difference belonging to the thing itself*" [154].[16] Inner necessity formerly meant "internal to appearance as governed by objective law." Now it means "internal to understanding." This new necessitation is the birth of yet another new universal and new process. It is the process understanding loves more than anything else in the world, more than the processes of nature that it seeks to ground. This is its own process of *explaining* or *clarifying, Erklären.*

Explaining or clarifying is the sophistical process in which distinctions are made "but not for real." Explanation is a charade in which distinctions are a pretense. Hegel proceeds to show how the explanatory process, which emerges dialectically from the breakdown of objective necessity, is at bottom tautological. This is fatal to what explanation intends, namely, to explain a phenomenon in terms of something deeper, to reveal something "new." On the positive side, tautology or circularity will generate self-consciousness as the self-differentiation of the self-same.

Understanding makes a distinction between law and force, between subjective formulation or theory and objective being. Force is supposed to be the objectively existing correlate of the law, the law's being-at-work. But force and law have the same logical structure and are therefore identical. The reason is that explanation "condenses the *law* into *force* as the essence of the law" [154]. Why does electricity divide into positive and negative? Explanation: Because that is its law. And why is that its law? Explanation: Because force divides itself into these two kinds of electricity. When we ask the understanding why something is the case, it pretends to show us the underlying ground and reason but in fact only repeats the fact that prompted the question in the first place, now under the cloak of a mysterious force. Why are human beings the way they are? Because of their genes. What are genes? That which makes us who we are. Why does opium put one to sleep? Because it has a "dormitive virtue."[17] Explanation, which natural consciousness tends to worship as revealed truth, is nothing more than the making of distinctions without a difference. As Hegel says in one of his early writings, it is ultimately the statement: "That is how it is."[18]

Tautology, however, is not mere repetition. It is a process of self-sublating, self-canceling difference. Explanation is the same positing and canceling of differences that defined appearance as the play of force [136]. Here, the play is the sophistic play of the understanding itself: "In the process, then, of explaining, the change and exchange [*Wandel und Wechsel*] that before was outside of the inner world and present only in the appearance, has penetrated into the supersensible world itself" [155]. Explanation undermines the august principles of the understanding, even as it uses them to "save the appearances." Now those principles are shown to have the same logical structure as the flux they were designed to ground and stabilize! The process of mediation that brings about this corruption of principles gives rise to a new law—and a strange world.

The Inverted World [156–60]

After the chapter on self-consciousness, Hegel's inverted world is perhaps the most commented on portion of the *Phenomenology.*[19] It is also the most cryptic. We first meet inversion in Hegel's Preface. There, natural consciousness and philosophic Science appear to each other as inverses, and Science seems to want natural consciousness to "walk on its head" [26]. The German word for inverted here, *verkehrt,* means both turned upside down and perverse or "twisted." Both meanings seem to be at work in Hegel's account of understanding's topsy-turvy world.[20]

The inverted world emerges from the shiftiness of explanation, that is, from the identity of explanation and the self-negating flux of appearance. At first, the shiftiness seems to infect only the subjective processes of the understanding itself, not the concrete actual world. But the inner world of the understanding is "the *inner being* of things" [156]. It is what the world, at bottom, *is.* What the understanding has experienced within itself is thus a new law that it sees as objectively governing appearances and constituting their essence. According to this new law, "Differences arise which are no differences," and "what is not self-same is self-attractive" [156]. Difference is no longer external to things as they are: it is now "inner difference" [157].

In its most general sense, inversion is simply contradiction or the dialectical change of something into its opposite. Every shape of consciousness we have seen so far has suffered inversion in this sense when it tried to transform its certainty into truth. In the present context, however, inversion has a more specific meaning. It is the change of the finite determinations of the first supersensible world into their opposites, the destabilizing and perversion of law. The inverted world is consequently a *second* supersensible world [157], a second "in itself" or essence, which is the *truth* of the first: "According, then, to the law of this inverted world, what is *like* in the first world is *unlike* to itself, and what is *unlike* in the first world is equally *unlike to itself*, or it becomes *like* itself" [158]. The inverted world is appearance or flux *made into a law.*[21]

It is important to stress that the inverted world is the truth of the first supersensible world. The understanding always thinks in terms of an inner world that duplicates and idealizes the outer world of appearances. The inverted world is the self-contradictory outcome of this duplication. It reveals that the sober understanding has been engaged in the antics of inversion all along.[22] Understanding wanted to grasp the actual world but refused to take that world on its own terms. In its incomplete idealism, it transformed the world of appearances into *another world* (the world of theory) in order to make appearance knowable. It took "low" sensuous things and lifted them into the heaven of pure thinkableness. Conversely, it took its "high" celestial principles and tried to put them to work in the world "down below." The inverted world makes clear that this twofold inversion—idealization of the impure and realization of the pure—leads to contradiction. All Beyonds lead to this self-negating result. The perversity of the inverted world is Hegel's way of showing us that, in truth, *there is only one world.*[23]

Since law expressed universality as mathematical formalism (equations), it failed to capture the whole of appearance in its world-picture or *Bild.* It was only the *immediate* raising up of appearance into universality. The inverted world completes the inner world *as* appearance [157]. It does so by doing what the first supersensible world failed to do: incorporate motion or flux, genuine otherness, into its structure. Again, this is the negative movement that Hegel identifies with the *self* [37]. As Hegel says, "The first kingdom of laws lacked that principle [of change and alteration], but it obtains it as an inverted world" [157]. Up to this point, universality was a process of mediation. But this process did not appear in the object of consciousness. Now it does. In a moment, we shall see how consciousness interprets this process.

Hegel's examples of inversion are initially what one would expect in the scientific world of the understanding. The inverted world changes sweet into sour, black into white, the north pole of the magnet into the south, and positive electricity into negative. In positing the first supersensible world (of sober law), understanding was obsessed with mathematical homogeneity: speed, space, time, and force were all magnitudes. In the second supersensible, inverted world, the scientist wakes up to a deeper aspect of his interest in nature: to the natural appearance of *polarity* and the natural unity of opposites. That is why the magnet, rather than electrical charge, is the prime example of inversion in science. The magnet, with its bound-together poles, is the observable, physical object in which opposites appear as inseparable.[24] It is the point at which theoretical physics becomes the study of opposites.

But then Hegel surprises us by shifting to higher, more spiritual ground. This is the Dostoevsky territory of crime and punishment [158]. In one spiritual instance of inversion, which recalls Macbeth's murder of his friend Banquo, the punishment of an enemy becomes a crime in which the murderer punishes himself. Macbeth acts on an "immediate law" (presumably, "an eye for an eye and a tooth for a tooth") and destroys his enemy, only to experience *himself* as a criminal who has, in effect, destroyed his bond with life and other human beings.[25] Macbeth's crime is like a force that evokes and solicits its corresponding corrective force, the force of moral retribution. Hegel's second example takes us to an even higher spiritual plane. In a reference to the many inversions that Jesus utters in the Gospels (for example, "the first shall be last"), Hegel says that what is despised in the apparent world, according to the first supersensible law, is honored in its inverted world, and vice versa. What is punishable under the first law merits pardoning grace [*Begnadigung*] under the second, "New Law."[26]

These spiritual instances of inversion make it clear that inversion is an historical phenomenon well before it is conceptualized in Hegel's dialectic of consciousness, and that it appears not only in theoretical physics but also in works of fiction and in the Bible. Gadamer points out that satire, for example, owes much to this idea (48). But it is with the teachings of Jesus, who turned the world upside down, that inversion receives its deepest and most exalted expression. As Hegel will say much later, Christianity, the teaching in which God *inverts himself* to become man, is the religion in which absolute spirit is "open" or manifest—not in concepts, but in images or representations [788].

Understanding regards the inverted world as a second supersensible Beyond, or more accurately, as a revision of its first Beyond. Formerly, the transcendent essence of things was an idealization of those things in universal law. Now, essence or the in-itself is the *opposite* of how the thing appears. It is a static, separate opposite that exists "off" in its own world. Hegel warns us against taking this "superficial" view of the inverted world, in which the opposing essence lies outside the appearances [159]. This is the view of natural, non-dialectical consciousness, which cannot "think pure change"

[160]. It is also the view of Kant, whose whole philosophy is a temple dedicated to *Verstand.*

According to the superficial view of inversion, what *appears* sweet to us is *in the thing itself* sour; or what *appears* to us to be the north pole of a magnet is *in itself* the south; or what *appears* punishable in "this world" may advance a man in the *other world* [159]. The superficial view is manifest in science when it tells us, "This table may *appear* solid, but we know that *in itself* it is mostly empty space." Or, "This rock seems to be at rest, but there's really a bunch of electrons whizzing around inside it." Or, more famously, "The earth appears to be at rest, but it is in itself orbiting around the sun." The Copernican Revolution is an instance of inversion superficially understood if it is taken to mean that one world-view was simply replaced by its opposite. So is Kant's Copernican Revolution in philosophy, which made the human knower rather than the object central to knowing but still had the subject on one side of the "fence of consciousness" and the thing-in-itself on the other. Kant failed to grasp inversion as the dialectical *motion* that connected subject and object.[27]

This, however, is not Hegel's last word on the relation that modern science has to inversion. Modern science, although it cannot think the Concept, is not always so superficial. In theorizing about the magnet, for example, science posits the unity of opposites in one and the same world: the world of appearances. Furthermore, philosophically minded scientists, like Leibniz, consciously posit opposites like mind and body, mechanism and teleology, active and passive force, and at least try to render their unity intelligible. At some level, the scientist knows that the world is paradoxical.

The superficial view of inversion infects the spiritual realm as well. The criminal who ends up suffering for his deeds blames society, his externally negating other, for the punishment he justly receives. He fails to see how his punishment is logically self-generated. So too, anyone who thinks that Jesus was speaking of a separately existing Other World as the polar opposite of "this world" misses the true depth of how true spirituality, for Hegel, reveals itself right here on earth.

All these external oppositions of two-world thinking are *gone* in the inverted world rightly understood: that is, as it is understood by the phenomenological observer. The world of appearance *is* the world of essence: essence and appearance are self-negating moments of a single process. Or rather, appearance, as *apophainesthai,* is the shining forth of essence. As I noted above, there is only one world. And inversion is its truth.

Hegel's main idea here is that inversion is the logical relation in which opposites are not external to each other but *contain and actively posit each other.* In the *Phaedo,* Socrates playfully compares pleasure and pain to two quarreling creatures that have had their heads tied together by the gods

(60B): where the one is, the other is sure to follow. Hegel makes the connection between opposites more intimate. One and the same thing or force contains opposites or polarities, not because of constant conjunction, but because each opposite necessarily contains and posits its other. Sour is sweet's own internal otherness. Without this otherness, there would be no such thing as sour. So too, the opposing poles of a magnet, as I noted earlier, cannot be separated. The south pole is the north's own otherness. And punishment is the fulfilled self-negation that crime bears within its own self. Inversion rightly understood is the inner difference or self-negativity that was implicit in every external distinction consciousness has made in the course of its experience. The logical process of inversion makes explicit that to negate is to posit and contain.

Inner difference obliges us "to think pure change, or *think antithesis within the antithesis itself*, or *contradiction*" [160]. In effect, it is impossible to isolate an opposite or "pole." The attempt to do so only evokes and awakens the opposite pole. Opposites *enspirit* or inspire each other [*begeistet*] [161]. To say that the north pole of a magnet is "in itself" south does not mean that it is south "in another world," but that it is really *in* the north pole itself, within it as a necessary part of its logical structure and identity. Opposites belong to a unitary process in which each cancels itself and affirms the other [161]. To use an image I referred to earlier, isolating a magnetic pole is like grabbing hold of Proteus, the Old Man of the Sea in Homer's *Odyssey:* the harder I squeeze, the more fluid and self-different he becomes. That is why the "clenched" immediacies of consciousness, all efforts to ward off logical motion, are vital to the begetting of that motion. Logical isolation is not a mistake to be avoided. It is rather the engine by which consciousness generates internal difference and brings it out into the open.

Again, it is important to emphasize that the inverted world is the truth of the realm of appearances. The first supersensible world took us beyond the appearances to a remote and sober realm of essence. The inverted world negates this negation of the appearances and so *returns* us to the appearances. From the perspective of the inverted world, things really are as crazy as they seem!

In the inverted world rightly understood, an opposite *contains* its opposite or has *inner* difference. Hegel's figurative way of putting this is to say that the inverted world has *overreached* [*übergegriffen*] the first supersensible world and "has it within it" [160].[28] This overreaching reminds us of previous overreachings: the process by which the Now "jumped outside itself" to become other Nows, by which the thing became other things, and force split in becoming a play of opposed forces. Inner difference, or the reciprocal containment of opposites, will now receive an evocative name: *infinity* [*Unendlichkeit*].

Infinity and the Birth of Self-Consciousness [161–65]

When we think of infinity, we usually think of unending on-goingness. Space, we say, is infinite, because there is no end of it.[29] For Hegel, infinity is self-sameness within self-differentiation, the positing of a difference that is no difference, and the containment of opposites in each other. It is the logical destiny of law: "through infinity, law completes itself into an immanent necessity, and all the moments of appearance are taken up into the inner world" [161]. This "immanent necessity" finally overcomes the mere "constant conjunction" or pseudo-necessity of natural causation, as it was conceived by the finite understanding.

Hegel's most accurate designation of infinity is *absolute Concept* [162]. This is his version of Heraclitus' *Logos,* the fire that enlivens and pervades all things. In infinity, thought beholds its own essence. Its object is its Concept, that is, its own activity and process of dialectical thinking. Hegel makes this crucial point in his Ode to Infinity:

> This simple infinity, or the absolute Concept, may be called the simple essence of life, the soul of the world, the universal blood, whose omnipresence is neither disturbed nor interrupted by any difference, but rather is itself every difference, as also, their supersession [*Aufhebung*]; it pulsates within itself but does not move, inwardly vibrates, yet is at rest. It is *self-identical,* for the differences are tautological; they are differences that are none. [162]

Absolute here refers to infinity as the self-differentiating One that has absorbed all otherness into itself. This is opposed to our ordinary view of the infinite as the perpetually incomplete. Hegel calls this *bad infinity.*[30] "Good" or genuine infinity is the completeness that results from opposites that posit and contain each other. Infinity cannot be contained by any finite determination, not because it lacks completeness or keeps on going but because, as the generator of inner difference, it is the immanent living source of all finite determinations or differences. Infinity is the dialectical process and whole, of which finite determinations and opposites are passing moments.

Especially interesting is the language of *life* and *blood.* These biological images remind us that conceptuality, for Hegel, is the opposite of what we would call abstract. In the previous chapter, I noted that the understanding's world of knowing lacked life. Life enters with infinity. Like the Concept, life is fluid and self-differentiating. Living things transcend their particularity. They die, but also procreate according to their kind and fill the world with universals or species. Moreover, a single living thing in its embryonic stage comes to be through a process in which difference (the articulation of members and organs) develops *from within.* Life, which comes on the scene at the beginning of Hegel's next chapter, does all this because the Concept, as universal blood, is coursing through its veins. Living things are higher than non-living because they are a more explicit manifestation of the Concept. And man is higher than other living things because he knows that he is alive. In this knowledge, he rises above life.

Continuing his ode, Hegel connects infinity with the whole path of consciousness taken so far:

> Infinity, or this absolute unrest of pure self-movement, in which whatever is determined in one way or another, e.g. as being, is rather the opposite of this determinateness, *this no doubt has been from the start the soul of all that has gone before* [my italics]; but it is in the *inner* world that it has first freely and clearly shown itself. [163]

As explanation, consciousness experiences its own tautological movement. This movement is *self*-consciousness. That is why explanation is so gratifying: because in explaining things, consciousness is really "in immediate conversation with itself" and "enjoys only itself" [163]. Explanation is the positing of distinctions that are no distinctions. But this very positing is the structure of self-consciousness. As a self-conscious being, I am aware of myself as other, and equally aware that this other is myself. Symbolically, I = I. I could not assert my identity, be self-conscious, without an initial splitting into two I's, without generating an inner difference with myself that I immediately cancel as a difference. Hegel brings I = I to dialectical life. He reads self-identity not as an abstract given but as a logical achievement, as the overcoming of a self-generated self-difference. It is the triumph of the infinite, rightly understood, over the finite—and of subject (which is negativity and flux) over static substance.

At the end of the chapter, we see what understanding sees when it peers into its inner world. This world is nothing other than appearance in its truth—appearance not as the original play of forces but as the pure, universal *thought* of that play [165]. What understanding experiences through the inverted world is the infinity that is "only *itself*." Earlier Hegel told us that understanding, which had posited a system of mediation or syllogism, would eventually experience the bound-together-being of its terms. Now this has happened. The system of three separate terms—two extremes connected through a mean—*collapses*. The extremes (understanding and its Beyond) have become identical; and the mediating "curtain" [*Vorhang*] of appearance has been taken away. Inner now means consciousness itself. But the tension or opposition within the system is preserved as the process of self-differentiation.[31] The reference to a curtain makes us think of what happens after the orchestra has played the overture: the actual play now begins.

This play is the turbulent drama of *man* as self-consciousness: the story that is *history.*

This process of infinitizing is the *self.* The self, or thinking subject, is a new logical structure. It is a new *syllogism,* in which the self "repels itself from itself" but at the same time cancels its self-difference. This is the deep meaning of I = I. With the curtain of appearance gone, consciousness, for us, becomes *self-consciousness.* As we now step behind the curtain, we ourselves fill what was once an empty Beyond. We replace the pseudo-depth of nature with the genuine depth of spirit and human life.

With the climactic entrance of the self, we reach the end of the first main section of the *Phenomenology,* the section entitled Consciousness. We have climbed the first three levels of Hegel's divided line (see diagram in Chapter 16): Sense-Certainty, Perception, and Understanding. But we are still far from the end of spirit's journey. At the beginning of this chapter, I defined the whole project of the *Phenomenology* as the quest for a self-differentiating One that knows itself as a self-differentiating One. Self-consciousness is this One, the One that experiences inner difference. But the self does not yet *know* itself in this difference. It does not yet know that this inner difference is essential to its being self-same.

The conclusion of Hegel's chapter leaves us with many questions. What does the self know when the curtain is drawn aside from the inner world that has been generated by the understanding? How will the self reconcile itself to the external world, which seems to threaten its newfound autonomy? How will the human One relate itself to other human Ones, other centers of autonomy?

As we now pass from consciousness to self-consciousness, let us note that the dialectic of experience works by way of extremes rather than degrees. Thus far in its journey, consciousness in its broad sense has been objective or merely theoretical. As self-consciousness it will leap to the other extreme. No longer a detached thinker, it will be immersed in the raw subjectivity of self-interest, action, and the drives of animality. Consciousness will experience a new force, whose name is *desire.*

SELF-CONSCIOUSNESS

Life is the faculty of a being by which it acts according to the laws of the faculty of desire.
KANT, *Critique of Practical Reason*

 7

On Life and Desire

WITH THE RISE OF SELF-CONSCIOUSNESS, THE *PHENOMENOLOGY* becomes a different kind of book. It is now explicitly about man as spirit's self-manifestation. Man as consciousness was a detached theoretician. As self-consciousness, he desires and acts. I noted in Chapter 1 that positing, for Hegel, is risk-taking. Perception, for example, exposed itself to death by refutation when it posited the thing as absolute. But from here on, risk, experience, opposition, suffering, despair, fear, and death are no longer mere metaphors for logical negation. They are real—real without ceasing to be logical.

How can this existential realm of felt negation bring us closer to absolute knowing—to philosophy in the form of *Science*? Hegel begins to answer this question early in his chapter, when he says that self-consciousness, *Selbstbewußtsein,* is "the native kingdom of truth" [167], the place where truth is *at home.* In his Preface, Hegel told us that his goal in the *Phenomenology* was to bring philosophy or the love of knowing to the point of actual knowing or Science [5]. To achieve this end, we must grasp and express truth "not as *substance* [or object] but just as much as *subject*" [17]. Subject here means self, or self-consciousness. This goal will be reached in the chapter entitled Absolute Knowing. The meaning and implications of truth as subject or self will emerge as we continue our journey. For now, it is enough to see that self-consciousness, the positing of the subject as absolute, is the first major step toward the completion of philosophy as Science or System. It is the first step toward man's realization that he not only can know divine truth but also *is* that truth.

Hearing the term self-consciousness, we think of our awareness of our unique selves, to which we are desperately attached. As self-conscious, I am aware that I am myself and no other: this singular I. This self-centeredness stirs my pride. But it can also bring on a feeling of profound isolation. In being self-conscious, I feel alienated. Consider the phenomenon of "feeling self-conscious." In this disquieting experience, my self-awareness is exposed. I am uncomfortably aware that others are aware of me, and, moreover, that they are aware of my being aware of myself as the one of whom they are aware. In my experience of feeling estranged from my own selfhood, self-consciousness is a suffering. Sometimes praise arouses this suffering. I receive a compliment, and I blush or stammer. I have been put on the spot, exposed. I become embarrassed that someone has made me aware of a virtue, trait, or achievement that is mine, embarrassed that my attachment to myself, and love of self, have been forced into the open and made public. The blush or stammer reveals that my self-centeredness is both my glory and my humiliation. These extremes within ordinary human experience will appear on a far grander scale in Hegel's chapter. Self-consciousness will begin in pride and end in mortification.

As a singular self-conscious being, I am inescapably the undivided center of the world—the absolute. External objects *come to me* out of a kind of dispersion and are focused in the point I call myself. This monadic self gathers the elements of experience and makes them into a coherent story—*my* story.[1] As I have stressed throughout our journey, shapes of consciousness are not psychological phenomena but claims to know absolutely, stages on the way to Science. Here, the claim strikes deep in my nature. My self-awareness is not a mere fact that I observe. It expresses the connection between my self-love and my knowledge of myself as the ultimate value and truth of all things. The mathematical formula for self-identity, I = I, fails to capture the boundless passion, the *violence,* that attaches me to my singular self. As a self-conscious being, I do not quietly say, "I am aware of my unity," but rather proclaim boldly, "I AM MYSELF!"

The preceding shapes of knowing belong to the section entitled Consciousness. As we know from Hegel's Introduction, consciousness in its broad meaning is the subject-object opposition. This is the consciousness that undergoes experience and moves from one stage to the next. But in its restricted sense, consciousness is the level of knowing at which the subject posits the object as absolute: the This, the thing, or force. As self-consciousness, the subject posits *itself* as absolute. This new stance takes us to a higher, and deeper, level of spiritual manifestation.

Self-consciousness is the beginning of the main drama of the *Phenomenology.* It is the center around which everything else turns. As we saw in the last chapter, self-consciousness proved to be the truth of consciousness. Let us pause to consider the meaning of this revelation. Consciousness in its restricted sense identifies the truth with objects. To say that the truth of consciousness is self-consciousness means that all knowledge is self-knowledge, and that all modes of knowing are modes of self-assertion, variations on the theme of "I AM MYSELF!" In the transition from consciousness to self-consciousness, the world of things is destroyed as the absolute: it loses its claim to independence. But thanks to the magic of determinate negation, it is also preserved within the more encompassing truth of self-consciousness. Objects are *for me.*

The centrality of self-consciousness in the *Phenomenology* is evident in the book's overall structure. The *Phenomenology* is divided into eight chapters. But Hegel overlays this numerical division with lettered sections that make the overall structure hard to understand.[2] After the Preface and Introduction comes the first major part of the book. Entitled Consciousness and labeled A, it consists of Sense-Certainty, Perception, and Understanding. After this comes the second main part, entitled Self-Consciousness and labeled B. Then something strange happens. There is a very long section labeled C, *which has no title.* It consists of four subsections: Reason (AA), Spirit (BB), Religion (CC), and Absolute Knowing (DD). The lack of a title suggests that this enormous stretch of text is a continuation of Self-Consciousness.[3] The drama that unfolds after the self-consciousness chapter supports this view. The dialectic of self-consciousness will reveal the fundamental problem that the rest of Hegel's book attempts to solve. In entering the realm of self-consciousness, we do not leave behind consciousness or the awareness of objects. On the contrary, the goal is to *reconcile* consciousness with self-consciousness: to grasp substance as subject without losing our hold on objective truth.

The chapter on self-consciousness has three formal sections: an introduction entitled "The Truth of Self-Certainty," followed by two sections labeled A and B. The A section is entitled "Independence and Dependence of Self-Consciousness: Lordship and Bondage," and the B section is "Freedom of Self-Consciousness: Stoicism, Skepticism, and the Unhappy Consciousness." These titles signal the shift from abstract theorizing to concrete human life, and from *nature* to *history.* I will treat Hegel's chapter in four of my own, dividing up the B section on freedom into one chapter on the stoic and skeptic, and another on the unhappy consciousness.

"The Truth of Self-Certainty" is frustratingly dense. It has three functions: to distinguish the new shape of knowing from the ones that came before it; to connect self-consciousness with *life* and *desire;* and to show that self-consciousness is the *Entzweiung* or splitting that produces two real, mutually opposed self-consciousnesses. Before turning to these themes, let me offer the following overview of where we are headed.

Self-consciousness is the dialectical birth of man as the being who is aware of his absoluteness as a thinking subject. The first stage of this subjectivity is the individual's intense awareness of his emptiness, insecurity, anxiety, and restlessness—his mere *Dasein* or being-there as this individual and no other. Man as self-consciousness inwardly proclaims, "I AM MYSELF!" But he has not yet proven to himself that he is worthy of this proclamation. Throughout Hegel's chapter, the individual strives to make his subjective certainty objective, to give concrete meaning and validity to his "I AM MYSELF!" In the end, he experiences the failure of all his attempts to make himself absolute. He becomes an *unhappy consciousness* that ultimately surrenders its selfhood to another. As a determinate negation, this self-surrender will give rise to a new shape of consciousness, and a new self-confidence. Just as consciousness had generated self-consciousness, so self-consciousness will generate reason, *Vernunft.*

Self-Certainty [166–67]

The previous modes of certainty all resulted in a contradiction between concept and object: between what the object was *for consciousness* and what it was *in itself.* This contradiction was the truth of the initial certainty. The truth of the sensuous particular or This was the universal (the expanded Here-and-Now). The truth of the thing, which was posited as absolutely independent, was the dependency on other things. And the truth of force was the dissolution of force into a flux of exchanged identities or roles: active and passive became each other.

But now we have "a certainty that is identical with its truth" [166], and a shape of consciousness in which "the object corresponds to the concept." In self-consciousness, *the subject is its own object.* In the language of force, I, as subject, am the active knower, and as object, the passive known. But the passively known I or object *is* the actively knowing I or subject. Self-consciousness is the unity of this opposition. The poles of the opposition contain each another, like the poles of the magnet in the inverted world. In being aware of myself, I am aware of myself as aware. I am *for myself* what I am *in myself:* a being that thinks or is aware. This mutual containment of opposites is the infinity that appeared in the last chapter [160]. Hegel again uses the verb overreaching (or overarching) [*übergreifen*], to describe the act by which self-consciousness transcends the finitude of opposite determinations. The I is explicitly self-related, or rather, *is* the very act of self-relating. It is "the *content* of the relation and the relating itself" [166].

The correspondence of object and concept leads to Hegel's assertion that self-consciousness is "the native kingdom of truth" [167]. The reader may be puzzled by the apparent finality of this pronouncement. If concept now corresponds to object, why are we not at the end of spirit's journey? Why must consciousness move on? These questions take us to the very heart of Hegel's book. The incompleteness of the self at this stage will help us see why spirit's progression is the drama of self-consciousness.

After identifying self-consciousness as the home of truth, Hegel tells us that self-consciousness "comes on the scene or steps forth" [*auftritt*]. It is a new *immediacy* that must be mediated and developed. The immediacy derives from the as-yet abstract self-identity of self-consciousness, I = I, together with the subject's new relation to objects. As self-consciousness, consciousness despairs of objects and turns toward itself. Objects are still there. But they only seem to exist as other than me. In reality, they *are* only insofar as they are objects for me—mere appearances.

In the turn away from external objects, consciousness becomes its own object. It is *self*-conscious. This awareness of itself is very different from the awareness of its previous objects. Self-consciousness, Hegel says, "is movement" [*Bewegung*]. This movement, which is non-temporal or purely logical, has two aspects or moments. In one sense, self-consciousness is movement because it is "the return from *otherness*," a withdrawal from the world of external objects [167]. But self-consciousness is also a movement *within itself*, a movement that is immediately brought to a standstill, since self-otherness is canceled in self-identity. Self-consciousness is both motion and rest. It is the "motionless tautology of: 'I am I'" [167]. In being self-conscious, I am a circle.

Let me try to spell out what Hegel means by this curious identity of motion and rest.

Self-consciousness posits a difference within itself between subject and object. We touched on this phenomenon in the last chapter. In order to regard or intuit myself, I must generate an inner separation or distance. I must "step back" from myself. Recall the dialectic of the Here in sense-certainty. Pointing to a fixed Here seemed to be immediate, that is, to involve no motion whatsoever. But I could not point to a fixed Here without jumping outside it in order to re-fer or "carry back" to it by means of other Heres. Pointing to the Here was a movement of referral and relating: a mediation. The same dialectic is at work in the phenomenon of self-consciousness. Being self-conscious is a movement, a transition into otherness. This is in fact the movement that pertains to consciousness as the subject's process of relating to an object. But in the act of self-intuiting, the difference that has been generated by the self is immediately *canceled*, or, as Hegel puts it, "what it [the self] distinguishes from itself is *only itself as* itself."

As self-intuition, self-identity is still formal and abstract, an unproved certainty. The cancellation of difference has happened, as it were, too quickly. It is not the cancellation of a *real* objective difference. Self-consciousness is a "return from otherness" because in turning toward itself the subject has withdrawn from the external world of objects [167]. And yet, in this state of withdrawal, the subject thinks this external world *as its own*. It is certain of *itself* as the absolute. The self-certainty of self-consciousness means that the self is certain of being the truth of external things, things other than itself. It cannot simply withdraw from these things into its formal self-identity, I = I. It must be unified with them if it is to be their truth. It must encounter, and grapple with, *real difference.*

Self-consciousness is a problem, because it has a double awareness and a double object. It is aware of itself, *and* it is aware of the external world. The opposition of subject and object that defines consciousness is preserved within self-consciousness, which must reconcile these two sides of itself: its relation to self and its relation to other, its *self-consciousness* and its *consciousness* [167]. Only through this reconciliation can self-certainty (I = I) become the truth that self-consciousness posits: that the *subject,* in its awareness of itself, is also the *substance* of things, that is, their persistent independence and being-there as things. Self-consciousness is not fully itself, not fully unified, until it is unified with the external world, the realm of real otherness.

The immediate form of this quest for unity is *desire, Begierde.* Self-consciousness *is* "desire in general" [167]. Desire is the negative force by which the self seeks to cancel the otherness of the external world in order to affirm itself as absolute. As Hegel says in the *Philosophy of Nature:* "Animal desire is the idealism of objectivity [i.e., objects are not real], so that the latter is no longer alien to the animal" (388). At the level of animality, desire is only appetite, only the desire for food, drink, sleep, and sex. Human desire will transcend mere appetite and become a spiritual, humanly distinctive need: the need for recognition by another self. Ultimately, human desire is the desire for another being capable of experiencing desire.

The Facts of Life and the Logic of Life [168–72]

Hegel's account of life is compact and sketchy. The more systematic treatment appears in the *Science of Logic* (761–74).[4] Here in the *Phenomenology,* Hegel develops the idea of life for the sake of illuminating self-consciousness, which defines itself in opposition to life. Life as organism will appear positively, as the general object for consciousness, at the level of Reason [254 ff.].

As Hegel told us in his Introduction, experience is so constituted that a shift in cognition produces a shift in the object of cognition [85]. In self-consciousness, the subject turns back on itself or becomes reflective. This produces a new, more complex object that has also "returned into itself." "Through this reflection into itself," says Hegel, "the object has become *life* [*Leben*]" [168]. The previous shapes of consciousness abstracted from life. Force approached life, but was not life. It was at work in things like electrical charges and falling bodies. Life is the scandal of the finite understanding because it exhibits qualitative difference and real change. Life is fluid. It resists reduction to the homogeneity of mathematical formalism.[5] Life emerged, we recall, when understanding *fell*, when infinity and inner difference came on the scene, and understanding went beyond its limits or "overreached" itself. Infinity and Concept were "the simple essence of life, the soul of the world, the universal blood" [162].

Life is perpetual flux—becoming. This flux is different from the earlier play of force. The latter was the sheer instability of becoming. Differences no sooner appeared than they disappeared. There was no coherent *being* that could internalize differences and express its unity in and through them. Living things, however, as opposed to non-living forces, are what they are precisely in and through their differences. They come to be and pass away; but they also stay remarkably themselves throughout all sorts of changes. Animals struggle to exist and to preserve themselves. Most important of all, they leave offspring, or produce themselves.[6] Life, as the movement of infinity, is restless. But unlike the play of force, it produces independent, self-preserving, self-replicating beings.

Life as infinity or inner difference is evident in morphogenesis. As an embryo matures, it becomes more internally articulated. Its distinctions are fluid in the sense that they all emerge from an organic unity and form a continuous whole. This fluidity, combined with "tight" organization, makes the living being at once vulnerable and tough. The unity of the organism is not that of thing-like One *and* Many, nor the force-like passage of One into Many and Many into One. It is a persistent unity in and through manyness: sturdy independence through fluid interdependence. More than any other phenomenon we have seen so far, life presents itself as Hegel's dialectical logic made incarnate. It is where the abstract-sounding terms seem concrete and "at home."[7]

Hegel's main concern in this section, however, is not with animals in general but with the rational animal, *man*. The reason is that the *Phenomenology* traces the evolution of consciousness. Life is the new object for consciousness, whose previous appearance was the rational understanding. The conscious individual now becomes aware of *himself* as organically alive. He discovers his body, and all the desires that go with it.

Life, Hegel tells us, is the *negative* of self-consciousness [168]. This takes us back to the tension between the self's awareness of its self-identity and its awareness of its object. This is the opposition within self-consciousness between self-consciousness and consciousness. Object, here, is no longer merely the thing I sense, perceive, or seek to understand. It is the object of my desire and concern: myself as a "living thing" [*ein Lebendiges*]. I am aware of my radical self-identity, I = I. But I am also aware of my living body, which is the object of my care and whose desires I strive to satisfy. This body is somehow me and not me. It is a personal Other that shadows my self-identity. In positing his famous split between mind and body, Descartes failed to grasp the depth and poignancy of this split. He failed to see that the mind-body split is a *wound* I bear within my being, a painful reminder that I lack unity and wholeness—that I am the dissonance of pure mind and bodily organic life.

The twentieth-century poet, Paul Valéry, describes this profound personal duality in one of his prose poems. He gives heart to Cartesian dualism. Writing to his living body as he contemplates the miracle of sleep, Valéry says:

> There is no more intimate marvel. My love toward you is without limit. I lean over you, who are I, and there is no communion between us. You await me without knowing me and I am what you lack that you may desire me.[8]

Self-consciousness craves unity. It craves to make its formal, abstract unity with itself actual. But there cannot be unity—I cannot be whole—unless my self-consciousness is reconciled to my living body. In its "deep" dialectical structure, my bodily life mirrors the self-otherness of my self-consciousness. Life, like self, articulates itself from within. It experiences *Entzweiung* or splitting. But it also mocks my self-consciousness with its apparent independence and there-ness. How, then, can I be a spiritual and at the same time bodily being? How can I rise above my natural, organic life and assert the claims of my absolute self-identity without committing suicide? It will take the rest of the *Phenomenology* to answer these questions.

Hegel now shows how self-consciousness logically evolves from organic life. He will provide, he says, not a full dialectical analysis of life but only one that is sufficient for the evolution of the self [169]. This evolution is one of the most baffling sections of the *Phenomenology.* Hegel's abstract language in these few paragraphs makes it difficult to identify the concrete "facts of life" on which self-consciousness depends. These are: relatively stable human individuals as parts of a family line, the on-going cycle of generations, the opposite sexes and their mutual attraction, copulation, death, the family, self-preservation, and desire as free-roaming appetite. As we shall see, Hegel's logic of life paves the way for the social nature of the self and the distinctly human desire for *recognition.*

The dense account of life begins with an image: "Essence is infinity as the being-sublated [*Aufgehobensein*] of all difference, the pure movement of axial rotation, its self-repose being an absolutely restless infinity" [169]. The image of axial rotation beautifully captures the motion-in-rest that is the *essence* of self-consciousness. When a sphere turns on its axis, like a spinning top, it generates different positions in space. But as it constantly moves away from a given position, it is always returning there and restoring its equilibrium, correcting itself. Rotation is a continually canceled self-otherness. In this motion that most resembles rest, the rotating sphere is the perfect image of self-consciousness as the tautology, I = I.[9]

But axial rotation is also a fact of life. When Hegel says that we are entering the *sphere* [*Sphäre*] of life, he is directing our phenomenological gaze to the rotating Earth as the cosmic place and stage of life (Harris, 1:322). As the Earth goes round and round, life goes round and round on the Earth's surface. Animals distinguish themselves from the body of the Earth, feed on the fruits of the Earth, and then disappear back into it. Earth, as the home of life, is also the home of self-consciousness, which is rooted in life, even as it transcends it. The spinning Earth is *time* [*Zeit*] that has acquired "the stable shape of *space* [*Raum*]." It is time that is *there* in bodily form. The Earth is the enduring *place of life*, the place where time does not merely go on but goes in cycles. These cycles are evident in the seasons, and in the living generations that come to be and pass away, and that are produced by the interrelated forces of sex and death.

Continuing his account of life as infinity, Hegel stresses that in order for life to be the continual cancellation of differences (an abiding flux), these differences must themselves have an enduring existence or survival [*Bestehen*]. Life must generate "members that have been rendered distinct and parts that are *for themselves* [or independent]" [169]. These members [*Glieder*] are individuals considered as creatures of genesis or the life-process: beings that maintain their survival by leaving offspring. Viewed in this way, humans, like other animals, are fleetingly independent, only passing moments in the flux of life. They are parents, who sacrifice their individuality for the sake of their children, who in turn become parents. In this cycle of coming to be and passing away, finite mortal individuals give rise to a living universal, a genus or *kind* [*Gattung*] that is the result of sexual reproduction or begetting [*Begattung*]. This universality, which the sexually mature individual bears within himself as a potency, is what Hegel calls "that simple fluid substance of pure movement within itself."

Human individuals, as "members" or "parts" of life, are independent and for themselves [170]. Like all organisms, they struggle to exist as individuals. But they are also *for another*. That is, life produces an *Entzweiung* or splitting of its members into two different sexes that need and attract one another. Sexual attraction leads to sexual union, in which difference is momentarily overcome. The sexes are like the opposite and mutually attracting poles of a magnet. In the next section, attractive being-for-another will be replaced by repulsive being-for-another. In the upcoming fight-to-the-death [187], the sexual *erōs* between male and female will give way to the *eris* or strife between opposing males.

Hegel now looks "more closely" at the two opposite moments of the life-process [171]. The first is the *Bestehen* or survival of beings that are for themselves through the consumption of the fruits of the earth. Food is our "inorganic nature." This is because digestion takes place at the sub-organic level of chemical breakdown and assimilation. In this aspect of our existence, we assert our individuality and suppress our inevitable subjection to the infinity of becoming, "the universal substance" of life [171]. We stave off dissolution and death. This attempt to deny the fluid self-differentiating process of life is futile, since death is an essential moment of the process. In spite of our effort to keep ourselves alive, we die. We prove to be passing moments of life as fluidity.

The second moment, which is opposed to the first, is that we live for another. That is, we seek pleasure in sexual union and (sometimes inadvertently) reproduce ourselves through the kind or genus (a family line). In the first, self-preservative moment of our organic life, we subordinate the universal medium of life to our individuality: we consume our environment as food. But in the second, procreative moment, we ourselves are consumed, undone as pleasure-seeking individuals, by the universal process of becoming, that is, by the kind or genus that is the result of sexual union. Procreation is not, at this stage, the individual's goal in sexual union. The goal is rather self-feeling or enjoyment. But the life-process turns this joy into something unintended though necessary for the continuation of life. The sexually distinct individuals (man and woman) are other than each other. But in sexual union, which naturally leads to conception, the kind or genus (the family) becomes an *other* to the singularity of both of them. It is something over and above them that cancels their singularity [171]. Having "kids" ties you down and ruins your being-for-self. In this way, the second moment of organic life is the inversion or *Verkehrung* of the first.

But sexual union is also a *self*-inversion. That is, the moment of sexual fulfillment, in which each individual experiences a climactic "flow" and "unity with itself," is also the production of a stable form: a child. Individuals lose themselves, in a sense die, in sexual climax. They experience a "general dissolution" of their difference. But this process transcends itself in conception. The sexual act produces independent sexually distinct beings, with which the whole process started.[10] And so, we get "the whole round [*Kreislauf*] of this activity that constitutes life" [171]. Life, then, is not the essence of living things (what we call a soul), or the stable independent form (the child), or the fluid process of life, or the sum total of all these. It is rather a circle of self-consumption: "the self-developing whole that dissolves its development [by producing a stable form] and in this movement simply preserves itself [the stable form can eventually reproduce]."

Hegel now points to "the universal unity" that transcends the immediate unity of singular individuals and contains all the moments of life within itself [172]. This is the "simple genus or kind" [*Gattung*].[11] In a given family line, members die off and leave progeny. They die *because* they have fulfilled their natural destiny, which is to procreate. Individuals pass away, but the family or kind survives. Life is the dialectical interplay between the ongoing life-process, which dissolves human singularity, and the stable products of generation. The genus or kind is the universal that results from this interplay. But the kind, as Hegel somewhat cryptically says, "in the movement of life itself, does not exist [*existiert*] for itself as this simple [kind]." The kind or genus, as a universal, points to consciousness as that *for* which life exists as this unity.

What Hegel seems to mean here is that although life produces universals (kinds), it is logically incomplete, since, in its merely organic mode, it does not *know* these universals. The concept of life is complete only in a living self-consciousness in which *life becomes aware of itself,* in a conscious subject that can grasp universals like genera and species, or subject and object. Life reaches its perfection in the living being who, in addition to being part of the life-process, *knows* that process.[12]

Self-Consciousness and Desire [173–77]

Self-consciousness, which now emerges from the universality of life, "is kind or genus for itself" [173]. It is, to itself, one of a kind, *sui generis.*[13] Like the organic kind or *Gattung,* it is a self-enclosed unity that endures throughout all its passing states (which are, in a sense, instances of itself) and contains all differences within itself. But self-consciousness not only mirrors life: it also identifies with it. It regards itself as the universal *end* for the sake of which everything in life exists and has value. It feels a *right* to be gratified. Before this point, the individual was a more or less un-self-conscious "member" and "part" of the life-process: a victim. Now he is more knowing, or rather, cunning. Having experienced the life-process, he refuses to be its victim. He is now the self-absolutizing egotistical individual who deliberately, knowingly, subjugates life to the satisfaction of his natural desires—like the man who has a mid-life crisis and leaves home in order to "live it up." Before, the individual lived. Now he wills to live. His desires are projects.[14] Animals strive to exist and follow their desires. But only man, properly speaking, asserts himself.

The I that sets out to "live it up" has only *itself* for object [173]. This I is "pure" [*rein*] in the sense of being undeveloped or abstract. It is ego pure and simple, the self-conscious version of the immediate This of sense-certainty. This immediate I, which is at first an empty universality, I = I, will "enrich itself" in the course of its upcoming experience and "undergo the unfolding which we have seen in the sphere of life." In other words, the I that absorbs all universality into its ego-world is no more than *this* I right here and now. In the course of experience, it will become, by analogy with the This, a passing moment in the universal *movement* and *process* of self-consciousness. Self-consciousness at this point may be said to know the facts of life, but it does not know the logic of life. It has yet to "catch up" to life as the dialectical interplay of unstable process and stable form. It does not know that singularity is *self-canceling.*

Earlier in this section, Hegel announced that self-consciousness "is desire in general [*Begierde überhaupt*]" [167]. The object of this desire is my living body [168]. That is, in my immediate awareness of myself as an infinitely self-valuing self, I live to gratify my natural appetites. Hegel now develops this identity of self-consciousness and desire. He returns to the theme of this whole introductory section: self-certainty [174]. The living self confronts an external world of living things. In its radical egotism, it identifies itself as the "negative essence" of those things. The egotistical self is certain of the nothingness of all things other than itself. It is, to itself, the entire genus or kind and is consequently "unkind" to other living things, which are no more than food for its self-certainty: "[the self] explicitly affirms that this nothingness [of other living things] is *for it* the truth of the other; it destroys the independent object and thereby gives itself the certainty of itself as a true certainty, a certainty that has become explicit for self-consciousness in an objective manner" [174].

Desire, for Hegel, is different from desire, as we normally understand it. We tend to think of desire as a stretching out toward an object different from ourselves—as the urge to have this object. The apple over there on the table is the object of my desire to eat. I pick it up and take a bite. I gratify my desire, fill a void. On this naturalistic view, the desire for knowledge is no different from my desire for an apple. "All humans," says Aristotle at the beginning of his *Metaphysics,* "by nature desire to know." The word for desire, here, is *oregesthai,* to reach or stretch out. For Aristotle, the fruit of knowledge, which determines my desire, is already there, waiting for me, as it were, on the table of the gods. I need only stretch out for it by engaging in philosophy.[15]

In the classical and medieval view, which supports the natural view, desire is defined in terms of its object. This object is *other* than the being that does the desiring. In general, the object is prior to the various faculties or powers by which we relate to objects. In the *De Anima,* for example, Aristotle discusses the faculty of vision in terms of color as the *object* of vision. At the beginning of his *Nicomachean Ethics,* he affirms an end or highest good for the sake of which we do all the things we do. Without such an end, he says, desire, *orexis,* would be "empty and futile" (1.2.1094A 21). For Plato, *erōs* is for the good and the beautiful. The lover desires that the good be his own forever (*Symposium* 206A). In medieval thought, God is the ultimate Beloved. Dante's Beatrice is the Other who leads him to God. Dante's love for this Other is a desire, not to possess or assimilate her for the sake of his self-certainty, but to be with her in the world in which she belongs, the heavenly City of the *Paradiso.*[16]

In modernity, the priority shifts from the object to the faculty or power, from *object* to *subject.* We do not love things because they are good: they are good because we love them. This inversion of ancient-medieval desire is most visible in Spinoza: "By the *end* for the sake of which we do something, I mean appetite" (*Ethics,* part IV, definition 7). Man, for Spinoza, is defined not by the natural end of his desire but by the desire itself, by man's *conatus* or striving for self-preservation. Desire, which is this striving insofar as it involves "mind and body together," is "man's essence" (*Ethics,* part III, scholium to proposition 9). For Hobbes, desire is infinite in the sense of infinitely ongoing—what Hegel calls "bad infinity."[17] There is no highest good, only "a perpetuall and restlesse desire of Power after power, that ceaseth onely in Death" (*Leviathan,* part I, chapter 11). That is why happiness, for Hobbes, is impossible.

For Hegel, as for his fellow moderns, the end of desire is not the object but *desire itself.* The desirous self stretches out *for itself* and for the proof of its self-certainty. It longs to make itself objective or real. There is a deep bond here between desire and nothingness. Non-being is dynamic. It is an active force, or rather, *the* active force. It is the engine and soul of all the cancellations and undercuttings we have witnessed in the dialectic of experience. In desire, I *feel* this force of negation as identical with my very self. Desire is the being-at-work, the raw energy, of my inner void or nothingness striving to make itself an objective something. I turn my attention, for a moment, away from all objects to my pure inwardness. What do I "see"? Nothing. But this nothing, for Hegel, is not a mere blank or absence. It is not a nothing toward which I can remain indifferent. This nothing is the *self-relating negativity* Hegel discusses in his Preface. There, Hegel asserts: "the negative is the self" [37]. The nothing I "see" when I look within, the nothing of self-intuition, is my infinite restlessness or anxiety. This is the core of my selfhood, which feels its difference from all objects and longs to destroy them in order to make itself the only reality. Desire is subjectivity in its raw, most immediate form. It is not a being *drawn out* by an object's apparent goodness, much less its beauty, but a being *driven from within* by a dynamic nothingness that compels me to fill the void that is myself and transform it into a something. This understanding of desire makes it clear that the self for Hegel is its own end.

In its immediate or natural form ("I want what I want"), desire will be self-defeating or tragic. It will perpetuate itself, just as it does in Hobbes' definition. But it will also transcend itself, as we shall see, in the desire for recognition. Consciousness will learn, through experience, that the void of selfhood can be filled, and that otherness can be overcome, only if the individual self is recognized as a self by another individual. This is the dialectical moment in which the "bad infinity" or infinite reduplication of desire becomes the genuine infinity of an opposite in its opposite, a self in its other.

Desire starts out as sheer negation and conquest [174]. It is the raw, violent negativity and hatred of otherness that is the basis of all fanaticism. We see this fanaticism in the French Reign of Terror, with its "fury of destruction" [589]. The desirous self is at war with the otherness that seems to contradict the self's certainty of being the absolute. The apparently independent reality of objects reminds me of my own intensely felt unreality as a creature of need. The apple is other than me. It is an object of consciousness. As *self*-consciousness, I am certain that *I* am substantial or absolute and that this apple, in itself, is nothing. But my certainty lacks truth. Eating the apple supplies that proof. It is my negation of external nature and the affirmation of myself as absolute. It is the moment of truth. By destroying the apple in consuming it, I prove what I really am, and what the apple really is. It is *for me,* and I am for nothing other than myself. The whole external world is like this apple: it is "food" for self-conscious appropriation, fuel for my affirmation of myself as the "master and possessor of nature."[18] Self-consciousness as desire thus recalls Hegel's praise of the animals in the chapter on sense-certainty: "they do not just stand idly in front of sensuous things as if these possessed intrinsic being, but, despairing of their reality, and completely assured of their nothingness, they fall to without ceremony and eat them up" [109].

Hegel is not denying that my desire to eat the apple is motivated by physical hunger. He is saying that conscious physical desire has its origin in a deeper truth about my selfhood and *its* desire or drive. It is this deeper truth that connects my desire for apples with my desire for knowledge. Thinking, for Hegel, is a kind of eating. In both activities, the self seizes upon something in the external world and makes it conform to its self-identity through a process of negation. In eating the apple, I destroy it, make it part of myself, and put it in the service of my physical sustenance and preservation. In thinking the apple, I destroy it as a particular in order to make it conceptual or universal: I make it conform to the self-identity of thought or Concept. I make the object intellectually *mine.*

But the connection goes beyond analogy. It is also genetic: the natural desire for apples is the necessary first stage of the self's ultimate desire, at this point unrealized, to prove that it is the truth of all things. Self-consciousness as desire thus recalls Hegel's goal in the *Phenomenology:* to complete *philosophic* desire by grasping and expressing truth as subject as well as substance [17].

Animals too have desire. But since they are not self-conscious, desire is not for them what it is for us. When an animal feeds, nothing is at stake for it beyond self-preservation. Man, by contrast, is the being whose self-certainty and self-identity are at stake. As self-consciousness, man is restless and insecure. He experiences *anxiety* over his being, his unity, his worth, and his relation to the external world.[19] This anxiety permeates every aspect of his natural existence. Eating, for man, is not mere feeding; sex is more than bodily pleasure and procreation; and sleep, spiritualized by contact with self-consciousness, "knits up the ravelled sleave of care" (*Macbeth* 2.2).

Let us return now to Hegel's text. As we noted earlier, self-consciousness, as desire, is certain of the nothingness of its other, that is, of its natural object out there in the world [174]. The self at this point is only "desire in general" [167]—not a specific desire for a specific object but an indiscriminate "I want." In this infantile state, the self wants all its natural desires satisfied.[20] It is immersed in time as the flux of life. In order to validate my self-certainty, make that certainty true, I must negate the object in order to reveal it as nothing and myself as the only something: I act on my desire and eat the apple. But I am not satisfied. When I am done eating the apple there is no more apple to eat. The proof of my self-certainty requires the negation of my other. If that other no longer exists, my selfhood has no "food" for negation and I am back where I started: stuck with unproven self-certainty. The point here is that even though the apple momentarily satisfies my physical hunger, the physical satisfaction I enjoy fails to satisfy the non-physical, spiritual desire of my selfhood. Self-consciousness is at odds with its own desire to negate the object. It posits that object—in a sense, resurrects it—in the very act of negating it. This is what Hegel means when he says that in the satisfaction of natural desire, self-consciousness learns that "the object has its own independence" [175]. To be sure, when I eat an apple, the apple is gone. But self-consciousness as desire needs apples in order to perpetuate its self-certainty. It feeds on its desire, and so must perpetuate its need. Eating apples leads me not to the end of desire, but to more apples and the renewed desire to eat them. This is the "bad infinity" of Hobbesian desire. Immersed in time as the sheer flux of life, the cunning appetitive self is never a self-same unity. It is always on its way to a future self-identical I that it seeks but cannot find.

As long as it stays at this level of desire, self-consciousness remains unsatisfied. In destroying the object, it keeps positing the object as independent. The animals may be wise in their desirous, negative attitude toward external things [109]. But they are not *that* wise. Their relentless acts of negation cannot satisfy a being that is self-conscious.

Another Self-Consciousness [175–77]

What the self learns from trying to affirm itself by gratifying natural desire is that such negation of the external other (eating) is incomplete, even tragic.[21] To consume the object (the apple) is merely to posit all over again both object and desire. The negation the self really seeks, the negation that would truly satisfy its desire, is one that the external object effects "of itself in itself" [175]. The object must be capable of engaging in *self-negation.* It must be *for itself* what it is *for me.* It must be an independent, abiding being that cancels its own independence, another being capable of desire: "*Self-consciousness achieves its satisfaction only in another self-consciousness*" [175].

What does the self truly desire? Not edible apples, but the golden apple of recognition [*Anerkennen*]. Having experienced the failure of natural desire, the self rises from mere bodily appetite to the spirited love of honor and victory.[22] At first, this desire will be one-sided: self-consciousness will want to *be recognized* by another but not to recognize that other in turn. This one-sided desire will give rise to a life-and-death fight for recognition and the relation of master and slave. In the course of long experience, the self will eventually overcome its egotism and realize that the recognition it desires must be *reciprocal* or *mutual.*[23]

Hegel does not mention recognition in the present section, much to the confusion of his reader. He gives only the purely logical "Concept of self-consciousness" [176]. Self-consciousness is logically summed up in three moments. First, the self is immediately aware of itself as a bare, formal "undifferentiated I." Second, this certainty of its unity with itself is actual only through desire as the negation of external objects. Third, self-consciousness is *duplicated:* its external object must be another self-consciousness, an independent being capable of negating its own independence (the future slave).

"A self-consciousness is *for a self-consciousness*" [177]. The logical structure of self-consciousness, in other words, cannot be grasped by looking at only one self. Self-consciousness is the gazing of two selves into each other. That is what it means for them to be *for* each other. In the concrete other who is "for me," the self overcomes its merely formal I = I. It beholds itself as a *real* other and thus experiences "the unity of itself in its otherness." The object is no longer merely an object—a *Gegenstand* set over and against me [*gegen*]. It is an objectively real subject. As subject, it transcends the natural object of desire, which is "only independent," that is, only an object for my gratification. The apple momentarily satisfies natural desire. But it is not something in which I behold the "apple" of my precious I.

With the identity of subject and object, and the satisfaction of self-consciousness in another self-consciousness, Hegel says, "we already have before us the Concept of *spirit*" [177]. In what follows, this idea will be developed and made concrete or actual. Hegel calls spirit the "absolute substance that is the unity of the different independent self-consciousnesses which, in their opposition, enjoy perfect freedom and independence: 'I' that is 'We' and 'We' that is 'I'." Hegel ends his introduction to the dialectic of the self with the opposition between Night and Day.[24] He tells us:

> It is in self-consciousness, in the Concept of spirit, that consciousness first finds its turning-point, where it leaves behind it the colorful show of the sensuous This-world [*Diesseits*] and the nightlike void of the supersensible Other-world or Beyond [*Jenseits*], and steps out into the spiritual daylight of the present. [177]

Present, here, refers to history, which is the actuality of spirit. In referring to the "I that is We and the We that is I," Hegel leaps far ahead in the journey of consciousness. He points to the full revelation of spirit *as spirit.* In this identity of self-consciousness and the Concept of spirit, we have further confirmation of what I proposed at the beginning of this chapter: that the *Phenomenology* is the drama of man as self-consciousness.

For Hegel, complete individual self-awareness requires other people. The individual is complete only insofar as he transcends his individuality, negates himself, and finds himself within a concrete universal self-consciousness. Spirit, as fulfilled or satisfied self-consciousness, *is* community or intersubjectivity. It is the I that has expanded into a We and, in this expansion, has "come home to itself." Community here is not a mere collection of individuals (the "general will" of modern liberalism) or the "government" that bears down on the individual self (also the product of modern liberalism).[25] Nor is it the natural interdependence of mere life and the pseudo-community of hive and herd. It is one's own individual innermost selfhood and subjectivity made substantial or real. In spirit as community or mutual recognition, I am concretely unified, not only with others, but also with myself. In the chapter entitled Religion, we find the definition of spirit I cited in Chapter 1. Spirit is "the knowing of its own self in its externalization; the essence that is the movement of retaining the sameness with itself in its being other" [759]. This is exactly what we have in the "I that is We and the We that is I."

In the move from consciousness to self-consciousness, we have gone from nature to man, and from abstract individuality (I = I) to community or mutual recognition (that is, prospectively). But we have not therefore ceased to concern ourselves with being and truth. Community, for Hegel, is not a mere fact, or a human expedient, or the cure for loneliness, or a means of gratifying natural desire, or the escape from a Hobbesian state of nature. It is a metaphysical accomplishment. Man as self-consciousness is *more of a being* than a This, a thing, a force, or an animal. And community, as universal self-consciousness, is *more of a being* than man as an isolated individual abstracted from his human context. Man, as concretized subjectivity, is what the This, the thing, force, and organism were aiming at but could not reach: the self-differentiating One that, in community, *lives* the knowledge of itself as a self-differentiating One (Chapter 6).

Community, in the *Phenomenology*, has three major forms: social-political, religious, and philosophic. As spirit advances, various kinds of social-political structures arise. These include the Greek world, medieval feudalism, ancient Rome, and modern civil society. All are examples of self-consciousness transcending its particularity in order to become universal. But community is not purely secular. It is also sacred or divine (in Hegel's sense of these terms). Spirit as a divine community among human selves appears as the Lutheran Community of the Faithful, which Hegel defines much later in the book as "God appearing in the midst of those who know themselves as pure knowing" [671].

Community in its most divine and perfect form is philosophy itself as absolute knowing or Science. Logic is pure thought communing with itself. It is the divine banquet or symposium where the Forms, drunk on rationality or selfhood, spontaneously organize themselves into the most sober of all wholes [47]. And phenomenology, as the prelude to Science, is spirit's perfectly rational *communion with itself* in its manifold appearances in history.[26] Science, the self-revelation of the Concept, binds the philosopher to the world of body and time, with which he communes in thought, and to other lovers of reason everywhere. In thinking the Concept, the philosopher does not flee from the world but rather unites himself with "the simple essence of life, the soul of the world, the universal blood" [162].

In our next chapter, we examine the logical movement of recognition. We will also witness the violent encounter of the two opposing selves. This is the fight to the death, in which self-consciousness, the hero of Hegel's philosophic epic, rises above life and life's desire.

There is such divine harmony in the realm of lifeless nature, why this discord within the rational?
SCHILLER, *The Robbers*

 8

The Violent Self

In Quest of Recognition

VIOLENCE IS CENTRAL TO HEGEL'S THOUGHT. IT PLAYS A KEY ROLE, not only in his philosophy of history but also in his logic, which is not a calm sequence of steps but the revelation of inner conflict. In his *Lectures on the History of Philosophy,* Hegel says: "There is no proposition of Heraclitus that I have not adopted in my Logic" (1:279). As we now approach the fight that lays the foundation for human history, one of these propositions stands out: "War is the father of all and king of all, and some he shows as gods, others as men; some he makes slaves, and others free" (fragment 53).

In our last chapter, we saw that desire is aggressive or violent: the impulse to negate. This impulse recurs throughout the journey of consciousness. In the upcoming fight, it defines the individual who is "for himself."[1] Later, desire as the *will to negate* will be historically manifest in the French Reign of Terror [582 ff.].

At the beginning of this section, Hegel makes explicit what he only hinted at in the last: that the true object of self-conscious desire is *recognition by another, desirous self.* He begins with the purely logical "movement [*Bewegung*] of recognition" and then proceeds to the actual experience of self-consciousness in the fight to the death. In this experience, the self begins to fulfill its logical destiny: its unity with itself [167].

Throughout the for-us part of this section, Hegel stresses the reciprocal nature of recognition [182–84]. This reciprocity, the basis of spirit as community, does not appear until much later in the *Phenomenology,* at the end of the chapter on morality. There, we witness "a reciprocal recognition, which is *absolute* spirit" [670]. Two opposing selves will be reconciled through confession and forgiveness. In the Christian phenomenon of reconciliation, the wine of infinity and self-negation is at last allowed to flow, from one self into the other and back again, as the two selves experience *universal selfhood.* This is the "I that is We and the We that is I."[2]

In the last chapter, I proposed that the *Phenomenology* is the drama of man as self-consciousness. The endpoints of this drama can now be more precisely defined. The drama begins with the fight for recognition in the present chapter and ends with the reconciliation of two self-consciousnesses at the end of the morality chapter [670]. Religion and Absolute Knowing, the final chapters of Hegel's book, further develop what this drama has accomplished. The initial fight and the eventual reconciliation of two self-conscious individuals are the endpoints of the "great arch" of the *Phenomenology.* This arch embraces the path by which spirit struggles to know itself in time. The result will be "God appearing in the midst of those who know themselves as pure knowing" [671].

The Logic of Recognition [178–85]

Hegel begins this section with a crucial statement: "Self-consciousness is *in* and *for itself* in that, and by the fact that it is in and for itself for another; that is, it *is* only as a self-consciousness that is acknowledged or recognized [*ein Anerkanntes*]" [178]. As I first noted in Chapter 3, something is "in and for itself" when it is logically complete, when its essence is fully manifest, specified, and actual. In the present context, self-consciousness is fully what it is—this existing self-conscious I—only in being recognized as such by another self-consciousness. "For another" here means "present to another as object." Self-consciousness is my awareness of myself as my own other. This self-otherness, which is necessary to my self-identity, is made actual or explicit only in the presence of another self who recognizes me, that is, who respects my claim to be a self. In the presence of this other concrete self, my inner or merely implicit self-otherness is made actual. His otherness as a being distinct from me is *my* otherness concretized and made real. It is the nature of self-consciousness, in other words, to be social.

The phrase "in and for itself" suggests independence, in German, *Selbstständigkeit* or "self-standing-ness." As we have seen, the search for a true *being* is the search for a truly independent or "self-standing" being, a true One. Man is that One. When the thing of perception became the relating of thing to thing, it lost the independence that was essential to its purported absoluteness. Relation was the death of thinghood, since in being related to other things, the thing "*is for itself, insofar as it is for another,* and *it is for another, insofar as it is for itself*" [128]. At its next level, consciousness came up with a new object, force, and incorporated relation into its concept of substance: it is the nature of forces to interact. But the independence of force vanished in the play of force: force became unreal [139–41]. Man as self-consciousness unites the for-itself and the for-another. The human self is independent or "for itself," but only insofar as it is for another self, that is, only insofar as it is recognized as independent by another self. Man as self-consciousness is not a thing: his being-for-another fulfills rather than undercuts his being-for-self or independence. As we shall see, however, man *is* a kind of force.

Hegel's word for recognition, *Anerkennen,* is related to the word for cognition, *Erkennen.* More than mere cognizance or acknowledgement, recognition denotes honor and respect. What I desire in desiring recognition from another is his awareness, not simply of my selfhood, but of the dignity and worth of my selfhood. I want another self to confirm my inward claim to be independent and non-derivative, an end that is not also a means. I want to be recognized as absolute. This desire, or rather expectation, is evident in ordinary experience. When two human selves meet, each recognizes the other as human. In meeting the other, I do not merely observe that he is human, or that he is this man as opposed to that one: I honor the selfhood and absolute independence in him as if it were a god. I see in him what I honor in myself.[3] This is an instance of the mutual recognition that self-consciousness, still in its nascent state, has yet to achieve.

Hegel proceeds to trace out the purely logical movement or process of recognition [178]. What is most characteristic of this process is that self-consciousness reveals the infinity that was generated at the end of Hegel's last chapter. This is the positing of opposites *in* each other. Self-consciousness, as infinite, has a fluid structure—like life. Every determinateness that appears within it is immediately its opposite: Other is also Same, and Same Other. Self-consciousness is therefore contradiction, contradiction that is actually lived and felt. As a self-conscious being, I see myself in an other, and the other sees himself in me. In our opposition, we are co-inherent.

The following points will serve as signposts along the way through the purely logical movement. First, recognition, as I have said, is not mere awareness but esteem or honor. Second, the two selves that are "for" each other are, as the manifestation of self-consciousness, *absolutely identical:* one and the same self is both one and two.[4] Third, absolute self-identity, I = I, is essential to the self: the other who confronts me falsifies this equation and puts an inequality in its place. Fourth, Hegel examines the process of recognition from the perspective of *one* of the selves before presenting it as the work of both. Fifth, although Hegel presents recognition as ultimately mutual, this result (as I noted above) is not achieved until much later in the book. Sixth, the for-us opening of the section corresponds to what in earlier chapters I called the logic of the object. It reveals the purely logical, non-temporal structure of an experience that unfolds in time.

From here on, everything is double. The duplicity inherent in self-consciousness is made literal in the appearance of *two self-consciousnesses.*

Let us call them **A** and **B**. Each is for the other in the sense that each faces or confronts the other: each *sees itself* as other. The first self, **A**, "has come outside itself" [179]. As **A**, I am aware of my selfhood as something "thrown," to use Heidegger's term, into the outside world.[5] Another self, **B**, has stolen it from me and confronts me with the theft, perhaps with no more than an arrogant look. In this first logical moment, there is a loss of self, an inequality or injustice that must be rectified. But then, infinity brings me to the second logical moment: in beholding **B**, I am really beholding my own selfhood. Since the selfhood I behold is my own, this other in whom I see myself must be non-essential, nothing but a reflecting surface of the essential selfhood that belongs to me uniquely.

My externalized selfhood mocks me in this other, who seems to be an I in his own right. I must act to set the record straight. In order to transform the certainty of myself as an absolute unity (I=I) into truth, I who am **A** must negate **B** [180]. I must regain the selfhood that I have lost in being externalized or "cloned." **B**, as other, is independent of me or self-standing, and so I must cancel his apparent independence. And yet **B** is *myself* externalized. To negate *him* is thus also to negate *myself.* Again, Hegel at this point does not tell us what negation means in the context of actual experience. He is simply generating the purely logical structure of recognizing Same-in-Other. In the upcoming fight for recognition, negating the other means killing him (in its first stage), and negating myself means risking my life in combat.

My double cancellation of **B**, says Hegel, results in a double *return to myself,* a double retrieval of my stolen selfhood [181]. First, in negating **B**, I take back the selfhood that **B**, as my other, had stolen. I become "equal" to myself. But second, the other self-consciousness, **B**, having seen himself in me (*his* other), gives my selfhood back to me. *He* sees his selfhood not in himself but in *me.* Why should he cling to what he sees as not in him in the first place? I thus get my selfhood back twice—I take that which the other gives—and let the other be an other. I let him "go free." Again, in the upcoming fight this will mean that I succeed in killing the other self. When Hegel describes this moment (which turns out to be a Pyrrhic victory), he repeats this language of letting the other go free [188]. Here, he restricts himself to the logical point: negation of the other ceases once selfhood is retrieved. Equilibrium, justice, is restored.

The dialectic so far has been one-sided, all from the perspective of **A**. Hegel now shifts to the fuller picture of recognition as the action of both self-consciousnesses: "For the other [**B**] is equally independent and self-enclosed [*in sich beschlossen*], and there is nothing in it that is not through its own self" [182].[6] Hegel goes on to say that the process of recognition "is the double movement of the two self-consciousnesses." As **A**, I look at **B**, who confronts me. As I look at him, I see not merely him but his *gaze.* I see that he is also an independent being who returns my gaze as a self in his own right. I see him, not as someone who exists "primarily for desire" but as a self just like me, as independent or self-standing. Each self sees the spontaneity or independence of the other in the gaze of the other. Whatever each makes the other do, therefore, the other must do of itself. We thus have *two* reflexive moments within the logical structure of self-consciousness: self-negation and reciprocity [183].[7]

The moral of the story is that recognition is not like eating apples (the satisfaction of natural desire), where I am active and the apple is passive. In recognition, each self is both active and passive. Each negates itself as it negates the other.

We have seen this phenomenon before. It is the reciprocity of force, "now repeated in consciousness" [184]. Force started out as split into two separate determinations: active force and passive force, soliciting and solicited [138]. In the play of force, the separateness of these opposites vanished: each was in the other (active in being passive and passive in being active). Two selves who see themselves in the other are thus like two colliding metal spheres. In collision, Body **A** and Body **B** make each other move. According to Leibniz, this happens in such a way that the being moved is also the spontaneous or self-generated *action* of each body: solicited and soliciting are the same. What Body **A** does to Body **B** *Body **B** does to itself:* its passion is its action, and its action a passion. But passion is a form of negation. It is a "being done to" that limits and cuts against the positive effort to be and to be active. At the moment of impact, as each body acts on the other, each also *negates itself* as it negates the other.

This dialectically revised version of Leibnizian collision is exactly what happens when two self-consciousnesses meet. Recognition between the two selves is the moment of *human impact.* The other jars or shocks me into my spontaneous awareness of self in other, as I do the same to him.[8] The other prompts me to feel the negativity of my own selfhood as an individual. The two selves are force made self-conscious. These individuals will be even more explicitly force-like when they meet: they will fight.

Force became actual or explicit in the play of force, where the extremes of active and passive, soliciting and solicited, became identical. Hegel defined the play of force in terms of the syllogism [141]. As we saw in Chapter 6, syllogism is mediation or rationality made explicit: it is logical thoroughness expressed as logical through-ness. By through-ness, here, I mean that the middle term expresses the flowing of opposites into each other. The play of force exhibited this syllogistic through-ness in that each extreme (active and passive) was itself "solely through the other" [141]. The middle term of the syllogism was therefore not a static middle interposed between the extremes, but the passage of the extremes into each other: their dialectical unity. The same thing happens in recognition. Each self is itself only *through* the other: "Each is for the other the middle term, through which each mediates itself with itself and unites with itself; and each is for itself, and for the other, an immediate being on its own account, which at the same time is such only through this mediation" [184]. More simply, when I recognize another self, I see this self both as a being in its own right and as grist for the mill of my self-identity. This other is a means to my self-identity precisely because he is not merely a means but also an end: another self. The other puts me in touch with myself by being *himself.* With the syllogistic structure of recognition, reciprocity is made explicit: the two selves "*recognize* themselves as *mutually recognizing* one another" [184].[9]

Of course, this is self-consciousness in its perfected, communal state. The initial meeting of selves will be violent rather than harmonious. The reason is that each claims to be absolute, to be the one and only glorious Self. Shakespeare's Prince Hal captures the situation perfectly when he says to Hotspur, that other Harry: "Two stars keep not their motion in one sphere" (*Henry IV, Pt. 1* 5.4). When the two selves meet, they indeed see themselves in each other. But they do not respect the other's selfhood. Offended by the vision of self-in-other, by the counter-gaze of the other, they do not yet know that their deepest desire is for mutual recognition, community, and friendship.

All of this has been, in Spinoza's phrase, "under a certain look of eternity." It is a logical snapshot of what has yet to unfold in time. We now turn to that unfolding, to how self-consciousness appears, or *comes on the scene.*

The Fight for Recognition [186–88]

Hyppolite calls human desire "the disquiet [*l'inquiétude*] of the self" (167). This disquiet is vividly displayed in the individual who now appears. We are now at the beginning of the individual's actual experience of being self-aware. The individual here embodies the raw immediacy of selfhood—desire that now has a spiritual rather than natural object. He is the human, self-conscious version of sense-certainty's This. Hegel calls this raw immediacy "simple being-for-self" [186]. Selfhood here is simple because it is "self-equal through the exclusion from itself of everything else." It is the mere *being* or fact of selfhood. Selfhood in its immediacy is the Hobbesian condition of uncompromising egotism and self-assertiveness. The hallmark of sheer being-for-self is the repelling of all otherness: to be for oneself is to be against all others. In the present context, the simultaneous affirming of self and repelling of otherness takes the form of aggression.[10]

This egotism, to which all otherness is an affront, is reflected in language. Only I can use the pronoun "I." To me, the other is not an "I" but a "you" (and therefore an "it"). The pronoun "I" is a sign of my glory as a thinking being.[11] But this other is a self. He too uses the pronoun "I." And even if he does not actually *say* the pronoun, I see, in his vaunting gaze, that he calls himself "I."[12] How dare he do that! How dare he usurp the sacred pronoun, and with it my very selfhood! The recovery of self-identity requires the negation of my non-identity in this other who confronts me. I must recapture the sole use of the sacred pronoun. As simple being-for-self, the individual acts in accordance with his Declaration of Independence—"I AM MYSELF!" His vaunting egotism is the soil out of which community and freedom will eventually emerge.[13]

With the fight for recognition and the master-slave dialectic that follows, the *Phenomenology* becomes explicitly historical. This fight is the dialectical origin of history. It is easy to go astray in formulating the role of history in Hegel's book. First-time readers tend not to realize its importance in the *Phenomenology.* More experienced readers, especially those influenced by Marx, sometimes fall into the opposite error. They over-historicize the fight for recognition and the master-slave relation, and make the *Phenomenology* into a socio-anthropology.[14] Hyppolite makes a helpful observation in this regard: "The struggle for recognition is a category of historical life, not a specific, datable moment in human history, or rather pre-history" (170).[15] The fight for recognition is not so much the temporal beginning of history (although in some sense it is that as well) as the principle on the basis of which all human life and history must be understood.

The temporal history of man must not be confused with the philosophic or logical history of consciousness, although the two are connected. To be sure, spirit appears as history. In his final chapter, Hegel will say that spirit "empties itself" into historical time [808]. But the shapes of consciousness, the figures in Hegel's "picture gallery," are eternal archetypes. They are forms of soul, which, having once appeared in ages that were ripe for them, continue to do so throughout the ages in varying contexts to varying degrees. Masters, slaves, stoics, skeptics, and unhappy consciousnesses all continue to be part of the human experience, just as sense-certainty, perception, and understanding continue to play their part in human efforts to know the truth of objects.[16] The shapes of self-consciousness, like many character-types to come, are not just passing phases in man's history. They are *universal figures* and *eternal possibilities* that embody necessary logical moments of absolute spirit [808].[17]

As we now return to Hegel's text, let us bear in mind that we are witnessing the primordial, archetypal War of Independence. For the first time, an individual confronts an individual [186]. Each self resists mediation and division, which would compromise the unity of the self. These selves, as radical singularities or Thises, are like colliding bodies or forces that simply repel one another. The two selves exhibit self-consciousness in Hobbes' "state of nature."[18] They are "for one another like common objects, independent shapes, individuals submerged in the being of *life.*" Each is to the other merely "an unessential, negatively characterized object." But the self-certainty each possesses is still only internal and unproved. The two selves at this point do nothing but regard each other negatively—give each other a look. They have not "come out" and translated their being-for-self into action. Each self, therefore, "is indeed certain of its own self, but not of the other, and therefore its own self-certainty still has no truth" [186].

For Hegel, I am not a true being-for-self until I am *actively for myself,* and I cannot be actively for myself unless the other is also *actively for himself.* I cannot prove my own worth until I have gotten **B** to prove his. The situation reminds us of Hegel's earlier analysis of Newton's Third Law: my fist cannot assert itself against the wall unless the wall asserts *itself* by hitting back.

To actualize my self-certainty as **A**, I must negate **B**, who is the obstacle to my affirmation of myself, *and no other,* as absolute. But I must also negate my animal attachment to immediate being or life, my impulse to self-preservation. That is why the struggle or fight [*Kampf*] must be combat rather than murder—an *affaire d'honneur* like that between Achilles and Hektor in the *Iliad.*[19] In attacking **B**, I intend to provoke a counterattack that exposes me to death. In the last chapter, I noted that part of the problem of self-consciousness is that I have a body. This body, by attaching me to the immediacy of life, drags down my certainty of myself as a high or worthy being, a being that is purely inward and absolutely self-identical.

Self-consciousness is submerged in the medium of life and is therefore at odds with life. It is at odds, tragically, with its own necessary condition: "Self-consciousness thus is what exists through refusing to be" (Hyppolite, 167). By virtue of my body (a mere thing), I am outside myself and not self-identical. Here, that negative relation to body plays a key role in the dialectic of recognition. In seeking to negate the presumptuous independence of my other, my rival for the crown of selfhood, I must *risk my own life* [187]. This is reciprocity in action. Murder or assassination would be one-sided, untrue to the logical structure of self-consciousness. What I want in fighting the other is not the death of his body but the cancellation of his claim. As I act negatively against him, I must prove my own claim to absoluteness and therefore must fight against the thingly part of myself. The love of glory is the scorn of life.

This observation leads to another: the "life-and-death fight" [187] is not something bad for Hegel. In one sense, it is Hobbes' state of nature, the war of each against all. But it is not "nasty," as Hobbes says, in spite of its violence.[20] This is an important difference between Hegel and Hobbes. For Hobbes, the state of nature (or civil war) is an evil to be avoided through the social contract. For Hegel, the primordial fight is the necessary first step in the education of consciousness toward freedom as self-affirmation. It is the first impulse toward genuine community and better things to come. The two heroic selves "must engage in this fight, for they must raise their certainty of being *for themselves* to truth, both in the case of the other and in their own case."

The fight to the death is not only necessary: it is also noble. Addressing individual readers and peoples in all times and places, Hegel says: "And it is only through staking one's life that freedom is won." He thus pays tribute to the connection between human dignity and spiritedness. In Chapter 1, I noted that spirit is spirited: it risks itself in making claims to absolute truth. Here, in the chapter on self-consciousness, we get a clearer picture of why risk is essential to spirit. In the *Republic,* Socrates talks about spiritedness or *thymos* as a middle part of the soul. This part mediates between the "lower" appetite and the "higher" reason (4.439E ff.). If it had a natural place in our bodies, that place would be the chest.[21] Spiritedness, the Achilles part of the soul, delights in victory and honor. It longs to prove its worth and to be recognized by others—to be "above." Hegel promotes *thymos* to the status of a fundamental drive and principle. No longer a mere part of the soul, this new version of spiritedness animates and defines the self at its most fundamental stage. It is the force that moves the self toward freedom. Hegel disparages the individual who is not willing to risk his life in order to be free, the mere "person" with property rights [187].[22] But he lacks "the truth of this recognition as an independent self-consciousness." And the reason is that he lacks the spiritedness that signals the proper estimation of human selfhood and freedom. The mere person is, in the wonderful phrase of C. S. Lewis, a "man without a chest."[23]

The goal of the individual, as Hegel describes it, is a kind of purification. The individual has a mixed being. His being-for-self, what he most prizes in himself and considers his true essential being, is "caught up" [*befangenes*] in all sorts of non-essential relations that spring from his "immediacy." As a living individual, a man needs to eat and drink; he experiences sexual desire (a major distraction from his being-for-self); he gets tired; he has personal quirks; and so forth. Such trifles distract the individual from his true vocation, which is to prove his worth as absolute. In staking his life, he proves that he transcends his natural being or immediacy. This is what Hegel calls "absolute abstraction" [186]. Later in the *Phenomenology,* we meet the "moral valet" [665], who sees in the hero only the same human foibles that afflict the general lot of mankind. The moral valet is blind, or rather blinds himself, to heroism and reduces the hero to mere life. In Hegel's first "real man," we see the exact opposite of the moral valet. We see the refusal of the individual to play the moral valet to himself.

In its result, the noble life-and-death fight is self-defeating. It "does away with the truth which was supposed to issue from it, and so, too, with the certainty of self generally" [188]. This is the negative moment of dialectical experience we have seen many times before: the effort to make good on a claim to truth *fails.* The individual who risks his life and succeeds in killing the rival self does not get the recognition he desired. In the death of his double he has accomplished what Hegel calls a merely "*natural* negation of consciousness." The other is now no more to me than an apple that has been devoured. The "movement of recognition" has been brought to a standstill, short-circuited. In engaging in combat, I have risked my life. But in killing my double, I have killed the reciprocity and fluid "play of exchange" [*Spiel des Wechsels*] on which recognition depends [188]. After the battle, "the two [either both dead, or one dead and one alive] do not reciprocally give and receive one another back from each other consciously, but leave each other free only indifferently, like things." As simple being-for-self, self-consciousness wanted to rise above nature. In destroying either the other or himself, however, the individual has sunk back into nature. He fails to preserve what he negated and thus fails to prove the nobility of which he was certain. The fight for recognition, when its result is death, reenacts the tragedy inherent in natural desire.

Master and Slave [189–96]

In the life-and-death fight, self-consciousness failed to achieve, in the language of dueling, "satisfaction" of its honor. It experienced the truth "that life is as essential to it as pure self-consciousness" [189]. I must not die in the fight if I am to satisfy my desire for recognition. Nor must my rival. We must both *stay alive.*

In this new shape of self-consciousness, the individual tries to save his simple being-for-self or egotism by saving his own life and reducing his rival to a conscious still-living *thing* or non-self. Self-negation and life now go together: one self emerges from the fight as independent, the other dependent. The former gets recognition as absolute from the latter, but does not return it. The victorious self is only *for himself.* The vanquished self, who cancels or yields his independence, is only *for the other.* The first figure is lord or master [*Herr*], the second bondsman or slave [*Knecht*].[24]

The master-slave relation is the first concrete human bond in the *Phenomenology.* In other writings, notably the *The Philosophy of History,* Hegel describes the various ways in which slavery as an institution has appeared in world history: in ancient Greece and Rome, and in the feudalism of the

Middle Ages. The master-slave relation manifests itself within a much larger social, political, and theological context. But this larger world of knowing does not appear at the present stage of spiritual unfolding in the *Phenomenology.* Social contexts will emerge later in the book: the world of knowing will be a world in the concrete sense of the term. Hegel will even speak of "three worlds" of spirit [581]. But here, in the master-slave relation, the self's world of knowing is extremely constricted. What Hegel focuses on is not the larger world in which there are masters and slaves—not world as an elaborated, organic community—but the individual master and slave. A world, strictly speaking, does not yet figure into self-consciousness at all. The absence of a real world as a dialectical moment is important to the education of natural consciousness. Natural or immediate consciousness is *singular* consciousness that has not yet risen to universality, that is, to selfhood manifested as a whole world. Hegel will show how natural, singular self-consciousness, the love of personal glory, grows beyond itself and becomes *universal* self-consciousness.

The negative result of the first fight was the collapse of the syllogism that defines recognition [188]. Syllogism, or articulated mediation, is now revitalized. In being an actual, no longer merely implicit being-for-itself, the master has a consciousness that "is mediated with itself through another consciousness" [190]. Furthermore, this other consciousness, which is dependent, is nevertheless "synthesized" [*synthesiert*], put together with, the independence that belongs to *things.* Thinghood is woven into the fabric of the individual's self-awareness. It is the essence of the dependent, or slave, consciousness: the slave *works on things* in order to satisfy the natural desire of the master. He is, in Aristotle's definition, a living tool.[25]

The logical elements of the syllogism that defines recognition are now all present. Recognition is actual. The system of mediation or through-ness is as follows. The master is related to himself only through being related to both the slave and the thing that constitutes the essence of the slave. He is for himself only *through* the slave, and *through* the thing on which the slave works. The master is related "immediately to both [order the slave to work, eat the pie he makes], and mediately to each through the other [ordering and eating remind the master who is boss]" [190].

This logical formulation must now be made concrete or experiential. We recall that in the life-and-death fight, once one or both of the individuals died, the two combatants let each other go "like things." This thinghood is preserved in the new relation of selves and refers to mere life. The slave became a slave because, in the life-and-death fight, he experienced Hobbes' fear of violent death and chose life. He chose life over the recognition of his being-for-self as absolute, life over honor. Death for him was "the absolute lord" [194]. Soon Hegel will dwell on this aspect of the fight. For now, we need only see that the slave is attached to life. He is attached to himself as a mere thing and is not for himself but only for another, for the *use* of another. This attachment to life, and to himself as a thing, is the chain, "from which he could not break free in the fight" [190]. The master, however, the self who succeeded in getting his opponent to prefer life to honor, "is the power over this thing, for he proved in the fight that it [life as thinghood] is something merely negative." The slave is only secondarily a slave to his master. Primarily, he is a slave to his own life and to the fear of losing it.

That is how the master relates mediately to the slave through thinghood or mere life. But the master also "relates himself mediately to the thing [and to thinghood] through the slave." What all this mediation means is the following. The slave works on things for the master but does not enjoy them. He makes the apple pie but does not get to eat it. The master has his natural desire satisfied through the slave's work. This work makes actual the fact that the master is for himself, the slave for another. Since the slave does not consume or enjoy what he works on, the thing on which he works remains, for him, independent. In the independence of the thing, the slave sees the chain that made him a slave: the independence of life as the thing-like other of self-consciousness.

Self-consciousness is now at a higher level. It is higher because the system of mediation (the syllogism) is preserved. The master-slave relation succeeds in doing what mere desire and the fight-to-the-death could not. Self-consciousness is desire [167, 174]. But desire is self-defeating or tragic since the object of desire is constantly posited by desire and so remains independent [175]. Desire as such is an incomplete *Aufhebung* or sublation. I eat the apple, and desire or dissatisfaction immediately reasserts itself. But the master does not encounter apples as independent things at all. He does not experience the apple as something that must be reached for and gotten hold of in order to be eaten. On the contrary, he has apples brought to him and even made into apple pies. The master now accomplishes what desire of itself could not when it involved only one individual: "the master, who has interposed the slave between [the object of desire] and himself, takes to himself only the dependent aspect of the thing and has the pure enjoyment of it" [190]. For the master, the object of desire no longer resists him as other or independent: it is not something he has to conquer. His eating of apples brought to him by the slave or made into pies is therefore different from what it was at the previous stage: it is pure enjoyment. The master leaves the independent aspect of the thing to the slave, "who works on it." Of course, this also means that desire is de-spiritualized for the master, who has become a constantly satisfied *consumer.*

As we know, recognition is logically complete only if what one self-consciousness does to another, that other also does to itself. This is the apparent victory of the master over the slave: "the other consciousness [the slave] cancels its own being-for-self, and in so doing itself does what the first [the master] does to it" [191]. The self that clings to life and becomes a slave gives up all authority for his actions; he yields his independence or self-determination. He does only what the master tells him to do, and is purely instrumental. The result is that "what the slave does is really the action of the master." The master is authoritative, not just because "what he says goes," but because in metaphysical strictness only he can be said to act. He is the essential, spontaneous side of the relation, and the slave is the non-essential —a re-action rather than an action.

Clearly, the slave does not do to the master what he does to himself, nor does the master do to himself what he does to the slave. Reciprocity is still incomplete. And so, mutual recognition, the end of self-consciousness, has not yet been achieved [191]. In spite of the master's apparent victory, self-consciousness has failed to posit an object that corresponds to its concept. The desire that matters remains unsatisfied.

But there is an even greater failure at work. This is the inversion or *Verkehrung* of the master-slave relation: master and slave have their truth, not in themselves but in *each other,* that is, in their opposites. The result of this inversion is that the master is debased and the slave ennobled. Let us see how this reversal comes about.

In the master-slave relation, the master, as I noted above, is essential, the slave non-essential. The master is wholly independent or for himself, the slave wholly dependent or for another. But the master wants a slave not in order to eat apple pies he does not have to make, but in order to confirm his claim to independence, his "I AM MYSELF!" The master's self-certainty is made true and actual, here, in a *non-essential or insignificant self* [192]. But recognition that comes from an unworthy, non-essential being, a mere slave, is no recognition at all. The master thus fails to have his self-certainty made actual, since the non-essential status of the slave undercuts the supreme worth of recognition. And so, as we have seen in previous shapes of consciousness, "this object [the slave, in whom the master sought to actualize his self-certainty] does not correspond to its concept" [192]. The object has turned out to be "something quite different from an independent consciousness," that is, a dependent or slavish consciousness. The truth of the master is therefore no truth at all, since it comes from a slave, a being who is incapable of confirming the master's self-certainty: "The *truth* of the independent consciousness is accordingly the servile consciousness of the slave" [193].

The slave consciousness, too, has its certainty in its opposite. It grows beyond its immediate condition: "as a consciousness forced back into itself, it will withdraw into itself and be transformed into a truly independent consciousness" [193]. Hegel proceeds to show us how the very things that make the slave a slave bring about his awareness of himself as *independent* of the master, or for himself.

This inversion of master and slave confirms an important point made by Hyppolite: "The path of mastery is a dead end in human experience; the path of servitude is the true path of human liberation" (174). As Hegel now turns to what the slave consciousness is "in and for itself," we come to see that the master's life, the life of constantly satisfied natural desire, is boring, static, and unmanly. Deprived of the suffering that would drive him into himself and make him reflective, and equally deprived of the challenges that would spark his *thymos* and drive him to greater heights, the master is dragged down to the realm of nature. In rising up as master, he is spiritually degraded. He becomes the slave of life and desire.

The three things that constitute the slave's bondage are *fear, service,* and *work* or labor. Each of these "chains" is in fact the slave's bond with independence and provides the dialectical seed of genuine mastery and freedom. Just as the master has his truth in the slave, the slave has his truth in the master, in "the independent consciousness that is *for itself*" [194]. In the last two paragraphs of the section, Hegel reveals the various ways in which the slave is for himself or independent. As we read this last part of the analysis, we must ask: How are the three chains intertwined? And in what respects is the slave aware, and not aware, of his truth as an independent self?

To address these questions, we must look at who the slave is from the slave's own perspective: what slave-consciousness is "in and for itself." In his obedient service [*Dienst*], the slave acts in such a way as to make the master the slave's essence and truth. This is the most obvious way in which slave-consciousness has its truth in its opposite: the being-for-self or independence of the master. But the slave qua obedient servant is not aware that this is his own truth and independence. His explicit awareness of his being-for-self comes from the other chain—*fear* [*Furcht*].

Fear, for Hegel, is essential to true education. Fear deepens us, forces us back into ourselves, and makes us acutely self-aware. Recalling Proverbs 9:10, Hegel says, in reference to the slave's initial fear of the master (in the life-and-death fight), that "the fear of the lord is indeed the beginning of wisdom" [195]. The slave's fear is experienced as negative. In having trembled before the opponent bent on destroying him, the slave trembled before Death itself, the "absolute lord or master" [194]. He has experienced dread [*Angst*] and utter dissolution [*Auflösung*]. His whole world has been shaken to its foundations. This is why his fear is also positive. It is the experience of the dialectical truth of self-consciousness, which is "pure universal movement," "the absolute flowing away of everything stable," "absolute negativity" [194]. Through fear, the slave has felt the negative essence that defines self-consciousness as movement or process. This process is "pure being-for-self" [194], the relation that allows me to say "I AM MYSELF!" In the fear of violent death, the slave has felt, profoundly, the bond between life and self-consciousness. He has experienced a piercing self-feeling—the feeling of himself *as an absolutely unified self-loving self.*

This is the subjective way in which the slave is aware of independence. The objective independence is, of course, the master himself, whom the slave feared and now recognizes as existing independently or on his own. In the master, the slave sees his subjective fear objectified: that is, the master is the object of his former fear of violent death. The slave's explicit awareness of self as self comes out in the other two chains that tie him to his master: service and work. In service, he does the bidding of another. In the inverted world of master and slave, service, like fear, is positive. In service, I give up my claim to all natural existence: to food and drink, procreation, even sleep. In stripping myself naked with respect to bodily nature and in working for the master, I experience my independence from nature—my spiritual, non-bodily being-for-self.

But even this is still only an implicit, not fully concrete experience of the dissolution or negativity that constitutes being-for-self. It is through work, *Arbeit,* that self-consciousness comes to be "in and for itself" or completely actual: "Through work, the slave becomes conscious of what he truly is" [195].

With the slave's work, we reach the peak of this first main part of Hegel's chapter (the part entitled "Independence and Dependence of Self-Consciousness"). The slave's work is more than the work of a slave. It is a prophetic figure of *thought itself,* "the work or labor of the negative" [19], which fashions the world in its own image, thereby establishing its absolute right to all things. In working on nature, the slave embodies the work of negativity. He breaks the mold of consciousness. Sense-certainty, perception, and understanding, were all modes of consciousness. They all displayed the cognitive "piety" toward objects. The slave destroys this piety. In work, he experiences the objective world as having an essence only insofar as it is remade by a human self.

Desire failed to get what it wanted. The negation of the thing (the apple) posited the thing all over again since desire always needs food for negation. In the master-slave relation, the dependent aspect of the thing fell to the master, who, as desire personified, gobbled it up, while the independent aspect fell to the slave, who made pies he did not eat. Ultimately, the dialectic reveals that it is the master whose sense of self is fleeting, since desire and its natural satisfaction are fleeting [195]. Desire and work are thus inverses of each other. Work is "desire held in check [*gehemmte*] and fleetingness staved off." Whereas desire consumes and reduces things to nothing, work "builds" or gives things form and lastingness. In this way, one of the things that made the slave a slave, the abiding independence of the pie he did not eat, turns out to be that in which he experiences his independence from the master, his *being-for-self* [196].

Work, like desire, is negative, but not in the same way. Desire negates the object by destroying its form. But work destroys the object's natural form in order to give it a new, artful form—a form congenial to man. It makes a mere object into a product of human labor, a thing that embodies the soul or selfhood of the human laborer. In Hegel's dialectical understanding of work, the slave, in making the pie, invests himself in the pie.[26] By yielding himself completely to labor and production and by sacrificing desire, he loses himself only to find himself in the object that for him remains independent. In the independent product of his labor, the slave sees his own being-for-self. The slave, in short, is the world's first artist and "master of the world," even if at this stage he fails to grasp the full significance of labor as spiritual accomplishment and self-overcoming.

It is important to grasp the intertwining of the three chains: fear, service, and work. Only together do these bring out the slave's being-for-self. The slave makes pies because he must do his master's bidding. And he obeys because, in the fight for recognition, he trembled before Death, the greatest Lord and Master. Without this fear, the slave's work would not be self-transformative. The dialectical moment of fear is preserved in the dialectical moment of work. Work transforms the thing by negating it (apples become the pie). In work, the slave too is transformed: he rises above his initial fear of death. But, to repeat, this would not have happened if he had not experienced fear. The thing on which the slave works embodies the violent attachment to life that made him a slave—the fear of death, the ultimate negation. In work, the slave "posits *himself* as a negative in the permanent order of things, and thereby becomes *for himself*" [196]. The external thing is thus no longer alien: it is the slave's own being-for-self. In the thing that he has made, the slave recovers the independence he lost in the life-and-death fight. He has *found himself again* [196].

In working for the master, the slave at first seemed to have only "an alien mind" [*fremder Sinn*], the awareness of himself only as one who does the master's bidding. But work transforms this immediate awareness into its opposite. Through work, the slave acquires "his own mind" [*eigner Sinn*]. He experiences a "rediscovery of himself by himself." For this rediscovery to occur, however, work cannot be simply work. The other two chains, fear and service, must also be present. In working, the slave does not forget what made him a slave, what it felt like to fear the Absolute Master. Nor does he forget that his life is service to another. In the end, master and slave have their truth in one other, but they have not escaped from their respective roles or from their one-sided relation. The master at this point becomes dialectically irrelevant: he is swallowed by his desires. And the slave, although his condition points to a new shape of consciousness, remains a slave—one who has a sense of himself, but not a will of his own.

Hegel wards off any sentimentalism regarding the slave's work and the discovery of "his own mind" by stressing the role of negativity in the slave's transformation. He thus makes us aware of the larger implications of slavery. The slave needed to be a slave in order to "find himself again." He is not some conceited artist, the Poet of Apple Pies, who "suffers for his art" (that is, for his vanity). Nor does he simply fear and serve another. Fear, work, and service—*all three* are necessary to the discovery of his independence. Indeed, they are necessary to the education, and liberation, of man as self-consciousness, to his mastery of the world through *Bildung* or culture and "formative activity" [*Formieren*] [196]. Without the three chains by which man surmounts his natural consciousness, the human self is a spoiled child, whose having a "mind of his own" [*eigner Sinn*] is no more than sheer *obstinacy* [*Eigensinn*]. This is "a freedom still enmeshed in servitude."[27] Negativity must be complete and devastating if selfhood, as "absolute Concept," is to make itself "the universal power [*Macht*] and objective being in its entirety" [196].

The master-slave dialectic leaves us with a master who is no longer a man, and a slave who, in his being-for-another, has experienced his being-for-self. At a more universal level, the slave reveals the self's *right to all things.* In the product of his labor, the slave recognizes his independence from the master. But he is still a slave and does not yet recognize this independence in himself apart from the thing. He has not yet discovered the work that has no product but itself—the work of *thinking.*

For freedom is not acquired by filling ourselves up with the things we desire, but is the demolishing of desire.

EPICTETUS, *Discourses*

 9

Freedom as Thinking

IN THIS NEXT SECTION OF HEGEL'S CHAPTER, WE MEET THREE distinctive character-types: stoic, skeptic, and unhappy consciousness. These figures are more overtly historical than those of the previous section. The stoic and skeptic belong to imperial pagan Rome. And the unhappy consciousness is manifested in the medieval Christian. But like the figures we met in our last chapter, the stoic, the skeptic, and the unhappy consciousness are not confined to a single temporal horizon. As eternal archetypes within spirit's absolute knowledge of itself [808], they reappear in various forms throughout world-history.

In spite of the overtly historical aspect of these new shapes of knowing, we must bear in mind that self-consciousness continues to be an isolated individual self-consciousness. The stoic, skeptic, and unhappy consciousness all presuppose a social, political, and religious context. But this context is not part of the analysis here. It belongs to a more advanced world of knowing, in which selfhood experiences itself as objective and universal, that is, as concretized within a community. Our three new shapes are far from the "I that is We and the We that is I" that is the logical destiny of self-consciousness.

In the present chapter, we take up the stoic and the skeptic: in the next, the unhappy consciousness.

The Dream of the Stoic [197–202]

As Hegel's title for this section indicates, the overarching theme that unites our three new shapes is *freedom*. The previous section was about independence and dependence. Now consciousness is at a higher level of self-assertion and self-sufficiency. Independence is low-level freedom, mere non-dependence on another. A thing can be independent, as we saw in the claim of perception. Freedom, by contrast, is actively self-positing and intelligent. Up to this point, the individual had been a warrior and either a master or a slave. Now he is a thinker and therefore free: he has a self-concept. As Hegel says in another context: "Freedom is just thought itself; he who casts thought aside and speaks of freedom knows not what he is talking of."[1]

Hegel begins by reviewing the difference between master and slave. These figures, as we saw, exchanged roles in a classic case of inversion. Each had its truth in the other. The independent or master self is "only the pure abstraction of the 'I'" [197]. The master did not receive the recognition he sought, since his verification was lodged in the non-essential being or slave. As I noted in Chapter 7, the destiny of self-consciousness is to be a self-differentiating One that knows itself as a self-differentiating One. For the master, this self-differentiation has not occurred concretely. His essence [*Wesen*] is only inwardly self-differentiating and fails to become objective. The master gives this or that order, and has this or that fleeting desire gratified by the slave. But he has no relation to things qua things, things in their independence. Nothing, for him, is objective or in itself. He does no work and so fails to make his selfhood real. Self-consciousness, we recall, was self-identity as the overcoming of self-otherness [167]. But the master does not generate any real otherness. He therefore slips back into unproven self-certainty —the formal and abstract I = I.

The slave, by contrast, develops real differences through work. This is the first step toward real freedom. He makes things and is the world's first artist, demiurge, and developer. In giving lasting form [*Bild*] to the world, the slave himself is formed and educated [*gebildet*]. Through work, attended by fear and service, he "goes into himself" or is deepened, as he "comes out" into the world in the product of his labor. The apple pie that is not consumed by the slave is the slave's selfhood made real. In work and its product, the slave recovers what he lost in the fight for recognition: his independence.

But in his newfound independence of mind, the slave is still a slave. He is aware that in spite of his independence not he but his master exhibits being-for-self [197]. The slave is the living contradiction of dependence and independence. The contradiction is focused in the independence of the thing the slave has made, and which he beholds. This thing leads a double life. It embodies the slave himself, who, through work, has invested himself in the thing and sees himself in it. It also embodies the master or consciousness that is independent or for itself. From the slave's perspective, these two aspects of the thing "fall apart" [197]. In the thing made, the slave beholds a subject and an object. Or rather, he beholds a subject that is an object (himself), and an object that is the genuine subject (the master). The slave does not put these two moments together. He does not think himself as the *substance* of the thing, even though he experiences himself *in* the thing. The reason is that he does not experience himself as substantial: he sees the master rather than himself as the essential or independent self. The slave does not see that, qua conscious worker, he rather than the master is the substance of things—the being that gives form, lastingness, and value to them.

We phenomenological observers see in the made thing what the slave does not. We see it as concretized subjectivity, selfhood that is in and for itself or is its own object. In other words, we see that what things are *in themselves* is what they are *for the self*—that the substance of things is their relation to the thinking subject or consciousness. We grasp the synthetic unity of the two moments (the objective in-itself and the subjective for-itself) that "fell apart" for the slave. The awareness of this synthetic unity is "self-consciousness in a new shape" [197]: the stoic.[2] Hegel describes this new shape in terms of the infinity that was generated by the understanding [160–61]. This is the "pure movement" of consciousness itself, the unbounded or free movement of thinking. The stoic, in other words, is the identity of thinking and freedom.

As usual, Hegel does not immediately name the new shape. He dwells instead on the universality and spiritual phase that the shape embodies. The stoic principle "is that consciousness is a thinking being [*Wesen*], and that something is essential for it, or is true and good, only insofar as consciousness conducts itself in it as a thinking being" [198].[3]

That thinking only now makes its appearance in the *Phenomenology* may surprise us. Were not all the previous shapes thinkers insofar as they were shapes of consciousness? Surely, the heroes of understanding, men like Newton and Leibniz, were thinkers. One difference, however, is that understanding, as a mode of consciousness (in its restricted sense), was interested in the substance and causality of *things.* It almost grasped that consciousness itself was the truth and substance of objects. Understanding, *Verstand,* was incomplete idealism. The stoic, by contrast, consciously affirms himself as absolute. He is thus the first positive step toward *complete* idealism, the full revelation of the thinking subject as the substance of things [17].

The decisive difference between the stoic and the heroes of understanding lies in the all-important word, freedom. The stoic is a world unto himself.[4] Occasionally, he may talk about nature, gods, and providence, but the real core of his teaching is self-sufficiency. The stoic asserts himself, and needs no Beyond. He recognizes himself as absolute. He knows that as a purely intellectual being he is infinitely worthy and needs no other, not even a god, to make his self-certainty real. Or rather, the stoic's integrity, concentrated in his boundless power of thought, is his god—the god within. The stoic is superior to the heroes of mere theory because he adopts a moral stance with respect to his thinking. He identifies the true with the good, and the good with freedom understood as autonomy. He connects knowledge or reason with man as self-consciousness. The stoic thus sets the stage for Descartes' imperious "I think, therefore I am."

Hegel's characterization of stoic consciousness is borne out by the two historical stoics to whom he alludes: Marcus Aurelius and Epictetus. The first was a Roman emperor, the second a former slave. Their radical inequality of station makes the point that the stoic is free "whether on the throne or in chains" [199].

In earlier chapters, I introduced a shape of knowing by pointing out what was attractive about that shape. In the case of the stoic, the attraction is clear. Life is full of suffering and uncertainty. In our dependence on external things and the play of chance, we are the slaves of hope and fear. We are victims, not of external circumstances but of our passions and imagination. The stoic refuses to be a victim. To counteract the enslavement to passion and imagination, and to the fear of violent death, he cultivates freedom from passion or *apatheia.* He makes himself a fortress of self-contained invulnerability, an impregnable self-same One. He does this by thinking. As Hegel puts it, the stoic "always comes directly out of bondage and returns into the pure universality of thought" [199]. This return involves "thinking away" both the external world and that part or aspect of the stoic himself that is bound up with externals: his own human singularity. These implicit negations will become important as we proceed.

The most remarkable thing about Hegel's stoic is that he is the father of pure conceptuality: thinking as Concept. Thinking, for the stoic, is not the thinking of objects but the thinking of *thinking* as the substance of objects: "in thinking, the object does not present itself in representations [*Vorstellungen*] or shapes [*Gestalten*] but in *concepts* [*Begriffen*]" [199]. The stoic's moral freedom, his mastery of passion, derives from his intellectual freedom. The stoic can effectively withdraw from his bondage to externals because his thinking abstracts from representations or images and returns to its own pure universality. Through the god-like power of non-representational thought, he is free from anxiety about this or that human fate, and from the terrors conjured by the imagination. Stoic consciousness reminds us that, for Hegel, representational thinking or imagination (the hallmark of natural consciousness) is spiritual bondage—Ariel in the cloven pine. This bondage resembles the enslavement to images we see in the cave dwellers of Plato's *Republic.* As the first appearance of purely conceptual thinking, the stoic is the gateway to Hegel's own logic as the spontaneous self-development of the Concept.

The stoic gives us our first glimpse of true freedom: "In thinking, I *am free,* because I am not in an other, but remain simply and solely with myself [*bei mir*], and the object, which is for me the essence, is in undivided unity my being-for-myself; and my movement in concepts is a movement in my own self" [197]. Thinking, for Hegel, is the purest and most intimate form of self-relation. In thinking, I am in my own presence. I am at home with myself, *bei mir*, as an inward or spiritual being.

We are reminded here of what Timaeus says about the divine cosmos in Plato's dialogue: that it was made to be its own best friend (34B). We also recall Aristotle's view that thinking is the highest form of happiness, since it displays, more than any other activity, *autarkeia* or self-sufficiency.[5] On the modern side, there is a connection between stoic freedom and Spinoza's definition of freedom in the *Ethics:* "That thing is said to be free which exists solely from the necessity of its own nature, and is determined to action by itself alone" (part I, definition 7). Pure thinking, thinking through concepts alone, meets this condition. It is spontaneous or self-determining as well as self-contained or "with itself."

Pure thinking and nobility of soul bring the stoic into close contact with Plato and Aristotle, for whom thinking is the highest freedom. To be sure, Plato and Aristotle are vastly more interesting, because more speculative, than the stoics. The Roman stoic does not even seem to acknowledge anything like contemplation. For him, philosophy is moral philosophy, and even this is practical wisdom rather than moral inquiry. But two things must be said on the stoic's behalf. The first is that the stoic, especially the Roman stoic, reveals spirit at this stage of its development because of the stark opposition he generates between inner and outer, self and world. As a generator of dichotomies, the stoic is the forerunner of the Cartesian dualism that defines the modern world. Plato and Aristotle are too advanced and metaphysically rich to capture this polemic stance that the self, as stoic, takes with respect to the external world. The speculative limits of the stoic are, in this respect, precisely his strength. Stoicism is the stark immediacy with which pure thought, as a *will to power,* asserts its claim as master of the world. In this way, the stoic sets the stage for the self-confidence of modern reason.

A second point is that the stoic is much closer than Plato and Aristotle to the universal problem of human existence or *Dasein,* as Hegel understands it. To the stoic, human life, the life he sees all around him but from which he escapes in thought, is a condition of intense, widespread anxiety, suffering, and spiritual homelessness or alienation. His entire moral system is designed to neutralize this condition. In his *Philosophy of History,* Hegel defines the world-spirit, in its Roman phase, as a forsaken Dido: with Rome, "the world is sunk in melancholy: its heart is broken" (278). In another work, he calls ancient Rome "the universal unhappiness of the world."[6] Plato and Aristotle do not connect philosophy with suffering. They speak to the few, whereas the stoic speaks to mankind. Stoic wisdom is accessible to people of modest intellectual gifts, and is eminently practical (especially in terrible times).

Recalling imperial Rome, Hegel notes that stoicism, as a "universal form of world spirit," came on the scene "in a time of universal fear and bondage, but also a time of universal culture" [199]. Stoic thinking is a response to a question Plato and Aristotle never asked: How can a human being be master of his fate under the worst, most potentially enslaving circumstances?

The *Phenomenology* does not end with the stoic and his pure thinking. We cannot jump directly from stoic freedom to Hegel's logic. Hegel emphasizes that the stoic represents pure thinking only in general, and that "its object is an *immediate* unity of *being-in-itself* [objects] and *being-for-itself* [the subject or thinker]" [197]. The stoic knows that "being and thinking are the same," to quote Parmenides. But he knows this only "as a universal essence in general, not as an objective essence in the development and movement of its manifold being."[7]

His godlike *apatheia* and awareness of suffering notwithstanding, the stoic enjoys a merely abstract freedom. It is true that the stoic does not have his essence in something other than himself. Nor is he simply the master's abstract I (the master was unthinking and did not know himself as free). Nevertheless, his freedom remains unreal, a mere dream. The source of this abstract, dreamy unreality is the stoic indifference to life: "Freedom in thought has only pure thought as its truth, a truth lacking the fullness of life" [200]. Stoic freedom is only a freedom in the mind, not "the living reality of freedom itself." The stoic flees from the world rather than being actively reconciled to it. And the world, for all its woes, has a concreteness and vitality that the stoic, in his dreamy self-sufficiency, lacks.

From the beginning, self-consciousness was at odds with life. It posited itself as absolute in the sense of radically self-identical. The self was pure self-relation, I = I, for which life was thinghood—an otherness begging to be negated by desire. Stoicism is a refined negation of life. In his *ataraxia* or unperturbed indifference, the stoic holds himself apart from life. He protects himself from the disordering influence of fear and desire, and strives to maintain his pure inwardness as absolute. The abstract non-living freedom of the stoic derives from the abstract character of his thinking. It is true that the stoic opens up the realm of pure conceptual thinking. But this thinking "has no content *in its own self* but one that is *given* to it." This is the closest Hegel comes to saying that there is still something servile about the stoic. The word "given" is the sign that stoic thinking, in spite of its purity (or rather because of it) has not succeeded in rising above natural consciousness, man's enslavement to the given.

Hegel's account of the stoic mixes praise and blame. The stoic is noble, right-minded, and temperate. We admire him and applaud his high regard for pure thought as the true self of each. Nor can we deny that in the midst of extreme misfortune stoicism makes sense. But the stoic, in addition to being cold, is also platitudinous. He is constantly telling us, "Be reasonable," but does not explain or even question what being reasonable means—what the true, the good, wisdom, and virtue *are.* Lacking this Socratic moment, he falls back on something for which Hegel has a special distaste: edifying discourse. As we hear in the Preface, in one of Hegel's memorable apothegms: "philosophy must beware of wanting to be edifying" [9]. It must beware, that is, of substituting the flattery of elevated feeling for the hard work of thinking.

The edifying tone of stoic discourse derives from the "incomplete negation of otherness" [201]. The stoic is above fear and desire. He is nobody's slave. He is indifferent to external things (including his own body) and their influence. But unlike the slave from the preceding section, he is also above the work of negation. This is what his thinking lacks. He is too high-minded and pure to do the dirty work of negating the world in thought.[8] And yet, his indifference to external things, his treatment of them as non-essential, necessarily implies that the world is in fact nothing—that it has been exposed by thought as thoroughly non-essential. Lacking that exposé, the stoic's self-certainty is a certainty lacking truth. The skeptic actualizes what stoic negativity merely implies: "*Skepticism* is the realization of that of which stoicism was only the concept, and is the actual experience of what the freedom of thought is" [202].

Hegel's account of the stoic is strikingly free of dialectical tension. It is mostly description. This lack of tension mirrors the placidity of the stoic himself. The transition to the skeptic is similarly undramatic. It consists simply in the fact that stoic freedom necessarily implies a negative work that the stoic himself has not carried out. The transition resembles the move within the thing of perception from the placid Also or medium to the "One that excludes" [114]. Both are moves from something posited to some condition that is *pre*-posited. Like the stoic, the skeptic is a gateway to Hegel's logic. The stoic gives thinking its principle of purity, self-containment, and spontaneity: the skeptic provides the equally necessary moment of unfettered negation.

The Work of the Skeptic [202–7]

Hegel's skeptic is the Imp of Contrariety. For him, thinking is actual and concrete only insofar as it "annihilates the being of the world in all its manifold determinateness" [202]. Like stoicism, skepticism is a claim to absolute knowing in the form of intellectual freedom. The skeptic does not merely go around negating things in thought. His spree of bubble bursting is the act in which he asserts himself and his thinking as master of the world. Skeptical thinking is a return to desire and work [202]. With the stoic, desire and work went underground. With the skeptic, they re-emerge in a more educated form.

The skepticism under investigation here is not the modern skepticism of Hume but the ancient Roman skepticism of Sextus Empiricus, whom Hegel discusses at length in his *Lectures on the History of Philosophy* (2:338–73). This is the skepticism (or Pyrrhonism, after its Greek founder, Pyrrho) that was admired by Montaigne and attacked by Pascal.[9] In reading Sextus, one is struck by the identical goals of stoicism and skepticism. Like the stoic, the skeptic aims at *ataraxia* or unperturbedness. His moral purpose is the same as that of the stoic: to liberate and pacify the human individual. The skeptic, however, is at war with *dogmatism,* that is, with all forms of certainty. The only certain truth for him is that nothing is certain. Unlike the stoic, the skeptic has a method. By practicing the logic of refutation, the skeptic achieves what he takes to be the highest human virtue and true freedom. This is the skeptic's famous *epochē* or "suspension of judgment," by which the skeptic achieves "mental tranquility."[10]

Thinking, for the skeptic, is the infinity of thought, just as it was for the stoic. The stoic captures infinity as intellectual self-containment and self-reference, the skeptic as the presence of opposites in each other (infinity as it appeared in the dialectic of understanding [163]). The skeptic, as I mentioned above, is the return to desire and work. In their earlier appearance, desire and work "were unable to effect the negation for self-consciousness" [202]. Desire posited its object all over again, and work produced an independent object that embodied the worker-slave's chain to his master. The skeptic is beyond these limitations. He approaches the world as a fully confident, freewheeling self-consciousness—a self that is supreme master, warrior, and exposer of the logical one-sidedness that inheres in every idea (time, place, cause, gods, etc.). Skeptical thinking is the new fight to the death, in which the skeptic always wins. Infinity, which first appeared in the understanding, is the weapon he uses to transform all determinations into their opposites—to show that every finite claim to know is self-contradictory.

In Hegel's deep reading of the skeptic, this dissolution of the world is the projection of thought's own self-negativity. Understanding had projected a changeless Beyond. Through the skeptic, self-consciousness projects its own obliteration of difference: "The differences, which in the pure thinking of self-consciousness are only the abstraction of differences, here become the *entirety* of the differences, and the whole of differentiated being becomes a difference of self-consciousness" [202]. What Hegel seems to be saying in this dizzying sentence is that skepticism enacts the potential for destruction that is inherent in self-consciousness as desire. Skepticism is the French Reign of Terror without bloodshed. Everything for it belongs, and always will belong, to a metaphysical *ancien régime.* The skeptical self negates the world, annihilates all established differences, and in this negation experiences nothing but itself. This is the negativity and otherness that define self-consciousness.

The skeptic's thinking is, in fact, the dialectical movement we have witnessed in all the previous shapes of consciousness, from sense-certainty up through the master-slave dialectic [203]. The skeptic reveals the negative truth at the heart of every certainty and every supposedly stable determination, even moral determinations and ethical laws that seem to be sovereign commands. Nothing is immune to skeptical deconstruction. Needless to say, the difference between Hegel's negations and those of the skeptic is that the latter are not determinate: they aim solely at destruction. Stoic thinking is purely formal or empty. It was dependent on a given content, that is, a content not generated by thought itself. The same formality or emptiness haunts skeptical thinking. Stoic and skeptic both depend on a content that is given rather than self-generated. The skeptic *finds* distinctions all around him and applies his skepticism to them. This is how his thinking spreads itself, like a virus: by "attaching the Concept in fact in a merely external way to the being constituting its content." The skeptic is not as free as he imagines. In spite of his resemblance to the hard-at-work slave, he is also like the master who eats food that is prepared by others.

In the earlier shapes of knowing, dialectic was something suffered. Now it is deliberately practiced, or rather perpetrated. For the skeptic, dialectic "is a moment of self-consciousness, to which it does not *happen* that its truth and reality vanish without its knowing how, but which, in the certainty of its freedom, *makes* this 'other' which claims to be real, vanish" [204]. Hegel adds: "What skepticism causes to vanish is not only objective reality as such, but its own relationship with it." In addition to gleefully destroying the steadfastness of things, the skeptic also gives up those tempters in the soul that lead us to place our trust in things: perception and dogmatizing, which the skeptic regards as sophistry. He pulls the rug out from under himself (the skeptic's final prank) and asserts himself as absolutely free. In this strange way, the skeptic is "with himself" in being negatively "with" the objective world, since his thinking is itself sheer negativity. The negativity or inherent nothingness of the world *is* the skeptic's selfhood and freedom. In negating the world, the skeptic preserves himself as the "stoic indifference of a thinking which thinks itself, the unchanging and genuine certainty of itself" [205].

We now move closer to the contradiction *within* skeptical thinking. Where, we must ask, does all the instability and negation that the skeptic exposes come from? Not from "something alien," as we have seen, but from consciousness itself. The skeptic posits himself as stoically detached from self-negation by being the impregnable spoiler of other people's certainties, the "god of refutation."[11] But as skeptical thinking, "consciousness itself is the *absolute dialectical unrest*" of *all* perceptions and dogmatic assertions. Skeptical consciousness is therefore not stoically self-identical at all. It is instead "a purely casual, confused medley, the dizziness of perpetually self-engendered disorder" [205]. Furthermore, the skeptic is aware of this dizziness and actively produces it in himself to keep dogmatism at bay. Like the relativist whose relativism turns against him, the skeptic must confess that his own consciousness is merely empirical or contingent, that he is a mere mortal like everybody else, prone to error and misplaced trust in the senses. He is what Hegel provocatively calls a "*lost* self-consciousness" [205]. But the skeptic, rather than abandoning the skepticism that led him here, reasserts his absolute self-identity and the universality of his certainty that all things are uncertain. He becomes thoroughly contradictory. By turns, he posits himself as master of the world and as the slave of contingency and animal nature, as god and as beast. Skeptical consciousness cannot "bring these two thoughts of itself together."

Hegel relishes describing the giddy whirl of skepticism. He seems to enjoy the spectacle in which the higher dialectic exposes the lower. The skeptic "pronounces an absolute vanishing, but the pronouncement *is*." He is the relativist for whom relativism is absolute. He perpetrates the very dogmatism he seeks to destroy. The theory of the skeptic, Hegel observes, is constantly at variance with his practice. He destroys seeing and hearing in thought but continues to see and hear, and to trust what he sees and hears. He destroys the fixity of ethical determinations but continues to live in accordance with them.

The result of this dialectic is that the skeptic experiences himself as *two consciousnesses* in one: an above-it-all universal consciousness and an individual consciousness afflicted with contingency, self-otherness, and animal instincts. He is both intellectual master and slave. The skeptic does not put these two selves together but is always going back and forth between them. If you point out to the skeptic one side of him, he will point out the other. Hegel compares the skeptic's split personality to two stubborn children, one of whom, out of sheer perversity, says A when the other says B, and B when the other says A [205]. In the skeptic, Roman gravitas degenerates into a degrading, and tedious, spectacle of immaturity.

In skepticism, "consciousness in truth experiences itself as internally contradictory" [206]. The skeptic is not one self but two: a changeable and an unchangeable consciousness. He experiences these two selves as constantly passing into each other. At this crucial moment in the *Phenomenology*, there emerges the spiritual shape Hegel calls the unhappy consciousness, "the consciousness of self as a dual-natured, merely contradictory being." The logical transition takes place because the skeptic, in spite of his duality, is *one and the same individual.* The skeptic experiences himself as the perpetual transition from changeable to unchangeable consciousness. But he does not think these two forms of consciousness within a single consciousness: the conflicting selves are not experienced as *in each other.* In other words, he has only an incomplete experience of the infinity or self-negation that defines his skepticism.

As an unhappy consciousness, spirit for the first time experiences itself as explicitly self-contradictory. It "knows that it is the dual consciousness of itself, as self-liberating, unchangeable, and self-identical, and as self-bewildering and self-perverting, and it is the awareness of this self-contradictory nature of itself" [206].

The unhappy consciousness experiences the two selves that have been dialectically generated by the skeptic—the changeable and the unchangeable consciousness—as, respectively, man and God. This consciousness is the unity of the human and the divine. But it does not experience this unity as the reconciliation of the human and the divine [207]. Like the stoic and skeptic, the unhappy consciousness will experience infinity, but only as an infinite yearning for an infinitely remote Beyond. Stoic and skeptic were efforts to reach freedom and to surmount slave consciousness. As an unhappy consciousness, the human individual will strive once more for freedom, man's ultimate goal. He will do so by seeking unity with the divine Other, with whom he struggles—and to whom he is in thrall.

Then, solitary, drift, inert,
Through the abyss where you would have me go
And, lost to your desire at last,
Ravish the waste for what you cannot know.
EDGAR BOWERS, "Adam's Song to Heaven"

10

Infinite Yearning and the Rift in Man

THE UNHAPPY CONSCIOUSNESS IS MAN ALIENATED FROM HIS ESSENTIAL selfhood, his I = I. Self-consciousness started out as desire [167]. What aroused this desire was the intolerable aspect of unassimilated otherness: the other *as such.* Desire desired the reduction of all things to the self's self-identity (I = I). The desirous self was violently for itself and against everything else: other things and, at a higher level, other selves. To establish its self-unity, it sought to negate otherness. Through this negation, the individual self struggled to prove that it was absolute, and that objects, and other selves, were nothing.

With the emergence of the unhappy consciousness, desire is transformed, and deepened. It is now the *infinite yearning* for an Other, who is changeless, pure, and utterly self-identical—the yearning for God. This Other is consciousness itself, but the unhappy consciousness is not yet aware of this truth. Understanding, we recall, projected the self-transcendence or beyonding of appearance into a transcendent supersensible Beyond—the restful kingdom of law (Chapter 6). The unhappy consciousness does something similar. It interprets the self-otherness that is necessary to self-consciousness as the *changeableness* that makes it *other than* the unchangeable supersensible Self.[1] Unhappiness, we must note, is a form of self-certainty. I am certain that as a changeable individual I am non-essential, the slave of my lower desires, and that this Other, the Master Self, is essential—the only self worthy to say "I AM MYSELF!" or, more accurately, "I AM WHO AM."

In the dialectical structure of self-consciousness, the self is both self-same and self-other (Chapter 7). I = I is the immediate cancellation of self-otherness. Hegel used axial rotation to illustrate this act [169]. Self-otherness is the "gap" that is necessary if I am to be aware of myself as object. I am on intimate terms with myself only because I am thrown back from myself, self-repulsed (like force). The unhappy consciousness experiences these two logical moments, self-identity and self-difference, as a "split" between a pure divine self and an impure human self. The former is universal and unchangeable, the latter singular and changeable.

The inversion of self-consciousness—man turned inside out—is the negative truth of self-consciousness and its certainty of itself. But since negation is determinate, something positive will rise, Phoenix-like, from the ashes of unfulfilled longing. Deepened by oppression and self-laceration, spirit, at the end of Hegel's chapter, will emerge in a new form. The slave discovered a new independence in being oppressed and forced back within himself. At the end of the chapter on self-consciousness, this discovery of independence within bondage is repeated at a higher level. Casting off his longing for union with an infinitely remote Self, individual man will rise up and become a modern "Renaissance man." Full of confidence in his resources of observation and action, he will posit himself as absolute. Consciousness will become *reason*, "the certainty that, in its singularity [*Einzelheit*], [human consciousness] has being absolutely *in itself*, or is all reality" [230].

As I noted in the preceding chapter, the paradigm of the unhappy consciousness is the medieval Christian. This is evident from Hegel's allusions in the text. The paradigm, however, does not exclude other interpretations. The unhappy consciousness is, most generally, man's unhappy relation to a transcendent Being or Truth he desires but cannot know. Kant, seen in this light, is a version of the unhappy consciousness.

The medieval Christian is, nevertheless, Hegel's archetype and historic *Gestalt* for the union of intimacy and estrangement that defines consciousness at this stage of its development.[2] One reason for this is that the Christian believer shows us what it means to take the absolute personally, not merely as Being, Mind, Truth, or the Unconditioned. God is *my* God. Also, Christianity posits a highest being that is unique and universal (monotheism), alive, intelligent and self-aware, individualized (like me), and the embodiment of a purity, constancy, and incorruptible wholeness I long for in myself. This wholeness is unattainable through my own efforts and exists only in a hoped-for Beyond. All these determinations belong to self-consciousness at its present stage and have been dialectically generated by previous stages. There is, in other words, a perfect fit between the logical requirements of consciousness at this point and the unhappiness of medieval Christianity, as Hegel understands it.

The historical origin of Christian unhappiness is a combination of the Jewish and the Roman spirit. In his *Lectures on the Philosophy of Religion*, Hegel spells out what each contributed to the formation of Christianity, and of modernity.[3] Through the Jewish spirit, man feels humiliation before the

God who is above him. And the Roman world, which Hegel calls the world's "universal unhappiness," "drives and presses human beings back into themselves," thus generating those intellectual escape artists—the stoic and the skeptic.[4] Here, in the chapter on the unhappy consciousness, the crucial aspect of unhappiness is the one that comes from the Jewish people, who are defined by "misery" and "a boundless energy of longing."[5]

The unhappy consciousness, as we shall see, presupposes a God that is incarnate as an actual individual: the man-God, Christ. We must not conclude, however, that the unhappy consciousness sums up the Christian experience for Hegel. Christianity takes three forms in the *Phenomenology* (we will review them in Chapter 16). At the current stage, it is tormented subjectivity. But later it will appear in the more positive forms of *faith* and *religion*.[6] The unhappy consciousness is primitive or nascent Christianity. Consciousness, at this stage of its religiosity, has an abstract relation to God as the essential self. It does not yet experience God as present *in* the religious community.

The problem of the unhappy consciousness, and of self-consciousness as a whole, is the estrangement of man from God. This estrangement is summed up in the text of Isaiah, who calls God the *deus absconditus* or "hidden God" (45:15).[7] Christianity seems to solve the problem of separateness at one stroke in the person of Christ as divine Mediator. But Christ, as a sensuous individual who vanishes in death, reproduces the very separateness that must be overcome. As Hegel reminds us, the dialectic of the unhappy consciousness is not about God as he is in truth, but rather God as he appears to consciousness at this stage of its development [211]. The unhappy consciousness is only nascent Christianity, pre-Reformation Christianity that does not yet know itself.

To appreciate the central role of unhappiness in Hegel's project, we must grasp the deep bond Hegel means to forge between the philosopher's love of wisdom, and man as a lost soul in search of a divine counterpart from whom he has been estranged.[8] For Plato and Aristotle, philosophy begins in wonder. For Hegel, it begins in misery. This misery derives from human self-consciousness. To quote Pascal, self-conscious man is both great and wretched. Self-consciousness (as I noted in Chapter 7) is our blessing and our curse, our glory and our humiliation. We are wretched in our egocentrism, our "hard" being-for-self.

In an early writing, Hegel speaks of the "need [*Bedürfnis*] of philosophy."[9] The phrase refers to both the world's need for philosophy and the philosopher's need for wisdom. This twofold need originates in *Entzweiung* or splitting—the experience that defines the unhappy consciousness. Philosophy, for Hegel, is always a response to an actually present world. Insofar as it merely exists, a specific world of knowing or culture is unreflective, even though it is a house or building [*Gebäude*] made by spirit itself (at the level of finite *Verstand* or understanding). Spirit, the human-divine source of culture, loses itself in the house it has built. It is like a poet who forgets himself by identifying with his poems, or a self-made man who derives no enjoyment from his achievements, wealth, and power. All the parts of spirit are present in the House of Spirit, but the absolute itself is not present. Spirit's productivity or world-building alienates spirit as an inwardly working, contemplative being from its outward productions. In its struggle to know itself through cultural house building, spirit generates a split between itself and the world, inner and outer, subject and object, essence and existence.[10]

This split is unhappiness in its most comprehensive form: the self-estrangement and homelessness of spirit in the world it has created. The task of philosophy is to enter into the static oppositions that appear in the House of Spirit and render them fluid—to transform architecture into *music*. Philosophy thus brings about a living unity in the minds, hearts, and lives of men and overcomes their spiritual homelessness. As Hegel puts it, "When the might of union [*Macht der Vereinigung*] vanishes from the life of men and the antitheses lose their living connection and reciprocity and gain independence, the need of philosophy arises."[11]

We may connect this with the labyrinth image I used at the start of our journey. The labyrinth is human history, which at first seems to make no sense. The Philosopher, Hegel, is the modern Theseus who takes us into this labyrinth and reveals the thread of *logos* that connects its various chambers. He shows us that history is the path by which the human spirit achieves complete self-knowledge and overcomes its alienation. Hegel reveals the logic of our desire. He slays the Minotaur of natural consciousness, which teaches us to fear negation, or logical death.

Hegel's goal is the overcoming of unhappiness, understood as alienation. In the *Phenomenology*, Hegel tries to show the path by which spirit, through suffering and work, generates and overcomes the unhappiness of *Entzweiung*. In the course of its Way of Despair, spirit comes to be at home with itself [*bei sich*] in the house it has built. In his book, *Hegel and Marx*, the historian Elie Kedourie emphasizes the poignancy and scope of Hegel's project. He defines the goal of philosophy for Hegel as "the healing of the rift in man." Quoting a letter to Schelling from 1800, Kedourie says: "Hegel's whole philosophical endeavor is to find how, under modern conditions, 'man can experience a *happy consciousness* [my emphasis], how he can feel at home in the world.'"[12]

What this happiness is, what it *means* to be at home in the world, will be revealed, obscurely, in Hegel's final chapter. Absolute knowing will reconcile man to man, man to God, and man to the external world.

A Logical Overview [207–14]

The unhappy consciousness is the truth of self-consciousness as a whole. It is the dialectical offspring of the skeptic, who emerged from the stoic, who emerged from the slave. Stoic, skeptic, and unhappy consciousness are characters within the section entitled "Freedom of Self-Consciousness." They are efforts to transcend slave-consciousness, and bondage to nature, through pure thinking, that is, pure inwardness.

Consciousness is now split, as I noted above, into a non-essential *changeable consciousness* and an essential *unchangeable consciousness* [208]. This split is the result of skeptical experience. The two consciousnesses are the embodiment of the two logical moments of self-consciousness and its I = I: self-otherness and self-sameness. Hegel refers to them respectively as the slave and master consciousnesses, now appearing within one and the same self [206]. In the master-slave dialectic, the master fell by the wayside. He was dialectically uninteresting because he neither worked nor suffered, and therefore lacked a principle of further development. With the unhappy consciousness, the master returns. He is reborn as the divine, super-independent Lord of changeable man, who is now more deeply wretched than the former slave.

Hegel does not call the poles of the opposition man and God but rather the changeable and the unchangeable. There seem to be several reasons for this choice. First, Hegel thereby highlights the purely conceptual character of the two selves, and of their opposition. Second, he makes possible an extension of the unhappy consciousness to non-Christian experience. Third, he avoids a potentially misleading emphasis on picture thinking, which interprets the man-God relation as the separation of two *beings* rather than the distinction between two opposed aspects of one and the same self. Fourth, "changeable" (singular) and "unchangeable" (universal) remind us that although the experience before us is one of overwhelming feeling and suffering, the larger drama is about the striving for knowledge. Through the unhappy consciousness, knowledge comes to be defined as the union of human singularity and divine universal truth.[13]

As an unhappy, inwardly split consciousness, the self, for the first time, *feels* contradiction. It posits or affirms its own inversion—selfhood turned inside out. The self here experiences the self-otherness and self-externality inscribed in the logical structure of self-consciousness. But it does not experience what Hegel calls the reconciliation, *Versöhnung*, of its inner and outer moments [207].[14] The language of reconciliation appears in the New Testament and especially in the *Letters* of St. Paul.[15] The term suggests that the separateness of these moments is not just a gap that must be bridged (like Plato's separateness between things and Forms), but an original "falling out" that must be surmounted, an offense that must be forgiven.[16] The unhappy consciousness is a kind of incipient mutual recognition: "The unhappy consciousness itself *is* the gazing of one self-consciousness into another, and itself *is* both, and the unity of both is also its essence" [207]. But consciousness at this stage dwells on the moment of separation and sheer otherness. Unity, for it, remains a Beyond, and the two selves do not yet see themselves as reconciled or rendered harmonious in each other.

Hegel's account of unhappiness is logically complex. It is also rich in allusions to the Bible and to the beliefs, practices, institutions, and history of medieval Christianity. Like the previous exposés of consciousness, the account begins with a for-us section [207–14], followed by the usual triple-tiered dialectic of experience. In its first phase (**in-itself**), consciousness experiences its relation to the unchangeable Other through "pure consciousness," that is, through the inward disposition of the *heart* [*Gemüth*] in relation to God as a remote object [215–17]. In its second phase (**for-itself**), it relates to the Other through its own desire and work [218–22]. In the third phase (**in-and-for-itself**), it destroys the satisfaction it found in desire and work, "mortifies the flesh," and, in a final act of surrender, puts its fate in the hands of a human mediator, or priest [223–30].

Hegel's behind-the-scenes overview is somewhat longer than its predecessors. Let us examine its main points before turning to the actual experience of unhappiness.

It is important to bear in mind here that the unhappy consciousness is *one self* that experiences itself as split into two separate selves. These selves, or rather sides of a single self, *must* be together (they contain each other) and *cannot* be together (they are exact opposites). Since the self experiences itself as split and painfully self-other, consciousness identifies itself with the non-essential, *changeable* side of the relation [208]. The individual assumes that no essential splitting occurs, or can occur, in the *unchangeable* self. He assumes, in other words, that God is *not* self-differentiating and therefore does not really suffer. This assumption constitutes the singular self's natural, non-dialectical conception of the divine: God is experienced as absolutely self-same and in no way self-other. The goal of the changeable, singular self is to be united with the divine Other. It can bring this about only by "freeing itself from the unessential, i.e., from itself" [208]. The unhappy consciousness does not have the luxury of stoicism. It cannot be indifferent to this Other, since the Other is its own absolute self-identity —the unity it is fated to crave. The recurring problem, as we shall see, is that the individual, whose peculiar self-certainty is the certainty that he himself is nothing while God alone is everything, cannot shed his being-for-self, the certainty of himself as a changeable individual. He cannot get past the "dear self."

To be united with the Other, I must be at war with myself: what was previously a fight to the death between two individuals, in other words, is now a fight within a single self. This fight "is against an enemy [*Feind*], to vanquish whom is really to suffer defeat" [209]. The enemy takes many forms: pride, lust, inconstancy, to name just a few. Ultimately, the enemy is my actual existence as *this* individual. My consciousness of myself "is only the grief [*Schmerz*] over this existence and action." As an unhappy consciousness, I rise up to God, who is everything, only to confront—myself as a sinful *This.* I cannot shed the inevitable fact that it is only an unworthy *nothing* that rises up.[17]

But in rising up, consciousness "experiences just this emergence of singularity [this-ness] in the unchangeable, and of the unchangeable in the singularity" [210]. This is the distinctly Christian moment of the unhappy self's experience, in which the unchangeable or God takes the shape of a singular man. We are reminded here that the two opposed selves, although experienced as mutually exclusive, are nevertheless *in each other.* For us, the appearance of singularity within the unchangeable is not a miraculous given but an appearance generated by consciousness itself. As in previous moments, in which experience generates a new object, consciousness here does not know what is happening "behind its back." It does not realize that it itself has given rise to its unchangeable counterpart, and that the singular this-ness it sees there is itself. As Harris notes (1:413–14), this miraculous "rising up" of singularity within the unchangeable is both the Incarnation and Christ's presence in the Host during the Catholic Mass.[18]

Even at this early stage, we can see the problem here. Singularity arises in the unchangeable. It is the logical result of the individual's reaching up toward God, thus mixing his this-ness and contingency with the universal, divine essence. But the divine individual, Christ, is pictured as *separate* from God himself, who is kept absolutely self-same. The medieval Christian, in this aspect of his experience, remains faithful to the Jewish prayer: "Hear, O Israel: the Lord our God is one Lord."[19]

Hegel now outlines the threefold way "in which singularity is linked with the unchangeable" [210]. These three relations mirror the three Persons of Christianity's triune God: Father, Son, and Holy Spirit. These Persons are the picture-form of the three logical moments: *in-itself, for-itself,* and *in-and-for-itself.* In the first relation, singularity and the unchangeable are mutually opposed, like ordinary objects: God is represented as the pure Being "who passes judgment on the singular individual." In the second, consciousness experiences God as a being who reveals *himself* as singular (the Incarnate Son of God). God, here, is "for himself" or self-conscious. In the third relation, God is experienced as spirit—God as he is "in and for himself" or logically complete.

At this third stage, finite consciousness "finds its own self as this singular [individual] in the unchangeable." In this joy [*Freude*], as Hegel calls it, the rift in man is healed: the human finds itself in the divine, and the divine in the human. Singularity and universality are reconciled in an act of co-inherence. The joy of reconciliation, however, will not come on the scene until much later in spirit's journey.

Hegel reminds us that what the changeable side of consciousness has gone through also happens on the side of the unchangeable "absolute" self [211]. But consciousness itself does not posit this reciprocal self-splitting and reciprocal agony. In its unhappy yearning, it cannot get past the sheer antithesis of changeable and unchangeable, inconstant and constant. It cannot think the human within the divine any more than it can think the divine within the human. Although consciousness indeed posits singularity in the unchangeable self, it does not grasp the inner necessity of this divine manifestation. As I mentioned above, the appearance of a divine individual is just that—an appearance or fact (Jesus' birth in Bethlehem). For consciousness at this stage, the Incarnation is not a necessary negative moment in the establishment of *God's* self-identity, his being in and for himself. It is represented, pictured, as "a contingent *happening*" [212]—a Gift. The result of this inability to grasp the dialectical nature of God is that the separateness of the singular individual and the universal, the changeable and the unchangeable, persists. Christ as an individual only intensifies the pain of separation from God—the experience of God, the universal unchanging self, as an unreachable Beyond.

Initially, the changeable consciousness wants to negate its singularity in order to be joined with the divine Other, the universal self. Once singularity is posited within the unchangeable, the changeable self directs its efforts toward union with this divine individual (Christ), who is the incarnate universal and divine Mediator between the human individual sinner and the pure universal Judge. In other words, the changeable self sees in the divine Mediator the ultimate object of human desire: union with the pure, unchanging Self. Christ embodies what sinful consciousness strives to become.

Hegel concludes the for-us introduction with a summary of the threefold dialectic I outlined above. Consciousness attempts to unite with the divine individual, through whom it hopes to secure unity with the unchangeable, universal self, in the following three ways: "as pure consciousness" (the inner motions of the heart), through desire and work, and as a consciousness "that is aware of its own being-for-self" [214]. This third stage is not the satisfaction of desire. It is, in fact, the individual's full realization that all his efforts to reach the hidden God on his own are doomed to failure.

Phase One: The Motions of the Heart [215–17]

Hegel now proceeds to the experience of the unhappy consciousness. In this experience, the finite human self struggles for union with the unchangeable transcendent Being as incarnate or "shaped" [*gestaltete*] [215].

Hegel observes that although the unhappy consciousness does not enjoy the presence of its unchangeable object, it is nevertheless, as a thinker, an advance over the stoic and the skeptic. The stoic renounces his singular selfhood in order to affirm his essence as pure thinking; and the skeptic's selfhood is nothing but an endless going back and forth between two opposite selves. Stoic thinking is abstract, and skeptical thinking merely restless. Neither has a root in the live, human self that does the thinking. The unhappy consciousness, by contrast, "brings and holds together pure thinking and singularity" [216]. It is the thought of *this particular individual.* The unhappy consciousness says "I" rather than "Man" or "Reason."

As the unity of pure thinking and singularity, the unhappy consciousness recalls the condition for absolute knowing: the ultimate unity of the individual knower and truth in its sheer universality. This consciousness is *certain* of itself, *knows* itself (albeit unhappily) as this union of opposites. It posits purity and universality in its changeable self (that is, implicitly or in a Beyond), and it finds singularity in the unchangeable. What it does not know is that the singularity it posits in the unchangeable is its own. As the tragic unity of the singular self and the universal (of man and God), the unhappy consciousness, more than any other spiritual shape, reveals the problem that must be solved if man is to achieve absolute, divine knowing.[20]

Hegel's positive formulation of the unhappy consciousness as the union of opposites is "for us." But it is perplexing. What is this pure thinking that Hegel is talking about, the thinking that puts the unhappy consciousness above the stoic and skeptic? And why does he emphasize *thinking* just before the stage at which the unhappy self approaches God through *feeling*?

Taking up the latter question first, we can say simply that in the very next paragraph Hegel will define "pure feeling" as a kind of thinking: an intellectual straining of the mind for contact with the divine. As for the former question, we should note that it was characteristic of medieval theologians like St. Augustine and St. Anselm to combine thinking and feeling, theology and the heart.[21] In the *Proslogion,* which contains the famous "ontological proof" for God's existence, Anselm rouses his longing for an ascent to God, who dwells "in light inaccessible."[22] Thinking here is joined with prayer and personal desire. To be sure, the thinking of the human individual does not succeed in reaching God. But it does succeed in appreciating God as infinite: "Therefore, Lord, not only are You that than which a greater cannot be thought, but You are also something greater than can be thought."[23] Anselm's thinking, though bold and energetic, is ultimately unhappy: "I strove to ascend to God's light and I have fallen back into my own darkness."[24] My point is not that all unhappy consciousnesses are also theologians, but that the medieval theologian brings to the fore, and articulates, what all unhappy consciousnesses have in common. They experience a clear awareness of their bond, as finite individuals, with the unchangeable and the infinite. Their human thinking, however much it falls short of the Concept, consciously, lovingly, touches on the divine.

In the first (in-itself) phase of his experience, the unhappy individual approaches God through his inward disposition or heart, *Gemüth.*[25] He feels but does not act. Or rather, his feeling *is* his act. This "infinite, pure inner feeling," as Hegel calls it, is a mystical, quasi-romantic relation to the unchangeable. Recalling the rite of the Catholic Mass, Hegel describes this union with the absolute as "the shapeless [i.e. tuneless] jingling of bells, or a mist of warm incense, a musical thinking that does not get as far as the Concept" [217].

Most interesting here is what Hegel has to say about thinking. The unchangeable, for consciousness, is itself pure thinking: God does not imagine or feel but rather thinks. Thinking is the perfection of his being—an Aristotelian insight preserved in Catholic medieval theology. God is intellectual light, and we who are exiled from God dwell in darkness. Moreover, consciousness knows itself as implicitly such a being. If only it could shed its desire and corporeality, it would be joined to God in an act of pure contemplation. The self, having recovered purity of heart, would "see God." Playing on the similarity between the words *Denken* (thinking) and *Andacht* (devotion), Hegel says that the ritualized mysticism of pure feeling (the Mass) is really "a movement *toward* thinking [*an das Denken hin*]."[26] This movement is *infinite yearning.*

Infinite yearning is inverted desire. It is negativity that the self directs, not against others but against itself. The goal of yearning is *mutual recognition.* The pagan philosopher longs to know the whole of all things, but not to *be known* by the object of his knowing. This is a direct result of his stoic-like shedding of his all-too-human singularity for the sake of universal thinking.[27] But for the unhappy consciousness, the ultimate goal and object is not a form, a force, a prime mover, or the structure of the universe. It is the perfection of my own selfhood. I cannot be united with the absolute unless the absolute is, like me, self-conscious and individual. That is why Christianity is necessary to philosophic completion: only Christianity posits the union of singular and universal consciousness (in the person of Christ). Only Christianity holds out the hope of completing self-consciousness as desire, that is, of mediating and reconciling the singular self and the universal self in mutual recognition. In its purely rational, non-mystical formulation, whose significance emerges only much later in our journey, this means simply that I recognize human community as God in the midst of man. I recognize community (more specifically, my social-political community) as the living universality essential to my human this-ness, and the community recognizes my this-ness as essential to its universality.

Pure feeling fails to take hold of its object, which remains a Beyond [217]. What Hegel seems to be describing here is the desire for unity with Christ, that is, with God in his manifestation as an individual. Hegel's remarks about bells, incense, and devotion call our attention to the Catholic Mass, where Christ is believed to be actually present in the Host.[28] In consuming the Host, the believer is mystically united with Christ as an individual.

It seems at first that the singularity of Christ will be the bridge to the unchangeable absolute. But this absolute resists reduction to singular this-ness, even as it manifests itself through singularity. In the person of Christ (both in the Incarnation and in the Host), the absolute is still a Beyond. At this first stage of experience, the failure to reach the absolute derives from the limitations of feeling. Feeling is ultimately only self-feeling. It *seems* to be more intimate than speech and conceptual thought, but in fact it is not. In devotional feeling, I am in contact, not with the universal, but with the very singular corporeal selfhood I long to transcend. This is how Hegel interprets the story in Luke's Gospel (24:3–5), where the followers who find Christ's empty tomb are told by two angels, "Why seek ye the living among the dead?" (Luke 24:3–5). If one searches for God as a singular This of sense-certainty, then one finds only an *empty grave,* that is, the God who has died [217].

Hegel's reference to the grave recalls his discussion, in other contexts, of the Crusades. Medieval Christianity sought God's presence in the Holy Sepulcher in Palestine, only to discover that the divine is not to be found in a sensuous This. The failure of the Crusades recapitulates on a grand scale the individual's failure to find God as a sensuous individual embodied in the Host.[29] God, as the universal pure being, has fled. Instead of unifying the singular and the universal, devotional feeling and crusading zeal have only separated them.

Phase Two: Desire and Work [218–22]

God, for the unhappy seeker, has fled. But in the "return of the feeling heart into itself," the individual feels his own actual existence [218]. This is like the slave who, in being "pressed back," discovers himself and acquires "his own mind." In being expelled from the divine, the feeling heart *becomes its own object,* and the self discovers its own being-for-self. "In this return into self," says Hegel, "there comes to view its second relation [to the unchangeable], that of desire and work." Logically, the transition to desire and work is the result of pure feeling that has "returned into itself."

The return to self produces a new relation to the realm of actuality, the world of things. In work and desire (or, as Hegel also says, enjoyment), the individual seems to have found a way to overcome his alienation in the Here-and-Now (his exile from God) by transforming the Here-and-Now, by being a worker in the vineyard of creation. He plants his crops, then harvests and eats them. This, for him, is a religious act—a reminder of his place in God's creation. But unlike the rite of the Mass, it is an act in which man does not passively receive but actively works and produces. Like the slave, he cancels the independence of outward things and gains a sense of himself. In this new relation, God appears in a new form. His singularity is now not Christ but *the world itself* as God's "offspring." The world bears the stamp of the unchangeable and therefore partakes of God's sacredness. I commune with God by enjoying and working on the things God has made, and which he has given to me as a natural being.

The actual world of things is now "broken" into two aspects. It is broken because its two aspects are not reconciled in a unity. As something separate from God, the world is a nothing, like me. But as something made by God, it is a "sanctified world," in which I see "the shape [*Gestalt*] of the unchangeable" [219]. One thinks of the beautiful Psalm verse, "The heavens declare the glory of God" (19:1), and of Paul's assertion that God's invisible nature is evident in the things he has made (Romans 1:20). But desire and work, as they appear in the unhappy consciousness, are ultimately incapable of accomplishing their goal. The reason is that the world is not experienced here as implicitly nothing: it bears the stamp of the unchangeable. In the end, it is God's world, not mine. So if the individual, unlike the slave, enjoys the things God has made (the fruits of the earth), and works on things to make them beneficial (through tilling the soil), this is only because God has given the individual all his faculties, talents, and transformative powers. Everything I am and do is the result of God's grace, which Hegel calls (in Miller's gloss) "a gift from an alien source" [*eine fremde Gabe*] [220]. The crucial point here is that consciousness, in working on the world, shares in that world's "brokenness" into a for-itself actuality and an in-itself Beyond. To be sure, I am the one who desires and works, but only insofar as I am *this* individual estranged from the divine. I am not, and cannot be, the real author of my transformations of the world. In desire and work, therefore, my self-certainty, like the world itself, remains "broken" [218].[30]

Throughout this section of the text, there is a deliberate, highly unorthodox conflation of Christ and world. Both are "shaped" manifestations of the unchangeable divine.[31] God *surrenders* his embodied shape, his actual individuality, in making a world that is the negated object of our desire and work. This self-surrender mirrors the sacrifice of God's Son for the benefit of man, which sacrifice is recapitulated in the Host, where God as Christ is "given up" to human consumption. God's surrender of his embodied shape is Hegel's dialectical way of saying, "Man proposes, God disposes." As we have seen, desire and work are modes of negative transformation. But since it is God's world, not ours, it is not our negativity that brings about the transformation. We are the ones who desire and put our backs into the work of the field. But the outcome of all this effort is produced, strictly speaking, by God's act of self-relinquishing.

Hegel now focuses on the specific character of the self-surrender that occurs in both the changeable and the unchangeable consciousness, in man and in God. He recalls the reciprocity of active and passive force in the chapter on understanding. Like the pole of a magnet in the inverted world [156 ff.], the human self "repels itself from itself" [221]. That is, it renounces its singularity and with it the worth and efficacy of its desire and work, which, in the end, *do nothing.* The individual self "gives thanks" for what is not really its own: it "denies itself the satisfaction of being conscious of its independence, and assigns the essence of its action not to itself but to the Beyond" [222]. And the unchangeable on its side surrenders its shape (as the world) to desire or enjoyment and work. The problem, however, is that each surrenders only what is superficial [221]. The reciprocity that is the goal of self-consciousness therefore remains incomplete in that both the changeable and the unchangeable consciousnesses "have withdrawn into the unchangeable."

The superficiality of the self-surrender on both sides of the man-God relation enters for the following reason. First, the individual, in fact, "has *willed, acted,* and *enjoyed*" [222]. That is, man knows that God has not done everything, and that even the act of thanksgiving is one that the changeable consciousness must call its own, however much it may want to credit God as the ultimate source of all good things. Man, therefore, has sacrificed only the surface show [*Schein*] of gratifying his self-feeling and being-for-self [222]. Second, on God's side, the self-surrender is even more superficial. Man at least acknowledged the Other as his source: he gave thanks to God and has sacrificed (if incompletely) his very actions and essence. But God, *as he appears within consciousness at this stage,* does not give of his substance.[32] This goes back to what I noted earlier: God's manifestation of himself as shaped or incarnate (as both world and Christ) is not essential to what God is. God remains One and aloof, safe from the unhappiness of *Entzweiung.* He remains an *unchangeable* consciousness.[33]

Hegel here touches on a problem St. Augustine reports in his *Confessions.* I do a good deed, or exercise self-control, or humble myself, only to feel pride in having done so.[34] This is the enemy with whom I am constantly at war—my "hard" being-for-self. In negating myself, I assert myself, since it is I who negate. The result of this second stage of unhappy experience is the unsuccessful shedding of this being-for-self. Singularity and universality have each "come out of themselves" only to go right back in. They remain in unreconciled opposition.

Phase Three: Self-Surrender [223–30]

The third and final phase of the unhappy consciousness emerges from this tragic experience. Feeling (the first stage) failed to reach the divine manifested as an individual: feeling was ultimately self-feeling. Through desire and work (the second stage), the unhappy individual posited a sanctified world and tried, simultaneously, to accept a kind of causality in God's world (thus allowing a limited form of inescapable being-for-self) and to divest itself of causality in an act of thanksgiving. But this act, like its desire and work, was inescapably its own. Consciousness failed to negate the "enemy" [*der Feind*] who stands between it and the divine Other—itself. In the third stage, consciousness experiences itself as incorrigibly actual or "in and for itself" [223]. In the course of its experience, it has learned that it possesses no acid strong enough to dissolve its hard individuality, which clings to it in every negation and every attempt at spiritual suicide. This is what Hegel means when he says: "But here, now, is where the enemy is met with in the shape that is most his own [*in seiner eigensten Gestalt*]."

The curious inversion that takes place here, under other circumstances, would produce happiness. After all, the individual has had proven to him, now beyond all doubt, that he is "true actuality" [224]. His "I AM MYSELF!" has been thoroughly confirmed. But this fulfillment is the deepest, most tragic failure for the unhappy consciousness, whose certainty consists in positing essential selfhood outside himself in a Beyond. The more real and particularized I know myself to be, the more ghastly I seem to myself, the more distant from God. My exquisite reality, now focused in the most degrading bodily functions (no doubt excretory), is exquisite misery. This misery is not just the awareness of my wretched individuality: it is self-disgust *united with* the perpetual thought of the pure, sacred Other, from whom I am estranged. The individual here confronts his stubborn this-ness as thoroughly impure. That is why "consciousness is aware of itself as this *actual singular* [self] in the animal functions," which, Hegel says, "are no longer performed naturally and without embarrassment" but rather become "the object of serious endeavor" [225].[35]

In the consciousness of its exquisite impurity and defilement (the appearance of the enemy "in the shape that is most his own"), the unhappy individual is nevertheless aware that in principle or implicitly, he is one with the pure unchangeable Other. This implicit longed-for unity is the source of the individual's wretchedness, since the individual sees himself in light of the pure Other, before whom he is unworthy. That is, the individual's miserable relation to himself "is *mediated* by the thought of the unchangeable" [226]. The logical transition at this point consists in the individual's conscious positing of a mediated relation to the unchangeable. The individual, in experiencing just how dirty and *non-universal* he really is, only now realizes that his self-negation is doomed to failure, that the only way he can divest himself of his filth is to surrender himself to the authority and action of a mediator or priest [228]. The priest embodies the mediated relation that the individual has to his unchangeable object.

At this advanced point in the dialectic of unhappiness, the *syllogism* that defines self-consciousness now becomes explicit in actual experience [227]. Through the mediating priest, and only through him, the changeable and the unchangeable consciousnesses come into contact with each other. This human mediator "presents the two extremes to one another, and ministers to each in its dealings with the other."[36] The priest is on the same level as the penitent. He is therefore someone with whom the penitent can deal, concretely and effectively. The priest is the penitent's bridge to God. In him, sinful singularity is cleansed (in confession and absolution) and made presentable to the unchangeable Other, just as in him the divine finds a path to the sinful individual—that is, from the standpoint of consciousness at its present stage.

The priest mediates only because the sinful individual divests himself of all being-for-self [228]. The penitent gives the mediator his freedom of decision, his responsibility for his actions, his property and money (as a tithe), and even his desire for clear thought expressed in a familiar language (he must be content with incomprehensible formulas in Church Latin). The individual also chastises desire through fasting and ascetic self-denial and self-laceration. In these acts of surrender, the unhappy consciousness "truly and completely deprives itself of inner and outer freedom, of the actuality in which consciousness is *for itself*" [229]. This is what it could *not* do in its direct relation to an absent God. The slave at least had a work and a mind [*Sinn*] he could in some way call his own [196]. But the unhappy self, in this final act of surrender, gives up its entire selfhood. It has made itself into a *thing* [229]. As Hegel observes, in one sense this surrender is a victory: the self-sacrifice that previously was hypocritical (acts of self-negation and gratitude are inescapably *my* acts) is now actually accomplished without deceit [*Betrug*]. I really do give up everything here, not to the God I cannot see, but to the actually existing priest that I can.

At this point, we must recall the whole drama of self-consciousness. Like all the previous shapes of consciousness, self-consciousness begins in mere certainty and ends in truth—the negative truth of spiritual suicide. This is the tragedy and despair that define the education of consciousness. Self-consciousness was initially desire or the effort to affirm itself by negating the world (and other selves). In the course of his complex unfolding, man as self-consciousness, having passed through the stages of combatant, slave, stoic, and skeptic, has been inverted as an unhappy consciousness. His essential selfhood is projected into a sacred Beyond. Here, at the end of its dialectical exertions, self-consciousness self-destructs. Its former pride has become abject humility, its being-for-self an abject being-for-another, its freedom bondage.

Hegel now reveals the light on the spiritual horizon. This is the determinateness or positive accomplishment of all the yearning, grief, and negativity. He reminds us that through its self-sacrifice, made directly to the mediating priest and indirectly to God, the penitent self "has also *implicitly* [*an sich*] obtained relief from its *misery*" [230]. It hopes for eternal relief in a future world, where it will both see and be seen, recognize and be recognized. Such relief can only come through the action of God himself, who alone can absolve the sinner from his guilt and annihilate his unhappiness.

But on the positive side, the whole process of mediation takes place because the priest embodies *God's universal will on earth.* The priest is the *unity* of the singular and the universal. This unity is what Hegel calls *reason,* the next stage of consciousness. As reason, the singular self posits its singularity as universal and becomes a genuine self-affirming *individual.* This comes about because the priest, as representative of the universal Church, has absolute certainty that he speaks for God, the universal. He enjoys a privileged, universalized individuality. This is perhaps Hegel's most astonishing thought in the entire chapter: that the medieval Church, the Christian Rome that oppresses the believer and takes away everything he has and is, is the birth of reason and the obliteration of the Beyond. The believer's freely willed alienation of his freedom, his self-negativity, is thus creative. It gives rise to a liberating force right here in the present.

We should note that what now arises for consciousness is only the *notion* or *Vorstellung* of reason [230]. This is the undeveloped intuition that the singular human individual has universal significance in the Here-and-Now. Hegel's enormous chapter on reason will trace the development of this intuition.

The unhappy consciousness, though hopeful, is still unhappy in its present or *Diesseits:* "for itself, action and its own actual doing remain pitiable, its enjoyment remains grief, and the cancellation of these in a positive sense remains a Beyond [*Jenseits*]" [230]. He is like the slave who sees himself in the thing he has made but fails to see himself as essential: "for consciousness, its will does indeed become universal and essential will, but consciousness does not take itself to be this essential will." By consciousness, Hegel means this particular stage of consciousness.

As for consciousness in its broad sense, which passes through all these stages, a new shape and certainty have arisen for it (through the unity of singular and universal in the priest). This shape, as I have noted, is reason. The new certainty is that the human individual "is all reality." With the dawn of reason, spirit experiences a renewed pride. The individual no longer yearns for an infinitely remote Other. Instead, he universalizes himself and makes *himself* into a god. The world is now transformed by the pride of reason. Formerly nothing but food for desire, it is now a field of opportunity, an arena for the individual's self-actualization and conquest.

Is reason, then, the end of all desire? Will it liberate man from all the things that make him a slave to unassimilated otherness—to the given, to natural consciousness, to the Beyond? Will reason bring man home?

REASON

To strive, to seek, to find, and not to yield.
TENNYSON, "Ulysses"

11

Idealism

HEGEL'S ENORMOUS CHAPTER ON REASON BEGINS WITH A BRIEF introduction entitled "The Certainty and Truth of Reason." I will discuss this introduction in my present chapter. In the following three chapters, I will take up reason's three stages: reason *in itself,* reason *for itself,* and reason *in and for itself.* These logical moments correspond to the three "shapes" described below.

The Transition to Reason [231]

Experience, for Hegel, is not just suffering. It is also work. The unhappy consciousness suffered because it desired, but could not reach, union with the pure unchangeable Other. In the end, however, it destroyed the hard being-for-self that separated it from God by handing over its inwardness and will to a mediating priest. The priest is the determinate product of the penitent's negative work. He embodies, implicitly, the self-certainty that Hegel calls *reason, Vernunft* [230].

In his introduction to the chapter on reason, Hegel reviews this amazing transition. The unhappy consciousness, he says, is a syllogism [231]. Its extreme terms are changeable singular consciousness (the penitent) and unchangeable universal consciousness (God). The middle term is the consciousness of the priest, who proclaims to God that the sinner has renounced himself, and to the sinner that God has forgiven him. The unhappy consciousness pictures this relation as taking place among three separate persons. But *for us,* the extremes flow into each other and become identical. We see that the awareness of the mediating priest is the immediate unity of singular selfhood and universal will. The priest proclaims, not only to the unhappy individual but also *to himself,* "the certainty of being all truth" [231]. As a singular self-consciousness in the Here-and-Now, he is the transition from a theological to a secular sensibility. He foreshadows Hegel's *Gestalt* for reason and the founder of the Age of Reason: René Descartes and his "I think, therefore I am."[1]

The unhappy consciousness is the truth of self-consciousness as a whole. Self-consciousness was a thoroughly negative force. This was evident in the violence of desire, the fight to the death, the master-slave relation, stoic withdrawal, skeptical annihilation, and the self-negating motions of the unhappy penitent. As reason, self-consciousness reverses its polarity: "its hitherto negative relation to otherness turns round into a positive relation" [232]. This positivity of reason is *idealism.*[2] Idealism is "the certainty of consciousness that it is all reality" [233]. In the words of Parmenides, it is the certainty that "thinking and being are the same."[3] But it is Descartes rather than Parmenides who embodies the idealism Hegel now has in mind. Thinking here means *my* thinking, the thinking of *this singular I,* which now has universal authority and worth. As reason, I do not merely think: I think for myself. *My reason is my freedom.*

Reason is the unity of consciousness and self-consciousness, the two preceding stages of consciousness in its broad sense. It unites the one-sided claim that sheer objectivity is absolute with the equally one-sided claim that sheer subjectivity is absolute. In reason's world of knowing, object and subject cease to be inimical to one another. In existential terms, man, as rational self-consciousness, is no longer a stranger in the world but regards it as his own. Casting off his role as penitent and pilgrim, he becomes a bold adventurer and a cultivator of his possibilities—a *modern.*

The Forgotten Path [232–39]

As I noted above, reason is the certainty that consciousness has of being all reality: "its thinking is directly actuality" [232]. No veil of appearance here, no curtain that hides transcendent Being, no supersensible world. Nor is the individual alienated from his I = I. Reason approaches the world confident that what it seeks it will find, and that what it finds will be its own self. The unhappy consciousness went beyond the stoic and skeptic in uniting thought and individuality. But individuality was its hell. "Alas," the penitent self lamented, "I am only me!" Reason turns this hell into a garden of earthly delight. "At last," the rational self exults, "I am an autonomous me—a thinking thing!"

The world at this point opens up and becomes new: "it is as if the world had for [consciousness] only now come into being" [232]. To borrow Descartes' first name, the individual is *rené,* reborn, and the age he belongs to is a *renaissance* or rebirth. In its previous stages, consciousness "did not understand the world; it desired it [the first appearance of self-consciousness] and worked on it [the slave], withdrew from it into itself [the stoic] and abolished it as an existence on its own account [the skeptic]." But through the creative suffering of the unhappy consciousness, consciousness lost the "grave of its truth" and became awakened to the world as *its* world. Reason is the now-positive expression of the certainty that defined self-consciousness in its initial burst of self-confidence: I = I or "I AM MYSELF!" The revised version of this battle cry is, "THE WORLD IS MINE!" Reason is past all the insecurity and angst of self-consciousness as desire. It "strides forward," Hegel says, and "plants the ensign of its sovereignty on every height and in every depth" [241].

Hegel speaks more directly here than he did in previous chapters about the path or way of consciousness. He emphasizes that reason has a history and even refers explicitly to the world-spirit or *Weltgeist* [234]. History is the path along which reason proves the truth of its idealism: the truth of the certainty that self and world are one. Truth, in other words, is the product of suffering and work. We have seen this work in the path that led up to reason. The work consists in overcoming *otherness.* In the course of the experience of consciousness (sense-certainty, perception, and understanding), the otherness and independence of objects vanished [233]. The *self* became absolute, and otherness was only *for consciousness.* But in the course of the self's experience, this otherness too vanished [233]. That is, the *mere* subjectivity of self-consciousness vanished. This vanishing of a vanishing gives rise to reason, which, as I noted above, unites the in-itself of consciousness with the for-itself of self-consciousness.

This sums up the path of the *Phenomenology* so far. Along this path, Hegel says, consciousness has *forgotten* where it has been [233]. Every stage of consciousness, as a new immediacy and "burst" of certainty, is a forgetting of the mediation that led to that stage. The *Phenomenology of Spirit,* the act by which the philosopher thinks through and *recollects* all the stages [808], is the cure for this amnesia. Descartes' "I think, therefore I am" (the identity of thought and being in the individual self) expresses the immediate certainty of reason. But this certainty will have to prove itself in order to become truth. It will have to do the actual work of finding itself in nature.

Hegel distinguishes the idealism that strives to prove itself from the transcendental idealism of Kant's *Critique of Pure Reason.* To understand what Hegel is getting at in this part of his introduction, we must look briefly at Kant's teaching.

For Kant, the term transcendental refers not to being as it is in itself (which Kant calls transcendent), but to the universal conditions of human knowing. These conditions transcend experience in being the purely subjective, sub-experiential ground of experience. Kant's idealism is the attempt to ground nature in the ordering power of thought, to make man the legislator of nature. Kant calls this his Copernican Revolution in philosophy.[4] We know external things, not as they are in themselves but only as they appear to us through our forms of sensuous intuition and thought: not as *noumena* but only as *phenomena.* We find intelligibility in nature because we put it there in the first place. Through our sensuous intuition, we represent objects in a manifold of space and time relations. Through our universal forms of thought, or categories, we think the spatiotemporal manifold as constituting the coherent order we call *nature.* In this way alone, Kant argues, can there be certain or necessary knowledge of nature—only if the knowledge of objects is *self*-knowledge.[5]

For Hegel, Kant's idealism is a universally shared *subjective* idealism.[6] According to this idealism, the world is "just in our heads" or *for us,* even if it is in all our heads in exactly the same way. This is the epistemological attitude I described in Chapter 1, the attitude that treats cognition as a tool and medium. Kant succeeds in imbuing the thing with thought or selfhood, but only at the level of *appearance,* only insofar as the thing is *for me.* A consequence of this limitation is that the self that underlies my representation of objects, the absolutely self-identical I, which Kant calls the *transcendental unity of apperception* (I = I), is precisely what I cannot experience as a concrete thing. The genuine subject never *appears.*

It is in this context that Hegel refers to the "forgotten path" I mentioned earlier. To know reason is not to critique it, or to treat it as a faculty or tool, as Kant had done, but to know its concrete history. The *Phenomenology* is the reconstruction of that history. Kant's idealism is a "bad" idealism [235] because it asserts rather than proves that consciousness is all reality. Reason, for Hegel, is not the abstract *thesis* of idealism but the concrete *manifestation* of reason, the striving of thought to make itself real through an encounter with the world.

Hegel nevertheless uses the terms of Kant's idealism to define reason: *category, schema,* and *the unity of apperception* (I = I). He puts new wine in old bottles. He reshapes the Kantian apparatus in order to bring out the history and living drama of actual reason, thus showing us what Kant failed to see in his own Copernican Revolution. The result is a rational *animism,* in which Kant's cognitive machinery comes to express the striving of man in time.[7]

The Kantian term that captures the universal thinkableness of the thing is *category.* In the *Critique of Pure Reason,* Kant presents his categories in a table. The four main categories are Quality, Quantity, Relation, and Modality.[8] This is not category in Aristotle's understanding of the term. It is not a predicate that refers to a thing as such.[9] On the contrary, category here must be understood in the context of modern doctrines of subjectivity. It expresses the certainty "that self-consciousness and being are the same essence, the same, not through comparison, but in and for themselves" [235]. Category, for Hegel, *is* the self—not as subjectivity cut off from objects but as implicitly united with them as their very substance.

The absolute unity of the self with itself (I = I) manifests itself in its relation to things (nature). Different categories are different modes of self-relation and self-difference. As Hegel says, "the many categories are species of the pure category [the I = I]" [236]. They are simply different ways in which selfhood is present in the actual world. Different categories are different "functions" of the spontaneous "I think," different ways of "I-ing" the world. We can sum this up by saying that reason [*Vernunft*] is higher than understanding [*Verstand*]. As we saw in Chapter 6, understanding could not think *inner difference*, which, for it, could only be self-contradictory (the inverted world). But now, at the level of reason, the differences the self finds in its objects are nothing but differences it finds in itself, i.e. categories. Thought itself is *self-differentiated* in order to be the unity in the midst of an objective manyness (the sensuous manifold of the given world). And so, we have a plurality of categories, each of which expresses the certainty reason has of being one with its manifold object. This plurality is objective difference grounded in subjective difference.

Reason, to repeat, is the self's positive relation to otherness (nature). The rational self does not *find* an external other but rather *posits* or *affirms* that other as, in principle, the same as itself. That is why "we can, strictly speaking, no longer talk of *things* at all" [236]. The absolute independence of the thing has vanished in the course of experience: things are now determinations of the self as category. But unlike self-consciousness as desire, reason wants, not to obliterate objects, but to preserve them as incarnations of itself.[10] There must therefore be some way of making the transition from the pure self or Concept to "external reality" [236]. This moment of transition from inner to outer is what Hegel, again borrowing from Kant, calls "the pure schema."

In Kant's *Critique of Pure Reason*, the schema is intermediate between the heterogeneous faculties of intuition and category, sensing and thinking. It is that through which a category is *applied* in a specific way to the sensuous manifold of intuition. This schema is *time*, or rather a *time-structure* that mediates between inner and outer, thought and thing.[11] Time, rather than space, is the mediator because time belongs to both outer and inner experience: both birds and thoughts "fly" in time. Causality is one of the time-structures that Kant discusses at length. It is one of the modes in which the sensuous world appears as an intelligible order, a *nature*. Causality, for Kant, is the irreversible order of the time-sequence. It is the universal ground of our saying: "this necessarily comes *before* that, and is therefore its cause."

In Hegel's appropriation of the term, schema is "the transition of the category from its concept to an *external* reality" [236]. Like Kant's schema, it mediates between pure thought and sensuousness, unity and spread-outness. As pure undifferentiated category, I am universal but not yet particularized and therefore not yet "in touch with" the particularity of real things and with my own individuality. As schema (in Hegel's sense of the term), I become "a singular individual"—*this* I, which is conscious of *these* things. As a rational individual, I am that *through which* a universal becomes real. The schema is like an image. It points to an other, that is, something other than consciousness [236]. But at the level of reason (the self's certainty of being all reality), this other is consciousness itself. Schema thus expresses the concrete relation I have with things as a concrete relation I have with *myself* as a thinking being. Ultimately, the schema, as a time-structure, points ahead to the more developed idea of spirit at work in *history* [801].

Like other stages of consciousness, reason is a syllogism. Its extreme terms are the sheer universality of the category and the sheer particularity of things. As we have seen, these two poles express a difference that is internal to the self: the original category or I = I, which splits into many categories. Differences in the thing are grounded in, and derived from, differences within thought itself. Schema is the middle term of the syllogism of reason. It mediates between pure universality and concrete particularity.

Because of its dialectical structure, reason will show itself as both *restlessness* and *tranquility* [237]: restless because of the inner difference and otherness it contains, tranquil because it is ultimately in communion with nothing but itself and its self-identity (I = I). Reason roams endlessly through the whole realm of things in their infinite variety. But it does so in the unshakable faith that all these things will ultimately express the identity of thing and self, the union whose name is category. Consciousness as reason is "this whole process itself," that is, the process by which the self reaches out endlessly into the external world as a particular self and appropriates that world in order to prove the absolute claim of its idealism and of its self-identity within otherness [237].

Understanding tried to make knowledge finite and restful, only to generate the extreme unrest of the inverted world. It gave birth to *infinity* as the cancellation of all difference and the identity of opposites. Infinity was the Concept as the life, soul, and blood of the world [162]. Self-consciousness was the unhappy experience of this infinity. It yearned infinitely for an infinitely remote Beyond. At the level of reason, infinity is reborn as something positive: *progress*. Reason is a "happy" striving. It enjoys its infinite project, its endless roaming about the world for ever-new experiences, ever-new differences, which always prove the unity of self and thing. Reason thus finds rest in motion. But it also finds motion in rest, since every experience is finite and therefore prompts further experience and adventure. In the language of force, reason's two sides, motion and rest, constantly *solicit* each other.

Unlike the stoic, skeptic, and unhappy consciousness, reason is worldly.[12] The logical ground of this worldliness lies in the at first purely formal and therefore empty claim, "THE WORLD IS MINE!" Category is the *cognitive hand* of the I = I. It expresses empty, indiscriminate *mine-ness.* But reason cannot attain the truth of its certainty if it simply keeps saying "mine." It must acquire filling, which can only come from the external world of things. The pure rationalism of reason, Hegel concludes, must therefore "be at the same time absolute empiricism" [238]. In historical terms, Descartes, the supreme rationalist, and Bacon, the supreme empiricist, necessarily imply each other.

The tension between the strictly rational and the empirical sides of reason can be seen in Kant. Kant's "pure reason" [238], Hegel says, immediately lapses into its opposite, empiricism, because of its very purity. What gives filling and content to the pure category but the actual world of sensuous objects? Kant's idealism, says Hegel, "becomes the same kind of self-contradictory ambiguity as skepticism." Kant's bad idealism, like skepticism, has two minds that it fails to unite: one is pure, the other corrupted by sensuous influence. Here, Hegel mentions the *bad infinity* we discussed in Chapter 7, infinity as indefinite on-goingness. Bad idealism keeps going back and forth between its two minds. It says, on the one hand, "Sensing, perceiving, and even understanding an object other than the self do not constitute true knowledge: true knowledge must be the self's unity with itself (Kant's unity of apperception) or self-knowledge." But on the other, bad idealism says, "If you want actual knowledge, knowledge that has a relation to real *things,* you must go out into the world of experience for it." The contradiction is the result of Kant's conception of the transcendental I as purely formal: the I does not generate its own content but takes it as external or *given.*

Hegel ends his introduction by distinguishing Kant's "pure reason" from "actual reason" [239]. Actual reason, *wirkliche Vernunft,* is reason that acts or goes to work. It does not rest content with an empty formality that begs for a sensuous experience that reason hypocritically also rejects. Actual reason "is not so inconsistent as that." Rather than starting out with the dogmatic assertion of idealism, actual reason embraces its encounter with the world of things. It knows that it must prove itself and is *driven* [*getrieben*] "to raise its certainty to truth and to give filling to the empty 'mine.'"

Kant's idealism comes into conflict with itself—it oscillates infinitely between pure formality and impure empirical thinking—"because it asserts the *abstract concept* of reason to be the true" [239]. This key term, *concept,* has the double meaning I noted in the dialectic of force in Chapter 5.

Concept can mean the mere notion of something, as opposed to its truth, or Concept in its high sense. The latter is concrete thought as the unity of thinking and being. It is the "good" infinity that Hegel had called "the soul of the world" and "the universal blood" [162].

Actual reason (reason that is at work in the world) strives to be Concept in this high sense, to be the soul and blood of the world. In Hegel's animation of Kant's cognitive machinery, Category (which I henceforth capitalize to signal Hegel's special use of this term) is selfhood striving to "schematize" and make its mark on the sensuous manifold or world. It is the self's *impulse* to be concrete universality or *Concept*. The German word for Concept, *Begriff*, comes from the verb that means grasp or take hold of [*greifen*]. Category is a grasping and grabbing—the cognitive hand I mentioned above.[13] As the Category personified and brought to life, the individual reaches into the great Grab Bag of the World and seizes one thing after another. Each grasp, each conquest, confirms his double certainty of being all reality, the certainty that says, "The world is *mine*!" and "I *am* the world!"

The Shapes of Reason

As I noted above, reason is composed of the three logical moments that recur throughout the *Phenomenology:* the in-itself, the for-itself, and the in-and-for-itself. These are, respectively, the affirmation of the object, the affirmation of the subject, and the affirmation of the unity of object and subject. At the level of reason, the shapes or *Gestalten* that incarnate these logical stages are as follows: reason as scientific observer, reason as the individual who makes himself real by opposing the actual world, and reason as the individual who is fulfilled in the actual world. The first level is passive or *theoretical*, the second and third active or *practical*.

These shapes embody the new attitude that the individual self adopts with respect to the *thing*. As we know, the goal of the *Phenomenology* is absolute knowing. This is the completion of philosophy in the form of System or philosophic Science [5]. The obstacle to this completion is the opposition between subject and object, self and thing. Reason is the attempt on the part of consciousness to overcome this opposition once and for all. The self must be a thing, objective and actual, without ceasing to be a self. And the thing must be thoroughly spiritualized, or permeated by the self, without ceasing to be a thing. Self and thing must be co-inherent. To use a term from a later stage of reason, they must experience an *interpenetration* [*Durchdringung*] [394].

In German, there are two words for thing: *Ding* and *Sache*. Hegel distinguishes them later in the chapter [410]. Generally, *Ding* is more determinate than *Sache*. It is the thing of many properties—the object of perception

[115]. Hegel had used *Sache* at the prior level of sense-certainty [91]. There, "thing" referred to the radical particular, the completely indeterminate This-whatever-it-is. Thinghood became more complex with the advent of force, and then life. For self-consciousness, things were the organic objects of desire (e.g. fruit). They were either gobbled up, or else transformed into products of human labor (by the slave). The stoic was indifferent to things. The skeptic proved that the stoic was right: he showed that all thing-like determinateness was riddled with non-being or otherness. Then the unhappy penitent experienced his singular I as a mere thing.

Reborn as reason, self-consciousness regards things as embodiments of itself. As reason evolves, so will the thing. In its in-itself, objective mode, reason takes the thing as a *Ding*. It observes the natural things and their wealth of properties. Observing reason takes special interest in *living* nature, since this mirrors the fluid movement that the self finds in its own thinking process. At the second, for-itself level of reason, the thing is imbued with human subjectivity. It is action, or the thing one *does*. In the third, in-and-for-itself stage, action becomes concrete in the product of human making, the *Werk* or "work." Unlike the slave, the self-actualizing, free individual consciously identifies himself with his products, which reflect his absoluteness. Later in the chapter, the work gives way to what Hegel calls the *Sache selbst*, "the matter itself." This is thing in the sense of one's affair, interest, or cause—the thing one takes seriously (in Greek, a *pragma*). Thing here is "my thing" as opposed to "your thing." It is the whatever-it-is I take up and make my own. The *Sache selbst* signals a major turning point in the emergence of truth as subject [17].

In the final stage of Hegel's chapter, reason finds the ultimate "thing that matters" in the *moral law*. Here, reason becomes full-fledged practical reason. Law, the universal Ought, is the objectively subjective and the subjectively objective. It is what each individual sees as universally binding or valid in itself. Moral law is the culmination of reason's drive to achieve an interpenetration of self and thing, subject and object. But law, as reason conceives it, is abstract. It is an Ought that the individual merely *sees* as valid within his own mind, an Ought that lacks reality. At the end of the chapter, law in this abstract sense disappears, and with it the presumed absoluteness of reason's individualism. Law in the abstract gives rise to law in the concrete. This Ought that also Is, is the actual, lived law of a people or nation, law as *custom*.

Reason at this point becomes spirit, *Geist*. Here, at last, there will be mutual recognition, a genuine "I that is We and a We that is I." The first historical manifestation of this recognition will be the Greek *polis* or city-state.

Nature should be Mind made visible,
Mind the invisible Nature.
SCHELLING, *Ideas for a Philosophy of Nature*

 12

Adventures of a Rational Observer

"THE WORLD IS MINE!" THIS IS THE BATTLE CRY OF REASON. Hegel uses an accident of the German language to make his point. *Sein,* in German, is both the infinitive "to be" and the possessive adjective meaning "his" or "its." From the standpoint of reason, *being* [*Sein*] is *its* (reason's) *own* [*Seinen*] [240]. Reason appropriates being through sensing and perceiving. But these differ from their earlier, pre-self-conscious forms. Previously, consciousness sensed and perceived. Now, as rational observer, it *sets out* to sense and perceive, *wills* to sense and perceive.

Observing is the act by which reason seeks the universal in the particulars of nature. This universal will take the form of *law.* Reason observes nature to find itself in the infinite variety of sensuous things. It does not know this about itself but only has a premonition of its deeper motive. When asked about his goal, the rational observer says, "I want to know about falling bodies, chemical reactions, animals, plants, planets, how the human body works, and much more!" Knowledge, for him, is directed toward "the essence of things qua things" [242].

The crucial difference here between reason as observer and the earlier forms of sensing and perceiving is that the observer is driven to find the *essence* or *Concept* of things. The empiricist can rail all he likes against the rational apriorist for daydreaming rather than getting to the meat of reality. But empiricism, no less than rationalism, is interested in the laws, principles, order, and general thinkableness of the material world. It is this thinkableness or universality that makes the world rationally *mine.*

The universality that reason seeks is reason itself. Reason is the self's desire to "find itself present as an [outer] shape and thing" [241]. As I noted above, it does not know that its endless observational adventure is the striving to find itself in the world, and *as* the world. Hegel forecasts the eventual failure of this project: "But even if reason digs into the very entrails of things and opens up every vein in them [!], so that it may gush forth to meet itself, it will not attain this joy [*Freude*]; it must have completed itself inwardly before it can experience the consummation of itself" [241]. In other words, thinghood as observation conceives it (thinghood as nature) is an inappropriate vessel for the self, whose true nature observing reason does not know. At the end of the section, the vessel bursts. In the section that follows, the self's effort to *find* itself as something real gives way to its effort to *make* itself real through worldly action.

Observing reason has three moments. The first is the observation of external nature, especially organic nature [244–97]. This phase echoes Hegel's earlier discussion of life in the chapter on self-consciousness.[1] Reason then ascends from nature to spirit or man. In this second moment, reason observes the self's own inner workings and behavior [298–308]. It seeks universality in the laws of logic and psychology. In its third phase, observing reason seeks the *unity* of spirit and nature, inner and outer, in physiognomy (you can read a man's mind in his face and hands) and phrenology (you can read a man's mind in the bumps on his head) [309–46].

Observing External Nature [244–97]

This section of Hegel's chapter is very long.[2] It shows Hegel's abiding interest in the question of nature, and in the theories of nature that existed at the time he was writing the *Phenomenology*. Reason's observation of nature has three main stages. In the first, reason describes natural things in their particularity [244–52]. In the second, it turns to the individual organism or *living whole* [253–82]. And in the third, it studies the greater whole: life in general in the context of its inorganic environment [283–97].

We recall that in its attempt to know the appearances, the understanding posited *another world:* a restful kingdom of law similar to Plato's realm of separate Forms [149]. Reason, by contrast, forswears the Beyond. It wants not transcendence but immanence. Reason observes the particulars of sense experience in order to find universality *within* them. Universals are now embodied universals, and particulars must have something universal about them in their very particularity. That is why reason gazes fondly at organic nature. Living things are like reason itself, which is the positive form of self-consciousness. As we saw in Chapter 7, life and self-consciousness mirror each other: both are spontaneously self-differentiating. Life is therefore more gratifying to observing reason's not-yet-conscious desire to meet itself in the realm of things. Life tempts reason to believe that living nature is the Concept made real.

Throughout his account of natural observation, Hegel emphasizes the *instinct of reason.*[3] As observer of nature, "reason operates only instinctively"

[246]. The instinct of reason is the restless intellectual desire to leave no stone unturned in observing the world of things in order to find reason in nature. The observer's various experiments, classifications, laws, and theories are the work of an unconscious desire for self-knowledge. Observing reason is a Ulysses who thinks he wants to keep going out into the world forever but really longs for a homecoming and a return to self. Ultimately, this instinct is the unconscious striving of scientific reason to be *practical reason.* This is reason that is its own conscious object and end.

A) PHASE ONE

In its first stage of observing nature, reason describes the things it finds in the world of objects taken generally. This describing is a purely subjective movement that is "not yet a movement in the object itself" [245]. Reason is like a wild animal on the prowl. It has an insatiable desire for the *new*—a new genus, or "even a new planet." In this experience of endless discovery, reason becomes aware of the difference between what is essential to cognition and what is true in itself [246]. This is how reason differs from the scientific understanding: it is *aware* that its ideas may be no more than mental constructs.[4] With animals, reason is on firm ground, since the marks by which we distinguish them (their claws and teeth) are also the means by which they maintain their independence from each other. Plants belong to a lower order of independence and so make reason less sure of itself. And chemical objects are confusing because they do not remain static and independent but vanish in their various combinations. Reason in this case does not know whether the various distinctions it posits within the object are really in the object or only in cognition.[5] In response to this doubt, it clings to fixity of determination, the static observation of the static differences in things (e.g., genus, species, and differentiae). It resists all objective movement or transition into other.

But there *is* movement in nature. The static determinations that reason sorts out in its purely descriptive phase are moments in a process of becoming [248]. Reason must therefore "move on." It now observes the movement in the object itself (which, unknown to reason, is also reason's own movement). It seeks the rational *law* that governs how things behave in the process of natural transformations. Law, as the pure thinkable or universal within sensuous particulars, gets reason closer to the Concept (truth as self-movement and subject). At first, law is reached through induction. It expresses a probability, whose sole ground is sensuous observation. Reason has not yet achieved "insight into the pure Concept" [250], which alone conveys inner necessity.[6] This sort of law is thinkable (minimally) and sensuous. But it is not yet the unity of the two. And so, reason strives to raise empirical laws to the level of the Concept by subjecting them to *experiment*

[251]. It attempts to bring out what is essential and to strip away sensuous clutter. Reason seeks "the *pure conditions* of the law." In this way, it tries to unite the ideal and the real, the *rationality* of law with the *actuality* of sensuous existence.[7]

Reason's effort to raise the law above its dependence on contingent, sensuous clutter only obscures the appearance of rationality in these particulars. Electricity, for example, starts out sensuously as the difference between resin-electricity and glass-electricity. In reason's effort to reach the ideal conditions that reveal the rational within the real through experiment, these become, intangibly, negative and positive electricity. These opposite forms of electricity vanish upon interaction, or are neutralized. The same thing happens with an acid and a base. When reason tries to rationalize the sensuous particulars through "controlled" experiments (which eliminate the supposedly non-essential), the result is "to cancel the moments or activated sides as properties of specific things, and to free the predicates from their subjects" [251]. The predicates (positive and negative electricity, or acid and base) become de-thingified as so-called *matters*, "which are neither bodies nor properties."[8] In other words, reason has failed to find an embodied universal.

B) PHASE TWO

In the hypothesis of matters, reason liberates law from its sensuousness and generates the universal as "a non-sensuous sensuous" or "an incorporeal and yet objective being" [252]. This new object reveals itself within the realm of the sensuous while at the same time being free of the sensuous. It is the autonomous *organism* [253]. A rabbit is not a property or a mere body. Nor is it an inert theoretical "matter" that emerges in reason's search for pure conditions. The rabbit is concrete, but not a mere thing. With this new object, there arises "another kind of observing."

In the turn to organisms, the observation of nature reaches its second stage. At first, reason seeks the laws that govern the relation between organic and inorganic nature [255]. This leads to "the *great influence* of environment," which reappears at the end of the section [297].[9] Laws of adaptation are meant to express a necessary connection between birds and the air, water and fish, hairy animals and northern climates. But in fact there is no such connection. As Hegel notes, "*there are* also land animals that have the essential characteristics of a bird, of a fish, and so on." Laws of adaptation fall inevitably into a mere statement of contingent fact. They fail to reveal logical connections, or the necessity rooted in the Concept. Hegel calls this Lamarckian adaptation of an organism to its environment a "teleological relation" [255]. Fish have gills *so that* they can live in the water; birds have wings *so that* they can live in the air. But unlike gills and wings, the relation of "so that" has no sensuous existence, and cannot be observed. It is *external* to the things it relates (water and gills, air and wings), and so is really "the antithesis of a law."

Laws of adaptation hover above organisms. They fail to express what is *in* them as the rational core of their being. Dissatisfied with this (non-Aristotelian) "external" teleology, reason turns to the Concept of an end or *Zweck*, which is in the organism itself and expresses its inner essence [256]. (As we shall see soon, reason will transform even this internal end into something external to the organism!) An organism is not simply the necessary result of external natural processes. It functions as a self-contained, self-preserving whole. To be sure, the organism interacts with its environment. For example, it cannot live without food. But this interaction is not determinative of the organism's behavior, form, and growth into maturity (the point at which it can reproduce). The organism spontaneously develops and *acts on* its environment. It is its own end: "The organism does not produce something but only preserves itself; or what is produced, is as much already present as produced" [256]. As its own end, the organism is a true individual. It points beyond itself to self-consciousness or *man.*

In his Preface, Hegel defined reason as "purposive or goal-directed activity" [*das zweckmäßige Tun*] [22]. With the organic end, reason therefore comes closer to recognizing itself in nature. But reason at this stage is only a drive or instinct. It does not yet know that what it seeks is itself. Hegel proceeds to examine how reason "finds itself" in the organic end or *telos,* "but does not recognize itself in what it finds" [257]. End, here, is the dialectical or logically fluid *Concept* that reason, as observer, will turn into something static and "above" the phenomena of life.[10]

Let us recall that reason is searching for necessity. This is the universal rationality within sensuous particulars. Reason thinks it has found this in the organic end, which expresses a necessity internal to the organism. This end is a "hidden" necessity that reveals itself to the observer only retrospectively, only in the wake of the process or activity that led to that end [257]. Only then does the end appear as having been there all along. In striving to accomplish its end, the organism seems to be going outside itself. But in fact its movement is a return to self. The rabbit goes out in search of carrots. It finds those carrots and eats them. The result is the rabbit's *Selbstgefühl* or *self-feeling:* its return to self as end. There is an apparent distinction between what the rabbit *is* and what it *seeks.* But this distinction is canceled in the rabbit's satisfaction in eating carrots.

Hegel concludes that the organism, as its own end, is "in its own self a Concept." That is, the organism's being-toward-end mirrors the Concept as the rational One, which differentiates itself from itself only to cancel that distinction and return to itself. The organism and self-consciousness are similarly constituted [258]. Each distinguishes itself from itself "without producing any distinction." Each is a circle. The rabbit desires carrots: observing reason desires knowledge. Moreover, each acts instinctively. In thinking the Concept of end or goal-directed activity as the truth of nature, reason comes home to itself. But, as I noted above, *it does not know this.* In its instinctive mode, reason distinguishes its self-consciousness from its consciousness, or awareness of objects as "out there" and distinct from the self.[11] It falsifies the circular character of being-toward-end by sticking to the distinction between essence and end. It thinks of the rabbit as *having* an end rather than *being* its own end (a merely formal distinction). And so, even though it eats the carrot of self-return and Concept, observing reason cannot achieve satisfaction. Its satisfaction is "shattered" by the antithesis of organism and end.

Since reason cannot think the identity of organic thing and end (the thing is sensuous, the end intellectual), it posits the end as "outside" the organism.[12] Reason here repeats the dichotomy of essence and appearance that we saw at the level of understanding. A further consequence is that reason thinks of organisms as having been assigned an end by "another intelligence" [258]. This is God as the Author of Nature. God knows the ends of things because he gave organisms their natural end.[13] His is the mind in which nature has its purposes. In sum, observing reason places the organic end *both* outside the organism *and* outside itself.

The problem of end, however, also lies with nature. The organism acts purposively. It is its own end. But as far as observation is concerned, the inner necessity this involves does not come on the scene until the organism has accomplished its end, say, in eating carrots. To use an even better example, we do not observe the end of a still-developing organism until that organism has reached its mature form. We do not *observe* the means becoming the end, the cause becoming the effect. The nature of the functioning organism "is to conceal the necessity [of the end], and to exhibit it in the form of a contingent relation" [259]. The rabbit's teeth develop to the point that the rabbit can eat carrots. In retrospect, we say that the teeth grew the way they did *so that* an end would be achieved, as if there were some intelligent "pilot" or *kybernētēs* at work in the inner process of nature, steering it toward its end. Once the eating takes place, and becomes the "food" of scientific observation, the end is clear. But this end was not observable while the teeth were growing. It was "hidden." Reason cannot find the rational connection between the non-purposive, observable processes that precede the end and the end itself. The end seems, almost miraculously, simply to appear out of seemingly mindless motions.

The result of this experience of observing reason is that the end is not visible until it has been achieved. It does not show itself as the beginning of development and activity. The end was "there all along" only for the designer-God or demiurge who made nature (the God who is the projection of our own rationality). The hypothesis of such a God occurs because reason cannot think end dialectically. It cannot see the end at work in the rabbit's actual *movement.* And so, the search for immanent necessity must go on. Reason must look deeper into the rabbit itself as a self-contained individual. It must look to "what belongs to the organism itself" [260]. This is "the action lying in the middle between its first and last stage." This is the organism's singular being-for-self bereft of any universality or purpose.

The problem now is that reason has generated a split between the singularity of the organism and the universality of its end. The organism as such has been "deserted" by the universal. Its activity is not even that of a *machine,* since this has a purpose [261]. It is only an activity like that of an acid or base. Reason therefore has two immediacies that must somehow be connected: the singular organism and the universal end. To repeat, the organism has in fact *returned into itself* with the arrival at its end (mature functioning). But reason does not see this return or dialectical circle. It "converts the antithesis" of singular organism and universal or rational end into an opposition suited to its own limited perspective.

This is the opposition between *inner* and *outer.* Faced with the problem of a real individual and an ideal end or universal, and unable to think their dialectical unity, reason connects these two poles through picture-thinking. It imagines an observable organic inner that is present in an observable outer. The resultant law is: "*the outer is the expression* [*Ausdruck*] *of the inner*" [262]. The observable inner here is the organism's life-force or *soul* which expresses itself in various organic functions or powers [265].[14]

Expressivity takes us back to *force.* One important difference is that expressivity now refers to living things rather than colliding bodies or electrical charges. Another difference is that organic expressivity is genuinely spontaneous. An individual life-force or soul does not need another to solicit its action. All it needs is a suitable environment for its *self*-caused development and activity. As with active and passive force, reason's distinction between inner and outer is purely formal [266]. In other words, whether we are talking about implicit and inner or explicit and outer, the *content* is the same. Expression is mere translation rather than real change. Reason posits the poles of inner and outer, but it cannot think their dialectical unity, or transition into each other. It cannot think the "pure change" that defines the Concept [160].

As Hegel explains, reason's new inner and outer each have their own inner and outer. Let us return to our rabbit.[15] It has its own life-force or soul. This force expresses itself, and is observable, in three distinct psychic powers or properties: *sensibility, irritability,* and *reproduction* [265].[16] Each expresses a logical moment of the Concept, which appears in "a being whose end is its own self" [266]. Through sensibility, the rabbit is something *in itself*, set apart from other natural beings. It *feels* the effects of the external world, as they impinge on its selfhood. Irritability is the rabbit's *being-for-self* or "elasticity." This is its tendency to react on the basis of its sensibility. The rabbit is *for itself* in being *for another* (that is, related to another). To shift our animal example, stir a hornets' nest and you will be the *other* on whom the hornets inflict their *being-for-self*. Finally, reproduction, the most important organic factor, is "the action of this *whole* [our rabbit] in the self-reflecting organism." Here, the rabbit is *in and for itself*: it not only is, and is related to an other, but also *produces an other that is itself*. The *outer*, physical medium in which the individual rabbit-soul expresses itself resides in the anatomical *systems* that correspond to each organic power: the nervous system to sensibility, the muscular system to irritability, and the visceral system to reproduction [267].[17]

But the rabbit also belongs to the whole ecosphere, which contains both organic and inorganic being. The rabbit is not only self-related but also other-related. This is the whole *outer* aspect of its being. The rabbit in relation to the whole of the organic and inorganic world belongs to the *third stage* of reason's observation of nature.

The outer aspect of the rabbit—the world that exists beyond the rabbit —also has *its* inner and outer [283]. The outer aspect of this larger world or ecosphere is the sum total of all life-forms in their outward shape together with the whole inorganic realm of the elements [284]. The inner aspect of the ecosphere is the "stream of life" that courses freely through all living things, and is indifferent to the particular shapes these things happen to assume [285]. This stream is not interested in the existence or non-existence of rabbits, and is indifferent "to the kinds of mills it drives." This inner of the outer, the universal life-process, transcends all static shapes. In its unpredictability (mutants) and penchant for bizarre combinations (the platypus), it defies all laws.

In both its inner and outer aspects, reason's new law—"the outer is the expression of the inner"—comes to naught. The inner and the outer, and their respective self-expressions, have similar problems. In both cases, reason seeks a law by which a self-same universal accounts for specific distinctions or differences. In both cases, the law is *quantitative* rather than qualitative or genuinely conceptual. Why? Because mathematics is the only way that non-dialectical reason, in its bond with understanding, can combine movement or fluidity with intelligibility. Observing reason knows that movement must be part of its world-picture (this is rooted in its instinctive search for self), but it does not know how to make the movement intelligible. The *inner* aspect of both the inner and the outer (that is, the inner soul of the rabbit and the inner "stream of life" that transcends the rabbit) is *for us* the fluidity or *movement* of the Concept [265, 285]. The *outer* of both the inner and the outer (anatomical systems and life's variety of shapes) represents the vanishing poles of this movement as static determinations or logical *rest* [265, 284]. But for reason, the fluid undifferentiated inner expresses itself in a determinate way by means of quantity, degree, and *number* [271, 285]. Differences of form are differences in the degree to which life expresses itself (as a "range" of higher and lower organisms). Number makes the life-continuum rationally discontinuous.

As we know from Hegel's general critique of mathematics in the Preface [42–46], mathematics in biology (a prime instance of schematizing formalism) is doomed to failure, insofar as it claims to get at the essence of things.[18] The mathematical is opposed to the truly conceptual or logically fluent. This is especially evident in the sphere of organic life, where all fixed distinctions are fluid and vanish in the life-process, just as they do in the movement that defines self-consciousness [171]. Reason posited the expression of the inner in the outer in order to secure a necessary connection between the thinkable universal and the strictly observable particulars of living things. Mathematics blocks rather than captures this necessity. It masquerades as the Concept.

Let us now see how mathematics emerges for both the inner and the outer of organisms. We start with the inner. The organic inner is expressed in the three properties I noted earlier: sensibility, irritability, and reproduction. Unable to find logical or qualitative connections among these, reason devises relations like this one: "sensibility and irritability stand in an inverse ratio of their magnitude, so that as the one increases the other decreases; or better, taking the magnitude itself as the content, as its smallness decreases" [271]. Echoing the earlier breakdown of scientific explanation, Hegel argues that this is a *tautology*. It is no different from saying "that the size of a hole *increases* the more what it is filled with *decreases*."

More generally, Hegel argues that static systems of *any* kind cannot capture the Concept of life. Formalism in biology turns life into anatomy: the study of the living organism insofar as it is *dead* [276].[19]

In analyzing the rabbit, reason fails to make its picture-thought of expressivity logically coherent: "the idea of law in the case of organic being is altogether lost" [278].[20] The same thing happens in the case of reason's depiction of the rabbit as an expression of *life in general.* Reason cannot mediate the extremes of sober static-system-of-life-forms and drunken fluid-stream-of-life: determinateness and indeterminateness. It cannot explain how an undifferentiated life-flow becomes the actual individuals and kinds of individuals we observe. In general, reason cannot make its object determinate without making it static, or fluid without making it vague. It is caught between mathematical formalism and mystic intuitionism.

Hegel notes in passing the differences between laws of observational *reason* regarding organisms and laws of the *understanding* [279]. The understanding was the movement or transition from the individual thing of perception to the universality of law. The true object of understanding was law itself in its presumed eternal self-sameness or rest. Explanation was the purely subjective movement between the restful kingdom of law and the play of individual forces [154]. But for reason, the object is life, which *is* transition. Individual forms mysteriously emerge from the universal life-flow, and vanish back into it. The laws of the understanding are only static universals (like Newton's inverse-square law). But the laws of reason govern inner development, growth, and transformation.

In using number to formulate laws of organisms, reason also reveals its *bond* with the abstract understanding. It reduces the fluidity of life to the static being of the inorganic. It makes the determinateness of living things rational at the expense of what they *are*. As Hegel says, mathematical formulae suppress the reflection-into-self or inwardness that distinguishes organisms from ordinary things of sense and perception [281]. They "extinguish" the Concept and make necessity "vanish" [280].

C) PHASE THREE

We now reach the third stage of reason's adventure as the observer of nature. Having explored the rabbit's individual inner and outer, we now turn to the realm *outside* the rabbit—the environment [283]. The realm beyond the individual rabbit has its own inner and outer. These are, respectively, the "stream of life" and the inorganic realm in which this stream presumably expresses itself.

As I noted earlier, reason seeks to make the stream of life determinate by means of *number* [285]. Organisms preserve themselves, and distinguish themselves from other organisms and from their inorganic environment, by virtue of their *specific gravity* or density (mass divided by volume) [288].[21] This physical inorganic property supposedly accounts for all the observable shapes of organisms, especially for their *cohesion* as individuals [287]. What Hegel tries to show is that specific gravity has no necessary connection to the cohesion of individual organisms, the resistance they exhibit in response to their environment. The real cohesiveness by which an animal preserves itself depends on the fluid connections of all the qualitatively distinct parts and powers of that animal. It cannot be a matter of more and less in what is only one property among others. The quantitative character of specific gravity, though clear and distinct, is at odds with the phenomenon it seeks to explain: organicity and the obviously *qualitative* differences both within and between organic beings.

Hegel uses specific gravity as a springboard to another dialectical relation that the individual organism has to the outer world [291]. Specific gravity, he claims, is the *inner* of inorganic beings—a free-floating variable that assumes different values and underlies their various shapes and properties. This is intended to account for why individual metals, for example, hold together and resist change, and why some metals do this more than others.[22] This, however, does not express anything essential to life. It is one property among others, not an organic inner.

The individual rabbit, by contrast, has a necessary relation to its organic outer or the life-process in general. As Hegel puts it, "the being-for-self [or individuality] of the living organism . . . has in its own self the principle of *otherness*" [291]. The rabbit has a living "outside" that is the direct result of its own relation-to-self. This is the genus or kind that emerges from the life-process. As we saw in Chapter 7, genus, *Gattung*, results from the act of sexual union, *Begattung* (that is, begetting). The individual rabbit shares the fate of all organic beings: it is mortal and eventually must die. But it also transcends its death through reproduction. Death and reproduction are intimately connected. In the language of force, the rabbit *repels itself from itself*, casts itself forth as an other.[23] The genus (the individual's self-transcendence) is the universality that the rabbit bears within itself and constitutes the rabbit's intelligible "unity" and "inwardness." Specific gravity and the living genus are both "free" in being completely indifferent to the various shapes we see. But the genus is free in a more radical way. It is not, like specific gravity, a static property that merely *is*, but life's "universal freedom"—life as the ungoverned and awesome "stream of life."

The self-transcendence of the individual organism in universal life or genus gives rise to "the *determinate* universal, the *species* [*die Art*]" [292]. Unlike inorganic bodies, the rabbit is in itself universal: it contains its own otherness. It is the sexual or procreative version of the singular Now that posits itself as negating itself, thus generating the Now of Nows [107]. Also like the self-negating Now, it gives rise to the "bad infinity" of one rabbit after another. The individual rabbit generates *but does not contain* this universal. And so, we have a vanishing singular rabbit and the universal life-process (the genus) that is not expressed in any one rabbit or number of rabbits.[24]

The species is the apparently stable *middle term* that reason uses to mediate between these two extremes. Individual rabbits are evanescent—like the individual forces of understanding. Just as the latter dissolve in the play of force [143], the former dissolve in the game of life. Individual organisms are not really substantial abiding beings when looked at in terms of their relation to the life process. What is real and substantial is the *species,* which is both universal and determinate.[25]

Hegel observes that if the universal life-process or genus *were* the movement from this universality to the actual individual through the species, "then the organic genus would be consciousness" [292]. By consciousness, Hegel means specifically the *understanding* (Harris, 1:531–322). Understanding generates the abstract concepts of genus, species, and individual. It propounds a static or immediate version of the dialectical syllogism, where a less comprehensive entity is subsumed by, or "under," a more comprehensive one. Observing reason fails to see this version of itself in the life-process. It translates the genus as thought or consciousness into a "dumb" classification of species according to specific gravity, i.e., a dead *number.*[26] This is the work of reason's picture-thinking, which persistently fails to recognize the dialectical Concept of life and thinks relation only as external to the things related.

The genus or life process is the *inner* of the organic individual (our rabbit). It does not manifest itself in an all-encompassing organic individual. Unlike Plato in the *Timaeus* (33A–B), Hegel does not think of the universe as the mega-animal that contains all other animals. Nevertheless, there is a "universal individual" that sustains the life of all organic individuals. This is the Earth [294].[27] In the Earth, universality has "an external actuality" and "falls outside the living organism." The Earth is where reason ends up because it cannot recognize thought itself in the relation of genus, species, and individual rabbit. It can imagine but cannot *think* the concrete unity of universal and individual.

We can now grasp the Concept of life as a *syllogism* [*Schluß*] [293]. One extreme is the universal life-process or genus. The other is this same universal individualized and brought to rest as the Earth. The middle term "is composed of both." The first extreme participates in this middle term as a species (the determinate universal), the second as a concrete single individual (the rabbit). In one aspect of the middle term, the organism is a specification of universal life: in another a mere outward life-form that comes to be and passes away on the great stage that is the Earth.

The outward shapes of life all arise as specifications of the life-process. In reason's mathematical formalism, this happens in accordance with the number (specific gravity) that determines the organism's various outward inorganic features (shape, color, etc.). The number that corresponds to specific gravity places each organism in the continuous chain of life.[28] This determination is the peaceful, self-contained life of the genus or life-flow that spontaneously differentiates itself into more and less. But as the genus nicely specifies itself by grades or degrees, it "suffers violence from the universal individual" [294]. Life evolves into many forms. But it does so only under the stringent conditions of climate, temperature, terrain, etc. It is "interrupted, incomplete, and curtailed on all sides by [the] unchecked violence [of the elements]." Earth is the ultimate externality.

The result of this stage of the dialectic is that life fails to express itself in its outer structured shape [295]. It has become entrenched in the inorganic realm of number, and in the violent contingencies of the Earth. The genus indeed differentiates itself into a seemingly infinite variety of shapes, which reason statically classifies. But life is not *itself* orderly; nor does it reveal its inner workings in these shapes. Nature is depicted or imagined by reason, but not thought. Its various forms are merely pigeonholed.

The problem, however, lies not just with reason but also with organic nature itself. Nature "has no history" [295]. It is not "self-systematizing development," not a process in which the middle term contains the extremes of the life-syllogism and develops them out of itself. The middle term that has this character is *consciousness.* Human individuals *know* themselves as parts of the universal process of *world-history.* But organic nature, the object of reason at this stage of its development, "falls from its universal, from life, directly into the singleness of *Dasein* or being-there, and the moments of simple determinateness, and the single organic life united in this actuality, produce Becoming only as a contingent movement." History, unlike organic nature, is the whole that is *for itself.* It is the work of beings that are conscious of purpose, and conscious of themselves as ends. Such beings individually are aware of themselves as universal and for that reason *contain* the universal.

Reason's instinctive goal in observing nature was to meet itself as the realization of the universal in the concrete particular. But its attempt to unify these extremes only drove them farther apart. Mathematics was the sure sign that the Concept was obscured rather than incarnated. Reason indeed saw itself in nature, but only as genus or "universal life as such" [296]. This is reason itself as the inner undifferentiated stream of thought. Reason sees the other aspect of itself, the arrangement of parts into a stable system, in the classifications that reason has devised. But this realized "system of life" has no immanent necessity. It is the result of the external necessities imposed on life by the Earth. Reason's two sides remain two sides. It has failed to think organic nature as a self-differentiating One.

Hegel now sums up the result of the whole dialectic. Reason's quest for a vision of itself in organic life results in a syllogism without a middle term. Genus or the universal life-process simply falls immediately [*unmittelbar*] into individuals and species formed ultimately by the random turbulence of the Earth [297]—Hegel's version of Plato's "wandering cause" in the *Timaeus* (48A). Reason cannot observe "life." It can only mystically *mean* or intend it as something akin to Bergson's *élan vital* or creative impulse.[29]

Echoing his opening to this section [240], Hegel plays on the word *Meinen.* As a verb, it is to *mean* or intend. As the possessive adjective, it refers to what is *mine.* Reason can meet its own (that is, itself) only through meaning *as opposed to* observing. It is like sense-certainty, which can mean, but not express, the sensuous This [97].

Observing reason, as we know, is imaginative. It approaches nature by means of picture-thinking [290]. The law, "the outer is the expression of the inner," was a prime instance of this thinking. The observation of nature becomes, in the end, the telling of anecdotes—what Plato called "likely stories." Reason thus enjoys an "unspiritual freedom" that consists in caprice rather than science. It sees in nature "the beginnings of laws, traces of necessity, allusions to order and system, ingenious and plausible [*scheinbare*] relations" [297]. In accounting for why organic forms are the way they are, reason cannot get beyond the "great influence" theory that Hegel criticized earlier [255]. And when it contemplates life in its immanent unity, it devises a life-form series based on *number* (specific gravity). This releases the qualitative aspect of nature into the realm of subjective *play* or the freedom of imagining. Observation is not the seeing of immanent order but a matter of "clever remarks" and "interesting relations"—what Hegel derisively calls "a friendly approach to the Concept."

Observing the Mind: Logic and Psychology [298–308]

In its previous phase, observing reason failed to find itself in a thing. Lost in the labyrinth of nature, reason brought about the opposite of what it intended. In the concept of Life, it made thinghood or reality inaccessible to reason. In seeking to make nature both real and rational, it transformed life into concept in its *lower* sense of mere subjective notion—something always meant and never observed.

This melting of thinghood into a vaporous intuitionism has a positive, productive result. As things dissolve into the mere concept of them, into something that is merely *meant,* Concept or self absorbs their thingliness. The "thing" or object that reason now sets out to observe is the behavior of *self-consciousness itself* [298]. In this second phase of observation, reason first posits the truth as residing in the formal laws of thought. These are the laws of identity, non-contradiction, and excluded middle.[30] Logic, here, is mental behaviorism, the study of "how we think." Reason then moves beyond formal logic to the more concrete study of psychology. This whole middle, inwardly turned phase of observing reason is very short-lived. The phase devoted to formal logic quickly passes into psychological laws, and the whole section quickly passes into the third and final stage of reason as observer.

It is not hard to see why, in its instinctive quest for self, reason makes this move from external nature to inner self. By observing the inner self, reason seems at last to have come home to itself and to have found the link between selves and things. It makes its own selfhood or inwardness into the "animal" of its consideration. Moreover, in observing my inner state and seeing that it is governed by laws of thought, I seem to have discovered in my own person the unity of individual and universal (or instance and law). This is precisely the unity that reason seeks.

Hegel's critique of positing the formal laws of thought as absolute is the opposite of what we might expect from his usual attacks on formalism [51]. The problem is not that these laws are merely formal but rather that they are content *without* form [300]! Grounding the truth of these laws in the observation of How We Think makes the laws a contingent fact or fluke of our inner constitution, a mere description of how we behave internally. This is one of the major stumbling blocks observing reason keeps hitting. Genuine thought and universality imply necessity. But particulars, although thingly and real, are contingent. In identifying the thinking self with observed laws of thought, reason de-rationalizes or unthinks itself: "But observing is not knowing itself, and is ignorant of it; it converts its own nature into the form of [mere] being, i.e., it grasps its negativity only as *laws* of thought" [300]. Instead of preserving universality within thinghood, the laws of thought, which are themselves objects of observation, erase this universality and reduce it to a mass of irrational fact.

The experienced inadequacy of the laws of thought (as rules of mental behavior) propels reason to look for the rationality of the inner behavior that is the larger context for logical laws: our psychological makeup or whole inner life. Observational psychology posits what observational logic could not: internal movement, life, otherness, and "restless movements" [303]. We look inside ourselves. What do we see? Not logical ducks all in a row, but (in the words of William James) a "booming bustling confusion" of this half-thought, that memory, this regret, that image. Observational psychology looks for the causality in the chaos, the law in the jungle of inner particulars. To do so, it turns to the outside world, to something *actual,* in order to explain an individual's inner state. It appeals to the "universal inorganic nature" that is observable in the individual's "given circumstances, situation, habits, customs, religion, and so on" [305].[31] The *law* of observational psychology, the universal at work in the individual, is the necessary relation that supposedly exists between the state of the external world and the individual's peculiar combination of personality traits, passions, and propensities.

This psychology posits a dualism between *two worlds:* the world as it objectively exists, and the individual's subjective way of responding to and even changing that world [302]. The former is the external world as given, the latter the world as reconstituted or "spun" by the peculiar inner makeup of the individual. Empirical psychology wants to say *both* that the individual represents the actual world that is outside him, *and* that he makes of it what he will [307]. Again, recalling the instinct that drives observing reason, we can say that reason here wants a concrete particularized embodiment of the self—the unity of self and thing. It thinks it has found such a unity in regarding the individual self as a filter that simultaneously represents and alters the universal milieu or actual conditions in which the self lives (social, political, religious, economic, etc.).

Ultimately, this fails because there is no necessary connection between the state of the world and the interior of any individual who is affected by that world: "the individual either allows free play to the stream of the actual world flowing in upon it, or else breaks it off and transforms it" [307]. An individual with a given socio-economic background might choose to conform to his culture. But he might just as well rebel against it, or set out to change the world. The supposed law that unifies universal influences and an individual's psychological response breaks down and becomes a matter of sheer chance. The term "psychological necessity," Hegel says, thus "becomes an empty phrase." This incoherence of observational psychology reminds us of the breakdown of necessity we saw at the level of the scientific understanding. There, too, necessity was "an empty word" [152], nothing more than the statement, "That is the way things are."

Observing Mind in Body: Physiognomy and Phrenology [309–46]

The failure of observational psychology to unite self and thing leads to the third and final stance of reason as observer. In the previous, psychological phase, the actual world of universal laws and customs and the self-contained individual went their separate ways. Hegel calls this the "mutual indifference" of inner and outer [309]. Now reason puts these two sides together in the self-contained individual. No more is there talk of an individual *and* the world that contains and influences him. Now the individual as such—this human individual apart from all external influences—is the expression of universality within a particular. He is the absolute, a world unto himself. The human individual is the immediate unity of the objective in itself and the subjective for itself. Actuality is no longer the external world of laws, customs, religions, family life, etc., but my own *body* [310]. My bodily organs—whether hand or face—become that in which I reveal myself, as a self, to direct inspection. In this third incarnation, observing reason is *physiognomy*, the "science" of reading an individual's inner state and personality in his physical characteristics. Here the inmost self becomes, in Hegel's provocative phrase, "a visible invisible" [318].[32]

Through physiognomy, reason tries to satisfy its need for an objective vision of itself, its desire to see itself as a thing, and a thing as itself. In this final observational phase, reason posits a distinction between an invisible inner spirit and the external organ that expresses that spirit.[33] It will try to unite these extremes in a way it deems scientific. Rather than dialectically relating inner and outer, thus revealing the Concept in its truth, reason will rigidly separate them and then try to establish unity as the external relation of mere *correspondence.*[34]

To get at how physiognomy understands itself, we must revise the way we look at our bodily organs. Mouth and hand are instruments I use to express myself: my mouth speaks, my hand works on something [312]. In speaking or working with my hands, I bring my inner spirit out into the open. As an expressive being, I am the self-conscious incarnation of *force.* But someone hearing or seeing me does not automatically know what I mean to express. He cannot observe my transition from inner to outer, any more than he can observe the action of force. He sees or hears only the result and product: a word with an intended meaning, or a wave that signals warning. Reason as observer wants more than this. It wants a science of "reading off" the inner spirit directly in the bodily organ. We must therefore not think of the hand, for example, as primarily an instrument for doing and making, but as containing directly observable *signs* of a human being's inmost disposition regarding his speeches and deeds—*signs that the individual cannot hide.*[35] According to physiognomy, we do not need to look at someone's actual life and deeds to know who he is in his depths. To read his heart, we simply inspect his face, hands, or handwriting—his *body language.*

As the sign of a secret interior, the organ reveals, not the actual work a man does but his intention: "We see from a man's face whether he is *in earnest* about what he is saying or doing" [318]. The problem here is the same one we saw in empirical psychology. Just as the individual may or may not conform to his culture, so too, he may or may not fit his facial gestures to his inner state. He may make his face into a mask [318] and be an Iago or a Tartuffe. People pose. And even a sincerely meant sign can unintentionally deceive. Furthermore, who we are is not necessarily reflected in who we *think* we are. We can be mistaken about our inmost motives and our hearts, just as the physiognomist can be mistaken about the motive he thinks he sees in the lines of our hand. Physiognomy succeeds as a science only if we always wear our hearts on our sleeves and possess self-knowledge, and if signs are always unambiguous. Only then will there be a necessary connection —a *law*—that connects inner and outer. But in fact, there is no more a necessary correspondence between my inner spirit and my outward bodily appearance than there is between my soul and my culture. Correspondences admittedly exist. But in the end, "There's no art to find the mind's construction in the face" (*Macbeth* 1.4).

Hegel's deeper critique of physiognomy has to do with what this pseudoscience regards as the essential or true spirit of a human being, namely, the intention all by itself rather than the individual's whole life [267–69].[36] This dualism of mind and body, intention and bodily part, is the ultimate undoing of physiognomy, which posits a radical inner (the intention), a radical outer (the body), and the hand or face as the middle term that is supposed to mediate these extremes. But instead of mediating, the presumed sign simply expresses an illogical juxtaposition of inner intention and outer bodily sign. The inner here has absolutely nothing to do with words and deeds. And the organ, as a mere *thing*, is detached from any spiritual expressivity (such as work or speech). At the level of empirical psychology, world and individual went their separate ways. So too, here in the claims of physiognomy, intention and deed also go their separate ways. The truth of physiognomy's certainty is the union of two things that, according to physiognomy itself, have nothing to do with each other.

Observing reason makes one final attempt to unite self and thing. This attempt is *phrenology*, or what Hegel calls *Schädellehre*, skull theory.[37] Phrenology claims to read a man's inmost spirit, the depths of his heart, in the bumps on his skull. It is physiognomy pushed to its logical conclusion. This is the moment in which observing reason *as a whole* experiences its truth as an absurdity. The absurdity consists in the judgment and affirmation that the actuality of spirit is—a bone.

The skull bone is attractive to observing reason because it is "a mere thing," indeed a "dead being" [329] that lacks "self-conscious movement" [323].[38] Unlike hand and facial organs, the skull has no action of its own and has nothing to do with "signing." It is *only* a thing—a thing, however, that physically receives "the internal action of the self-conscious being operating outwards only against its own body" [325]. Bumps on the skull, in other words, are the protuberances and "impacts" formed by an individual's psychic energy and personality (via the nervous system) and have nothing whatsoever to do with his free will. In the language of gamblers and con artists, these bumps are the ultimate "tell." The actuality of man or spirit is not his speech, or his deeds, or what is expressed in his hands and face, but *just this telltale bone.*

The problem with this view, apart from its being offensive to any sane human being ("The real you is your skull bone!"), is that phrenology is incoherent. It cannot point to any necessary causal connection between spirit and skull, inner and outer. Bumps, like signs, are open to interpretation. This is the same problem we have seen before. Reason as observer wants a union of self and thing but cannot get away from its basic dualisms. It posits a radical heterogeneity of inner and outer, and then tries to find correspondences between them. It confuses causality with juxtaposition.

It seems odd that Hegel would devote so many pages to this boneheaded theory. Phrenology, however, plays a crucial role in Hegel's Science of experience.[39] It is the perfectly logical culmination of the instinct of observing reason, the drive to find spirit in a thing. As Hegel notes, "Observation has here reached the point where it openly declares what *our* concept of it was, namely, that the certainty of reason seeks its own self as an objective reality " [343]. In phrenology, in other words, observing reason *becomes self-conscious.* It sets out to find itself as pure mind in a blunt thing. Furthermore, the manifest absurdity of phrenology makes us aware of the not-so-evident absurdity in other, apparently scientific efforts (like those of physiognomy) to read the nature and workings of the human spirit in the human body (for example, in an individual's body-type or DNA).

This coming to self-consciousness of observing reason has a "double meaning" [344]. The first meaning is that reason as observer, having realized its truth in the absurdity of phrenology, has hit bottom and rebounds from its unsatisfying union of self and thing. Reason now turns to a form of thinghood that can accommodate its newly discovered self-consciousness. This is the transition to the next section, where reason moves from dead thing to living deed: "Consciousness no longer aims to *find* itself *immediately,* but to produce itself by its own activity" [344].

The second meaning deals with the duplicity within phrenology itself. The phrenologist does not deliberately set out to identify spirit, or mind, and bone. There is in him a naïveté that is the work of "a profounder self-consciousness of spirit." The phrenologist realizes that something as sublime as spirit or mind cannot be literally reduced to a bone. And so he leads a double life. He sees the absurdity of what he says and tries to whitewash his teaching, *hide it from himself,* with technical sounding "explanations," in effect, scientific mumbo-jumbo [345]. Hegel's discussion reminds us of earlier end-of-chapter accounts of how consciousness, once it catches a glimpse of its error, runs away from truth and blinds itself to what it has seen.

Hegel ends with the ironic marriage of depth and shallowness. Depth is present because phrenology is the Concept itself in its negative phase: the Concept as *split* [*entzweit*] into the extremes of inner and outer, thought and thing [346]. In phrenology, inner and outer have been radicalized as *mere* inner and *mere* outer, living intention and dead thing. Phrenology's ignorance of what it is doing in attempting to unify these opposites in the skull bone is a spiritual revelation. Phrenology makes explicit the *gap* that must be bridged if idealism is to reach its truth, the estrangement of self and world that must be overcome. But skull theory is also shallow because it reveals the Concept in an utterly non-conceptual way: through *picture thinking* that leads to absurdity [346]. In phrenology, spirit combines a noble truth with a disgraceful expression of that truth. It is like its fellow ironist, nature, who, Hegel observes, wittily combines in the male organ the high power of reproduction with the low act of pissing [346].[40]

With the irony of nature and spirit, the adventures of the rational observer come to an end. This is the last theoretical shape of consciousness we meet in the *Phenomenology* until we reach absolute knowing. In the shapes to come, we are in the realm of human praxis and passion. In its very next phase, reason will be reborn as a new breed of idealist. This idealist is animated, not by instinct but by conscious desire and will.

The spirit helps me, suddenly I see counsel
And confidently write: In the beginning was the Deed!
GOETHE, *Faust*

13

The Romance of Reason

REASON NOW BECOMES A ROMANTIC. IT APPEARS AS A TRIO OF heroic archetypes dear to the German romantics of Hegel's day: the disenchanted scholar, the criminal with a heart of gold, and the high-minded preacher of noble intent. In this for-itself, subjective phase of reason, I feel the prompting of my inmost self as the drive to self-actualization. I go out into the world, not to observe but to act—to *make* rather than *find* myself [344]. The world, for me, is ambiguous. It is an oppressive other that stifles my desire for happiness with its piety, laws, selfishness, and hypocrisy. But it is also the medium in which I seek my reality and fulfillment.

The upshot of the unhappy consciousness was that the self succeeded in making itself into a thing [231]. This determinate negation produced idealism, my certainty of being all reality. Something similar happens in the transition from phrenology to active reason: "Self-consciousness found the thing to be like itself, and itself to be like a thing; i.e., it is aware that it is *in itself* the objectively real world" [347]. Phrenology, the pinnacle and pit of observing reason, failed to satisfy reason's idealism. Reason wants to meet itself in the external world [241]. But when the phrenologist observes spirit in a bone, this objectivity or thinghood of spirit does not in turn observe him: no *living thing* returns his gaze. This lack of reflexivity in the object is unsatisfying to reason, which craves an objective experience of itself as alive and conscious. Reason therefore seeks a new object: another human self that *recognizes* the individual in search of actualization. Reason's paradigm for this search is Faust, who seeks to make his selfhood real, to see himself in another, by seducing the innocent Gretchen.

Desire and recognition form a close bond between active reason, as it first appears, and self-consciousness. Active reason is self-consciousness at a higher level. It is the middle stage of reason as idealism. But it is also a new beginning, just as self-consciousness was a new beginning. Revealing the larger drama that is at work here, Hegel tells us that reason as a whole repeats the dialectical movements of consciousness and self-consciousness [348]. Reason as observer repeated the stages of consciousness: *sense-certainty, perception,* and *understanding.*[1] Now in its active mode, reason "will again run through the double movement of *self-consciousness* [my emphasis] and pass from independence to freedom." The moment of independence is reason at its present stage. This is reason that is restricted to the individual and his opposition to other individuals. Freedom comes in the next section. There, reason will appear as a jungle of self-actualizers before culminating in *universal reason* as the source of the moral law.

Ever since his birth as self-consciousness, the individual was driven to make himself substantial. He was subject seeking substance. Selfhood is a no-thing striving to be a some-thing. At first, the self was desire, and the world was only food for negation. The self waged war on thinghood: in the case of the unhappy consciousness, the thinghood of its own *body.* Reborn as reason, or positive self-consciousness, the individual is certain of his *unity* with the world. Objectivity is now good, something to be desired in a positive sense. Ultimately, the individual subject desires *inter*-subjectivity. This is mutual recognition or community, the "I that is We and the We that is I" [177]. A community of selves is the fulfillment of the individual self. Only through community is the individual present to himself as objective or real.

The concrete manifestation of human community, and of the universal reason it embodies, is *ethicality.* We enter this realm at the beginning of the chapter entitled Spirit. Ethicality, *Sittlichkeit,* derives from *Sitte,* the German word for custom. Its Greek counterpart is *ēthos.* Custom is living law: the Ought that also Is. It is the substance of a "free people or nation," a *Volk* [352].[2] For Hegel, as for the German Romantics of his day, the historical paradigm for ethicality was the ancient Greek *polis,* which Hegel describes at the beginning of this section.[3] Life within the *polis* is *das Glück,* happiness [353]. As Hegel's language implies, Greek ethical life is the historical Eden from which modern man has fallen.

Ethicality is obviously not confined to antiquity. Modern individuals, too, live within an ethical context: they belong to families and are subject to the laws of their state. All the forms of self-asserting individuality we meet in the present chapter presuppose ethicality. But ethicality has not yet emerged as the social substance in which individuals are fulfilled. It has not yet been dialectically generated out of the more immediate forms of consciousness that show why ethicality is necessary.

Hegel portrays ethicality as a heaven on earth. In the life of a free people, "the Concept has its complete reality" [350]. A people or *Volk* embodies *mutual recognition.* In the communal body, I experience my being-for-self in other independent beings. This is reason actualized as the unity of self and thing, inner and outer. It is the parity of selves that overcomes the one-sidedness of the master-slave relation. Reason in this communal form is "the fluid universal substance." A people or *Volk* is substantial or thingly because it is concretely *there* as an actual historical entity: it has body. It is universal because all the individual members are bound together by the same customs and therefore have the same *soul.* And it is fluid because it is a self-differentiating One (see opening of Chapter 6) that is at home in its Manyness as an organic system of life. This One is the communal spirit that flows out into its members and back into itself. Ethicality "shatters into many completely independent beings" [350]. It is like light that bursts into "stars as countless self-illuminating points." These starry citizens dissolve, happily, in the very moment in which they appear. They regard themselves and their independence or being-for-self as vanishing moments in the ethical substance of their city-state. They are willingly self-sacrificial. In the language of Spinoza, they regard themselves as passing *modes* of a glorious social *substance.*

Ethicality does not include the "need of philosophy" I discussed in Chapter 10. The reason is that there is no alienation. In Greek ethicality, truth is lived, not sought for. The philosopher, Socrates, comes on the Greek scene as part of Athens' tragic *decline.* He is the subjective moment of intellectual unrest and is fundamentally at odds with the life of contented custom.[4]

Hegel lays particular stress on reciprocity. As I sacrifice my individual selfhood to the community, the community, as "the might of the entire nation," sustains the most natural aspects of my individual life, for example, my need for nourishment [351]. In a reference to Adam Smith's "invisible hand," Hegel observes that in working for myself I am also working for the good of the whole. Ethicality, as I noted above, embodies mutual recognition. When I meet my fellow citizens on the street, I see in them the free being I know myself to be: "I regard them as myself and myself as them" [351]. The ethical community is idealism's dream come true: the unity of self and thing in the *polis.* Hegel ends his Ode to Ethicality with "the wisest men of antiquity," who "have declared that wisdom and virtue consist in living in accordance with the customs of one's nation."[5]

But ancient wisdom, like ancient ethicality, is incomplete. Reason "*must* withdraw from its happiness" [354]. The fall from Eden, which modernity inherits in the form of alienation, is inevitable. Why this is so can be summed up in one word: *given.* Custom, however vital and sustaining, however much it makes the citizen a "star," nevertheless keeps him in the cave of natural consciousness. Custom is "spirit in the form of [mere] being." It is something given in the sense of unquestioned. Ethicality, in its paradigmatic Greek appearance, is not a whole but a collection of independent, warring, city-states. There is Athens, and there is Sparta. Each has its own customs and character, its own soul, and uncritically believes that its way of life is absolute. An individual in any one *polis* is bound to his community through "a solid unshaken trust" [355]. He is not aware of *himself* as absolute by virtue of his individuality. He is not self-conscious, not at the point of declaring, "I AM MYSELF!" Lacking this moment, mutual recognition is indeed lived and enjoyed, but it is not comprehended. It is therefore not fully lived.[6]

The fall from ethicality occurs for the individual when he discovers the absoluteness of his individuality or being-for-self. Trust is lost: "Isolated and on his own, it is [the individual] who is now the essence, no longer universal spirit" [355]. Self-consciousness is not entirely absent from the ethical whole. But it no sooner arises than it is submerged in the communal soul and becomes trust. Self-consciousness is the human dissonance that custom perpetually and vigilantly resolves, the serpent that keeps getting stepped on. Once the individual eats from the tree of self-consciousness, he experiences his former Eden as something opposed to the infinity he now finds within himself and which must have its day. Eden ceases to be a home and becomes the Establishment. The individual, now alienated from all laws and customs, regards himself as "his own living truth" [355]. He is "sent out into the world by his own spirit to seek his own happiness" [356].

As Hegel presents it, ethicality is an earthly paradise that is, paradoxically, both lost and not yet attained. Self-consciousness *both* "has withdrawn" from the ethical condition *and* "has not yet realized it" [353]. Hegel's discussion of this point is confusing. The movement of self-consciousness in relation to ethical Eden can be described in two different ways, more as an either-or than a both-and. The individual can be imagined either as starting out in the mere subjectivity of impulse or desire and transcending these in the substance of ethical community, or as starting out in the ethical condition and breaking away from it [357]. In the first version, the individual transcends his natural impulses and moves toward an ethical condition. In the second, what is transcended is the more or less enlightened view (the "false idea," as Hegel calls it) that consciously *posits* natural impulses as absolute and thus rebels against custom.

Clearly, Faust represents the latter version. This way of looking at the individual, and at ethicality as a lost Eden, is more familiar to us moderns, and is therefore the path followed here in the *Phenomenology*. It also fits the journey of consciousness as a Way of Despair, or, in this case, a way of disillusionment. Faustian renunciation presupposes an already existing ethicality. But from the perspective of consciousness at its present stage of development, ethicality is unsatisfying and stale. The individual does not "find himself" within an ethical whole. He does not yet experience community as his own work and substance. Active reason is thus precisely what Hegel says it is: the *beginning* of the individual's "ethical world-experience" [357].

We see what the modern idealist does not: that in his very individualism he is striving for a return to Eden. This new Eden will be based on self-knowledge rather than trust or right opinion. It will be experienced not as a piously observed given but as the work and fulfillment of individual self-consciousness. This grounding of community in the individual subject, rather than in an unquestioned social substance, is the "higher shape" of *morality* [*Moralität*] [357]. Morality will be the culmination of Hegel's chapter on spirit. Although higher than ethicality, it is, as we shall see, also far more problematic.[7]

Hegel ends his sweeping introduction with his usual preview of things to come [359]. In the first stage of active reason, the rational individual is obsessed with his singularity and private happiness. Negative experience of this "happiness" brings reason to its next level. In the second stage, the heart is universalized as a *law* of the heart. At the third and final stage, the individual suppresses his singularity or ego for the sake of an ideal "good in itself." In the course of experience, he learns that action is not for the sake of this higher disinterested cause but is its own end, that the world *as it exists* is good. He no longer opposes the world but expresses himself within it through his special talent. The world at this point will be *civil society* or the social marketplace.

Desire Revisited [360–66]

The first shape of active reason is Faust, the hero of Goethe's famous poem. Hegel called it "the one absolutely philosophical tragedy."[8] Faust consciously enacts the transition from the skull of science to the flesh of experience. He goes from Baconian knowledge to knowledge "in the Biblical sense" (Hyppolite, 283). Faust is the prototype of the fall from ethicality and the father of all rationally self-conscious individuals who, in their singularity, are *for themselves.*[9]

Only Hegel could make illicit sex this hard to understand, so hard in fact that it is difficult to tell that the account is even about sex. But it is. Reason's "Faustian moment" must be connected with life, self-consciousness, and desire, as these first appeared in the section entitled "The Truth of Self-Certainty." There, too, Hegel's abstract terms made it difficult to see that the account was about "the facts of life."

The first stage of active reason (rational self-consciousness in its raw immediacy) is the effort to be real as *this singular bodily I* with no intrusive, stifling universals or principles. It is the erotic version of sense-certainty.[10] Hegel's title for this section is "Pleasure and Necessity." The word pleasure, *Lust,* is somewhat misleading. Faust does not seek pleasure indiscriminately:

he is no hedonist. Nor is he Don Juan: he does not seek the conquest of one woman after another. He falls in love with Gretchen and wants the pleasure of union with her, and her alone. He wants an "I that is We and a We that is I" that consists of only two people who become one flesh outside the ethical context of marriage.[11] What he wants most, on Hegel's reading, is the pleasurable *awareness* of himself in and through another. He wants "the vision or intuition [*Anschauung*] of the unity of the two independent self-consciousnesses [himself and Gretchen]" [362].[12]

Reason is self-consciousness made positive. As reason, the individual is certain of the unity of self and thing, inner and outer. This is his idealism, and the imprint of the self on the world is the Category. As rational self-consciousness, I act, make things, speak, and desire because I seek self-realization as the unity of self and world. This has two meanings: I seek to make myself real, and I seek to know myself in making myself real. My self-knowledge and my worldly action are inseparable. In Faust, this unity of knowledge and action is at its most immediate level, like the singular This of sense-certainty. Hegel calls it "the poorest shape of self-actualizing spirit" [363]. In unethical romance, which is based entirely on feeling, I come to know myself, feel my singular selfhood, as absolute through union with another self that recognizes me as absolute. My goal, as I noted above, is to see myself "as another independent being" [360], and to see another self-consciousness as myself [359]. Sexual union consummates this romantic (and implicitly spiritual) desire for an interpenetration of selves. Romantic *erōs* parts company with all universals and deifies the singular ego. As we shall see, the universality that Faust and Gretchen reject ultimately destroys their happy purpose. The Faustian project turns out to be no more stable than the fleeting sensuous This.

In Goethe's poem, Faust is disenchanted with science, and with all that is calm and celestial. Tired of being a detached scientific observer, he craves the tumult and excesses of the non-scholarly life. Faust turns away from "the heavenly seeming spirit of the universality of knowledge and action," that is, from science and ethicality [360]. He yields to the Earth-Spirit or *Erdgeist,* who tempts Faust with the forbidden fruit of experience with all its intense pleasures and pains. Faust makes a pact with the devil, Mephistopheles, who grants Faust's wish in exchange for his soul. He falls in love with Gretchen, whom he seduces, abandons, and unintentionally ruins. The pious Gretchen betrays both her family and her religion. In order to be with Faust, she accidentally poisons her mother, intending only to "knock her out." She becomes pregnant, is subjected to public disgrace, and eventually goes mad and kills her baby, for which she is condemned to death. Instead of the romantic vision of lovers united, Faust witnesses the horror he has inflicted on the beloved, whom he has tempted to commit crimes of her own.[13] The tragedy of Faust (in the version Hegel knew) begins with the desire for unleashed singularity and ends with Gretchen's brutal fate. It begins in *pleasure* and ends in *necessity.*

Faust is not merely a romantic who yields to a life of feeling: he is the rational, scientific individual who renounces universality in favor of this life. At first, the principle of his idealism is the general "to be is to feel." But after seeing Gretchen, he feels the more specific desire for self-unity through union with the beloved. Hegel quotes the lines in which Mephistopheles relishes the ease with which the hater of reason and science can be ensnared.[14] The lines no doubt embody the view of Goethe himself, who was a passionate student of physical science. They certainly appeal to Hegel, who often decries the destructive consequences of romantics and their deification of feeling. Once self-consciousness has renounced the "highest gifts of man, it has handed itself over to the devil and must perish." Faustian consciousness plunges into life and indulges its self-feeling. All else is nothing but a "lifeless mist" compared with the individual's luscious this-ness [361]. The individual here is not interested in accomplishing anything beyond the immediate realization of his singularity. He wants only to enjoy union with the beloved, to "seize the day" as one plucks ripe fruit that is ready to hand. He wants his own private Eden or heaven on earth. This is an Eden without God, marriage, work, thought, sacrifice, or prohibitions—an Eden without consequence.

Active reason recapitulates the dialectic of self-consciousness, which first appeared as desire, *Begierde* [174]. As we recall, desire was the drive to destroy and assimilate. It was like eating. Now at a higher level, desire is only in part destructive, as Hegel points out [362]. It aims to destroy not the object in its totality but only the object's *independence.* Faust changes Gretchen into the medium of his self-actualization. In Goethe's story, he gazes at Gretchen and conceives the desire to be with her. In Hegel's reading, he feels the certainty that defines idealism: the prospect of his singular selfhood made immediately, feelingly real. The realization of this certainty is the pleasure of union—a pleasure all the more satisfying because it is outside the context of marriage. What drives Faust is not animal instinct, or the will to destroy, but the desire for *knowledge,* the real and fleshly knowledge he has never experienced. He does not merely seek pleasure but seeks it as *absolute knowing,* as the gratification of reason's drive to be one with the bodily world. As we saw above, Faustian reason craves an *Anschauung,* an immediate vision or intuition, not of the beloved simply but of "the unity of the two independent self-consciousnesses" [362].[15]

Rational desire is similar to self-consciousness in its fight for independence. That fight, we recall, ended in the master-slave relation. Seduction, too, is a form of conquest. In seduction, one self gets another to surrender autonomy or independence. The difference is that in rational desire (desire as Category or positive self-assertion) the self wants to overcome an opposition or difference (male vs. female) through *union* rather than to find its independence as *one side* of an opposition (master as opposed to slave).

The fulfillment that Faustian self-consciousness seeks is short-lived. Pleasure or immediate gratification passes immediately into its opposite, universality in the form of a *family.* Sex has unintended consequences. It transcends itself. On the positive side, sexual climax gives the self a powerful, even godlike feeling of itself as objective and real. It produces a mind-destroying "rush" of self-feeling that is absent in, say, metaphysical speculation. But the negative side to this act follows hard on the heels of positive enjoyment. In the sexual act, self-consciousness is assimilated into the universal process of *nature,* which has no regard for my dreams of "being one" with the beloved. As we saw in Chapter 7, life is the process in which an animal cancels or negates its singularity. Driven by sexual desire, the animal engages in begetting [*Begattung*], which leads to the genus or kind [*Gattung*]. Faust's union with Gretchen reduces him to the status of a generic male. In the circle of life, lovers become passing moments—*parents* [362]. The joy of sex gives way to the truth of sex: coming to be and passing away, the endless cycle in which offspring displace their parents and, when sexually mature, produce offspring who will displace them. In natural begetting, singularity is destroyed in the very moment that it is fulfilled. In other words, sexual climax is a form of death.

This self-cancellation would be stable, fruitful, and happy if the end were family. In marriage, husband and wife *will* to be superseded by their offspring. This is precisely the universality, and self-sacrifice, that Faust rejects.[16] Universality is not only nature. It is also society. Like nature, society is the realm of uncontrollable consequence. Faust's union with Gretchen sets off a whole chain of events within the ethical realm, events that lead to Gretchen's tragic destruction, which is Faust's *work.* The lovers are the prey of a universality they can experience only as an irrational and all-crushing Fate or Necessity [363]. In seeking to be beyond good and evil, Faust unleashes on the beloved forces vastly more potent than his pitiful attempt at erotic self-actualization.

In the unfolding of Faustian experience, pleasure becomes necessity. Goethe's story shows what happens to the lovers. But it does not show why the tragic reversal, considered as a stage of universal consciousness, is rational and necessary. This is the task of Hegel's logic of desire. Faust's position undercuts itself in the course of experience. The pleasure of illicit sex, taken as the absolute, generates its opposite: the necessity that destroys pleasure. The truth of Faust's certainty is evident in the fate of Gretchen, who falls under necessity's crushing blow.[17]

The dialectical path from pleasure to necessity is dense and hard to follow. Its central theme is the *abstractness* of romantic feeling. Faust wanted to escape from the dry bones of science and morality. He broke with the human community and asserted his this-ness through a quest for intense self-feeling. But this self-feeling, like sheer this-ness, is abstract. So is the romantic ego that cuts itself off from the genuinely concrete objective relations within ethicality. Pleasure is abstract because it is purely formal: it lacks content. The self that makes pleasure its absolute has no content but is the sheer nothingness of undeveloped immediate singularity. Sexual enjoyment of the beloved is the merely *immediate* unity of the for-itself (subject) and the in-itself (object). It is "the abstract Category" of mine-ness. The irony of this pleasure, as I noted above, is that it seems to be the most real thing of all—the godlike "rush" of one's singularity—whereas in fact it is the *nothingness* of singularity.

Having stressed the abstractness of Faustian desire, Hegel proceeds to show how the necessity that destroys the lovers is the abstractness of Faust's desire made objective. In Hegel's words, "This essence [the universal that opposes the romantic idealist] is nothing else than the concept of what this individuality in itself is" [363].

Faustian romance results in a tragic *logical projection.* As reason, the self projects itself onto the world. It puts its imprint on the world, just as Kant's pure self (I = I), as Category, puts its imprint on, or schematizes, the sensuous manifold. Faust, as Category, makes his selfhood real through his sexual union with Gretchen. As we have seen, this selfhood is nothing but unbridled singularity, selfhood without content, the mere *being* and "thrust" of the singular self. Faust is a "circle" of abstract, formal relationships (the logical structure of mere feeling). Hegel speaks of a circle here because, although Faust wants immediate unity with the beloved, there is *mediation* in the reality or thinghood that reason seeks (unlike the "dead" thing of observing reason) [363]. In other words, Faust joins immediately with another living self in order to return to himself, to *mediate* his self-unity through sexual "relations." There is nothing in his certainty beyond this empty self-relation through union with an other. In gratifying his desire, he not only fathers a physical child. He also "has cast forth this circle of abstractions from its confinement within simple [i.e. immediate] self-consciousness into the element where they are *for* self-consciousness" [363]. Simply put, Faust's desire, once gratified or rendered objective, makes the world into an abstract, inimical other. His "I must have and enjoy" makes the world into the realm of an equally abstract, and brutal, "This must be!" The world thus becomes the mindless, irresistible force of *necessity* [363].

The Faustian self wanted to go from dead theory to vibrant life. This was its certainty. Its *truth* is the exact opposite: "the consciousness of its own lifelessness" [363]. The Faustian project was reason's attempt to transcend phrenology: the truth of spirit in a skull. In the end, the skull returns as a symbol of the "dead actuality" to which Faust's certainty has been reduced. Faust did not escape the skull of phrenology but only deepened its meaning.

Faustian experience ends with the phenomenon of inversion: the moment in which pleasure becomes necessity. As I noted above, the truth of Faust's certainty is actualized in the consciousness of Gretchen.[18] Having experienced the blow of necessity, this consciousness is uncomprehending. It is a riddle to itself and does not see what we see, that its suffering is the direct result of the sweet self-feeling to which it yielded. It therefore experiences its fate as a "sheer leap into its antithesis" [365]. Necessity, for it, is abstract and meaningless, "the merely negative, uncomprehended *might of universality*, on which individuality is smashed to pieces." This tragic consciousness, the inability to find oneself and one's heart in necessity, is the culmination of Hegel's story.

The inability of this shape of consciousness to grasp the unity of opposites that defines it generates the next stage of active reason. For itself, consciousness has been destroyed. But in itself or implicitly (that is, for us), it "has survived this loss" [366]. In its tragic inwardizing and *awareness* of the contradiction between heart and necessity, the self has united these opposites in a new shape.

The Tyranny of the Heart [367–80]

In its first phase, active reason sought the pleasure of forbidden love only to find necessity as its brutal truth. Reason now combines the opposites of feeling and necessity in the *law of the heart.* The heart assimilates universality. It produces heartfelt necessity. The heart no longer merely feels and yearns, as it did in the case of Faust. It now dictates what ought to be, and prompts action in the face of a corrupt world. Abandoning its role as seducer, consciousness becomes a rebel humanitarian. Hegel's lurid title suggests that reason will again suffer inversion: it will begin with "the law of the heart" and end in "the madness of self-conceit."

The influence of Rousseau is strong in this phase of active reason. Rousseau played a key role in the advance of Romanticism, which extols feeling over thinking. In various writings, most impressively in *Emile,* he praises the inherent goodness of nature and blames society for human corruption. Most important for this part of Hegel's chapter, Rousseau preaches the natural goodness of sentiment as opposed to reason.[19] His teaching is closely allied with Pascal's famous saying: "The heart has its reasons, which reason knows not at all."[20] Hegel strongly disagrees with this statement. Reason, as philosophy, not only knows the heart but also knows it better than it knows itself. Hegel's analysis of the sentimental moralist offers powerful support for this claim.

This moralist is a manifestation of phenomenal reason, as was Faust. Reason here is not the faculty of reasoning. Nor is it philosophy. It is Category: the force or primordial will to power, by which individual selfhood imposes itself on the world and claims the world as its own. Reason is idealism, my certainty that my selfhood is one with the substance of the world.

Rousseau embodies the certainty that there is a law of the heart, and that this law is absolute. The self-negating result of this certainty is dramatized in Schiller's early play, *The Robbers,* to which Hegel alludes at crucial points of his account.[21] Karl Moor is the prodigal son and rebel, who lives out the law of his heart and suffers the consequences of his idealism. Estranged from his father the Count, Karl lives in the woods of Bohemia as the leader of a band of thieves, not suspecting that his brother Franz, the "good son" who stayed home, is plotting his downfall. Karl too has plans of downfall. He and his band swear to wreak terror on a cruel and tyrannical world order. The idealistic Karl is eventually undone by the contradiction between his evil deeds and his noble heart. In the final scene of the play, he laments: "Oh, fool that I was, to suppose that I could make the world more beautiful through terror, and maintain the laws through lawlessness." His final act is one of humane feeling: he hands himself over to a poor man who will receive a large ransom from the authorities for catching the robber alive.[22]

This second phase of active reason transforms the necessity that destroyed Faust's project into something good, a goodness of heart. Heart here means *my* heart. Like the previous certainty, this one places the absolute in a single, self-assertive individual. But this new shape is richer, since it expresses the universal [367]. Whereas Faust's world of knowing had only two people in it (himself and the beloved), the world of the sentimental moralist embraces all of humanity. This moralist posits the law of his heart as an end to be realized in the world. Experience will determine whether this end corresponds to the initial certainty, whether *object* corresponds to *concept* [368].

As in the previous stage, the heart of the individual poses itself by opposing an actually existing world. The quandary of reason is that the self cannot make the world its own without going out into the world, thereby becoming an other to its own self. Until reason finds a way of making this union of the self with its opposite intelligible, it will be tragic and incoherent. The heart, taken as absolute, brands the external world of non-heart as unfeeling and evil. The world consists of oppressors and oppressed. The existing laws oppress individual hearts everywhere. Humanity suffers under the yoke of this social necessity [369]. What Faust had to discover through experience, the rebel sentimentalist takes as his starting-point.

Our new hero wages war on the existing laws, which contradict the law of the heart, and on the suffering of humanity. He is not careless, like the adolescent Faust, but earnestly pursues a noble goal: the welfare of mankind [370]. Faust wanted only his own pleasure. But the sentimentalist, in pleasing his own heart, is sure of pleasing all hearts everywhere, for the good is posited as the law or universality of the heart. Hegel lays particular stress on this point: that the heart of the individual expresses the undivided unity of himself and universal humanity. Because of this presumed immediate unity, the sentimentalist is uncritical of himself. He is *ungezogen* or impudent, a "bad boy" who passes himself off as the voice of mankind and the virtuous savior of downtrodden man.

The individual who makes the law of the heart absolute foreshadows the man of conscience, whom we meet later in the *Phenomenology.* The heart, *my* heart, is the ultimate judge of all ordinances both human and divine [371]. It does not matter that these ordinances sometimes happen to coincide with the law of the heart. What matters is whether the heart itself feels itself gratified in the law. The well-intentioned bad boy regards existent law, regardless of its content, as having no authority. He therefore actualizes the law of his heart by negating the illusory authority of existent law.

And so, the individual embarks on the path of experience and "carries out the law of his heart" [372]. A problem immediately arises, since this law, in being realized, ceases to be a law of the *heart.* In being externalized, the inward heart is falsified. The situation resembles the formation of a club. A visionary establishes a club that realizes his dream. The members all agree on the laws of this club. But then the club takes on a life of its own. It *has being* and becomes something other than the visionary's beautiful dream: an establishment. Now his vision is an external reality to which he must be subject as to an alien necessity, which demands obedience. The law of the club, which originated in his heart, now impersonally dictates to him: "Rules are rules."

The romantic rebel is just such a visionary. He is at odds with the actualization of his own law, which, once realized, no longer reflects and embodies the mine-ness of his personal vision, or rather the warm intensity of his personal feeling. Dialectically, the individual, through action, has become universal. He has started to grow up, to free himself from the confines of his mere singularity [372]. From here on, the individual will be plagued by this contradiction from which he cannot escape: the vision of actualization that perverts what it is supposed to express, namely, the natural goodness of the law of the heart. Like Faust, the romantic rebel is his own worst enemy.

At the first level of his experience, the apostle of the heart feels the sting of actuality. The outer, impersonal being of his actualized law contradicts the inner and personal character of his heart.[23] He now proceeds to the deeper level at which the actualized law of the heart "turns against him"

[373]. In realizing this law, he has experienced himself as the contradiction of individual and universal. He must find a way to preserve his individuality (which is essential to his certainty) in the face of this contradiction. His solution is to attribute the failure of the actualized law to the hearts of *other people.* I know my heart: in Rousseau's words, *je sens mon cœur.* And I know that my heart was good when it set up its law. My project failed, I felt a contradiction, because the hearts of others are bad.[24] I did not really fail. Those wretches who I thought shared my vision and my feeling—it was *their* hearts that betrayed *my* heart and brought its noble designs to ruin! They usurped my project, made what my heart intended into what their heart intends.[25]

The established laws are, for me, transformed in this experience. They are not dead after all, but are enlivened by the bad hearts of the very people I wanted to save, the people who, as I believed, did not find themselves in the law but suffered under its yoke. Those "under" the law regard the law as universally binding, as their living law. The sentimental bad boy does not realize that this actualized universal *is* his truth, that the law of the heart cannot be actualized without a cancellation of the law of the heart [374]. He experiences the truth of his certainty as an internal contradiction, a contradiction *within* his heart and not merely between his heart and the outside world. He sees what he has engendered, knowing he has engendered it, yet cannot bring himself to acknowledge it as his own. "No," he says, "that can't be me—and yet it is!"[26] The split within the self drives the idealist to distraction [375], as the heart experiences its actualization as the perversion [*Verkehrung*] of itself.

At this point, the individual holds both sides of his contradiction (inner law and outer world) to be his immediate essence [376]. He must escape from this contradiction, save the absoluteness of his heart. As Hegel observes, the "heartthrob for the good of mankind therefore passes into the ravings of insane self-conceit" [376]. The bleeding-heart rebel, whose ideological father is Rousseau, foists the perversity he has experienced in himself onto others. He manufactures a conspiracy theory. Here, Hegel echoes the speeches in which Karl lashes out against the universal order as the work of "fanatical priests" and "bloated despots," who have perverted the law of the heart [377]. They have done this out of sheer selfishness, that is, out of individuality that is "alien and accidental." And yet, what could be responsible for the transformation of this selfish desire into a universal order except the heart, not the heart of one man but the hearts of many? Let the Establishment be as perverse as one pleases; it is nevertheless stable and has stood the test of time, which is more than one can say for the private untried law of the rebel humanitarian. The Establishment is real, universal, perverse, *and* it is the work of other people's hearts.

The heroic individual learns from this experience that the world is the actualization of people's hearts, and that his good-heartedness, which was supposed to be the absolute, is a will-o'-the-wisp—a mere intention [377]. The heart learns "that its self is not real, and that its reality is an unreality." One cannot keep the heart safe from the taint of egotism and take refuge in Rousseau's "society makes us bad," for society is itself the work of the heart. The bad heart is not something accidentally bad. On the contrary, the very singularity of the heart, which is the supposed absolute of the rebel humanitarian, is, qua singular individual, "perverted and perverting" [*verkehrte und verkehrende*].

The logical result and truth of the rebel's initial certainty is that all hearts are selfish, and that there is no actualized order of the heart that is immune to resistance by the hearts of other people: we are all bad boys at heart. The heart, as this particular heart, breeds war when it takes itself to be the absolute: "The consciousness that sets up the law of its heart . . . meets with resistance from others, because it contradicts the *equally particular* laws of their hearts" [379]. Throughout Schiller's play, Karl wrings his hands over all the discord in the world, not realizing, until the end, that he has generated the inner ground of this perpetual conflict as a war of every heart against every other heart. Hegel's analysis thus shows that if you start with Rousseau's absolutizing of sentiment, you will end up with Hobbes' state of war.[27]

The experience of the rebel humanitarian redefines what consciousness thinks of as the world. Originally, the world was the sphere of oppressor and oppressed. Now it is a war of egotistical geniuses, each striving to grab hold of reality and make it conform to his agenda, each justifying his action by appealing to universal self-interest.[28] The world has become what Hegel calls the Way of the World or *Weltlauf* [379]. No longer an Establishment you can point to, it is now the "natural law" of self-interest, which courses through the spiritual veins of individuals everywhere.

The Ideologies of Motive [381–93]

In the final stage of active reason, individual and world are what experience has made them. Having suffered the consequences of assertive individuality, heroic idealism now *suppresses* individuality and takes the high road of virtue [*Tugend*]. The idealist, no longer a bad boy, submits to "the discipline of the universal" [381].[29] He makes the cancellation [*Aufhebung*] of individuality the principle of his action. This self-certainty generates a third opposition within active reason: that between disinterested Virtue or Nobility and the self-interested Way of the World, between the good in itself and the dog-eat-dog law of nature.[30] Logically, this corresponds to the distinction between essence and existence or being-there [*Dasein*].

Our new romantic hero—the Knight of Virtue [386]—wages war against selfishness.[31] Unlike the real battles of the knights of old, however, his fight tends to be merely ideological, a battle of words. Also unlike them, he is not religious, even though he is characterized by faith. His faith is not in God but in the natural goodness of the human heart, and the ultimate triumph of this goodness [383]. The Crusaders belonged to the medieval world of the unhappy consciousness, the world in which man experienced himself as alienated from his true, unchangeable selfhood. But the modern Knight knows nothing of repentance. He breathes the pure air of rational self-confidence. For him, self-interest is a vice but not an original sin. Man can, through his own efforts (that is, without divine grace), turn away from self-interest and be fully himself.

The first two shapes of active reason were easy to identify (Faust and Karl). The archetypes for the Knight of Virtue and the Way of the World are much less clearly established in Hegel's text. As Harris suggests, the Knight is probably best summed up by the Marquis of Posa—the idealistic Knight of Malta, who plays a central role in Schiller's *Don Carlos* (2.74, note 77).[32] The Marquis espouses the view that "virtue has its own worth" (act 3, scene 10) and makes many lofty speeches throughout the play. He tries to turn his childhood friend Carlos away from the latter's self-interested love for the Queen (his mother-in-law) and toward the loftier, universal goal of leading the Flemish armies against his father, Philipp II, in order to establish a new, more humane political order. Ultimately, he sacrifices his life for the young prince. The spokesman for the Way of the World, according to Harris, is Machiavelli (2:55).[33]

Both identifications make sense, given Hegel's general descriptions. The Marquis and Machiavelli are excellent examples of the opposed ideologies that mutually define each other at this stage of active reason.

Hegel outlines the logic of this third form of romanticism in light of the previous two [381]. In the Faustian experience, an immediate or raw singularity (the sensualist) opposed an equally immediate universal (nature and society). In the law of the heart, the individual was the unity of individual and universal, heart and law, while the world embodied their split or opposition. In this third phase, hero and world *each* contain both the unity and the opposition of these logical poles. The virtuous Knight opposes *in himself* the individuality or egotism he finds in the selfish world: he makes the good essential and his individuality or self-interest non-essential. And the advocate of the Way of the World mirrors the logical structure of the Knight by being his reverse image. He opposes *in himself* anything that is purely good: he makes his individuality essential and makes everything that is "true and good in itself" non-essential, or subordinate to his self-interest [381]. Each is "a movement of law and individuality toward one another, but a movement of opposition." For virtue, law [*Gesetz*] is essential: for the world, self-interest.[34] Both sides mirror the conflicting claims of *reason*. The Knight posits a strict distinction between the Ought of virtue and the Is of the world, between the ideality of law and the reality of individual action. In the course of experience, this distinction will vanish.

Like Karl, the Knight is a reformer who speaks and acts as though he has imbibed the teachings of Rousseau. But he is not a bomb-throwing revolutionary.[35] He knows better than to set about reforming the world or Establishment through sheer opposition. For him, true reform must go to the very root of evil and bring about a *change of heart* or conversion. The Knight is a modern preacher of virtuous intent. He regards the world as corrupted by individuality or egotism, but not naturally corrupt. He is no cynic. On the contrary, for him, the dog-eat-dog world has a noble interior or natural goodness that has not been allowed to come to light. The Way of the World or *Weltlauf* is a race or course (from *laufen*, to run).[36] From the Knight's perspective, it is a stream running in the wrong direction, against its natural tendency. The Knight wants to reverse the flow of the stream, bring humanity back to its originally good intentions. It is important to realize here that the struggle between Knight and World is a war between opposing ideologies. The chivalrous way preaches, not against wicked actions per se but against selfish motives. And the worldly way, on its side, preaches against the sort of head-in-the-clouds nobility that the Marquis fanatically champions in Schiller's play.[37]

The Knight cannot make the world virtuous (that is, unselfish) through direct action. Action is part of the world. It proceeds from the very individuality or egotism he wishes to defeat. His attack on individuality must therefore be indirect, that is, cunning.[38] The Knight simply "makes room" for the dormant goodness of the world to emerge on its own [381]. By opposing the Way of the World through his own self-sacrifice, through his show of altruism, he tries to inspire the world to come to its senses and experience a change of heart.

The Knight, as Hegel portrays him, is a modern idealist. His virtue is not the concrete virtue of ethical life but a personal ideal that lacks reality. Ancient virtue was strength of character. It existed in and through actual deeds and had its roots in the "substance of the *Volk*" [390]. Unlike the idealist's virtue, which is a Rousseau-inspired goodness of heart, ancient virtue, Greek virtue in particular, did not involve romantic striving. It was the unity of being and goodness, essence and appearance. This unity is the Eden from which we fell when we became self-conscious or dual.[39]

As a mode of consciousness in its broad sense, idealistic virtue is a claim to know the absolute. As a mode of idealism, it is certain of being all reality. This certainty is expressed in the saying, "Virtue triumphs." In the course of the Knight's experience, virtue will suffer defeat and the world will triumph. Hegel reminds us that the certainty of virtue has been logically generated from the previous two stages [382]. The dialectical origin of virtue is individuality or egotism, which asserted itself in the *erōs* of Faust and the impudence of Karl. Virtue turns against both these forms of self-interest.[40] It actualizes itself, becomes *for itself,* by setting out to *cancel* its own origin.

The Knight of Virtue strives to reform the world's interior, to reverse its wayward course and bring out its "true essence." He makes a show of suppressing his individuality in order to get the world to suppress *its* individuality, for individuality is "the principle of perversion" [383]. The Knight knows that he must negate a negation, convert a perversion or *Verkehrung.* But what he is converting the world *to* is merely ideal, something that cannot be actual and which must remain an in-itself or good intention. Hegel calls this "abstract universality" [384]. Given the individuality of all concrete action (all action is the action of a self-interested I), there is nothing in the phenomenal world to justify the Knight's certainty. His certainty is mere belief or faith [*Glauben*].[41] Virtue can only *believe* in the good. And since the Knight seeks to suppress his own individuality, he must similarly suppress any joy or pleasure he might take in his idealistic striving, for all such joy is part of the world he fights.[42] In his fight against selfishness, the Knight must be careful not to fight in order to win, which would be selfish. He must fight, perversely, against the realization of his own ideal.

This abstract idealized good, as something that is merely willed or intended, is nothing on its own. It gets whatever reality it has from being opposed to the reality of the world, the perverse reality that virtue seeks to conquer [384]. According to Hegel, this good is only a being-for-another, that is, a being *in relation to* another. This is the logical designation of a good, which, as the in-itself, lacks independent substantiality.

With what weapons, then, do virtue and world, ideal and real, fight each other? What exactly is the mode and character of their struggle? The weapons are "gifts, capacities, strengths" [385], that is, not actualities but potentialities. Hegel calls them collectively the *universal*—the "passive tool," which individuality can use for either good or bad. Natural gifts are the universal weapons of both virtue and the Way of the World. They include things like quick-wittedness, organizational skill, charisma, and rhetorical ability. As for the battle itself, we must remember that although the Knight rebels against the Way of the World, he does not, like Karl, rebel against the established laws. His fight is more refined, even cunning, as we shall see. Moreover, the Knight, unlike Karl, fights to suppress his own selfish motives. Let us now see how this curious fight between disinterested virtue and self-interested world unfolds in experience.

Virtue and world fight each other with the exact same weapons: the universal gifts, capacities, and powers, which individuals are free to use for good or ill. Since this is the case, how can virtue be certain that it can and will triumph over self-interest? What is virtue's *secret weapon*? It is none other than belief in the power of good, the faith that "the good is in and for its own self, i.e., that it itself brings itself to fulfillment" [*sich selbst vollbringe*] [386]. As a scion of Rousseau, the Knight believes that the human heart is naturally good, and that it will therefore be susceptible to a show of gifts properly used, to the Knight's example of suppressed egotism. This is the weapon that virtue has "held in reserve" and uses in its ambush on the world "from the rear." Virtue thus intends to educate the world, awaken it to its selfless interior and a belief in "the good in itself," that is, the inherent goodness of self-sacrifice.[43]

The appearance or show of virtue as a shining example of gifts well used is amusingly captured in Hegel's reference to *Spiegelfechterei*, literally fencing in a mirror, what we call "shadow-boxing" [386]. The Knight of Virtue cannot take his fight seriously. He can only pretend to be fighting his opponent, since he believes that the good is "in and for itself" and brings *itself* to fulfillment. The Knight must be careful, in his use of gifts, not to displace or usurp the good itself, which, he believes, is at work both in him and in his opponent. As a virtuous Knight, I might use my organizational skill to promote the public good. In doing so, I imagine that some deluded advocate of the principle "every man for himself" is watching me. I advertise myself as an inspiring example of virtue, preach the goodness of what I am doing, since my goal is not to act but to convert. My Machiavellian opponent uses the same organizational skill to make money or gain power. I say to him in my mirror fencing, "Look at me! This is who you really are—this is the proper use of gifts!" My certainty is that virtue will prove inspiring and that, in seeing my example, the worldly other will "remember" who he is and change his attitude. In this mirror-fencing, I must be careful not to damage my own gift, which is an expression of the good, nor my opponent's, which is a potential for good. I must *care for* everyone involved.

In spite of this projection of a noble image, the fight that uses the weaponry of gifts is itself very real, since gifts do not remain mere potentials but are actually *used*. My selfless use of a talent is not just an exemplar to be seen. It is also in the world, or rather in society, as a concretized universal, a gift that has been allowed to *be* through the agency and filter of my individuality. My *show* of a gift well used is also the *reality* of a gift well used. This transcends my goal, which is to move the other with a noble show, thus soliciting the appearance of selflessness in him. Intending to actualize one thing, I succeed in actualizing another. I am more successful than I think I am, or rather, than my certainty will let me be. By engaging in my mirror-fencing for the sake of my opponent's change of heart, I actualize a real good.

More generally, when I look at the world I had supposed was riddled with egotism, I see examples everywhere of gifts well used, universals that have been "animated by individuality" and have become beneficial to others. How, then, can individuality be something bad, let alone perverse? In attempting to fight on behalf of a good that is merely willed or intended, the Knight finds the good *in the world* as the actualization of a potential.

In the actual world of individuals using their talents, the Knight sees his certainty refuted. He sees that self-interested action is beneficial to others. This *actual good* "is inextricably interwoven in every manifestation of the Way of the World" [386]. For virtue, therefore, "the Way of the World is invulnerable." In the fight against worldly self-interest, virtue learns that the world is already that which it would solicit the world to be—that self-interest, as an actualized universal or gift, is also *good.* The fight to produce a change of heart in others thus becomes a fight against oneself. In fighting the world, virtue must protect the world from virtue's own assault on the world! That is to say, in fighting the world as if it were an enemy, virtue is really at odds with itself. It must will its own defeat and protect the enemy's weapons, his use of gifts, "against its own attack" [386].

Hegel now shifts our attention to the perspective of the world, or enemy, in order to highlight the triumph of reality over idealistic virtue. Self-interest, because it is not idealistic, has nothing to lose. It has no faith in some dreamy in-itself but lives fully awake in the realm of the actual. Nothing for it is "enduring or absolutely sacred" [387]. It is therefore immune to inspiration by the Knight's noble mirror-fencing. The cunning "rear attack" on self-interest is futile, since, for the Machiavellian Way of the World, which is "alert and self-assured," everything is an explicitly present object: there is no "in itself" but only a "for me." Self-interest holds up its own mirror to the Knight and says: "Here's who *you* really are!" If the Knight chooses to fight self-interest through action, he *becomes* self-interested and loses all credibility. If he identifies himself with nothing more than his good intention, he accomplishes nothing because he has nothing objective or real to *show* self-interest. Either way, the world wins.

The end of the Knight's experience is what we would have expected from the start. In romantically positing a good that is merely implicit or in itself, a mere intention, virtue makes itself unreal. It cannot sustain its purely verbal distinction between goodness and world. Virtue, as the Knight understands it, is abstract. We are no doubt surprised that the Knight has to learn by experience that the world, which courses along on the stream of self-interest, is also the realm of actualized good. But that is what the idealism of the good in itself and its attendant demonizing of individuality produce: the naïve forgetting of selfishness as the means by which the universal is made alive and effective.

Hegel is quick to point out that the world does not triumph over virtue as over something real. What it triumphs over is the *nothingness* of so-called virtue, which appears in the Knight's pompous, self-important speechifying or rhetoric [390]. This rhetoric exhorts us to fight against selfishness, an oppressed humanity, and the abuse of gifts. It is a lot of words that appeal to the heart but not to reason, words that "edify but raise no edifice." The Knight's mirror-fencing is here exposed as a mere *talking* in front of a mirror. His edifying discourses inflate his self-importance and "make his head big" to himself and to others [390].[44] It is in this context that Hegel sharply distinguishes between ancient virtue, which was real, and modern romantic virtue, which is merely imagined and idealistic. In the prevailing culture, Hegel observes, all this inflated rhetoric has become a *bore.*

In the final moments of this section, we witness the transition from the Knight of Virtue to the next, higher stage of reason. Through the Knight's self-negating experience, consciousness learns that the good in itself is a dead end and cannot be the absolute. It learns, to the defeat of its certainty, that the good is made real in human society through individual action: that the good and individuality, which the Knight wanted to keep separate, are unified. Consciousness, Hegel says, drops the abstract concept of a "good in itself" like an *empty cloak* [391]. The image captures what experience has revealed: that the good in itself is a ghost. Hegel must mean here that *universal* consciousness drops the cloak and moves on to a higher stage. As finite manifestations of universal consciousness, the Knight and his opponent remain, we must imagine, entrenched in their ideologies. What they learn through their encounter with one another is no sooner learned than forgotten.

Just as consciousness learns that the good in itself is a ghost, it also learns that the much-maligned Way of the World is not as bad as it seemed. In fact, the way of self-interest is better than self-interest thinks [392]. Virtue, as we saw, proved to be an abstract moment in a greater whole. This whole, or society, is a movement in which individuals, by using their gifts, give reality to the universal and are effectively good. Similarly, self-interest is an abstract moment of the same process: it tends to the common good. In their mutual conflict, each party becomes his opposite or suffers inversion. The selfless Knight becomes a pompous narcissist, and the world of self-interest becomes the locus of gifts well used, the universal in act: self-interested action benefits society. Virtue posited a strict distinction between essence and appearance, universal and individual. But through the use of gifts, a universal potential became actualized in an individual. The motion of the struggle with the world revealed the poles that were supposed to be strictly distinct as united in a more comprehensive process in which the poles negated themselves. As Hegel puts it, the movement of the struggle showed the unity of the in-itself (universality) and the for-itself (individuality) [392]. The Knight and his opponent thus reenact in the human sphere the dialectic of *essence* and *appearance* that we saw at the level of understanding.

What this means in concrete experience is that selfishness is never mere selfishness, so long as it acts. Being is always a being-for-another and is never merely for itself: the world, or society, is an interconnected whole. In action, selfishness transcends itself. It manifests the universal in the realm of actuality. The Machiavellian preacher can persist in his cynical Way and assert that all action is merely self-interested. But that would only mean that no one knows what action is [392]. Action is not simply *my* action. It is the manifestation of a universal working through me, since to act is to use a universal talent or gift. This manifested universal shows itself in the fact that when I act in my own self-interest, I also serve the common good and contribute to society. This is the Smithean "invisible hand" that is at work in the sphere of ethicality [351].

With the disappearance of the pompous rhetoric of virtue, and of the reductionist explanations of self-interest, the Romance of Reason comes to an end. The individual no longer opposes himself to the world but fulfills himself in and through it. The world, as the field of action, has become good. Consciousness has learned that action does not point to some unrealized and unrealizable good, to which individuality should bow, but *is its own end* [393]. Action itself is the good as individualized universality. The cultivation of gifts, capacities, and strengths becomes the end itself. Through the dialectic of experience, the self has become a talented individual among other talented individuals. With individuality now conceived as the process of self-unfolding [393], a community arises. It is the community of those who put their self-interest to work and happily *do their own thing.*

But do your thing, and I shall know you.
Do your work, and you shall reinforce yourself.
EMERSON, "Self-Reliance"

14

Rational Animals and the Birth of Spirit

THE THIRD STAGE OF REASON UNITES WHAT THE PREVIOUS STAGE had separated: self-interest and the good. The Knight of Virtue vanishes, along with his ghostly good in itself, and the Way of the World triumphs. Neither the dreamy Knight nor his steely-eyed opponent grasps the true nature of human action. Neither sees what their mutual struggle in fact reveals: that the good is *self-actualization,* the process in which individuals become real, and more than merely selfish, through their use of universal gifts, capacities, and strengths. In the present section, reason celebrates this process. It posits individual human doing [*das Tun*] as absolute.

As observer, reason was *in itself* or objective. It strove to find itself in the things of perception. Active reason was *for itself* or subjective. It posited itself as absolute by opposing the world. In its third phase, reason is *in and for itself,* both objective and subjective. It is now not simply active but *self-actualizing.* Action is the unity of subject and object, being-for-itself and being-in-itself. To convey the intimacy of this union, Hegel uses the word *Durchdringung,* interpenetration. Action is "the self-moving interpenetration" of the individual and the universal—that is, of the individual and his property-like gifts, capacities, and strengths [394].

At the beginning of the last section, Hegel noted that active reason repeats the two stages of self-consciousness: independence and freedom [348]. The independence of reason was the individual's effort to assert himself by opposing the world. But now, through action, the individual transcends his romanticism and becomes spontaneous or self-moving: subjectively absorbed in something objectively real. This self-motion or self-determination is reason's *freedom:* "Action or doing [*das Tun*] is in its own self its truth and actuality, and the setting-forth and expression of individuality is, for action, the end [*Zweck*] in and for its own self" [394]. As passive observer and active hero, the rational individual merely found himself in the world. As a self-actualizing doer and maker, he *is* a world.

Reason, as we know, expresses itself as Category. This is the unity of being and self-consciousness [235]. The Category is the spontaneity of the self, the act by which the self projects itself onto the world and makes the world its own. At this stage of reason, the Category, which has been the soul of everything reason has done, "has become aware of itself" [395]. Man, as Category, now acts. In acting, he knows himself as spontaneous or self-determining. He knows that the world is real insofar as it is his own work. Action is self-consciousness liberated from the desire to negate and made happily objective. The individual at last is autonomous or absolute and needs nothing beyond his own power. He does not need to master another in order to be free. He is not a slave who makes things that reflect somebody else's selfhood. He neither stoically flees the world nor skeptically destroys it in speech. And as a manifestation of rational self-confidence, he does not need God. Moreover, as we have seen, the individual has risen above the shallow "abstractions and chimeras" of reason in its previous phase [394].

The godlike autonomy of action is captured in Hegel's image of the circle. In action, consciousness "has cast away all opposition and every condition affecting its action; it starts afresh from itself, and is occupied not with an other [for example, an imagined enemy], but with itself" [396]. Action is a circle that "moves freely within itself in a void, which, unimpeded, now expands, now contracts, and is perfectly content to operate in and with its own self." It is not a transition into otherness but the actualizing of a potential, a coming into one's own. Action is the translating [*Übersetzen*] from not being seen to being seen by others and displayed [396]. Self-actualization reminds us of force and its utterance. The human individual at this stage *is* force—force that has become aware of itself as force. Like the living organism, however, which we encountered at the level of observing reason, this human force does not need an other to solicit its action: it is *self*-soliciting, or its own cause and reason.

Hegel does not limit the range of what counts as an action. An action is whatever an individual invests himself in *qua individual* and makes his own. There is no hierarchy, no standard according to which one kind of action is better than another. Action includes professions, specialties, and interests of all kinds: carpentry, cooking, the sciences and arts, writing on Hegel, law, medicine, or business. All these *technai*, as the Greeks called them, are valid modes in which individuality flourishes or experiences itself as absolute. From this standpoint, the pastry chef no less than the philosophy professor whirls unimpeded in the heaven of his natural gift.

This world of self-actualizing individuals is very familiar to us. H. S. Harris calls it "the way we live now" (2:77). It is modern *civil society*, in which

"I am what I do, and you are what you do."[1] As Hegel says in the *Philosophy of Right,* civil society is the realm of diversity or difference [*die Differenz*]. In it, "each member is its own end, everything else is nothing to it" (White, 147). We are all equal in this world because we are all equally absolute. Each of us is objectively self-absorbed, individually at work in the circle, or rather sphere, of our interests and abilities. We assert our individuality and resist assimilation into a greater whole. Whether or not we are conscious of the fact, many of us do identify this aspect of our lives with the essence and fulfillment of our lives, with the good. Hegel's analysis of action offers us an opportunity to examine the nature, and limits, of this thoroughly modern view of human life, freedom, and happiness.

Action, in the present context, does not include *everything* human beings do. Action, here, is whatever constitutes my self-actualization as the practitioner of a *technē*. It does not include ethical action, as Aristotle discusses it in his *Nicomachean Ethics.* For Aristotle, action, *praxis,* is the exercise of moral virtues like courage and liberality. These virtues are necessary to happiness in the context of the *polis* or city-state. But the modern self-actualizer does not think of himself as part of an ethical whole. He is not an embodied universal, in whom the social substance manifests itself, but a world unto himself. His larger "world" is only an ensemble and collision of human atoms endowed with energy (the capacity to do work). We moderns find action in this sense appealing *because* it is not moral or political. Within our private spheres of action and interest, nobody tells us what to do. In Leibniz' phrase, we are monadic *little gods*[2] who happily express ourselves beyond the reach of laws, customs, and moral virtues—without, however, becoming criminals like Faust or Karl Moor.

This highest phase of reason has three stages. In the first, reason manifests itself as the realm of individuals who severally "do their own thing." In the second, reason becomes *universal selfhood* in the form of a moral legislator [419]. In the third, reason *tests* rather than makes moral laws. As these two law-centered modes prove themselves to be abstractions, consciousness passes from reason to spirit: from abstract law to the living law of custom.

The War of the Works [397–407]

Hegel gives the first phase of self-actualizing reason an odd title: "The spiritual animal kingdom and deceit, or the 'matter itself.'"[3] This kingdom that combines the high and the low, the spiritual and the animal, is Hegel's designation for modern civil society, the realm of rampant difference or diversity. In what follows, we will see how this realm generates deceit [*Betrug*]. We will also explore the meaning of Hegel's impossible-to-translate phrase, *Sache selbst:* the "matter itself" or "real thing."

One of the most striking aspects of phenomenal reason is its animality. Animality was evident in observing reason, which was initially driven by an *instinct* to find itself in the material world [245–46]. At the current stage of reason, we are animals not through instinct but through the free exercise of our natural gifts, capacities, and strengths. It is in this sense that we belong to the spiritual animal kingdom, *das geistige Tierreich.* When I actualize a talent, whether for investment banking or playing the bassoon, I am happily in my element. I am like the fish that swims, the bird that flies, or the lion that hunts its prey. I do what I do because I can. Other human beings, whose skills and interests differ from mine, do the same. We are all immersed in our individual techno-element, caught up in the seeming concreteness and self-containment of our individuality at work. We are rational animals in the wild kingdom of unimpeded talent.

Self-absorption is the basis for human interaction in civil society. In the animal kingdom, animals interact by preying on each other. In the *spiritual* animal kingdom, humans do the same. Others, as we shall see, appropriate or "feed on" my work by taking an interest in it and making it their own. I do the same to them. The spiritual animal kingdom is spirit in Hobbes' state of nature, spirit that has not yet achieved ethicality as a genuine I that is We. Individuals in this condition "recognize" one another's interests and accomplishments. But this is not the mutual recognition that was the object of self-conscious desire, since individuals here are to each other always a means and never an end.[4] As modern societal animals, you and I recognize each other, not as fellow rational beings but only as competitors in the marketplace of talent. We live a life of *perverse sociability.*

Hegel begins the dialectic of action with the Concept and certainty of self-actualizing reason [397–404]. This certainty is then set in motion and unraveled in the experiential process, which liberates all the pent-up negativity that is implicit in action [405–18]. There are three stages to this process. We may briefly designate their respective topics as the *work* (in the sense of the oeuvre or product of work), the *matter itself* or "real thing," and finally the interplay of individuals in the societal game of mutual *deceit.*

The account of reason's certainty elaborates what we have already seen: that action, in its circle-like self-sufficiency and self-containment, is posited as absolute. Hegel begins his main discussion by telegraphing the eventual failure of this claim. In the hard school of experience, self-actualizing reason will learn that action posited as exclusively *my* action is abstract and universal: that action in this sense produces, not solid individuality but "merely the empty thought of this Category" [397]. In more concrete terms, Hegel's analysis will show that our effort to make ourselves "little gods" by identifying ourselves with our natural talent and private interests results in our leading lives that are not lives at all. Like the previous heroes of individualism, the modern self-actualizer makes himself unreal—a ghost. His expression of self will be a loss of self.

The claim of the self-actualizer is that the activation of his gift or talent is the ultimate reality, the concrete unity of subject and object in which he absolutely knows himself and furthermore knows the world as himself. Self-actualizing reason thinks of itself as thoroughly positive, as the simple translation (as we saw above) from the night of the possible into the daylight of the real. But as Hegel proceeds to show, both action and the talent that is its source are negative. Translation is in fact change.

We begin with what Hegel told us at the beginning of his chapter: that consciousness, as it journeys forth, forgets where it has been [233]. This forgetfulness is the source of renewed immediacy. At his present stage, the rational individual is in immediate possession of a natural gift or talent, which, once activated, reveals the interpenetration of self and world, subject and object. This mere possession of the gift, the gift prior to action, is a "simple in itself," a given potentiality. *We* see that what reason takes as immediate is in fact the result of the previous mediation, that self-actualization as the good emerged dialectically from the Knight's battle with the Way of the World. But mediation is negation, which is always preserved and never left behind. Here, it is preserved as the specificity of my natural gift. Hegel calls this a *determinateness* [398]. Recalling Spinoza's dictum, "every determination is a negation," we can say that having *this* gift means not having *that* one. Hegel calls this determinateness "an original determinate nature." The word nature implies that we are in the realm of the immediate or given. Insofar as my talent is implicit or dormant, my individuality, which I identify with my talent, is also implicit. As Hegel says, it is in the realm of mere being. Because talent is determinate, being manifests itself as a "range of being," that is, a range of talents or human potentialities that exclude each other [399].[5]

As a talent-animal, I do not, however, experience my determinateness as a limitation to be overcome. My talent is not a cage but a wing. It does not confine but liberates. Its determinateness carves out the world in which I am simply myself, potent and free. In the self-contained sphere of action, "consciousness is a relation purely of itself to itself: relation to an other, which would be a limitation of it, has been eliminated." The individual lives and breathes the element of his native gift. He sees the whole world through the specific coloration of his techno-medium and originality [399]. Like animals that breathe the breath of life into the inanimate elements they take in, thus animating the whole in which they live, so too individuals have a reciprocal, symbiotic relation to their distinctive talent or gift, which is their world. My talent inspires or breathes into me, and I breathe life into my talent.

This positive aspect of action is only what action is implicitly, before any real action has taken place. But action itself "is itself nothing else but negativity" [399]. It is process, movement, becoming [*Werden*]. In action, one step succeeds and therefore negates another.[6] The song or poem I set out to compose comes out gradually. As it comes out, my potentiality is gradually canceled in being actualized.[7] Choices are made, which are both determinations and negations: this note, *not that one,* this word, *not that one.* This is the negation I mentioned above (the determinateness of talent), now appearing in the context of process. In other words, the process of acting further explicates, and indeed is the same as [398], the determinateness inherent in the gift that allows me to act. Moreover, as the song or poem gets written, my selfhood cancels its mere inwardness and comes out into the open in a specific form. My potential or talent is a resource that is distributed and exhausted in the course of use: "when individuality acts, determinateness [my specific skill] is dissolved in the general process of negativity or in the sum total of every determinateness" [399]. In other words, when I use my talent, my individuality vanishes in the fluid interaction of all talented individuals in civil society. I become a ripple in the talent pool.

Action seems simple at first: the immediate unity of subject and object (me and my talent). But action has a complex interior. In the activation of a gift, dormant distinctions and oppositions are awakened and come out into the open: negativity is awakened. Action reveals differences as moments of action [400]. First, there is the opposition between the object, the proposed end, and what was there in the first place as given.[8] Second, there is an opposition between the proposed end and the means I adopt in achieving this end. This is the moment of transition from the given (already existing wood, words, musical tones) to the sought for (table, poem, song). Third, there is an opposition between end as merely proposed and end as achieved. This latter end is the *Werk* or work as product. Once the work is brought to light, it is no longer simply my own but exists "out there" as my other. My action is now complete. In the work, I confront my individuality as external and real. In the totality of its moments, action [*Handlung*] "does not go outside itself, either as circumstances, or as end, or means, or as the work" [401]. Action contains, and therefore sublates or transcends, all its oppositions and distinctions.

The circle of action raises the possibility of a *vicious* circle. If action alone makes explicit for me who I really am, then it seems that I know myself only after I have acted, only when I am in the presence of my work. How, then, can I begin to act, since I must know before acting what I can only know afterwards?[9] The self-actualizing individual does not worry about this sort of thing but is *thoroughly practical:* he gets down to business and immediately acts [401]. The theoretical paradox about making a beginning only highlights the absoluteness of action, which has its starting-point not in some external situation that dictates whether, or how, I will act but in my own selfhood. My beginning is my talent operating as an impetus or force. To begin to act, I have only to take an interest in something. Action is thus completely spontaneous, circular, and non-reactive: "the entire action does not go outside itself, either as circumstances, or as end, or means [talent], or as the work that has emerged from these" [401]. Strictly speaking, I am not "free to act." My action *is* my freedom, which is my radical self-determination or creativity.

The for-us dialectic now focuses on the work [*Werk*], the concrete result and truth of my action. The work is specific or determinate: this business venture or poem, not that one. In the specific quality of the work, individual consciousness discovers its own specificity. It manifests itself as this talent, not that one. Consciousness itself, however, is universal and is the awareness of objects generally. Having channeled itself into specific productivity, consciousness now "steps back" from action. It recovers its inherent universality and is free to compare works as well as the individuals whose works they are [402]. It can compare, for example, the sonnets of different poets and say: "This poet has a more inventive nature than that one." But although it can make quantitative, non-essential comparisons, it cannot make meaningful qualitative ones. It cannot say: "This sonnet or poet is bad, that one good." The essence of action is to express an individual's selfhood. Beyond that, action is nothing. Since, for reason in its current form, the good *is* self-actualization, insofar as something is an action at all—that is, someone's embodied selfhood—it is good.

As for how I respond to my own work, "feelings of exaltation, or lamentation, or repentance are altogether out of place" [404]. Being talented means never having to say you're sorry. Once I grasp what action really is, I see that it can neither rise above nor fall below an expectation, since the sole content of the action is my "original nature." Action expresses nothing but my technically "colored" selfhood. I *am* my originality or native talent—a self-made man, as the saying goes. What I produce is myself, not some extraneous ideal against which I measure my success. Action is self-validating. Hegel puts this in terms that remind us of the projected goal of self-consciousness [177]: "[The self-actualizing individual] can have only the consciousness of the pure translating [*Übersetzens*] *of himself* from the night of possibility into the daylight of the present" [404]. True to the certainty of idealism, reason affirms that action alone is real (since it is embodied selfhood), and that all else is mere seeming [*Schein*]. As a doer and maker, the individual seems to experience the joy of homecoming that reason was seeking all along [241]. In the world in which actions alone are real, he "*experiences only joy in himself.*"

Action embodies a claim to absolute knowing. The individual acts, not in order to do and make things but to behold and "meet" himself in the things done and made. This reminds us of Faust, who wanted a self-intuition made real in an other. Reason longs for the return to self and thinks it has experienced this in the subject-object unity that action embodies. As we shall see, this return is precisely what fails to happen. The undoing of doing and making begins as soon as the action is finished, when there is a *work*. Having set forth the concept consciousness has of itself as a self-sufficient producer, Hegel now turns to experience [405], which will reveal the contradiction between the concept of action and its reality.

The work "is the reality that consciousness gives itself; it is that in which the individual is explicitly for himself what he is implicitly or in himself, and in such a manner that the consciousness for which the individual becomes explicit in the work, is not the particular, but the universal, consciousness" [405]. When it is not absorbed and channeled in producing a work, consciousness is universal—as it has been all along. Simply stated, thought or awareness transcends all determinations *and has no determination or form of its own.* Consciousness "goes beyond itself as the work, and is itself the non-determinate space [*Raum*], which finds itself unfilled by its work" [405].[10] Consciousness can never be fully expressed by a determinate object, even one that has been produced by consciousness. It is the field or space of all being, since there is no object that is not an object for consciousness.

Clearly, there is a problem here. Reason posited action as the unity of universal (talent) and individual (*my* talent).[11] But in the determinate work that *is* (the particular table or poem), consciousness as universal does not find itself, since the worker is more comprehensive than his works. How, then, can there be a work that is not determinate but universal, a work that reflects and embodies consciousness in its universality? How will individuality, which posits itself as universal in talent, "know how to satisfy itself" [405]? The answer to this question is the *matter itself,* the *Sache selbst,* which the dialectic will soon generate.

Universality, here, refers to universal consciousness as the open field of being. This is also the field in which individual consciousnesses themselves appear as beings: civil society as the marketplace of talent. As Hegel told us earlier, once my work is finished, I recover my universality as the ability to contemplate and compare other works and other workers. But *they* occupy the same space of conscious comparison with respect to *my* works. While I am acting or in process, I determine and shape a given material, invest it with my selfhood as talent. But once the work is "out there" or public, it is *anything anyone wants to make of it.* It is, Hegel says, "in the determinateless space of being" [405]. In the marketplace of talent, anyone can compete, and be seen. My work, in being *for me,* is also *for others.* In producing my techno-child, I generate a hostage to fortune. And since this techno-orphan is myself externalized, I have, in fathering it, exposed myself as well as my work to other people's originality and projects of self-actualization. My being-for-self becomes a being-for-others. That is, it becomes its opposite.

Let us look at this self-negation more closely.

Action is a becoming, and the work that has come to be negates that becoming. The work [*Werk*] is not a movement. Moreover, action is *my* action. But as we have seen, the work, in being for me, is also for others. It has been "thrown out" [*hinausgeworfen*] into existence or being-there. For me, the work embodies my selfhood. But for others, it is "an alien actuality"—a spiritual *commodity* [405]. When action was only implicit or in its concept, talents were not opposed to each other. They were only diverse: I am a poet, you are a song-writer. But in the marketplace of talent or talent-pool, different works and workers invade each other's "space" and negate each other's originality. What to me was a poem that embodied *my* individuality is to you lyrics for a song that embodies *your* individuality.[12] Perhaps a third individual then takes this song and composes a parody of it or puts it in his play. I may exact my revenge by writing a poem deriding those who use other people's works for their own purposes. Of course, that is what I too am doing in writing such a poem.[13] As little gods, we are all beasts that feed on each other's creativity. This modern feeding frenzy is not the result of merely practicing arts, which of course the ancient Greeks also did, but of making this practice absolute, of failing to posit an *ethical whole* in which what is mine can be yours without ceasing to be mine.

This dialectic reminds us that as a self-actualizer I want to live in the privacy of my own talent, even though I produce public works. Other people are at first nothing to me and play no part in my world of knowing. But the work, once produced, makes me aware of other self-actualizers who dwell and jostle in the marketplace of talent. Since my work is alien to them, they must make it their own. They must make *my* work the unity of *their* selfhood and the world. My goal was to posit myself as an end, to *make myself.* But in producing a work, I have made myself into the means of other people's self-actualization. In this self-negating process, my work, in being a work, loses what makes it characteristic or, as we say, "special" [*eigentümlich*]. It has perished, not because people do not pay any attention to it, but precisely because they *do.* I am in the paradoxical condition of being offended when others say, "My, your work is interesting," which I interpret as a predatory gesture. And yet, I cannot deny that this work, which others appropriate, is nevertheless mine. I am in the same position that Karl Moor was in when others appropriated what was supposed to be the law of *his* heart.[14]

In this inversion of my original position (the mutual negation of works and workers), I experience myself not as abiding but as vanishing. What I have done (or rather, what I have made myself) is undone by "the counterplay [*Wiederspiel*] of other strengths and interests." Strength, here, is *Kraft*, force. And indeed, the play of individuals at work resembles the earlier play of forces. In that play, force lost its substantiality and became a mere ripple in the restless sea of appearance. The same thing happens here. In seeking to actualize myself in my work, I make myself unreal, both for myself and for others.

Reason's certainty was that being and action were the same. The work, which perishes, reveals the truth that contradicts this certainty. In producing my work, I learn that being and action *fall apart*, that the work cannot preserve the process by which I produced the work. I become aware of the antithesis of being and action [406]. Being here refers to two things: my universal talent, or the determinate nature that simply *is*, and the work that simply *is*. These are, respectively, the beginning and endpoint of action, which is movement or becoming, the transition to reality or thinghood. To say that being and action fall apart is to say that there is no necessary connection between my labor and the work itself (which embodies my talent). In seeking to actualize myself, I have in fact regressed to the stage of a Knight-like idealist: my selfhood, whether initially only possessed as a potential or eventually embodied in the work, is something only thought or intended, a non-actual in-itself [406].

The self wanted to make itself real in a static being or thing, which was actualized talent. But no mere being or thing can express selfhood, which is not a static content but a living "self-identical form." This form is present not in the work but in the action [406]. I am not my products but my spontaneous activity or freedom, to which no static being, however grand and well-crafted, is adequate. In the static work, consciousness thus experiences "its empty concept of itself" as the truth of its initial certainty.[15]

In the separation of being and action, the distinctions we saw earlier, which were harmonized and held captive within the sphere of action, are now liberated from their all-mastering sphere [407]. Like the work itself, which *is*, these former "slaves" now *are*. Moreover, in the thingly realm of being, they are indifferent to each other or independent. In particular, actual means and intended end are now indifferent to each other. The work is not the necessary offspring of my technical labor but only something contingent or accidentally related to action. In other words, it is purely accidental whether my chosen means succeed in achieving my intended goal. Is this the book I should be writing, the one that matches my talent and interest? Are these the right means for writing the book I intend? All this is purely a matter of chance.

The negative result leads to an important question. Is there a thing that *would* be adequate to the spontaneity or sheer action of the self, a thing that would reveal not static content but active form? The matter itself will be that thing: the "real thing" that embodies the very *form* of my selfhood.

The Thing That Matters [408–15]

With the matter itself, or what matters most, we reach the second stage of the modern self-actualizer's experience of himself. As we have seen, the work, which was posited as essential, vanishes and becomes contingent or non-essential. It proved to be the negation of my selfhood. But since the work vanishes or becomes insignificant (works and workers negate each other's originality), the self-negation it embodies also vanishes [408]. The work is thus the negation of a negation, a "vanishing of the vanishing" [409]. This is the positive result or determinate negation of the preceding experience. What vanishes here is the impervious, non-spiritual "out-there-ness" of the work, the merely natural thinghood that stands opposed to self-consciousness.

Originally, action was for the sake of the work—a mere means. This relation is now inverted. Consciousness steps back from its works and posits the action rather than the work as absolute. The action itself is now "the true work" [409]. In Hegel's words, "consciousness is reflected out of its perishable work into itself, and preserves its concept and its certainty as that which *is* and *endures* in face of the experience of the contingency of action" [409]. Reason still posits the unity of subject and object. But this unity is no longer expressed in a product. It is revealed in a new, spiritualized thinghood that Hegel calls "the matter itself"—*die Sache selbst.*[16] This is the Category as the sheer spontaneity or action by which the self unites with being. In the matter itself, the Category emerges in its pure state. Liberated from the confines of static thinghood, it is now more fully "aware of itself," more manifestly self-conscious. The self no longer needs products to be concrete but is self-concretizing: its action as such *is* its work. Action is transformed, more deeply spiritualized, in the transition to the matter itself. No longer requiring bodily movement, it is the form rather than the content of the self: the act of *taking an interest in something,* thereby making it essential or important. What matters is not my work, but my effort or, as we may also call it, my *sincerity* and *concern.*[17]

It might seem that the matter itself is merely subjective, and so constitutes a logical regression. But this is not the case. Taking an interest in something is not a mere desire or whim. It is the subjective act by which the object of my interest, my *cause,* becomes concrete and real *in itself.* This is what we mean when we say that something is important or serious, that it *matters.*

Miller translates *die Sache selbst* as "the heart of the matter," and *Sache* by itself as "the matter in hand."[18] *Sache* is thing, but not the thing apprehended by sense-certainty and perception [410]. The German *Sache* is what the ancient Greeks called a *pragma,* the thing with which one has to do (from the verb *prattein,* to do, practice or achieve). It is one's affair or business. *Pragma* is the origin of our "practical," and indeed, this is the moment in the *Phenomenology* when consciousness becomes, or at least approaches, practical reason. At first, practicality will refer to whatever I happen to take an interest in (whether cabinet-making, writing about Hegel, or global warming), whatever I am "into" or make "my thing" or "my cause."[19] This private or isolated practicality will contradict itself. It will develop into the more mature public practicality of ethical law.

The matter itself is thinghood that has been thoroughly imbued with selfhood. Human interest, *my* interest, is like a spirit or breath that I infuse into the pores of a topic or event, thus making that topic or event alive, real, and universal. This new "thing" is not only different from thing in its old sense—the thing, *das Ding,* as it appeared to perception. It is also that in which things in the old sense have their true meaning [410]: a thing is a true thing, something real, insofar as it is *for me,* insofar as it is matters or is important to a thinking subject. The *Sache,* in other words, does not cancel out the objectivity of the *Ding* but rather absorbs it into a higher unity. Hegel notes that the dialectical movement of the matter itself will repeat the transition from sense-certainty to perception [410]. The *Sache selbst* will be dialectically transformed from being *my* thing into being *our* thing. The individual self, the abstract human *This* of reason, will be transformed into the *universal* selfhood of spirit and ethicality.

In the matter itself, the interpenetration of self and object now becomes objective [411]. Consciousness has for its object the *unity* of subject and object. Furthermore, it has this unity not in some external work but (as I noted above) in its own act of paying serious attention to things that matter or that interest it. Consciousness, here, does not receive but bestows value and reality. It no longer needs the external blessing of works well done but locates the absolute in its sheer *taking an interest* in something—in making, as we say, an "honest effort" and being devoted to one's cause.

The matter itself embodies a new certainty. It is therefore a new immediacy that cries out for mediation. Consciousness is certain of finding its substance in the matter itself but "has not yet developed into a truly real substance." (This substance—the truth of the matter itself—will be ethicality.) The immediacy of the present stage consists in reason's positing the matter itself as a simple universal that contains rather than develops its various moments: the individual as *this* individual with *this* particular talent or interest, as well as his end, means, action, and the reality achieved in his work. The most important opposition contained in the matter itself is, of course, that between subject and object. The matter itself is both *my* thing and my *thing.*

All these moments are free-floating elements that consciousness can emphasize or suppress at will. Their indifference to one another is the source of what soon becomes deception, *Betrug.* The matter itself is an all-purpose abstract predicate that can be applied to any of these moments, since each moment is that in which I have invested myself. The matter itself, says Hegel, "is not yet a subject" [411]. What he means is that the *Sache selbst* is not yet the completely self-identical *self* that controls and interrelates all the moments. At the present stage of immediacy, it is a static genus, of which all the moments are species or instances, different aspects of "being interested" in something.

Consciousness at this point becomes *honest* or *respectable* [*ehrlich*] [412]. I am honest—authentic or "real"—when I am personally invested, when I throw myself into something and make my best effort, regardless of the outcome. Thus am I "true to myself." Our self-actualizer now does well by meaning well. This is his Knight-like idealism [412]. I intend the matter itself as my ultimate reality or absolute, just as the Knight of Virtue intended his good in itself. But unlike the Knight's in-itself, the matter itself is present in something here and now. I do not practice fencing in a mirror but take up something concrete that interests me—*whatever that happens to be.* As we know, reason is the individual's will to satisfaction, his will to power. Reason is satisfied to the extent that it finds itself in an object. At the previous stage of its experience, it tried, and failed, to find itself in its works. But in the matter itself, reason *knows how to satisfy itself* apart from works [405]. The key to this self-satisfaction is knowing how to make every aspect of the matter itself into what matters to me.[20] As Hegel puts it, "Whichever way things turn out, [consciousness] has accomplished and attained the matter itself, for this, being the universal genus of those moments, is the predicate of them all" [412].

I now become a virtuoso at transforming every defeat into a victory. If I try to put my stamp on a committee meeting by speaking up, and my point only makes the discussion worse or goes nowhere, well, at least I spoke up and showed my sincerity of interest, and *that's what matters.* If I write mediocre poems, at least I did my best, and *that's what matters.* I wrote what I had in me and was therefore authentic or real. And as for those other self-actualizers who appropriate my poems, they would not have been able to do this if I had not written the poems in the first place. My undoing at their hands is really *my doing,* and those thieves and plagiarists are therefore also in a sense my poems, something I *made.*[21] This last sentiment, Hegel says, is that of "bad boys who enjoy getting their ears boxed because they are the cause of its being done" [412].

In this new interpenetration of self and being, subject and object, my selfhood is not my accomplishment but my *resolve* [*Entschluß*]. Every outcome, even no outcome at all, is now incorporated into what I consider real, since the real is what I intend and make the object of concern. If I fail at something, then I re-name my failure "that of which I was capable." The failure becomes my badge of honor. If some money comes my way, then it was because I deserved it. If the president makes a decision that improves the situation in the Middle East, I say to myself: "Of course that succeeded: that was *my cause:* it was exactly what *I* would have done!" If he makes a bad decision, I say: "It's exactly the cause I opposed!" Formerly, I showed my originality in my work. Now I show my authenticity—a subtler form of originality—in my interest. As a self-actualizer, I give myself the right to intrude anywhere in the world of human events and make the reality of a situation what I want or do not want, intend or do not intend. Everybody's business is my business. Thus do I show myself and others that I am a real human being who takes a serious interest in things by making them his own.

This concern or being real can maintain itself only because the matter itself can be found in any one of its moments or aspects. Consciousness separates these aspects and does not "bring together its *thoughts* about the matter itself" [414]. Again, the matter itself is a free-floating predicate, the simple universal I can use to describe my work, my action, a shabby action, no action at all, an impossible action, and even other people's actions, which I can easily transform into being mine simply by taking an interest in them or claiming them as embodiments of my will. My honesty is omnivorous. It feeds on anything, even my failures and other people's successes.[22]

The individual who is honest, cannot, however, engage in this sleight-of-hand and not know it, since the various aspects of the matter itself are obviously intertwined [415]. Surely, I know that the matter itself, or what is important to me, is something I in particular find important, that my *thing* is also *my* thing. I also know that what I posit as mattering to me matters as something important in its own right since the matter itself is no mere whim or desire but what I take seriously as having universal worth and interest. In other words, the "concerned" individual cannot fail to know that the matter itself is both subjective and objective. Therefore, when he puts forth one aspect of the matter itself, he is also aware of the other that he suppresses. At one time, I say, stressing my personal involvement: "This is what *I* find interesting." At another, I say, stressing my objectivity: "This isn't just what I'm interested in: this is important, I tell you!" Both are lies, or rather abstractions. So-called honest consciousness, individuality in civil society, is thus "not as honest or respectable as it seems." By shifting its ground, it tries to hide from itself the fact that it cannot articulate, and does not know, *how* the subjective and objective sides of the matter itself are related, *how* they interpenetrate. It willfully deceives itself or, as Hegel has said at previous stages, runs away from the truth.

Artful Dodgers [416–18]

The sleight-of-hand we have just seen results from the various moments of the matter itself, which are aspects that consciousness shuffles rather than thinks through or mediates. This shuffling reveals the opposition and contradiction in the varied contents of the matter itself. But a shuffling also goes on in the realm of form [416]. Form here means *relation.* The matter itself is both for (or related to) me and for (or related to) others. This double relation recalls self-consciousness. In the phenomenon of self-consciousness, I am both for myself (an object to myself) and also for others (an object to them). When self-consciousness first came on the scene, it gave rise to a fight for recognition. Here something similar occurs. But instead of physical combat there will be what Hegel calls "a play of individualities with one another in which each and all find themselves both deceiving and being deceived" [416].[23]

Deception [*Betrug*] results from the duplicity or double-sidedness inherent in the matter itself. In positing the matter itself as absolute, consciousness must posit both sides of the opposition the matter itself contains: individuality and universality. But consciousness posits them only one at a time, since it runs away from thinking through their opposition or contradiction. It flips the two-sided coin of the *Sache selbst* rather than grasping both sides. At the level of form, the fundamental opposition that appeared within the content of the matter itself—between its subjective and objective sides (individual and universal)—is split into one side or "face" that is *for me* and the other that is *for others.* Consciousness will alternate between making the one or the other essential to its certainty of itself. This alternation results in mutual deception, which spells the downfall of the matter itself as rooted in a single consciousness.

To illustrate Hegel's drama of deceit, let us suppose that I have taken an interest in something and made it my *Sache* or cause. I proceed to set my plan into motion and show my seriousness [417]. To recall reason in its scientific mode, let us say I am a molecular biologist who wants to do an experiment designed to locate the gene responsible for self-consciousness.[24] My interest or effort makes this project into an objective reality, a *Sache selbst.* From my point of view, I am taking up something universally important—a *cause.* My fellow biologists also take it in this light and therefore conclude that I am not self-interested but "objective," that it is not *my* project but *the* project. And so, they appropriate it, either by engaging in their own experiments or offering help with mine. At this point, I express my irritation at these invaders of my techno-space. In Hegel's spatial formulation, I have gone out of where they mean me to be [417]. I show that I am interested in my thing, my project, not because it advances science, but because it is *mine.*

My colleagues thus feel that I have deceived them by presenting a false show of objective interest. But in fact they too are deceivers, since what they really want is to see and show [*sehen und zeigen*] *their* action, not the matter itself. They are guilty of the same deceit of which they accuse me.[25]

Having seen what they take to be my true colors, my colleagues conclude that since I am nothing but a self-interested whiner, the field of research I opened up is legitimately open to everybody, especially them. They can subtract me from the equation and treat me as someone who is not interested in the project as something universally important. But again they are mistaken, since I have gone out once more from where they think I am. I now go back to the *universal* side of the *Sache selbst,* the side that shows the matter itself as something purely objective and open to all. I show my current position or "colors" by interfering in what my colleagues are doing with what used to be my project. That is, I do to them what they did to me. If I cannot re-appropriate my gene experiment, then I can at least *take an interest* in their work, give it my official stamp of approval or disapproval, and maybe publish my opinion of it in *Genes Are Us.* Moreover, to continue the pathology of appropriation, even when I praise my colleagues' work, I am praising myself for being a generous human being who has resisted the temptation to damage their work by criticizing it [417]. I am, to myself, the Great-Souled Biologist.

As for my colleagues, they think, or rather pretend to think, that I have deceived them by interfering, that once again I am only being self-interested. But in fact they too are motivated by self-interest, which they display in criticizing *my* self-interest.[26] Their claim to be disinterested is contradicted by what they actually do. They bring what is now *their* gene-experiment out into the open, make it public, and thus show that they want attention and want to interest others in *their* accomplishment. What the dialectic of deceit shows is that actualization, doing something that expresses my selfhood, is never simply private: "Actualization is, on the contrary, a display of what is one's own in the element of universality whereby it becomes, *and should become* [my italics], everybody's *Sache* or 'thing'" [417].[27]

Hegel continues to characterize this deceit in which a purely subjective interest masquerades as disinterested objectivity. It is the deception of oneself as well as others to take human action as either *purely* self-interested or *purely* objective. The deception repeats, now within a single consciousness, the false opposition we saw earlier between the self-interest of the Way of the World and the Knight's good-in-itself. The two-faced coin of the *Sache selbst* will not permit such one-sidedness. Anyone who opens up an interest or topic "soon learns that others hurry along like flies to freshly poured-out milk, and want to busy themselves with it" [418]. What these human flies discover about my milky topic is that it is not just *the* topic of interest but also *my* topic of interest, that I have invested my selfhood in it. On the other side, if some advocate of the Way of the World thought he had discovered in my interest only my egotism, he too would be mistaken, since I have made my interest objective, brought it out into the open as something available and interesting to everyone.

What consciousness learns in the experience of this mutual deception is that individual and universal, subjective me-ness and objective this-ness, are *both* essential to the matter itself [418]. It learns that my action cannot be mine alone, and that what is for me must also be for others. The matter itself must be "the action of all and each." This is what Hegel calls "spiritual essence." It is selfhood that has become universal or communal in *ethical law.* The matter itself is thus transformed, or rather revealed for what it is in truth. It ceases to be what is important or valuable to me as a singular self, and becomes what is important or valuable to *us* as rational beings. The various technical powers and individual interests fail to do justice to the universality of consciousness because they interest only the individuals to whom they belong (and their self-actualizing parasites). But the ethical law, in being mine, is also profoundly ours. It embodies my awareness of myself as universal, and of an interest that is universal. And so, in one of those amazing ironies that populate the *Phenomenology of Spirit,* Hegel generates the beginnings of ethical community from the drama of deceit, from the perverse version of community that exists in modern civil society.

Earlier, Hegel said that the matter itself was initially not a subject but only a universal and abstract predicate that accompanied its various aspects or moments. Now, the matter itself has become "substance [objectivity] interfused with individuality [subjectivity]." That is, the opposition between the open or universal "space" of being and individual mine-ness is overcome by a higher unity, of which both these opposites are moments. These once-separate terms now "coalesce into simple individuality, which, as this particular individual, is no less immediately universal." More simply, when I look into my reason, I see, not my special powers and distinctive natural talent, but universal *laws* that are binding on everyone. I see in my individual reason the universal reason in which all individuals participate. To act in accordance with these laws is what it really means to act, since it is only in ethical action that subjectivity and objectivity are completely and permanently fused.

Ethical law embodies the universal "self-identical form" of selfhood. It is the full flowering of the Category. Formerly, the Category was only the *formal* side of my selfhood, the act as opposed to the resultant work and *content* of my selfhood. It was only the thought or certainty of the unity of self-consciousness and being. But now the Category is both form and content [418]. It is the genuinely autonomous and fully actual sphere of practical reason.

It is not a talent that uses tools outside itself for the sake of an end outside itself. Nor does it require the filling and impetus by some chance individual interest. The Category, as practical reason or "wisdom," absorbs all these previous distinctions, those arising both as content ("purpose, action, and reality") and as form ("being-for-self and being-for-another"). It embodies the self-sufficiency, power, and freedom of expression that the individual self-actualizer sought but could not achieve.

Hegel's two concluding sections on law—reason as lawgiver, and reason as testing laws—constitute the momentous transition to spirit, *Geist.* We will take up these two forms of reason, and the transition to spirit, in the following sections.

Reason Gives the Law [419–28]

The first thing that strikes us about Hegel's two concluding sections on law [*das Gesetz*] is that they are so brief, especially when compared with Observing Reason, which was gigantic. The second is that the argument is not especially difficult. In the first section, reason posits what it takes to be unconditional rules for ethical action. Hegel easily shows that these rules necessarily involve conditions. In the second, reason tests laws to determine their moral validity. The standard is logical self-consistency. Hegel shows that, according to this purely formal standard, any moral content can be justified.

The transition to spirit occurs when consciousness realizes that making ethical laws depend on what an individual immediately posits as universally binding is a form of "tyrannical insolence" [434]. If the law is to be truly lawful, it must be beyond the pretensions of individual reason. This is the lived law of *custom, Sitte,* made concrete in a people or *Volk.* It is the form of spirit that Hegel calls *ethicality, Sittlichkeit.* Its archetype is the world of ancient Greece, which we meet in Hegel's next chapter. Indeed, ethical substance now comes on the scene as the fulfilled *Sache selbst* [420].[28] But it is not yet ethical substance as something fully actualized, as it is in the Greek world. It is a still-abstract ethical *essence* (or "meaning"), which has not yet been made real in a *Volk* [439]. Simply put, at this concluding stage of reason, the individual is still in charge. He regards himself as absolute, even though he now knows an ethical realm that transcends the spiritual animal kingdom. This realm is that of common sense or "healthy reason" [422]. It knows, simply or without reflection, "what's right."

Let us review. Reason is the certainty the individual has of meeting himself in the world of things. This certainty of the unity of self and thing is the Category [235]. Phrenology failed because the skull was a dead thing, a mere *Ding,* in which self-consciousness could not meet itself. The works of self-actualization were also dead. They were products of the self but not embodiments. The self is not a thing but an act, and until reason finds a thing that embodies this act of self-assertion, it will not find itself. The *Sache selbst*—the matter I make real by taking an interest in it—was the first move in this direction. But the subjective and objective sides of the *Sache* displaced each other rather than coalesced. In ethical law or "what is right," this coalescence finally takes place. Law is the genuine *Sache selbst,* the enduring interpenetration of subject and object. It is important or serious, not as a mere interest or personal cause but as that which embodies my will as universal practical reason.

At this point, individuality *as such* has dissolved in the negative process of mutual deception. Authenticity, or sincerity of purpose, failed as the basis for objective seriousness and truth. In the process of experience, consciousness always *falls up.* When opposites dissolve into each other or become identical, they do not cancel each other out but coalesce into a higher, more concrete universality. Thus did the vanishing of the sensuous This become the concrete universality of the thing with properties. In the process of mutual deception, the opposite poles of the for-me and the for-others, individual and universal, coalesce into the higher universality of ethical law. The self loses the ambitious, resentful individuality of the spiritual animal kingdom and becomes a *universal self* [419]. It falls up.

As I noted above, this universality does not yet take the form of a determinate human community with defining laws and customs—a *Volk* or concrete "I that is We." That transition will take place at the *end* of the dialectic of law. The universal selfhood that now appears is still an ideal or thought, a universality that the individual *finds within himself.* Hegel wants us to understand this "practical wisdom" in reference to the Greek world, to which he obliquely refers in this section [420]. But law, in the present context, is not yet that world. It is still an abstract in-itself that is "perceived" by the individual as such. The emphasis is on the *validity* of the law, not action in accordance with the law. The law is not yet the ethical life of an actual community. It is not a custom but a commandment [*Gebot*] or moral maxim, and so manifests itself as a *Sollen* or *ought to.* The brief dialectic that Hegel presents here is the *transformation* of this abstract Ought into an Ought that also Is, or ethicality. With the rise of ethicality, we finally reach the level of *spirit:* reason as community that is for itself.[29]

The law signals a greater self-sufficiency and freedom than we had in the techno-space of the spiritual animal kingdom. The ethical realm, like the selfhood it embodies, is self-differentiating: it gets its content not from the outside world, or from natural talent, but from itself. As the perfect union of being and selfhood, the law both *is* and *has value or worth* [*es ist und gilt*] [420]. The object of reason has thus become the True [*das Wahre*].

The *Sache selbst,* formerly a matter of sincerity, has become the universally important ethical *substance.* In the law, consciousness is "at home with itself" [*bei sich selbst*]. At this new stage of certainty, I both cannot and do not want to go beyond this substance. I cannot, because the ethical good is "all being [*Sein*] and all power [*Macht*]." It is the element of my life. I do not want to, because it embodies my will. In the ethical medium, I meet myself. This medium, like self-consciousness, is self-differentiating. It spontaneously divides itself into various laws—*masses,* as Hegel calls them [420], each of which expresses the unbreakable unity of being and selfhood. These ethical "masses," which Hegel mentions later [437], are the different city-states into which Greek ethical substance or world naturally divides itself. Each of these masses itself divides into various aspects of ethical life. When the Greek world comes on the scene in Hegel's next chapter, there will be two such aspects: the *family* or private life and *politics* or public life. The first is presided over by Woman, the second by Man.[30]

Ethical *consciousness,* as it now appears, is a mode of certainty, a new claim to absolute knowing, that is dialectically on its way to the level of the Greek *Volk.* It is not yet political. The ethical reason now before us is a new immediacy, a mere certainty that still lacks truth. The immediacy consists in reason's treating ethical laws as simply *given.* This reminds us that we are in the realm of natural or non-dialectical consciousness. Ethical certainty is like sense-certainty [423]. A given law is an ethical This intuited by our natural reason. Like the sensuous This, it simply *is* [91]. With the emergence of law, consciousness rises to a higher level of being honest or "real." Honesty now takes the form of "healthy reason" or common sense, which "knows immediately what is right and good" [422]. Reason, in this form, knows *particular* laws as right and good: the law has content. The rational individual, here, is what the French moralists call the *honnête homme,* the decent and sensible man who follows the plain teachings of natural reason. In the experience of such immediately intuited laws, healthy reason will prove to be abstract. Determinate laws, far from being absolute, will show themselves to be merely contingent, a matter of "situation ethics."

Hegel picks two examples to illustrate this point: truth-telling and love of neighbor. Both embody Kant's *categorical imperative.* This is a rule of action that is in no way conditional or hypothetical, in other words, that does not have the logical, hypothetical form "if, then."[31] The law is an unconditional Ought or *Sollen.* This Ought is no mere counsel but expresses obligation or necessity. As a rational being, I am not advised but compelled to follow ethical laws. It is precisely this necessity or absoluteness that will be lost in reason's experience of the law.

"Everyone ought to speak the truth" [424].[32] Hegel shows that what is meant here is not what is actually said. Healthy reason commands me to speak the truth. But I can speak the truth only to the extent that I *know* the truth. That is, I can speak it only *on condition.* But that is not what the law said, and the law is what it says. In adding this condition of knowing the truth, I am, in effect, violating the law. Revising the law to include the condition will not save the law's absoluteness. It would only make the law explicitly situational: "Tell the truth, depending on what you know at the time."[33] Nor can I save the law by making it depend on the logically prior law: "Know the truth!" That would deprive the original law of its presumed immediacy and independence.

The second example is: "Love your neighbor as yourself" [425].[34] Hegel's analysis highlights the fact that in real life I follow moral commands in order to do good. To love someone actively is to do him good: *real* good, not my fleeting impression of good. Recalling occasions on which people (parents, for example) do harm in the name of love, I realize that I must not simply love people, but love them *intelligently* or wisely. This adds a condition to what was posited as unconditional. Moreover, effective, genuine do-gooding is best handled, not by me but by the universal action of the state [425], which can offer substantial help to, say, the poor, the disabled, or young people who need a sound education. My individual action cannot add much to this power for good and might even get in the way. Whatever an individual can do to love people by actually helping them is thus a matter of chance. Once again, the presumed absolute necessity of an ethical law, *because it is taken as something immediate,* has become a matter of mere contingency, something that may or may not be good, depending on the circumstances. My attempt to love my neighbor by actually helping him becomes the mere intention to help him, the mere *sentiment* of benevolence [425]—a non-action.

In both of Hegel's examples, the problem is not the law per se but positing a determinate law as a blanket universal that is assumed to be true apart from other laws and from how that law is applied and lived. What good is an ethical law if it cannot effectively dictate real action that is in accordance with the law, if it cannot be followed?

Immediately given laws fail to be laws because they "stop short at Ought" and "are not laws [*Gesetze*] but commandments [*Gebote*]." Their content cannot be absolute, since law is universal and individual laws are determinate or specific (and therefore conditional). This is the same problem we saw earlier in the *work,* which could not capture the universality of my selfhood as talent. The authoritativeness of the law must therefore reside in the law's universal *form*—in lawfulness. The law must be self-identical: always what it is and never what it is not, regardless of content. The ethical nature is not a specific content but only a standard or measuring-stick for deciding whether a given content can be a law or not [428]. With this move, we go from reason as giving laws to reason as *putting them to the test.*

Reason Tests the Law [429–35]

Unlike the first stage of reason in relation to the law (ethical common sense), the second stage leads to an explicit critique of Kant's moral teaching. It proceeds from Kant's claim that the moral validity of a maxim consists entirely in its *form,* in the maxim's being *free of self-contradiction.*[35] The absence of self-contradiction shows that the law is truly universal or truly a law. The individual here uses his reason, not to intuit the truth of a determinate law but to test prospective laws. In the previous stage of experience, we too tested laws. But what consciousness does here is different. It does not test a law to see whether its *content* is morally valid but rather tests only for formal self-consistency. Kant presents this test in a series of moral thought-experiments. He urges us to test a maxim (or prospective law) by imagining what the world would be like if everybody followed that maxim—if, as he puts it, the maxim were to become "a universal law of nature."[36] Kant then takes us through examples of possible maxims to show us how they give rise to self-contradiction, that is, to a situation in which my will comes into conflict with itself.[37]

The problem with testing the law in this way is that a purely formal measuring-stick never gets to the content of a given maxim. Hegel's argument is that a specific content, so long as it remains simply itself, an "isolated determinateness," will obviously prove itself to be self-consistent *and therefore ethical* [430]. Is it ethical to have private property, or not to have it? Hegel shows that both property and non-property can be shown to be either self-contradictory or self-consistent, depending on how these are taken, whether as simple or as analyzed into their moments [430].

Hegel first takes up the denial of private property or communism. He reveals that when its concept is analyzed into its moments or aspects, a contradiction results. According to the concept of communism, all goods are held in common. The problem is that this means two conflicting things: that everyone gets what he needs, and that everyone has the same amount of everything. If I need a house, this cannot possibly mean that I need it only for today. I need it for the duration of my whole life. According to the concept of communism, therefore, the house must be mine *universally.* But my need for a house conflicts with the stipulation that anyone else who needs it right now should therefore have it. Need is an emergent inequality that conflicts with permanent equal distribution. Conversely, if goods are distributed equally and permanently, then they cannot address individual emergent needs. The law "Goods should be held in common" is in tension with itself. It fails the test for moral validity.

The law "Goods should be privately owned" also contains a contradiction. The contradiction stems from the individuality of the owner and the universality of the thing owned [431]. Strictly speaking, a thing, say a house, cannot be owned in the sense of held on to forever. There will come a time when I, as owner, am gone, and the house will pass to someone else—or else be destroyed. Owning something means precisely not statically and permanently having it. Others, to be sure, recognize my house as mine. But that does not make me the eternally exclusive owner of the house. In acknowledging my right of ownership, others simply acknowledge a universal or general right of ownership for a certain period of time. Once I die, or if I plan to sell my house, the house is potentially everybody's and anybody's—a dialectical echo of communism.

These contradictions spring from the one-sidedness of reason, which treats an abstract moment as the whole and ignores the motion of real life. So long as we treat private ownership and public ownership as abstract *simples*, each ideology remains self-consistent—a valid law. But when we analyze them, each reveals its contradictoriness or moral invalidity. A purely formal test is therefore unhelpful. Indeed, it is immoral, since it can be used to justify or to condemn anything.

The presumed honesty of these two forms of ethical certainty, intuiting the law and testing the law, is thus not as honest as it seems. Both in fact are guilty, as I noted earlier, of "tyrannical insolence" [*Frevel*] [434]. In the first form, since the content of the law proves to be contingent, the law is whatever an individual says it is: he arbitrarily *lays down his law* as universal. The individual may call his caprice insight, but that is just a cover for his self-will. In the second form, the individual who tests prospective laws in order to see whether they are in fact laws insolently puts himself above all laws. He presumes to "move the immoveable." Once again, laws are reduced to "an alien caprice." The point of the test was to determine whether a maxim has the unshakeable authority and eternal self-sameness of law. But it is precisely the process of the test that undermines the authority of lawfulness.[38]

The problem here is that ethical consciousness, as it first appears, manifests itself as "only a *willing* and *knowing* by this individual" [435]. The substance of the ethical, as reason conceives it, is merely subjective. The two abstract approaches to ethical law vanish. They have shown their abstractness in the arena of experience.

The Fall of Reason and the Rise of Spirit [436–37]

Testing the law provides the transition from reason to ethicality, the first stage of spirit. It is the second negation of the "matter itself" (the first was the move from a private to a public or universal self). By testing prospective laws, and realizing that this undermines lawfulness, the individual discovers something greater than himself: law as the Not-to-be-Tested. In the very act of rationally violating the law, he discovers that law, if it is to be law, must be acknowledged as immovable and something in its own right.

Ethicality *inverts* the relation of law and individual that was present at the level of reason, and hence inverts reason itself as individual self-assertion. I do not contain ethical substance: it contains me. "I am," says Hegel, "within the ethical substance" [437], that is, within a living ethical community. Consciousness has returned into the *universal,* which contains and dwarfs the individual. The vanishing of reason's individualism gives rise to the consciousness of ethical substance, the Ought that also Is, as absolute. Self-consciousness has developed and matured into *communal self-consciousness* or the concrete ethical awareness of an actual people [435].

The law, or rather custom, is "an eternal law that is grounded not in the will of an individual, but is in and for itself" [436]. It is not a commandment that *ought to be* but a universal that "is and is valid." To obey the law is therefore not to obey a master whose commands are arbitrary, since customs embody thoughts that belong to consciousness itself. Nor does the individual merely believe in [*glaubt*] the laws he holds dear, since belief, Hegel says, is in an *alien* essence. On the contrary, the ethical self "is *immediately* one with the essence through the universality of its self" [436]. This universal selfhood is the Category, which has become the concrete unity of thinking and being. The custom of a *Volk* is concretized universal selfhood. It is also *organized.* The sense-certainty of reason, which randomly intuited this law and that one, gives way to an articulate living system that resembles the organization and gathering of properties in the perceptual thing. In our next chapter, this ethical "thing" that is a determination of the more comprehensive ethical substance will be the ancient Greek *polis.*

Reason rose from the ashes of the religious unhappy consciousness. It thought it could dispense with the divine and was completely secular. With the emergence of law as something both actual and beyond the reach of skeptical questioners, the divine re-enters the *Phenomenology of Spirit.* But this divine is something affirmed by an actual people or *Volk:* it is not the supersensible Beyond of the understanding, or the Unchangeable Self of the unhappy consciousness.[39]

Stressing the ethical *non*-alienation of man with respect to the divine, Hegel says that the difference between self-consciousness and essence is "perfectly transparent" [437]. In other words, there is an acknowledged difference between man and the divine, but this difference appears as a manifold divine *presence* in the various "masses" of Greek ethical life. These "masses," as I noted above, are the various Greek city-states: the political individualities or *spirits* that bring to life the ethical substance of Greekness.[40] They have their divine counterparts and patrons among the gods, in whom custom is grounded. The ancient city *identifies itself* with its divine patron: Athens, for example, with Athena.[41] These are not the perishable and insecure *petits dieux* of modern self-actualization but the beautiful Olympians who abide or simply *are.* In a recollection of lost Eden, Hegel calls these beings that are the divine essence of political life "unsplit spirits" [*unentzweite Geister*] and "unblemished celestial shapes," who, in their very differences, preserve "the undefiled innocence and harmony [*Einmütigkeit*] of their essence" [437]. As Harris observes, Hegel's "deliberately idealized sketch" of the Greek gods and city-states is both ironic and bittersweet (2:132–33).[42] It foreshadows the tragic *fall* from ethical Eden that will take place in the chapter on spirit.

But for now, Hegel emphasizes the glorious thing that law, *Gesetz,* has become, namely, "the unwritten and infallible law [*Recht*] of the gods" [437]. The word *Recht,* which can mean law or right, recalls what the Greeks called *themis:* that which is right because it is right, not because an individual has tested it and found that it is right. To illustrate his point, Hegel quotes Sophocles' *Antigone,* which plays a central role in the next chapter. In the words of Antigone, the *nomima* or laws of custom "are not for today or yesterday, but live on forever, / And whence they appeared, no one knows" (456–57).[43]

Laws, from this now-concrete ethical perspective, are immune to personal insight and testing. They are also immune to any effort to *derive* them [437].[44] As an example of the "ethical disposition" [*Gesinnung*], Hegel returns to property.[45] If someone leaves an object or money in my keeping, then I acknowledge it as his. The object or the money *is* his property. I acknowledge this "*because* it is *so.*" And it is so because it is the established custom of my community and expresses a concrete relation I have to a fellow citizen. Thieves are those who break with the community, not those who violate some abstract ideal of reason. If I proceeded to *test* the law of private ownership, then I could easily justify keeping what is entrusted to me by shifting my moral perspective [*Ansicht*], by sophistically redefining what is "mine."[46] I thus remain logically consistent with myself and "pass" the test. As an ethical individual who lives in a concrete human community, I *avoid* treading this "unethical path" [437]. I have no ethical qualm or Cartesian doubt that would even suggest the need for a test.

The emergence of piety seems to be a regression in the education of consciousness. How can *not* questioning be higher than questioning, piety higher than reason? Reason's mission, we recall, was to unite subject and object, self and world, and thus *bring man home.* That is what reason, in its individualism, failed to do. From the standpoint of modern enlightenment (which we meet in Hegel's next chapter), pious ethicality is obviously unsatisfying. But from the standpoint of man in search of concrete human community and a spiritual home, it is Eden. Ethical Eden is, however, only the beginning of spirit's journey. We have yet to see how individuality and thinking re-emerge, as they must, in spirit's various worlds of knowing. We must see how ethicality and piety lead, in the end, to the *perfection* of reason.

At last, we reach the end of our adventures in the Land of Reason. Every phase of consciousness is a world of knowing. But only now, with spirit, whose precise nature we have yet to discover, is selfhood *there* as an actual world [438]. Only now do we have the living whole, of which everything so far has been a part. The object-oriented modes of consciousness, the self-negating modes of self-consciousness, and the self-assertive modes of reason—all these are possible only within the social whole that is the work of spirit as universal selfhood. It is to this all-encompassing whole that we now turn.

SPIRIT

And whoever thinks another a greater friend than his own fatherland, I say that man is nowhere.
Sophocles, *Antigone*

 15

Ethical Life
Laws in Conflict

Reason is spirit, *Geist*, "when its certainty of being all reality has been raised to truth, and it is conscious of itself as its own world, and of the world as its own self" [438].[1] Spirit is the spirit of a *community*. In the phrase of Montesquieu, it is "the spirit of the nation." What for reason was a mere ideal, is for spirit a living reality: a concrete unity of self and world in an "I that is We and a We that is I." This unity first appears as the ancient Greek world—the Golden Age and ethical Eden from which man historically fell.

The transition from modern reason to the city-states of ancient Greece reminds us that the *Phenomenology* does not simply mirror the course of world history. The Greek world, Hellas, is the logical result of the previous phase of experience. It is the *truth* of reason's *certainty*. Although this world is in the distant past, it embodies the concrete unity of self and world that modern reason sought but could not achieve. Spirit *is* reason that is actual in world-history.

Hegel's chapter on spirit is the longest of the eight chapters in the *Phenomenology*. It is also more overtly historical than previous chapters. This makes it easier for us to identify the shapes that consciousness assumes and to know what Hegel is talking about. But for consciousness, the world is not yet the historically emergent whole. It is only a series of finite versions of that whole: the Greek world, the Roman Empire, modern culture, the Enlightenment, etc. History as temporal unfolding is not *for consciousness* until the very end of Hegel's book. Only then does spirit realize that its truth is its history. Moreover, only then is spirit able to give a rational *account* of that history [808].

Spirit has three stages: **Ethicality** (the Greek world and the Roman Empire), **Culture** (French society of the seventeenth and eighteenth centuries), and **Morality** (Kant's Moral World-View).[2] In its first phase, spirit is objective or *in itself:* it is only implicitly self-conscious or subjective. As ethicality or *Sittlichkeit,* it is manifest in the living law of custom, *Sitte.* In its second phase, spirit is *for itself* or explicitly self-conscious. The individual, here, is his own object, and is aware of himself as always outside himself or self-estranged [*sich entfremdete*]. As a culture creature, he experiences himself as artificial rather than natural. In the third phase, spirit is *in and for itself,* the unity of its objective and subjective moments. Here, the individual overcomes his self-estrangement through moral certainty, which has its origins in Luther's turn to the inner voice of conscience. This inward turn is the origin of the modern world.

Hegel introduces spirit by reviewing the path of reason. Reason's object was the Category, the unity of self and being. As passive observer, reason posited this unity as something *in itself,* something that simply *is.* It seized on the objective side of the Category. Then reason turned to the subjective aspect: it became active. Man, as a lone individual, asserted himself. He was a romantic hero who was *for himself* and against the Establishment. Finally, reason posited the Category as *in and for itself.* This was the concrete unity expressed in the individual who actualized himself by using his natural talent. Eventually, the Category appeared "in its universal truth" as the *Sache selbst* or *what really matters* [438]. The true *Sache* was revealed in ethical law [420]. But law, which matters to everyone or universally, turned out to be abstract. It was merely formal, a spiritual essence without substance or reality. The individual placed himself outside this essence by arbitrarily laying down laws or testing them. He was not *in* the absolute he posited: his self-consciousness was detached from his consciousness of an absolute object (the law). In sum, reason's effort to meet itself in the world failed.

Spirit, as an I that is We, does what reason could not. It is the substantive, living unity of consciousness (awareness of *being*) and self-consciousness (awareness of *self*). In ethicality, as it now comes on the scene, ethical substance (lived community) is aware of itself as the good made concrete; and the individual experiences himself as *in* this social substance. As I noted in my Prologue, spirit is fully developed selfhood. It is selfhood that has outgrown the aggression of desire, infinite longing, romantic megalomania, private self-actualization, and reason's hybris in testing ethical laws. Spirit is selfhood that finds itself in human community and mutual recognition. In spirit, the ethical essence of reason is an actual world [439].

This world appears as a people or *Volk.* It is the Greek nation, Hellas, which manifests itself as a multiplicity of warring cities bound together by common ancestry, gods, language, and customs. These are the "masses" or ethical "bodies" into which the Greek substance divides itself. Each city expresses *congealed ethicality.* Each proudly exhibits, according to its character, Greek-ness as a whole.

In his opening remarks, Hegel continues the glowing depiction of Greek ethical life with which he introduced active reason. Ethical substance, which is present in each *polis,* is "the universal work produced by the action of all and each" [439]. It is the goal and purpose of the individuals who live within this substance, and who identify with their city: the *polis* is not "the Establishment." What natural talent was to the modern achiever, ethical substance, Greek-ness, is to the ancient Greek. It is his abiding and life-sustaining element. The difference is that this social-political substance, as it appears in a given city, binds individuals rather than separates them. It does so through shared custom. The community is a "work" that does not vanish in a "play of individualities." The *polis* abides as something satisfying to the individuals that make it up.[3] Ethical substance participates in both motion and rest. In its objective aspect, it reigns supreme as the unmoving Law of the Land. But on its subjective or self-mediating side, it is a living resource, a wellspring that flows out benevolently to all its members [439]. The *polis* demands absolute loyalty, but it also sacrifices itself to its individual members as the "universal being," which each member "tears at" [*zerreißt*] and makes his own. These two aspects of the city (fatherly demand and motherly self-sacrifice) flow into each other. I respect the ethical whole, my city, as the life-giving ground of my individuality and identity. It is something my fellow citizens and I do not merely obey but constitute through our interaction. We sacrifice ourselves to the city, and it sacrifices itself to each of us. This reciprocity or flow is what makes ethical substance "actual and living" [439].

For these reasons, spirit is "self-supporting, absolute, real being" [440]. It is the whole of which *all* the previous shapes of consciousness are moments. But spirit is not just the effect of what came before: it is also the cause.[4] The journey of consciousness is the work of spirit, which "analyzes itself" and "dwells" with each of its manifestations. Spirit preserves its vanishing moments. In positing itself as something objectively real, spirit preserves the modes of *consciousness.* In focusing on itself as subjective or for itself, it is *self-consciousness.* In expressing the immediate awareness of the unity of these two moments, it is *reason.* When this unity is posited as something that actually exists, spirit comes forth *as spirit.*

The first phase of spirit, Greek ethicality, is spirit that is "in its truth" [440]. As Hegel's title indicates, spirit here is "True Spirit." Truth, in this context, is what Socrates called "right opinion" or political orthodoxy. Reason in its lawful or universal mode was spiritual essence, an ideal that lacked existence and truth. Essence now exists: the moral Ought also *is* in the concrete form of custom. But custom is immediate or unreflective [441]. Greek ethicality is spiritual truth that is concretely lived *but not deeply known.* In ethical Eden, man, in spite of his many hardships, is happy or at home in the world: he has not eaten from the modern Tree of Knowledge, and is immersed in the element of civic and family life.[5] Life, suffering, and death *have meaning.* War has meaning, as we shall see, and is by no means excluded from ethical life.

Immersed in the immediacy of custom, spirit, too, must undergo experience, the process by which the immediate is mediated. It will surmount mere truth, that is, *trust* in the social substance, in its relentless drive to self-knowledge. In its previous shapes, consciousness went from certainty to truth. In the unfolding of spirit, this polarity is reversed. Consciousness will go from *truth* in the present section to *certainty* in the concluding section on morality [596], from the ancient virtues of character (ethical *substance*) to the modern testimony of conscience (moral *subject*).[6] Nevertheless, certainty will still be the engine that propels the dialectical motion in this section. This certainty will appear in the willfulness of Antigone and Creon.

Spirit's first step beyond the garden of custom and toward self-knowledge will be a new version of formalism with respect to the law. Law will be posited, once more, as a universal abstract essence. But unlike the formalism of reason, law will be enforced on a grand scale throughout the world. This is spirit that has become imperial Rome. At this stage of its development, spirit is inwardly split [*in sich selbst entzweite*] [442]. Rome generates the rift in man that we saw in self-consciousness (Chapter 10). This is the split between the universal and the individual aspects of spirit, here appearing as the split between universal empire and individual happiness.

The split generated by Rome is further developed in the modern, self-alienated world of *culture* [*Bildung*]. Ultimately, it appears as the conflict between the otherworldliness of faith and the secular "insight" of the Enlightenment. The culture world will destroy itself in the French Reign of Terror. At its highest stage, spirit is *morality.* Morality is the great unifier that affirms all oppositions and tries to harmonize them in a coherent Moral World-View. Its highest manifestation is conscience, *Gewissen.* Conscience seems to unite the natural goodness spirit lost in its fall from ethical Eden and the once forbidden fruit of knowledge, *Wissen.* It is "spirit that is certain of itself" [442].

Greek ethicality falls because it cannot incorporate the serpent of knowledge into the garden of custom, piety, and trust. Modernity falls because man eats from the Tree of Knowledge and becomes, as we shall see, perverse, self-alienated, and ultimately life-denying as a so-called *beautiful soul* [658]. Hegel's chapter on spirit thus lays bare the fundamental problem of the modern world: how to reconcile *substance* and *subject,* to infuse life with knowledge, and knowledge with life. The problem may be put in terms of this question: How is it possible for human community to be concrete and life-affirming without being provincial and self-ignorant, and to be knowing or enlightened without becoming abstract, antisocial, and "torn"? How, in other words, can we recover Eden without ceasing to be self-conscious? And how can knowledge, which resulted in our expulsion from Eden, become the element in which we live and find our happiness?

The practical problem of modern life is the same as the theoretical problem of completing philosophy in the form of Science. Both involve overcoming the split between substance and subject. Philosophy, for Hegel, cannot *invent* a solution to this problem (as Fichte had tried to do). It does not project a utopia but must follow the lead of world spirit, as it struggles to know itself concretely. History must generate an experiential or lived solution before philosophy renders that solution self-transparent or scientific. As Hegel tells us in his last chapter, the absolute must be felt before it can be known [802]. In the long chapter on spirit, we witness spirit's struggle to experience absolute knowing as the unity of life and knowledge: to live what it knows and to know what it lives. This unity will finally appear at the end of Hegel's chapter in the Christian phenomena of forgiveness and reconciliation [670].[7]

Things to Come [444–45]

Hegel begins his analysis of ethicality with a sketch of its logical structure [444–45]. The sketch centers on action, *Handlung.* Action will tragically destroy the acting individuals, the *polis,* and the entire Greek world.

Spirit is both ethical substance and the awareness of that substance as absolute (in one's customs). In its "simple truth," spirit is consciousness, that is, the subject-object opposition. As *consciousness,* spirit "forces its moments apart from one another" [444]. As *self-consciousness,* it unites them. Consciousness is the subject-object distinction. In ethicality, this distinction is between the individual member of the community and the community itself, which is the individual's abiding substance and truth. The opposition between the two moments emerges through the individual's action. In acting, I experience communal substance as something over and above me. Action is *my* action, the subjective action of an individual self-consciousness, as opposed to the objective "standing-there" of the community. But I also *join* my awareness of self to the communal substance that is my end and purpose. My goal is not to rebel against an Establishment (Faust and Karl), or preach nobility (the Knight), or succeed as a talented individual, or flash my authenticity. It is to *be ethical.* As an ethical agent, I experience myself as both distinct from and immersed in this substance. I am, as we say, "in the spirit" of my community. To act is to *champion* ethical substance (the community) and its truth. Prior to this championing act, ethical substance is, in a sense, asleep. My action awakens this substance and makes it actual.

But this actualization of ethical substance is, alas, also its downfall. The ethical world-substance, Hellas, divides into a multiplicity of political "masses" (see [420]). These are the various cities that make up the *Volk:* Athens, Sparta, Thebes, etc. There is no modern *state* or political *self* that governs this multiplicity. Hellas is a grand and colorful political *thing:* an Also with many political "properties" or "matters" that exist in different geographical places [115]. Moreover, each of these political masses is itself a political *thing* with properties [446]. Whereas the thing of perception had many properties, the political "thing," the city, has only two: "a human law and a divine law" [445]. In other words, the political "thing" is not really an Also but an *opposition.* This opposition is the source of the city's destruction.

Human law presides over civic loyalty and participation (in the Greek Assembly and in war). It is the realm of the public and *male.* Divine law presides over family loyalty. It is the realm of the private and *female.* Prior to the individual's championing action, these masses, or spheres of life, are harmonized within the ethical whole. Everybody does what he or she is supposed to be doing. But in the individual's action, which goes beyond voting in the Assembly and taking care of one's children, they come into conflict and contradict each other. Each champion takes one ethical moment, the one that suits his nature and character, and defends it as absolute. Through its ethical champion, that moment *comes to life* or asserts itself. The champions know what they passionately defend, but only partially. They have "a deceived knowing" [445]. In action [*Handlung*] that becomes a completed *deed* [*Tat*], the individuals discover, too late, their presumption and one-sidedness. They suffer the contradiction between their knowing what is ethical, and what is ethical "in and for itself." The archetype for this conflict is the opposition between Antigone and Creon in Sophocles' play.[8] This tragedy shapes and governs Hegel's whole account of the ethical world.

Tragic action is not limited to the individual champions. It is *ethicality itself* coming to life and revealing its self-conflict. In tragic action, ethicality becomes self-conscious: aware of what it really is. Self-consciousness becomes spirit's actuality and truth. Hellas *dies* of its late-acknowledged contradiction [445]. In that death, there arises a supplanting world whose actuality *is* its self-consciousness: the world of imperial Rome.

Ethicality goes through three stages. In the first, it is a beautiful harmony of opposites: individual and universal, divine law and human law, family and state, Woman and Man. In the second, these opposites are pitted against each other and destroy ethical harmony. In the third stage, the Greek world, as I noted above, gives way to the Roman Empire. Here, ethical life becomes the anti-life of *legalism.* I am no longer real as a human being with concrete human relations—a husband, father, friend, and citizen. I am instead reduced to the blank atomicity of a colorless anonymous *person* [477].

Life as Harmony [446–63]

In the *polis,* human and divine law, city and family, Man and Woman exist in a state of beautiful balance [462]. Hegel's word for this balance, *Gleichgewicht* or equal weight, fits his description of laws as masses [421]. Greek ethicality is a system in dynamic equilibrium, the harmonious result of opposing and complementary ethical forces and "areas" of life. Hegel's goal here is twofold: to spell out the differences between human and divine law, and to reveal the process by which "each preserves and brings forth the other" [463]. The latter reminds us of the reciprocity we saw in active and passive force.

As we saw above, spirit, in its ethical simplicity or consciousness, divides itself into a human and a divine law. It is "ethical perception" [446]. At the level of reason, we had ethical *sense-certainty* [423]. This was the certainty that a moral maxim was simply true because of what it asserted (i.e. practical wisdom). In ethical perception, the self now distinguishes between its two regions of ethical life: divine law and human law, family and state. These are the "properties" of ethical substance. The ethical thing is not a *Ding* but a *Sache.* From the standpoint of ethical *action,* this "thing" is a situation or "case" [*Fall*] in which civic and family duties unite. The "law of singular individuality" applies to the family, the "law of universality" to the state or government. Each of these ethical "masses" "remains spirit in its entirety" [446].[9] To be within one realm is also to be within the other. As a family member, I am also a citizen. As a citizen, I have an obligation to raise a family.

At the level of spirit, individuality appears in a new light. It is no longer the self-consciousness "of a singular, contingent consciousness" [447]. Within Greek ethical substance, there are no unhappy consciousnesses, romantic idealists, or private self-actualizers. Universality has permeated the single individual, just as singularity has permeated universality. The individual is a citizen and family member. And the universal is manifest in the city's specific character and customs, in the city *itself* as a single individual.

The opposition between human and divine law constitutes the double life of ethical spirit. Human law is spirit conscious of itself in public custom and in the proclamations of the government, which has an authority [*Gültigkeit*] that is "open and lying in the light of day [*an dem Tag*]" [448]. Divine law is spirit as it appears in the family. Whereas human law belongs to the daylight of the conscious, the divine law of family belongs to the nocturnal realm of the *unconscious*—the realm of feeling and intuition [450]. These two realms are soon identified, respectively, with Man and Woman.[10]

Hegel starts with the human law and proceeds dialectically to the divine. Human law is ethical spirit as the government [*Regierung*]. The government governs the individual, who, as individual, is for himself [449]. But the ethical individual is not for himself as an isolated self-actualizer but belongs to the concrete private realm of the family. This politically sanctioned realm of apolitical private life has its own authority and truth. It is the *inner essence* of spirit [449], which the city is bound to acknowledge and respect. Political power, in governing, discovers and discloses its own opposite. In pressing its power on the singular individual, it feels the counter-pressure of the life governed by a power other than that of the city. This is the ethical version of Newton's Third Law.

In distinguishing these two realms, Hegel observes: "each of the opposites in which the ethical substance exists contains the entire substance, and all the moments of its content" [450]. City and family each have absolute authority over me. Family and *polis* are equally authoritative and mutually recognize each other. The difference is that the government rules me from the outside and family from within, the former by custom and proclamation, the latter through consanguinity and the wordless bonds of feeling. This twofold loyalty embodies the double relation that ethical spirit has to itself. Through civic interaction, spirit communes with itself mediately, through family ties immediately. The former self-communion is the realm of *action,* the latter that of simple *being* [450]. As citizen, I act; as husband and father, I am. As citizen, I am in motion and busy; as husband and father, I am at rest or "at home."

Hegel now turns to his fascinating account of the ancient family. His goal is to show that the family, which is a natural rather than civic community, is also ethical, that it is not based purely on natural feeling or love [451]. To find an "ethical principle" of the family is crucial here, since each law of ethical life contains spirit as a whole [446]. The family is no less ethical than the state: in a sense, it is even more so.

Natural relations are based on desire and particularity. Ethical relations, by contrast, posit their good and purpose in the whole to which an individual belongs. As a man, I love my wife. As a husband, however, I have a duty to her. As a natural father, I am fond of my children. But as their ethical father, I must see that they are properly cared for and educated. In the family, natural bonds are mixed with ethical duties. What we must find, however, is the purely ethical act by which the family distinguishes itself from the city *and* rises above nature. This distinctly spiritual deed of the family is the *burial of the dead* [451].

We reach this conclusion by reflecting on death itself. We observe that at no point during a family member's life is he complete or summed up, for at each point of life he is this particular individual subject to these particular changes of fortune. The family member is complete, and universal, only in death [451]. In death, the individual, after a life of change and turbulence, "concentrates himself into a single completed shape [*Gestaltung*]" and rests in "the calm of simple universality."[11] Only then is he a proper object of ethical action within the family. Death is the individual's ultimate *Aufhebung.* It is the dialectical transition from singularity and contingency to universality. In death, the gradually emerging song of my life is at last completed. My infinite differences at last become my unified concept. Burial makes this *Aufhebung* actual. In burial, the individual becomes fully a member of the family, which claims him as its own. And he, in turn, becomes the *daimōn* or spirit who watches over the family and avenges wrongs done against it.

Death simply happens in the course of nature. It is arbitrary and irrational. Burial, the distinctly ethical deed of the family, wrests the death of the loved one from irrational nature. It pays tribute to him as more than an individual who has died and honors him qua family member. But the burial rite is more than tribute. It also dispels the illusion that the death of the loved one is irrational and has nothing to do with conscious choice [452]. If this were true, the individual would not be a universal but only one more particular that pointlessly appeared and then vanished. He would be, in Homer's phrase, "food for dogs and birds." Burial is the act by which the family enters the natural process of death and spiritualizes it, that is, lifts it above nature. In this deliberate sublation or "taking under," the family gathers the loved one into itself. Death is thus made active and conscious. Burial protects the loved one from nature by keeping away beasts that would disfigure and defile the body through natural appetite. It is also the final *marriage,* the solemn act by which the family "weds the blood-relation to the bosom of the earth, to the elemental imperishable individuality" [452]. In burial, the loved one is not only spiritualized but also transported. He becomes a potent spirit or *daimōn,* a member of the immortal community that reigns over the Lower Regions and their destructive forces. At the next level of the dialectic, these primordial forces, with which the deceased is now in league, will be incarnated as his Erinys or fury [462].

To sum up, burial, in Greek ethicality, is "the perfect *divine* law, or the positive *ethical* action toward the individual" [453]. It is the only such law. Every other obligation toward him belongs to the daylight realm of the city.

Having presented the two laws and lives of spirit, Hegel explores their "differences and gradations"—the pervasive work of consciousness—and shows their interaction and transition into each other [454]. He begins with the government or ruling power. The government is the "simple *self* of the entire ethical substance" [455]. It is where the communal essence is "revealed in the sun" and has its "actual vitality." The city is the power that gives the family its being and its being-for-self or independence. As political rule, spirit generously grants individual families their private spheres. But the city is also a "negative unity" that brings different families together into a common whole by making them aware of their dependence on the city's all-encompassing sphere.

Families tend to isolate themselves from their civic whole. The expedient the *polis* uses to counteract this tendency is *war.* War doesn't just happen: it is necessary to the *polis.* War counterbalances the generosity of the *polis:* the city's promotion of family subgroups within the political whole. Through war, the *polis* upsets its own established order, temporarily rescinds the independence of individuals and their subgroups, thus making them aware of the greater whole. Through family, individuals enjoy their bond with nature. In war, however, the *polis* reminds them of who they ultimately are as spiritual beings that rise above nature. It forces them to confront death as their lord and master [455]. Hegel's language here recalls the educational role of fear in the life and death struggle of self-consciousness. I am free to the extent that I rise above nature. In fearing death, and by surmounting this fear in combat, I experience what it means to be a citizen. It is here that human law experiences its transition into the divine law. In sending me off to battle, the *polis* forces me to confront my mortality, the eventual loss of everything time-bound and finite, and the prospect of another, eternal world—the realm that is under the earth.

Divine law, as we know, governs the family. Its internal differentiation will culminate in a transition into human law. The relations here are husband and wife, parent and child, and brothers and sisters or siblings [456]. Husband and wife manifest mutual recognition through their love for one another. This love, however, is natural rather than strictly ethical. It is only the image [*Bild*] of an actual spiritual presence. The concrete presence is the *child* of the parents' union.[12] As we saw above, the family is a mix of natural feeling and ethical duty. Only one family relation is *purely* ethical: that of brother and sister [457].[13] Brother and sister are intimately related without any admixture of desire or sibling rivalry. They are to one another "free individualities." In the mutual recognition of brother and sister, spirit reaches a sublime equipoise within itself. It is a happy unity of opposites.

"The feminine, in the form of the sister," Hegel says, "has the highest *intuitive* awareness of what is ethical" [457]. The sister represents the family in its relation to the unconscious and eternal divine law.[14] She is inner being and feeling, as opposed to outward proclamation and civic interaction. The feminine, whose archetype is the sister, is loyal, not to the public gods of the city but to the private gods of her household, what Hegel calls, borrowing a term from Roman culture, the Penates.[15]

When we review the relations Woman has to other family members, we find that only the relation to *brother* is purely ethical, that is, free of any admixture of desire.[16] The loss of her brother, unlike that of other blood relations, is therefore irreparable, and her duty to him is the highest. Here Hegel recalls the speech in which Antigone gives poetic utterance to the sister's perspective on the family. As she descends into the tomb that is also her bridal chamber, the place where she marries Death, Antigone tells the chorus that she could, if she wished, get another husband or child, but never, since her parents are dead, another brother (909–12).[17]

The brother-sister relation is also the point at which the family loses its independence and experiences its transition into government [458]. The brother eventually leaves the family and becomes part of political life. That is, he leaves the unconscious realm of feeling and enters the sunlit realm of deeds and deliberations, the realm of human law. The sister, or else the wife and mother who remains after the father dies, is then "the head of the household and the guardian of the divine law." Thus do brother and sister reveal the ethical difference between Man and Woman. The brother-sister bond is ethicality in its immediacy. It is an intimate union of opposites, in which the sister (as Woman) stays within the family and its divine law, and the brother (as Man) represents the transition from divine to human law [459].

The male-female difference within Greek ethicality expresses both the *difference* between the two realms of spirit and their *passage* into each other. The husband is "sent out" by the spirit of the family to be independent of the family and to join the world of action and actuality, to be a public or practical man. Whereas the family fulfills his natural need, the city fulfills his spiritual need.[18] Family and city imply each other. Only together are they absolute [460]. In sending the husband out into the assembly and marketplace, the family acknowledges that only through its contact with the practical world is family something actual. So too, the city as the realm of public life respects the divine law that is guarded by the family as the ultimate source of the human law's "power and authentication." The two laws flow into each other, each acknowledging the other's sway in a moment of mutual recognition. The terrestrial, sunlit realm of the city draws its strength from the mysterious realm of the dead; and the nocturnal Underworld has its effect only in the conscious world of the city.

What reason wanted but failed to achieve is summed up in the ethical world [461]. Everything objective has been spiritualized, even death. The unsatisfying skull of phrenology is replaced by the deeper rationale of burial rites. The meaningless "given" of observing reason is replaced by custom, which is embodied in the lives and deeds of individuals. The seeker of love's delights finds an abiding pleasure in the family. And what used to be the brute necessity that destroyed happiness is now the smooth passage of the male from family to political life. The law of the heart is actualized as the hearts of my fellow citizens (the *polis* is not an Establishment). Self-sacrificing virtue is not an empty ideal, a noble intention, but is actually at work in family and city. Virtue now gets to enjoy what it has produced. Finally, the *Sache selbst,* which for reason embodied only abstract commandments, here takes on genuine content. It finds its validating standard, not in moral constructs but in deeds and real community as the Law of the Land.

The ethical world is the restful equipoise in which spirit is at home [462]. This beautiful harmony is sometimes disrupted by criminality. But justice, *Gerechtigkeit,* restores harmony, thereby making the ethical order both self-correcting and alive or vigorous. Thanks to retributive justice, the ethical harmony regularly tunes itself and keeps itself in shape, taking harsh measures when these are needed. Crime is the passing dissonance that enhances the harmony of the whole. Invigorating justice has a dual nature that fits the double life of spirit. On the one hand, it is the power of the universal over the individual who, in committing a crime, has broken away from the universal. On the other, the individual is himself the agent of the Underworld and lives on in the members of his family, especially in his sister. The greatest wrong he suffers is that of being denied burial, and the greatest deed of those in whom he lives on is to defeat the natural order that would destroy him [462]. The just deed of a Creon is to defend the city from private interest, of an Antigone, to defend her brother from the ravages of nature.

This is what the "true spirit" of ethicality is in its concept, prior to an individual's championing deed. Greek ethical life is *in itself* a world unsullied by discord. It is a syllogism in which the extreme terms of human and divine law display themselves by peaceably passing into and soliciting each other. The middle term and concrete embodiment of this passage is *marriage* [463]. This union is not merely physical. It expresses both the static difference between human and divine law and the movement from the one to the other: the Male movement from political life down to potential death in battle, and the Female movement upward from the subterranean divine law to the daylight deeds of burial rites.

In the next section, this beautiful reciprocity is destroyed by the very elements that constitute it. Equipoise will become strife.

The Tragedy of Action [464–72]

Greek ethical life is spirit in its immediate truth, its state of nature. In the *Philosophy of History,* Hegel discusses the "happy," positive relation the Greeks had to nature.[19] Here in the *Phenomenology,* this relation appears as the individual's immediate identification with family and city. Ethicality falls because of this immediacy [476]. As a claim to absolute knowing, it posits, but does not think through, the oppositions that define it. Immediacy and nature will show themselves in ethical action. This action [*Handlung*] is determined by the individual's character. Character is the fixed nature or stamp that becomes the individual's suffering or *pathos.* Character, in other words, is Fate.[20]

Hegel's analysis of the fall from ethicality is steeped in Greek tragedy. (We will return to tragedy in the context of the Greek art-religion [733].) The Greek Age, for him, is essentially tragic, as it was for Nietzsche. In tragedy, great individuals, through their strength of character, bring about their own downfall. This downfall is a transition from ignorance to knowledge. Sophocles' *Oedipus the King* is a good example of tragedy in this respect, since it revolves around what Oedipus knows, and does not know. In fact, the story of Oedipus resembles the story of consciousness in the *Phenomenology.* Oedipus and consciousness are both *driven to know themselves.* They find self-knowledge through the inversion of what they thought they knew absolutely. Both learn through suffering.[21]

It is the *Antigone,* however, that provides the paradigm and *Gestalt* for the fall of Greek harmony.[22] This play reveals all the tensions within the ethical world. In his *Aesthetics,* Hegel calls it "the most magnificent and satisfying work of art of this kind" (2:1218). The *Antigone* is the perfect tragedy because the conflict is brought about, not through private passions (like the jealousy of Othello) but through the necessary transgression of law and the conflict between two *rights.*[23] In Sophocles' play, Creon and Antigone *act* as champions of the law: he in proclaiming that the body of Polyneices (brother of Antigone and enemy of the city) remain unburied, she in defying the proclamation by burying her brother.

The negative self-experience of the "true spirit" begins with self-consciousness [464]. Greek ethicality, in positing community as the absolute, suppresses self-consciousness or individual being-for-self. The laws of city and family treat the individual per se as no more than "a shadowy unreality," a vanishing moment in a greater whole. This is the negative side of being immersed in one's ethical community. As Hegel puts it, the individual has not yet come forth as someone in his own right. His use of the term right, *Recht,* foreshadows the upcoming clash of rights between Antigone and Creon. It also looks ahead to the Roman phase of ethical spirit, where spirit expresses community as "the condition of legal right," *Rechtzustand* [477].

As Hegel's title for this section indicates, we are moving from the ethical *world* [*Welt*] to ethical *action* [*Handlung*].[24] It is helpful to compare this action with that of the rational achiever in the spiritual animal kingdom. Both are the work of self-consciousness and being-for-self. Both are instances of negativity. Both generate an opposition between doer and thing done. Both proceed from a natural given: techno-action from talent, ethical action from character. Finally, both are self-destructive. The crucial difference lies in the nature of this self-destruction. Unlike techno-action in civil society, ethical action is tragic. It involves noble individuals: character is of a higher spiritual order than *technē* or expertise. And it summons great powers that transcend the individual (city, family, and the Underworld). Most important, ethical action, unlike techno-action, produces *guilt, Schuld.* What this guilt is, and why it is necessary to ethical action, will become clear as we proceed.

In action, individual self-consciousness shows itself: "the deed [*die Tat*] is the actual self" [464]. In this deed, the ethical world is actual or real. But action, as the action of an individual who is for himself, "disturbs the restful organization and movement of the ethical world." In action, human law and divine law no longer counterbalance and authenticate each other, but undermine each other. They become warring powers. Action is the negative moment of self-consciousness that brings about the dissolution of the ethical whole. Through ethical championship, the singular individual, previously contained by the ethical whole, now becomes the abyss that swallows that whole [464].

Action solicits the greater force to which both realms of ethical life are subject. This greater force is *Fate* [*Schicksal*]. At the stage of absolute knowing, this Fate will be revealed as *world-history.* Fate, for Hegel, does not invade the ethical whole from the outside. It is not the work of gods. On the contrary, Fate is the inner necessity that springs from an individual's character.[25] The conflict we witness in the *Antigone* is not between passion and duty [465]. Nor is it the individual's inner conflict over which duty he should obey. On the contrary, the tragic individual is determined or "fated" to follow one law or the other, city or family, by character as opposed to either feeling or "free will." There is no wavering or deliberation here ("*Should* I bury my brother?"). Ethical consciousness *knows* what it has to do, and does it. This immediate firmness, as Hegel calls it, is the ground that ethical spirit has in nature, where nature has the specific function of making one protagonist male, the other female. Strictly speaking, Creon and Antigone do not *choose* to act, as though they had "options." He acts as a male loyal to the civic law, she as a female loyal to the family. It is this sexual division of labor that most clearly reveals the rootedness of "true spirit" in the immediate realm of the natural.[26]

Character compels ethical consciousness to claim as absolutely right only one aspect of the law [466]. Antigone and Creon—champions, respectively, of divine and human law—regard each other as having no right whatsoever. Each views only his or her particular law as absolute. Each therefore regards the conflict as unnecessary, as no more than "an unfortunate collision" between right and non-right [466]. One of the ethical consciousnesses forces the other into subjection. The other tries to outwit its opponent, to conceal that it has acted according to its own law. This is what we see in Sophocles' play. Creon compels family members not to bury their dead, and Antigone buries her brother and tries (at least initially) to get away with it.[27] In claiming to be absolutely right, each demonizes the other. The female champion of divine law sees in her opponent only "the violence of human caprice." And the male champion of human law sees in his opponent only "self-will and disobedience."[28] Again, these are the very accusations that Antigone and Creon hurl at each other in the play (441 ff.), where the tension between the two sides of ethicality is dramatized as a primordial "battle of the sexes."

Ethical action makes explicit the antithesis between the *known* and the *unknown.* This distinction corresponds, as Hegel notes, to the earlier distinction between the conscious and the unconscious within ethical substance [467]. *Known* here refers to the absolute insofar as it is known by consciousness: *unknown* to the absolute insofar as it is not known [467].[29] What first appeared as two-part harmony between human and divine law now emerges as a clash between two versions of right. Whereas law is ethicality in its objective wholeness, right is the individual's ethical consciousness with respect to law. Whereas the law *is,* right [*das Recht*] "takes its stand" or "insists" [*besteht auf*] [468]. It is ethical consciousness that presses an absolute right, not knowing that it champions only a partial right. As the protagonists press the right that fits their specific character, and that each knows, they are destroyed by what they do not at first know but come to know through suffering. Creon comes to know the right of family; and Antigone comes to know the right of the city. As ethical self-consciousnesses, each claiming an absolute right, they are ultimately destroyed by "the divine right of essential being," that is, by the right of the *whole* essence of ethicality. Their presumption to know absolute or divine right is destroyed by the recognition of their ignorance of absolute right. Antigone and Creon presumed to know immediately what can only be known mediately, that is, as a dialectical unity of opposites.

Hegel distinguishes ethical consciousness from consciousness in its pre-ethical sense (where the object was absolute apart from consciousness), and ethical action from the action of self-actualizing reason. The distinction helps us see why ethical consciousness is an extremist, why, from its perspective, it knows the whole or the divine and *cannot be wrong.* Unlike consciousness in its earlier sense, ethical consciousness has "drunk from the cup of substance" and become utterly one with its object (ethicality as law). For this consciousness, self and world are not independent of one another: both are immersed in ethical essence or "meaning." The ethical self is no unhappy consciousness that yearns for objective reality. It acts rather than yearns. But this action is not that of the rational achiever. Like the achiever, the ethical agent acts only on the basis of what he knows. But unlike him, he produces something that "cannot suffer any perversion of its content." The ethical deed does not have multiple interpretations. It is what it is: this particular ethical content and no other. Nor is it arbitrary, like reason's capricious positing of laws. As an ethical agent, I am not a rebel or vigilante (Karl) but an agent of the actual ethical law, which I both know and champion. My action makes real what I know to be right, and nothing beyond that [467].

The ethical essence that the individual claims to know and enact is, however, twofold. Divine right is present in both city and family (even though, from the family's point of view, the city is only the work of men). Ethical essence, as Hegel puts it, insists on its right to manifest itself in these two opposed ways—insists, that is, on the right to appear in its totality [468]. This is the divine right that transcends what Antigone and Creon know. Each knows (in the sense of recognizing as absolute) only one side of the law, and consequently neither knows the whole of divine right. Nor can they know the whole, since within ethicality each is stamped with a character that determines their allegiance: one character male, the other female. Within ethicality, nature determines one's vision and will. Antigone and Creon are fated to collide, determined by their natural allegiance to identify the whole of divine right with the side of divine right that each knows. To act ethically is to be beautifully and courageously one-sided.[30]

The doubled essence of ethical right is also the essence of self-consciousness [468]. That is, ethicality is at work not only in my simple allegiance to what I know is right, but also in my own splitting as a self that is aware of itself. Action is self-awareness made actual. When I act, I am aware of myself as acting. In a sense, I "see" myself acting. Action is my inwardness made external. In this self-splitting, I lose my immediate relation to ethical life, which suppressed my individuality. Action is mediation or non-immediacy. As an agent, I am *this* individual, aware of myself as distinct from the ethical substance. And as an individual who takes sides, I am not ethical but *for myself.*

Hegel wants us to consider, however, not so much the process of acting as the result of *having acted.* Ethical action here resembles techno-action, since it produces a work or result as something over and against the acting self [468]. This is the actual *deed* [*Tat*]. We must think of Creon and Antigone as looking at the actions they *have* committed. They acted, as I noted above, solely on the basis of what they knew and recognized as absolute right. In retrospect, they see the tragic result of their action. They see that their perspective on absolute right was only a perspective, that it was partial rather than complete knowledge. It is this retrospective realization of ignorance (the dark power of the Not Known) that transforms their action into guilt. This guilt must not be confused with modern "moral responsibility" (my actions are *my* actions) (Hyppolite, 360). Guilt is no mere awareness of ownership. It is the realization that my action was ignorant, and that in acting I falsified the very right I presumed to champion and represent.

The second tier of this negative moment is that I realize in retrospect that my action, in addition to being guilty, was also a *crime* [468]. Not only did I not know the whole of what I claimed to champion, thereby incurring guilt: I also violated the side of right that I did not recognize as right. Simple ethical consciousness, as Hegel calls it, "has turned toward one law, but turned its back on the other and violates the latter by its deed." The result of this dialectic of action is universal and devastating. All human action is guilty insofar as it proceeds from fixity of character, which spurs me to do what is right but also sets a limit to what I know or recognize as right. Action is necessarily one-sided and is therefore at odds with complete knowing, which is two-sided. Action is ethical blindness, and full knowing, in this ethical context, is only the awareness that this blindness is my own. There is no escape from criminality (which here refers to Antigone's defiance of Creon's edict). As Hegel puts it, the only innocence would be non-action. It would be like "the mere being of a stone, not even that of a child."

Ethical consciousness acts. In the wake of action, it "learns from the deed the developed nature of what it *actually* did" [469]. Again, the theme here is the tragic consequence of a one-sided insistence on right. This insistence was the result of a one-sided knowledge. Antigone and Creon are ethical forces that solicit one another, thereby bringing the whole of ethical essence to light. Contrary to what each thinks, their collision is not an "unfortunate collision" but is grounded in the very nature of ethical essence. In action, one of the two laws that define ethicality is fulfilled. In being fulfilled, it summons or, in the language of force, solicits its other as the law that has been violated. Creon's proclamation (the fulfillment of human law) presses down on and thereby provokes Antigone's burial of her brother (the fulfillment of divine law). Through the actuality and full result of these acts, both individuals, who act according to the right they *know*, are forced to encounter the right that they did *not* know.

The transition from knowledge to the discovery of one's ignorance is beautifully captured in the story of Oedipus, who realizes only after his acts that he has unwittingly murdered his father and married his mother [469]. In discovering who he is and what he has done, Oedipus is compelled to acknowledge his crime and guilt as the truth of his actions. His non-knowing or ignorance is embodied in a power that shuns the light of day and ensnares him [469]. This dark power is the unconscious right of family ties, of which Oedipus was ignorant when he killed another man in anger, solved the riddle of the Sphinx, became king, and married the widowed queen.

Antigone, however, is a more complete example of tragic ethicality. Unlike her father, she *knows who she is* (that is, who her character and lineage make her). She is aware of the law she insists on violating [470]. Her guilt is therefore "more inexcusable" than that of her father Oedipus. The full revelation of ethical action consists in the individual's realizing that his other, whom he has violated and provoked, is his own actuality and truth. Creon is the truth of Antigone, and Antigone is the truth of Creon. Each is made to feel the right of the other and in that way come to know this right. Action, which is essentially tragic, results in a reversed perspective, an *inversion* of the individual's original position. In ethicality, knowledge of the whole truth of ethicality comes about only through suffering the truth of one's actions. Quoting Antigone, Hegel says: "Because we suffer we recognize that we have erred" (926).[31] In the words of the chorus in Aeschylus' *Agamemnon*, learning comes through suffering (177).

With the dawning of this self-knowledge, the protagonists experience a tragic version of mutual recognition, *and are destroyed.* To see one's truth in one's opposite is to realize one's guilt and crime. Having put the entirety of their selfhood into the one-sided right they knew and acted upon, they can now no longer live within a substance they have experienced as transcending this one-sidedness. There is no place for them in a world that goes beyond their character-driven allegiances. Antigone commits suicide, and Creon exiles himself. For Hegel, both individuals do this in response to their recognition of guilt. In the wake of their guilty actions, they experience a "return" to ethical right by acknowledging their guilt. But this right is no longer embodied in character, which Creon and Antigone now surrender. It appears as a mere ethical sentiment [*Gesinnung*] [471], the *pathos* into which character has dissolved. It is an ethical position to which no *act* corresponds.

In the conflict between Creon and Antigone, the ethical whole has committed suicide. It has pitted its two great powers, human and divine law, against each other and has been torn apart. As finite moments of the whole of ethical right, Creon and Antigone, having invested themselves completely in their partial rights, are destroyed because their *pathos* or suffering is also their character and natural stamp—who they are necessarily. When it becomes clear through action that one side of ethicality destroys the other, that ethicality itself is unstable, neither individual can survive [471]. At this point, Hegel observes that each realizes that both suffer equally and are equally guilty. He is thinking of the lines that follow the ones quoted above. As Antigone descends into her tomb and bridal chamber, she says: "But if Creon and his people do wrong, let the evils they suffer be no more than the injustice they are doing me" (927–28).

This recognition of equal doom is important to what is now revealed. The tragic experience of Creon and Antigone shows that both ethical powers [*Mächte*], human and divine law, along with the individuals who call them into action, are equally essential. For this reason, they are "without a self" [472]. There is no selfhood, no dominant monad, in Leibniz' phrase, that belongs to ethical right *as a whole* and therefore to the individuals who presume to act ethically. There is only character, which is necessarily one-sided, and its corresponding *pathos.* Ethicality is substance without selfhood. When the two champions act and pit one ethical power against another, ethical right has a self, but only one that is broken up into opposing sides (Antigone and Creon). In order for "absolute right" to be fully manifest, both sides must be destroyed. In this twofold destruction, ethical substance comes forth as "the negative power that engulfs both sides, that is, as omnipotent and righteous *Fate* [*Schicksal*]" [472].

The Fall of Ethicality [473–76]

Hegel now spells out the downfall of Greek ethicality and its transition into the crushing power of Rome. He focuses on the clash that precedes the actions of Creon and Antigone [473]. This is the war between Antigone's brothers, Eteocles and Polyneices. The former defended the city; the latter attacked it in an attempt to gain political power.

The clash of brothers is the conflict between family, which is grounded in natural bonds, and the city. These are the two great powers and "masses" of ethical law. That there are *two* brothers shows how contingent or arbitrary nature comes into conflict with political hierarchy or exclusiveness. As Hegel puts it, the ethical necessity of unity conflicts with the natural accident of duality [473]. In the end, ethicality wins, as spirit triumphs over nature. This is also the triumph of the universal over the individual. The brothers kill each other on the battlefield through "reciprocal action." In the death of both brothers, the natural ground of the conflict is destroyed. Individuality "destroys itself." The universal "spirit of the community" then asserts its right over and above the claims of natural individuals who make the city into an arena for sibling rivalry. Creon, who represents the government or political rule, honors Eteocles, the city's defender, and punishes Polyneices, the city's enemy, by denying him burial.[32]

In this solution, however, the city (or universal power) only succeeds in knocking off "the pure peak of its pyramid" [474].[33] Denying the rite of burial to Polyneices only provokes the confrontation between human and divine law. It starts another, deeper war, which the city *cannot* win. In denying the right of burial, Creon (as the city) awakens the lower Powers that find their agent and instrument in the living. *Polyneices is now an avenging Fury in his sister.* He comes back from the dead, in spirit, to punish the city for its violation of divine right. In presuming to govern the dead as well as the living, Creon learns that "the publicly manifest spirit" has its roots in that underworld of unconscious nature [474]. The side of the law that Creon championed thus comes to know itself in its other. It experiences a tragic inversion. The city is now destroyed for having dishonored its own roots in the family, and in the family's divine right, which lies at the base of the royal pyramid.

As Hegel moves toward the conclusion of this section, he reminds us that the story-aspect of what we have observed only appears to be a contingent happening. In its depths, the conflict is not just between individuals but is, more deeply, a necessary conflict of universals within the nation as a whole [475]. These universals are Man and Woman. Human law is the male aspect of the community. It is effective in the actual government of the city (which excludes women from the Assembly). It rules by subduing the right of families to be something apart from the city. The realm of families and their separate household gods is the feminine side of the community. Whereas Man is the force for unity, Woman is the force for multiple households. These two forces oppose each other. The manly force for unity is by nature oppressive. If there is to be an ethical community at all, this force must exist, since unity depends on immersion in a communal spirit. This immersion cannot be secured unless the community interferes with the happiness of the family and absorbs individuals into the universal whole. But in pressing down on the family, civic law generates "an internal enemy"—Woman [475]. Woman is "the eternal irony of communal essence." She is ironic because she cannot take the civic law and its Assembly of males seriously as an absolute.

Woman, in Hegel's portrait, champions the force of vigorous male youth over that of prudent old age. She favors the son who becomes lord of his mother, the brother as one in whom a sister finds her equal, and the youth of another family, who marries her daughter. All this is the world according to Woman's point of view within the ancient city. It is precisely the private perspective and world that the community as a whole, represented by Man, must suppress if there is to be a concrete unity. Through his politically repressive attitude, Man makes Woman into his enemy.

The principle of privacy and separateness is evil [*böse*], since it undermines the ethical unity on which both family and city depend. This principle of corruption, as Hegel calls it, would be powerless if the community itself did not acknowledge and promote youthful manhood as the power and military might of the whole [475]. In other words, the city, for reasons that are alien to Woman, seconds Woman's private worship of male youth. But it does so in a way that disrupts the family and gives Woman further ground for resentment. The city is *for others,* that is, has a relation to other cities, from which it must defend itself. It is, in this respect, like the thing of perception: it is for itself insofar as it is for others, and for others insofar as it is for itself [128]. War is the actuality that makes political identity explicit. In war, the principle of singular individuality, which the city sought to suppress, is put into the city's service.

War is the ultimate truth of the ethical community. In war, the male youth, Woman's idol, "now has his day and his worth is openly acknowledged." He has been co-opted, wrenched from the family, by the universal. But war, as the realm of male excellence, is also the realm of chance. The being and unity of the community, in other words, depend on strength and luck. The city is not self-sustaining. It does not depend on the inner, self-necessitating work of its own ethical spirit. For this reason, "*it is already decided* that its downfall has come" [475]. Just as the "national spirit" or city consumed and absorbed families and their divine guardians, so too an all-encompassing "*universal* community" now consumes cities along with their "living spirits" or gods [475].[34] Athens and Athena "go down" together. Individual cities are now *aufgehoben* within the more encompassing whole that they produced through their mutual conflicts.

This power that consumes cities and cancels their independence is *Rome.* Rome is Fate in a new form—Fate detached from character. It is the new spirit of a new world order. Hegel portrays the transition from the Greek to the Roman spirit as a *descent into the underworld.* Whereas the universality of Greek ethicality was a vibrant whole in which the individual found his substance, the universality of Rome is "bereft of spirit and dead." It is alive only in the single individual qua single, the individual as a human This.

For Greek ethicality, the law was given or immediate. It was determined by the natural difference between male and female. This natural immediacy is the "germ of corruption" that causes spirit to fall [476]. As the equipoise of opposites, Greek spirit enjoyed two forms of "rest": the unconscious rest of family and the restless rest of civic interaction. Hegel's emphasis on rest highlights the connection between Greek harmony and the natural goodness of Eden. The *action* or anti-rest of individuals reveals the conflict with this harmony, the contradiction between *spirit* as political community and *nature* as the right of family. Rome is the loss of naturalness and rest. Individuals here are no longer at home within the substance of the community, which is no longer a spirit that dwells within them. Hegel's concluding image is that of shattering or bursting. The living, natural whole that once was the spiritual home of man—Hellas and its distinctive city-states—is shattered [*zersprungen*] into "many points or atoms" [476].[35] With the rise of imperial Rome, the singular human being is absolute—and alone.

The Degradations of Personhood [477–83]

Ethical Eden made man happy at the expense of his self-consciousness or individuality. Happiness was immersion in the communal substance. In its Roman phase, spirit posits individuality as absolute, not in the abstract manner of reason but as the principle of an actual world. In this world, individuality appears in two forms: the individual bearer of legal rights and the emperor. Individuals gain absoluteness by losing their character. They become *persons*, human atoms who enjoy legal status or *Rechtzustand* [477].[36] That which makes the individual absolute, here, is the very thing that degrades him. The individual ceases to be a family member and citizen, and is transformed into a property owner. Right of ownership is now the basis of mutual recognition. Whereas ethical man is and acts, the person *has*.[37]

The Roman phase of spirit is the transition from Greek immediacy and naturalness to modern self-consciousness and artificiality. The next major phase of spirit is culture or *Bildung*. Its defining characteristic is *alienation* [*Entfremdung*]. In the few pages Hegel devotes to imperial Rome, we witness the dialectical emergence of this alienation, which haunts the course of modern history and man's quest for happiness.[38]

Greek ethicality lacked self-consciousness. It had a male self and a female self but no *single self* or dominant monad that held it together. Rome is the selfhood that corresponds to this new and higher unity. Here, there is no male law and female law. There is just law, and all persons are equal before it. Rome as a new shape of spirit came on the stage when cities negated each other in war. It was the all-consuming *fatum* that was vastly more powerful than Fate as character. Hegel now identifies this *fatum* with self-consciousness. Rome is ethicality that has been *reflected into itself* or made self-conscious. The might of Rome bears down on cities and individuals alike. It is the restless I that appeared in the chapter on self-consciousness, now made into an actually existing world.

The transition from Greece to Rome signals a shift from *substance* to *subject* [17]. In its first appearance, self-consciousness or being-for-self was aggressive. It manifested itself as a fight to the death. Here that aggression is replaced by what Hegel calls brittleness [*Sprödigkeit*] [478, 482], which stands in sharp contrast with the beauty and fluidity of Greek life.[39] Whereas ethicality made the community real and the individual a passing "shade" [477], Roman legality makes the individual real and community unreal. The lack of real community is reflected in the brittle simplicity of human points. The dignity of these points or atoms consists in nothing more than hardness or resistance to intrusion, in the negative "Do not violate my property!" There is no Greek fluidity in the self-conscious individuality of Rome, no passage of the individual into communal substance, and no fluid interaction between city and family [478]. Moreover, mutual recognition is only abstract or formal: I respect your legal right to your property, and you respect mine. All relations in this new world of knowing are external—just what one would expect from mutually repelling human atoms. The model for Roman life is the world as Lucretius depicts it in his poem, *On the Nature of Things*. We are hard selves moving meaninglessly in a void, united only through the external force of the emperor.

As we saw in Chapter 9, self-consciousness as stoic and skeptic sprang from Roman soil. Hegel now takes us back to these shapes and gives us the actual world to which they belong. At the end of the section, we also meet, once more, the unhappy consciousness, which is the *truth* of Rome.[40]

The stoic represented a "flight from the actual world" [479]. Rome's legalism embodies this flight. It mirrors the stoic's attempt to find freedom in pure thought. Just as the stoic, in his abstract freedom, is the ghost of a fully alive human being, so too, the person who enjoys legal standing is a stripped-down self that is "not tied to a richer or more powerful existence." The stoic takes the legality that pervades his Roman world of knowing and distills it into an abstract principle that governs his life (pure thought). Moreover, just as stoic abstraction was actual in the skeptic's annihilation of order, the abstract legalism of Rome is actual or at work in the disorganization and confusion of Roman life under the empire [480]. Since I am no more than a person before the law, the content of my life is left completely to my passions and caprice. The law does not form or train me: it simply protects my rights. It is abstract. In general, for Hegel, abstract means "lacks content." The lack of content in Rome's legalism is evident in the concept of property, which can be anything whatsoever. The law is completely indifferent to what my property happens to be. From the formal legal standpoint, the only thing that matters is that what is mine, is mine.[41]

The power that holds all the human atoms together is concentrated in yet another atom or monad, "alien to them and bereft of spirit as well" [481]. This is the emperor: "the Lord of the World."[42] All other atomic humans are empty and impotent. He alone is "absolute power and absolute actuality." They have property rights under the law, but the dominant monad possesses things themselves in abundance. He is, in Shakespeare's phrase, "the universal landlord."[43] He is the true owner of the whole, whereas others have what they have only on rental.

The emperor's substance is his power. But he is powerful only insofar as he lords it over the lower monads. He is like the master, whose truth is in the slave. Apart from the slave-monads, the emperor is "a non-actual impotent self," impotent because he lacks self-control.[44] Like them, he has no inherent form or organizing principle. The content of his selfhood is nothing but a storm of violent passions, which he has the means of gratifying on a grand scale. These "spiritual powers" and "elemental beings" roam and fight in the seething underworld of the emperor's soul.[45] For this reason, the Lord of the World is also the world's most abject slave, all the more a slave for thinking of himself as "an actual living god." He is the *ungeheure* self-consciousness, the Self that is both titanic and monstrous [481].[46] His soul is that of Rome herself.

The emperor becomes fully aware of who he is by destroying the selfhood of his subjects [482]. His negative relation to them embodies the purely negative relation they have to each other. These individuals learn that he, the master self, is the only true self, who alone has substance, power, and content. But their selfhood is not authenticated in his. He keeps his substance and authority all to himself and does not let it flow out into others. As we saw, this master consciousness, a slave to its passions, cannot enjoy its surpassing wealth, power, and prestige. In finding its actuality only in destruction, it ends up throwing away its own self-consciousness.[47] The emperor is outside of or *beside himself* [*außer sich*]. His mind is not his own. We think of the distraction and pathological brooding of Tiberius, the madness of Caligula and Nero, the gross excesses of Commodus, and the melancholy of Marcus Aurelius.[48]

In the master-slave dialectic, the master fell by the wayside. The partial *Aufhebung* or sublation occurred in the slave, who finds himself in his work [196]. Having described the degradation of the Roman "master" consciousness, the "absolute being," Hegel now turns to the slave or person-consciousness that is "driven back into itself" [483]. This consciousness, unlike that of the world's master, is reflective. It is reflective because it is not the master and has been prevented from having any inherent actuality. This consciousness is not beside itself. It *thinks*. This thinking generates the three shapes of self-consciousness we met earlier: stoic, skeptic, and unhappy consciousness. All three manifest thinking as a flight from the world and the world's madness and contingency.

The unhappy consciousness was the truth of the stoic and skeptic. But that truth was limited by the one-sidedness of consciousness, which at that point was locked inside its mere subjectivity and did not connect its unhappiness with the actual world of Rome. That connection is now apparent. The Roman slave-consciousness or dehumanized person sees in the master-consciousness the "universally acknowledged authority," in which it has no share whatsoever [483]. The selfhood of the person is alienated from all worth and power. The individual sees selfhood as actual, but not in himself, only in the Imperial Self, which arrogates to itself all worth and power. The former slave at least had his work. But the Roman person, qua person, has no work in which to contemplate himself as essential. The only actual selfhood is that of the emperor, from whose selfhood all other selves are alienated. The individual thus experiences selfhood as the *perversion* [*Verkehrung*] of selfhood—as actual selfhood that is outside itself.

Selfhood, as the unhappy consciousness of mere persons, is alienated from itself [*sich entfremdet*] [483], alienated, that is, in the actual here and now. In its Roman phase, this self-alienation is something suffered. But in the determinate negation of this suffering, spirit posits self-loss and self-alienation as necessary to its goal of achieving universal selfhood. Alienation becomes its *project.* This next shape of spirit is the world of *culture,* which heralds the beginnings of modernity. Culture, *Bildung,* is the process by which I give myself form, *Bild.* The process involves self-negation. As a thinking individual imbued with the spirit of culture, I re-make myself by destroying everything in me that is immediate and natural. I systematically destroy the principle of ethical Eden in order to constitute a new order. The world that spirit was given is now replaced by the world that spirit makes for itself.

Cast your sight down, and see how far you have turned.
DANTE, *Paradiso* 27

16

Interlude

WE ARE NOW AT THE BOUNDARY BETWEEN THE ANCIENT AND THE modern worlds of spirit. At this advanced stage of our journey, let us pause before moving on. Where are we in Hegel's book? What remains? And what is the shape of the whole journey of consciousness? In this chapter, I will briefly address these questions. Also, since Christianity is central to Hegel's treatment of the modern world, it will be helpful to distinguish its three appearances in the *Phenomenology of Spirit.*

A View of the Whole

Reading the *Phenomenology* is often so difficult that the whole tends to disappear in our struggle with individual words, sentences, paragraphs, and transitions. The forest vanishes, and we are left with gnarly trees. When this happens, we must go back to the simplest formulations of Hegel's project. We should remind ourselves that Hegel's goal is to transform philosophy as the love of knowing into actual knowing [5]; that the key to this transformation is the dialectical nature of selfhood; that logic, for Hegel, is a logic not of thought merely but of being and life; and that spirit, selfhood that is concrete and universal, comes to know and to be itself through suffering, which is the experiential process of self-positing, self-negating, and rising up.

Diagrams provide another aid to seeing the whole. The First Diagram (facing page) shows the stages of the entire journey of consciousness. It shows us where we've been and what remains. The diagram simply follows Hegel's table of contents from top to bottom. But since the *Phenomenology* is an *ascent* to divine knowing, a more telling picture would start at the bottom and work its way up. It would resemble the divided line of Plato's *Republic* (6.509D ff.), or Diotima's love-ladder in the *Symposium* (210A–212C). Read vertically, Plato's line depicts the ladder by which the

First Diagram: An Overview

Consciousness. The truth is a *thing.*
- a) as an immediate One [This]
- b) as a mediated One [thing with properties]
- c) as a dynamic One [force]

Self-Consciousness. The truth is the *self.*
- a) as natural being-for-self [life and desire]
- b) as independent being-for-self [warrior and master]
- c) as free being-for-self [stoic, skeptic, unhappy consciousness]

Reason. The truth is the *unity of self and thing.*
- a) unity as observed in nature [empirical science, logic and psychology, physiognomy and phrenology]
- b) unity as imposed through action [Faust, Karl, Knight]
- c) unity as self-actualization [techno-action, law giving, law testing]

Spirit. The truth is a *world.*
- a) as ethical substance
- b) as self-alienated [culture] ←WE ARE HERE.
- c) as a moral universe [morality and conscience]

Religion. The truth is the *unity of Man and God.*
- a) through nature [natural religion]
- b) through art [Greek religion as art]
- c) through divine self-manifestation [Christianity]

Absolute Knowing. The truth is the *unity of Man and God, Time and Eternity, rendered conceptual as Science.* It is TRUTH.

---

soul makes its ascent out of the cave of opinion and toward the sunlight of wisdom.[1] It has four parts: imagination [*eikasia*], trust [*pistis*], understanding [*dianoia*], and intellection [*noēsis*]. Hegel's *six-part* divided line has its "bottom" in the cave of natural consciousness, and its "top" in the sunlight of absolute knowing. The Second Diagram (next page) illustrates what such a line looks like with all the subsections omitted.

Natural consciousness, we must note, is not a stage of the journey but the condition from which consciousness must be converted. At the level of absolute knowing, the subject-object distinction that defines consciousness is obliterated. Replacing it is the absolute identity of thought and being. This identity is developed in Hegel's *Science of Logic.* In the diagram, this Science appears above the line and corresponds to the Platonic Good, the source of being and intelligibility. Logic fills out and articulates what has been achieved through experience: the condition in which thought has been purged of illusion and is now open to the whole.[2]

Second Diagram: Hegel's Divided Line

SCIENCE OF LOGIC

6. ABSOLUTE KNOWING ↑	the human-divine Logos of the Whole
5. Religion	concrete unity of man and God
4. Spirit	universal self as world
3. Reason	unity of self and thing
2. Self-Consciousness	the self
1. Consciousness	the thing

NATURAL CONSCIOUSNESS

The straight line is, of course, inadequate to the true shape of the journey. Thinking, for Hegel, goes in circles. Moreover, each successive stage of the journey is not only higher than the previous stage but also more encompassing. Higher stages contain lower ones. Absolute knowing is the most encompassing circle. It contains every preceding stage and every opposition that has appeared along the way. It is the circle of circles. The Third Diagram (facing page) depicts the levels of our divided line as a series of concentric circles. The circles represent the major worlds of knowing. The arrows remind us that a given world defines itself through self-mediation or dialectical motion. The dashed curves represent the transition from one realm to the next. The resultant spiral depicts the whole journey from consciousness to absolute knowing.[3] And the outermost circle, the circle of circles, is the eternal contemplation of spirit's past. In his final chapter, Hegel will call this recollection [808].

To attempt pictures of this, or any, sort is to realize the unpicturableness of thinking. Our circle diagram portrays an ever-expanding domain in the form of a spiral. But it fails to capture the transition from one circle to the next as the result not of a going around and out but of a turning inward. When a mode of knowing is refuted, it falls up, as I noted in Chapter 14. But it does this by being driven back into itself. That is, experience is a process by which a mode of knowing becomes reflective. We could try to re-draw our circles, this time adding vectors or spokes that show motion away from, and back, toward a center. But this would only produce a picture that was cluttered and confusing.

Pictures help. And it is in our nature to be "greedy for images," as Socrates describes himself in the *Republic* (6.488A).[4] Pictures capture aspects

Third Diagram: The Circles of Knowing

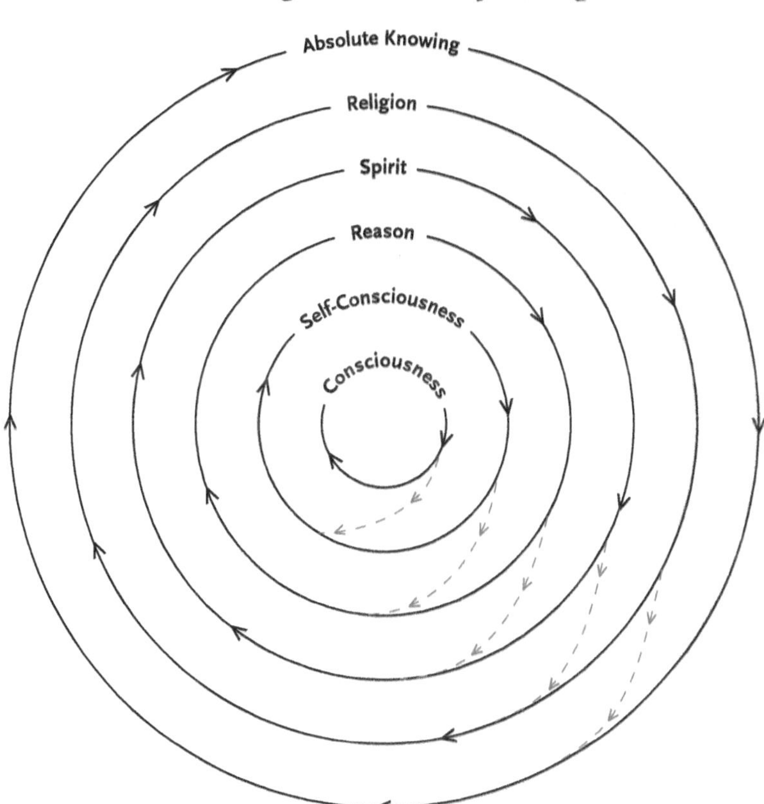

of thinking, but they do not capture thinking itself. They help us but also introduce false notions of what we seek to picture. To learn this lesson from our three diagrams is to re-live the lesson of phrenology. Pictures are skeletons. They help us to see static structures. Some are more revealing than others. But they can also indulge the illusions of materialism, or the schematizing formalism Hegel attacks in his Preface [50 ff.]. There is no diagram that shows what thinking itself is. There is no visible thing—neither our body nor any line we might draw—that captures the invisible nature of spirit or mind.

Let us now turn from pictures to the motion that connects the stages of consciousness and makes the journey continuous. This motion is mediation, *Vermittlung.* Mediation in the *Phenomenology* is the self-negating process of experience. By "thinking itself through," consciousness makes its ascent up Hegel's divided line. Experience or mediation, in other words, is not merely passive. It actively generates the stages of consciousness; or, as we may also say, it generates its own suffering. As we saw in Chapter 5, Hegel inherits this identity of action and passion from Leibniz' account of active and passive force.

In his Preface, Hegel speaks of the abhorrence of mediation [21]. This abhorrence derives from the fear of death. Truth, for Hegel, comes only through negation, and negation is a kind of death. In "tarrying with the negative," the philosopher looks death or non-being in the eye. His patient dwelling with the negative is the magical force [*Zauberkraft*] that transforms death and non-being into life and being [32]. Dialectical thinking overcomes the fear of death by incorporating death. In grasping this connection between truth and negation, and between negation and death, we begin to see why Christianity, with its doctrine of the God who suffers and dies in order to rise again, thus reconciling man and God, provides Hegel with the authoritative image for philosophic *logos.*[5] As Hegel says in his *Philosophy of History,* the essence of Christianity is mediation (377), the process in which the loss of self produces the finding of self.

The journey of consciousness begins in the immediacy of natural consciousness and ends with mediation as the unity or reconciliation of man and God. By now we have witnessed many examples of mediation in the rise and fall of various worlds of knowing. Some falls were more significant than others. The most tragic was that of the Greek world. To say that these worlds of knowing are mediated is to say more than that they came to be and passed away, or negated themselves. In this negation or death, they also revealed themselves, as they became articulated and shapely. As Hegel tells us in his Preface, mediation is "self-moving self-sameness" [21]. It is identity spelling itself out and thinking itself through, identity that reveals itself in the process of othering.

It is clear from our second diagram that culture, the second level of spirit, is on a very high rung of Hegel's ladder. Let us recall how we came to be at this advanced stage.

In the dialectic of sense-certainty, perception and understanding, objectivity loses its claim to truth. Despairing of external objects, consciousness turns to itself and becomes self-conscious. Self-consciousness is "the native kingdom of truth" [167], and the rest of the *Phenomenology* is the story of man as self-consciousness. The self now realizes that its search for truth is also a quest for freedom and happiness. With self-consciousness, the *Phenomenology* comes to be about the good (or freedom) as well as the true. But in its uneducated subjectivity, the self eventually despairs of *itself* and becomes an unhappy consciousness. It yearns for a God—a pure Self—that it can never reach.

Reborn as reason, consciousness renounces all this suffering and self-negation and becomes positive or self-affirming. The rational individual seeks his happiness in this world rather than in some atemporal Beyond or in God. He tries repeatedly to bring about the unity of self and world. But in the dialectic of law reason generates its opposite—piety. Law becomes something eternally abiding and profoundly mysterious. It is transcends reason, yet appears in the actual world.

At this point of Hegel's divided line, the divine re-appears. It is the not-to-be-tested Law that governs the Greek family and city-state, the law that *is.* As spirit, universal selfhood manifests itself as an actual world, law as custom. In this world, individuality is the opposite of what it was for reason. It is not free-roaming and abstract but immersed in communal life. It is selfhood that has "drunk from the cup of [ethical] substance" [467]. Selfhood here is not self-consciousness or being-for-self but *character.* This is individuality that is thoroughly conditioned by the natural distinction between male and female. The finitude of character is a tragic limitation of human knowledge. It brings the ethical world to ruin.

With the fall of the Greek world, the individuality that was suppressed in political community asserts itself as the world of Rome. No longer defined by character, individuals are now persons with property rights. They are intensely aware of their individuality. But personhood and legal standing are also the source of rigid formality, merely external relations, inner disorder, and emptiness. Community is replaced by the Lucretian chaos of human atoms moving in a social void. There is only one true self, the emperor. In him, individuals experience themselves as cut off from their selfhood, meaning and worth. They are unhappy or alienated from themselves. Unlike the subjective unhappiness we met earlier, this unhappiness is a whole world of woe.

And so we arrive at culture. Culture is the determinate negation that emerges from the universal unhappiness of Rome. It makes Roman alienation into something positive. The individual here willingly negates or alienates his nature in order to become cultured or formed, thereby making himself substantial and worthy of recognition.

The Appearances of Christianity

My attempt to review the whole of Hegel's book brought us to Christianity as the religion of mediation or rationality. The ascent of spirit reaches its penultimate moment in the *Phenomenology* in religion, the highest point of which is Christianity. In Hegel's rationalization of Christian faith, Christianity becomes a sort of John the Baptist to philosophy as the Word Incarnate. It is the poem or *Mythos* that points ahead to the divine *Logos* of philosophic

Science, the rational unity of man and God. In the move from the penultimate stage of religion to the ultimate realm of absolute knowing, Mediator or Person (the Holy Spirit) becomes mediation as Concept.

Christianity has three appearances in the *Phenomenology of Spirit:* the unhappy consciousness, faith, and religion. The following is a brief account of how they differ from one another.

The **unhappy consciousness,** as we saw, was purely subjective, a religious romantic. It was trapped inside its misery, infinite yearning, and efforts to reach God on its own. Its attempt at works came to naught. In its despair and alienation, it handed itself over to ecclesiastical authority as mediator when all its efforts failed. In this critique of early medieval Christianity (and indirectly of Catholic romantics in his own day), Hegel sets the stage for the liberation of Christianity that comes with Luther and the Reformation.

The second appearance of Christianity is **faith.** It occurs at our present stage, the stage of culture. Through faith, man reaches a higher level of his relation to God. Faith is unhappiness that knows the perversity of the cultured City of Man and looks ahead to future happiness in the City of God. The believer still longs for God as the one true Self. He is alienated, still unsatisfied in the *Diesseits* or This World. But he interprets his longing and his being-in-the-world positively, as the progressive casting off of his fallen nature. Moreover, he affirms his faith *as an individual,* unimpeded by institutionalized mediators. Seen through the eyes of faith, life is not only a Vale of Tears but also a purification and pilgrimage. The believer looks beyond his unhappy present to an actual Kingdom where, in an utterly transformed condition, he will be happy with God.[6]

We will have more to say about faith when we turn to culture and the battle between faith and reason. For now we simply note that faith, though still subjective, directs its attention to something objective or actual without the mediation of ritual and priesthood. It is higher than the desperate unhappy consciousness.

Finally, Christianity appears as **religion** in the chapter that bears this name. It has three phases: oriental nature-religion, Greek art-religion, and manifest religion or Christianity [683]. Just as faith is higher than the unhappy consciousness, religion is higher than faith. It is faith that has shed its subjectivity and become objective or actual. In his discussion of culture, Hegel calls faith "a flight from the real world" [487]. Religion by contrast is man's consciousness of God as present. In religion, spirit thinks itself *as spirit,* that is, as divine manifestation: "The self-knowing spirit is, in religion, immediately its own pure self-consciousness" [677].

Religion is not just higher than faith: it is also higher than all the stages that have appeared up to that point. In the chapter on spirit, Hegel presents three worlds: the ethical world, the culture world, and the moral world.

Religion is higher than all three. The reason is that in its three merely social manifestations, spirit makes an objective, concrete whole *but does not see itself in that whole* [677]. It is conscious of this social world or community as the object it has produced. But this object does not contain or reflect spirit's consciousness of itself as the divine source of the world. To use an image from Chapter 10, spirit does not self-consciously occupy and animate the house it has built. As religion, especially manifest religion, spirit becomes self-conscious, aware of itself as the pure thinking that has made the world. In Hegel's final chapter, this divine self-awareness is the philosophic, purely conceptual grasp of the whole—Science.

Christianity makes its final appearance in the closing lines of Hegel's book. The *Phenomenology* is "conceptually grasped history," and history, in its actual existence, is the Golgotha or Skull Place of absolute spirit [808]. In his Introduction, Hegel compared the journey of consciousness to the Stations of the Cross, that is, the Passion of Christ [77]. The *Phenomenology* is thus the logical reconstruction of God's suffering in time. It is the process by which God comes to know himself—and fully *be* himself. In an early work, Hegel posed as the ultimate goal of philosophy what he called "the speculative Good Friday."[7] This is the philosopher's re-thinking of the death of God. In the *Phenomenology of Spirit*, Hegel accomplishes this goal.

It was culture itself [Kultur] that inflicted this wound upon modern humanity.
Schiller, *On the Aesthetic Education of Man*

17

Culture as Alienation

Culture is the most historically vivid entry in Hegel's picture gallery. Here we meet the idols of modern society: power, wealth, prestige, utility, sophistication, and wit. Of particular interest are the diseases of *language* that afflict man as a creature of culture: flattery, chatter, and nihilistic banter. This part of Hegel's account is a stunning instance of philosophy as pathology.

This middle section of the long chapter on spirit has three parts: "The World of Self-Alienated Culture," "The Enlightenment," and "Absolute Freedom and Terror." In this chapter, I examine part one; in the next, parts two and three.

Bildung is a central term in Hegel's book. In his Introduction, Hegel defines the *Phenomenology* as "the developed history of the education [*Bildung*] of consciousness itself to the level of Science" [78]. The verb *bilden* means "give something form or shape."[1] In its most general sense, *Bildung* or culture is spiritual formation.[2] In Hegel's present chapter, it has three basic meanings. It is: a) the process by which individuals become cultured or civilized and thus worthy of recognition, b) civil society or the milieu in which these individuals live, and c) civilization as the universal process by which European civil society developed over the course of centuries. Historically, culture begins with the fall of Rome and the rise of Christianity.[3] Its highest embodiment is seventeenth- and eighteenth-century France. In this middle section of the chapter on spirit, we witness the dialectical path by which French society, in its progression from early feudalism to monarchy, culminates in two devastating negations: intellectual chaos (or nihilism) and the social-political chaos of the French Revolution.

Bildung is human development or self-making. It is progress in the realms of the scientific, economic, and aesthetic. In its present context, culture is precisely *not* the formation of man as a moral being.[4] Modern European society proceeds from Rome's disintegration of ethical community and the virtues of character, and from the production of isolated human atoms.[5] The absence of an ethical whole is the soil out of which culture grows. In the course of the dialectic, culture will reveal itself as perverse and manic. Morality, the *German* world of spirit, will be the determinate negation of culture—and its antidote.

The three stages of spirit in Hegel's chapter show an historical progression. Spirit's first world is Greek (true spirit that is objective or in itself), its second French (alienated spirit that is for itself), and its third German (spirit in and for itself). Later, Hegel will present a triad that underscores the importance of Rome: he will distinguish three worlds of *Self* [633]. History is the unfolding of the tensions within man as self-consciousness. Since Greek ethicality is spirit as substance rather than subject or self, it is, strictly speaking, pre-historical—Eden before the fall. The worlds of self begin with Rome. The Greek world is the prelude to the great fugue of history. The three "subjects" or themes of this fugue are Rome, France, and Germany. These nations embody three forms of self: the *legal* self or person, the *cultured* self, and the *moral* self.

In my Prologue, I noted that the focus of our study would be the self and Hegel's identification of man and self-consciousness. Self-consciousness was suppressed in the Greek life of substance. It came to the fore as the principle of a world and of human life with imperial Rome, the first world of self or subject. But in the Roman world, man's self-consciousness was his misery. Here, at the level of culture, self-consciousness becomes the creative energy of self-formation. Culture, or refined subjectivity, will give us a further opportunity to explore what it means for man to reveal himself by saying "I."

Alienation

As Hegel's title for this section indicates, culture is "self-alienated spirit." This contrasts with the true or substantial spirit of ethicality. To understand the title, we must examine two closely related terms: externalization [*Entaüßerung*] and alienation or estrangement [*Entfremdung*]. Although their meanings often overlap, one can observe the following general distinction. Externalization is the process by which the self experiences itself as outside itself and therefore other than itself. It is the first stage of the process by which the self gains access to itself by making itself into an object. Alienation is the "stronger" term (Hyppolite, 385).[6] It is the process by which the self externalizes itself in such a way that it does not recognize itself in its externalization and is therefore thrown back on itself and rendered self-conscious.

We have seen many examples of these processes. Greek ethical life is the paradigm of non-alienated externalization. Ethical individuals are at home in the world. They see themselves in each other and in their community, as well as in their gods, customs, and institutions. Spirit itself is a *good* externalization. It is "the knowing of its own self in its externalization; the essence that is the movement of retaining the sameness with itself in its being other" [759]. I quoted this passage earlier (Chapter 1) in describing spirit as fully developed selfhood, selfhood that has come to terms with the duality inherent in self-consciousness.

Alienation first appeared with the slave. The slave unites alienation and work. He makes things for the master and so becomes external to himself, an object. As a worker, he invests himself in the thing he makes. This thing embodies him. In externalizing himself the slave is also alienated. He sees in the product of his work not his own selfhood but that of the master, whom he fears, obeys, and serves.[7]

The paradigm of alienation is the unhappy consciousness. Consciousness here splits into two selves that are external to each other, one impure, the other pure. The impure self yearns for God as the true Self from whom it has been estranged. Unable to alienate its corrupt nature on its own, the unhappy consciousness ultimately alienates itself by handing over its life, wealth, free choice, and salvation to the Church. This subjective or private self-alienation becomes a world of alienation with pagan Rome. The emperor is the master Self, in whom other individuals experience the loss of self.

Alienation also appeared at the level of reason. Faust experienced his knowledge and rectitude as alienated from life. He tried to undo this self-alienation through seduction (Faust's version of *work*) only to generate a far worse alienation in the brute necessity that destroyed pleasure. Karl experienced alienation when he tried to actualize the law of his heart. He was driven to frenzy when he could not recognize himself in the band of thieves he himself had created. Finally, the modern self-actualizer tried to make himself real by "outering" himself in his achievements. But he became self-alienated. His works were appropriated by other self-actualizers, who made what was his theirs.

Rome is alienation writ large: the misery of the world. Culture transforms this misery into an active principle. Self-alienation is now consciously posited, *willed,* as the necessary means to the individual's happiness and universal significance. Politically, alienation appears in the contract theories of Hobbes, Locke, and Rousseau. Rousseau in particular (in many ways the central figure in Hegel's analysis of culture) stresses the concept of alienation in his *Social Contract.* There he defines the meaning of the verb *aliéner* as hand over, sell, or transfer (I, 4). To alienate is, in Latin, to make *alienum* or other. As a noun, *alienus* is a stranger or alien. To alienate is to make what is mine no longer mine, to make it a stranger to me. The modern authors mentioned above all assume, contrary to Aristotle, that man is by nature asocial. They hypothesize a *non*-communal state of nature, in which man has a natural right to all things. In entering civil society, man gives up or alienates this right. He destroys himself as a natural being in order to gain worth as a social being. In Rousseau's formulation, man renounces his "natural liberty" in exchange for "civil liberty" (I, 8).[8]

For Hegel, alienation is, most generally, a *logical function.* It is the pervasive instability and unrest of the culture world, where everything is defined by its opposite, or finds its meaning outside itself. Culture will begin in the certainty that its oppositions and distinctions are rigidly fixed. In the course of experience, it will discover the truth: that all opposites in the culture world solicit and turn into each other, as do active and passive force.[9]

A House Divided [484–87]

Hegel begins his analysis with a dense summary of the transition from ethicality to culture. The summary focuses on the terms discussed above (externalization and alienation). He also traces the main stages of the drama to come, as culture moves from its universal origin in self-alienation to its breakdown in the French Revolution.

Ethical substance, which manifested itself in the Greek *polis,* suppressed the antithesis that defines self-consciousness [484]. As citizen and family member, I experience no opposition between my selfhood and my world. My substance is my community, whose customs I experience as having their origin in the gods. In order to be united with this substance and find my essence or meaning in it, I do not need first to alienate myself from myself. I am not an unhappy consciousness at war with a sinful nature. Nor do I need to engage in any work to develop a substantial world from within myself. I enjoy a natural ethicality. All this changes with Rome, where self and world, inner and outer, are experienced as outside each other and antithetical. The individual has rights he did not have as a Greek. But he has no essence or inherent meaning. He is emptied of meaning *so that* he may be a person or property owner. Man now experiences his interiority as a nothing. This nothing is his self-consciousness. The only something is the harsh, unfeeling world of abstract legal right. This world has no determinate content, but is the arena of raging elemental passions. It is the reappearance of self-consciousness as *desire.*

This harsh actuality, *Wirklichkeit,* is in fact the work, *Werk,* of self-consciousness. The Roman person suffers the loss of meaning. But from the for-us perspective, he *constitutes* his existence or *Dasein* as meaningless [484].

The inimical external world is not simply there. It has been put there, made the harsh thing it is, through spirit's process of self-externalization. In the Roman world, substance and actuality are not simply given but are the result of *negative work.* The loss of self is the work and essence of self, the process of externalization and alienation whereby spirit makes itself into a world in order to make itself real. Rome is selfhood made manifest as the loss of selfhood, as the "alienation of the personality" [484]. This loss of self is productive or creative. As selfhood loses itself, it makes a world. What was merely *for us* in the Roman world becomes explicitly *for consciousness* in the world of culture. Cultured man views himself as perpetually outside himself: he is always to himself a project.

The Roman spirit in this way gives rise to the *Christian* consciousness of the Here-and-Now as the world in which the self is estranged. This is the mutual estrangement of inner essence and outer actuality, meaning and life. The self of culture thus has a double or divided consciousness [485]. As actual, it is aware of its present or actual world. As pure, it is aware of its interior thoughts, desires, ideals, values, etc. In making man a stranger in the Here-and-Now, Rome compelled him to turn inward in his search for meaning. This turn results in the projection of a Beyond—meaning cut off from reality.

To these two modes of consciousness, there correspond two *worlds* that spirit develops or "cultivates" [*bildet sich*] [486]. These are, in St. Augustine's terms, the City of Man and the City of God—the world of the Here-and-Now and the heavenly Beyond. Again Hegel returns to the Greek world, the eternal reference point of world-history. He reminds us that the Greeks had no Beyond, and that the deceased lived on in his family.[10] He also stresses that the modern world of culture defines itself as the opposition of essence and actuality, meaning and life. Insofar as the world is actual or present, it is without essence or meaningless; and insofar as it has an essence or is meaningful, it is not present. In the culture world, "Nothing has a spirit that is grounded within itself and indwelling [*inwohnenden*]; but each is outside itself in something alien" [486]. Opposites are precisely not harmonized and balanced, as they were in the Greek *polis,* but fight each other right from the start. As Hyppolite nicely observes, modern man is tormented with having to live in one world and think in another (382).[11]

We see that the same spirit manifests itself as the opposition between the City of Man and the City of God. But culture consciousness does not. For it, one must take sides: choose between the actual world and the pure world of transcendent essence. This is the ground of the conflict between secularism and faith. Their opposition recapitulates the confrontation between Antigone and Creon, where Antigone prefigures the man of faith and Creon the enlightened secularist. Like their ancient counterparts, the Christian believer and the secularist fail to see themselves in each other. Experience will show that they are in fact the revelation of one and the same self-consciousness, and that both are concerned with "enlightenment."

Ethicality divided itself into divine and human law, and into knowing and non-knowing. Its dissolution was the return of these opposites into their primal unity—the self as "the negative power of this antithesis" [486]. At the level of culture, this engulfing, destructive power of the self appears as "pure intellectual insight." This insight "completes culture." Both the Greek world and the world of culture are ultimately undone by the negativity of the self. But whereas ethicality dissolved in Fate (or character), culture dissolves in pure insight [*Einsicht*], which "apprehends nothing but self and everything as self, i.e., it conceptualizes [*begreift*] everything, wipes out the objectivity of things and converts all being-in-itself into being-for-itself."

Insight, here, is clearly not what it was for Plato and Aristotle: the intuition of a Form. It is not a looking at but a *seeing through,* the intellectual acid that dissolves its objects and reduces them to the self understood as intellectual process. This seeing through or unmasking is typically French. It is evident in the cynical maxims of La Rochefoucauld, who sees through virtue and exposes its hypocrisy and self-interest.[12]

Secular consciousness, which promotes insight, is the enemy of all stable essence, especially the transcendent essence of Christian faith. In the Enlightenment, this hostility of insight toward faith becomes the project of engendering widespread disillusionment [486]. The Enlightenment seeks to unsettle the believer's peace of mind, the tranquility he finds in picture-thoughts and in the prospect of happiness with God. Having annihilated meaning in the realm of actuality, insight as enlightenment "upsets the housekeeping of spirit in the household of faith." It does so "by bringing into that household the tools and utensils of *this* world." The Enlightenment invades the infinite but empty space of the Christian Beyond and fills it with the finite thinking of the Here-and-Now. Pure insight in this way generates its own Beyond in the blank "absolute Being" of deism and in utility. By destroying a personal God, and by replacing the good with the useful (a form of "bad infinity"), enlightened man re-creates an empty Beyond, a world that lacks both substance and meaning.

This double annihilation (of actual objects and of the picture-objects of faith) becomes a reality in the French Revolution. The revolution overthrows both the existing regime and the Church that supported that regime. It is also the birth of *absolute freedom* [486]. The Terror is the final self-destructive truth of culture. Once the fire of the Terror consumes itself, spirit is purged of its self-alienation. It abandons culture and enters the higher realm of *moral consciousness.* How this amazing transformation takes place, how pure insight becomes pure terror, which in turn gives rise to *morality,* will be the theme of our next chapter.

As we have seen, the world of self-alienated spirit is really two worlds: the actual world of societal life and the inner world of thought or essence. The latter is the world spirit builds "in the aether of pure consciousness" [487]. It, too, is self-alienated or double. One side of this thought-world is *faith.* The other is pure *insight.* The first is Christian picture thinking, the second pure conceptuality (intellectualism). Historically, these come on the scene together because each defines itself by opposing its other. They manifest themselves in the eighteenth-century war between *faith* and *reason.*

In the present section, Hegel treats the actual or lived side of culture. Here, culture manifests itself as the opposition between state power and wealth. In the next section, he proceeds to the inner aspect of culture, where culture reveals itself as the opposition between faith and insight. The dominant voices for lived culture will be Rousseau and Diderot. The former provides Hegel with the depiction of society as anti-natural and self-alienated. And the latter, in his revolutionary novel, *Rameau's Nephew,* expresses the ultimate breakdown of modern society in the chaotic language of its central character.[13]

The Metaphysics of Lived Culture [488–95]

Before getting to the concrete objects of state power and wealth, Hegel first gives a difficult for-us account of the dialectical nature of the culture world. The account is easier to follow if we keep in mind that the spirit of culture is the exact opposite of the ethical spirit. Instead of being indwelling, it is self-alienating or outside itself.

Culture is the work of individuals who divest themselves of their personality [488]. A simple example is civility or *politesse.* As a social being, I suppress all sorts of things I might naturally want to do or say in order to do and say what is socially acceptable. I give up my particular being-for-self or state of nature and *make myself universal:* I conform. My equality with everyone, Hegel observes, is not like the Roman equality of legal right. Legal standing requires no work and does not depend on self-alienation. It is not antagonistic toward nature but tolerates and even justifies all sorts of characters and natures: it lets nature run amok. Here, in the anti-natural culture world, I must win my universality, prove myself. Whereas my universality as a property owner simply *is,* my universality as a member of civil society or culture is one that has *come to be* [*gewordne*]. It is a cultivated or developed universality.

Self-consciousness is the desire for recognition. In the culture world, recognition takes the form of social status. As a culture creature, I have worth and actuality only by virtue of my *Bildung* or self-formation. My goal is to *alienate my nature* [489]. Cultured individuality molds itself [*bildet sich*] into what it inherently is. It does not have an essence. Or rather, its essence is to make its own essence. Only in this way does it have actuality and power [*Macht*]. As a respectable man or *honnête homme,* I am somebody, not by virtue of my natural endowments but only insofar as I use my talents and my will to re-make myself and destroy every vestige of my natural being.[14] In the culture world, therefore, the worst thing one can be is a *kind* of being, an *espèce,* which recalls the subhuman species or kinds of the animal kingdom. Hegel here quotes directly from Diderot's novel, where the nephew calls *espèce* "the most horrid of all nicknames; for it denotes mediocrity and expresses the highest degree of contempt."[15]

When self-consciousness first emerged, the individual sought recognition or honor in a fight to the death. That fight is now replaced by cultural re-formation. Instead of seeking honor by risking my life in combat with a worthy opponent, I pursue wealth, improve my social standing, and gain prestige as a cultured individual who goes to the opera, reads the latest books, quotes Rousseau, and makes witty remarks at social gatherings. My *thymos* is sublimated, turned from combat to socially acceptable forms of competition, all of which constitute my war against *myself* as a natural being.

Culture is a dialectical interplay of individual and societal whole. This whole or milieu is substance imbued with the spirit of self-alienation. The process by which the individual cultures himself is the same as that by which the culture world makes itself actual [490]. From the individual's point of view, society is something already out there, a field of possibility and advancement. In this respect, the world is something the individual feels he must master and make his own. But in fact his self-advancing ambition is the work of society as a whole, whose spirit drives it to enrich itself by inspiring the self-interest and industry of the individual.

The logical moments of culture are our old friends, the *in-itself* and the *for-itself.* These moments will be objectified, respectively, as *state power* and *wealth* [494]. The former will be associated with wholeness and integrity, the latter with fragmentation (wealth is the societal "pie" we all want a "piece" of). State power is the universal or shared object that abides, wealth the object of self-interest that comes and goes. Consciousness will try to make one good and the other bad—one essential, the other inessential. This attempt will fail, since opposites in the culture world are self-alienated and thus have their meaning not in themselves but only in each other. The opposite moments of culture, the in-itself and the for-itself, "enspirit" [*begeistet*] each other, that is, give each other life and self-awareness [491]. Culture "is really the perversion [and inversion] of every determinateness into its opposite." It is through such perversion, or immediate transition into other, that the culture world maintains itself. Whereas the opposite moments of Greek life (government and family) asserted themselves within the context of harmony and balance, the analogous moments of culture assert themselves through mutual force-like solicitation and conflict (between different social *classes*).

Hegel explains the wholeness-in-opposition of the culture world through an obscure analogy with the four elements of body: air, water, fire, and earth [492].[16] Just as these elements and "humors," through their conflict, sustain the natural world, so too a dynamic interplay of opposed spiritual moments sustains the world of culture. In its objective moment, culture or society is an abiding universal authority, the *general will.* As a cultured individual, I must conform to this will. But culture in its guise as civil society is also a resource and fund for the play of individual talents, interests, and ambitions. In Hegel's formulation, culture in this moment *sacrifices itself.* This is the subjective or fluid side of the culture world. In the first moment, society says: "Respect my rules!" In the second, it says: "Come and get it!" The first is the spirit of bourgeois conformity, the second that of acquisitive individualism. This is only one of many ways in which modern life is a condition of fragmentation or torn-ness.

These moments first appeared in the sphere of ethicality [439]. In its objective moment, ethicality was the government, in its subjective moment the family. The former demanded virtue and self-sacrifice and was thoroughly ethical. The latter promoted the amassing of wealth and the satisfaction of desire, and was ethical only in burial rites. The spirit of the modern culture, however, is not Fate but self-consciousness [492]. That is, the individual experiences himself, not as having a fixed character but as a *singular self* that either yields or indulges his singularity, either conforms or appropriates.

In order to illuminate how self-consciousness becomes the substance of culture, Hegel begins with the individual's representation of the two moments of the culture world as *thoughts.* These thoughts—*values,* as we call them—are Good and Bad [493].[17] In their self-alienation, these thoughts concretize themselves in the culture objects of state power and wealth.

Good and Bad are, respectively, the in-itself and the for-itself moments of culture. The in-itself is universality. This is the authoritative voice of the general will, the spirit of conformity, without which individuals would still be in a state of nature. Universality here is the value called *Good.* From the perspective of societal conformity, particular interests are non-essential. The for-itself moment is culture in the mode of self-interest. Culture in this moment excites our singularity, our standing out from the social body taken as an integrated whole. This fragmentation or self-interest is represented in the thought or value called *Bad* [493]. Good and Bad, here, do not mean virtuous and non-virtuous. The opposition within culture is not between ethical dispositions but between "mind sets" through which our individuality "relates to" society.

The inner thoughts of Good and Bad, because they are inner, have their reality in something outside themselves. They are, as thoughts or essences, *self-alienated* [494]. The Good is externalized or self-alienated as state power [*Staatsmacht*], the Bad as wealth [*Reichtum*]. These objects are the result of values that *posit* their external actualities. To grasp the being-at-work of alienation within culture, it is not enough to see that the values Good and Bad are "applied" to state power and wealth. We must see that these objects are congealed essences, projected idols of culture consciousness. They are what selfhood, in its self-alienation, has made them.

State power is the "universal work [*Werk*]" of individuals. It is also, significantly, "the absolute matter itself" [494], or *Sache selbst,* the "real thing" or "cause" that expresses the individual's sense of himself as universal and meaningful. Like the work that appeared in the spiritual animal kingdom, this communal work *hides* the process of its coming to be in the ultimate static product. In their day-to-day life within the culture world, individuals *forget* that they are the basis and author of this world. They experience this world as their abiding, given *substance.*

Hegel is referring here to Rousseau's notion of the social whole as brought about through the *general will.*[18] This will embodies the suppression of particular or natural will and the formation of an artificial public will.[19] It is an *Aufhebung* that cancels the individual in order to preserve him in a higher, civilized form. As part of the general order, I breathe the pure socializing air of universality. I respect the general will as an in-itself that simply *is,* forgetting that this will was the result of singular natural wills that negated themselves. I experience society, in its in-itself moment, as over and above me.

Consciousness will discover that state power and wealth have the same dialectical structure and are therefore identical [494]. Both are universals made real through the activity of individuals who are for themselves. Just as individuals create the general will, so too they create wealth as that which benefits society as a whole. Consciousness will start out by making the in-itself moment (state power) good and the for-itself moment (wealth) bad. Both determinations, as we shall see, are present in each of the moments. In striving to amass wealth for myself, I am unconsciously producing the universal wealth that creates jobs and puts bread on other people's tables. I *mean* to be selfish, to play the angles and use society for my own ends. But the spirit of society has its own angle: it begets the illusion of self-interest that excites my working for the good of the whole. This is the secular providence, as we may call it, of Adam Smith's invisible hand, the forerunner of Hegel's cunning of reason.[20]

In state power and wealth, self-consciousness beholds its own inherent duality of objective in-itself and subjective for-itself [495]. The individual does not know this. He thinks of power and wealth as separate from him, as objects he can either choose between or leave alone. This is his freedom of judgment [*Urteil*]—the experience of the values Good and Bad as "free-floating." At first, the individual regards state authority as good and wealth as bad. But, as I noted above, each determination, being self-alienated, contains both logical moments of in-itself and for-itself. The individual's experience of culture will now bring this duplicity to light.

Nobility and Contempt [496–506]

The dialectic of judgment proceeds from the duality of self-consciousness. The self-conscious individual is the unity of two opposed moments: objective in-itself and subjective for-itself [496]. He judges things as good or bad depending on whether he finds them to be like or unlike himself: likeness to self is good, unlikeness bad. But as Hegel observes, the determinations of in-itself and for-itself are logically unstable: what is judged good for me is also judged to be good in itself, and what is judged good in itself is also judged as good for me. The immediate judgments, which try to make one object good and the other bad, are therefore unstable and will turn into their opposites.

Hegel proceeds to show how consciousness, in judging state power and wealth, finds *in each object* both a likeness to itself and an unlikeness. Such judgments are therefore abstract and incomplete expressions of spirit (selfhood that is both in and for itself). When consciousness considers state power, it finds itself only partially reflected. The individual, as a myopic middle-class merchant, finds his universality and substance, the in-itself or worthy aspect of self-consciousness, but not his individuality as such, his being-for-self [497]. He therefore experiences state power (the government) as something that oppresses him. He judges this power to be unlike himself and therefore bad [497]. Wealth, by contrast, now reflects the for-itself or happiness-seeking aspect of the self and is therefore judged as good: "it leads to the general enjoyment, is there to be made use of, and procures for everyone the consciousness of his particular self."

But this reversed judgment is just as abstract as its opposite. When the individual, now as a myopic civil servant, uses his in-itself aspect as the criterion for judging good and bad, he discovers that state power reflects his own individuality as something inherently worthy, the aspect of his self-consciousness that is in itself and thus good [498]. In this experience of state power and wealth, I am glad there is a stable organized government that reflects the stability and universality I feel in myself. Wealth is now judged to be bad because it is unlike myself. In experiencing it, I confront *my selfhood* as something other, non-essential, and transient.

The dialectic shows that state power and wealth must be judged together, and that the in-itself and for-itself aspects of consciousness imply each other and are both essential. Neither wealth nor power can be judged as simply bad. Simply put, merchants who wish to stay in business must be law-abiding, and civil servants must surely see the universal benefit of wealth. When *we* judge the two former one-sided judgments, we see emerging two more fundamental and concrete "shapes of consciousness" [499]. Each is aware of both the in-itself and for-itself aspects of selfhood, and therefore concretely judges the whole of the culture world or society. One shape of consciousness or social type is itself good, the other bad.

These two types are, respectively, the *noble-hearted* [*edelmütige*] and the *base* or "low-bearing" [*niederträchtige*] [500].[21] Each has its own "mind set" and "self-image" (to use our current lingo of self-alienation), against which it judges the now-unified culture objects of state power and wealth. The noble self sees in these objects a likeness to itself. It respects and serves the public authority (the status quo) because it recognizes in this authority its own universality, essence, and inherent worthiness. The noble self also regards wealth as having been generously bestowed on it by the state power it respects. It connects its being-for-self or pursuit of happiness with those who dispense wealth. Its nobility thus takes the double form of respect and gratitude.

Base consciousness takes a contrary view of government and wealth. In these objects, it sees only an unlikeness to itself [501]. It experiences the *ressentiment* of the have-nots. The resentful individual sees in government only oppression and is always on the brink of revolt. He hates authority and "obeys only with a secret malice." In wealth, which he struggles for but only meagerly receives, he experiences a bitter reminder of his ignoble being-for-self and constant state of need. What little enjoyment he has passes quickly, and he soon returns to himself as an always desirous humiliated nothing. He loves wealth but also hates it for how it makes him feel. He envies the rich and in no way regards them as benefactors. Their gifts are wounds and insults.[22]

These two shapes first appear as separate. In the course of the dialectic, they will become each other. Noble consciousness will become selfish and contemptuous, and base consciousness will take on a kind of nobility. Noble consciousness, which Hegel treats first, will prove to be only the façade of culture, the pretense of inherent worth. Contempt and self-interest will take us to the deeper, more advanced stage of "pure culture." There, culture *celebrates* its perversity and torn-ness.

State power, we must note, is not simply "out there" as an inherently worthy object. It is *made* worthy, *given* its essence, by the selfhood of individuals. State power is something that the noble consciousness confronts and respects. But it receives its living selfhood from those who respect it. The noble self is positively related to this power only insofar as it is negatively related to its own ends and desires, only insofar as it alienates itself [503].[23] This negative work is "the heroism of service." It is the virtue of self-sacrifice on behalf of the ruling power or Establishment. Through this negative work of the noble consciousness, state power is actual. If respect were withdrawn, the state would lose its power. In service to the state, the individual self and the state *both* become actual. Hegel here begins the dialectic that mirrors the historical transition from medieval feudal administration to the modern French monarch.[24]

State power is at first only the impersonal embodiment of law: the Establishment. It is not yet a self-consciousness, that is, a *monarch* [505]. The identification of power with impersonal law thus represents an imperfect stage of both statehood and the individuals who serve it. At this stage, the noble individual indeed achieves recognition: others respect his authority and honor him for his public service. But he is only a "haughty vassal," whose self-sacrifice or negative work is incomplete.[25] There is not yet a personal lord who infuses power with selfhood, and who responds gratefully to those who serve his being-for-self and yield their hearts as well as their deeds. In the monarch, statehood and individual service become complete.

Since state power in its early, feudal stage lacks self-consciousness (i.e., is not a man), it also lacks will. Those who serve the state offer counsel [505]. But there is no absolute will, no sovereign power that can oppose counsel and decide what is best for the general good [506]. This is the modern analogue to the absence of a single Self in the ancient city-state. There we saw a family self and a governing self, but no self that ruled the whole. Monarchy, for Hegel, is essential to the being and unity of the modern state. So long as there is no monarch, there is no fully actual state power.[26] In the absence of a directive universal self and will that could silence eager counselors, society is the disagreement among the various classes or "estates" [*Stände*] over what is best. These classes are at this stage no more than special interest groups, whose self-interest or entitlement is the measure of what they consider good for all. Hegel calls their endless debate over the general good *chatter* [*Geschwätz*] [506]. Seriously intended, it is ultimately *talk* that replaces *action*.

Even the most extreme self-sacrifice in the public interest, that which threatens the vassal with death, leaves the vassal in a natural, self-interested state. His service is never enough to make his voice in council meetings more than the expression of his private opinion about the general good. In spite of his public service, he still feels within himself the force of self-interest and defiance. This taints him with the potentially revolutionary attitude of the lower, contemptuous self.

The vassal is thus incompletely noble or self-sacrificial. Death in the act of service would resolve the contradiction. It would be the complete alienation of being-for-self and complete devotion to the state as the in itself or universal. But, as in the earlier fight to the death, the individual would not be around to enjoy the fruit of his accomplishment. The problem of the noble consciousness is therefore this: how to die to self, completely alienate one's natural being, and so become fully universal and noble-minded, without experiencing physical death. The solution is—*language.*

The Self as Language [508–10]

Hegel's brief discourse on language is one of the most illuminating moments in the whole *Phenomenology.* Here we see the intimate bond between language and selfhood. Up to now, language had occurred, but it was not negative work, not self-alienation [508]. It was merely the form of a given content, a tool for conveying meaning. In law, command, and counsel, language had power and authority. It dictated and advised. But only now does it have worth [*gilt*] as language. Before this moment, speech only *prompted* deeds. It now *is* a deed: the authoritative deed of the self. Speech is now the creative force [*Kraft*] that "accomplishes what has to be accomplished."

The speech-deed before us is *flattery* [*Schmeichlerei*]. Through flattery, noble consciousness dies to self, thus completing its nobility, and creates the "unlimited monarch," that living Idol of the culture world [511]. Language in this productive guise will mediate the two sides that stand in immediate relation to each other—universal state power and individual noble consciousness—and make them into a spiritual whole.

Before turning to flattery, Hegel dwells on language as the unique revelation of the pure I. Language, he says, is the "*Dasein* [or being-there] of the pure self as self" [508]. Language here is live speech—speech as the process of utterance or "outering" [*Äußerung*]. It is the being *there* of the *in here.* In the act of speaking, I bring my inwardness out into the open for another. To be sure, I express myself in other ways as well: in gestures and in non-verbal actions. Such expressive body language was the object of physiognomy, which tried to find the pure self in bodily manifestations or meaning-traces. But these are like the corpse that remains after the soul has fled: the dead after-effect of a fugitive cause. Only language, as process, *preserves* the self in its expression and presents the self as self. Language alone is not trace but presence.

In speaking, I reveal myself as this particular I to another who hears and understands. In being for myself, or in my own presence, I am also for others. The self-actualizer was frustrated when others took his product and made it theirs. In the deed that is speech, I experience the opposite phenomenon. Here, I want what is mine, my inner thought and meaning, to be yours as well. My speech is *my* speech, the expression of this singular I. But it is also the field of universal meaning in which all I's who speak the same language have a share. Language preserves the unity of individual and universal that is conveyed by the word "I."[27]

Language is an *infection* that passes from speaker to listener [508]. To speak is to infect another with my self-consciousness, thus lifting him, along with myself, into the field of universal self-consciousness. As my speech is heard and understood, as it passes from me to you, it dies away. Its actual being-there or *Dasein* dies away. But this death is accomplishment and new life: it is the fluidity of meaning.[28] In vanishing, my speech becomes the actuality that it is. It constitutes itself as shared meaning in passing from me to you. This is another way of saying that language is the only expression of self in which inwardness is preserved in its vanishing. The dialectic of language is thus the same as that of the sensuous Now. Language is "a self-conscious Now" that cancels its singularity and transforms itself into universal meaning. In speaking, I negate the inarticulate privacy of mute intention.[29]

Hegel's discourse on language ends with the syllogism. The extremes here are state power and the nobility. Prior to the event of language, these confront each other as two unyielding sides of an opposition [509]. State power is an objective in-itself that is not yet a subjective for-itself. And the nobles, who want to be inherently worthy (in accordance with their self-image) through service to the state, keep falling back into their *mere* being-for-self. Language, as the middle term, bridges the gap. Through flattery, the state acquires selfhood or being-for-self. And the nobles are able to divest themselves of their otherwise persistent being-for-self (or selfishness) and become inherently noble-minded. Language, the basis of the culture world, reveals what all middle terms, for Hegel, have in common: fluidity. The middle term is not a static *tertium quid* but rather the passage of extremes into each other. Language makes lived culture into a "spiritual whole" [509].

From State Power to Wealth [511–16]

Through the power of language, noble consciousness transforms the proud vassal's "heroism of silent service" into "the heroism of flattery" [511]. Flattery imbues state power with selfhood and personality. It concentrates state power in an individual endowed with universal meaning. This individual is the "unlimited monarch." Through flattery, the nobles alienate their individuality or being-for-self and invest it in the monarch as the universal work of all. They become courtiers. The personality of the monarch is evident in his being given his own distinct *name:* there is only one "Louis XIV." The monarch is a glorified Monad cut off from everybody else, a "unique atom that cannot impart any of its essential nature."[30] As the self-consciousness and will of state power, the monarch can say "*L'état, c'est moi*" (Hyppolite, 405). He also knows that the nobles are there to serve the state as embodied in his person. But they are not merely his servants. They are also human ornaments that group themselves around the monarch's throne and constantly tell him who and what he is. Their flattery is the foil for his gem-like ego and the source of his sunny eminence.

As we have seen, state power, through flattery, becomes self-conscious and for-itself, just as the nobles, in sacrificing their being-for-self, take on the in-itself character of state power. Language as the middle term of the culture syllogism unites the two extremes by making them pass into each other. In other words, the monarch, in being flattered, loses his power, which in turn passes to the nobles [512]. By giving flattery, the latter relinquish their high opinion of themselves: their being-for-self. But in being swayed by flattery, the monarch relinquishes actual management of the state and the execution of state power.[31] His title becomes "an empty name."[32] As the nobles inflate the sovereign ego, he inflates their pockets and invests the nobles with influence and power. The monarch, as the personification of state power, becomes the dispenser of wealth, that "low" idol of culture consciousness. Both courtier and monarch are debased in this transaction. The nobles become *clients* of a monarch turned *patron.* Their pride becomes arrogance, their love of honor the love of status. Dialectically, the in-itself side of the culture world has been reduced to the love of private gain, and the for-itself or self-seeking side has become something valued in itself.

At this point, the heroism of flattery, which was initially sincere, becomes a façade for the projects of self-interest [513]. Noble consciousness wanted to renounce being-for-self for the sake of the common good, the in-itself aspect of society. But through flattery and royal munificence, this consciousness has become in truth the "setting aside and rending [*Aufheben und Zerreißen*] of the universal substance." This language of tearing foreshadows the fragmented or torn individual whom Hegel soon describes. Noble consciousness thus degenerates into its opposite and becomes aware of its impure, self-seeking motives. The distinction between noble-mindedness and contempt, between "high" and "low" forms of consciousness, disappears. Now there is only one kind of human being: the one who is *for himself.*

Through the nobles, who have had their pockets filled by the monarch, cultured self-consciousness is transformed. It now appears as the love of wealth. But wealth is still a "subjugated" [*unterworfen*] universal, that is, a universal that is kept under the control of the state as the true universal. Wealth has only just come on the scene and is not yet a full-blown idol. The nobles enjoy wealth, but they have not put their souls into it and do not feel the full extent of the unlikeness between it and them [514]. They feel little if any degradation in the riches they get from the monarch, since they are "in the universal," part of the scheme of things, and are grateful for what they receive. Nor would the monarch ever think of saying "*La richesse, c'est moi!*"—even though Mr. Moneybags (to quote Marx) is precisely what the monarch has become.

Just as state power needed to be enspirited, made self-conscious, in order to become fully what it is, so too wealth "requires to be ensouled" [515]. Formerly, wealth was only one of the idols of culture. Now it becomes the supreme idol or Golden Calf—the good. No longer merely what I selfishly seek in order to satisfy desire, wealth is an end in itself. It develops a spirit and will of its own—a *self-consciousness* [515, 516].

At this point, the essential relation within culture shifts from the monarch and his courtiers to rich merchants and their poor clients. Wealth undermines state power as the absolute value. With the emergence of wealth as the absolute, human beings no longer take their bearings by the distinction between high and low. There is now nothing to look up to or respect. The dominant passions become contempt and arrogance. Wealth generously gives itself to individual being-for-self (no more hypocrisy about the in-itself worth of public service!). It liberates self-interest. Unfortunately, it liberates some (the wealthy) to make slaves of others (the poor). Society thus regresses to a state of nature—to *barbarism*, as Hegel calls it in an early writing.[33] The self-alienation that occurs at this point is far more drastic than that of the nobles, since man now alienates himself, not in another living self-consciousness but in a dead thing.[34]

The relation between merchant and client, as I noted above, is the modern version of that between master and slave. The merchant *has* wealth. He therefore only imperfectly feels what it means to place one's essence in wealth and to *be* what wealth itself is: a degraded, meaningless universal. It is the dependent client, culture's counterpart to the slave, who, lacking wealth, embodies wealth in its spirit of fragmentation. This is the base consciousness we met earlier. His model is the young Rameau from Diderot's novel.

Rameau's Nephew: Language and Perversity [517–25]

In the culminating moment of lived culture, Hegel draws extensively on Diderot's wildly imaginative work, *Rameau's Nephew.* The novel is a reported conversation between a gentlemanly "philosopher" and the outrageous nephew of the famous composer and harmonic theorist, Jean-Philippe

Rameau. Hegel's use of this "underground novel" in the *Phenomenology* is perhaps his most masterful appropriation of a literary work. In what follows, I will refer to only some of the ways in which the nephew sums up the perversity of the whole culture world.[35]

Like wealth itself, the client circulates through society and has no fixed "home." He is, in Hyppolite's words, a "vagabond parasite" (412). The client goes from one patron and job to another and is always at the mercy of chance. Also like wealth, he is *for another*, a means and never an end. He is constantly outside himself or self-alienated, since he "belongs to another" [517], namely, his rich benefactor. The proud vassal had a certain degree of fulfillment in his self-alienation and noble service. Not so for the client, whose I is always at the mercy of someone else's fickle I, and whose sustenance depends on trivialities like being in the right place at the right time, or being amusing [517]. Vassal and courtier enjoy recognition, but the client goes unrecognized and humiliated. When he receives a benefit, his gratitude is really "the most profound dejection" and "extreme rebellion." His contempt for his benefactor goes hand in hand with his self-loathing, his awareness of himself as a low *thing*.[36]

In the self-conscious degradation of the client, the pure I experiences itself—as well as "everything that is called law, good, and right"—as disrupted and destroyed. This condition is one of *Zerrissenheit*, fragmentation or torn-ness. We have seen this split before in the phenomenon of self-consciousness. Here that split engulfs the whole world of culture, which is now embodied in the base client: "All self-sameness [*Gleiche*] is destroyed, for what presents itself is the purest dissimilarity [*Ungleichheit*], the absolute non-essentiality of the absolutely essential, the being-outside-itself of the being-for-self: the pure 'I' itself is absolutely disintegrated" [517].[37]

The unhappy consciousness also felt this split. But unlike this consciousness, the worldly client does not yearn for a changeless transcendent God. Instead, he affirms his own self-identity, thus achieving a perverse form of heroism. He rebels inwardly against the whole culture world and its hypocrisy, and refuses to bow to the vulgar patron he both needs and despises. The client feels the contradiction of the pure I as an independent, thinking subject *and* a thing-like object that belongs to another. He rises above this contradiction and proudly asserts his "I AM MYSELF!" His selfhood, Hegel says, is "absolutely elastic" [518].[38]

Hegel now turns to the rich benefactor. As we have seen, wealth is not merely the material object but a spiritual *value*, the low idol of culture. In the benefactor, wealth manifests itself not as rebellion but as *arrogance* [*Übermut*] [519]. The rich man knows, as well as the client, that self-interest is purely contingent and transient, and that wealth has no inherent meaning. But he delights in being the source and dispenser, the very god, of contingency (*fortune* in both senses of the term). He is arrogant rather than proud because, unlike the master we encountered earlier, he knows that he is not better or more courageous than his underling but only more powerful by virtue of his wealth.

In his arrogance, the rich patron believes [*meint*] that "by the gift of a meal" he has acquired another human being's selfhood [519]. He thinks that this other has inwardly submitted to him. But he is mistaken. In Hegel's ominous portrait, when the rich patron looks down on his dependent, he ignores the latter's inner rebellion and contempt for all law and order. Wealth is a drug that anaesthetizes the patron to the resentment and tearing of self-identity that he causes in the client. He stands on the edge of an abyss, "in which all stability and substance have vanished," and sees in his client, not an abyss, but a barely human *thing* that is at the mercy of his whims. In his arrogance, the benefactor himself becomes thing-like, since he lives for material wealth. He is, in Hegel's closing epithet, a "spirit-forsaken superficiality" [519].[39]

State power became actual through the language of noble flattery. Something similar happens in the case of wealth. Here, however, flattery is *ignoble* [*unedeln*] [520]. The flattery of wealth and the wealthy glorifies what is unworthy and meaningless. But the deeper and more revealing language in relation to wealth is not that of flattery but of indignation or rebellion [*Empörung*] [520]. This revolutionary language, the language of the humiliated client and his shredded identity, is "the perfect language and the authentic existent spirit of this entire world of culture." It is *culture* aware of itself as thoroughly contradictory and perverse—as a world without integrity.

The language of indignation and torn-ness is evident in the young Rameau.[40] The nephew's language embodies "pure culture" [521]. This is culture unmasked, culture that is actual not in state power and wealth but in witty, self-lacerating language. In his wild exhibition of identity within difference (through bizarre bodily gestures, multiple personalities, and mood-swings), the nephew reveals the self-contradictory truth of the world to which he belongs. His speech *is* that world made self-conscious and self-knowing. The nephew sees through everything. He sees that all the rigidly adhered to distinctions in this world—state power and wealth, the social values of good and bad, noble and base consciousness—are unstable. In his shameless confessions about money, vice, and self-advancement through bootlicking, he says what all people would say if they were not such hypocrites.[41]

The nephew's chaotic language is the revenge that the resentful self takes on society for having oppressed and degraded it—for having alienated it from its self-identity. As culture's version of the unhappy consciousness, the nephew, in his self-loathing, also exacts a perverse vengeance on himself. His self-destructive language is a "universal justice," in which the incoherence of the culture world at last rises to the surface of experience and shows itself for what it really is: a spiritual unity that maintains itself through the transition of opposites into each other [521]. What consciousness now posits as absolute is neither state power nor wealth but the "universal talk" that reduces everything to nothing and thereby asserts its power over the whole world. Pure culture, manifested in the language of client-consciousness, is nihilism.[42] Such language is a witty game that the pure self plays with itself, the game dramatized in the bizarre conversation between Diderot's philosopher and the jester-like nephew.

At this moment of the dialectic of culture, language itself becomes the absolute, a world unto itself. Once again, language is the middle term of a culture syllogism. The language of pure culture, however, is more complete, closer to the truth, than the previous syllogism that united noble consciousness and state power. This time language reveals culture in its bare contradictoriness, as the absolute unrest of opposites that are always turning into each other [521]. The language of pure culture "overpowers everything; it is solely with this alone that one has to do in this actual world."

The respectable individual (as Hegel calls him) is the philosopher who speaks with the young Rameau. In his bourgeois placidity, this philosopher is the perfect foil and "straight man" for the nephew's jokes. He tries to maintain order and the distinctness of opposites like good and bad, honorable and shameful, high and low. But the more truthful nihilist (who embodies the Concept) reveals the sheer fluidity of all these value judgments and dissolves their seriousness in a flurry of wit.

Following Diderot, Hegel emphasizes the *musical* character of the nephew, who lives resentfully in the shadow of his famous uncle. The nephew, with his madcap gestures and speech, embodies the fluid, promiscuous, Dionysian spirit of music. This is music's sophist-like ability to imitate everything and anything, and to combine what it pleases: music as a "Bohemian rhapsody." Quoting the philosopher from Diderot's novel, Hegel says that the nephew, in his demonic mimicry, mixes "thirty arias, Italian, French, tragic, comic, of every sort" [522]. He goes from the infernal regions of contempt and abjectness "to the highest pitch of admiration and emotion; but blended with the latter will be a tinge of ridicule which spoils them."

The respectable individual, needless to say, shrinks from this promiscuous union of clashing styles and idioms. He wants to maintain the decorum and stability of music, and thus the value judgments of culture itself. But all his attempts to school the nephew are doomed to failure. The nephew knows he is perverse and shameless. There is nothing the bourgeois philosopher can call him that he hasn't called himself, and nothing he can point out that the nephew doesn't already know [523]. If the philosopher insists on the distinction between good and bad, the nephew agrees, adding that the distinction is fluid, that all identities are unstable, and consequently that good and bad are *also* identical. In the dull uninspired speech of Diderot's philosopher, all this philosopher shows is that he is a mere vanishing moment in the more encompassing (and truthful) vision of the nephew. The latter's speech is not only scintillating and witty. It is also an exposé of culture and its hypocrisy. The destabilizing nephew is, in speech, a microcosm and forerunner of what the French Revolution will be in deed.

The philosopher also thinks he can refute the nihilist nephew by adducing an example of virtue. Here Hegel repeats his earlier reference to *espèce* as the worst insult: "to represent the existence of the good and noble as an isolated anecdote, whether fictitious or true, is the most disparaging thing that can be said about it" [524]. To say "I once knew an honest man" is hardly a refutation of perversity. Moreover, the respectable philosopher cannot claim that he himself is free of the culture world, since, as a self-interested individual, he is part of that world. Referring to the final moments of Diderot's novel, Hegel says that even Diogenes in his tub is dependent on the society he cynically derides. Nor does it make sense to advise society to throw off its development and return to a Rousseau-like state of nature—to "the simplicity of the natural heart." Reason cannot, without denying its reasonableness, recommend a regression to "the wilderness of nearly animal consciousness." There is no defense against the perverse and truthful voice of pure culture, at least none that *this* world can offer. . . .

The witty speech of the nephew is the dialectical origin of a new shape of consciousness. In the awareness of the vanity of all things, the self rises above vanity. Logically, this is the moment at which the alienation that defines culture *alienates itself,* as Hegel told us it would [491]. Through pure culture and its witty talk, the self becomes liberated from the objects that made it perverse and vain. This does not mean that the worldly nephew undergoes a personal conversion. Indeed, at the end of the novel, after tearing himself and society to pieces, he goes off to the opera, telling the staid philosopher, "He laughs best who laughs last." *We* see in his talk the transcendence of vanity by the pure self that is above the world and its distinctions. We see that the witty nephew has unwittingly generated the self as *universal* thought, as self-consciousness that has come to know what it is in itself. This is the pure I that transcends power, wealth, and wit alike and turns its gaze "to heaven" [525].

Faith and Reason [526–37]

Culture in its broadest meaning is the alienation of actuality and essence, life and thought. Having examined actual or lived culture, we now turn to culture as thought. This is the moment of "pure consciousness." Disenchanted by wealth, power, and nihilistic wit, the pure I now experiences a return to itself. It becomes *reflective* [526].

The realm of pure consciousness stands beyond the actual world [527]. It is the Beyond that is dialectically generated by that world, the Beyond *of* the actual world. Consciousness here is defined as a flight from this world and all its vanity, turmoil, and impure intentions—brilliantly summed up in the nihilistic nephew. This flight is faith, the Christian belief in a timeless Kingdom of God. Hegel emphasizes here that faith, as a form of immediacy, is but the first step of a more complete negation of the actual world. Faith is a mode of thought [529], but thought that is *not yet Concept.* It is thought that is still bound up with the finite things of this world. As a consequence, faith thinks the Beyond in thingly pictures or representations [*Vorstellungen*]: in a God as three separate Persons and a supersensible Kingdom patterned after earthly kingdoms. The thinking that characterizes faith is thus, so to speak, impurely pure.

Hegel distinguishes the believer from both the stoic and the unhappy consciousness. The believer is different from the stoic because his thinking is not merely formal but *has content* [527]. His Beyond may be unreal, but he nevertheless imagines this Beyond as actual *in itself,* if not yet actual *for him.*

In the previous chapter, I distinguished three forms of Christianity in the *Phenomenology:* the unhappy consciousness, faith, and religion. Hegel now reminds us that faith is intermediate between the first and the third forms [528]. Unlike the unhappy consciousness, faith is positive. It is not infinite yearning that hands itself over to an external authority but rather the individual's certainty of his implicit union with God. This shift from external to internal authority comes on the scene with Luther's Reformation and the positing of conscience as absolute.[43] But faith still suffers the self-alienation of the culture world to which it belongs. In actively pursuing its fulfillment in a Beyond, it embodies the alienation of *essence* from *existence,* meaning from life [528]. In this respect, faith retains the subjectivism of the unhappy consciousness. As we shall see, religion will overcome mere faith and its alienation of essence and existence. It will be God manifesting himself on earth in and through the actual world of peoples and their communities and institutions—in history.

Like everything else in culture, faith defines itself through opposition. It flees society not only because of the vanity of worldly things, but also and more importantly because of the vanity of clever, worldly thinking. Faith opposes this thinking. The oppositional or aggressive aspect of faith appears in Pascal's polemic against Descartes and Montaigne in his *Pensées.* Pascal is no doubt Hegel's paradigm for the cultured post-Reformation believer. Faith is an alienated consciousness [529]. As faith-thinking flees the world, it takes with it this other to which it is opposed and through which it defines itself. This other is *pure insight,* or acuity. Its historical paradigm is Voltaire, who directs his biting wit against the "positive thinking" of otherworldliness and naïve faith.[44] This acuity derives, ultimately, from Descartes, who identified truth with clarity and distinctness. With the emergence of insight, pure consciousness splits. It is now the dyad, faith-and-reason.

Faith and insight are two complementary sides of universality: culture in its mode as inward thought or reflection. For the former, the universal is a positive stable *essence,* for the latter a negative *process.* Whereas for faith the universal is an imagined object, for insight it is the negative work of the self: "pure thought as the absolute Concept in the might [*Macht*] of its negativity, which eliminates everything objective" [529]. In sum, faith corresponds to *consciousness,* and insight to *self-consciousness.* In its reduction of everything to the process of selfhood, insight turns against the stable objects of faith. It seeks to destabilize the believer's peace of mind—to replace the "rest" of faith with the "motion" of purely conceptual thinking. Like desire, insight negates everything objective. It strives to destroy the imagined objectivity that faith posits and to reduce all irrational faith-objects to the conceptual purity of the not-to-be-pictured self. Faith and insight each have their strength and weakness. Faith has objects, but not a conceptual insight into them. And insight, though purely conceptual, has no content but the pure self. In our next chapter, in the dialectic of the Enlightenment, these two opposed moments will become identical.

As forms of pure consciousness or inner reflection, faith and insight both flee the actual world. This flight, as a determinate negation, is conditioned by *and contains* that world [530]. Faith and insight will reveal themselves in three ways. Each is what it is on its own, in relation to the actual world it negates, and in relation to its pure counterpart or other. Hegel now proceeds to examine these three aspects. He begins with faith.

From the perspective of the believer, the aspect of being in and for itself belongs to only one being, God [531]. This Being is a Trinity of Father, Son, and Holy Spirit. As we saw in our discussion of self-consciousness, faith does not attend to the logical process by which these three Persons (or personified moments) give rise to each other, thus forming a coherent whole. Instead, it treats them as "a tranquil diversity and their movement a [mere] happening" [531]. God the Father is God as the "simple eternal substance" [532]. In passing over into a mortal form and thus sacrificing himself, he is the Son. And the return of the Son to the Father, the re-establishment of their original unity, is represented as the Holy Spirit. Hegel adds that this mediation of God with himself is also the mediation of the individual believer with the transcendent God [533]. As the believer passes beyond the actual world in thought, God descends to that world and becomes "a participant in the self-consciousness of the believer." The believer calls this participation *grace.*

The second aspect of faith is its relation to the actual culture world, whose vanity the believer seeks to flee. Here Hegel sharply distinguishes the believer's relation to the actual world from that of the disrupted self, which is "a clever consciousness of its perversity" [534]. The believer avoids such intellectual vanity. He seeks to overcome the actual world not in witty speech but in "the obedience of service and praise [of God]." The believer is thus engaged in a perpetual process, since his union with God in his Kingdom remains a Beyond. His life is not a fulfillment but a pilgrimage.

The third aspect of faith is the relation to faith's other, pure insight [535]. This aspect "is really the true relation in which faith here appears." It is what most brings faith to light as belonging to the opposition-driven world of culture. Hegel will develop this opposition between faith and reason in his account of the Enlightenment.

Whereas faith had for its object the Being who was in and for himself, pure insight has for *its* object nothing but self-consciousness itself [536]. Insight abolishes everything that purports to be in-itself. In its acid of rationality, it dissolves all external objects and reduces them to human self-interest and self-projection—to being-for-self.

When insight first appears, it is "not yet realized." It is only the "pure intention" to make the world rational [537]. This rationalization cannot be left to geniuses. Like everybody else in modern civil society, geniuses "cheat and struggle over the essence of the actual world." They are part of the spiritual animal kingdom. Insight, however, in the purity of its intention, must rise above this struggle. Its intention is not to actualize a particular self, or to promote an ingenious personal vision, but to make insight "the property of every self-consciousness" [537].[45] Just as faith is essentially communal or universal (it is for everybody), so too is insight, which seeks *universal enlightenment.*

Pure insight defines itself in the imperative that ends this first part of the dialectic of culture. The imperative is addressed to all human beings everywhere: "be *for yourselves* what you all are *in yourselves—reasonable.*" Or, as Kant, quoting Horace, declares as the motto of enlightenment, "*Sapere aude!* [Dare to know!] Have courage to use your own reason!"[46] In the next chapter, we will witness the devastating consequences of this well-meaning imperative.

Grace comes somehow violent.
AESCHYLUS, *Agamemnon*

 18

From Pure Insight to Pure Terror

The Darkness of the Enlightenment

WITH THE ENLIGHTENMENT, SPIRIT CONTINUES ITS FRENCH PHASE. The Enlightenment, we recall, is insight seeking to make itself universal, the possession of all mankind. Insight opposes the picture-thinking of faith. In the section now before us, insight will wage a full-scale war against what it takes to be ignorance and prejudice. It will identify faith [*Glauben*] with superstition [*Aberglauben*].[1]

When we first entered the realm of spirit, I noted that the fundamental problem of modern man for Hegel is that of infusing life with knowledge and knowledge with life (Chapter 15). This is the existential version of uniting subject and object. As a mode of pure consciousness, faith liberates man from the vanity of culture by turning his gaze to a future world, where life is knowledge. In this world, man enjoys the vision of God magnificently depicted in Dante's *Paradiso.* The Enlightenment by contrast wants the heaven of insight, the unity of life and knowledge, in the Here-and-Now. It seeks to free man from his dependence on the Beyond and to "transplant heaven to the earth below" [581], thus putting an end to all alienation.

This attempt gives rise to what Hegel calls "the greatest world-event of our time," the French Revolution.[2] In seeking to liberate man from his bondage to external authority, and to make reason a reality, the Enlightenment leads to the Terror of 1793. Instead of a heaven on earth, we get a hell. But thanks to the regenerative power of negation, this hell is in fact a purgatory. Its fires purify even as they destroy. As spirit in its French phase purges itself of its rational madness, a higher form of practical reason rises from the ashes. This is morality. It is founded on Luther's Reformation, which compelled man to look within his own conscience for the divine authority that makes him a truly spiritual being. Kant's Moral World-View is the rational development of Luther's inward turn. With the turn to conscience and the inner man, spirit ceases to be French and embarks upon the German phase of its adventure.

In this chapter, we explore the path that leads from pure insight to pure terror. We will also examine how, in the wake of culture, the Moral World-View comes to light.

The Animus of Insight [538–62]

In the previous section, Hegel told us that faith and insight had to be looked at in three ways: by themselves, in relation to the lived world each seeks to transcend, and in relation to each other [530]. Having outlined in that section insight as it is in itself, he now takes up insight in its relation to the actual world and faith.

As we know, pure insight has no objects of its own. Objectivity is all on the side of faith. The only object insight has is—faith itself. Against this object insight directs "the force [*Kraft*] of the Concept" [538]. This is the irresistible might of Descartes' clarity and distinctness. But insight and faith spring from a common source. Both are instances of pure consciousness, which opposes "the impure intentions and perverse insights of the actual world." Insight thus has a positive goal: to reform the world and bring about a true *Bildung* or education. In the two remaining parts of the chapter on culture ("The Enlightenment" and "Absolute Freedom and Terror"), we witness how this positive goal becomes ruthlessly negative.

The impetus of the Enlightenment derives from the conversation between the placid *philosophe* and the turbulent nephew [538–40]. Diderot now appears as author and recorder. He is the "third consciousness" who, in writing, seeks to enlighten his readers and "clear up the confusion" of the culture world that the nephew embodies [539]. Writing stabilizes live speech and makes it public. Such stabilization is all the more salutary when the spoken word is the "arguing and chattering" of the perverse realm of culture. By collecting and thereby unifying the often-insightful utterances of the nephew, Diderot lifts the reader above the perverse actuality of the culture world.[3] These utterances transcend self-interest and idiosyncrasy, and become something available to everyone: "individual judgment is resolved into the universal insight" [540].

But the enlightened *philosophe* author has no insights of his own: all content is on the side of the perverse nephew. This is where faith comes in. Whereas enlightenment is nascent and empty, faith is long-standing and full of content. Insight must be invented, whereas Christian faith has been around for centuries and *is*. Pure insight thus "only manifests its peculiar activity in so far as it comes on the scene in opposition to faith" [540]. To become king, insight must subvert a king.

The Enlightenment is consciousness in one of its negative modes. Other such modes included Roman skepticism and the practical negations of Faust, Karl Moor, and the Knight of Virtue. The Enlightenment is superior to these, since it is the work of universal spirit rather than isolated individuals [541]. It is the world turned against itself in an act of universal re-making or *Bildung.* Its goal is the diffusion of insight.

As we saw in the preceding section, faith and insight are two aspects of the same pure consciousness [541]. They do not know themselves as aspects. Each takes itself as the absolute, and does not see itself in the other. This not seeing is the ground of their conflict. It recalls the lack of mutual recognition in the case of Antigone and Creon. Most generally, the war of faith and reason is a conflict between *image* and *concept.* Faith is pure thought without conceptuality, the imagining of God. Insight is the thinking of everything, especially God, in purely conceptual non-imaginary terms.[4] For faith, the essence of everything resides in its pictorially represented *objects.* For insight, the only essence is the human *self* or thinker. Since content is on the side of faith, insight must fill itself by feeding parasitically on what it opposes [541]. It is a form of *desire,* as this first appeared in Hegel's chapter on self-consciousness.

In order to attack faith, insight concocts a conspiracy theory. It depicts faith not as a genuinely inner condition but as something external and forced, "a tissue of superstitions, prejudices, and errors." This mass delusion is the work of an evil priesthood in cahoots with secular despots [542]. The priests, in their cunning self-interest, embody the *impure* insights and intentions of the perverse culture world.[5]

From the perspective of insight, faith manifests three evils: a mind tainted with error, deceptive priests, and a despot who supports their deception and tyranny. Insight does not directly attack the second and third but focuses its attention on the first. This is where it finds common ground: in the individual who is *potentially* rational.[6] Insight wants to awaken the individual to his inherent rationality. The Enlightenment in this way hopes to defeat the conspiracy of clerics and despots by breaking the spell *from within.* With the removal of prejudice, according to insight, the mind will naturally "see."

Insight has a contradictory relation to faith as the naïve thought of God [544]. It wants to transform faith into itself, certain that once the veil of illusion is removed, believers will "see the light." But insight also finds the believer offensive, since, by giving himself to an imagined God, the believer foolishly renounces his being-for-self or self-conscious individuality.[7] Insight is thus both the friend and the enemy of unenlightened fools. It must elicit reasonableness, evoke the believer's true self. But it must also oppose the God to whom the believer slavishly gives himself.

Faith and insight thus occupy the same spiritual "space" of pure thought. *We* see that they flow dialectically into each other and are, respectively, the objective and subjective sides of the same dialectical coin (the Concept) [545]. But insight interprets this fluidity one-sidedly, as the simple mind's receptivity to its project of awakening. Since insight regards faith as insight that has been clouded over, it believes its triumph over faith will be smooth and silent, a covert operation not unlike that of the Knight's rear-attack on the Way of the World [386]. Hegel first compares this process to the expansion of a perfume through the non-resisting atmosphere. He then abruptly switches the image to an *infection* that insinuates itself into the body and begins to spread—the very image he used earlier to describe language as the spreading of self-consciousness [508].

In fact, insight does spread like this through the modern world. This infection of light shows itself, not in occasional symptoms but as a true *epidemic.* Purely conceptual thinking, as "an invisible and imperceptible spirit," reaches the inmost, noblest regions of human life. Faith itself can be infected, tempted to seek a reasonable ground for itself. Insight is sure that the idol of faith in a picture God will be smashed. In the words of the perverse nephew: "one fine morning it [insight] gives its comrade [faith] a shove with the elbow, and bang! crash! the idol lies on the floor" [545]. A nudge is all it takes to bring about faith's self-destruction! To insight, it seems that the process of enlightenment will be no more than the shedding of a skin; that Christianity will end up, like so many other idols, in the junkyard of history; and that the merely imagined Savior will be replaced by a worthier idol—"the new serpent of wisdom raised on high for adoration."[8]

But insight is one-sided in this view of its project. It hides itself from itself, conceals its irrational offense and ill will [546]. The developed process of enlightenment will be anything but smooth and silent. Having spread like a silent cancer, it will break out furiously against faith. In this antagonism, insight is really at war with *itself,* since the Concept for it is everywhere and everything. Nothing is outside it. Insight cannot attack faith, therefore, as though it were something substantial and real without contradicting itself. In seeking to transform its certainty into truth, insight will be the very perversity it sought to rise above. Its claim to be truthful and disinterested will be revealed as "a lie and insincerity of purpose" [547]. This "fall" of reasonableness mirrors the transition we saw in the last section from noble to base consciousness.[9]

The contradiction within insight is rooted in the *Category* [548], which first appeared at the level of reason. The Category was the certainty that subject and object were the same, that the thinker himself was the substance of the world.[10] Insight is a higher version of reason as Category. Whereas reason was limited by its individualism, Enlightenment expresses the *concrete universality* of reason's dominion in the world. From the exalted position of "the absolute Concept," which insight champions, the non-rational has no truth whatsoever: everything that is, is rational. When insight fights faith, therefore, it fights with the otherness inherent in its own self: "what pure insight pronounces to be its other, what it asserts to be an error or a lie, can be nothing else but its own self; it can condemn only what it is itself" [548]. This self-opposition is the work of the Concept as it is in truth: self-identity within self-difference. Insight fails to know that it has the same dialectical structure as the perverse, self-lacerating nephew.

The only object that stands over and against insight is faith. Not recognizing itself in this object, insight accuses faith of error [549]. This error consists in the believer's not knowing that his own consciousness is the source of his presumed absolute Being. The believer has not found God but only invented him. Insight says to the believer: "It's all in your mind!" This is a partial truth. God as a spiritual being is necessarily of the mind. For the believer, man and God are the same spiritual substance. The believer believes that his consciousness is implicitly one with God, that his mind will one day "see" God. But this does not make God a chance invention or mental construct.

When insight says to the believer, "It's all in your mind," it fails to see that this is also what is expressed in the Concept: "Everything real is purely conceptual." In other words, "what enlightenment declares to be an error and a fiction is the very same thing as enlightenment itself is" [549]. Both faith and enlightenment express the certainty of the Concept. This is the certainty that what is real is what is pure in the sense of intellectual or non-bodily. What insight calls error is thus insight itself. Enlightenment wants to school faith in the "new wisdom" but in fact does not tell faith anything new. The believer already believes that his object is not some material thing outside him but "a pure essence of [his] own consciousness," an object in which he finds himself.

The delusion of insight in matters of faith is evident from the standpoint of the religious community [549]. Believers believe that God works through them, that obedience and action are essential to God's presence on earth. They also experience God as the very spirit of their community.[11] In this community, the believer is united with absolute Being. God would not be present as *the spirit of the community* if the community were not itself active in bringing this about. He comes to be present as spirit through the community's "bringing forth" of God from its own consciousness [549]. God is an inner, not an outer being, a being that is present "when two or more are gathered in [God's] name" (Matthew 18:20). But absolute being is not *merely* the product of a human bringing forth. It is, says Hegel, also "in and for itself," or actual.

So far, we have seen the first moment of the accusation insight levels against faith: "It's all in your mind." We now turn to the *second* aspect of insight's relation to faith: that of faith as an offensive other and the product of deceptive priests. Insight here accuses the believer of taking into his mind a God who is alien to the mind—an imposture and changeling rather than a trueborn child of reason [550]. This is the exact opposite of the first accusation (that the Christian God is a mental construct). Hegel exposes the contradiction by stressing the reaction of faith itself. Faith regards as "completely foolish" the charge that believers are the victims of deceit, since it has also heard the accusation "It's all in your mind." What insight accuses as being "alien to consciousness" is what it had also accused of being "the inmost nature of consciousness itself" [550]. To faith, enlightenment thus reveals itself as "the conscious lie." In contradicting itself, enlightenment shows not only that it does not know what it is talking about but also that its intent is malicious. Faith sees that insight is a sophist, and that the accusation leveled against priests is really insight's unwitting accusation of itself.[12]

We must now look more closely at how faith itself exposes the perversity of the Enlightenment [551]. Three moments of the believer's God must be considered: God as the pure object of thought (God as he *is*), God as the ground of faith, and God as the being to whom the believer relates through acts of worship and service.

In the first moment, insight accuses faith of materialism. Insight, we recall, has no object of its own: it is only the intellectual acid that analyzes or dissolves determinate being. There is only the self (the home of pure concepts) and the rest of the world. For insight, therefore, the only solid object faith could possibly have is a sensuous thing in the form of statues, sculptures, a piece of bread, and a human shape [552]. Thus does insight misrepresent what faith represents to itself as the divine. As Hegel puts it, enlightenment defiles faith's spiritual objects—eternal life and the Holy Spirit—with the view of sense-certainty [553]. Even if believers use objects of sense to express their faith, they certainly do not think they are worshiping them.

In the second moment, God is the ground of faith. Here again enlightenment plays the sophist. It willfully construes the believer's faith in God as belief in chance historical events, thus bringing faith down to insight's own level of bodily thinking [554]. In this second moment, faith appears as mediation. This mediation is the work of God as spirit, that is, God as the being who bridges the gap between God and man. Faith is not only the thought of God (the first moment): it is also the thought of one's relation to God as the source of faith. In believing in God the believer knows or is certain of himself in this relation. He does not disappear but rather "finds himself" in God. Insight misrepresents this mediation by reducing the ground of faith to the naïve belief in mere sensuous, contingent happenings. But as Hegel observes, "it does not occur to faith to fasten its certainty to such evidences and fortuitous circumstances." True faith is (or should be) indifferent to facts about the historical Jesus. If faith does appeal to such grounds, "then it has already let itself be corrupted by the Enlightenment."

The third moment deals with action [555]. The believer acts by sacrificing himself to God. In his effort to be spiritual, he gives up his natural self-interest or independent being-for-self. Enlightenment's attack here hinges on the "twisted" manner in which it depicts the believer's purpose and end. Purpose here is intention, and end the object for the sake of which I act. The believer's *purpose* is to be genuinely self-sacrificial. His *end* is union with God. Enlightenment construes these as self-otherness or hypocrisy. It foists upon the believer *its own* belief in self-interest as the principle of all action (an echo of the Way of the World in response to the Knight). Enlightenment cannot imagine genuine self-sacrifice, which it considers irrational. It refuses to accept the believer's outward actions, his giving up of property and money to the poor and to the Church, as evidence of a pure heart, and regards such actions as foolish [556]. As Hegel wittily observes, the Enlightenment's charge against the believer for trying to prove his inner state through outer deeds of abstention is, in the exactly opposite case, like accusing a man "who, in order to eat, has recourse to actual eating" [556].[13]

As for the accusation regarding the end of action, enlightenment finds it morally wrong to give up sensuous pleasures just in order to give them up, "without receiving anything in return." The believer has no reasonable end. But in thus accusing faith, pure insight exposes its own materialistic, impure view that only things like "butter and eggs" are essential [556]. Insight, as we know, is a form of pure consciousness. It promotes the transcendence of mere bodily pleasure and monetary gain as belonging to the vain culture world. But when faith actually goes to work to accomplish this transcendence, insight objects. In objecting, it reveals its latent cynicism and hypocrisy. Insight only pretends to be concerned with transcendence. In fact, it regards this effort as superfluous and foolish, "and even wrong to be in earnest about it." The upshot of this third moment is that insight, in attacking its presumed enemy, really "belies itself" [*verleugnet sich*], both as pure insight and as pure intention. It becomes its opposite.

This concludes the threefold way in which enlightenment, in opposing faith, opposes itself. But there is also insight's positive claim to produce a better man, world, and God [557]. Let us assume that enlightenment has overcome the prejudice and superstition of faith. "*What next?*" Hegel asks. "*What is the truth enlightenment has propagated in their stead?*"

Hegel now revisits the three preceding moments, this time attending to the positive teachings of the Enlightenment. In the first moment (God insofar as he *is*), enlightenment avoids the error of faith: thinking of God in terms of wood, stone, bread, and human shape. It does so by emptying the concept of God of *every determinateness* [557]. This is its only recourse, since all objectivity for insight is, apart from faith, the realm of sense-objects. All content is regarded as belonging to the vulgar imagining of God, which is the ground of superstition. Reason's God must therefore be "a *vacuum* to which no determinations, no predicates, can be attributed."[14]

We now turn to the second moment, that of God's relation to the individual knower. For faith, this relation was rich in spiritual content. But having subtracted all content from God, the enlightened rationalist inevitably returns to the sense-world as the ultimate object of determinate knowledge. He thus returns to the level of consciousness as *sense-certainty* [558]. But whereas sense-certainty was an immediate, unthinking affirmation of the sensed world, a merely natural consciousness, insight embraces sense-certainty as a *result,* that is, as something enriched and rationally confirmed by the previous logical movement. Insight is sense-certainty that has been educated, *gebildet.* Sensuous this-ness is now on a firmer footing. Indeed, at the level of insight, it is absolute truth [558].

In the third moment, the moment of individual action, insight replaces the believer's action of worship and service, his deeds of self-transcendence, with *utility* [560]. Utility is modernity's way of affirming beyond-ness *within* ordinary experience. A useful thing both *is itself* and *transcends itself* by being *for* something else. Insight concocts a theology to support the view that things are absolute and true insofar as they are useful. It makes God the author of nature—in that sense makes him *useful* to nature—and interprets nature as the God-given object of man's mastery and possession [559].[15]

According to insight, utility is the bond of the whole world, where everything is both user and used, end and means, where "everything is at the mercy of everything else" [560]. Nothing is good in itself or noble. The noble is meaningless. Within this use-world, man's place is ambiguous. On the one hand, man, as a natural consciousness, is good. Hegel is thinking of Rousseau here when he says that man is good insofar as he "has come from the hand of God." The world exists for man's pleasure and delight: man "walks the earth as in a garden planted for him" [560]. On the other hand, man has also eaten from the Tree of Knowledge. He, alone of the animals, can go beyond himself, transgress the limits of his natural good. But since this is the Eden story as retold by reason, there is no original sin, repentance, and Savior. In order to right ourselves, we have reason—the most useful tool of all.

Furthermore, just as man uses, he is also used. Utility is now the bond of human community. In yet another appearance of Adam Smith's invisible hand, the individual serves others by serving himself. What was formerly part of the corrupt culture world insight now sanctions as the bond of rational community. There is no deceit because there are no noble illusions: everybody knows that everybody is both user and used, end and means. This is the rational, disillusioned, way to look at the world.

Utility is the dialectical unity of the *in-itself* and the *for-another:* a this for the sake of that. It thus manifests the Concept. A thing is what it is insofar as it is useful. This double essence derives from the double essence of insight's Supreme Being, the vapid God of reason [559]. This is where secular enlightenment, in fashioning a natural religion, *mimics religion* in attempting to correct its errors. The Christian God raises the believer, but also reminds him that he is nothing without God. The believer is both elevated and humbled, made aware of a sameness (he is in-himself loved by God) and a difference (he is *for* Another). The God of reason performs a similar function by being utility itself. God as nature continually creates and destroys, bestows in-itself-ness and then takes it away—makes man an end and also uses him as a means within the economy of the whole. In its first appearance, culture had called the in-itself good, the for-another bad [559]. But insight, in its rage for conceptuality, prefers to drop these figurative forms of speech in favor of "the purer abstractions" of in-itself and for-another.

Let us sum up where we are at this point. Insight has found its absolute in the useful. Regarding all things as useful establishes the right and truly rational relation of things to one another, of things to man and God, and of God to man. Religion itself becomes "supremely useful," since "it is pure utility itself" [561].[16] This is Hegel's interpretation of what moderns like Descartes, Spinoza, and Rousseau mean when they say that all things come from God. They mean that all things come from the divine essence, which is eternally itself, while continually producing finite things. God is *useful* as the infinite source of these things: the in-itself source of what is for-another.[17]

This three-fold enlightened view of God is clearly abhorrent to people of faith [562]. But in addition, faith hears in the presumed wisdom of enlightened thinking and its deism only the platitudes, "God is absolute and unknowable" and "Only the finite is knowable." Deism, the modern utility God, knowledge as limited to sensuous things—all these sound empty to faith, because they are.

Faith Unsettled [563–73]

The conflict between faith and reason can be put in terms of right [*Recht*] [563]. Faith has the *divine right* of being always self-same. It is the identity, the steadfastness and in-itself-ness, of pure thought. Faith is faithful. It is faithful, moreover, to a self-consistent, enduring content. Enlightenment, by contrast, our "new serpent of wisdom," slinks and wriggles in the medium of otherness (the "slippery" side of the Concept). It has "only a human right as against faith and for the support of its own truth; for the wrong it commits is the right to be *non-identical,* and consists in perverting and altering." The division into divine and human rights strongly echoes the conflict between Antigone and Creon. There, as in the present case, although one right is higher than another, both must be recognized. Faith is the right of consciousness (objectivity), enlightenment the right of self-consciousness (subjectivity) [563]. Enlightenment wrongs faith but does so, paradoxically, with right.

It is important to realize here that faith and insight are not externally opposed, like two warriors gazing at each other across an abyss. Insight engages faith by opposing it, and in that sense enters into faith: to negate is also to embrace and invade. Enlightenment opposes faith but does so with "principles that are implicit in faith itself" [564]. It twists the meaning of faith; but the ground of this twisting lies in faith itself, which has within it an otherness it does not recognize. At first, faith sees only wrongdoing. It does not see that it affirms itself only by separating what is also combined. Enlightenment, in spite of its ill will, functions as a sort of Socrates to faith: it reminds faith of its *other* elements when it tries to cling to just one. As faith clings to self-sameness, the serpent of reason keeps pointing out otherness. The perversity of the Enlightenment is thus also a revelation—one that will succeed, if not in converting faith, then in destroying its comfort and satisfaction.

Enlightenment, however, is in the dark about itself. It too fails to bring its separate thoughts together. It no more sees itself in its other than does faith. Again, the central character here is the almighty Concept, the whole of which faith and insight are parts. These parts do not see themselves as parts. Insight confronts in faith the givenness of the Concept itself, Concept as an object [565]. But it does not know that it is looking at the other, equally necessary moment of itself—the moment of self-sameness. As Hegel puts it, enlightenment is the Concept in its *unconscious* movement or self-otherness.

Earlier, we looked at the Enlightenment from the perspective of faith—as the rationalism that willfully misrepresents faith. But the Enlightenment also contains truth. It reveals to faith the moment of *self-otherness* that faith fails to acknowledge in itself. This self-otherness or logical fluidity is the work of the Concept, which insight champions but only imperfectly understands. Faith may assert itself with a divine right of self-sameness. But it is the overarching power of negation and self-otherness that combines both aspects of the Concept as a transition of the one into the other: to negate is to embrace. Enlightenment, as this power of negation, thus enjoys an "absolute right" over the non-dialectical simplicity of faith [565].[18]

To clarify how the Concept manifests itself in insight's battle against faith, Hegel returns for a third and last time to the three moments of faith. He reveals how the stark opposition between faith and reason contains an underlying unity that neither faith nor reason understands. In this last part of the analysis, faith and insight grow closer together and "get on the inside" of each other. Enlightenment will reveal its identity with faith; and faith, infected by its other, will become a form of enlightenment. Each gets into a tangle of same and other. This tangle is the work of the Concept, which manifests itself as the simultaneous separation and identity of opposites.

In attacking faith's first moment (belief in an objective God), enlightenment claims that the Christian God is simply a product of the believer's own mind [566]. When faith objects, claiming that its God is something purely in itself, enlightenment calls attention to the *second* claim that faith makes, that God comes to be something *for the believer* through the believer's own actions of worship and service, that God in this sense indeed comes *from* him. Generally, faith separates logical moments that belong together: the in-itself and the for-consciousness. Enlightenment only reminds faith of its other claim, thus correcting the one-sidedness of faith. But enlightenment does the same thing it faults in faith: it separates what it should also combine. In order to trap faith in a contradiction, it accuses the Christian God of being a mere product. It refuses to admit that God could be *both* a being in itself *and* something brought forth by action. As we saw, enlightenment also makes the exactly opposite accusation, namely, that faith's picture-God is utterly alien to the believer's mind. The same tangle of Same and Other appears within faith, which simultaneously affirms God as the being in whom the believer finds himself and the being that is "unsearchable" and "unattainable."

The tangle of Same and Other also arises in the case of the materialism that enlightenment ascribes to faith [567]. Faith obviously does not worship *things.* But it cannot deny that material things are part of the believer's picture-oriented relation to God. Nor can it deny that it believes in an historical, sensuous happening (the Incarnation) as an essential part of its faith. But enlightenment too avoids putting the moments of the Concept together to form a whole. It does so here by denying that the sensuous world has anything of spirit in it at all. The world for it is only sensuous.

Next, Hegel takes up the second moment, God as the ground of faith [568]. Again faith falls prey to its picture thinking. Unable to "think necessity," that is, conceptually, faith admits that it is purely contingent, something that happens to come from God. It forgets this contingent, non-essential aspect of itself when it takes up its first moment: the claim that through faith the believer knows the essential Being. But again, in reminding faith of its one-sidedness, enlightenment reveals its own. It takes the birth of Jesus as only an historical fact having no connection with absolute being.

Finally, insight and faith reveal their mutual one-sidedness in the sphere of action [569]. Enlightenment, as we know, finds it wrong to give up pleasure and property. Faith agrees with this, at least in part. It agrees that sacrifice must be the giving up of something acknowledged as good, something it would not make sense to part with. The believer shows the goodness of pleasures and material goods by holding on to some while giving up others. To give up some of these things just makes the believer "all the more self-centered and stubborn." It only shows that sacrifice takes place on this side of the Great Divide and fails to be a way of reaching God. Sacrifice is therefore ineffective and merely symbolic [569].[19]

The other element of action is purposiveness. Here the tangle of Same and Other manifests itself in the opposition of particular and universal [570]. Enlightenment rightly accuses faith of wrongly believing that specific instances of self-sacrifice prove that one has achieved a universal or total self-sacrifice. In response to God's complete surrender of his Son, the believer must free himself from all sensuous influence. But no specific actions can accomplish this. There is, in short, a dissonance between the universality of the believer's purpose (complete self-sacrifice) and the inevitably incomplete (because individual) character of action. Here enlightenment, once again, is one-sided in charging faith with one-sidedness. In its non-dialectical thinking, it separates what it should also combine: inner intention and outer action, universal and individual. It treats these opposites as though they had nothing to do with each other, as though the intention by itself were essential [571].

But in spite of enlightenment's lack of self-knowledge, it succeeds in gaining "an irresistible authority [*Gewalt*] over faith" [572]. The reason is that there is nothing the Enlightenment affirms about faith that is not in the believer's own consciousness. By revealing the self-otherness inherent in that consciousness, enlightenment seems to destroy the beauty of simple faith, "to pollute its spiritual consciousness with mean thoughts of sensuous reality." The result, however, is not pollution but purgation. What enlightenment has really destroyed is the separation that exists in faith-consciousness between its two ways of thinking. Faith distinguishes sensuous experience and spiritual experience, the dreamy perceptions of its picture thinking and the wakeful perceptions of sense-objects. Both perceptions are non-conceptual, that is, not rational. In this divided state, faith maintains its certainty at the cost of self-knowledge. Through the accusations of enlightenment, which faith now sees are based on its own claims, faith is made aware of its doubleness. The believer wakes up to the undeniable reality of his Here-and-Now. He realizes the infinite distance between where he is and where he wants to be.

At the beginning of the account, faith was full and insight empty. Now the roles are reversed. Enlightenment has interpreted faith as having no other content than sensuous thinghood. It accused faith of being a closet materialist. Faith as picture thinking is powerless to fend off this charge. Enlightenment is right to remind the believer of those aspects of his faith that involve sensuous existence. In Hegel's words, enlightenment "illuminates that heavenly world [of faith] with ideas belonging to the world of sense, and points out this finitude that faith cannot deny" [572]. Faith here is expelled from the heaven of its certainty. It collapses into a state of listless internal movement within itself [573]. By reducing spirit to matter, enlightenment has transformed all reality into the wakefulness of sensuous *things.* Everything that faith, in one aspect of its thinking, had projected into a heaven is now given back to the earth.

Faith clearly cannot rejoice in this return. What is a homecoming to insight is to faith an exile. Faith still looks to heaven. But that heaven has been emptied of all spiritual content. Enlightenment has convinced faith that it cannot make its spiritual objects determinate without reducing them to sensuous thinghood. The believer, infected by enlightenment, is thrown back into the world of sense, where he feels alienated and restless. The certainty of faith has thus become pure yearning [*reines Sehnen*] [573]. Faith has become enlightenment. It is forced to acknowledge that its God, like the god of deism, is "an Absolute without predicates." The difference is that whereas rational enlightenment is *satisfied* enlightenment, faith is *unsatisfied* enlightenment.

The satisfaction of insight is, however, only a surface phenomenon, a passing mood. To see why this is so, we must remember that faith and insight are intimately bound together as necessary aspects of the Concept. The yearning and unhappiness of faith is also the yearning and unhappiness of spirit, "which mourns over the loss of its spiritual world" [573]. The dissatisfaction of faith "bleeds over" into enlightenment and infects it with yearning. This yearning stems from the inherent shallowness, the unsatisfying bread and water, of the empty God of deism, progress without purpose, and the degradations of mere utility. In what follows, enlightenment will rid itself of this residual nostalgia for a World to Come, this blemish of yearning on the face of rational certitude [573].

The Two Enlightenments and Utility [574–81]

The Enlightenment wanted to unsettle faith. It succeeded. Enlightenment "lit up" the spiritual objects of faith, not by rendering them conceptual but by transforming them into the daylight things of the sensuous Here-and-Now. It thus took possession of the Kingdom of God.

As we saw in our previous section, negation is containment, an *embrace* of one's opposite. In their dialectical encounter, faith and insight "get on the inside of" each other. *We* saw what the warring parties did not: that faith and insight were equally necessary moments of the Concept. Faith and insight inject their "poison" into each other. Insight infects faith with the restlessness of *self-consciousness,* and faith infects insight with its dependence on an absolute other as the object of *consciousness.* Faith becomes aware of the undeniable Here-and-Now. Insight becomes aware of its bondage to a Beyond, which it has not yet fully absorbed. To this extent, insight shares in the restless "to and fro" movement experienced by faith.

Picture thinking is the most obvious form of consciousness. When I picture something, I put it "out there" and before me in the "space" of consciousness. This is what faith does in picturing God and a Kingdom of Heaven. Concepts, by contrast, are internal to me. A concept is not an object-like thing I picture "out there" but the movement of my own thought.[20] Concept *is* my act of thinking. At its present stage, insight absorbs into itself—that is, into *the* self—the consciousness mode of faith. This happens "beyond consciousness" [574]. The Other, which faith posited as something out there and immediately given, now appears within pure insight itself. At first, objectivity was all on the side of faith, and self or non-object was all on the side of insight. Now both moments appear within insight.

Insight, in short, makes itself actually what it is through self-differentiation and self-splitting. To repeat, this self-splitting is the Concept in its higher, dialectical sense, which works behind the back of insight. This process resembles the morphogenesis of living things, which become real to the extent that they manifest self-differentiation. Insight now has an object: *itself in the form of an object* [574]. This is its absolute being. This being is both thought and non-thought, self and thing. It is a "pure thing." But since insight is unconscious of what conceptual thinking (dialectic) really is, it does not know how to think this object in its wholeness. It can only think the sheer opposition of its two opposing moments: thought and thing. This inability gives rise to a civil war within the Enlightenment, to *two Enlightenments.*

Insight now experiences its former battle with faith as a civil war *within itself* [575]. Insight, as we know, is the drive to negate and "see through." When faith ceases to be a full-fledged opponent, it turns this drive against itself. The warring parties continue their Antigone vs. Creon posture and fail to see themselves in each other. But the schism that occurs within insight, far from being a defect, shows the *superiority* of insight to faith, which shuns division and stays self-same. This is old Hegelian wisdom: to be self-split is to contain otherness, to be Concept-like and thus *victorious.* The schism within insight makes it "refined" [*geläutert*] [575].

Hegel now reveals the double nature of insight's absolute Being [576]. On the one hand, this Being, as thought itself, transcends all finite things. It *is* only insofar as it is neither my individual (finite) *self*-consciousness nor anything sensed. But insofar as this Being is thought of as external to me, yet *for* me, it must reveal itself in the realm of ordinary sense-experience. Being must be infinite and empty, and yet also a source of finitude and fullness. This is the duplicity that inheres in the "pure thing" of insight.

What insight thinks of as its absolute Being depends, Hegel stresses, on the starting-point of its two "cultural developments" [*Bildungen*] [578]. If insight begins with the intellectual side of the "pure thing," then it calls the absolute *God,* the first cause of all things. If it begins with the sensuous side, then it calls the absolute *matter.*[21] Matter here results from the process of abstraction. It is what is *left over* when we take away a thing's color, taste, texture, and so forth [577]. Pure *thought* and pure *matter* mirror each other's lack of predicates or determinations, and *are* each other. This is the identity of inner and outer that insight posits but does not comprehend.[22] If these two "cultures" or Enlightenments were to set aside their rigidly held starting-points, they would meet. Enlightenment as *deism* starts with God as the inscrutable primal cause, on which finite things ultimately dependent. Enlightenment as *materialism* starts with sensuous things and abstracts all their qualities in order to get the absolute as matter.[23]

We now reach the crowning moment in this section: the transformation of insight's "double essence" into the single essence of *utility* [579]. Utility is *the truth of enlightenment.* It is that in which "pure insight completes its realization" [580]. Utility was present earlier, when insight struggled against faith. But there it was only a weapon that insight used to reduce the pretensions of faith to feet-on-the-ground reasonableness. Here, the useful becomes *absolute,* not a means but the ultimate end of reason.

Utility is the logical outgrowth of the need to unify thinghood and selfhood. The two conflicting sides of the "pure thing"—in-itself and for-me, thing and thought—coalesce. The useful is neither thinghood by itself nor thought by itself but the unity of thing and thought. Utility expresses "the universal" that is common to both God and matter [579]. It is the mind's experience of its own *inner motion* or *instability* in an actual object. A thing is just a thing. But a useful thing goes beyond itself and is therefore unstable or transfinite. Yet in this very instability a useful thing remains a thing. The hammer is what it most is when it is for something else: its being-in-itself is its being-for-another. Utility is thus the perfect God-substitute for those who seek transcendence but hate religion. In Hegel's image, utility is "simple rotary motion," a going out into otherness that always returns to self. The hammer, as a useful thing, is what it is, stays within itself, only by being for another, that is, by going outside itself. In going outside itself, it "stays within itself" in that it remains a hammer: "it is absolutely *for another*, but equally is for an 'other' merely what it is in itself" [580]. This axial motion of the useful is also the motion of thinking, the motion we first saw as *self-consciousness* [169].

When insight first came on the scene, it was conceptuality, "reasonableness," without an object. Or rather its only object was faith, which insight opposed. In the useful, insight now has an object to which it is positively related. To faith, sentimentality, and so-called "speculation," to make the useful the absolute is a scandal [580]. But utility is in fact a victory for insight. It is the internal restlessness of spirit, the desire for a Beyond, made into a rational, down-to-earth *thing*. The "blemish" of yearning, which insight experienced through its contact with faith [573], has been removed. The Beyond is now no longer a transcendent Better World but rather the self-transcendence of *this world*, of things insofar as they are useful.

Insight has found itself in an object—but only in an objective form [580]. *We see* the dialectical, truly rational form of the useful, but insight does not. In a curious turnabout, insight, in finding its object, has become a form of *Vorstellen* or picture thinking as opposed to conceptual insightfulness! It is thus *satisfied* with utility but does not know why. In fact, this satisfaction itself is only relative and passing. To the extent that useful things are only useful *things*, insight still finds itself confronted by an external world [580]. The thinking subject, man as self-consciousness, has not yet been infused into that world. Through the useful, the world is *for* him but does not yet reveal itself *as* him. This final phase of insight will occur in the next section. There, the positive object of insight will, like Pandora's box, release its latent negativity, the negativity of the self as *desire*.

Hegel ends this middle section of his chapter on culture with a summary [581]. The motion of enlightenment began with the nephew, who embodied the vanity of culture. Pure consciousness, of which faith and insight are parts, fled this vanity by turning within. Insight *purges* faith of its assurance that God is present in the way that objects are present. It reduces the God of faith to the unknowable first cause and to indeterminate matter. But insight has not yet sufficiently purged itself of a lingering hope for a Better World. It does in the useful. The useful is the God of secular insight. For consciousness in its broad sense, the whole world is now objective in being useful to man. This includes not only the real world of objects but also the ideal world of thoughts, which, like hammers, are now *true* to the extent that they can be *used*.

Culture's first "world of spirit" was its moment of self-*certainty* [581]. Culture expanded into existence like nature, which brings forth an infinity of individuals. But there was not yet a universal—a commonality or *genus*—to hold together these self-interested and ultimately perverse individuals. In its "second world," the culture spirit finds its *truth* and universality in pure thought as faith in a Being that is in itself and infinitely worthy. This spirit is explicitly self-opposed in the battle of faith and insight. The Enlightenment transforms the God of faith into the vacuous Supreme Being of deism. The "third world" is that of the useful. Utility is the union of self-certainty and truth. It expresses man's certainty of himself in a concrete way, his self-certainty *in this world* of actuality. The world *is* insofar as it is for man.

Spirit's adventure of self-discovery began with the Eden of Greek ethicality. But then spirit became self-conscious and unhappy. As Roman, it was thrown back on itself and exiled from its Here-and-Now. Modern culture cultivates man as a being who rises above his nature or givenness. But this project of culturing makes man always outside himself or self-alienated, only and always "on his way." Faith offers a hope for escape but at the expense of the Here-and-Now. Insight, through the Enlightenment and the useful, brings man back to the Here-and-Now. It *seems* to give man his homecoming and return to Eden, the state in which man's inner and outer worlds "are reconciled and heaven is transplanted to earth below" [581].

Terror as the Truth of Culture [582–95]

Hegel's title for this section is "Absolute Freedom and Terror." Here we reach the truth of the whole culture world. Throughout spirit's journey, man as self-consciousness has tried to posit himself as absolute, to be fully himself and subject to nothing outside himself. When self-consciousness first appeared, it was desire. This is man's impulse to make himself independent and free through the destruction of external things. The impulse is also man's desire to be God, the desire inherent in man by virtue of his being self-conscious and *self-centering.*

In being self-aware, I am an object to myself and therefore self-opposed or self-negating. This relation to self is the paradigm and source of my relation to everything other than myself, my relation to the world. To think is to bring the object within the sphere of my self-consciousness. That is why self-consciousness is not only the truth of consciousness but also "the native kingdom of truth" itself [167]. Self-consciousness is not the self apart from the object, but the self as having *within itself* the opposition of subject and object. It is the self-differentiating One and, as such, is identical with the Concept as the form of all rationality. As I have regularly observed in the course of our journey, man, for Hegel, does not just know the truth: he *is* the truth. Desire is the most primitive form of self-awareness, because in desire I experience the raw negativity of my relation to everything other than me. I want to destroy, eat, the external world and put myself in its place.[24]

I have gone through all this to remind the reader that the *Phenomenology* is primarily the logic and the story of self-consciousness as desire. I also want to emphasize, at this critical moment of the drama, that all the practical-historical happenings or phenomena we meet in Hegel's *Phenomenology* are for the sake of absolute knowing, the completion of philosophy in the form of Science [5]. The historical emergence of man in his fullness is identical with the dialectical emergence of thought or truth in its fullness. Both embody the triumph of the Concept over alienation and picture-thinking.

In this third and final stage of culture, man as self-consciousness and desire bursts forth violently. Desire, the sheer will to negate, appears as fanaticism. The French Revolution, in particular the Reign of Terror, is the individual now made universal, at last asserting his absolute right over all things—his *absolute freedom* [582].[25] As I stressed above, this is also the Concept's right to be all things, the right championed by the Enlightenment. The French Revolution is the Concept making itself real by releasing the full force of the negativity implicit in self-consciousness. Man's earlier efforts at self-assertion were feeble by comparison. These were individual combat, stoic withdrawal, romantic yearning, vigilante rebellion, middle-class morality, vanity, otherworldliness, and the calm pursuit of the useful. All that is past. Now man asserts his individuality, not as this singular object-like self (my self as opposed to your self) but as the universal *process* of self-consciousness, as pure *subject.*

The path from pure insight to pure terror begins with the useful, the positive side of the Concept. We then proceed to Rousseau's general will, and from there to the desire-like annihilation of the culture world. Let us look more closely at this path.

The Enlightenment found its congenial object in utility [582]. The useful expresses the certainty that the world exists for the sake of the self or man. This certainty is the "inner revolution" that is the seed of "the actual revolution of the actual world." It is a seed because the useful is only an object and thus fails to express the Concept as subject. Since negativity is still implicit, so too is self-consciousness, which is the negativity I outlined above. In short, the useful expresses the certainty that the world is *for me* but not yet that it *is* me (*"Le monde, c'est moi!"*). Insight has not yet established its interiority, the pure motion of thought, as the reality of the world. It has only implicitly transplanted heaven to earth below. The return to the ethical Eden of the Greeks is still an end to be achieved [582]. The French Revolution will be that attempted return.

The useful offers only "an empty show of objectivity" [583]. It only seems to be a predicate of the world qua external. In fact, it is the world insofar as it has been completely taken over, invaded, by self-consciousness. As useful, the world is actual only in being *for me.* The useful, as Hegel has already shown, has the same dialectical structure as self-consciousness. It *is* self-consciousness as object. In beholding the useful, I am really gazing at myself as the unity of subject and object. In the useful, I have become the essence of actuality, the Concept made real.

The world is now the possession of the self, of the individual not as passive spectator but as active force, indeed as the creative force that has shaped, and continues to shape, the world of culture. In the instrumentality of the useful, the self sees its own practicality or being-at-work, its world-creating, world-transformative power. It sees the useful as the image of the will. With this revelation of the subjective nature of the useful, a new shape of consciousness arises. This is "absolute freedom" [584]. In absolute freedom, man discovers that the world is not merely his tool but his very act of willing.[26] Man now grasps that his self-consciousness as an individual, his certainty of himself, is the essence of the entire culture world, that "all reality is solely spiritual [i.e. the work of self-consciousness]." The world, for this new shape of consciousness, is simply "its own work" [584]. It is only what man wills and, moreover, wills universally.

It is important to distinguish absolute freedom (or will to power, as we may call it) from the efforts of the modern achiever (Chapter 14). The achiever used his talent to make his selfhood real. He was locked inside his contingent individuality, which he tried but failed to make essential. He failed because in his obsession with products he failed to actualize the form, act, and negativity of his self-consciousness. Man was not spirit but only a spiritual *animal.* At spirit's present stage, by contrast, man appears as "the universal subject" [583]. This universality has emerged from insight's having successfully risen above vanity and idiosyncrasy and become the active individuality of all human beings everywhere. Simply stated, enlightenment, like faith, is for everyone.

Absolute freedom—the absolute *as* freedom—is the condition in which the individual affirms his universality or uncompromised worth as thinking subject in the realm of actuality. This freedom takes the form of Rousseau's general will, which is "the will of all individuals as such" [584].

For Hegel, Rousseau was the first to posit freedom as the absolute. He thus paved the way for Kant's moral philosophy and the later German Idealists (Fichte, Schelling, and Hegel himself).[27] In his *Social Contract,* Rousseau seeks the conditions under which government can be just, given man's natural freedom. He finds the answer in the general will.[28] Through the general will, the individual obeys laws that he himself has authorized. Law in this sense is not external to the individual but emanates from him. It is the very expression of his freedom. In obeying laws that emanate from the general will, I obey only myself, my individuality as a universal. The general good is my good, and my good is the general good.[29]

Hegel observes that "this undivided substance of absolute freedom ascends the throne of the world without any power being able to resist it" [585]. That is, freedom is the spirit that pervades and takes possession of the modern culture world and reveals itself as the source of all the social spheres or "masses" into which that world is divided. Once laws and institutions are revealed as nothing but selfhood made objective, there is no going back, no way to retrieve the absoluteness of objectivity as such. The spreading of freedom through society is just like the spreading of enlightenment in the realm of thought. Positive teachings and institutions, whether of Church or State, are powerless to fend it off. The spirit of freedom is infectious, undeniable, and terrible. For Hegel, there is nothing to which we are more tightly bound, not even life itself, than freedom. To deny its supremacy, once that supremacy has been revealed, is to deny oneself.

The onset of absolute freedom, in the form of the general will, is the destruction of anything that could oppose that will as a prospective absolute. The otherness or difference inherent in objectivity has been completely destroyed [586]. There is no Beyond of any kind. All the alienation that was present in the culture world has vanished. As we saw, the God of faith was de-constructed by enlightenment. God was reduced to the unobjectionable but vacuous *Être supreme.* Now even that vestige of divinity has been "exhaled," Hegel says, like a "stale gas."[30]

The only opposition remaining is that between individual and universal consciousness. This opposition is canceled or *aufgehoben* in the general will [587]. Selfhood is now experienced as a process in which individuals come outside themselves to form a communal or public consciousness only to return to their individuality. The universal expresses and embodies the individuality of each. Therefore, the action of individuals, by which they make their selfhood objective, is really the action of the whole or state, the being-at-work of the laws. To act in accordance with the law is to *be* the law. The individual is no Karl-like rebel alienated from an unfeeling Establishment. He is rather a non-alienated *citoyen.*

We now reach the critical moment of Hegel's exposition, the moment in which the self pays the price for its radical subjectivity. In order to will nothing but itself and thus be absolute, the will must be utterly non-positive. Indeed, positivity was bondage and non-freedom. It was the rule of objects like God, Church, and Regime. As Hegel puts it, consciousness "cannot achieve anything positive, either universal works of language or of actuality, either of laws and general institutions of *conscious* freedom, or of deeds and works of a freedom that wills them" [588].

At first, the general will might seem like a buttress for conservatism and the status quo. Seeing my will embodied in institutions and laws would seem to make me perfectly happy with the existing regime. This is far from being the case. Insofar as such things are positive or established, they are given; and as given they do not embody me as universal self-consciousness and will. The situation is like that of the achiever, whose individual works could never embody the sheer universality of consciousness. Not even specific laws I give myself, and which are expressions of the communal good, can embody "the universal work itself" [588]. Action too is limited in this way. It cannot give rise to something positive without being limited to the positing of *this* individual, who excludes all other individuals. The general will dare not develop and expand into an articulated whole (that is, a concrete societal world) without ceasing to be free. If freedom is to be absolute or universal, it cannot have any content whatsoever but must be the expression of sheer willing. As Hegel now puts it, "there is left for it only *negative action;* it is only the *fury* of disappearance" [*die Furie des Verschwindens*].[31]

The negativity implicit in the general will is now released. This is the opposition within consciousness between universal consciousness as something abstract and individual consciousness as actual and concrete [590]. The universality that guards freedom by refusing to expand into a concrete whole becomes both empty and self-opposed. Having destroyed the institutions and human representatives of the *ancien régime,* the Revolution turns against its own representatives. It pits abstract principles of Liberty, Equality, and Fraternity against the equally abstract or stubborn individuality of revolutionary heroes like Danton and Robespierre, both of whom were guillotined.[32] Both these extremes are rigid, cold, and uncompromising. In this advanced stage of upheaval and turbulence, the spirit of *la Liberté* turns against the only thing left to destroy: the mere *life* of individuals who, through their ideological willfulness, are traitors to the cause of freedom.

The sole work of universal freedom is thus *death* [590]. It is the work of the sheer Universal putting to death the sheer Individual. Since this individual is regarded as having no claim to universality at all, his death "is the coldest and meanest of all deaths, with no more significance than cutting off a head of cabbage or swallowing a mouthful of water." It is not even, strictly speaking, an execution, since no specific crime has been committed. Death is but erasure.

The "wisdom" of government is at this point summed up in one word: "Death!" This syllable embodies absolute freedom that refuses to mediate itself and give itself content. The Revolution, through the work of men like Danton and Robespierre, indeed sets up a government. But this government expresses nothing beyond sheer force, the right to do anything and everything. Since everything positive is considered suspect and bereft of universality, the New Republic can manifest itself only as a self-interested *faction* [591]. No regime, under this view of government, can be universally valid. And so, the Republic invokes its own overthrow by another faction. The very existence of an established government is proof of its "guilt." Thus is generated the battle among revolutionaries themselves, who, after all, are only individuals. Since there is no positive law and no criminal acts, it is enough that someone be suspected of a criminal intent in order for him to merit "cold, matter-of-fact annihilation."[33] The direct result of absolute freedom, in other words, is that universality seeks the death of the very people who champion that universality.

In the Reign of Terror, spirit learns the true meaning of absolute freedom [592]. Freedom, here, is universality without content: abstract freedom. The abstraction from all determinate content is the source of all the fanaticism and murder.[34] Empty willing, which affirms the abstract principles of "Freedom, Equality, and Brotherhood," is only world-destruction and the erasure of all life. The Terror is freedom that has become objective to itself. Spirit here sees the transition of its initial, positive certainty into a horrific negative truth. The actualization of self-consciousness as absolute freedom is thus the utter annihilation of self-consciousness. What was supposed to be preserved in the general will—the individual—is in fact destroyed.

In place of the mutual recognition promised by the general will, we have the fear of violent death, the "absolute master" [593]. The Republic indeed becomes an articulated whole. Society reconstitutes itself. But individuals obey the "laws" of this new arrangement only out of fear, and the new order is vulnerable and unstable.

This return to an Establishment and positive law seems to suggest that spirit goes back to ethicality and starts all over again [594]. But in ethicality (the Greek *polis*), there was a reciprocal relation between inner self and outer world. The individual was fulfilled in law as custom; and the community was actual in the words, deliberations, and deeds of its individual members. Such reciprocity is no longer possible in the culture world, where, through the negative work of absolute freedom, universal and individual are mutually alienated. The French Revolution and its mortal Republic thus constitute "the most elevated [*erhabenste*] and last" stage of culture, that Second World of Self. The culture spirit can only watch its concrete forms vanish in the fury of self-consciousness: honor and wealth, the language and insights of the perverse nephew, the heaven of faith, and the utility of the Enlightenment. The end of culture is nothingness, the void, made objective as terror and death.[35]

But suddenly, amid all this blackness, a ray of light appears, the welcome work of determinate negation. This Nothing that has come on the scene is not an alien Nothing like the necessity or Fate that destroyed the ethical world. It is rather the dynamic nothingness of self-consciousness as sheer universal *willing* (the enlightened version of desire). Hegel puts this in a deliberately paradoxical way: the Nothing unleashed in the French

Revolution is "the pure positive because it is the pure negative" [594]. The individual has been swallowed and negated by universality in the form of violence. But this universality is *his own selfhood.* In this crucial dialectical turn, the negativity of the universal becomes positive. It transforms the individual from being an abstract point into an expansive *inner* world. The crucial word here is "pure." *Sheer* willing has become *pure* willing. Let us see what this means.

Through the ravages of the French Revolution, the self learns not to look for itself in the realm of immediate existence. The self turns away from its merely political or outer view of freedom. This is the view that gave rise, through Rousseau's general will, to revolutionary government on the one hand, and individual ideologues like Danton and Robespierre on the other [594]. Thus purified of its political rage for freedom, the self reaches a higher *inner* unity of individual and universal, a higher will. This is the "pure will" of Kant's moral philosophy. As a pure moral will, self-consciousness appears as "the pure knowing of essential being qua pure knowing." It is selfhood communing with itself. The will, here, is no longer immediate or natural, *like desire,* which is obsessed with negating the external world. Instead, the now moral will expresses the universality of the individual who wills universally binding moral laws. Content no longer poses the problem it did for the general will, since the individual will here wills not a specific content but the *universal form* of moral judgment. This is Kant's categorical imperative.

Hegel now states the dramatic conclusion of his long chapter on culture: "Absolute freedom has thus removed the antithesis between the universal and the individual will" [595]. In the first major transition of the culture world, lived or actual culture passed into a realm of pure thought (faith and insight). Now, in this second inversion, absolute freedom, having annihilated the whole culture world, passes into yet another realm of pure thought. This realm is spirit's Third World of Self. Spirit now leaves France and enters "another land" of self-knowing. This is the realm of morality as the higher freedom. It is where, through Luther, spirit gave birth to the *German* Revolution.[36]

Heaven, as it is called, does not lie beyond the grave. It already surrounds us here and its light is kindled in every pure heart.
FICHTE, *The Vocation of Man*

 19

Pure Willing and the Moral World-View

THE TRANSITION FROM CULTURE TO MORALITY IS ONE OF THE MOST stunning inversions in the *Phenomenology*, as we go from revolutionary fanaticism to the moral will. We are now in the upper regions of Hegel's divided line (see Chapter 16). On the other side of morality is religion, and after that, absolute knowing.

Spirit, we recall, is selfhood as community or world [438]. Its three stages are ethicality, culture, and morality. These embody the three stages of the Concept: self-sameness or unity, self-otherness or opposition, and unity within opposition. Alternately, they are identity, difference, and the identity of identity and difference. *Ethicality* is spirit in its moment of self-sameness and objective immediacy, spirit as *consciousness*. The ethical individual experiences the customs of his concrete community (the *polis*) as his substance and truth. *Culture* is the Concept at its middle stage of dichotomy or self-splitting. It is spirit in the mode of *self-consciousness*. The cultured individual makes himself other than himself. He alienates his natural being in order to gain universality and worth as a social being. *Morality*, the third stage of spirit, is the Concept at *its* third stage. It unites the objectivity or substance of the ethical world with the subjectivity or individuality of culture. Morality is thus spirit at the level of self-affirming *reason*.[1]

Ethicality was spirit in its *truth* [473]. The individual found his fulfillment in a non-reflective relation to the spirit of his community: in *trust*. Custom was the sacred object of his consciousness. As the title of the present section indicates, morality, by contrast, is "spirit that is certain of itself."[2] In the overall dialectic of spirit, the individual comes to see that the absolute resides, not outside the individual but in his "pure knowledge" and self-certainty [596]. As Hegel dramatically puts it, moral self-consciousness "has become master [*Meister*] of the opposition within consciousness itself [between subject and object]." Morality heals the rift in the culture world.

It seeks to recover the spiritual health and harmony of the Greek *polis* by grounding these in an inner sense of absolute "rightness"—in absolute freedom that has become *positive.*

At this stage, the individual experiences moral self-certainty as the core of his being. He finds his vocation and absolute in *duty,* the absolute Ought or *Sollen* [599].[3] Duty here refers not to dutiful acts but to the inner ground of action, the all-demanding imperative to act morally. Duty is higher than custom because it is an inner authority, the sacred "call" of my inmost self. It is higher than culture because it transcends the opposition of faith and insight. Morality, in short, is the enlightened version of piety.

The moral law first appeared at the third and highest stage of reason. Law was the universal human *thing* or *Sache selbst,* the "work of all and each" [418]. But morality, with its pure Ought, was not yet present. The individual could not shake off his naturalistic will to assert himself qua individual. By testing laws, he put himself above them and subverted their lawfulness [434]. This experience of subversion generated the *sanctity* or inviolableness of law—law's complete independence from human reason. The sacred, which reason had forsworn, re-enters the *Phenomenology* with spirit. In ethicality, it is Greek *themis* or Right, in culture the Christian supersensible Beyond. In morality, the sacred takes the form of pure duty: the Ought.

In this section, Hegel initiates us into the Moral World-View, *die moralische Weltanschauung* [600]. More accurately rendered Moral World-Intuition, the phrase defines morality as an act of *Anschauen* or intellectual "seeing." In its moral "seeing," the self claims to have immediate access to the absolute. This view is summed up in the three postulates put forth by Kant in his *Critique of Practical Reason* (Pluhar, 155 ff.).[4] They are *God, freedom,* and the *immortality of the soul* (ibid., 168).

Hegel will treat freedom as a moral given rather than a postulate. In place of freedom, he lists as a postulate what Kant calls the highest good or happiness. In this revised version of Kant, the *first postulate* is the ideal harmony of duty and *external* nature, of duty and the fulfillment of duty. The *second postulate* is the ideal harmony of duty and *internal* nature (my sensuous impulses and desires). And the *third postulate* is God as the ideal being that wills, and in willing sanctifies, specific duties.

As Hyppolite notes, morality, for Hegel, is not confined to Kant's moral teaching, but expresses the broader phenomenon of *moralism* (470). The *Phenomenology* is about experience as the path to absolute knowing. The shapes we meet along this path are universal attitudes that have welled up in the course of history. These are the immediate appearances or phenomena of spirit. A shape may find its authoritative expression in a philosophic doctrine. But Hegel's primary focus is experience as the process of positing and suffering. The Moral World-View is an advanced stage of this process. Kant is the systematic voice of the Moral World-View. But the view itself is not so much a philosophic teaching as a way of viewing the world and a way of life. Hegel will show that moralism is, in truth, exactly the opposite of what it intends. The high-minded attempt to ground world and man in pure duty, to *live* in accordance with Kantian morality, will result in hypocrisy.

Hegel's account of morality, like that of culture, is very long. In this chapter, I take up the Moral World-View (sections a and b). In the next, I explore conscience and the romantic human type known as the *beautiful soul* (section c).

Morality and Its Postulates [596–600]

Hegel begins with a quick review of spirit, as it has appeared thus far [596]. He sets forth the path to moral consciousness as the process by which the individual is *purified* and rendered universal. In the Greek *polis,* the individual was universal through his immersion in his ethical substance. His individuality as such was suppressed. After Hellas falls, this suppressed individuality affirms itself as absolute. The individual becomes universal as the Roman legal person. But this person, though absolute, is abstract, empty, and meaningless. Expelled from ethical Eden, man is no longer at home in the world. At the stage of culture, he seeks his "substance and fulfillment" in a heavenly Beyond. Culture further develops man's Roman alienation. Eventually, in the French Revolution, it overcomes the split between heaven and earth, between essence (or meaning) and actuality (or real life). Through the Terror, spirit comes to know the world as its own, as nothing but the manifestation of the self's will to power. By annihilating the world, as it currently exists, spirit comes to know itself as the true master of the world. Spirit then returns into itself, or becomes reflective, and is certain that its moral self-knowledge is the substance and truth of all things—that morality is the true freedom.

This hard-won knowledge is not speculative or for its own sake. It is rather my intuition of myself as a moral agent—a being that *acts.*[5] Morality affirms the supremacy of practical over speculative reason: it affirms *moral certitude* as absolute knowing. This affirmation is central to the teachings of Kant and Fichte.[6]

Moral selfhood is more advanced than selfhood in its previous forms [597]. Moral self-knowledge is both immediate and mediating. It is immediate because the moral individual, like his ethical counterpart, obeys an unquestioned given: duty. But moral awareness is higher than the natural immediacy of character, since it is defined by knowing rather than not knowing [597]. Like culture and faith, morality is "absolute mediation." As a moral, self-reflective being, I make myself other than myself, by analogy with the cultured individual and the man of faith. But my process of self-othering is neither negative nor otherworldly. I cancel my immediate, natural being in order to affirm the universality I find within myself as a moral being. I am not self-alienated but positively self-transcending or noble. I do not flee my Here-and-Now, nor do I experience my essence in something other than myself (a Kingdom of Heaven). In my awareness of duty or the Ought, I have within myself that which transcends the sensuous Here-and-Now. The whole meaning of my life is immediately present to me in my "intuited pure certainty" of myself. This moral knowing and willing constitute the absolute freedom that the French Revolution generated but failed to grasp. The moral self "is absolutely free in that it knows its freedom, and just this *knowledge* [my italics] is its substance and purpose and its sole content" [598].[7]

Hegel proceeds to show what it means to adopt the Moral World-View. Self-consciousness "knows duty to be the absolute essence" [599]. It has for its object its own immediate knowledge of the Ought and is "locked up" [*beschlossen*] within itself. But from within this self-certainty, the individual is also aware of the external world as his other. Since the worldly out-there adds nothing essential to his moral in-here, the individual "behaves with perfect freedom and indifference toward this otherness" [599]. Precisely because the morally self-certain individual is free of the outside world, this world is free of him and his good will. It has become "a complete world within itself with an individuality of its own, a self-subsistent whole of laws peculiar to itself, as well as an independent operation of those laws, and a free realization of them." This freely operating, lawful, and self-sufficient realm is *nature*. The Moral World-View consists in the intuited relation [*Beziehung*] between the two autonomous and mutually indifferent realms of moral value and natural fact—in logical terms, between "the being-in-and-for-itself of morality and the being-in-and-for-itself of nature" [600].

At this point, Kant's three moral postulates (as revised by Hegel) come into play. Hegel first shows how these postulates dialectically imply each other (a). Then, in the next section (b), he shows how morality consciously violates its own distinctions. The third postulate, God, will sum up the self-contradictory nature of all the postulates, and of the very act of moral postulating.

The First Postulate: Duty and the External World [601–2]

For the moral individual, duty is the essence of action. This inner certainty grounds and gives meaning to action. But the individual is also aware of nature or the external world, which he has assumed to be completely independent of moral value. Duty is the Ought that commands me, absolutely, to fulfill my duty. But to act is to enter the realm that is indifferent to moral intent: the realm of Is. The self thus learns by experience that the world "may let it become happy, or perhaps not" [601]. It learns that a good will does not necessarily meet with good results, that, in fact, good people sometimes fare badly and the bad prosper. Happiness here is not the gratification of natural desires but the joy of seeing my moral purpose fulfilled. It is "the happiness [*das Glück*] of accomplishment and the enjoyment of completion."[8]

To illustrate Hegel's point, let us assume that I tell the truth in order to fulfill my duty and bring about my moral purpose, the good. Experience teaches me that this effort sometimes succeeds and sometimes does not. Sometimes I only make matters worse by telling the truth. Or I tell the truth and no one believes me. In addition, I see other people who embody "non-moral consciousness" achieving their goals through amoral or even immoral means, if not through outright lies then through little dissimulations and truths withheld. Their impurity succeeds where my purism fails. They are happy: I am not. This rankles, since accomplishment is essential to duty: morality commands me to *do* my duty. It seems unjust to me that these others, who follow the Way of the World, should fare so well, while I, the Knight of Duty, am imprisoned in my good intentions and denied the joy of fulfillment [601]. At a later stage of experience, this resentment will become full-blown envy [625].

The moral individual "cannot forgo happiness and leave this moment out of its absolute purpose" [602]. Actions belong to real human beings, who want to see their purposes fulfilled. Like the achiever at the stage of reason, the moral agent seeks self-actualization in his effort to actualize duty. His moral effort belongs inescapably to the realm of nature, which is also the realm of deeds. Morality cannot therefore be indifferent to nature but must incorporate nature (the world) into its moral outlook. And so, on the basis of the individual's experience of the world's injustice, morality propounds its First Postulate. If morality is to make sense, there must be a *harmony* between the moral and the natural, between duty and happiness as moral fulfillment.[9]

To say that harmony is postulated means that moral reason demands it.[10] This ideal harmony consists in a *future* coincidence of duty and nature. Moral reason demands a world in which the Ought *is*. This demand is not psychological, but is rooted in the very concept of duty. Without a postulated future identity of Ought and Is, the moral Ought would be a contradiction, a command incapable of being carried out.

The Second Postulate: Duty and the Internal World [603]

Hegel now moves on to what he calls "a whole circle of postulates" [603]. Up to this point, nature was the external world of things and actions. But nature also contains my inner desires and sensuous impulses, which pull me away from what I ought to do. These constitute the otherness I encounter *within* myself.[11] As Hegel puts it, "pure thought and the sensuous aspect of consciousness are in themselves a single consciousness."

Aware of this moral dissonance, morality puts forth a Second Postulate. It demands another harmony—the unity of my "reason" and my "sensuousness" or inclinations—in order to make sense of its world-view.[12] The unifying idea here is the individual's *infinite progress* toward moral perfection [603]. In my actual Here-and-Now, I am a clash of opposites: pure will and sensuous impulse. The harmonious unity of these opposites is a not yet accomplished goal. But this goal must also be infinitely distant, something that I must *never* reach. For if I did reach it, "this would do away with moral consciousness." I am a moral being only insofar as duty rises above sensuous impulse. The Knight of Duty (as we may call him), like the Knight of Virtue, demands an opposition, something to fight against. If the fight were to stop, he would cease to be moral. The ideality of the ideal *that ought to be real* must be protected from the real. This is the paradox and perversity of moral purism. On the one hand, the unity of duty and desire must remain an ongoing task if morality is to be preserved. On the other, since duty demands nothing less than perfection, the unity must be thought of "as something that simply must *be,* and must not remain a [mere] task" [603].

As a moral individual, I may try to console myself with the fact that infinity is a long way off. Why should I concern myself with contradictions in some dim indefinite future, when duty commands me to be as good as I can be right now? But this is cold comfort. A contradiction within "perfected morality" would be a contradiction *within morality itself.* It would damage the purity of being moral and render absolute duty unreal [603]. I cannot therefore take refuge in an imprecisely moral Here-and-Now. Once again, *I need a postulate* in order to save my moral view of the world from self-contradiction.

The Third Postulate: God [604–11]

So far we have two moral postulates. The first demands a harmony of morality and nature—a final purpose of the world [604]. The second demands the harmony of duty and sensuous impulse, the ultimate unification of the individual. These postulates correspond to the first two moments of the Concept. The first demands an objective unity, a unity at the level of being-in-itself. The second demands a subjective unity, a unity at the level of self-consciousness or being-for-self. These logical extremes do not yet have the middle term that unites them. This middle term is *action.* When I try to do my duty, act morally, I come up against two forms of otherness: external nature (which is indifferent to my moral designs) and my own sensuous nature (which pulls me away from duty). The Third Postulate, which corresponds to the third level of the Concept, will posit a harmony that is *in and for itself.* This is the harmony of the first two harmonies. Its name is God.

To act morally is to act in accordance with specific duties. "Be dutiful!" is not helpful when it comes to the concrete moral demands of life. We know that the moral purist does not place his absolute in the specific moral content of any law. To do so would be to abandon pure duty for the sake of something that is not duty. The absolute must be, not a determinate set of duties but the *form* of dutifulness, the pure Ought. And yet, in order to answer duty's call, to act morally, I must regard specific, determinate duties as absolutely morally binding, since there is no such thing as action in general. The Third Postulate of morality is the attempt to avoid this contradiction and make moral action possible.

Morality, or enlightened piety, posits duty as sacred. The problem is this: How can specific duties come to be sacred, that is, absolutely compelling? If *I* were to treat as sacred any specific moral duties, I would be guilty of what Kant calls *heteronomy.* That is, I would be an idolater, who defiled the pure form of willing with specific content and ulterior motives. But in order for my specific duties to have the moral force of duty itself, which they must, they too must be sacred. The moralist's way out of this dilemma is to posit a divine consciousness that can do what he, the moralist, cannot: a Being who sanctifies specific moral laws, thus saving moral purism from either paralysis or idolatry.

God is the Third Postulate of morality. God, and only God, makes specific moral laws sacred. He "knows and wills them as duties" [606]. For this divine consciousness, both the content and the form of moral duties are sacred. God unites the particular and the universal. He is therefore "the same as the concept of the harmony of morality and happiness." The Third Postulate contains the first and brings it to a higher level. God is the being who not only overcomes the split between universal form and specific moral content, but also ensures that morality is ultimately victorious. As Hegel puts it, "This [consciousness] is then henceforth a master and ruler of the world, who brings about the harmony of morality and happiness, and at the same time sanctifies duties in their multiplicity" [606]. In speaking of God in this way, we must remember that the moral individual does not do his duty *because* it is God's will. That would be another version of heteronomy, action for the sake of something other than the moral Ought. The absolute remains pure duty, which is the lawfulness or form of the law. God is simply required, postulated, as the Being who keeps morality from falling into contradiction.[13]

The Third Postulate also envelops the second: the harmony of duty and sensuousness. In acting, the moral agent is aware of himself as "completely individual," someone who has his own particular goals and impulses [607]. He knows that the validation of his actions lies not in himself but in the other, divine consciousness, which alone renders his specific duties morally sacred. In short, the moral individual is aware that this Other is pure, and that he himself is impure. In postulating a sacred Other, the individual becomes the moral equivalent of the unhappy consciousness. In Kant's phrase, he feels his *unworthiness to be happy.* He is aware that his moral striving is always haunted by egotism and sensuousness. Happiness cannot therefore be something earned and necessarily produced, something the moralist deserves. It must be contingent and gratuitous, a gift of God's *grace* [608].[14]

In spite of his impurity, the moral individual nevertheless experiences himself as pure insofar as he makes pure duty his essence [609]. In that sense, he *is* perfect. This thought of himself as a pure will is identical with his thought of *God* as a pure will, "a being that is postulated *beyond* actuality." From the perspective of the Third Postulate, God sees the quality and extent of my pure willing: he knows my heart. He "gives full weight to [my] imperfection" and "bestows happiness according to worthiness, i.e., according to the merit ascribed to the imperfect moral consciousness" [609].

God is not a being the moral purist merely happens to believe in. He is the being the moralist *demands* if his world-view is to make sense. The moralist must maintain, without contradiction, his own perfection or worthiness to be happy and his imperfection or unworthiness. He does this by postulating a divine consciousness that unifies the perfect and the imperfect by directly intuiting the extent of both and, in effect, pardoning his sins.

With the Third Postulate, "the Moral World-View is completed" [610]. It is completed because God unites the two poles of moral purism: duty and nature or actuality. In this final phase, the individual locates pure duty not in himself but in God. Duty is therefore not valid in and for itself but acquires its worth only in a transcendent Being that is *imagined* or *represented* [*ein Vorgestelltes*]. This Being, though non-moral in the strict sense (God has no duties), is morally perfect insofar as he embodies a will undefiled by sensuousness. On the one hand, the moral individual thinks of his present actuality as an impediment to his moral state. On the other, thanks to his notion of God, he also thinks of his imperfection as superseded or *aufgehoben* [610]. In theological terms, the individual, keenly aware of his guilt, postulates a God who looks upon the heart and sees beyond sins. Moral imperfection makes sense if I postulate a God who sees my good intentions and grants happiness accordingly.

Hegel now paves the way for a more self-reflective moralism. He notes that the completion of the Moral World-View does *not* mean that moral consciousness has its own concept as an object, that it grasps the unity of duty and nature [611]. Its object is not itself as a concrete whole but duty as an abstract essence. Moral consciousness thus "rolls onward, without being the concept that holds [its] moments together." Hegel is here thinking of Kant, who, from Hegel's perspective, makes distinctions between inner and outer, self and nature, form and content, without thinking them through, and who invents postulates as he happens to need them. Such thinking is abstract in two senses. First, it does not think the concrete whole to which these moments belong. And second, the moralist, like the stoic, interprets freedom as merely "the freedom of pure thinking," as opposed to a *living* freedom. This second abstractness makes nature a separately existing other rather than the otherness of its own self. Only in the last stage of moral intuition [*Anschauung*], where God is postulated as a Being who derives his being from thought, does self-consciousness itself become aware of itself as the origin of objective being. Only then is the conjunction of being and thinking said to be what it really is: an act of representation or imagining [*Vorstellen*].[15]

The postulate approach to morality springs from the individual's awareness that his moral absolutism is contradictory without ideal harmonies, especially God as the Great Harmonizer. Having experienced the process of postulating, the individual now realizes what it means to postulate. He feels his power of willing something into being—of willing a God into being—and so reaches a deeper self-knowledge.

A Higher Moral Certainty [612–15]

Now aware that all moral objectivity is a projection of its own self, moral consciousness expounds its world-view "in another shape" [612]. The transition here corresponds to the shift from Kant's objective or realist view of duty to the subjective or idealist view put forth by Fichte (Harris, 2:428–29).[16] In this more knowing, self-certain version of the Moral World-View, the self begins with the intuition of itself as an "*actual* moral self-consciousness" [612]. Duty or the Ought is still the essence of this consciousness. But it is now conceived, or rather intuited, not as an objective standard but as the subjective moral *drive* that defines my true selfhood and unifies the in-here and the out-there.[17]

As a morally aware individual, I now know the external world, nature, as actual only to the extent that it conforms to my moral will. Genuine being is that which I produce through moral action—that which is "in keeping with duty." In other words, I consciously posit my own actual moral self-awareness as the essence of the world.[18] I know the world as real only insofar as it is a moral world, as an externality that I master and contain.[19] This was implicit in the previous shape but was posited less forcefully. Having grasped postulation as my own creative power, I now experience an intensified self-certainty—a genuine knowing rather than a cautious moral faith in ideal harmonies.[20]

This heightened moral self-consciousness is nevertheless burdened with the subject-object opposition implicit in consciousness. It *pictures* or *represents* the unity it finds within itself, the unity of morality and nature, and therefore regards it as a distant goal. It thinks of the unity "as *object,* and is not the Concept, which has mastery over the object as such" [612]. The more self-aware moral consciousness is thus still burdened with a Beyond, an ultimate unity that "falls outside of it." This is the direct result of its failure to be dialectical. The new shape intuits and contains but does not *think through* the unity of its opposing moments. That is why the unity remains a Beyond.

In the first moment of its experience, the higher moral shape asserts its pride or self-exaltation: "There *is* a moral self-consciousness" (namely, *my* moral self-consciousness). In its second moment, in which the self represents its own self as a Beyond, the individual revises his self-understanding. Humbled by the awareness of the imperfection he finds within himself, he now asserts the opposite of his initial position: "There is no moral, perfect, actual self-consciousness" [613]. And since there is no moral realm *at all* unless there is an actual moral self-consciousness, the more extreme conclusion follows: "There is no moral actuality."

In its third moment, the moral self, aware that it is a *single self,* posits an ideal or perfected self-consciousness that unifies duty and nature or actuality [614]. In this way, it tries to avoid the contradiction involved in being at once moral and non-moral, perfect and imperfect, proud and humble. This ideal self is God, who embodies "perfect morality." This perfected moral condition contains the first two moments, since it preserves actual moral self-consciousness but as a Beyond that *ought* to be actual [614].

At the end of this first section, Hegel observes that the first two moments are posited as having truth only in relation to each other. Pure duty and actuality (nature) are no longer "free" but are bound up with each other [615]. Duty is thought of as implicitly in harmony with nature; and nature is "raised above its actual existence" by being thought of, *imagined,* as implicitly good or moral. As for my inner duality, I am actually non-moral or imperfect but implicitly moral or perfect. My perfected state is something not experienced but merely *imagined.* I do not actually know myself as a moral being. Fortunately, God knows me better than I know myself. Hegel's formulation here sets the stage for the sophistry to come: I am not an actual moral self-consciousness, but God *lets me pass for one* [*dafür gelten gelassen*].

The Dance of the Moral Sophist [616–30]

Hegel now proceeds to the phenomenon of *Verstellung,* dissemblance or displacement. He shows how the moralist, in struggling to maintain his position, uses the postulates of morality as strategies for dodging his inherent contradiction.[21]

This second section of the Moral World-View begins with a summary of the more forceful shape of moral certainty [616]. At this exalted level, the individual regards himself as the moral master of the world (Fichte's Absolute Ego), who actively gives rather than passively receives reality. Here, "consciousness *itself* consciously produces its object." It does its duty and directly intuits itself as morally active.

It might seem that the individual has at this point attained "peace and satisfaction," that the Beyond has been erased. But this is not so. Duty or perfected morality is still conceived as the infinitely distant star that can be approached but never reached. That this star is my own perfected selfhood does not make the star any closer. For the individual, the morally perfect world remains a Beyond—a projected Ought or *Sollen.* It is posited on the one hand as objective or in itself, and on the other as something that exists only because the self postulates it. It is like the case of someone who insists that he believes in God but also insists that God is only an idea in his mind. Unable to grasp the dialectical unity of the two moments of duty, objective in-itself and subjective for-me, the moralist distinguishes them only to shuffle them.

The Moral World-View "is, therefore, in fact nothing other than the elaboration [*Ausbildung*] of this contradiction that lies at its ground" [617]. As we shall see, the moralist's purism is his undoing. In making pure duty sacred, he worships something that both must, and must not, be actual.

We now turn to the consequences that flow from the contradiction between the two opposed aspects of duty: the in-itself and the for-me. The moral purist, we must note, engages in conscious *Verstellung* or shiftiness. Aware of his contradiction, the purist will try to save his world-view by sliding back and forth between the moments of in-itself objectivity and for-itself subjectivity, thereby showing that he is serious about neither of them [617]. His shiftiness is like the mutual deception we saw in the spiritual kingdom of animals. There, the "respectable" individual claimed at one time that his interest in a given *Sache* was important in itself, and at another that it was so only to him [415–18]. He showed that he was not as serious as he claimed to be. Something similar happens in morality. Moral seriousness (a pious form of respectability) will be what Hegel calls a "swindling movement" [*schwindelnde Bewegung*].

Before taking up this movement, we should note Hegel's passing reference to Kant's "whole nest" of contradictions [617].[22] In the *Critique of Pure Reason,* Kant sought to expose the antinomies of reason in its speculative employment. When speculative reason attempts to know the absolute, Kant argued, it necessarily ends up proving both sides of a contradiction.[23] But where speculative reason fails, practical reason, for Kant, succeeds. In the concept of duty, I have *legitimate* contact with the absolute. In the present section of the *Phenomenology,* Hegel turns the tables on Kant. He shows how the practical realm is no less riddled with antinomies. This is Hegel's first big step in showing that moral, intuitive knowing necessarily points beyond itself to the very thing Kant had denied: the completion of philosophy in the form of *speculative* knowledge or Science.

Hegel starts out with the first assumption of the moral idealist, that there is an actual moral consciousness [618]. This assumption is based on my immediate intuition of myself as a moral being that transcends mere nature by virtue of his moral will, a being capable of action. Hegel then shows what happens to this consciousness in connection with the three postulates of the Moral World-View.

THE FIRST POSTULATE

We begin with the First Postulate: the harmony of duty and nature. The origin of this postulate is the perception that the external, actual world is morally indifferent and only implicitly moral. Such harmony is posited as an ideal of moral reason. It must be ideal or non-actual since duty is a striving, not an accomplishment. The outside world is not already moral. If it were, I would not have to act. On the contrary, duty commands me to make the world a better place, to make the natural world into a moral world. But the moral self here is a being that does not merely contemplate action but *really acts.* In acting morally, I produce the very harmony I posited as merely ideal. I make the ideal real. As Hegel puts it, "the *place* [*Stellung*] [given to actuality] is dissembled or *dis-placed* [*verstellt*]." That is, the original "placing" of actuality in the realm of the non-moral is now the very actuality *of* the moral. Moreover, since the morally active individual knows his action as his own, he also feels the joy of fulfillment. Hegel sums up the situation as follows: "Action, therefore, in fact directly fulfills what was asserted could not take place, what was supposed to be merely a postulate, merely a beyond" [618]. Moral action is thus undone *as moral* precisely because it is successful *as action.*

What fascinates Hegel is not the contradiction per se but the individual's presumed seriousness, his moralistic tone of sincerity. Morality is largely defined by this tone. In going back and forth between the in-itself and the for-me, the moralist shows that "he is serious about neither of them" [617].

Now, as we shall see, he is serious about neither his real moral action nor his ideal postulates.

In acting, the individual displaces the postulate according to which perfected duty is an infinitely distant ideal. He shows that his initial assertion of a disharmony between moral purpose and reality was not seriously meant [619]. Apparently, it is not the transcendent ideal but this-worldly action that the individual takes seriously. But there may still be a way to save morality as an ideal, and prevent action from becoming too serious. The individual can regard his deed as only *his* deed, a mere contingency quite incidental to the higher moral purpose, which is the moralization of the *whole world.* This way of looking at action would have the following result: "Because the universal best ought to be carried out, nothing *good* can be done."[24] The moralist thus tries to save morality as an ideal by depriving individual action of its moral value. Rather than inspiring moral action, the universal goal of morality in fact discourages and stifles it.

Rebounding from this unwanted result, the individual, in a second displacement, reinstates action as something he does take seriously. He asserts that since every action embodies duty as such, or is the expression of a pure will, action, however limited in content, has formally accomplished its entire purpose [619]. But this is in turn displaced by the view that since actions exist in the morally indifferent realm of nature, it is not really action that matters but rather *duty as such.* This, however, contradicts the individual's intuition of himself as an active or actual moral being. The individual thus shifts *yet again* and reinstates the view that there ought to be action and that the moral law ought to be realized as natural law [619].

But if action translates morality into actual nature, then nature "does not have a different law from that of morality" [620]. Nature becomes the Ought realized. Once again the moral individual is shown to be dishonest, since his position leads to the obliteration of morality as the pure Ought. Morality as an ideal vanishes in the moment it has contact with reality: it becomes its other. Indeed, if nature is the realm of moral accomplishment, the realm in which what ought to be *is,* then the moral law would be *violated* by efforts to change the world through action. My moral gallantry or knightliness would be a desecration. Hegel draws the inevitable conclusion: "Because moral action is the absolute purpose [*Zweck*], the absolute purpose is, that there should be no such thing as moral action" [620].

This dizzying series of displacements has its origin in the dialectical nature of duty [621]. Duty is an Ought or *Sollen.* But an Ought is an ought-to-*be.* It is, by definition, the drive to otherness in the form of nature: a *movement.* In a sense, the Ought wills its own destruction insofar as its goal is to be not merely ideal but real. Duty expresses the unity of inner self and outer world. It necessarily *contains* nature as the opposite with which duty is ultimately identical. This, we recall, is the true or genuine infinity [160]. But morality, whose truth is intuitive, wants nothing to do with opposites that contain each other. In spite of the manifestly paradoxical, self-canceling nature of duty, the moralist insists on the absolute distinctness of the Ought and the Is. That is why he is reduced to moral sophistry. He can save his moral idealism only by shifting from one side of his opposition to the other: from the ideal to the real, and back again.

Moral consciousness thus lives the dialectic of duty in an inauthentic way. Beginning with the disharmony of duty and nature, it proceeds to undercut the seriousness with which this disharmony is put forth by experiencing action as the harmony of duty and nature. But it does not take action seriously either, since the goal is not merely something good but the highest good, which transcends and deflates all individual action [621]. As Hegel puts it, "what [consciousness] really holds to be most desirable, to be the absolute, is that the Highest Good be accomplished, and that moral action be superfluous."

THE SECOND POSTULATE

Even this is not the end of moral displacement. Consciousness now displaces or dissembles its *cancellation* of moral action [622]. This leads to the moral individual's appeal to the Second Postulate. The result of the previous experience was that the individual, who was apparently deprived of the power to act morally, returns into himself. Recoiling from action as an encounter with external nature, he now re-interprets morality in terms of a battle *with himself.* He shifts his ground, concedes that his moral purpose is not the unity of the Ought and the external world but rather the harmony of his moral reason with his sensuous impulses. This is now the moral ideal the individual strives for but never reaches—the ideal that stays ideal.

We begin, as before, with an individual who claims to be actually moral—a moral force in the world. This individual claims that his moral purpose in acting is pure, that his actions are not influenced by his lower, sensuous nature [622]. But this claim is really a subterfuge. For what makes action actual, if not the spring of sensuous impulse? I do my duty because I am inclined to do so. I would not have acted if I had not wanted to act. Duty may command, but it is inclination that impels and stirs. My sensuous nature is for this reason the "instrument" and "organ" of moral realization. It is the middle term by which inner command flows out into existence.

Again Hegel highlights the tone of seriousness or sincerity. The morally active individual knows about the sensuous springs of action, since he has felt them. But to admit this would be tantamount to denying the Second Postulate, according to which I am only implicitly the harmony of duty and impulse or inclination. Moral consciousness therefore concedes that impulses are not to be eliminated but only *made conformable* to duty. That is, sensuous impulse is only an "empty shape," whose filling and true spring come from duty itself [622]. But impulse, as part of the spontaneous realm of nature, has its own "laws and springs of action." It does not need to be prompted and filled by duty in order to incite. The moral individual *knows* that this is the case and so does not take his moral action seriously. Instead, he puts forth a deceptive "reading" of what goes on inside him. He does so to save the Second Postulate, which, like the First Postulate, *prevents* morality from becoming real in the Here-and-Now while at the same time *demanding* that it be real in some indefinite future.

The individual's apparent seriousness about his postulate is in fact another lie. That is, morality, when posited as absolute, becomes hypocritical. It only *seems* that the postulated unity of moral reason and sensuous impulse is the seriously meant goal of morality. In fact, the individual cannot be serious about this goal, since the perfection of morality, if achieved, would *destroy* morality [622]. As we have seen, morality makes sense only in the context of what is opposed to morality. I know that I am a moral being, attentive to the call of duty, because I feel an inner pull away from what I *ought* to do and toward what I am *inclined* to do. If I did not experience an opposition to duty, I would not know duty, for duty *is* the transcendence of nature. The moralist is therefore not serious about his highest goal, as stated in the Second Postulate. He shows this lack of seriousness by making his highest goal impossible to reach, that is, by placing it in an infinitely distant future [622].

The search for what moral consciousness does take seriously must therefore go on. At this point, it seems to take moral *progress* seriously [623]. But this proves to be just another dissemblance. How can I take my moral progress seriously if I think that every step I take toward my goal is a step toward the annihilation of morality?

Nevertheless, for now at least, the individual takes refuge in progress or moral gradualism. With this "intermediate state," Hegel returns to the individual's worthiness to be happy [624]. The morally progressive individual is aware of his imperfection and so of his unworthiness to be happy. He cannot demand happiness as something he deserves but must instead hope for it as a gift from above. This sounds at first like a morally respectable position. But to hope for happiness in this way is to believe that happiness has absolutely no rational connection with moral worth, that happiness and worth are entirely separate. The paradoxical conclusion here is that the individual, *because he is a moral purist,* shows that he is concerned "not about morality, but solely about happiness as such without reference to morality" [624]!

Hegel now combines the belief in moral progress with the foregoing detachment of happiness from morality [625]. The ground for the First Postulate was the moralist's lament: good people fare badly, and the bad prosper [601–2]. But this purported disharmony is a lie. According to the postulate of moral progress, there are no "good" or "bad" people. There are only people on the way and in between. Since no one is either moral or immoral in the strict sense, there is no experience of good people faring badly. Moreover, since happiness has been detached from morality, the lament of the moral purist is not as objective as he claims. It is, on the contrary, simply the *resentment* he feels that certain people (namely, those who are not like him) should be happy [625]. His judgment that they should *not* be happy, Hegel observes, "is an expression of envy [*Neid*] that assumes the cloak of morality." As for the pronouncement that certain other people *should* be happy, this too is simply the result of a sensuous impulse masquerading as moral reason. It is a mere "friendliness" [*Freundschaft*] toward others and oneself.

THE THIRD POSTULATE

Moral consciousness acknowledges its moral imperfection [626]. This is implied in the assertion of moral progress. But, as we saw earlier, there is no morality unless there is *perfect* morality. Since the individual knows he is impure, morality must find its perfection in *another consciousness*. This is God as "a holy moral lawgiver." Here, moral displacement occurs at the level of morality's Third Postulate. In its dissemblance, moral consciousness will show that it is ultimately not serious even about God.

This last phase of the Moral World-View begins with the moral individual in the trenches of real life. Life is full of moral situations, each with its own peculiar demands. This complexity gives rise to the need for many specific duties [626]. As we saw earlier, the individual does not regard these duties as essential to his Moral World-View. Only duty as such is essential. And so, God is postulated as the consciousness that does what the individual cannot: sanctify duties in their specificity or determinateness.

Here we reach the displacement that sums up all the other displacements and lays bare their source. Moral consciousness, in postulating the Holy Lawgiver, draws a distinction between this Lawgiver and itself. But there is in fact no such distinction for moral consciousness, since consciousness itself is for itself the measure of all things and the source of the Lawgiver himself: "the moral self-consciousness is its own absolute, and duty is absolutely only what it *knows* as duty" [626]. Hegel continues: "what is not sacred [for moral self-consciousness] is not sacred in itself, and what is not in itself sacred, cannot be made sacred by the holy being." The distinction between myself and another consciousness is therefore not seriously meant but is immediately canceled or displaced. If *I* cannot sanctify a given duty, then the God I consciously posit and postulate cannot either.

Moreover, the standard of moral purity must apply no less to God than to me. For this other consciousness, as for me, duty is valid only as pure duty, duty that has no specific content [627]. Apart from specific duties, then, God must sanctify duty itself. He grounds morality. But if this is the case, then morality does not have its ground in the concrete moral individual, who partakes of sensuous impulses. Only God, who is free of sensuous impulse, can be a truly moral being.

This absence of sensuous impulses in God, which seems at first to be a solution, is problematic, since morality has a necessary relation to nature [628]. As Hegel puts it, "the *reality* of pure duty is its *actualization* in nature and sense." The moral individual is imperfect because he has a positive relation to nature: he wants what he wants and goes with the flow. To be moral, he must adopt a wholly *negative* relation to his natural impulses, *not* go with the flow. Here is where the problem arises for the God of morality. God, who is above the "*struggle* [*Kampf*] with nature and sense," has no negative relation to nature but only a positive one. This was exactly what was designated as *immoral.* I might try to avoid this unwanted conclusion by positing a God who has no relation to nature whatsoever. But then God would be no more than "an unconscious, non-actual abstraction in which the concept of morality, which involves thinking of pure duty, willing and doing it, would be done away with." He would be the gaseous Supreme Being of the Enlightenment. The final result of all these rationalizations is that the demand for a "purely moral being" must be abandoned.

The God of morality is the synthetic unity of all the contradictions we have seen so far [629]. He brings all the extremes "closer together" and so most clearly reveals the perpetually displacing, self-contradictory character of morality. It is this ideal of moral perfection that ultimately induces despair in the individual, leading him to abandon the Moral World-View and to seek his certainty in the more interior and self-sufficient shape of *conscience.*

As Hegel now proceeds to show, the God of morality is not only absolutely unreal, as the previous dialectic has shown. He is also posited as absolutely *real.* This follows from the individual's awareness that his everyday morality is impure—a fleeting image of the true morality [630]. The impurity here takes the double form of natural impulses and the concrescence [*Konkretion*] of many specific duties in every real-life situation.[25] *Pure* morality must therefore have its reality "in another being." In this reversal of its former position, individual moral consciousness is unreal and merely implicit, while God as the "second consciousness" is real and explicit.

Moral consciousness thus goes back and forth between God as an ideal "thought-thing" utterly removed from actuality, and God as the peak of moral actuality. Morality *thinks* or rather *imagines* God as real, places him within moral consciousness, and at the same time regards him as "really real" or independent of consciousness. God, in this way, most clearly exhibits the self-contradictory character of moral postulates in general: the contradictory unity of the objective in-itself and the subjective for-me. Morality set forth its postulates in order to render its world-view coherent—to explain how pure duty can be actual without ceasing to be an ideal or perpetual ought. The idea of God was supposed to be the harmony of harmonies that made the Moral World-View truly synthetic and harmonious. But the God of morality is not a solution. He is the *problem* of morality writ large, the contradiction of morality projected into a Beyond.

The Awakening [631]

In the last paragraph of this section, Hegel stresses the "syncretism" [*der Synkretismus*] of all the contradictions in morality [631].[26] God is the synthetic idea that both unifies the Moral World-View and brings it to ruin. He embodies the unstable distinction between "what *must* be thought and postulated" as essential and (since duty alone is the true absolute) what must be thought of as "*not* essential." This fundamental incoherence derives from morality's ambivalence regarding actuality, which morality takes at one time as the *tainted* realm of inclination and circumstance, and at another as the *pure* realm of perfected morality.

This contradiction within morality is evident right from the start in the dialectical nature of duty. Duty is the Ought. But the Ought points beyond itself to the ought-to-*be* of moral accomplishment, moral purpose. The moral ideal is the striving to be real. But how can the Ought become an Is (which it must) without being undermined as an Ought? The whole point of the three postulates was to answer this question. But the postulates merely project the original problem into a supersensible Beyond. This Beyond or God, rather than sanctioning and inspiring moral action, in fact undermines it.

In its nascent state, moral consciousness affirmed duty as the absolute. It then realized that postulates were necessary in order to unify duty and nature. Eventually, the moralist realized that his own thinking was the origin of his postulated harmonies and re-shaped his world-view accordingly. He took as his starting-point, not duty as an object-like standard, but his own concrete experience of himself as an actual moral consciousness, a moral master of the world. Then, knowing that he was the source of all his distinctions and projected harmonies, consciousness kept displacing the real and the ideal, the in-itself and the for-me. Finally, in the course of experience, the moralist acknowledges what he was doing all along. He "comes to see that the placing-apart [*Auseinanderstellung*] of these moments is a dis-placing [*Verstellung*] of them, and that it would be hypocrisy if, nevertheless, [he] were to keep them separate" [631].

The moralist, however, is not Rameau's nephew. In spite of his hypocritical rationalizing, he does not celebrate contradictions and self-otherness. On the contrary, the essence of morality is integrity and self-sameness. Moral consciousness therefore "flees" from the untruth that the previous dialectic has brought to light. It flees "with abhorrence back into itself." The new shape it assumes is that of "pure conscience." The conscientious self rejects the pseudo-objectivity, sophistry, and complications of the Moral World-View—which Hegel now re-names the Moral World-*Representation* [*Weltvorstellung*]. It does so "with scorn." It takes refuge in being "the simple spirit that, certain of itself, acts conscientiously regardless of such ideas [of the Moral World-View], and in this immediacy possess its truth." It is significant that Hegel calls this new shape *spirit.* As the final manifestation of spirit or *Geist,* conscience and its ensuing dialectic will reveal most clearly what it means to be spiritual.

Hegel ends with a hint of things to come. Moral consciousness flees from the contradictions of the Moral World-View. It scorns the hypocrisy of distinctions that are no distinctions, and the transcendent God who is both real and unreal. But these contradictions are no cloak that morality can simply cast aside. They are instead "the development of moral self-consciousness in its moments," the reality and essence of that self-consciousness [631]. Conscience, our new moral shape, does not see that it has its origin in this series of displacements. It does not know that the hypocrisy it flees is bound to reappear, and that its high-minded scorn is "the first expression of hypocrisy."

The conscientious individual rejects the supersensible Beyond and places the divine wholly in himself. He will claim to *be* God. In our next chapter, we will explore the meaning and implications of this astonishing claim.

I, knower: possessing the secrets
of all action and not stirring,
while the hero strides out of my door
outward-resolved, as if breaking off with me.
Rilke, *Uncollected Poems*

20

Conscience and Reconciliation

Hegel's Divine Comedy

Hegel's goal in the *Phenomenology* is the transformation of philosophy, the love of knowing, into actual knowing [5]. It may seem surprising, in light of this theoretical goal, that the moral-practical realm should be so high on Hegel's divided line, so close to absolute knowing. We must remember, however, that knowledge, for Hegel, is self-knowledge. In the course of the education of consciousness, man comes to know the truth as subject, as well as substance. He comes to know that he *is* the truth, and that self-consciousness and Concept are the same. Man discovers this in moral experience because here, in moral *willing,* he affirms his selfhood as universal and absolute.

Conscience, *Gewissen* (from *wissen,* to know), is the perfection of morality. It brings man closer to the identity of man and God in the concept of *absolute spirit* [670]. Conscience takes moral self-certainty to its extreme. It is individual selfhood, or personal inwardness, that is self-absolutizing. The Kantian moralist posited an objective, quasi out-there absolute in the form of moral law. The conscientious individual rejects this worship of law. His absolute is himself and his act of willing. This act is his law. As Hegel puts it, quoting Jacobi, "it is now the law that is for the sake of the self, not the self for the sake of the law" [639].[1] Conscience is hyper-moralism. It conflates the Kantian distinction between individual and universal, natural inclination and duty. The man of conscience experiences his *nature* as in itself *moral.*

Schiller's "beautiful soul," or *schöne Seele,* provides the human type for conscience, as it first appears in the *Phenomenology.* In his essay "On Grace and Dignity" (1793), Schiller presents the beautiful soul as the model of "perfected humanity."[2] This soul is so morally refined that, for it, duty and inclination are identical: "With a lightness, as if nothing but instinct acts out of him, he [the beautiful soul] carries out the most painful duties of mankind; and the most terrible sacrifice that he extracts from natural drive [*dem Naturtriebe*] looks like a freely willed effect of just this drive." Schiller continues: "It is thus in a beautiful soul that sensuousness and reason, duty and inclination, harmonize, and grace is its apparent expression."[3]

As we shall see, conscience is logically unstable. Schiller's "perfected humanity" will prove to be a false paradise. Conscience, which manifests itself as a *community* of beautiful souls, will unravel. The logical poles that it unites, singular and universal, will fall apart and oppose one another. Hegel will personify this opposition as a falling-out between an "acting consciousness" and a "judging consciousness" [665]. The latter embodies universality, the former singularity (that is, individuality as *this* particular self).

The opposed consciousnesses both turn out to be hypocrites. Conscience will bring on an even greater hypocrisy than the one it sought to avoid in the Moral World-View. Once the poles of conscience, the Doer and the Judge, confess their hypocrisy to each other, they experience forgiveness and reconciliation, *Versöhnung* [670–71]. In this sublime moment, all the tragic reversals of the *Phenomenology* are transmuted into "divine comedy." Selfhood, which up to now had been greedily guarded and defended (or torn to shreds in the culture world), is at last allowed to flow. It becomes universal. Individual self-consciousness comes outside itself and sees itself in the other.

In Chapter 8, I referred to the "great arch" that embraces the drama of self-consciousness in the *Phenomenology*. This arch had its beginning in the fight to the death between two warriors striving for recognition [187]. Reconciliation will now provide the end. The bond among individuals is not custom, law, or the social contract, but mutual forgiveness and communal self-knowledge. This is the *mutual recognition* that self-consciousness wanted all along: the "the I that is We and the We that is I" [177].

The Transition to Conscience [632–34]

At the end of the dialectic of the Moral World-View, moral consciousness, realizing the immorality of its position, fled from it "with abhorrence back into itself" [631]. This inner flight is the birth of conscience. The experience of hypocrisy is a purgation. In his inward turn and inward suffering, the moralist discovers a more radical self-certainty, and a new and higher claim to absolute knowing. Such inward turns or self-reflections occur regularly in the *Phenomenology*. They are moments of spiritual gestation that precede the next spiritual appearance or "burst."

The moral individual, reborn as a person of conscience, is no longer locked up inside a solipsistic devotion to duty. He is no longer paralyzed by the awareness that no matter what he does he will never be worthy of happiness, and that duty, once made actual through deeds, ceases to be pure. For him, outer and inner, action and thought, Ought and Is, are no longer opposed. Instead, he experiences himself as the absolute point, or "center of force," from which moral deeds freely flow. He no longer looks above himself, off toward the unreachable ideal of Pure Duty, but rather finds the unity of Ought and Is in himself and his act of sheer willing—in his *freedom.* He does not need to think before he acts, since there is no external measure of his actions, no law to which he must conform. His acting is his moral knowing, and his knowing is his action. Moral World-Intuition has become intuition, *Anschauung,* as the direct, immediate knowledge of moral essence. Here is a knowledge that needs no postulates.

The conscientious individual is a moral will to power. For him, the logical poles of individual and universal, self-consciousness and duty, are identical: "[Self-consciousness] is itself *in its contingency* [my emphasis] completely worthy in its own sight, and knows its immediate singularity [*this* I right here and now] to be pure knowing and doing, to be the true actuality and harmony" [632]. The singular I here experiences itself as God on earth. It is, in Nietzsche's phrase, a *creator of value.*[4]

Hegel regularly looks back before moving on. Such retrospective glances are especially important in these upper regions, as spirit approaches the end of its journey. Here, at the beginning of the dialectic of conscience, Hegel reviews what he calls the *three worlds of self* that have appeared in the chapter on spirit [633]. These worlds (which I introduced in Chapter 17) help us to understand why morality is the culmination of this chapter, and why conscience occupies so high a place in the *Phenomenology.*

Spirit is selfhood that manifests itself as a community or *world.* It first appears in the *Phenomenology* as the Greek nation or *Volk.* This is not a world of self. It is founded on custom, not self-conscious individuality. The Greek individual has reality and truth in the family (represented by the female) and in the state (represented by the male). He is an individual only to the extent that his self-consciousness or being-for-self is immersed in the social substance. The conflict between Antigone and Creon in Sophocles' play dramatizes, as we have seen, the contradiction between these two spheres, and the tragic un-tuning of Greek harmony. The first world of self is Rome, which replaces character and its attendant virtues with the legal person and property rights [476]. This is self-consciousness in its most dehumanized, abstract form.

The second world of self is culture. Its pinnacle is eighteenth-century France. Culture was manifest, or *there,* as perversity and self-rending. It is man in the condition of cultivated self-estrangement. The cultured individual seeks happiness in the destruction of what is natural about him: in self-betterment, sophistication, bourgeois morality, the accumulation of wealth, and social climbing. He is summed up in Rameau's nephew and his "torn" or shredded personality. In its truth, culture is nihilism and revolution, the pure negativity of the Reign of Terror.

Morality, the third world of self, is sheer willing that has become pure willing. It is the Phoenix that rises dialectically from the blood and ashes of the Terror. It negates the previous negation. Having experienced itself as Greek, Roman, and French, spirit becomes German, in fact, a Kantian. Morality posits pure duty as the stable essence that gives meaning to human actions and lifts man out of his self-interest and perversity.

The problem with morality, as Kant's Moral World-View, is that it conceives of duty as purely formal or empty. Conscience, or hypermoralism, fills this empty duty and makes it real. It brings the Ought down from its heaven and puts it to work in the earthy realm of Is. Conscience is immediate, concrete moral action that is at the same time concrete moral knowing. The historical archetype for this moral will to power is Napoleon, whom Hegel once called "this world-soul on horseback."[5] Whereas the Kantian moralist is paralyzed by the disparity between impure particulars and pure universal duty, conscience is at home in the concrete moral situation, the moral *moment.* Since it acknowledges as real only what it has brought forth or created, conscience "is existence or *Dasein* itself" [633]: it makes its world and acknowledges as real only the world it has made. The Kantian moralist was an unhappy consciousness, who experienced the pain of being incompletely moral, of never measuring up to the moral law. He was not worthy of happiness. His postulates failed to secure a harmony of morality and nature. The conscientious man, as he first appears, feels no such existential angst. If I am certain of being the law in every concrete moral situation, then I never feel that I am a sinner, that I am unworthy. To act is to succeed as a moral being. Conscience is, in Hegel's words, "concrete moral spirit" and "a self-actualizing being" [634].

Conscience and the Man of Action [635–54]

Hegel now takes us on a journey into the soul of conscientious man. In what follows, we must keep in mind that conscience, *Gewissen,* is a form of knowing, *Wissen.* In a concrete case of moral action, the conscientious individual knows what is real and true. He is not plagued by the doubt that his thoughts might be abstract, that they might be detached from reality. There is no disparity for him between thinking and being, intention and action. On the contrary, the world has value and true being for him only insofar as he *knows* this world [635]. Conscience is the direct immediate intuition [*Anschauung*] of what is right in any given moral situation. It is like sense-certainty, which was the immediate intuition of the sensuous particular [91]. As moral intuition, conscience does not survey and sort out the various duties that enter into a case of "What should I do?" Conscience simply knows and acts. For the conscientious individual, the complexities of a moral situation are demolished [635]. Moreover, the man of conscience does not waver between placing morality in himself and in a supersensible Being [636] (the contradiction of the Kantian moralist). He needs no divine Other. He is self-sanctioning, and is his own God.

The moralist was paralyzed by his distinction between duty and reality [637]. He could act only if he could do so for the sake of pure duty. But this is impossible. I cannot do my duty without having specific goals and purposes in mind, without wanting to succeed and be happy. The desire for happiness defiles pure duty with naturalness and self-interest. The result is that "I do *not* act." For conscience, the case is very different. Conscience is a mode of human *Dasein* and being-in-the-world as well as a mode of thought. It "knows that it has its truth in *the immediate certainty* of itself." Knowledge, here, is not of an object distinct from myself. It is rather the knowledge that whatever I know to be right *is* right. Conscience is the immediate *knowing that I know.* Its essence is what Hegel calls *conviction* [*Überzeugung*].[6]

Conviction is not opinion, which is merely subjective. "That's my opinion," means, "That's how it seems to me." Conviction, by contrast, is the immediate identification of the subjective with the objective, the individual with the universal. In conviction, I experience myself as absolutely right.[7] This identity of subject and object is the essence of the beautiful soul, as Goethe understood it. In a letter to Schiller, Goethe writes that he was inspired to invent a character that embodied "the noblest deception" and the "subtlest confusion" of the subjective and the objective.[8] This inspiration became the focal point of the chapter entitled "Confessions of a Beautiful Soul" in Goethe's novel, *Wilhelm Meister's Apprenticeship.*[9] There, a female beautiful soul boasts: "I was always led and guided by an impulse or drive [*ein Trieb*], following my own persuasions [*Gesinnungen*] with freedom, and knowing neither limitation nor remorse."[10]

Conviction, to repeat, is not subjectivity by itself but the immediate unity of subjectivity and objectivity. This unity occurs *within* the self-absolutizing subject. It is different from the interpenetration of subject and object we saw in reason's *Sache selbst.* There, the individual attached himself to a specific content. Conviction, by contrast, is radical, purely formal (or empty) subjectivity that claims to be immediately objective.

In his Preface, Hegel said that his goal was to present the truth not as *substance,* but equally as *subject,* as the work of self-consciousness [17]. Conscience is precisely the attempt to grasp the truth in this way. The conscientious person is not a philosopher. His thinking (or rather, intuiting) is not theoretical but practical. Nevertheless, he is essential to the appearance of philosophy in the form of Science or *Wissenschaft.* Hegel tells us in his final chapter, that worldly experience and *feeling* necessarily precede philosophic knowing [802]. Prior to the philosophic, purely conceptual grasp of truth as subject, there must be a phenomenal burst upon the world-stage, an unreflective appearance of the radical identity of subject and object. Conscience is that appearance.

Hegel proceeds to show how duty, no longer the absolute it was in Kantian morality, is nonetheless preserved as a moment in the hyper-moralism of conscience. He cites the saying of Jacobi that I mentioned earlier: "It is now the law that is for the sake of the self, not the self that is for the sake of the law" [639]. Duty, in other words, has no meaning apart from the willing self. It no longer stands over and above the self. Hegel stresses the point I made earlier, that conscience is not mere subjectivity but rather the identity of subjectivity and objectivity. But if duty—the in-itself, as opposed to the subjective for-itself—no longer makes morality objective or real, then what does?

Duty is no longer essence, but is now mere being [639]. It is not a what-it-is but only a that-it-is: a fact. Duty has become a vanishing moment or aspect of morality. But if I am really the unity of individual and universal, then objectivity must somehow be present in my moral experience. If it is not the impersonal Ought of duty, then what is it? Hegel's answer is: *being-for-another,* that is, being in relation to another self-consciousness. My moral conviction has its objective moment in the sheer *fact* that others recognize my deeds as moral. Objectivity or reality is not *what* they recognize as moral in my actions but only *that* they recognize them as springing from my inner conviction or authenticity—my commitment.

This recognition is a crucial turning point in the analysis of conscience. It is the dialectical origin of moral intersubjectivity or the community of moral selves. Unlike the Kantian moralist, the conscientious individual needs others to provide the objective universality of which he is subjectively certain. Since everything in conscience is subjectivized, it is no surprise that this would be true of universality as well, which is no longer impersonal self-less duty but the living acknowledgement by other selves. Duty has not disappeared. It has rather been transformed into a *subjective* universal, a community: "Conscience is the communal element of the two self-consciousnesses, and this element is the substance in which the [conscientious] deed [*Tat*] has lastingness and actuality, the moment of becoming recognized by others" [640]. Clearly, recognition here means, not that other people are merely aware of my conscience-grounded deeds but that they acknowledge them as good—that they respect as absolute the *right* of my conscience.

Unlike the moralist, the conscientious individual acts [640]. He can do so because others recognize his deeds as moral. Their recognition makes him real: "The action is thus only the translation of its *particular* content into the *objective* element, in which it is universal and recognized, and it is just the fact that it is recognized that makes action [*Handlung*] actual" [640].

When someone claims to do something from conscience—say, not go to war because he is a "conscientious objector"—he assumes that his decision will be universally recognized, that his action (or, in this case, inaction) has its ground in conviction, which is the expression of his freedom. Again Hegel is at pains to show how conscience casts off the self-imposed shackles of Kantian morality. What I do from conscience "has standing and being-there" [*Bestand und Dasein*]. The conscientious individual is thus free from the moralist's lament that good intentions come to naught and good men fare badly [640]. He is above the moralist's resentment and envy, and experiences moral accomplishment. His world is not the private realm of moral striving but the public realm in which deeds done from conscience are recognized as having worth. This is the first, positive level of the experience of conscience. In the upcoming dialectical development, a less naïve, darker side of conscience will appear.

Hegel reminds us that the moral situation is a complex of various particulars and conflicting duties. The conscientious individual approaches this situation as a knower. He is self-certain and self-absolutizing [642]. Since this knowing must be universal, conscientious action seems to require that I know the situation inside and out, in all its details and complexities. That is what we normally mean when we say that someone is conscientious. But since I am aware of myself as a particular *finite* knower, I realize that I cannot know all these details and circumstances, which spread out into infinity [642], and therefore cannot act conscientiously. This is the first sign of a disparity between conscience and reality.

At this early stage of its experience, conscience has a way of coping with the disparity. As a conscientious being, I admit that I cannot do justice to all the details of a moral situation. Nevertheless, I am to myself the Napoleonic creator of value, the God who wills what is right. Sifting through circumstances and details is certainly important if I am to be conscientious. But this is not essentially what it means to act from conscience. Sifting is only a moment or aspect, something I do only "for *others*," that is, in view of others [642]. My knowledge of all the particulars is necessarily incomplete. But it is sufficient to *my* knowing what I need to know in order to be self-certain and to act. My incomplete knowledge is thus complete and absolute insofar as it is mine. Knowledge, for conscience, means *my* knowledge, however limited such knowledge happens to be.

That knowledge for conscience is essentially complete even when it is materially incomplete leads to the next major step in Hegel's analysis: "Conscience does not recognize the absoluteness of any content, for it is the absolute negativity of everything determinate" [643]. This abhorrence of finite content (the very stuff of life), with its correlative yearning for a sublime but gaseous infinity, is the origin of the beautiful soul.

Conscience, like pure duty, is formal. Its formality lies in the self's act of willing and being decisive, not in some objective lifeless essence (pure duty). Conscience discovers this formality when it is confronted with an infinite host of circumstances and must at some point *cut off* its inspection and deliberation. The conscientious individual must act. He is able to act, as we saw above, because the knowledge sufficient to his action is whatever his knowledge happens to be at the time. What is essential is that it be his. Conscience, therefore, is not guided by anything it sees in the moral situation. What, then, prompts it to act in the specific way it does? Hegel's answer is: impulses and inclinations, that is, the individual's natural rather than moral consciousness. The content that determines how the individual acts is his own immediate certainty, "conceived as content." In short, the self-absolutizing individual, the man of conscience, acts out of caprice or willfulness [*Wilkür*], which Hegel calls "the contingency of his unconscious natural being." This is the only thing left in his subjectivity that has content.[11]

In the *Phenomenology,* Hegel reveals the *logos* that animates and connects concrete character-types. Plato would have called them kinds of soul. We should regularly ask ourselves if we know, or have read about, people like the ones Hegel describes. The type we have just met may be familiar to us. He is the one who is always morally superior because he sees the heart of the matter, the moral *Sache selbst.* Others are blinded by abstract moral principles and endless deliberations: but not him. He does not need to look in order to see, since his seeing is his willing, which is self-validating. And if he changed his mind tomorrow about some moral issue, it would make no difference to his moral certainty: he has absolute knowing *in each moment* of his moral judgment and action, and is therefore free to "cook the books." He is the man, moreover, who cannot tell the difference between his principles and his whims, since these have become identical. His whims, the creatures of his subjectivity, are all elevated, in his mind, to the level of divine insights. This is exactly the confusion of subjective and objective that Goethe captured in his female version of the beautiful soul.

As Hegel now tells us, the individual's "caprice gives [duty] its content and can associate every content with this form and attach its conscientiousness to the content" [644]. He cites the example of someone who accumulates wealth for himself and his family, knowing full well that it might also be his duty to be charitable and care for others in need. This man makes the pursuit of wealth his duty because it is the content of his certainty of himself as conscientious, because he *wills* this aspect of the moral situation and not the other. Other people may find fault with his choice and criticize him. They may call him a selfish and violent capitalist, while he clings to his duty to be independent in the face of others. And what they call cowardice is, for him, a conserving of goods and the refusal to ignore his own needs and those of his family.

Duty, here, is empty. It is a free-floating value that can be attached to any moral content whatsoever: to the "cowardly" capitalist and to the "courageous" socialist. What validates the individual's choice is not a specific duty but conviction. If we assume that others who criticize the capitalist *know* this, and justify their actions in the same way, then even though both parties disagree on the content, they must agree on the moral rightness of both sides. I may disagree with the conscientious objector's decision to avoid going to war, but I nevertheless respect the testimony of his conscience and the authenticity of his conviction.

Hegel sums up the preceding account by pointing to what he calls "the blemish of determinateness" [645].[12] The reference to a blemish [*Makel*] highlights the aesthetic temperament of the person of conscience. It also points out his tendency to confuse the true with the beautiful.[13] The pure knowing of conscience, as we have seen, is free of content, just as it is free (ultimately) from sifting through the details of a moral situation. Conscience "absolves itself [*absolviert sich*] from any determinate duty that is supposed to have the validity of law" [646]. In this indifference to content, we begin to see the disparity between pure knowing and the realm of concrete action, the two opposite poles that conscience is certain of having unified. This disparity will eventually give rise to the beautiful soul, who is so exquisitely sensitive to the "blemish of determinateness" that he renounces action and life.[14]

Conscience is a pure knowing that is "immediately a being-for-another" [647]. It is, in other words, communal. This being-for-another is other people's recognition that what I do, I do from conscience and conviction rather than caprice. Recognition, here, is reciprocal. Others recognize and respect my moral conviction, and I recognize and respect theirs. This mutual recognition is "the element whereby conscience stands directly in a relation of equality with every self-consciousness; and the meaning of this relation is not a law bereft of self, but the self of conscience" [647].

Once the conscientious individual acts, however, he gives determinate content to an action. To act is to do *something*. This content is distinct from his selfhood or pure inwardness [648]. The situation is like that of the *spiritual animal kingdom* or civil society. As a society animal, I try to make my individual selfhood real by using my natural talent. But when I generate this reality that is supposed to embody me, it ceases to be mine. Other self-actualizers come along and make it theirs.

Something similar happens in the case of conscientious deeds. These are valid only insofar as they embody my act of willing. The problem is that once I have acted, once my selfhood has discharged its creative energy, my action is "out there" like an ordinary product of human making. It is separate from me and exists in the realm of "mere being." My deed, once my selfhood or willing is withdrawn from it, "is therefore not necessarily recognized" [648]. It becomes multivalent, capable of having imposed on it *anybody's* interpretation regarding my motive. A disparity thus arises between the individual who acts and the communal universal consciousness that is supposed to recognize this action, between me and other people. The reality of my action, its having been done, produces a moral no-man's land, a spiritual region of *doubt* as to the morality or immorality of the action.

As Hegel puts it: "Others, therefore, do not know whether [my] conscience is morally good or evil, or rather, they not only cannot know, but they must take it to be evil" [649]. They must take it as evil [*böse*] because my conscience and knowing are *mine,* not theirs. A moral content that is authentically yours is precisely *not* authentically mine. Mutual recognition exists only so long as conscience is looked at from the side of form (the act of willing). But once a specific content enters, as it must if action is to take place, then the community of mutually recognizing selves breaks down and splinters. It resolves itself into particular consciences at odds with each other. Each man's will is autonomous. It is "free from the *specificity* of duty, and from duty as possessing an *intrinsic* being." When it comes to deeds done from conscience, only subjectivity counts. My conscience must therefore reject as immoral what another conscientious individual does, since "it is something expressing only the self of another" [649].

The breakdown of community results from the externality of deeds. My deeds are not only mine: they also *are.* Other consciences are free to chalk up my motives for these deeds to mere individuality, to my "pleasure and desire" [650]. But it is not the morality of the outward deed, or of a specific duty, that I want others to recognize. It is the presumed *absolute knowing* embodied in my moral conviction. I want my *selfhood,* or authenticity, to be recognized. In this recognition, conscience seems to find its stable resting point and concrete universality. The *Dasein* or being-there that my conscience intends, and wants others to recognize, is the objective embodiment of my most inward, intuitive knowledge—of the self qua self. This embodiment is *language* [652].

Language has appeared at key moments in the journey of consciousness. It expresses the universal. Sense-certainty, in its effort to suppress universality and language, discovered that "language is the more truthful" [97]. Language was prominent in the French world of culture, where the monarch derived his power and existence from the self-alienating flattery bestowed by the nobles [508–11]. In that context, it was "the *Dasein* of the pure self, as self" [508], the concrete medium in which individuals *cancel* their individuality and produce a concrete universal. Hegel now repeats this idea: "Language is self-consciousness that is *for others*" [652]. It is selfhood standing in its own presence. But unlike the self-alienating language of the culture world, the language of conscience is the authentic expression of the self: "it is the spirit that has returned into itself, is certain of itself, and certain in itself of its truth, or of its recognition [of that truth], and which is recognized as this knowing" [653].

Through language, the conscientious individual makes his self-certainty or conviction real, objective, and universal. Conviction, in order to be universal, must declare itself: "Whoever says he acts in such and such a way from conscience, speaks the truth, for his conscience is the self that knows and wills. But it is essential that he should *say* so, for this self must be at the same time the *universal* [communal] self" [654]. Language solidifies the mutual recognition of individual consciences by making their convictions or authentic interiors reciprocally transparent. In saying, "This I did from conscience," I acknowledge my continuity with other conscientious people. I also show that I am worthy of being acknowledged in turn. By declaring my conscience, I rise above the possible accusation that I have acted out of mere pleasure and desire. "You know who I am," says the man of conscience, "and I wouldn't be telling you that I acted from conscience unless I knew who *you* were."

The Beautiful Soul [655–58]

Hegel now presents his loftiest depiction of conscience. It is the prelude to the tragic beautiful soul, the rise before the fall. Hegel's portrait takes us beyond the aesthetic realm of Schiller to the theological, mystic realm of Novalis, as conscience is now explicitly revealed as the God within. Hegel's remarks here seem to have been lifted straight from the final pages of the unfinished novel *Henry von Ofterdingen,* where the old Sylvester calls conscience "the vicar of God on earth" and "the divine primal man."[15]

"In the majesty of its elevation [*Erhabenheit*] above determinate law and every content of duty," conscience is free to make *anything* the content of its knowing and willing [655]. Echoing Novalis, Hegel calls conscience "the moral genius that knows the inner voice of what it immediately knows to be a divine voice."[16] And since conscience knows its absolute rightness in action and existence, it is "the divine creative force [*Schöpferkraft*] that in its concept possesses the spontaneity of life." Conscience knows itself as absolute. It is "in its own self divine worship, for its action is the intuition [*Anschauung*] of its own divinity." Conscience, in other words, is spiritual narcissism.

As we have seen, the person of conscience, although self-absorbed, posits a *community* of mutually recognizing consciences. This community is engaged in "divine [self-] worship" [656]. It renders actual, or historically present, the narcissism of the conscientious individual. There are various forms of this community. Its overtly religious form has its roots in the German movement known as *pietism,* which was anti-theological and sought the absolute, or God, in inwardness and feeling.[17] Quakers would be a modern-day example. But there are other versions as well. The community of beautiful souls can be a group of friends who retreat from the world, share intimacies and sublime feelings, and form their own quasi-religious romantic cult of inwardness. Rousseau depicts such a community in *La nouvelle Héloïse.*[18]

The individual must speak. He must declare his conscience to others, just as they must declare their conscience to him. The mutual declaration is their bond with reality and the praxis of their aesthetic *religion* of conscience [656]. Hegel now spells out the narcissism of this communal speech: "The spirit and substance of their association are thus the mutual assurance of their conscientiousness, good intentions, the rejoicing over this mutual purity, and the refreshing of themselves in the glory of knowing and uttering, of cherishing and fostering, such an excellent state of affairs" [656]. Implied in this communal self-congratulation is the arrogance of feeling superior to people who place morality in specific duties. In other contexts, Hegel refers to this indifference to all moral content as romantic *irony.*[19]

However obnoxious this community may seem, it is nevertheless the first appearance in the *Phenomenology* of a community based on knowledge or inwardness. The community of beautiful souls has "only a *hidden* life in God." These souls do experience something genuinely divine: pure subjectivity or self in the form of conscience. The problem is that God is present only in the minds and hearts of the individuals who make up this pious community. Inwardness has not yet dared to "step out" into the realm of concrete existence, that is, real life. Consequently, it is spirituality that is not yet *spirit.* Conscience indeed gives rise to a community, and a religion. But at present, this is only a religion of pious feeling and empty intuition. It is not yet religion in its concrete, objective form, religion as it appears in Hegel's next chapter.[20]

The community of consciences promotes rather than mitigates the introversion of the person of conscience, who is now a beautiful soul in all but name. This moral aesthete is intensely withdrawn. His radical loneliness is the direct result of conscience as self-worship. Conscience is the God within. To be in touch with this God, I must turn within myself, away from all externality. This inward turn was prepared, and necessitated, by the conscientious individual's abhorrence for all determinate content, which he regarded as a blemish. The essence of conscience shifts at this point from conscientious action to introspection, the other "pole" of conscience.

The beautiful soul gazes at the godhead that is itself. But it also peers into an abyss: selfhood or subjectivity bereft of all objectivity or this-ness. Conscience has discovered that all the determinate features of concrete moral life, the differences that make up life in general, have vanished and become mere abstractions, unrealities [657]. This is the price that conscience pays for its introversion and its disdain for determinateness or finitude. "Refined into this purity," Hegel says, "consciousness exists in its poorest shape, and the poverty that constitutes its sole possession is itself a vanishing."[21] Conscience, the ultimate self-certainty, proves itself to be "the absolute untruth that collapses internally."

Hegel describes this collapse in terms of consciousness and self-consciousness. In its withdrawal from all stable being and thinghood, conscience is only *self-consciousness.* The equally necessary moment of *consciousness,* by which Hegel means consciousness of an object, is submerged [657].

The beautiful soul is the exact opposite of the "beautiful individuality" for which Hegel praises the ancient Greeks.[22] The Greeks made themselves actual through display or appearance: in games and poetic competition. They *lacked conscience,* as Hegel observes in various writings, and were at home in the world.[23] The glory of the Greek *polis* was that it embodied concrete human community and life. Its defect was that this community was based on trust rather than self-knowledge. Greek life had *substance* and truth but not *subject* and self-certainty. Self-conscious individuality was suppressed on behalf of family and state. In the beautiful soul, the situation is reversed. Customs, family, laws, life, action, everything that belongs to the realm of consciousness, now count for nothing. The individual is alone with himself, enthralled by his inner purity, which is also the "black hole" of selfhood. In Greek life, self-consciousness was submerged in the daylight life of consciousness. For the beautiful soul, consciousness is submerged in the night of *self*-consciousness.

The moral genius is at last explicitly identified as "an unhappy, so-called *beautiful soul*" [658].[24] Hegel describes this character type in great detail. His vivid description recalls the death of Novalis by consumption and the mental breakdown of Hölderlin.[25] The most telling feature of this soul is its unrest. The beautiful soul, Hegel notes, is a reappearance of the unhappy consciousness [658]. That soul too was profoundly restless. Repulsed by its changeableness and carnality, it yearned infinitely to be united with God, the true and unchangeable self. The unhappy consciousness was "the consciousness of self as a dual-natured, merely contradictory being" [206]. This contradiction was the individual's consciousness of sin, and of God, in one and the same consciousness. When the unhappy consciousness thought of itself, it immediately thought of God, before whom it was impure. And when it thought of its sinfulness, it immediately thought of God, who was pure. The unhappy consciousness moves restlessly between these two poles.

The beautiful soul is even more self-contradictory and unhappy, more restless. The unhappy consciousness yearned for what it took as a stable if infinitely remote object, an unchangeable God. But the beautiful soul experiences the instability of *all* objects. This includes the inner God that it worships: its own selfhood. The beautiful soul experiences *itself* as the God it can never make objective and present. It is not that the beautiful soul has no consciousness of objects. It is rather that every object that rises to consciousness (every possible worldly concern) immediately disappears or dies. Consciousness is continually being drowned in pure introspection, self-worship, and feeling. When the beautiful soul tries to rise to consciousness, make itself objective, it fails. Gloomy introversion defeats it, sucks prospective objects back into the "black hole" of selfhood.[26]

The beautiful soul does not even try to act. But it does try to speak, to "confess" its inner beauty and thereby make itself objective and real as a self. This speech is the only externality, the only "world" the beautiful soul has. But conscience, in its aesthetically refined form, has lost the power [*Macht*] to make its speech objective and stable. Speech has become mere sound. And as the beautiful soul engages in this pathetic attempt to utter itself and communicate what it feels, it only hears this speech, which is itself, as an echo that dies away [658]. The image Hegel conveys here is worse than that of life as a continual funeral. It is life as a continual spiritual abortion.

Hegel's account of the beautiful soul emphasizes this soul's impotence. This is the *inversion* of the originally Napoleonic aspect of conscience. The beautiful soul "does not attain to actuality" and "lacks the power to externalize itself, the power to make itself into a thing, and to endure [mere] being" [658]. Again Hegel refers to the abhorrence of determinateness. The beautiful soul "lives in dread [*Angst*] of besmirching the splendor of its interior through action and existence." The only "object" it succeeds in producing is the "hollow object" of its own self, which has degenerated from moral insight into self-feeling. Its only action, Hegel says in another echo of the unhappy consciousness, is that of yearning [*Sehnen*]. The beautiful soul longs for the infinite and abhors the finite. But without content, infinity is only an edifying gas. The beautiful soul, in the end, becomes this gas: "it vanishes like a shapeless vapor that dissolves into thin air." Its pathetic vanishing is the result of a stubborn refusal to compromise purity of heart with worldly contact. The beautiful soul is miserable on principle. It enacts, and suffers, what Hegel took to be the spirit of romanticism in its life-denying mode. It is this romantic longing that the *Phenomenology of Spirit* will eventually transform into Science.[27]

The Doer and His Judge: Evil and Forgiveness [659–68]

The beautiful soul is conscience that has yielded to the Siren song of pure knowing, conscience as self-contemplation. This is the universal aspect of conscience, made actual in the self-worshiping community of beautiful souls. But this is only one side of conscience as the immediate unity of thought and action. Having followed the path of pure thought or universality to its logical conclusion (romantic evaporation), Hegel now takes up the other side of conscience, the side of individuality or being-for-self. Conscience, he says, "has to be considered as acting" [659].

As we proceed, we must keep in mind that for conscience as a beautiful soul, *all* action is sinful or guilty. Action as such has "the blemish of determinateness" and is defiled by self-interest. To act at all is to be guilty.[28] We must also remember that the opposition that now emerges between the Doer and the Judge concretizes and explicates the opposition *within conscience itself* between its two logical moments: thought and action, universal and individual.

The problem of action appeared earlier, in the realm of ethicality. In the conflict between Antigone and Creon, we saw that all action was guilty because it was finite and one-sided. Antigone and Creon championed one side of the law but violated the other. The tragic outcome was the result of noble purpose joined to partial knowing. At the higher level of morality, action will again be finite and guilty. The source of the conflict, however, is different. The problem is not the clash between opponents who champion one side of law and fail to know the other, or a battle of the sexes. It is rather the dissonance between knowledge *as such* and action *as such*, between inner and outer. Action will be evil, not because it violated a law, but because it *is*, and *is determinate.* It is more blameworthy than it was in the *polis* because there is no component of ignorance. Conscience *knows* that only pure willing is good. The evil of action is therefore not crime but *hypocrisy.* Strictly speaking, the "sins" of Antigone and Creon are examples, not of evil but of what the Greeks called *hamartia:* missing the mark, or error.[29]

Let us recall two crucial facts about the self-worshiping community of conscience. First, community was necessary in order for conscience to make itself concretely universal. Second, it consisted, not in deeds but in declarations of conviction, in speech. As long as I play by the rules of this religion of inwardness, I am one in spirit with my pious friends. I am "in" the universal and lifted above my merely natural being, my willfulness and desire. I am good because I am purely inward and unworldly.

But in declaring my conviction, I become aware of myself as an individual distinct from other individuals, a singular being-for-self. I am aware that *my* conscience, which I make clear to you in speech, is different from *your* conscience, which you make clear to me. This is "the antithesis [*Gegensatz*] of individuality to other individuals, and to the universal" [659]. Hegel now takes up what he calls the movement [*Bewegung*] of this antithesis, which had been there all along but only now comes to light.[30] The antithesis recapitulates, and renders more acute, the conflict between pure duty and private purpose that appeared in the Moral World-View.

The individual who acts is no ordinary individual. He is a person of *conscience*, who has presumably renounced his worldly existence in favor of purity of heart. In choosing to act, to yield to his willfulness and desire, he betrays not only the community to which he belongs but also *himself* as an inward, spiritual being. He has prostituted himself. Conscience tried to rise above the Moral World-View by positing the immediate unity of duty and inclination, spirit and nature. In the dialectical experience of conscience, this unity breaks apart. The breakup takes the form of a falling out between the Doer and the Knower, the Man of Action and the Man of Introspection. These opposed types personify, as I noted above, the two logical moments of conscience: individuality and universality. The beautiful soul, who embodies the universal consciousness of the community, regards action as the betrayal of pure inwardness. He judges this action as evil because it affirms individuality over universal duty [660]. Moreover, since the one who acts claims to do so out of conscience (and conceals his self-interest), to be in conformity with pure duty, his action is judged as *hypocrisy.*

This hypocrisy or concealment of self-otherness must now be "unmasked" [*entlarvt*] [661]. Its truth must be revealed, its darkness brought to light. The beautiful soul, who previously appeared as effeminate or "soft," now becomes a hard-hearted Judge. In this new role, it seeks to unmask the hypocrisy it sees in the other: "it must be made apparent that [acting conscience] *is* evil, and thus its existence [*Dasein*] made to correspond to its essence" [661]. Hegel reminds us that evil, in order to be successful, relies on the mask of good. As La Rochefoucauld says, "Hypocrisy is the homage that vice pays virtue." In hiding his true motives, the conscientious Doer not only deceives others but also hides from *himself* [661]. He engages in bad faith and self-deception. In order to act, and not feel guilty about acting, he must lie to himself.

The dialectic now focuses on the phenomenon of judgment, *Urteil* [662].[31] The essence of conscience now expresses itself as an opposition between "the acting consciousness" and "the judging consciousness" [665]. The former is evil insofar as it contains a disparity between its self-interested motive and the universal, to which it claims to conform.

As Hegel stresses, the unmasking of hypocrisy and the restoration of the unity of conscience cannot be the work of either the Doer or the Judge taken alone [662]. The Doer, from his one-sided position, cannot heal the wound of conscience. He cannot simply assure the other of his good intentions, since "this other does not believe [his assurance] or acknowledge it." It would be like saying, "You've got me all wrong: I acted from conscience." This does not restore the identity or friendship of the two consciousnesses, which is essential to conscience as universal or communal. It does not expose the self-interest and hypocrisy that had in fact taken place *and are still there.* It has not brought concealment as such to light. Moreover, the Doer cannot deny that in acting from his conscience he necessarily goes against the conscience of others and, in effect, wrongs them (by being self-interested). Nor can the universal consciousness (which speaks for the community), from its one-sided position, unmask and abolish hypocrisy: "In denouncing hypocrisy as base, vile, and so on, it is appealing in such judgment to its *own* law, just as the evil consciousness appeals to *its* law" [663]. The Judge speaks, as he must, from his own personal perspective. Judgment thus legitimizes rather than rises above the one judged. Only *together* can these individuals heal the wound of conscience and restore the unity of "theory" and "praxis" that conscience *is.* This whole problem, we must note, derives from the intense personal subjectivity of conscience, from conscience as the expression of Lutheran authenticity.[32]

The Judge speaks on behalf of the moral community. He presents himself to the acting individual as one who does *not* act, as a pure self that only thinks and apprehends. Nevertheless, he wants his judgment to be taken as an outward sign of his inner purity, as having the force and value of an actual *deed.* He wants to prove himself to others, not through real deeds but "by uttering excellent sentiments" [664]. The Judge is a hypocrite. He is an even bigger hypocrite than the one he judges, since he makes a pious show of being above hypocrisy. His "virtue" and "piety" consist in revealing the evil and hypocrisy of other people. In the experience that follows, the Judge will fall under the stern injunction of the Gospel: "Judge not, that ye be not judged" (Matthew 7:1). This does *not* mean, "Don't make moral judgments," but rather "Don't condemn others: we're *all* sinners."

The result of this stage of the dialectic is that both the Man of Action and the Man of Pure Thought are hypocrites. Both abuse the *language* of conscience. The former masks the self-interest of action by declaring that he has acted only from the purest, most disinterested motives. The latter masks the self-interest of his *inaction* under the cloak of pious speeches about how moral sentiment is higher than all action, and how people who act—worldly, vulgar people—ought to be ashamed of themselves.

The Judge goes beyond the preoccupation with the Doer's internal inconsistency and hypocrisy, his knowledge [665]. He is obsessed with condemning action as such. All Doers everywhere, not just those who have betrayed the community of beautiful souls, fall under the guillotine of moral judgment. Judging at this point is revealed as a type of behavior, a praxis and pathology that has appeared on the stage of history, along with the deeds of real heroes. The Judge, generalized in this way, now appears in his worst light. He becomes the resentful debunker of heroes, of men like Napoleon who asserted themselves, dared to act, and therefore *sinned.*[33] The moral Judge sees in action nothing but selfishness and the complete absence of any universal significance or nobility. Action, for him, is only individual or self-interested: it is *only* sin. He can engage in this sort of reductionism because he willfully ignores the actual result and historical meaning of the action and focuses exclusively on its inner intention and motive.

As we know, for people who go down this road of motive-mongering, there is no deed and no person however great that cannot be chopped down to size and made small. If an action results in fame, as it certainly did for Napoleon, then the debunker-Judge ascribes its motive to the base desire for fame [665]. "No action can escape such judgment," since all action is the action of an interested individual, and an action done only for the sake of duty "is an unreality." Here Hegel gives his version of a French saying: "No man is a hero to his valet; not, however, because the man is not a hero, but because the valet—is a valet."[34] He explains that the valet knows the hero only "as one who eats, drinks, and wears clothes," that is, as a merely *natural* being. The Judge, who represents conscience in its purest form, has sunk to the level of this valet.[35]

Through the moral valet and his jaundiced view of heroes, *history,* the realm of great deeds, becomes the negative object of moral judgment, which scorns as petty and self-interested not simply the active but the heroic or grandly active. It refuses to admit the existence of what Hegel calls "world-historic individuals," *individuals* who embody the *universal.*[36] As H. S. Harris observes, the reconciliation with which the entire chapter on morality ends "will take us from the standpoint of moral judgment in its final shape to that of historical judgment proper" (2:504). Of course, such historical judgment is, at this point, only *for us.* It will be *for consciousness* at the level of absolute knowing. Historical, as opposed to moral, judgment practices *rational forgiveness.* It is pure thought that lets Napoleon be Napoleon, that is, lets him be both self-interested and universal or great. Historical judgment forgives Napoleon because it understands him: *Tout comprendre, c'est tout pardonner.*[37] When Tolstoy, in the Second Epilogue to *War and Peace,* attacks Hegel's "great man theory of history," and Napoleon's claim to greatness, he is being a moral valet masquerading as a philosophic historian.[38]

The judgmental individual has shown himself to be base [666]. As a moral valet, he wants his *word* of condemnation to be admired as a *deed* that is higher than all deeds. He is conceited and hypocritical—the Napoleon of Inwardness. The Doer *sees* this about his Judge, who has sunk to the level of this evil consciousness. He now feels a bond with the Judge and finds him to be "identical with himself." In response to perceived equality in sin, the Doer confesses his sin. He does so, not to humiliate himself, or, we might add, to express regret that he had acted, but in the hope that the Judge, whom he now recognizes as his brother in spirit, will do the same.

This whole spiritual drama depends on the power of language. The active, worldly consciousness confesses not so much his sinfulness as his equality or parity with the hypocritical Judge. His speech reveals that he has seen himself in his other, and expects this other to respond in kind, to *complete the speech* in which spirit has its immediate being-there or *Dasein* [666].

The Judge's immediate response to this "I who have dared to act am finite and therefore wicked—and you?" is stubborn refusal [667]. The Judge wanted to unmask the hypocrisy of the other but not to be at his level, not to unmask *himself.* He thus continues to repel the other and to be offended by him. Here Hegel gives his dialectical analysis of what the Bible calls "hardness of heart" and "stiff-neckedness."[39] Hardness here is pure being-for-self. Contracted to a point, the Judge rejects community and continuity with the other, who has made himself transparent. The roles of Doer and Judge are now reversed. It is the evil consciousness that shows a communal spirit, and the "spiritual" beautiful soul that refuses to reveal itself. The sinful Doer is "open," the pious Judge "closed."

The beautiful soul "confronts the confession of the penitent with his own unrepentant character, mutely keeping to himself and refusing to throw himself away for someone else." Hegel calls this hard-heartedness of the Judge "the highest indignation or rebellion [*Empörung*] of the spirit that is certain of itself" [667]. This indignation is the obstacle that spirit must now overcome. In rejecting the other's self-sacrifice, the Judge sins against the Holy Spirit. He prevents himself from knowing that spirit "is master [*Meister*] over every deed and actuality, and can cast them off, and make them as if they had never happened." This is the Christian spirit of forgiveness and reconciliation, which counsels us to love others, forgive them so that we may be forgiven, and to "die to self" so that we may truly live. Thus do we live "in" the spirit.

The Judge fails to recognize that in refusing to join the other in confession (which is not abasement but truth-telling), he falls into contradiction

[667]. He condemns the other, not realizing that his failure to respond, his silent, implacable No!, is responsible for that other's inability to complete his confession and have his sin (the inevitable finitude of action) taken away.

In the next phase of his experience, the Judge *feels* his contradictoriness. As a beautiful soul that does not act, he "cannot attain to an objective existence or *Dasein*" [668]. This soul hides its self-knowledge, its bad conscience, and remains an ideal point of unexpressed selfhood. It simultaneously wants to express itself (for that is the desire of all selfhood) and refuses to express itself. This contradiction produces agony. The beautiful soul "is disordered to the point of madness, wastes itself in yearning and pines away in consumption."[40] In a sense, it does surrender its hard being-for-self, but only pathologically: by becoming a being on the brink of death [668].

Reconciliation and the Birth of Absolute Spirit [669–71]

Dialectical movement began with the action that betrays the universal. This solicited the judgment that condemned the action. Then the Doer made his confession, hoping to solicit a reciprocal confession from the Judge. Everything now hinges on the Judge, or rather the phenomenon of *moral judgment,* which is about to be superseded by the spirit of forgiveness manifested in religion. It is the Judge, the embodiment of pure thought, who will untie the knot of conscience by completing the speech of the penitent Doer.[41]

Throughout this final stage of the dialectic of conscience, Hegel explicitly draws on the Christian teachings of confession and forgiveness, or the remission of sins. There is, however, no transcendent God in the picture at all. The drama of the two individuals, the Doer and the Judge, takes place *wholly within the order of human existence.* Spirit, here, is not a being separate from these individuals but the substantial relation that they share as real existent selves, or would share if the Judge only "showed himself." It is God at work in time, God as a living universal.[42]

Hegel now reveals the dialectical process in which the hard heart of the pious, judgmental community is broken [669]. This is the path of a beautiful soul that does *not* collapse internally and succumb to consumption and death. It has already appeared in the individual who has confessed his sin, that is, the *finitude* of his worldly action that is in dissonance with the *infinity* of his inward thought. The Judge need only do the same: endure the process of destroying his hard being-for-self. In this act, the Judge discovers that "the wounds of the spirit heal, and leave no scars behind."[43] He experiences forgiveness, the determinate negation that lets being, *with all its faults and blemishes,* be. The Judge's forgiveness, here, does not mean: "I forgive you: now don't do it again!" In the famous words of Pope: "To err is human, to forgive divine." In forgiveness, we discover how divinely satisfying it is to be human, to recognize ourselves in those whom we are tempted to condemn as sinful.[44] As beings who, in order to live, must act, we cannot hope to be purely moral. But we can and must forgive others for failing to be so, thus meriting forgiveness in return. Indeed, we must *go on* forgiving them! In doing so, we let ourselves, and others, be human. Forgiveness in this sense establishes our bond with all of humanity throughout the ages. It reconciles us, in particular, to those we are tempted to think are *not good* because they appear *great.*

The problem of conscience is the disharmony of inner thought and outer action, knowing and doing, knowledge and life, dramatized in the two opposed individuals. The equalization or leveling of these individuals occurs once the Judge does what the acting consciousness has already done: confess his hypocrisy or self-otherness. In mutual confession, thought and action, the two poles of conscience, are themselves reconciled. The human phenomenon of forgiveness and reconciliation is, in other words, the "philosophic symbol" of a logical accomplishment or overcoming (Hyppolite, 524).

In mutual forgiveness, the evil consciousness freely gives up the absoluteness of its action, and the judging consciousness, which now admits to seeing itself in the other, freely gives up the absoluteness of pure thought.[45] Both admit that they have been one-sided, and that thought and action do not repel each other but are opposites that contain each other. The two consciousnesses recognize thought and action as moments of a greater whole [669]. Thought is now allowed to be external or worldly, and action is allowed to express thought or knowledge. Each drinks in the spirit of its other.

This resultant unity of selves is the work of mutual self-sacrifice: "just as the [evil consciousness] has to surrender its one-sided, unacknowledged being-for-self, so too must this other set aside its one-sided, unacknowledged judgment" [669]. Mutual confession and forgiveness, which is about to take place, is the mutual surrender of one-sidedness. The acting self, in confessing its sin, "throws away its actuality," supersedes its singular being-for-self, and thus shows itself as *universal* [670]. Similarly, the judging self, in confessing its sin, lets go of its judgment, in which it was merely for itself or subjective. By cooperating in this way, the two individuals experience selfhood in its most genuine form—selfhood as spirit, *Geist.*

At the beginning of the drama of self-consciousness, individuals engaged in a fight to the death. They desired recognition, not knowing that this must be mutual. The reconciliation of the two sides of conscience, thought and action, is this recognition. It is the resolution of the fight to the death, and of the drama of self-consciousness.

Conscience was universal in language. Indeed, it *lived* in the realm of language. At first, this was only the language of purely subjective conviction. Now language appears as the medium of reconciliation: "the word [*das Wort*] of reconciliation is spirit *that is there*" [670]. This is selfhood that is at home in being external to itself or *in the world.* As Hegel puts it in the chapter on religion, "spirit is the knowing of its own self in its externalization; the essence, which is the movement, of retaining the sameness with itself in its being other" [759]. This is what the language of reconciliation accomplishes. It reveals mutual recognition as the identity-within-difference that defines the Concept. Since this identity of opposites is experienced and actually exists, it is "absolute spirit," spirit that manifests itself in history [670].

In his final and very difficult paragraph, Hegel elaborates on what the dialectic of conscience has accomplished. The reconciliation of the two individuals is not just a human drama, a happening in the world. It is the moment in which all the "tragic" oppositions that have appeared in the *Phenomenology* are "comically" reconciled: inner and outer, thought and action (or theory and praxis), essence and appearance, subject and object, self and world, individual and universal—in other words, all the oppositions of Kant's Moral World-View. This is the moment in the *Phenomenology* when God is experienced, no longer as a supersensible Beyond or a postulated idea, but as the historically present spirit of human community. Morality, for this reason, is the first chapter of Hegel's book that has a happy, indeed triumphant, ending.

The triumph consists in the self's having vanquished all otherness with respect to itself. The Moral World-View tried to harmonize opposites by way of postulates. These proved unstable (was God a being, or only a thought?). Conscience rejected the mere harmony or external relation of inner and outer, and the postulation of an ambiguously external God. It assimilated *nature* (drives, feelings, actions, etc.) *and God* into self-consciousness. Conscience was not a harmony but an identity of opposites: the identity of duty and nature (Schiller's beautiful soul). In confession and reconciliation, the self posits and embraces otherness as *its own otherness.* Instead of an immediate, and therefore unstable, union of inner and outer, thought and action, there is *mediation:* the inevitable sinfulness of deed and damning word is overcome in mutual forgiveness grounded in the intuition [*Anschauung*] or seeing of self in other. Like the Concept, the pious community of consciences is first absolutely self-identical, then self-split, then identical in its self-difference. It abandons itself only to come back home.

Having described this mediation in terms of individual human types, Hegel shifts to the *spirit* that each embodies (the spirit of thought and the spirit of action). Absolute spirit is the unity of these two opposed spirits that exchange their identities or roles: universal duty and singular self-consciousness [671]. The roles are exchanged because, in confession, the Judge admits to being a singular sinner, and the Doer, having admitted that his action is sin, cancels his singularity and returns to the universal. These roles correspond, respectively, to the *continuous* and the *discrete.* The Judge represents the "pure continuity of the universal," that is, the community. The Doer represents the "absolute discreteness" or singularity that stands apart from community and asserts itself.

Each side of this opposition is a *self.* Spirit, as a whole, in other words, is in *both* the Doer and the Judge. Their unity exists in their speech [*Rede*], that is, in the language of confession and forgiveness. But although they are united in this way, these two spirits (the active and the contemplative) remain distinct. This is true to the experience we have seen. The two selves that have appeared are different. One locates its absolute in action, the other in pure thought (which tempts the self to hard-heartedness). This difference reflects the twofold manifestation or appearance of spirit in the world at large. There are Doers, and there are Knowers or Thinkers. There is Napoleon, and there is Hegel.[46] Each of these spirits [671] is an absolute or self-sufficient mode of being self-absorbed or turned inward—of being "in oneself" or *in sich.* Each is absolutely self-certain. For this reason, the active and the contemplative sides of spirit are both *universal,* not only for us but for themselves [671]. Each posits itself as absolute and is certain of being all reality, and each is *right.* The self-certain individual who acts and the self-certain universal that knows are both ways of affirming the self as absolute.[47] Each is the *whole self,* the whole human realm, from the perspective of either individuality or universality. Each regards objects as nothing more than determinations of the self, as objects of the self's *will* in one case, and of its pure *knowing* (or awareness of pure duty) in another. When the two individuals oppose one another, it is spirit coming to know itself as the opposition and unity of these two different ways of being self-related and self-determining.

These two selves "fill out the whole range of the self" [671]. Once forgiveness has occurred, the acting side of conscience contains the whole range of human action and desire, and the inward side thinks or contemplates this world *without envy or resentment.* Thought contains rather than repels humanity as it is, especially when that humanity aspires to greatness. It gives honor where honor is due. To repeat Harris' valuable insight, this is the moment in which *moral* judgment is transformed, for us, into *historical* judgment. The latter sees the play of passion and self-interest but refrains from condemning it. It lets Napoleon be Napoleon by understanding *who he is* as a world-historical individual.[48] This reformed Judge may even feel a certain fear and pity for such human beings, whose passions drive them to act, since, as Hegel emphasizes in his *Philosophy of History,* heroes have no private life and come to unhappy ends.[49] The Judge is now what Hegel calls in that work "the free human being" [*der freie Mensch*], who "is not envious, but gladly recognizes what is great and elevated, and rejoices that it *is*" (31).

In the last sentence of this momentous chapter, Hegel recalls the communal nature of selfhood or self-consciousness:

> The reconciling *Yea*, in which the two 'I's let go their antithetical *Dasein*, is the *Dasein* of the 'I' that has expanded into duality [*Zweiheit*], and therein remains identical with itself, and, in its complete externalization and opposite, has the certainty of itself: it is God appearing in the midst of those who know themselves as pure knowing.

The I, here, has become an "*actual* I." It has been liberated from its hard, unyielding being-for-self. The magic that accomplishes this is *language*, which is the existence or being-there of the self. In becoming communal, the self is a free and really existent spirit. Spirituality no longer consists in life-denying judgmental inwardness, and the world is no longer God-forsaken and vain. Thought and action, self and world, now bless rather than curse each other. The I of the beautiful soul, writ large in the aesthetic-religious community of moral narcissists, now gives way to a very different I: "God appearing in the midst of those who know themselves as pure knowing." This is the universal *Church* that celebrates "God in our midst." The praxis of this community is the forgiveness of sins. We have here the transition from Morality to Religion.

The reconciliation of the Doer and the Judge overcomes all the oppositions we have seen so far in the journey of consciousness. But the journey does not end here. It proceeds to Religion and Absolute Knowing. Morality becomes religion because, as we have seen, the judgmental community of consciences has become a community that experiences God in the forgiveness of sins. Morality has produced "pure knowing" as the knowledge of the divine [671]. This knowing, Hegel tells us, is at this point in the mode of *consciousness:* it is aware of the world as in need of constant forgiveness. The purely inward community of reconciled beautiful souls must now spell out for itself *what* it knows about the divine, which Hegel only now calls *God.* God must be its object. The community must become reflective or self-conscious. Religion, the prelude to absolute knowing, will be the *speculative moment* that goes beyond the praxis-orientation of morality. It is the awareness of the divine as absolute *being* and absolute *truth.*

As Hegel says in the next chapter, religion is the *self-consciousness* of spirit: spirit aware of itself as spirit [672]. This is the human community that contemplates God as the divine essence of the whole world of nature. Religion will contemplate this essence in *pictures,* not concepts. Just as the knowledge of "God in our midst" must become the knowledge of God as being and truth, the religious imagining of God must become logic or Science. This is necessary in order for spirit to grasp itself as the *movement* in which tensions are both overcome and preserved. This movement is truth as subject.

At the end of Morality, knowledge and human community are united. Human community consists of pure selves whose divine knowing is the recognition of how human we really are. In forgiveness, we are divinely human. Religion will now consider everything in human experience from its divine point of view. It will *think* (or rather represent) reconciliation as the relation of God and world. Religion in this way gives the concept "God" objective content and meaning. Once this absolute content has been revealed in the historical unfolding of world-religions, it will be rendered logical. This is the task of *absolute knowing.*

RELIGION

[Religion] is the region in which all the riddles of the world, all contradictions of thought, are resolved, and all griefs are healed, the region of eternal truth and eternal peace, of absolute satisfaction, of truth itself.

HEGEL, Preface to the *Lectures on the Philosophy of Religion*

21

The Depiction of God

AT THE END OF THE PREVIOUS CHAPTER, FORGIVENESS GENERATED the mutual recognition that *is* absolute spirit [670]. Spirit was the reconciled community of consciences. Hegel, who is careful with the word God, used it in the culminating sentence. The I that remained self-identical in its self-otherness was "God appearing in the midst of those who know themselves as pure knowing" [671]. Hegel is being precise. Having experienced the divine aspect of humanity in mutual forgiveness, the communal self now turns its gaze to the divine object that is all being and truth, *the object it calls God.*[1] It now sees everything from this absolute or divine perspective. Morality has become religion.

Religion signals a major transition in the *Phenomenology.* It transcends the entire realm of spirit in its mode of consciousness, that is, self-certainty manifested as a *world* [438]. Religion, Hegel says, is "the self-consciousness of spirit" [672]. In other words, God is the object of religion but not *merely* an object, as he was in previous stages of development. In addition to being divine substance, he is now also *subject* or self, God as spirit or mind, who is actual, and who knows himself in and through the finite humans who collectively know him.[2]

At previous stages, consciousness suffered the tragic defeat of its various claims to know. In the dialectic of conscience, tragedy was overcome in the "divine comedy" of reconciliation. The "reconciling Yea" of the Doer and his Judge overcame all opposites: individual and universal, essence and appearance, life and knowledge, action and thought, inner and outer, human and divine. Religion makes this reconciliation the principle of a new and higher unfolding. It is not a one-sided abstract certainty that refutes itself but a concrete *whole* that experiences itself historically or in time [679]. The reason is that, in the reconciliation that appeared at the end of the last chapter, selfhood affirmed its self-otherness. Unlike the ironic beautiful soul, religion is not inwardness that is adversarial or judgmental with respect to the external world. Determinateness or finitude is not a "blemish" but a manifestation of God's creative power. Religion affirms the reconciliation of finite and infinite at the highest possible level. A specific religion is therefore not a mere claim to know. Religious spirit knows itself as existing *within* absolute truth. What it seeks is the perfect *form* of that truth: "an expression adequate to its essence" (Hyppolite, 537). The history of religion is spirit's search for this form. The search ends with Christianity, the religion of mediation, which depicts absolute truth as the reconciliation of man and God within human community.[3]

Although a Lutheran community based on forgiveness and reconciliation appeared at the end of the last chapter, Hegel does not proceed directly to Christianity. Religion is a whole new *realm of experience*, which must be given its own logical development. This development is necessary in order for Hegel to reveal the problem that Christianity (almost) solves: that of reconciling the inwardness of *spirit* in its self-comprehension with the external world of *nature*.[4] Spirit must find a way of coming out into nature *as* spirit. It must find a "body" that is adequate to its "soul."

The chapter on religion is the most overtly schematic in the whole *Phenomenology*. Its overall, historical layout is easy to follow, as Hegel takes us through **Nature-Religion** [A], **Art-Religion** [B], and **Manifest Religion** (sometimes translated Revealed Religion) [C].[5] Nature-religion appears in Persia, India, and Egypt, and the religion of art in ancient Greece. Manifest religion [*die offenbare Religion*]—religion that is explicit or "open" [*offen*]—is Christianity, the religion of modern Europe.[6] Logically, these stages are the work of the triune Concept. In nature-religion, spirit knows itself in a strictly objective or thingly way, as spirit that is *in itself*. In the Greek religion of art, spirit is *for itself*, as the artist gives the divine the shape of humanity or self-consciousness. Finally, in Christianity, religion is logically complete or *in and for itself*.

Each stage of religion expresses the self-knowledge of an actual people or *Volk*, which experiences itself as "in" God. Nature-religion expresses the spirit of societies that suppress freedom by means of caste-systems. Art-religion expresses the freedom and "beautiful individuality" that flourish in the world of ancient Hellas. And Christianity expresses the spirit of the modern world, whose principle is the infinite freedom of conscience. *We* see that there is only one spirit animating both religion and world-history [678], but religion does not. In the course of its development, religion, having initially separated spirituality and the actual world, will overcome this split. Christianity, in positing the Incarnation, will be the ultimate reconciliation of God and man, spirit and nature. Religion, in this reconciliation, experiences its "perfection" [678].[7]

Religion, for Hegel, is all about expressivity. That is why art plays a prominent role in the chapter. Expressivity, here, is no longer that of an isolated individual, whether a slave-laborer, a modern self-actualizer, or a moral purist. It is rather the self-expressive knowledge of a spiritual community or Church. This expanded, universal I—the divine I—was absent from the previous stages of Christian consciousness. To be sure, there was the unhappy consciousness and faith. But they embodied religion as mere subjectivity and feeling.[8] At the present stage, faith takes its communal and bodily expression more seriously. It welcomes rather than flees nature and portrays nature as the utterance of the divine, as the mirror of God (the divine essence).

Christian images have been with us from the start. The stages of consciousness on its Way of Despair were like the Stations of the Cross [77]. Consciousness "died" at each stage only to be "reborn," Christ-like, in the next. The Concept, like the Holy Trinity, was composed of a fatherly in-itself, a filial for-itself, and a spiritual in-and-for-itself that expressed identity-in-difference or the "reconciliation" of opposites. At the end of the present chapter, we see why these images are the perfect metaphors for dialectical truth, why truth has a "Christian" form.

The upshot of Hegel's account is that religion grasps absolute truth, but only in an image or *Vorstellung:* something placed, *gestellt,* before, *vor,* the mind's eye. As religion, spirit presents itself to itself through pictures, stories, and symbols. This self-depiction or artistry is essential to religion.[9] But figure must rise to Concept, religion to philosophy in the form of Science [787]. This will be absolute knowing, the top of Hegel's ladder (see Chapter 16).

Hegel's account of religion is long and fascinating. It is crucial to an understanding of why religion (Christianity, in particular) is essential to the evolution of philosophy into Science. I will devote a chapter to each of religion's three stages. In the present chapter, I will examine the nature-religions of Persia, India, and Egypt; in the next, the art-religion of the Greeks; and in the one after that, manifest religion or Christianity.

Rethinking the Whole [672–83]

The most difficult part of Hegel's chapter on religion is the introduction. The crucial distinction at work here is that between *consciousness* and *self-consciousness.* The tension between these two poles defines religion, and is the reason why religion must undergo a development. Consciousness corresponds to *existence.* It is the awareness of concrete, finite things that are there in the natural world. Self-consciousness corresponds to *essence.*[10] This is religion's inwardness or spirituality, its awareness of God's infinite *depth.*

Religious consciousness separates these two moments of its awareness. It thinks of itself as apart from the world, as sacred rather than secular. But in order to express itself, religion must use the world that is present to consciousness, the world of nature. The historical-dialectical journey of religion is spirit striving to unite, and ultimately to identify, these two aspects of its awareness.

Previously, God appeared "only from the standpoint of consciousness" [672], only as a divine object or spiritual *substance.* But now, religion does what the previous shapes did not. It grasps absolute being as in and for itself or logically complete, in other words, *as God.* In the definition I cited earlier, religion is "the self-consciousness of spirit" [672]. It is spirit that is, for itself, *subject* as well as substance.

Consciousness had a kind of religion in the understanding and its supersensible Beyond [673]. This holy of holies [146] was "bereft of self," an empty universal. In the final phase of **self-consciousness**, the Beyond was the source of infinite yearning and misery. The unhappy consciousness tried but repeatedly failed to be one with God, the Unchangeable Beloved. Then came **reason**, which was godless and had no religion. The rational individualist sought only his own gratification in the Here-and-Now [673]. Religion reappeared at the level of **spirit**. In Greek *ethicality,* it was "the belief in the terrible, unknown night of Fate and in the Eumenides of the departed spirit" [674]. In *culture,* this spiritual darkness became light, as the faithful individual looked ahead to new life in the Kingdom of Heaven [675].[11] But the Enlightenment attacked faith and reduced the Christian God to the indifferent Supreme Being, "which is neither to be known nor feared." It reinstated the understanding's empty supersensible Beyond. Finally, religion appeared in *morality.* At that point, God was once more meaningfully related to man. He was neither empty nor indifferent. But the Moral World-View could not free itself from the Enlightenment's reduction of everything to the subjective, finite self. God was no sooner posited as real than he was "taken back into the self," that is, treated as no more than a useful idea or *postulate* [676].

In the religions of ethicality, culture, and morality, spirit failed to see itself in the world it had made. It did not yet know itself as spirit, and was therefore not religion in the strict sense of the term. Conscience, the highest level of morality, is the first appearance of religion as the *self*-consciousness of spirit [656]. Conscience overcomes the duplicities of the Moral World-View. It assimilates all opposites, or, as Hegel puts it, "brings itself, as well as its objective world in general, into subjection, as also its picture-thinking and its determinate concepts" [677].[12] Spirit is now "a self-consciousness that communes with its own self"—a sacred community or Church. Religion knows that the highest truth is one that encompasses everything and, moreover, is both alive and self-aware. This truth is God, who "contains all essence and all actuality." God, for religion, is not a postulate.

But as religion, spirit "is not in the form of free actuality or independently appearing nature" [677]. Religious spirit thinks reality or nature only from the standpoint of *self*-consciousness or pure thought. It absorbs actuality or nature into the sphere of thought, in a sense, imprisons it. This absorption of nature into thought is the dialectical inheritance of conscience, which, even in its communal or fulfilled aspect, remains inner. In principle (or in its concept), religion, prior to its development, is like force that has not yet expressed itself. But just as force, to be force, had to express itself, religion as the pure thought of being must cancel its inwardness and express its certainty and infinite depth in finite forms.

The pure inwardness of the religious spirit generates within religion a distinction between consciousness and self-consciousness [678]. Religion distinguishes between the active world outside the religious community and the reflective world within. The Christian Church, for example, thinks of itself as *in* the world but not *of* the world. There are two spirits: the Sunday spirit of worship and the working, secular spirit of the other days of the week. In Augustine's formulation, there is the City of God and the City of Man. *We* see that "there is indeed one spirit of both," but religion, as I noted earlier, does not. Religion will be "perfected" when the two separate moments of its awareness—the spirit of Sunday and the spirit of everyday life—become one.[13]

The separation between consciousness and self-consciousness explains why religion engages in *Vorstellen* or picture-thinking [678]. This is religion's attempt to express infinity in finite terms, to think God by means of things. Picturing is the work of finite consciousness, and what is pictured is the infinite depth of divine self-consciousness.

Depicting the divine involves a double injustice [678]. On the one hand, the actual world of nature does not receive its full right [*Recht*], since it is demoted to the status of a mere image or symbol. Nature, here, is no more than a guise or suit of clothes [*Kleid*], something external to spirit.[14] On the other hand, so long as nature is only something finite, only an objective *thing*, religious self-consciousness does not have its full expression. This finitude of expression means that religious spirit takes on "a specific shape." It becomes actual as a specific religion among other specific religions. Hegel goes on to say: "If [spirit's] shape is to express spirit itself, it must be spirit itself, it must be nothing else than spirit, and spirit must appear to itself, or be in actuality, what it is in its essence" [678]. Spirit, as religion, is both subject and object. It is what does the expressing and also what is expressed. If religion is to be fully itself, these poles must be identical. This identity occurs in Christianity, where God becomes man or, alternately, spirit becomes *nature.* Christ is a "free actuality" in that he is spirit as really existing. Not a mere symbol for God, he is God himself, divine self-consciousness made incarnate (that is, mortal). Christianity is manifest religion because it posits a God who fully manifests himself or comes out into the open as a living, historical self.

Hegel's for-us introduction is most centrally about the relation between religion and history. Religion preserves all the stages we have seen so far: consciousness, self-consciousness, reason, and spirit (in its immediate or objective phase) [679]. The *Phenomenology* has so far traced the path by which these stages form a purely logical, non-temporal sequence. Religion makes the stages into a totality or whole that unfolds *in time.* As Hegel emphasizes, "Only the totality of spirit is in time, and the shapes, which are shapes of the totality of *spirit,* display themselves in a temporal succession" [679].

History is diverse because this whole, which is spirit, manifests itself from different points of view. Now at a higher level, spirit takes each of its logical moments in turn and makes it the determining characteristic of spiritual expression. In this way, spirit is the spirit of India, or the spirit of Greece, or the spirit of modern Europe. Each of these world-spirits is spirit itself from a certain point of view. Religious spirit experiences itself as a temporal unfolding within a larger unfolding—a history within world-history. Since it separates its (sacred) self-consciousness or inwardness from its (secular) consciousness, religion does not see that it *is* the expression of actual world-spirit at a specific stage of its overall development. Indian religion, for example, does not see that it is the expression of India in its actual existence. To repeat, religion does not yet know that there is only one spirit and one world—that the sacred and the secular interpenetrate.

As I noted above, each religion contains the whole of religion or divine self-consciousness and expresses this whole from a specific point of view. Nature-religion is spirit determined or specified by *consciousness,* art-religion by *self-consciousness,* and manifest religion or Christianity by *reason,* "for in it spirit appears as it is in-and-for-itself" (Hyppolite, 544).[15] It may seem odd that reason, which for itself was godless, should correspond to Christianity. But from a logical point of view, this makes sense. Reason (as Category) is the unity of consciousness and self-consciousness. As the interpenetration of essential self and phenomenal world, reason sets the stage for the greater interpenetration to come: God's unity with man and nature in the Incarnation. Christianity thus gratifies the rational individual's desire for happiness. It shows the individual that he cannot be happy *in this world* without a God who becomes man.[16] Christianity, in other words, manifests reason in its higher form.

Religion recapitulates even the subdivisions of the main stages already traversed—at least for religion at its first level [679].[17] Nature-religion will recapitulate the three stages of consciousness. The Persian worship of light as divine presence will be the religion of *sense-certainty* [686], the Indian worship of thingly plants and animals that of *perception* [689], and Egyptian structuralism the religion of *understanding* [692].

Religion is the dialectical process or becoming [*Werden*], in which spirit reaches perfection by experiencing each of its specific self-depictions to the fullest [680]. To be what it is, religious spirit must do justice to its contents or logical determinations, each of which must be made into its own world. Religion is not a sum of parts but a whole of wholes. The movement that constitutes religion is, like previous movements, away from immediacy and implicitness (being-in-itself) and toward mediation and explicitness (being-for-itself). The goal is the attainment of the *shape* [*Gestalt*] in which spirit "intuits itself, as it is" [680]. In this consummate shape (Christ), the inner self-consciousness of spirit rises to full consciousness, or becomes actually present. *For us,* Christ is a religious *symbol* for spirit at work in time and history. Hegel will make this explicit at the end of his book [808].

Religion is not a one-sided, abstract certainty that refutes itself in striving for the truth. It is a concrete whole, or rather a whole of wholes, that manifests itself historically and undergoes a positive unfolding. Hegel gives a complex geometrical description of this unfolding [681]. As we know, Hegel's logic goes in circles. Up to now, the circles of "consciousness, self-consciousness, reason, and spirit" [679] were arranged in a linear sequence to form *one continuous strand or string.* When consciousness "turned on itself" or came full circle, a new circle began: self-consciousness. There was a logical knot or node that was both the end of one circle and the beginning of another. And so, we get a linear sequence of four tangent circles in all. From left to right they correspond to consciousness, self-consciousness, reason, and spirit:

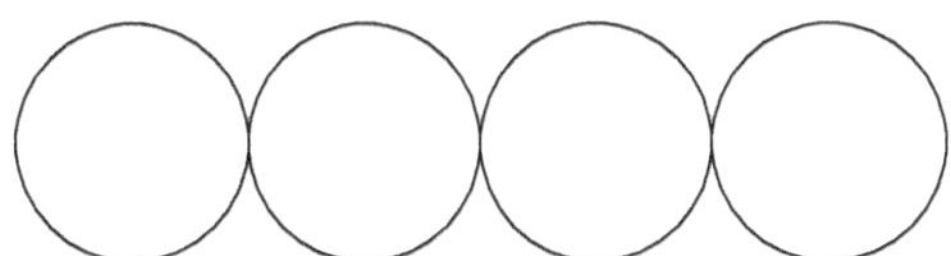

This sequence is now "broken at these nodes, at these universal moments, and falls apart into many lines." Rather than being arranged in sequence, these lines are now "gathered up into a single bundle [*Bund*]." They become four *radii* of the concentric circles that correspond to the various stages of religion. Religion is the circle of circles that unfolds in historical time. As the religion-circle "grows," each of its logical moments or "radii" also expands or grows.

To see how this works, let us consider the example of nature-religion. As we know, every religion, since it is a concrete whole, contains the moment of *self-consciousness*, even the pre-Greek religions that are not defined by self-consciousness. In the dialectic of nature-religion, spirit will go through three stages: the religions of light (Persia), of plants and animals (India), and of craftsmanship (Egypt). As nature-religion develops, or goes from one stage to the next, its circle expands. So does the radius that corresponds to its moment of self-consciousness. That is, as nature-religion goes from the worship of light to the worship of plants and animals, it becomes more self-conscious. This is evident in the Egyptian craftsman, whose experience generates self-consciousness as the defining feature of the next main circle (the Greek art-religion). The radius that corresponds to consciousness also expands. As nature-religion "grows," it becomes more aware of the wealth of nature. It goes from the inorganic to the organic and eventually to the all-embracing nature of man.[18]

The movement begins with religion in its immediacy. This "is only the *concept* of religion" [682]. At this stage, God is immediately present in nature as light. God, here, corresponds to the This of sense-certainty. He is mere being or presence. He illuminates the shapes in the natural world and gives them spiritual meaning, but he is not yet a creator, not yet the one who, in making the world, *creates himself.*

Hegel ends his general introduction with a sketch of things to come. Religion will first take the form of nature-religion. Here, spirit knows itself in an immediate way, as a natural object that is simply *there* [683]. In its second form, spirit knows itself "in the shape of superseded or sublated naturalness" [*aufgehobnen Natürlichkeit*]—that is, as art. The third and final stage combines the first two, thus overcoming their one-sidedness. Spirit now "has the shape of being in-and-for-itself." At this stage of manifest religion, consciousness and self-consciousness are identical. Christ is God made man: divine, universal selfhood that has become immediately present as nature.

In the closing sentences of his introduction, Hegel reminds us that the perfect shape of religious spirit (the figure of Christ) is nonetheless a shape, that is, something finite. Christianity, the perfection of religion, portrays but does not think through the unity of God and man. To be fully manifest, spirit must transcend its picture-thinking and "pass over into the Concept" [683]. Only then will spirit grasp itself, "just as we now have grasped it." In this moment, Christ, the divine Word or Logos, will become *logos* in the sense of dialectical logic. Religion will become philosophy.

A) THE RELIGION OF LIGHT [PERSIA] [684–88]

Having discussed what he calls the "pure Concept" of religion, Hegel proceeds to concrete religious embodiments or shapes [684]. Each shape, as the expression of absolute spirit, contains *all* the logical stages of consciousness that have appeared so far. The whole of religion is contained in each of its "parts." The series that is about to unfold thus displays the various aspects of "a *single* religion, and, moreover, every single religion." This does not mean that all religions are the same. Oriental religions that posit an incarnation, for example, should not be confused with Christianity, which grasps incarnation as absolute truth [684].

In his dense account of "lower" and "higher" shapes of religion, Hegel stresses that the truth of a specific religion expresses the actual world-spirit to which that religion belongs. Religion expresses "the *actual* self" of a *Volk* or people. That is why, in oriental religions (for instance, Buddhism), the rudiment of an incarnation "has no truth." It is because the Orient lacks the actual experience of reconciliation in its social-political life. A specific religion does not expresses selfhood generally, or the selfhood of an individual, but the concrete self of an actual world. Higher religions reveal more truth because they are the self-consciousness of higher, more spiritually developed cultures.

Nature-religion is religion in its immediacy. Light is the most immediate form of this immediacy [686]. It is the sheer presence or being-there of God. The religion of light is that of Zoroastrianism, the religion of Persia and the ancient Parsees.[19]

Self-consciousness is like night, and consciousness like day. When I look inside myself, I am in the dark, a dark so profound and impenetrable that I might despair of ever being able to see my true self and bring it to light. When I direct my vision out into the world, I am in the light. I see *things.* But where am *I* in this daylight world of things? Where is the I that sees? This is the problem of the *Phenomenology:* how to bring the dark of self-consciousness to light, to make the self appear and be the very substance of the world of things. At the beginning of the present section, Hegel recalls these images of day and night, light and dark. Before undergoing a phenomenal development or coming out, religion is in the dark about itself. It is immersed in the "night of its essence," that is, in self-consciousness [685]. The dialectical development of religion will be the daylight in which religious self-consciousness becomes conscious, or aware of itself as an object.

The Zoroastrian religion of light is religion at the level of *sense-certainty* [686].[20] This makes sense. Light is not a thing but the power by which things are made to appear and be present. What could be more God-like, more a spiritual presence, in the natural world than light? In the language of Descartes, things are real to the extent that they are "clear and distinct," and light confers this quality. Light keeps itself above things as their Lord and Master, even as it deigns to fall on them like an act of grace. It is also infinite *power:* the "pure, all-embracing and all pervading light of sunrise."

The religion of light combines the immediacy of both consciousness and self-consciousness, as these stages appeared earlier. It combines truth as sheer presence (sense-certainty) with truth as Lord and Master (from the master-slave relation). Light, in its simplicity or self-sameness, reveals spirit in its most immediate relation to itself [686]. It is "the shape of shapelessness."

But light presupposes and posits the *dark* as its resistant other. In order to be the all-mastering God (who mirrors the Persian king), light must therefore be violent. It must conquer the "will" of things to be opaque and resistant to illumination. Light must manifest itself as "torrents of light" and "streams of fire destructive of [all] structured form [*Gestaltung*]." Light's sole destiny and drive is to spread, that is, to dissolve all things and, in illuminating them as distinct shapes, *destroy* these shapes and reduce them to its awe-inspiring simplicity. For this reason, spirit as light "moves aimlessly about . . . without stability or intelligence, enlarges its bounds to the measureless, and its beauty, heightened to splendor, is dissolved in its sublimity" [686].

Light *falls upon* things, in both the positive and negative sense. But this glorious *substance* does not "descend," Hegel says, into its own depths to become *subject* [687]. In remaining above the multiplicity of the shapes it illuminates, light fails to express the difference within self-consciousness. It is *too* sublime. The One of Zoroastrianism has many names but is not itself many. It is only "clothed" [*gekleidet*] with many powers and attributes.

The differences illuminated by God as light must become real differences of God himself. Only then will nature manifest spirit's self-consciousness or being-for-self [688]. Light must not be the despot who affirms himself by depriving all others of their substance and being, for then God would break the vessels of his power. Spirit must transcend light. It must be the divine life-source that "sacrifices" its aloof simplicity or being-in-itself so that it may be present in the things it causes to endure.

B) THE RELIGION OF PLANTS AND ANIMALS [INDIA] [689–90]

To be present in this more developed way, spirit moves from sense-certainty to religious *perception* [689]. Light becomes Life, or rather the entire realm of living things. Just as perception sought the truth in the one thing with many properties, spirit posits itself as the divine One revealing itself in "the numberless multiplicity of weaker and stronger, richer and poorer spirits." These "spirits" cover the entire range of natural living things: plants and animals. This is the pantheism of India.[21]

Hegel's brief treatment of Indian religion traces the shift within Indian culture from peace to war: from the "passive resistance" of plant-life to the "hostile movement" of animal-life. These opposite moments correspond to the two aspects, respectively, of the perceptual Thing: the passive medium or Also, and the negative One [114]. *Flower religion,* the worship of "innocent" plants, is the undeveloped stage of Indian spirit, the stage at which this religion is in-itself and carefree (like modern-day hippies). But the other moment of this nature-worship expresses the "destructive being-for-self" of "guilty" animals [689].[22] In *animal religion,* the Indian spirit becomes conscious of its animalistic essence. It manifests itself as a perpetual war among "antagonistic national spirits who [like wild animals] hate and fight each other to the death."[23]

Persian light was not a sufficient manifestation of God. In destroying things other than itself, light (as fire or the blaze of glory) destroyed the medium of its own subsistence: the shapes of nature. The transition to the next stage was not temporal but logical: plants and animals allowed spirit to express itself through self-differentiation or infinite variety. Indian religion leads to a similar self-transcendence. Spirit—the universal spirit that is still searching for its perfect expression, still trying to overcome the split between its consciousness and its self-consciousness—absorbs the endless conflict of its Indian phase and rises above it. It reveals itself in a higher historical shape. This shape is the dialectical result of Indian hatred that has *consumed itself* [690].

Egyptian religion is the determinate negation of the self-destructive spirit of India. God tried to express himself, experience himself, first as light, then as plants and animals. Now he becomes the spirit of "the one who labors" [*der Arbeitende*]. Just as Indian aggression repeated the stage of the self-conscious combatants, Egyptian productivity will repeat the work of the slave.[24] The Egyptian "master of works" [*Werkmeister*], as Hegel calls him, rises above the "abstract being-for-self" of India. He also rises above the equally abstract, immediate in-itself of Persia [690]. His movement or work is "not merely negative, but tranquil and positive." He makes things—wondrous things that express divine meaning. But his activity will be "conditioned" or be-thinged [*bedingte*], and therefore imperfect. It will be the formation of a brute material already there and ready to hand, something that is not itself spirit.

C) SPIRIT AS CRAFTSMAN [EGYPT] [691–98]

Religion is spirit struggling to depict itself to itself. This effort is also spirit's drive to self-creation. Religion is divine self-intuition seeking to become divine presence. Spirit knows itself as spirit, but only in a self-conscious, self-absorbed way. It is aware of itself, and aware of the actual world. But it is not yet aware of itself *as* the spirit of the actual world. Until that point is reached, spirit lacks being or actuality and is not fully God. As Egyptian master-craftsman [*Werkmeister*], spirit begins to get an inkling of itself as a being that makes itself real by producing itself.[25] This self-production will become more fully revealed in the Greek artist [*Künstler*]. It will be perfectly revealed when God is posited (and knows himself) as a creator [*Schöpfer*].

As the Egyptian craftsman, spirit "produces itself as object but without having yet grasped the thought of itself" [691]. This work, however wondrous, is like that of bees building their honeycomb—something purely instinctive. That is why the craftsman, in spite of his artfulness, occupies the realm of nature-religion.

Persian religion was spiritual sense-certainty, and Indian religion spiritual perception. The Egyptian religion of the craftsman is the spiritual version of the *understanding* [692]. Pyramids and obelisks manifest spirit as structured (and self-structuring). These rigid structures are like the rigid formulae and laws of the scientific understanding. A sign of their abstractness is that pyramids and obelisks *have no curves.* They are structures "in which the incommensurability of the round is destroyed."[26] The pyramid, as a lifeless crystal or abstract form, is the fitting repository for the dead [692].[27]

In Egyptian architecture, structured body lacks the form of living soul. Form fails to express life, especially the life of the craftsman himself, who "has not yet appeared [in the product]" [693]. Artistry must therefore find a way to unite form and life, bodily structure and soul, the made and the maker. In a first effort to infuse architecture with life and the spirit of the curved, the craftsman incorporates the forms of plants into his structures [694]. Plants here are not gods, as they were in India, but only ornaments.

Desiring to express itself more fully, spirit as craftsman proceeds to depict animal forms, which convey the "shape of individuality" or being-for-self [695]. The craftsman knows that the animal shape is something *he* has produced in stone, that the animal per se is not a god. He sees himself in the animal nature, not in the violent animality that exists immediately, but in animality that has been artistically wrought and that embodies the human self qua worker. In Hegel's words, the wrought animal is "the hieroglyph of another meaning, of a thought" [695].

This vision of the unity of animality and thought raises the artisan to his next level: the depiction of the *human* form. But this form is only an outward bodily shape. It lacks the interiority or soul that expresses itself through language. The form sounds but does not speak. Hegel is here referring to the so-called statues of Memnon, which produce a tone when the rays of dawn fall on them. These statues only wear the outward shape of self-consciousness or man.[28] Spirit has not yet penetrated the object itself. Moreover, this shape is made out of *black stone,* in which Egyptian spirit hopes to capture its inner, night-like self-consciousness [696].[29] But this material "inner" fails to capture living selfhood. "Inside" the statue's outward shape there is nothing but the dark, immobile shapelessness of stone. Self-consciousness is not expressed but *covered.*[30]

Egyptian spirit has portrayed itself in the forms of plants and animals, and in the outward form of man. Both ways contain the moments of inner self-consciousness and outer consciousness [697]. But each fails to unite them. Spirit, working through the master-craftsman, attempts to express the tension the craftsman now sees within himself between inner and outer, self and thing. It does so in the Sphinx, which combines the outward shapes of animal (nature) and man (spirit).[31] With its human head and face emerging from the body of a lion, the Sphinx represents spirit's effort to free itself from animality, to *speak* and thereby show itself as spirit. But inner thought cannot escape the inarticulateness of nature. In the Sphinx, spirit experiences itself as an ambiguous, "self-riddling essence" [697]—an enigma in which the opposite poles of spirit *mate* but do not pervade each other. The enigma of the Sphinx gains further expression in Egyptian hieroglyphics. In this pictorial, non-living language, spirit reveals itself as "a profound, but scarcely intelligible wisdom." Egyptian spirit is, to itself, a monumental mystery.

Hegel's chapter on religion plots the course of spirit seeking to meet itself in the world—*like the self-certain I at the level of reason* [241]. In the human face of the Sphinx, the craftsman beholds himself as a self-conscious being: "spirit meets spirit" [698]. In this self-realization, all the monstrous, animal shapes of Egypt dissolve. The Sphinx is slain by the heroic spirit of a new and higher world of knowing.[32] In this new world—Greek ethicality—the human essence receives its due. Spirit will now find rather than lose itself in its "outering" or self-expression. It will celebrate the harmony of a "lucid, intelligible existence." No longer a master-craftsman, spirit becomes—*artist* [*Künstler*].

Through Apollo and Dionysus, the two deities of the Greeks, we come to recognize that in the Greek world there existed a tremendous opposition, in origin and aims, between the Apollonian art of sculpture, and the non-imagistic, Dionysian art of music.
NIETZSCHE, *The Birth of Tragedy*

22

The Greek Phase

THE EGYPTIAN CRAFTSMAN WENT BEYOND NATURE. HE INFUSED matter with an intelligent form, with *thought* in the outward shape of man. But he could not make thought and nature interpenetrate. His failure was explicit in the Sphinx, whose man-animal form tells the craftsman: "*This* is what you do not understand." Having failed to reach a true intimacy between thought and nature, spirit no longer tries to unite these by means of an artificial synthesis [699]. It does not combine what it finds "out there" with what it finds "in here," but rather *makes a world out of itself.*[1] The craftsman has been transformed into "a spiritual worker."

Hegel now launches into his amazing account of spirit's Greek phase: religion in the form of art. The artwork goes through three stages: the **abstract** work of art, the **living** work of art, and the **spiritual** work of art. Abstract art appears in statues of the gods and hymns; living art in religious festivals and games; and spiritual art in the language of epic poetry, tragedy, and comedy.

The actual world-spirit, whose essence art-religion depicts, is Greek ethicality [700]. Ethicality [*Sittlichkeit*] was the immediate stage of objectively appearing spirit. It was "true spirit" [444]. Greek spirit is *true* as opposed to self-*certain* because it lives in the medium of substantial custom [*Sitte*] rather than subjective knowledge (morality and conscience). In Persia, India, and Egypt, individuals were dissolved by Light, or killed off in tribal warfare, or subjected to a caste-system. In the Greek world, they are substantial and free. They recognize their *polis* as embodying "their own essence and their own work." Greek individuals are not beautiful souls: they *live* beautifully.

In the Greek religion of art, ethical spirit rises above, and withdraws from, its happy reality [701]. Elevation and withdrawal here correspond to religion as the *self*-consciousness of spirit. The *polis* immerses the individual in custom and makes him content. The individual trusts custom as the unchangeable aspect of a god-given, settled way of life. He sacrifices himself, happily, to the rights and duties of his political home. But this self-sacrifice has its down side. In the life of custom, the individual "has not yet grasped the unrestricted thought of his free self" [701]. Art gratifies the individual's need for subjective freedom and the transcendence of mere custom. The artistic individual turns away from trusting the *polis* to trusting himself and his creativity: he is actively self-certain. As a dutiful member of the *polis*, he experienced "light-mindedness" [*Leichtsinn*]. He was content. But in rising to artistic production, he experiences "unrestrained joyfulness." This joy was absent in the Egyptian craftsman, whose works were impressive but not beautiful—tasks rather than delights.

But Greek joy has its dark, or rather troubled aspect. The artist rises above "true spirit" and becomes self-certain. He is serene in his self-sufficient activity. But in this serenity, he experiences beautiful ethicality as mortal or passing away. He sees the tragedy of life, in which beautiful things fall. The Greek artist looks back at the glory that has been and commemorates it. Through the soul of the artist, spirit "mourns over the loss of its world, and now out of the purity of self brings forth its own essence which is raised above actuality" [701]. Greek spirit, in other words, does not simply mourn but transmutes its grief into a beautiful ideal.

Historically, the pursuit of ideal beauty through art flourishes when the actual spirit of Greece is both at its peak and degenerating.[2] The confrontation we saw earlier between Antigone and Creon shows that beautiful ethicality was inherently unstable all along and had to pass away, that tragedy was not merely an art form but the very soul of the *polis*. In place of ethicality, there will be the crushing power of Rome. This post-Greek era—spirit after the fall from ethical Eden—will be self-consciousness made into an actual world. The Greek artist laments the tragic loss of lived beauty. But he is not an alienated unhappy consciousness. He identifies with his city, which joyfully embraces his art and makes it universal in festivals, games, and dramatic spectacles. His gods do not make him feel unworthy, nor are they infinitely far away. In the human shape of the gods, the artist celebrates the *unity* of god and man.

The tragic sensibility of the artist is nevertheless the dialectical seed of the unhappy consciousness and its infinite grief. In the closing passages of his introduction to art-religion, Hegel describes the Greek artist in Christian terms. He reminds us that Greek art, the pursuit of ideal beauty, is on its way to the religion in which God manifests himself as man. In Christianity, the suffering artist becomes a suffering God. The greatest "artwork" will be man's salvation: the reconciliation between man and God.

"Absolute art" comes on the scene with the Greeks. Before this, art was only the "instinctive fashioning of material" [702]. The Egyptian craftsman was imprisoned in static structures and fixed animal natures. He was unfree. That was because his actual world, whose spirit he expressed, lacked the "free ethicality" of the Greeks. But spirit will also transcend art in order to reach "a higher presentation [*Darstellung*] of itself." This is the figure of Christ, God made man. As art, spirit brings forth into the day a substance (the artwork) from the creative night of its self-consciousness. But in Christ, spirit brings forth a substance that *is* its self-consciousness, a substance that is subject. It will then "have its very Concept for its shape" [702]. Spirit will meet spirit, not in a Sphinx-like riddle, but in mutual recognition. In the Incarnation, artist and product will "know each other as one and the same."

Art emerges, as we have seen, when ethical spirit withdraws from its outer existence and becomes self-conscious and self-certain. It is spirit that brings itself forth as object [703]. Spirit's activity is "pure form" because the ethical individual, through obedience and service to the *polis,* has exhausted all his finite obligations—all specific ethical content. He has done his duty and is free to enjoy artistic activity.[3] As subject or self that has been liberated from political substance, he is now active on his own.

Hegel calls this pure form "the night in which substance was betrayed" [*verraten*]. This night is the pure subjectivity or individual selfhood that is the source of art. But it also refers to the night on which Jesus was betrayed in the Garden of Gethsemane. The artist, like Antigone, cannot help playing Judas to the "true spirit" of the *polis.* Both embody the subjective moment of ethicality in the form of self-assertiveness. But the night of subjectivity is, in religious art, also creative. In betraying the substance of ethicality in reflection and self-fulfillment, art gives that substance new life, a life in which ethicality is "resurrected [*aufersteht*] as a shape freed from nature and its own immediate existence [as mere custom]" [703]. This shape is the work of art. Just as this art gives new life to merely natural existence, so too God, in becoming man, will break the bonds of nature in the Resurrection.

In falling from its ethical existence, spirit experiences sorrow [*Schmerz*]: it mourns over its lost world of custom.[4] The artist has been chosen by spirit to be the *vessel* [*Gefäß*] into which spirit pours this sorrow [704]. The spirit of divine expression masters the artist and drives him to seek ideal beauty. This is the artist's *pathos,* the origin of tragedy as an art form.[5] The artist sacrifices himself to his art and loses his freedom. This corresponds to the first stage of art, in which the statue fails to capture the artist's labor pains [709]. But his individuality re-asserts itself in drama, the higher stage of art. In tragic poetry, where suffering is made beautiful, the artist masters the *pathos* that masters him. He makes it into the very stuff of creativity, as the tragic hero, played by a live human being, replaces unfeeling marble. The tragedian pours into this hero the sorrow that spirit poured into *him.*

Having wrestled with the problem of how to give shape to the "shapeless essence" of his pure self-consciousness, the artist idealizes the spirit of suffering. He makes suffering into "a work [*Werk*], universal spirit individualized and depicted [*vorgestellt*] [704].

The "vessel of sorrow" is another recollection of Gethsemane. There, Jesus freely accepts the "cup" of the suffering willed by the Father, whom Jesus recognizes as "universal power" and authority. In the Incarnation, God is the tragic artist who makes himself into a tragic hero. This hero—Jesus as the perfect embodiment of an ethical or "good" human being—suffers and dies for the sins of humanity. His *pathos* or Passion is not something depicted on a theatrical stage, but rather the real drama in which God makes himself man. Philosophically interpreted, this will be the drama in which spirit sacrifices itself on the altar of time as world-history [808].

a) The Abstract Work of Art [Statue and Hymn] [705–19]

The abstract work of art is the statue of a god that stands in a temple [705]. It seems odd to call this concrete object abstract. The term becomes clearer when we consider that the statue represents the god insofar as he is remote or abstracted from where mortals live, the god in his awesome sanctity (Harris, 2:586). In the course of the dialectic, this abstractness will be overcome. The god will come down from his pedestal and join the community of religious self-conscious individuals.

The nature-worship of Persia, India and Egypt was the religion of *consciousness.* Greek art is religion at the level of *self-consciousness.* The gods now have human form, that is, the form of self-consciousness. The Greeks celebrate their humanity and see in their gods the ideal expression of their political character. Previously, self-consciousness was associated with night and darkness. Now, with the Greeks, selfhood comes out into the spiritual daylight. The Greeks are self-conscious, not because they desire to destroy all things (self-consciousness in its primitive form), but because they see themselves in everything, including their gods.

The statue or "first work of art" [705] is a static, lifeless object that is simply and immediately there, like the Thing of perception.[6] It will eventually give rise to the fluid hymn or sacred song. Statue and hymn are the two poles of abstract art. Their opposition foreshadows Nietzsche's "contrast between Apollonian and Dionysian art" in the *Birth of Tragedy* (Hyppolite, 551). The statue captures spirit as pure object, the hymn spirit as pure subject or self-consciousness (music has no outward shape). Each is abstract in a sense different from the one I mentioned above: each is one-sided and abstracts from the spiritual whole. In the dialectic of abstract art, the two poles move toward one another. Their movement is the act of worship or the *cult* [*Kultus*], in which the artist and the work of art are one [705].

The Greek statue transcends Egyptian craft. The god's beautiful shape is not an inhuman crystal that shuns the roundedness and "incommensurability" of living things. Nor are the shapes of plant and animal present in an artificial synthesis. Art in its higher form is "the pure Concept," the *genuine* unity of opposites, which appears in the god's human shape. This shape is the result of a double metamorphosis in which thought and nature, understanding and life, interpenetrate. The straight lines and flat surfaces of the pyramid evolve into the beautifully rounded features of the god. As they do so, what was previously only a plant or animal form has infused into it the intelligence that the Egyptian craftsman intended (but failed to achieve) with his mathematical shapes [706].

Hegel recalls the black stone, in which the Egyptian craftsman fashioned human and animal forms. This stone also undergoes a metamorphosis. It becomes white marble, as the night of self-consciousness is brought out into "the light of consciousness" [707].[7] In its Egyptian phase, spirit is *inside* this black animality, struggling to come out from under its cover. It is the "indwelling god," which emerges in the transition from Egyptian to Greek art. Animals are preserved as *symbols* of the god: the eagle of Zeus, and the owl of Athena. The emergence of bright beings from previously dark stone leads Hegel to portray the Olympians as having evolved from a dark, primordial past—an elemental *nature,* over which they triumphed, as over their dark former selves. This former life of chaos and violence is "the unethical realm of the Titans" [707]. Unlike these Titans (the primordial forces of Heaven, Earth, Ocean, Sun, and volcanic Fire), the gods are individuals. They have personalities and are beautiful. They are not the spawn of nature but "lucid ethical spirits of self-conscious nations or tribes [Dorians, Ionians, etc.]."

The Greek statue is spirit at rest. As a finished beautiful work of art, the statue escapes from nature's indiscriminate production of one individual after another. But it also breaks free of ethicality as a mere manifold of different duties and individuals [708]. The statue gathers this ethical manyness and represents it as a beautifully shaped, sacred One. In the statue of Athena, which stands in the Parthenon for all to see, the Athenians contemplate themselves as constituting one beautiful *polis.*

But the statue is logically one-sided. It captures only the serene moment of the artist. The other, equally necessary moment is the artist's experience of himself as active and restless, as a spiritual wrestler in the grip of his *pathos.* This is the pure form of self-consciousness. While the artist is making the statue, he is in motion and personally involved. When he finishes, he is at rest and uninvolved. He has given the statue individuality, but not *his* individuality [708]. If the work is to be truly inspired or ensouled [*beseelte*], it must contain the artist's creative breath, animation, and feeling. It must be a whole that *contains* its coming-to-be or genesis [708]. The truly inspired work will gather up into itself both artist and spectator, whose individualities will not be forgotten but expressed and enjoyed.

The artist looks at his product and "learns through experience" [*erfährt*] that he failed to produce "a being like himself" [709]. Self-consciousness is absent. Other people who see his work take joy in it, and admire his artistry. He too can step back and admire. But there is *too* much joy at work here—nothing but joy. The statue, with its unfeeling marble and untroubled expression, does not reflect the artist's "painful labor" of shaping himself into an artist, and the "strain and effort" of production. The image of the god, in failing to be sufficiently human, also fails to express *spirit.* This is the first sign that if God is to appear, he must, in creating, also be a God who suffers.

The god must experience "another mode of coming forth" [710]. The marble god had beautiful shape but not the expression of living self-consciousness (the fluidity of the Concept). Now, through the religious artist, the god breaks through the marble and becomes flesh and blood. He sings. This musical language is the "higher element" of artistry because the artist's individuality and effort to be one with the divine are preserved in the work. The stream of sacred song, the hymn, is the expression of the feeling and *pathos,* with which the individual acknowledges the god. Sculpture can depict suffering figures, but it cannot express suffering itself. Only music and poetry can do that. The hymn to the god is inspired *in itself* (it literally has breath in it). Singer and listener are not admiring onlookers but active participants. In culture, language was "the being-there or existence of the pure self qua self" [508]. Hegel now says the same thing in terms suited to artistic inspiration: language is "the soul existing as soul" [710]. Sacred song is the inner that is also outer, fluid self-consciousness that is *there.* In the hymn, individual and community—and artist and artwork—are one.[8]

The hymn was necessary because the statue was too objective or static: it captured beautiful form but not active self-consciousness, not the artist himself. Sacred song is equally abstract or one-sided. It is too subjective or self-involved, too steeped in the singer's feeling. Also, as a temporal art, song is only "a vanishing existence." [713]. The cult or act of worship is spirit's attempt to overcome this one-sidedness, to unify rest and motion, object and subject. It is the *movement* of the two extremes toward each other [714]. In this dialectical movement, the aloof god in static objective form and the human singer in his self-conscious, self-absorbed fluency will "mutually surrender their distinctive characters" [714]. Each will sacrifice itself to the other.[9]

This mutual surrender occurs in the actual deeds [*Handlungen*] by which the cult makes itself real: the deeds of worship. These are the sacrificial pouring of wine and the burning of slaughtered animals. In such deeds, the devotee gives up his possession and enjoyment of these goods to the god. He dies to self. But the god "dies" too: "The animal sacrificed is the *symbol* of a god; the fruits consumed [bread and wine] are the *living* Ceres and Bacchus themselves" [718].[10] These are the "ancient Eleusinian mysteries," into which even the animals are initiated [109].

The fruits of the earth, bread and wine, are the gods themselves in objective form. In cult sacrifice, the human individual, in relinquishing some of his individual possessions, becomes one with the god. And the god, who must already have sacrificed himself in principle, casts off his objective form and relinquishes it to man, who joyfully partakes of the god by eating bread and drinking wine. In this way, cult worship makes a concrete whole out of what was previously abstract or one-sided. Hegel emphasizes that this mutual self-sacrifice is but a pale reflection of what Christianity will offer. In the cult, man does not acknowledge the depth of his evil [715]. His impurity is superficial, and what he sacrifices is minimal compared to what he keeps for himself. Nor does a god himself die, but only his outer form: "The mystery of bread and wine is not yet the mystery of flesh and blood" [724].

The cult's deeds of sacrifice are still at the level of mere subjective devotion [726]. There is still something secretive and unfulfilled about them, something that has not yet come out into the open. This defect is overcome when the cult rises to the level of a religious *festival* [719]. The subjective enjoyment (in eating and drinking) that resulted from worship in its earlier stage is not something that abides. It is not enough like a statue. Artistic subjectivity must therefore take a more lasting, as well as public, form. It does so in the construction of temples that are for *mortals* as well as for gods, and in the accumulation of riches, which are both a tribute to the god and also for the city itself in time of need (for example, the gold on the statue of Athena in the Parthenon). In the religious festival, the city celebrates itself as divinely founded, protected, and rewarded for its tribute—as "belonging to the god." Individuals here do not make sacrifices in the hope of being purified for a future happy state, as they did in the cult, but see and enjoy the god's largesse in the Here-and-Now.

b) The Living Work of Art [Bacchants and Athletes] [720–26]

The result of cult worship was *satisfied* self-consciousness [721]. The spirit of the god entered the spirit of man, who enjoys the god in the form of bread and wine. At first, this human-divine intimacy is steeped in natural immediacy, in nature itself as the Earth-Spirit.[11] The union is *too* intimate. Enjoyment of the divine, here, is the complete immersion of the self-conscious individual in Ceres (the goddess of grain) and Dionysus (the god of wine). The individual has become "enthused." That is, he is in the god [*theos*], and the god is in him. The spirit of Ceres (or Demeter) is that of a silent maternal nurturing and yearning [723]. The spirit of Dionysus is the further development of this yearning. Eating bread is a quietly fulfilling way to be one with one's god. But drinking wine arouses and excites. It is the more explicit union with the god through intoxication, wandering, and wild gestures and utterances. The "frenzied females" or followers of Bacchus embody nature, not as a quiet Earth Mother but as a masculine *force* [721]. They are "the untamed frenzy [*Taumel*] of nature in self-conscious form" [723].[12]

Clearly, the cult, by which spirit as artist sought to overcome the opposition between statue and song, has produced a fluid whole that is unstable and unconscious, that is, drunk. We must bear in mind that it is not just the bacchants that are giddy and drunk. It is also Bacchus himself, the god who has been poured into them. This god is spirit as artist, spirit that is incarnate in its followers. As Hegel now puts it: "This undisciplined giddiness of the god must bring itself to rest as an *object*" [725]. Man must somehow drink in the god while incorporating the sobriety of statues.

The Greek art-spirit does this in the youthful, beautifully formed and forceful *athlete.* In the athlete, the natural force of Dionysus rises to the level of formed struggle. In the festival at which athletic competitions take place (the cult that has come out into the open), man celebrates and honors himself as a *living work of art:* "Man thus puts himself in the place of the statue as the shape that has been raised and fashioned for perfectly free *motion,* just as the statue is perfectly free *rest*" [725]. The winner in athletic competitions is honored and decorated as if he were a god. Like the statue, he stands for all that is beautiful and godlike in his people or tribe. Unlike the statue, he is actually one of them.

But the two extremes of the living work of art, bacchants and athletes, fail to bring about religion's goal: the overcoming of the split between consciousness and self-consciousness [726]. Each side contains both these moments but does not allow them to interpenetrate. Bacchic enthusiasm (the extreme of musicality or the hymn) is too absorbed in the night of self-consciousness, and the athlete is too corporeal—too much a naked object in the daylight of consciousness. Because of his corporeality, the athlete, although he is the "glory of his particular people," fails to capture his people's distinctive character, customs and spirit. But the more serious problem is that bacchant and athlete lack *language,* the "perfect element in which inwardness is just as external as externality is inward."

Spirit as religious artist was a sculptor, a singer, a worshipper, a bacchant, and an athlete. Now the statue of the god *really* comes to life, and music expresses the artist's *pathos* in an articulate and thoroughly concrete *Vorstellung* or representation. This happens in the *spiritual work of art.* At this highest level of its Greek phase, spirit expresses its inwardness in the language of epic poetry, tragedy, and comedy.

c) The Spiritual Work of Art [Epic, Tragedy, Comedy] [727–46]

The ascent to the spiritual work of art corresponds to the Greeks' heightened awareness of themselves as a unified people. This awareness is first present in the *epic* and the songs of Homer. In the sheer magnificence of his gods, his heroes, and his stories, Homer reminded the Greeks that, in spite of their differences, they were all related.[13]

The ascent to language and national unity is the dialectical result of spirit's experience of itself as an athlete or "beautiful fighter" [726].[14] The athlete was spirit as "complete corporeality." His body and motions swallowed up and obscured what they were intended to express, namely, the specific ethical character of his tribe. But this defeat is also a victory. By pouring itself into the athlete or living work of art, spirit purged itself of its nature-like differentiation into ethical types. Many different beautiful tribes are now ready to become one beautiful *nation:* Hellas. The nation "is, therefore, no longer conscious in this spirit of its particularity but rather of having laid this aside, and is conscious of the universality of its human *Dasein* or being-there" [726].

The Greek language is the medium in which the Greeks experience themselves as a united people or *Volk,* a people that consciously embodies the ideal of "universal humanity" [727]. Before Homer, the Greeks already spoke Greek. But it was Homer's poetry that made Greek a *work of art,* to be admired by all. Language is the *dwelling* [*Behausung*] of spirit, the "temple" where spirit is most at home. Since this dwelling is the home of human beings who honor themselves as divine, language is also the medium that gathers all the beautiful Greek cities into a single pantheon or collection of gods, a "collective heaven" [*Gesammthimmel*]. In the gathering of their individual city-gods on Olympus—the home of Zeus, Athena, Apollo, Artemis, etc.—the Greeks see the perfect image of *their* divine collectedness into *Hellas.*[15]

I. THE EPIC

Language expresses thought or universality. It is thought that is *there.* The epic, "the earliest language" in which Greek spirit expresses itself as divine, embodies thought or universality in a specific form: that of *Vorstellen* or picture-thinking. This picture-thinking is "the synthetic linking-together of self-conscious and external *Dasein* or being-there." The epic is a story that connects heroic individuals who are imagined as having really existed and acted. It is universal because it contains the whole world: gods, men, nature and the underworld. In its enthralling rhythmic narrative, the epic makes a fluid, articulate whole out of what was, in the preceding dialectic, inhumanly static (the statue) or simply drunk (the bacchant) or mutely corporeal (the athlete).

The universal world of the epic comes to be through the action of the singer or bard [*der Sänger*]. Homer, for Hegel, does not *write* the *Iliad* and *Odyssey* but rather *sings* them to a captive audience.[16] "Homer" is the spirit that is present in the *rhapsōidos* or rhapsode who performs the Homeric songs.[17] The singer's *pathos* is not "the stupefying power of nature" (the Earth-Spirit of cult worship) but Mnemosyne, "recollection" or "inwardizing" [*Erinnerung*]. In his epic songs, Homer imaginatively "remembers" a bygone age [729]. In the *Iliad,* he recalls events of the Trojan War that center around the wrath of Achilles. Homer's Muse, not Homer himself, is the source of the song. She is the divine spirit that enters Homer, who is merely "the organ or instrument that vanishes in its content."

The epic is a *syllogism* [729]. Its logical extremes are universality and singularity. Universality appears in the world of the gods, who, as ideal essences, abide and reign supreme. Singularity is present in the inspired singer, Homer, who is neither hero nor god. The middle term, individuality, combines universality and singularity. Concretely, this is "the nation in its heroes." It includes great Achaeans like Achilles, and great Trojans like Hector. These exalted human individuals partake of both the universality of the gods and the singularity of the singer.[18] They are god-like men.

The epic emerges dialectically from the primitive religion of cult worship. The human-divine relation that was only implicit in the cult is, in the epic, *presented* to consciousness in the form of stories about gods and men [730]. As we saw in Hegel's discussion of ethicality, the contradictions inherent in the Greek world came to light through action, *Handlung.* Creon acted when he championed the city by forbidding the burial of Polyneices; and Antigone acted when she championed the family by disobeying Creon's edict. Here, in the epic, the action is that of the *singer* or bard himself. Homer is the "self-conscious essence" whose act is that of singing a world into being. This world consists of the human-divine relations we see in the *Iliad.* The *content* depicted is the Trojan War, in which mortal heroes and deathless gods participate. Within the story, Achilles is the central figure. But the story itself, or rather the song, emanates from Homer, who is the self-consciousness of the Hellenic *Volk.* Homer's song, which exists in the live performances of Greek rhapsodes, reveals the dormant tensions in the ethical world. It "disturbs the rest of the [ethical] substance and excites the essence so that its simplicity [*Einfachheit*] is divided and opened up into the manifold world of natural and ethical forces" [730].

To illustrate this arousal of ethical conflict by the poet-singer, Hegel ingeniously enlists Homer himself. In Book 11 of the *Odyssey,* the cunning Odysseus continues to sing his songs of adventure to the enraptured Phaiakians, who will eventually bring the hero home. In his tale of a descent into the Underworld, Odysseus digs a trench, fills it with the blood of a slaughtered animal, and lets the shades of the underworld drink the blood in order to speak. He wakes the dead. So too, the singer of epic songs, who pours his life-blood into his performance, disturbs the self-satisfied simplicity of cult worship and awakens "the manifold world of natural and ethical powers" [730]. Like Odysseus, he *wakes the dead.* He brings forgotten heroes and events to new life. This life is not that of satisfied worship [721] but of heroic striving and conflict.[19]

Hegel now reveals the inconsistency of the epic in its portrayal of gods and men. This inconsistency is the direct result of the attempt to connect the divine and the human, the universal and the individual, by means of picture-thinking. In the case of the *Iliad,* there is a "business" [*Geschäft*] that has to be taken care of: fighting the war at Troy. Two different agents are involved in this fight: men and gods. The former represent the side of self-conscious individuality (the Greeks assembled at Troy): the latter, the side of "substantial powers" (the gods who help the Greeks).

As often happens in Homer's poems, a hero will accomplish some great feat. But from the other side of the same action, it is not the hero but the god who acts. Homer's epic *mingles* the agency of men and the agency of gods in one and the same act. The epic does not explain what the god, as opposed to the hero, contributes to the action. It simply presents the action as *completely* human (heroic) or *completely* divine (miraculous). Heroes appear as divinized men, and the gods appear as humanized deities. On the one hand, the "universal powers" are personified as man-like gods. They are presented naturalistically, as characters that act freely (and contingently). On the other hand, they are no more than the power and strength that belong to the heroic individuals themselves. And so, "both gods and men have done one and the same thing." Since from one side of epic presentation heroes do all the work, the seriousness the gods show toward action is "a ridiculous superfluity." And since from the other side the gods do all the work, the serious effort of heroes is equally useless [730]. Gods have power over men. But men also have a god-like power over the gods. They are the "mighty self" that appeases the gods with gifts, offends them with unholy deeds, and in general gives the gods an occasion to be active and real.[20] At the same time, the gods also remain aloof as the substantial universals—the abiding ethical ideals that mortals honor.

The epic gods also exhibit an inconsistency with respect to themselves, individually and in relation to each other [731]. They are "the eternal, beautiful individuals," who are free from care and death. But they are also particular gods who have human-like interactions and desires. They are unchanging ethical ideals that behave as if they had natural self-interest. In their quarrels with one another, the gods, who are supposed to be serene and god-like, exhibit "a comical forgetfulness of their eternal nature" [731].[21]

When a god fights a god in the *Iliad,* one invincible being goes up against another. Usually, this is only the god's desire to show off, and the mock-serious effort to fight dissolves into play [731]. But sometimes the god has a serious purpose. Zeus, for example, seriously intends to give honor to Achilles, and he must deal with other gods who get in his way. In agreeing to Thetis' request to honor her son (Achilles), Zeus knows that he will not be able to prevent the death of Achilles' best friend, Patroclus (which draws Achilles back into battle), or the death of his own mortal son, Sarpedon, whom Patroclus kills. These things happen because they must. Zeus, here, is confronted by "the pure power of the negative." Like the mortals who honor him, he must bow to the higher, impersonal power of Fate or destiny, which "hovers over this whole world of picture-thinking." Fate has no purposes. It is only "the conceptless void of Necessity—a mere happening." In the face of this Necessity, the gods lose, in part, the serenity that makes them gods. They become sorrowful, like Zeus when his mortal son is about to die [731].[22]

For the gods and men of Homer's stories, and for Homer himself and his listeners, the force that hovers over everything is a conceptless void, Fate. But *for us,* it is "the *unity* of the Concept" [732]. Negativity unifies. Homer's *Iliad* portrays a hero who feels and gives voice to this unity that brings everything together in one encompassing truth. This hero is Achilles, who is painfully aware of Fate as *his* Fate. He is the self-conscious hero who "in his strength and beauty feels his life is broken and sorrowfully awaits an early death." Achilles and his wrath provide the true *middle term* of the epic syllogism, the point around which the whole story of gods and heroes turns [732].[23] As the middle term, he is a unity of opposites or extremes, the tension between godlike glory and mortal life.

Achilles leaves the fighting after being dishonored by Agamemnon. He is a vibrant individuality that has been "banished to its extreme" of non-actuality or inaction. Achilles thus embodies the *problem* that compels the epic to become tragic drama. He embodies the disunity of the extremes of a necessity bereft of selfhood (Fate) and selfhood that has removed itself from all action (the singer).[24] Both of these moments are banished from the action of the poem itself. They hover, but are not actually there in the presentation or content of the story. As Hegel now says, "both extremes must draw nearer to the content." They must enter the actual story that connects gods and men. Necessity must no longer skulk in the background: its workings must be dramatized and embodied. And the singer, whose action disrupted the simple substance of ethicality, must get involved. He must become a tragic *actor.*

II. TRAGEDY

Tragedy is "higher" than the epic [733]. Its language gathers, unifies, and renders more intelligible what the epic left scattered and gloriously spilled out. In other words, tragedy is a more explicit appearance of the *Concept,* the logical unity that connects extreme terms through a middle term to yield the dialectical syllogism. The extremes are tragic necessity (or Fate) and individual selfhood. In tragedy, language is no longer narrative, and the story is no longer simply imagined in the listener's mind. Tragedy presents the story and characters directly. Heroes now appear on stage and speak, and listeners become spectators. Heroes are "*self-conscious* human beings who *know* their rights and purposes, the power and the will of their specific nature and know how to *assert* them."

Just as the epic is the live singing of a story, tragedy is not the written work but the live play that can be understood and enjoyed even by an illiterate audience. The artist here is the *actor,* into whom the playwright has poured his spirit [733]. The actor is the bard who has come out of hiding in order to appear as a character. He impersonates a human being who knows how to give eloquent expression to the *pathos* that masters and defines him. Tragic actors are live human beings who impersonate heroic figures of a glorious past. The actor is essential to the mask he wears in a performance. He is not like the sculptor who vanishes in his works, but the *live articulate presence* within the work of art. He is the means by which spirit attempts to bring its self-consciousness (and tension) into the daylight of consciousness.

Tragedy is a live motion that takes place in the medium of language spoken by live human beings. In the epic, the Concept, the source and unifier of logical movement, lurked in the background of events. Things seemed merely to happen. But tragedies, as I noted above, more explicitly manifest the Concept. They are more overtly dialectical, and present a unified action that centers on a single individual—the tragic hero.

Tragedy takes place in the same world as the epic: the bygone age of gods and heroes. The general outlook of the epic is preserved in the Chorus of elders, whose speech embodies the picture-thinking of the Homeric world [734]. This speech represents the commonly held belief in man-like deities who occasionally interact with men. The "wisdom" of the Chorus appears in the form of prayers and moral pronouncements. It reflects the thought of the people who are watching the play [735].

The main feature of the Chorus is that it is powerless—a disunited group of elders at the mercy of their king or government. They constitute a human collection "bereft of self" [734]. The Chorus' sentiments, prayers, allegiances, and reactions change depending on the situation that confronts it. In their picture-thinking piety, the elders pray first to this god, then to that one. When they do see some overall scheme at work, some divine plan that is (for us) the work of the Concept (the negative force that unifies), they experience this as an "alien Fate." Their response is a mixture of *fear* and *pity*.[25] The fear is of higher powers, of their own internal strife or disagreement, and of all-powerful Necessity. Fear begets an ignoble desire for "ease and comfort," and an equally ignoble desire to appease angry gods. Pity enters when the Chorus expresses compassion for those who suffer. But this pity is merely sentimental. It consists in the elders' feeling sorry for those who, like themselves, suffer under the blow of mindless Necessity. They do not see the suffering as the necessary result of a character's deed and *pathos.* Nor do they grasp Necessity as having its origin in "the absolute being," that is, a god [734].

The situation is very different for the tragic hero. In him (or her), spirit appears in "the simple splitting [*Entzweiung*] of the Concept" [735]. From the standpoint of social substance or ethical life, spirit appears as the split between the two powers of family and political activity. This split was evident in Hegel's earlier account of ethicality in the chapter on spirit. Tragedy ensues when these powers are pitted against each other, as they are in the confrontation between Antigone and Creon. Antigone and Creon are tragic heroes who "put their consciousness into one of these powers," thus making these powers truly active. As we know, the basis of ethical action is character, which is determined by the natural difference of male and female. Antigone defends the female right of the family, Creon the male right of the government.

What is new in the account of this tragic collision of rights is that tragedy is now regarded as a play performed before an audience at a *religious* festival. It is spirit as community beholding itself. Tragedies now embody spirit's self-consciousness and self-presentation. That is why tragedy, as a manifestation of Greek religion, is "purer" and "simpler" than ethicality that is simply lived [736]. In tragedy, Greek spirit is aware of its self-contradictory essence.

The content of tragedy is the split within ethical substance between family and state power [736]. This split reduces the array of gods presented in the epic to an opposition between two gods. In the *Oresteia,* these are the Furies and Apollo, who preside, respectively, over family and government. In the upcoming dialectic, these divine powers will be resolved into the single power of Zeus, who in turn eventually dissolves into the unconscious force of Necessity or Fate. In the dialectic of tragedy, the gods gradually *disappear.* In comedy, they will vanish into human self-consciousness.

As we know from Hegel's earlier account of ethicality, ethical substance divides itself into knowing and not knowing [737]. Antigone and Creon each knew or acknowledged only one side of the law and championed it to the exclusion of the other side. Each acted ignorantly, since action on the basis of character is finite or one-sided. Here Hegel brings in the Oracle or priestess of Apollo, the god of light and the son of Zeus. This "god that knows" [740] seems to be the source of absolute truth. But the Oracle, as we know, is deceptive. It told Oedipus, for example, that he would kill his father and marry his mother, but did not tell him who his real parents were. The god of light deceives mortals by bringing one truth to light and leaving another in the dark. Just as he deceived Oedipus, he also deceived Orestes when he told the hero that it was right to avenge his father Agamemnon by killing his mother Clytemnaestra. Apollo, here, is no different from the three witches who ensnare Macbeth by telling him his future [737].

Given the slipperiness of divine prophecy and the partial nature of human knowing, it makes sense to *mistrust* supernatural voices and visions. The skeptical Hamlet, for this reason, is superior to the gullible Macbeth [737]. He does not trust the apparition of his dead father but "tarries with revenge." He knows that a "revelatory spirit" might just as well be the *devil.* Hegel's shift into Shakespeare territory is no accident. Hamlet's mistrust of the ghost foreshadows what will now take place in the dialectic of Greek tragedy. The tragic hero will discover, through suffering, that oracles are not to be trusted, and that it is not the gods and Fate that matter after all but rather his own self-certainty as a human individual.

All tragic heroes eventually discover that their knowledge is partial, or rather, that there is an opposition between self-certainty and "objective essence" or truth [738]. To illustrate this tension, Hegel focuses on the *Oresteia* of Aeschylus, which, unlike the *Antigone,* explicitly dramatizes the opposition between two divine powers. The two powers at work here are the bright power of Knowing (represented by Apollo) and the dark power of Not Knowing (represented by the Furies). In obedience to Apollo, Orestes acts: he kills his mother, who slew his father. In so doing, he awakens the Furies, who pursue him. Orestes unwittingly transforms his self-certain knowledge of what is right into the divine Power that defends the opposite right: the female right that Orestes failed to acknowledge. He suffers *inversion:* his pious deed becomes a crime and brings to life an avenging adversary. Both powers, Apollo and the Furies, have equal right and enjoy equal honor from Zeus [738]. Zeus, in other words, is their necessary relation in the form of a picture-thought [739].

The dilemma of the tragic hero limits the divine cast of characters to three: Apollo, Furies, and Zeus [739]. Tragic action, which is the work of the Concept, reveals opposition—a Two. Apollo and the Furies embody the ethical tension or Two-ness within Orestes' action. Zeus represents the resolution of this tension in the ethical whole. The hero's tragic deed replaces the "spread" of gods we see in the epic with a divine Two that is under the control of a governing divine One.

Hegel's account of tragedy interweaves a distinction on the side of ethical *substance* (family and state) with a distinction on the side of the acting ethical *subject* (knowing and not knowing). Antigone, for example, acted in accordance with the right she knew and acknowledged, the right of family. Creon acted in accordance with the right he knew, that of the state. Each was determined by character (male or female). Each took a stand with respect to one side of ethical substance. Nevertheless, each consciousness "contained" the powers of Knowing and Not Knowing. Each character knew one aspect of ethical substance and failed to know the other.

Hegel's emphasis, here, is on the deceptiveness of supernatural voices. The things that gullible mortals take for absolute truth are really "warning signs of deception, of an absence of self-possession, of the singularity and contingency of the knowing" [740]. The real truth is contained in the *whole* of ethical substance—which whole the acting consciousness or hero cannot subjectively contain. To act from character is to be unable to think the whole. Antigone and Creon are both right, and both wrong (because one-sided). The result of their opposition is their downfall. The downfall demonstrates the fundamental unity of both sides. It reveals that the sides Antigone and Creon took are not absolutes, as they thought, but only vanishing moments in the ethical whole.

As the tragic figures dissolve and perish, order is restored. This restoration is evident at the end of the *Oresteia,* where Orestes is absolved from crime, and the Furies are incorporated into the ethical and political life of Athens. Ethical tension resolves into ethical calm. But this calm is really a death [740]. The tension is not preserved but rather drowned in forgetfulness: either in the Lethe of the "upper world" or in that of the underworld. The tragic figure that survives (Orestes) is absolved from his crime and experiences "peace of mind." But this, too, is a kind of death, or rather oblivion. In this oblivion of the tragic figures, the ethical substance itself *goes to sleep.* It returns to the unquestioning condition of people who do what they are supposed to do as family members and citizens.[26] The main result of this pseudo-resolution is, in the case of Orestes, that Apollo and the Furies, who were summoned into action and being by the hero's deed, also go to sleep or become oblivious.[27] Having acted against each other, they return to "the simple Zeus," who is their origin, substantial whole, and *Fate* [740].

Hegel now dramatically asserts, "This Fate completes the depopulation of Heaven" [741]. Tragic tension or opposition, as we know, reduces the Homeric gods to two: Apollo and the Furies. But these two divinities, as picture-thoughts or human-like individuals, at the end of the *Oresteia* retreat into their non-active, substantial whole. They vanish as divine agents. Each still stands for one aspect of ethical substance, but neither *does* anything. Since their action has vanished, so does their individuality. This vanishing begins the disappearance of picture-thinking in Greek religion, and the onset of rationality. Apollo, the Furies, and even Zeus cease to be Homeric figures and become divine aspects or thoughts—Ideas. (This reduction is especially evident in the plays of Euripides.) Tragedy, in other words, moves the Greek gods closer to the abstractness of Roman religion, where the gods are only symbols. In being more overtly conceptual than the epic, tragedy is also more philosophical. Hegel now makes this point explicitly. The reduction of the gods from many to three, and then from three to One, is just what the Greek philosophers demanded, namely, a god that was *not* a man-like individual but a single-formed, non-deceptive Essence. Hegel is no doubt thinking of the critique of the Homeric gods found in Plato's *Republic,* where Socrates argues that the god "would least of all have many shapes" (2.381B6).

Heaven has been depopulated, since the divine essence is no longer "mingled" with individuality [741]. Homer has been banished from the tragic city. Zeus is still present, but only as "the simple Zeus" or all-purpose Divinity, the supreme indivisible Power that permeates ethical substance. Zeus, who resolves all tension, is present in each side of the ethical content or *substance* (family and state). He is also present in each side of the ethical form or *subject* (the Apollo-realm of clear knowing and the Furies-realm of oaths and things concealed). This is not only how tragedy appears for us. It is also the perspective of the characters in the play and of the audience. In the *Oresteia,* we all see Apollo and the Furies as passing moments of the concrete whole, of the dramatic movement or plot. At the end of the drama, Apollo and the Furies leave, and we are left with the city by itself. The *abiding* theological consciousness of all the human characters is the vague sense that some universal Zeus or Fate hovers over all of nature and all of human life. As the Chorus says, toward the beginning of the *Agamemnon:* "Zeus, whatever he may be, if this name pleases him in invocation, thus I call upon him" [160].

Zeus, the simple unity to which all the gods have been reduced, is indistinguishable from unconscious Necessity or Fate [742]. Like Apollo and the Furies, he stands for something (the inescapable force in human events) but does nothing. The only real selfhood in tragedy is that of the human characters. They alone act. They do not recognize any selfhood in the events they have either witnessed or participated in. They see no mindful, guiding force—no providence. Necessity is only something to be feared.

This unconscious Necessity finds its self-conscious aspect in the individuals who are watching the play and are *aware* of Necessity. Heroes, gods, the clash of ethical rights—all these vanish, as we have seen, in the divine substance of Fate or Necessity. But we spectators are, in fact, the supreme "substance" in which all these appear and then vanish: the "spiritual unity into which everything returns" [742]. Divine substance (the "simple Zeus") is only an aspect of our own awareness: a "character" in the play.

Hegel seems to be inviting us to leave the stage for a moment and imagine the entire theater that contains both the play and the audience. This living theater—where mortals bring on gods, heroes and their Fate for their own benefit and entertainment—is the power of self-consciousness or self-beholding. It is the greater whole in which tragedies are produced—the subjectivity that contains and posits various "shapes," and makes them appear and disappear. The audience knows, moreover, that the play is *for them.* This fact is dramatized at the end of the tragedy when the Chorus draws a human moral for all to hear and heed. At the end of the *Antigone,* for example, the Chorus uses Creon to illustrate what happens to proud individuals who dare to be gods. They make us aware of our human perspective on a movement that presumably transcended our perspective and was the work of the divine. Tragedies are *about* gods, but they are *for* man, who uses the gods to tell stories and to entertain an audience at a religious festival.

Tragedy involves two perspectives: that of the Chorus, which speaks but does not act, and that of the hero, who acts as well as speaks. We are like the Chorus, since we merely watch a play about beings higher than ourselves. Insofar as we share the viewpoint of the Chorus, we experience fear and pity: fear before the alien power that threatens us all (our mortality), and pity or sympathy [*Mitleid*] for individuals who, like us, fall under the crushing blow of Necessity. The Chorus holds this view because it still distinguishes between self-conscious individuality and the Fate that seems to hang over the heads of men [742]. Chorus and audience do not yet see that this Fate *is* the negative force of self-consciousness.[28] They fail to see themselves in Necessity. If they *could* see selfhood in Necessity, they would see that Fate is really history as the being-there and necessary unfolding of self-consciousness. They would have absolute knowing.

But there is also the perspective of the actor who plays the part of the tragic hero. He knows that no heroic action has taken place at all, that he only pretended to be Oedipus or Orestes. He knows that to be an actor—in Greek, a *hypokritēs*—is to be a *hypocrite.* Furthermore, the audience knows that he knows. The truth of tragic performance is that the belief in higher powers is a pretense. The human beings behind the masks are the ones who do everything—evidence that human self-consciousness rather than divine substance is the ultimate source of events. In this dialectical moment, in which actors and audience are aware that tragedy, as Aristotle asserts in the *Poetics,* is an imitation, the hero who appears on stage "splits up into his mask and the actor, into the person in the play and the actual self" [743].

Everybody knows that plays are only plays. But the actual self-consciousness of the actor undercuts the whole tragic view of human life. The supremacy of the gods, the awesome power of impending Fate, the dignity of heroes and their exalted *pathos*—all these are a noble pretense. Human self-consciousness, embodied in the actor behind the mask, is the underlying truth of what the mask signifies.

Now that the tragic mask has begun to slip and to reveal the man behind it, this hypocrisy itself must be allowed to come forth.[29] It must be exposed and presented in a new kind of drama. This new drama, which joyfully exposes the noble pretensions of gods and men alike, is *comedy.* In comedy, the tragic actor throws away his mask and steps forth as himself. Human self-consciousness presents itself "as knowing itself to be the Fate both of the gods of the Chorus and of the absolute powers themselves" [743]. There is now no longer a distinction between "high" characters and "low," between privileged nobility and disenfranchised commoners. All are low. The tragic hero gets down off his high horse and joins the Chorus, who now represents "universal consciousness." In comedy, we know that the play is not only for us but also about us. We are allowed to be on stage as ordinary, flawed human beings.

III. COMEDY

Hegel now takes us from the noble world of Aeschylus and Sophocles to the raucous realm of Aristophanes.[30] The entire movement of the Greek art-religion consists in the gradual unification of the human and the divine. The human-divine unity became more intimate, and intelligent, with the spiritual work of art: the art of poetic *language.* In the epic, the gods related to man as characters in a story: they were picture-thoughts or embodied essences. In tragedy, they lost their individuality and became abstract Ideas. Now, in the most famous comedy by Aristophanes, they become a chorus of female *clouds:* free-floating thoughts, "which can be filled with any content you like" [746].

The result of the dialectic of tragedy was that man or self-consciousness became the Fate of the gods.[31] This is the principal aspect of Greek comedy [744]. The gods are now only beings for imaginative play. Man can do with them whatever he pleases and say whatever he wants: there is no such thing as blasphemy. The gods are vanishing properties, mere roles that the substantial actor takes on. When a god appears on stage, like Dionysus in

Aristophanes' *Frogs*, and tries to be serious, the actor playing the god lets his own ordinary humanity show through the mask and the performance.[32] He displays the irony of a "universal essence" trying to be something on its own. He exposes divinity as a pretense. The actor "plays with the mask." That is, sometimes he acts in character, sometimes not. In Aristophanes' plays, an actor will occasionally even address the audience as his fellow Athenians. He thus shows that the character he is playing is "not distinct from the authentic self, the actor, or from the spectator" [744].

The epic, as we saw, was a syllogism, in which the middle term, represented by the individual heroes, mediated between the two extremes of universal gods and the singular non-essential singer [729]. Comedy inverts this syllogism (Hyppolite, 554). Now the singularity of the comic actor (the higher version of the singer) is essential. Singular self-consciousness has become the middle term, in which the universal gods and individual heroes vanish. Gods and heroes alike are reduced to ordinary humanity.

Comedy is funny. But it also has "its more serious and necessary meaning" [745]. This serious meaning has to do with the two ways in which an individual relates to the "divine substance." One way has to do with *nature* and the cult mysteries of Ceres and Bacchus. The other has to do with *ethicality:* state and family (the opposite poles in tragedy).[33] Comedy exposes what is implicit in both these serious meanings. It reveals that man is the Fate of the gods.

As we saw earlier, the result of worship is satisfied consciousness. Nature seems at first to be a force beyond us: the objective form of the god (in bread and wine). Cult worship brings us closer to god through mysteries surrounding nature. But nature is not really independent from us. We *use* nature in our ceremonies, *adorn* ourselves with garlands, and *consume* the bread and wine. All this makes us feel good. Cult worshipers are like the animals Hegel talked about in sense-certainty. Indeed, Hegel there referred explicitly to "the ancient Eleusinian Mysteries of Ceres and Bacchus" [109]. The animals "know" that nature exists to be consumed, that it is an object of desire. So too, cult worshipers, in experiencing their god in nature, do so for their own enjoyment. Their actions show that it is not they who exist for the sake of the gods, but the gods (in natural form) who exist for the sake of them. In comedy, we become aware of this ironic *inverted world.* The specific comedy Hegel intends here is Aristophanes' *Frogs,* which at one point gives an extended portrayal of the rites of Bacchus.[34]

The serious *ethical* object that comedy takes up is state and family (the two powers in tragedy). But since, with comedy, actual self-consciousness or self-certainty has come on the scene, there is also the element of "pure knowing, or the rational thinking of the universal." Comic characters are not pious creatures of custom. They think for themselves, and take pride in this. With the onset of individual thinking, state and family, the two pillars of custom, degenerate. They dissolve into the Demos or People, outrageously depicted in Aristophanes' *Knights.* Demos is vain, powerful, moody, old, deaf, and full of all sorts of desires. Above all, he goes in for enlightened, progressive ideas and thinks he is wise. Demos is a spoiled beauty that loves being courted and fought over by fawning politicians. He is also a fool, who eventually discovers that he is a fool.[35] This fits Hegel's description of Demos, "which knows itself as lord and ruler, and is also aware of being the intelligence and insight that demand respect" [745].

But the paradigm Greek comedy is Aristophanes' *Clouds* [746]. Socrates appears as a paid professor who dispenses wisdom in his Thinkery. Strepsiades goes there in order to learn how to elude justice and avoid paying the debts incurred by his son, Pheidippides. At one point, Socrates summons his divine Ladies, who appear before Strepsiades as a chorus of clouds. At the end of the play, the son gives his father a beating, using Socrates' "logic" to justify his action. The outraged father, regretting his impiety toward the traditional gods, burns down the Thinkery.

As we know, the dialectic of the spiritual work of art consists in the gradual de-individualization of the Homeric gods, the reduction of the gods to pure essences. The *Clouds* takes the final step. It shows what happens when "rational thinking," whose *Gestalt* is Socrates, lifts the tragic Chorus' ethical maxims and right opinions about duty "into the simple Ideas of the Beautiful and the Good." Like modern skepticism, ancient rationalism knows that ethical right opinions are subject to dialectical vanishing, that the "old ways" are not absolute. Comedy presents these newfangled Ideas for what they are: *clouds* that are no more substantial than the Homeric gods they have displaced [746].[36] Socrates' rational clouds are all that is left of the gods. Lacking any real substance or content, the "simple thoughts" of the Beautiful and the Good, wrenched from their ethical ground, can be given any sort of filling—just as clouds can take on any sort of shape. Young and old alike, liberated from traditional piety, can use these cloud-thoughts to serve their own self-interest—either to beat one's father or flee from debt.

Before the emergence of comedy, Fate and self-consciousness were separate. Fate was "empty repose and oblivion." Now they are united [747]. Comedy reveals actual self-consciousness, the individual self, as that in which gods and nature *vanish.* Self-consciousness, however, does not vanish but "preserves itself in this very nothingness." In comedy, man experiences his own selfhood as "the sole actuality." He enjoys himself rather then feeling at the mercy of alien powers and overarching universals. This individuality enjoying itself is the consummation of the Greek religion of art. Greek art consisted in the effort to represent the divine. Ultimately, this was spirit's effort to present itself to itself. As long as the divine was merely *represented* to consciousness, god was remote from man. This remoteness appears in the statue, in the athlete, in the epic, and in tragedy. But in comedy, separateness is finally overcome, not unconsciously, as in cult worship and bacchic enthusiasm, but consciously in the identity of the human actor and his role, and of the audience with the play itself [747].

In comedy, the audience beholds the reduction of everything to the human self. It sees that the human self is absolute, or, in the words of the sophist Protagoras, that "man is the measure of all things." As Hegel says in his *Aesthetics,* the various fools we see in Aristophanes' plays always retain their self-confidence. They exhibit "the smiling blessedness of the Olympian gods, their unimpaired equanimity, which comes home in men and can put up with anything" (2:1222). At the end of his discussion of the Greek art-religion, Hegel strikes a similar note. In comedy, the Greeks completely lose their fear of the gods and Fate. Nothing is alien to them. They are reconciled to misfortune, to suffering, to the moral decline of their city, even to their downfall in the war with Sparta. They experience a "spiritual well-being and repose [in self-certainty], such as is not to be found anywhere outside of this comedy."[37]

Greek comedy is happy consciousness. But it is also gallows humor. From the perspective of the rationalized Demos, there are no more gods to fear. In Luther's formulation, *God is dead.* And human life has no divine significance whatsoever. In the third and final stage of religion, the manifest religion of Christianity, Greek comedy will find its "counterpart" and "completion" [752]. Happy consciousness will become *unhappy* consciousness, with its infinite grief and infinite longing.

For now we see through a glass, darkly; but then face to face.
PAUL, Corinthians I

23

Christianity, the Figure of Science

CHRISTIANITY, FOR HEGEL, IS THE TRUTH OF RELIGION. IT IS "absolute religion" [759]. Religion, we recall, is the self-consciousness of spirit, man's awareness of God as *subject,* and as the divine essence of all things [672]. It makes the logical moments of spiritual unfolding into an actual whole that unfolds in time. Religion is the divine self-understanding of an historical people or *Volk.* This self-understanding is figurative rather than conceptual, depicted rather than thought.

Religion reveals the work of the triune Concept, the universal form of thought and truth. Three-ness is more explicit in the religion chapter than in previous parts of Hegel's book. The three logical moments of the Concept are *Identity, Difference* (the splitting into opposites or self-alienation), and the *Identity of Identity and Difference* (the reconciliation of opposites). In the overall scheme of the *Phenomenology,* these moments appear, respectively, as consciousness, self-consciousness, and reason, which correspond to the three stages of religion [Chapter 20].

The Concept was also at work in the three stages of consciousness: sense-certainty, perception, and understanding. Religion preserves these shapes and raises them into their absolute or divine forms. In nature-religion, the Persian religion of light worshiped God in his simple self-identity. It was divine *sense-certainty.* The Indian religion of plants and animals worshiped God in the logical moment of self-difference or self-antagonism. God was an object of *perception,* a thing with diverse properties. Finally, God was an Egyptian craftsman, who used his *understanding* to reconcile thought and nature in monumental structures.

The Concept was even more prominent in the Greek art-religion. Once again, spirit went through the three determinations of consciousness, this time at the level of self-consciousness. Abstract art was the self-conscious version of divine *sense-certainty.* The man-god unity was experienced immediately in statues and hymns. The living work of art was the *perception* of God, who appeared as a divine Thing with properties. He was present in bread and wine (Ceres and Bacchus), and in the beauty, strength, speed, and skill of the athlete. In keeping with the second moment of the Concept, God was different from himself: he took on bodily form in order to unite with man.

Finally, in the spiritual work of art, God appeared in the universality of *understanding* or thought. Here, spirit rose above Egyptian understanding by taking the self-conscious form of language. The god-man unity was portrayed in the form of stories that united the Greeks in the ideal of universal humanity. These stories were Concept-driven *movements* that went from natural unity, through conflict and "tearing," to ultimate resolution or reconciliation. The *Iliad* depicted a "play of forces" that involved both gods and men. Ultimately, Achilles is reconciled: to Agamemnon, to the father of his hated enemy (Priam), and to his Fate. In tragedy, the play of forces became an actual *play.* The forces or powers of Apollo and Furies were roused into opposition with each other but then were reconciled in Zeus, who became Fate—the force of mindless happening. Laws, in the form of rights, collided with each other but then lost consciousness in the sleepy comfort of ethical substance. Comedy *inverted* this restful kingdom of laws. Audience and actor now remove the "curtain" [165] that separates the undying gods and mortal men. Gods become their opposite, and mortals enjoy the blessed laughter of the gods. Just as the abstract understanding found its truth in self-consciousness [163], so too the Greek art-religion finds its truth in comedy, where man enjoys himself, in all his folly and degradation, as the truth and measure of all things.

The work of the Concept continues, more explicitly, in Christianity. Formal divisions are absent in this part of Hegel's chapter. But the three moments of the Concept are nevertheless present in the Trinity of Father, Son, and Holy Spirit.[1] These "persons," the product of Christian picture-thinking, preside over the three stages of Christian self-consciousness. In the first stage (Identity), God is "with himself"—a pure universal essence. He is aware of himself but not yet alienated from himself. This is God before the creation of the world. In the second stage (Difference), God is *there* as a sensuously present human individual (Jesus of Nazareth). He is the other of the divine paternal essence. Finally, in the third stage (Identity of Identity and Difference), God knows himself in this other. He is reconciled to his own otherness in the form of nature (the actual world). Each of these moments is a stage of communal self-knowledge.[2] Each is a mode in which Christian consciousness, from our scientific perspective, worships itself as a community in which God is revealed.

The three stages of consciousness will be evident in the community's relation to Christ.[3] The immediate followers of Christ know him as a sensuous This. They have divine *sense-certainty.* At the next level, they know him as a sublated or resurrected This [762]. Having gained universality through his death and rising, Christ becomes an object of religious *perception.* Finally, at the third stage, God is known as the spirit of the religious community. This knowledge corresponds to thought or *understanding.* Here, God is known as an incarnate universal.

Hegel's chapter culminates in a dialectical interpretation of the Bible, starting with the creation and ending with the death of God (in Christ). In its negative aspect, the death of God, the loss of divine *substance,* produces infinite grief. But as a determinate negation, it is the moment in which God becomes a divine *subject* or self-consciousness made actual in the community of the faithful [785]. At last, spirit knows itself as spirit. This knowing [*Wissen*] is the penultimate moment of the *Phenomenology.* It sets the stage for Hegel's transformation of religious knowing into absolute knowing.

Hegel's Heresies

Before continuing our journey through the text, it will be useful to summarize the main points of Hegel's unorthodox view of Christianity. This will help us to see how the Christian religion paves the way for absolute knowing or Science.

Hegel's heresies, as they might be called, are as follows:

1. God is not a person and consequently does not love man.
2. God becomes fully God by becoming man. Only then is God subject as well as substance. As Hegel writes in the *Encyclopaedia:* "God is God only so far as he knows himself: his self-knowing is, further, a self-consciousness in man and man's knowledge *of* God, which proceeds to man's self-knowing *in* God" (*Philosophy of Mind,* 298).
3. In order to be a knowing self-consciousness, God must be, like us, evil as well as good.
4. The Bible is picture-thinking that must not be taken literally: it is not "revelation."
5. Jesus, whoever he was historically, is a religious picture-thought that must be transcended, and a logical *moment* of God as spirit. Hegel sometimes identifies Jesus with the *world,* as God's offspring.
6. Ultimately, God is embodied, not in Christ, but in the Christian community.
7. Man is united with God, not through faith in God's act of grace but through the community's works of mutual forgiveness.
8. The absolute truth of Christianity, or rather manifest religion, is open to everyone, regardless of any specific faith. That is, manifest religion is not *a* religion but religion itself. It is humanity's public

consciousness of its union with God. All human beings must forgive each other's finitude, one-sidedness, and selfishness.[4]

9. The Incarnation and Resurrection are not past events but the picture-versions of determinate negations and logical aspects of the divine essence.
10. There is no immortality of the soul, and no resurrection of the body.
11. There is no Beyond or supersensible Kingdom of Heaven. The belief in such a Beyond is a sign that God and nature, and God and man, are still alienated from one another or unreconciled.
12. The truth of Christianity is grasped only by philosophy in the form of conceptual knowing or Science.

From Greek Levity to Roman Grief [748–53]

In the opening paragraphs of "Manifest Religion," Hegel shows how spirit moves from the Greek art-religion to the secular world of imperial Rome, and eventually to the unhappy consciousness.[5] Unhappiness, here, is not confined to the individual, as it was in the chapter on self-consciousness. It is now the condition of a whole world that yearns for the appearance of God in a new form—the unhappiness of *spirit.*

Hegel reviews religion in terms of the relation between substance and subject [748]. In the nature-religion of light, man or self-consciousness vanished in God as an "awful substance." In the Greek art-religion, spirit "has advanced from the form of substance to assume that of subject" [748]. Art-religion, Hegel says, is a gradual "incarnation of the divine essence"—a *Menschenwerdung* or "man-becoming." The humanization of the divine will be completed in the man-God, Christ.

The Greek humanization of the divine began with the statue, which had only the outward shape of man. The cult brought man and god, subject and substance, closer together. The spiritual work of art, through language, made the self even more apparent and embodied. Comedy is the inversion and truth of art-religion. It destroys every trace of the awful or terrifying substance, and drowns the divine essence in light-mindedness or levity [*Leichtsinn*].[6] This levity is contained in the proposition: "The self is the absolute essence" [748]. That is, the human self is the truth of the gods. As Hegel puts it, divine substance has "sunk down" to the level of a mere predicate of human selfhood. In the laughter of mortals, who are openly skeptical about the divine, spirit experiences itself as subject or *self-consciousness.* It has "lost its *consciousness.*" That is, spirit no longer acknowledges the divine as an object or substance. Since ethicality has dissolved, spirit sees nothing outside of actual human selves that has any meaning. The world is only a world for self-consciousness.[7]

The actual, historical world that embodies the comic proposition, "The self is absolute essence," is that of imperial Rome [749].[8] We are perplexed to hear that Rome, in its might and seriousness, is the actualization of Greek comedy. This makes sense, however, when we remember that Rome is now being considered from the standpoint of religion. Worship of the gods has become the worship of an ordinary man who sits on the throne and is treated like a god: the emperor. This secular worship is Greek comedy made into an actual religion (Harris, 2:652). A good example of this comic man-god is "the divine Augustus" (as Octavian Caesar was called). Augustus could be called comic because he was not a monster like the emperors who came after him (Tiberius, Caligula, and Nero). Moreover, he inaugurated a period of relative calm that allowed Roman citizens to enjoy being what the Roman world-spirit had made them—formal persons with legal rights. This period, which Hegel called "the boredom of the world," is the Roman version of Greek levity [750].[9] It precedes the onset of widespread grief and longing.

The comic proposition, "the self is the absolute essence," expresses the Greek ascendancy of man over God. Imperial Rome will invert this proposition to read: "the absolute essence is the self." This tragic inversion expresses the reduction of the divine to mortal humanity. It takes the form of the "hard word" that "God is dead."[10] This word or saying sums up the unhappiness of the unhappy consciousness [752]. But Roman spirit will also invert the tragic inversion of comedy. It will give rise to a new, *divine comedy,* in which the two natures of God and man, awful substance and mortal subject, will unite—not in a pretend-god who sits on the throne, but in the God who incarnates himself by creating the world.

This complex dialectic begins in the actual, secular spirit of Rome, particularly in the cynical worship of the emperor. With the emperor, who embodies Rome, divine *substance* returns as the supreme essence in which individual selves are dissolved. But this return of an awful substance is not a return to nature-religion. The reason is that the Roman world is defined just as much by self-consciousness as it is by consciousness. The emperor is a godlike substance because other self-conscious individuals have made him into one. Self-consciousness "surrenders itself consciously" to this secular god. Self-alienation will be further developed in the modern culture world. There, individuals will alienate their natural being in order to be social animals, the rich will sell their souls, and fawning nobles will inflate the royal *Moi.*

As we know, each stage of religion grows out of its corresponding milieu or social world. The Greek art-religion belonged to the ethical realm. This realm gave way to Roman "legal standing" [750]. Rome made an actual world out of the comic proposition, "the self is the absolute essence," by making the self a bearer of rights. Greek ethical life filled its members with the spirit of community—a lived universality, in which "simple individuality" was submerged [*versenkt*]. In Rome, this individuality rises up and asserts itself. Its "levity" says: "I am a person with rights!" But this refinement of the individual into a person also spells the loss, or rather evacuation, of all ethical content. The Greek nations celebrated themselves in a pantheon of richly individualized picture-gods. But the Roman pantheon contains only "abstract universality, pure thought." Rome asserts the force of universality by destroying the independent shapes of nations. It thus gives individuals a new independence by making them persons *in and for themselves.* But this personhood, which makes everyone equal before the law, is "disembodied" (or abstract) and "bereft of spirit" (since personhood cannot be the ground of human community).

The individual eventually comes to feel the emptiness of his legally exalted status, the void that has been created by the loss of substantial life. His response is to turn *within,* away from a world grown meaningless [751]. This response is that of the stoic, who asserts the absolute independence of *thought* [197]. The skeptic spells out the negativity implied by stoicism. And the unhappy consciousness represents the inverted truth of stoic indifference. The unhappy consciousness, to repeat, is no longer limited to the individual believer. It expresses the grief of the whole pre-Christian world, of *spirit* that longs for rebirth.

The unhappy consciousness knows that its life is meaningless, that it cannot be happy either in the actual world of persons or in the inner sanctum of pure thought [752]. *We* see that the unhappy consciousness is "the counterpart and the completion of the comic consciousness that is perfectly happy within itself." As a comic consciousness, man was certain of himself as the absolute. Now he suffers the tragic consequences of this self-assertiveness. The divine essence has abandoned man and has become a Beyond. In leaving the earth, God has "died," and man experiences only "the complete *alienation or estrangement of* [divine] *substance.*"[11]

The loss of Greek ethicality is man's Roman fall from the historical Eden. As the tragic lover Francesca says in Dante's *Inferno,* "No greater grief there is than to recall the happy time in present woe" (Canto 5). The unhappiness of the unhappy consciousness consists in the painful awareness of what it has lost [753]. Trust in the laws of the gods is gone, oracles stand mute, statues are but stones, and hymns empty words. The cult of bread and wine (Ceres and Bacchus) offers no spiritual food and drink, and games and festivals no more make us feel vigorously one with the divine. As for the Muses, their tales of glorious deeds of gods and men have been crushed by Roman self-certainty and no longer have the power of spirit. The works of Homer, Aeschylus, and Sophocles become, for Rome, what they are now for us: "beautiful fruit already picked from the tree, which a friendly Fate has offered us, as a girl might set the fruit before us" [753]. Drained of their once-living spirit, the beautiful artworks of Greek Eden, where man walked with God, are no longer acts of divine worship. They are now only a "veiled recollection" and belong to a world we visit only in imagination.[12]

But that mysterious girl who gave us the fruit: what of her? Hegel, in a lovely rhetorical turn, notes that she is more than the nature that made the fruits of art, more than Greek soil and trees and weather. "In the gleam of her self-conscious eye and in the gesture with which she offers [her fruits]" we see the spark of a life that transcends ethicality [753]. The girl's self-consciousness is the *inwardizing* [*Er-innerung*] of fruits that were previously experienced as only fruits of an external, finite world—fruits of consciousness. In the girl's self-conscious eye, we behold our own inwardness, which has yet to make itself into a new spiritual world. Feeling the loss of Eden and the Muses, we sigh in melancholy recollection, like Hölderlin's Hyperion. But recollection, as the German word *Erinnerung* suggests, is also an inwardizing. Our looking back points ahead to a higher version of Eden, to an actual world in which spirit *will know itself as spirit.* This new world will be "comically" recollective rather than sad. Its spirit will know that the fall from ethical Eden (eating from the Tree of Knowledge) was necessary for man's spiritual "ascent."

The Birth of Christianity [754–58]

All the conditions are now in place for the birth of spirit that knows itself as spirit [754]. This will be the appearance of the true God as a self-conscious human being. All the negations that have occurred, which are now summed up in imperial Rome, have already generated this new manifestation of the divine in principle or in its Concept. In what follows, we shall see how the negativity of the unhappy consciousness becomes a *determinate* negation.

Religion is spirit's awareness of itself as a self-conscious object. This objectivity was absent in conscience. In Greek art, spirit has come forth. The productions of art form a *circle* that embraces "the forms of the externalizations of absolute substance [or God] [754]." These forms are the statue, hymn (the "pure language" that does not get beyond the self), cult worship, athlete, and poetic language. Rome has made this Greek pantheon of divine self-expressions into universal *thought* that expresses self-certainty. The Roman pantheon houses the forms of this self-certainty: the de-humanized Person, the detached Stoic, and the restless Skeptic. It also contains the "devastating ferocity [*Wildheit*]" of passions that have been unleashed in the absence of ethical restraint and piety (see [481]). These Roman types form a "periphery of shapes that stands, expectant and urgent [or pressing], around the birthplace [*Geburtsstätte*] of spirit as it becomes self-consciousness" [754]. The unhappy consciousness "permeates them all" and "is their center." This communal "pressing" is the *birth-pang* [*Geburtswehe*] of spirit itself as it struggles to come forth as a newborn shape. This child of spirit is "the simplicity of the pure Concept, which contains those forms as its moments."

In Hegel's version of the Bethlehem story, unhappiness is not merely passive and expectant. It is the painful *act*, the dialectical-historical process, by which God becomes man. Jesus is the child of our longing, the Son of Man (as he is called in the Gospels). With the onset of infinite yearning *as an actual condition of the whole world*, desire, for the first time, has become fruitful or productive. No longer an honor-seeking drive to subdue and enslave, or a Faustian drive to destroy another's independence through sex, or a French drive to destroy the whole world for the sake of abstract principles, longing is now the dialectical creative source of an actual coming to be.

The Incarnation is the unity of spirit's two sides: substance and subject [755]. It is the process in which both alienate themselves. God as substance becomes human, and man as self-conscious subject becomes divine. These self-alienations are already present in Rome. God has "fallen" to the level of human selfhood (he is "dead"), and individuals have sacrificed themselves to the divine substance of the emperor. With the birth of Christianity, these motions become one. In externalizing himself, God as substance becomes self-conscious or united with man; and human selfhood, by externalizing itself, becomes implicitly substantial or one with God. Both motions unite to form *spirit* as the unity of subject and substance, man and God. In the *Vorstellung* of the Nativity story, spirit, Hegel notes, has an *actual* mother but only an *implicit* father [755]. The reason is that self-consciousness or man has an actual existence and being-there, whereas divine substance, prior to its incarnation, is otherworldly and abstract—a mere thought.

The true meaning of Christianity consists in the double self-alienation I described above. There was a religious-intellectual movement around the time of Christ that embodied only *one* side of this self-alienation. It was known as Gnosticism, from *gnōsis*, a Greek word for knowledge. In his *Lectures on the Philosophy of Religion*, Hegel tells us that Gnosticism arose "from the need to *cognize* God" (3:196). Here in the *Phenomenology*, he says that in Gnosticism self-consciousness grasps "only *its own* externalization" [756]. That is, Gnosticism subjectively thinks various stages of divine unfolding, but it does not ground them in anything historical and actual, or even in anything portrayed as historical. In its effort to be intellectual rather than religious in the strict sense, it spawns theory-driven mythologies that seem, in part, to foreshadow or mirror aspects of the Holy Trinity. It speaks of a

Father-like divine Being, who, in himself, is "unknowable, uncommunicative, and inconceivable," and of a Son-like Logos, which reveals itself in various ways.[13] But ultimately, Gnosticism is a subjective dreaming that "merits neither belief nor reverence; it is no more than the dark night and self-delusive raving [*Schwärmerei*] of consciousness" [756].

Gnosticism dissolves the objective moment of divine self-externalization in subjective thought. It lapses into imagination and abstract dreams. If we are to avoid this merely subjective theology, we must attend to how spirit has actually arisen in the course of history, where history is spirit's necessary (as opposed to merely factual) development [757]. This is precisely what we have done in the *Phenomenology.* We have attended to how spirit's self-knowledge has logically arisen in the realm of consciousness or concrete existence.

By contrast with Gnosticism, Christianity is an historical movement grounded in the universal belief in an actual historical event. It is not an esoteric teaching dreamed up by an intellectual few but "the *belief of the world*" [758]. Christianity believes that absolute spirit has made itself into a self-consciousness that is also an object of consciousness. It believes "that spirit is immediately present as a self-conscious being, i.e., as an *actual man,*" whom the believer "*sees, feels,* and *hears.*" The first believers did not imagine Jesus but rather believed that the man who actually stood in front of them, who spoke and ate with them, was God. Christ embodies the simple immediacy of divine *selfhood.* This selfhood is not merely thought, as in Gnosticism. Nor is it brought forth, as in the religions of nature and art. On the contrary, God is now immediately and sensuously beheld as "an actual, particular man." He is historical. Only at this point can we say that God "*is* self-consciousness" [758].

The Humanization of God [759–66]

Christianity is "the absolute religion." Its "simple content" is the Incarnation or, more accurately, the "humanization [*Menschenwerdung*] of the divine essence" [759]. In other words, God has taken the form of an actual self-consciousness. Christianity is absolute because it is the religious awareness of God as *spirit.*

It is in this context that Hegel defines spirit: "For spirit is the knowing of its own self in its externalization; the essence, which is the movement, of retaining the sameness with itself in its being other [*Anderssein*]." Prior to religion, all the modes of certainty that appeared in the *Phenomenology* were *lost* in their otherness: they suffered contradiction. In their finitude or one-sidedness, they were the victims of *infinity:* the logical transition of opposites into each other that was latent in each shape [163–64]. Religion, by contrast, embodies the spirit of reconciliation (which it inherits from conscience). In overcoming all one-sidedness, it *embraces* infinity as the union of opposites: being and thought, substance and subject, infinite God and finite nature. Religion is thus higher than all the worlds of knowing that precede it. In the absolute religion, God becomes man. Dialectically, this means that the spirit of reconciliation, which is the principle of all religions, is now made explicit or "open." God, the divine essence, does not merely confront his other in nature or in man. He knows himself as God *in* that other, and that other knows him.[14] Mutual recognition, the essence of self-consciousness, is now a divine and not merely human event. It is absolute truth.

As we have seen, the Christian God is not a Gnostic fantasy. He has been born as an actual human self. The divine essence or "Father" externalizes itself as a man or "Son." In recognizing themselves in each other, they constitute God as the mediator or "Holy Spirit." This coming forth of God as spirit is another way of saying that God is manifested or revealed [*geoffenbart*] [759]. What God is, is now known [*gewußt*]. Christ, as the object of belief, is not God's prophet, or an appearance as opposed to a supersensible essence. He is not one of God's abstract predicates like "the Good, the Righteous, the Holy, the Creator of Heaven and Earth, and so on." These titles hide God as the substance who is also subject. Christ is God made known as this particular man. God is no longer alien to man. In Christian belief, "the divine nature is the same as the human, and it is this unity that is beheld [or intuited]."

Contrary to what believers might think, the Incarnation is not God's *coming down* from his "eternal simplicity."[15] In seeming to come down—to abase itself by taking human form—the absolute being "has in fact attained for the first time to its own highest essence" [760]. Man is not lower than God but is rather the fulfillment of God.[16] Hegel puts this central point in terms of the Concept, thus reminding us that Christ is not only an object of belief but also the fulfillment of *thought itself.* Christ is divine truth—divine *reason*—that bears the unmistakable mark of immediate sensuous this-ness. He bridges the gap that was first generated by the understanding: the "separateness" (to use Plato's term) between supersensible essence and sensuous appearances: "Thus the lowest is at the same time the highest; the revealed that has come forth wholly on to the *surface* is precisely therein the most *profound.*" This is no mystical teaching but a conceptual truth. The Concept is fulfilled in its particularized human instance—the figure of Christ.

The divine essence is God as substance, God as he is *in himself.* In becoming the Word made flesh, this essence is not less intellectual. On the contrary, Christ embodies, as we have said, thought itself or reason.[17] Christ *manifests* or *opens up* the divine essence, or God "as he is." He appears immediately to the senses. But *what* he is (spirit), is accessible only to pure thought:

"God is attainable only in pure speculative knowing alone and *is* only in that knowing, and is only this knowing itself, for he is spirit; and this speculative knowing is the knowing of the religion that is manifest" [761]. Christianity teaches that the highest destiny of *all human beings,* educated and uneducated alike, is to *see God,* not with the eyes but, as befits God's essence, with the mind.[18] This would be impossible unless God was the universal Self to which our selves could be joined. Jesus is the picture-thought that corresponds to this unity. That Christ is God made man means that man can now see himself in God. Christ is *this* self but also the *universal* self, the self in which all human beings are one with God [761]. This universal fulfillment of selfhood is what manifest religion knows. It is the joy, *Freude,* that all the unhappy shapes in the world had been longing for and *pressing* into historical being-there, the joy that now "seizes the whole world."

The knowledge of spirit that this joy embodies goes through stages [762]. These parallel the life, death, and resurrection of Jesus (which in turn parallel the history of the Church). As I noted at the beginning of this chapter, the threefold Concept is revealed in the three stages of consciousness: sense-certainty, perception, and understanding. Hegel now shows how these represent stages of the spiritual comprehension of Christ.

Christ is first known as an immediate This: Jesus of Nazareth, with whom the disciples eat, drink, and converse. He is "this individual self-consciousness," as opposed to the "universal self-consciousness" that will appear later [780]. The disciples do not yet recognize Jesus as the spirit of their community. To them, he is a singular divine *man.* This is Christian *sense-certainty.* God's shape does not yet have the universal form of the Concept [762]. In order for this form to appear, sensuous shape and individuality must be sublated. That is, Christ must die in order to rise again in a new and higher form.[19] In his risen or sublated form, Christ becomes a universalized This—an object of religious *perception.* This is the transformed, renewed Christ whom the disciples see after the Resurrection. But this shape does not yet have a fully manifest universal form. Only after Christ "ascends into heaven," leaves the disciples, is God known as spirit. God will then be an object of religious *understanding,* a purely intelligible essence that is incarnate and actual in the community of believers.

"This singular man," the immediate shape in which God reveals himself, suffers the dialectical movement of the sensuous This [763]. In that earlier movement, the This passed away. It mediated itself and became a universal. So too, Jesus (the divine This) passes away or dies. This is the second, negative moment of the Concept. The disciples' relation to Jesus also changes. It ceases to be an immediate seeing and hearing, and becomes a *having* seen and *having* heard. For Hegel, the death of Jesus is a second resurrection. Jesus first "rose up" as an object for consciousness. In dying, he cancels this objectivity, which prevents him from being absorbed by the community of his followers. He now rises up "in the spirit." Only in this way, only by dying to his particular shape, can God manifest himself, and be known, *as* spirit. In the death of God as a particular man, divine selfhood remains actual. It is now the "universal self-consciousness" of a community that is one with God.

Throughout his account of Christianity or manifest religion, Hegel interweaves the modes of "for us" and "for consciousness." The reader must be careful to distinguish these perspectives. For orthodox believers, Jesus was a man, God's son, who lived, died, and rose from the dead. He did all this long ago and in a distant land. We scientific observers, however, must not confuse this sort of having-been with the logical moment of having-been, the moment that does not take place in space and time [764]. We must be careful not to think that picture-thinking gives us the truth itself. The account of Jesus we find in the Bible is the imperfect, merely sensuous form of grasping the mediation of the divine particular. It lacks the form of thought.

Such picture-thinking is, nevertheless, the mode in which spirit is aware of itself at this moment of its historical unfolding [765]. Spirit is *necessarily* pictorial, or rather self-depicting, before it is intellectual or self-conceiving. Hegel makes the crucial point that Christian consciousness, precisely because it pictures Christ rather than thinks him, "is still burdened with an unreconciled splitting [*Entzweiung*] into a Here-and-Now [*Diesseits*] and a Beyond [*Jenseits*]." Christian picture-thinking has the "right" content but the "wrong" form. The *conceptual* form of divine truth emerges through "a higher *Bildung* or cultural development [of consciousness]." *Bildung*, here, refers us to the modern culture world, the world in which faith and insight, picture-thinking and pure conceptuality, clash. As we saw earlier, the Enlightenment (as the insight of the world) produced an empty Supreme Being, and faith (as the belief of the world) could not sustain its sensuous imagining of spiritual content. In the Enlightenment, Christianity undergoes a purgation. Having been invaded by insight, it begins to learn that it can sustain itself only by raising its intuitiveness and imagination of God "into the Concept" [765]. When this happens, religion will be *for itself* what it already is *for us.*[20]

To get at the true meaning of Christian spirit, we must attend to the developing consciousness of the Christian community—to the divine *content* of this consciousness [766]. This conceptual content constitutes the real "life of the community." Hegel again cautions us against confusing this content with the result of empirical historical research. The point is not to reconstruct the factual history of the Christian community, or to unearth the so-called "historical Jesus." This is only the pre-rational *instinct* to get to the Concept. It confuses the temporal and contingent origin of immediate existence with the non-temporal and necessary "simplicity of the Concept" [766]. Such an approach is a "recollection bereft of spirit."

The First Moment: God as Pure Essence [767–72]

Hegel now spells out the conceptual content of Christian spirit. This is the absolute content that will be fully realized in absolute knowing. The logical stages of Christian belief are also the stages of God's (or Mind's) self-comprehension as spirit. God is a Beyond only in the picture-thinking or imagination of believers. In truth, he is the spirit of self-knowledge at work *in* the community of those who know God as spirit.

The content of Christian consciousness (God as spirit) is a syllogism. The terms of this syllogism all pass into each other. The first term corresponds to God as "pure substance" [767]. God, here, is a disembodied essence apprehended by thought. This is God "before" the Incarnation and "before" the creation of the world.[21] But since God is spirit, he also is the *movement* from this first moment. He "descends" to a singular existence and "passes into otherness." The awareness of this divine passage is the middle term of the syllogism. It is also the passage from divine self-intuition into divine *picture-thinking* [767]. Christ, in other words, is not a being but a figure for a pictorial mode of thinking the divine. The third moment or term is the reconciliation of the two extremes of universal substance and singular existence—of intellectual intuition and picture-thinking. Here, singular existence "returns" to divine self-intuition to become divine *self-consciousness.* These three moments "constitute spirit."

Picture-thinking is the middle stage of spirit's self-comprehension, the stage of other-being. But it also characterizes the whole syllogism [767]. Pictures *mediate* between the actual self of the believer and God, who is "pure thought." What we have just presented as a dialectical syllogism the religious community pictures to itself as a contingent *happening* in which the Father begets the Son, who is one with the Father through the Holy Spirit.

The Christian *religion* is different from the unhappy consciousness we met in the self-consciousness chapter, and from the "believing consciousness" we met in the chapter on culture [768]. In the former, spirit experiences itself as a divine substance for which it yearns infinitely. It does not see itself in this substance and is therefore restless and unsatisfied. In the latter, spirit pictured God as the otherworldly Being, with whom man would some day be happy. But spirit's picture-thinking lacked "the certainty of self-consciousness" that existed for the enlightened enemies of faith. Faith too was unhappy. It was "unsatisfied Enlightenment" [573]. Christian religion is, by contrast, a happy consciousness. The reason is that the content of Christian communal thinking is God as he is present in the community itself. From the perspective of religion (which, we recall, is spirit that has passed through the stages of morality and conscience), God is not only the divine substance: he is also the unity of that substance with the religious community. This conception of the Christian God, we must note, would not have been possible without Luther's turn to God as the inwardness of conscience or religious self-certainty.

In the first moment of the spirit-syllogism, God is pure substance or, as Hegel also calls him, pure essence [*Wesen*]. Here, God is an object of pure thought. But this essence must also be *actuality.* God as spirit must be real, or rather self-realizing [769]. Unlike force, spirit does not need an other to excite or arouse it [137]. On the contrary, it is genuinely spontaneous and self-mediating. Its essence is not to remain an essence (a separate Platonic Form or Kantian thing-in-itself) but to "other" itself. Soon, this self-othering will be identified with the act of creation [774]. *We* see that the self-othering of the divine essence is a logical necessity, but the Christian community does not. For it, essence is the Father who "begets" the Son as an independently subsisting other. The devout community makes separately existing "Persons" out of moments that become each other in a purely logical or non-temporal way.

The three moments in question are essence and two forms of being-for-self [770]. Essence is the paternal, substantial moment of spirit. The first being-for-self is the other of essence, pictured as Jesus, who represents otherness *as such.* The second being-for-self is the knowledge that the divine essence has of itself *in* the other. This is the dialectical recognition that was expressed in Hegel's earlier definition of spirit [759]. As Hegel says: "in this externalization of itself, [essence] is only with itself [*bei sich*]."

Once more, Hegel revisits language as the existence of selfhood and spirit. The divine essence that knows itself in its externalization is the *Word, das Wort.* This is the Logos that Jesus incarnates. It appears at the beginning of the Gospel of John: "In the beginning was the Word [*logos*], and the Word was with God, and the Word was God." In the act of speaking, I alienate my self-consciousness in order to make it real, out there, and universal. I do not speak into a void but address my speech to other self-conscious individuals who make my selfhood real by hearing and understanding my speech. The divine exhalation of the Word works in exactly the same way. Divine speech, for Hegel, is no different *in form* from human speech. The difference is that divine speech is not communicative but creative. In Hegel's description, the Other that the divine essence spontaneously begets "is the word which, when uttered, leaves behind, externalized and emptied, him who uttered it, but which is as immediately heard [*vernommen*], and only this hearing [*Vernehmen*] of its own self is the *Dasein* or being-there of the Word" [770].

God is the being who creates himself. This self-creation is not an intellectual intuition (which is only one of God's moments). It is rational and discursive. In fact, it is the dialectical form of language as such.

The three moments of God as spirit are not independent "Persons" but distinctions that are "resolved as soon as they are made." The true God is not a being but a circular *movement* that resolves substance into subject and subject into substance [770]. God is Logos. This divine Logos will be made fully manifest or open in the conceptual thinking of philosophical Science. Hegel elaborates on how the picture-thinking of the Christian community falls short of a proper understanding of spirit. Such picture-thinking, as we saw above, has the true content but falsifies it by giving the moments of the Concept the naturalistic form of Father and Son [771]. It thus deprives spirit's conceptually fluid moments of their necessary relation to each other. Such naturalistic representations are especially troublesome here since spirit is supposed to transcend nature.

Hegel's critique of the Trinity as three coequal divine Persons indicates where Hegel stands with respect to the Enlightenment's attack on faith. Picturing spirit's moments as three Persons, although essential to this stage of spirit's self-expression, is the sort of thinking that made faith vulnerable to attack by insight. Insight is the rational "drive" to destroy all picture-thinking. But this drive led insight, in its rage against superstition, to identify faith with imagination and irrationally destroy the *content* as well as the form of Christianity [771]. Insight reduced the absolute content of Christianity to "an historical *Vorstellung* and to an heirloom handed down by tradition." Orthodox Christianity and the Enlightenment alike fail to see that the inwardness of faith *is* "the Concept that knows itself as Concept." Once the content of Christian picture-thinking is conceptually laid bare, there is nothing to which the Enlightenment can object. Christianity has been made perfectly rational, even to non-Christians.[22]

The first moment of spirit must not be understood as a substantial divine Father who gives rise to a substantial divine Son. This picture-thinking falsifies what divine essence really is [772]. Essence is not a stable independent substance but an unstable moment in the fluid *logos* that is spirit. The divine essence is God's "simple oneness, which therefore is equally essentially an othering [*Anderswerden*] of itself." This is Hegel's logical description of God "before" the creation. It is God standing in his own pure presence. God is a "trinity" of moments, but actual otherness has not yet occurred. God, in his purity, posits a difference that is immediately canceled, a difference that is really no difference. In figurative terms, the relation of God as pure essence to his other (being-for-self) is "a *loving recognition* in which the two sides, as regards their essence, do not stand in an antithetical relation to each other." "Father" and "Son" see the same essence in each other and, in the Spirit that unites and identifies them, rejoice. Christ is not yet the Word by which all things were made. He has not yet been "born."

The Second Moment: Creation and Fall [773–79]

The divine essence, as the essence of spirit, must make its self-otherness *real.* God as pure essence is self-canceling. He gives rise, necessarily, to a self-otherness that is substantial and that exists [773]. God creates nature or the world. In terms of religious consciousness, this is the transition from the abstract thought of God to his pictorial representation.

Hegel reminds us yet again that we must not accept Christian imagery on its own terms but must rather give this imagery a conceptual decoding. Creating [*Erschaffen*] is "picture-thinking's word for the Concept itself in its absolute movement" [774]. Creation is the self-realizing of divine essence. To say that the world was created out of nothing is to say that it was produced by the Concept. The world "emerges," non-temporally, from the dialectically tense relation that essence has with itself. In its immediate appearance, the world is God's radical other. It is what he is not. God is pure essence: the world is pure existence. God is universal: the world is full of particulars. God is spirit: the world is corporeal. God creates: the world is created. The world, at this stage of its existence, is nothing but a passive *being-for-another.* God posits an other, but does not yet recognize himself in this other.

So far, the world or nature is God in his *Geworfenheit* or "thrownness" [775]. But in creating a world, God also creates *himself.* The world is not only God's radical other. It contains *subjects* as well as objects, and is the birthplace of God's self-awareness as man. In its newborn stage, divine self-awareness is not yet fully *self-conscious.* The self is conscious, and it distinguishes the world "out there" from itself. But it is not yet spirit that is self-asserting or "for itself" [775]. This newborn self can therefore be called *innocent* or guiltless, but not *good.*

Clearly, Hegel is engaged in a dialectical, and highly unorthodox, decoding of the story of creation found in the book of Genesis. Adam and Eve before the "fall" represent the first stage of God's knowledge of himself *within* nature.[23] Just as the divine essence necessarily created a nature (spirit's other), so too subjective awareness starts out as merely natural. A natural being is one with itself. It feels no anxiety or inner tension. As the archetype of *natural consciousness* (now revealed in its absolute form), Adam and Eve do not feel "the rift in man" (Chapter 10). They experience themselves as other than the external world, but have not yet eaten the forbidden fruit of self-consciousness and self-tearing. They do not yet feel *other than themselves.* The divine essence "came down" in the sense that it fulfilled itself through an act of self-othering. Man, in order to become fully self-conscious and rise to spirit, must do the same. He must "fall." Creation and fall, here, are logical necessities that have nothing to do with free will.[24]

Newborn divine consciousness does not "grow up" all at once. It goes through stages in order to become spirit. Spirit knows itself in its self-externalization or self-otherness [759]. But at first, spirit must suffer self-consciousness as a negative moment, a moment of sheer self-otherness or self-alienation. Since man at this point of his imagined history is steeped in the immediacy of his natural world, his self-otherness—the first experience of himself as self-conscious—takes an immediate or natural form. Man becomes *self-centered* or proud. He experiences an *Insichgehen* or "going into self" [775]. This inward turn is not a contingent happening, as it is portrayed in Genesis, but rather the necessarily first stage of *knowing.*

In Genesis, Adam and Eve eat the forbidden fruit, and their eyes are opened: they become self-conscious. Their merely sensuous consciousness "changes abruptly into thought" [775]. That is, natural innocence sublates or cancels itself. Thought, here, is not the act of thinking [*das Denken*] but *a* thought [*Gedanke*], *the thought of good and evil.* This thought is the birth of self-consciousness. It involves good and evil because Adam and Eve know that they have done something wrong. Logically, this means that spirit knows the difference between being naturally one with oneself and one's world or self-identical, and being at odds with oneself and one's world or self-different. Good and evil are *opposed* to one another because thought is still "conditioned" [*bedingt*] by the sensuous things [*Dinge*] from which it has emerged. To this picture-thinking, good and evil are thus analogous to separately existing sensible *things.*[25] The Bible's version of all this takes the pictorial form of a man (Adam) who lost his happy self-unity when he ate the forbidden fruit of good and evil, and was expelled from a beautiful garden. In presenting this "true content" as a story or mere happening, picture-thinking deprives truth of its logical necessity and, to that extent, falsifies it.[26]

The unhappy consciousness distinguished between an essential or unchangeable self and a non-essential or changeable self. Since its awareness expresses the contradiction between these two selves, the unhappy consciousness identified itself with the latter [208]. The same thing happens here. The immediately existing self, in turning within (toward itself rather than toward God), experiences itself as having become unlike itself: twisted or perverted. It has lost its natural self-sameness. This consciousness, therefore, "is essentially only evil" [776]. But since it posits an opposition between good and evil, there must be some Good Consciousness, from which it has turned. Having become thoughtful (in an elementary way), the actually existing consciousness posits a *realm* of thought in which the opposition between good and evil takes the form of a battle between a good and an evil consciousness, between God (and the "good angels") and Lucifer (and the "rebel angels"). This "war in heaven" is imagined as happening *before* the creation of the world. Lucifer, the "very first-born Son of Light," was the first to turn inward and become proud. When he "fell," another (namely, Christ) "was at once created" [776].[27]

But this effort to "explain" the origin of evil by going "back" in the sequence of imagined events only leads to an infinite regress of originally evil *beings.* Evil is not the attribute of a fallen being who freely turned from God but a dialectical and necessary moment of God as spirit. Hegel will return to the conceptual grasp of Evil when at the third level of Christian awareness [780].[28]

In the thought of good and evil, man experiences his estrangement from God, the Good Consciousness. Man, as the being who turned inward or toward himself, is evil, since "evil is nothing other than the self-centeredness or going-into-self [*Insichgehen*] of the natural *Dasein* of spirit" [777]. To be evil is to be selfish, and to be good is to be selfless. Since man experiences himself as an actual self-consciousness that is evil, he also posits (or pictures) an actual self-consciousness that is good. Out of his Evil condition, which torments him, man posits a Savior who will resolve the human dissonance and make man good.[29] This can happen only if God renounces his pure self-otherness, comes down from Heaven, and becomes really other than himself as an actually existing self-consciousness—as Christ. For picture-thinking, this act of self-abasement embodies God's *goodness.* God's *evil* is pictured as "the wrath of God."[30] This presents devout picture-thinking with its greatest problem: the origin of evil. Hegel will solve this problem by making evil the necessary otherness within God as spirit.

Man's "sin," his having fallen away from God, demands a twofold "alienation or estrangement of the divine being" [778]. Spirit's two poles must be reconciled. These are man, as "the [actual] self of spirit," and God, as the "simple thought" of spirit. Man and God have moved away from each other and must now be re-united. *Two movements are at work here.* In one, man "dies to self" as a penitent unhappy consciousness. In the other, God sacrifices himself for man. In the former movement, God is essential and man is non-essential [778]. God is the purpose of man, who tries to rise up to God in an act of repentance. In the latter, man is essential, and God is non-essential. That is, man is the purpose of God, who wishes to save man through an act of grace. Both movements (or mortifications) come together in the death on the cross. This, rather than the birth in Bethlehem, is the true Incarnation. It is the moment when God becomes fully human. In the death on the cross, man and God are united and reconciled. The two opposed natures dissolve into each other in the moment of death. But they still lack the "middle term" of *Dasein* or being-there, that is, an abiding *life.* God and man are united, as yet, only in their mutual vanishing. The middle term, the abiding life of spirit and reconciliation, will appear in the third moment of Christian spirit. It will be the Christian community itself, in which spirit "dies every day, and is daily resurrected" [784].

We must not think of the movement at work here as taking place between two "separate and independent beings" [779]. This is mere picture-thinking. God and man, essence and actual selfhood, must confront each other, not as beings but as thoughts or concepts. Each side of the opposition contains the whole opposition and must resolve the conflict *through itself.* From the standpoint of religious picture-thinking, God makes a free motion toward man, and man makes a free motion toward God. But in fact these motions are logically necessary. Essence (God), the side of thought or being-in-itself, must cancel its own unreality and become for itself as an actual self-consciousness (man). The Incarnation was not an option that depended on what man did. It was the necessary self-realization of divine essence. It is not, therefore, man as an independent being who alienates himself from God, but God who alienates himself from himself. In dying to his mortal other, God overcomes his self-alienation. He negates a negation.

The determinateness of this negation now comes to the fore. In the death of God as an abstract essence or mere thought, this essence is infused into the realm of "immediate *Dasein.*" Spirit is "poured forth" into nature.[31] In Hegel's words, the death of God is "the resurrection of spirit" [779].[32] It is the transformation of the self's singularity and self-centeredness into universality. This universality, which is the natural or worldly presence of spirit, is the Christian community.

The Third Moment: God as the Spirit of Christian Community [780–86]

In the previous stage of Christian consciousness, Christ died as a singular man. More precisely, in Christ, God and man died together and became one. But in this death of God as a finite shape, God "rose up" in a new form—that of universal self-consciousness [780]. In Christ's death on the cross, believers are one with Christ. They, too, die to the recalcitrant singularity or selfishness that alienates them from God.

The third stage of Christian consciousness is the perfection of Christianity as the manifest or absolute religion. It is the knowledge of God as spirit or universal selfhood. The religious community takes Christ into their midst and celebrates his daily presence. In his first moment, God was pure essence or thought. In his second moment, he is the object of picture-thinking. In the third, he is spirit or "self-consciousness as such" [780].

Before taking up the communal appearance of God, Hegel returns to the theme of picture-thinking. He does so because the spiritual comprehension of God is precisely the transcendence and "death" of this picture-thinking. As we have seen, God is not God without his other (man and creation in general). God, as divine essence, necessarily creates the world or sublates himself. Up to this point, otherness was pictured as existing outside of God. It was in nature as an indifferent object, or in man as the being who became selfish, or in Lucifer as the primordial spirit who fell and then was replaced by Christ. But spirit is the absolute whole to which nothing is external. It reconciles opposites by absorbing them. Everything that picture-thinking regarded as external to God is really internal to him—including and especially evil.

Understanding also wrestled with otherness. It eventually discovered that opposite poles of a magnet, for example, had to be identical in order to be different—that the self-identical was self-repelling, and the self-repelling self-attracting. In other words, it learned that opposites necessarily posited and contained each other. This was the infinity of the inverted world [156–57]. The current opposition is that between good and evil. Up to now, these poles represented an either-or situation. Picture-thinking depicted man as being able to "turn" freely, either to selfishness (evil) or selflessness (good). Hegel now argues that good and evil are not freely chosen alternatives but logically necessary moments of God as spirit, *and that God himself must be the origin of evil.*

Picture-thinking itself plants the seed of this unorthodox idea. It asserts that God becomes his opposite, man—that the natures of the human and the divine are not separate. If picture-thinking went only that far, it could continue to believe that the Incarnation was contingent upon man's fall. But picture-thinking also declares that God, *from the beginning,* externalized himself as his Son [780]. This implies that God's self-externalization is not contingent but necessary, that God is essentially self-conscious or inwardly turned. But this inward turn is the selfishness that religious awareness calls evil. In creating a world, God "gave of himself." His creation was the unselfish gift of spirit. But in creating, he also retreated back into himself, separated himself from the other he had created (he absconded). In other words, good (as selflessness) and evil (as selfishness) necessarily imply and contain one another. They behave in exactly the same way as the north and south poles of a magnet.

Picture-thinking separates good and evil, thus making it impossible to grasp their unity. The "problem of evil" therefore continues to haunt this thinking. Religious consciousness does make an effort to connect good and evil by asserting that good *eventually* "comes out of" evil (through God's providence). Christ's sacrifice *eventually* made good on Adam's debt through sin. But this still separates the moments of spirit and fails to grasp the necessary unity of good and evil. It asserts that evil is only *in itself* or implicitly good.

Good and evil are united and reconciled only in their Concept: "self-centered being-for-self is simple knowing, and simple [being] that is self-less is equally pure self-centered being-for-self" [780]. Differently stated, to be evil or selfish is to *lose* oneself, and to be good or selfless is to *find* oneself. This teaching is contained in the Gospel of John, in the parable of the grain of wheat, which bears fruit only if it goes into the ground and dies (12:24). Christian picture-thinking fails to see the true meaning of this parable. Good and evil are not alternative choices but "sublated moments" within spirit, which is their totality. The truth is that good and evil are each same and different, identical and opposed. We grasp their natures only in the dialectical movement that connects them.

As Hegel now straightforwardly says, spirit has become universal self-consciousness or spirit's *community* [*Gemeinde*] [781]. Christ told the disciples that he was "in their midst" whenever two or more of them met in his name (Matthew 18:20). This being-in-their-midst is made actual in Christ's death. But it is not yet actual for the religious community, which, as the evil pole of the man-God relationship, must experience reconciliation with God. This development of communal self-consciousness is the movement we must now go though. God has done his part in dying for our sins. Now we must do ours if we are to join him in spirit. In what follows, Hegel will show how the community, in its thought and daily spiritual work, *absorbs* the events that picture-thinking portrayed as happening outside the community. He will show how God's death and resurrection occur within the community itself.[33]

Universal self-consciousness is at first "natural spirit" [782]. Natural spirit here refers to the thought that nature is good, that it is corruptible but not inherently corrupt. This thought amounts to the denial of so-called "original sin." It belongs to the Eden-spirit of the ancient Greeks, who experienced themselves as in harmony with nature. Christian spirit preserves this natural attitude to the extent that nature, man's nature in particular, is thought of as originally good, or rather innocent.

To become fully self-conscious, spirit must "withdraw" from this assumption and "go into itself." This inward turn has already happened in itself or implicitly. Man became selfish and alienated himself from God. As a selfish being, he is evil. But what must now take place in the communal self is the *conviction* "that natural *Dasein* is evil." That is, man must be evil not just *in himself* but *for himself*. He must convince himself, *believe*, that evil is an intrinsic part of creation, not an accident—that this is what he is up against in his effort to be a spiritual being that is reconciled with God.

Evil is "the self-centeredness of the natural existence of spirit" [777]. This definition, which was for us, is now for religious consciousness.

At the stage of picture-thinking, man's turn to self was evil. But being inwardly turned is now regarded as a necessary moment of *knowing*—the moment of pure self-identity or self-consciousness. Man's second inward turn, his conviction that he is evil by nature, is thus positive or good. As the negation of a negation, it is the first step in overcoming evil as selfishness. In terms of the religious community, the forgiveness of sin that we already saw at the level of conscience presupposes the confession of sin. This conviction or knowledge of one's natural or "original" sinfulness (that is, selfishness) is "the first moment of reconciliation" within the community itself [783]. It is the first step in the process of "dying to sin."

So far, this positive inward turn is only immediate, like the selfish nature that it overcomes [783]. The inner conviction that one is evil is only the implicit overcoming of sin, the *thought* of a movement toward good but not the movement itself. The actual movement that overcomes sin is the *reconciliation* or *forgiveness* that takes place daily in the community itself [784]. We have seen this phenomenon before in conscience [670–71]. The difference is that reconciliation now grasps itself as religion, which aspires to a speculative knowledge of God as absolute being [761]. In other words, the individual self experiences and knows his reconciliation with other human beings, and with God, as the overcoming of the split between spirit and nature.

That the community knows this about itself is the direct result of its picture-thinking approach to God as man (the person of Jesus). The religious community now *mediates* and *spiritualizes* this picture-thinking [784]. It takes the story of Jesus out of the pictured past and transplants it in the on-going present. It applies the main events of that story to itself. At this moment, the Church, in its gradual process of reforming itself, goes from being *Christ*-centered to being *spirit*-centered.[34] When Jesus died, God was reconciled to man and nature. The community now takes this to mean that it itself embodies the divine spirit of reconciliation. The birth of God is now the formation of the community as the birth of spirit. The death of God ceases to refer to a natural death and becomes the spiritual "death to self," the death that is a rebirth of selfhood as the community's universality. As I noted earlier, the community itself becomes the substantial medium in which divine spirit "dies" every day and "is daily resurrected" (in the mutual forgiveness of sins, that is, of selfishness).

What was formerly presented as a naturalistic story about God "is here shifted into self-consciousness itself, into knowledge that preserves itself in its otherness" [785]. Birth and death, in being de-naturalized, have been rendered spiritual. Picture-thinking has returned to its origin, which is selfhood or Concept, and being has become knowing. The death of religious picture-thinking preserves and overcomes all the oppositions that religious consciousness struggled to overcome from the very beginning. Spirit now experiences itself as containing rather than excluding its otherness. The death of Christ is grasped as the overcoming of all being-for-self. The individual self has blossomed into a universal self or community. The universal has ceased to be a mere thought or essence and has become actual. The unhappy consciousness, which was formerly taken to mean, "God is dead," now has the meaning of "simple self-knowledge" in the form of I = I. It is now *known* and *interpreted* as the loss of substance that is also the disclosure of subjectivity or self-certainty. This is the meaning of losing oneself in order to find oneself (Matthew 10:39). It is the knowing that is the "inspiration or in-spiriting [*Begeisterung*], whereby substance becomes subject" [785].

At this stage, spirit knows itself as spirit [786]. It has itself for its object. It is self-knowing and self-realizing or actual. Hegel puts all this in terms reminiscent of Aristotle. Spirit is *mover, moved,* and *movement* all in one. It is self-relating subject moving through the medium of substance—God *recognizing himself* within the natural world.

We have at last reached the goal of religion: to bring spirit to the level of having itself for object. This was also the goal of reconciling God as pure essence with nature or existence. The Concept of spirit that had emerged as the result of conscience was that of reconciliation [786]. There, spirit emerged as the knowledge of itself in its other. The Doer and his Judge, both hypocrites, renounced their hard being-for-self, forgave each other's sin and enjoyed mutual recognition. This recognition "bursts forth" in a joyously affirmative "Yea!" The religious community, which has transcended the worship of God as Son in the worship of God as Spirit, now *beholds* or *intuits* this Concept.

Not Home Yet [787]

Religious consciousness posits a split between the inner, sacred world and the outer, secular world. It distinguishes between the City of God and the City of Man, between Sunday (for Christians) and the other days of the week. Hegel now returns to this split. He shows that even for religion in its absolute form, there is still a Beyond.

The community "is not yet perfected in this its self-consciousness" [787]. It has not completely transcended picture-thinking. We got a foretaste of this claim when Hegel said that spirit merely beholds or intuits the Concept of itself [786]. Spirit, as manifest or absolute religion, is a "devotional [*andächtige*] consciousness" that still thinks of God as the sacred Other outside of space and time. It has successfully "divested itself" of naturalness and experiences an intimate bond with God. But it does not *identify* with God. It remains devout. Earlier, we saw that two movements of self-externalization were at work in manifest religion: God came down as man, and then man, as the religious community, rose up to God. The community does not see that these are *one and the same movement.*[35] Devout consciousness still regards itself as able to "rise up" only through God's grace: "Just as the individual divine man has a father in principle and only an actual mother, so too the universal divine man, the community, has for its father its own doing and knowing, but for its mother, eternal love which it only feels, but does not behold in its consciousness as an actual, immediate object" [787].

The reconciliation between God and man, since it is only at the level of the heart, is thus incomplete, still at the level of picture-thinking. Man is not yet home. Just as the earlier forms of manifest religion looked back to an historical Jesus, the community now looks ahead to full union with God. The actual world of nature, God's creation, is not yet reconciled to God. Nature has not yet experienced its *transfiguration* [*Verklärung*] as history.[36] The ultimate reconciliation of man and God, nature and spirit, will take place at the final stage of Hegel's *Phenomenology.* This is the stage of absolute knowing, the stage at which every trace of a Beyond is destroyed. With absolute knowing, man as self-consciousness finally comes home.

ABSOLUTE KNOWING

In the world you have anxiety; but be confident, I have overcome the world.
John 16:33

24

Speculative Good Friday

The Top of Hegel's Ladder

WITH THE RISE OF ABSOLUTE KNOWING, THE JOURNEY OF CONSCIOUSNESS reaches its end. But what does "end" mean here, and what *is* absolute knowing? What is Hegel's goal in the *Phenomenology of Spirit,* and how has that goal been achieved? Where are we—as thinkers and as human beings—at the end of Hegel's book, and where do go from here? In this chapter, I will address these questions.

Hegel's eighth and final chapter is by far the shortest in the book.[1] It is also the hardest to understand. This is due largely to the chapter's frustrating concision. In a mere sixteen pages of German text, Hegel recalls the whole journey of consciousness, shows how absolute knowing emerges from the unity of religion and moral action, and then explains why time is necessary to the unfolding of the Concept. Chapter and book end with world-history as the Golgotha or Skull Place of absolute spirit.

The goal of *my* chapter is twofold: to guide us through the "dark wood" of Hegel's text, and to highlight the fundamental problems Hegel claims to have solved. This will be the penultimate stage of our journey through the *Phenomenology of Spirit.* In my concluding chapter, which serves as an epilogue, I will say what we have most to learn from Hegel, and return briefly to the themes of selfhood and desire.

Prelude to the Finale

Hegel's goal in the *Phenomenology* is the transformation of the love of knowing into actual knowing [5]. We are now about to achieve this goal. Absolute knowing is Science, *Wissenschaft* [798]. It is not the fully developed body of Science but the pure "ether" of conceptuality, the *element* in which Science exists and develops [26, 805].[2] Throughout the journey of consciousness, the Concept has been *for us.* Now it will be *for consciousness.* Consciousness will at last come to recognize itself in its history.

Before proceeding, let us briefly review the place of the *Phenomenology* in Hegel's System. The *Phenomenology* is the introduction to this System, which consists of Logic, the Philosophy of Nature and the Philosophy of Spirit or Mind. It examines thought as consciousness or the subject-object opposition. Logic, the Science of *pure* thought, transcends this opposition.[3] It is the Science to which Phenomenology is most especially an introduction [37]. The Philosophy of Nature and the Philosophy of Spirit constitute the two "real" philosophic Sciences, real in that their subject matter exists or is concretely *there.* Nature covers both inorganic and organic being. It is the realm of necessity. Spirit covers the complete range of human experience, and is the realm of freedom.[4]

Phenomenology appears in the *Phenomenology* of 1807, and Logic in Hegel's other great book, the *Science of Logic* (1812–13).[5] The System or "circle" of knowledge appears, in outline form with lecture notes, in the *Encyclopaedia of the Philosophical Sciences* (1830). This includes the so-called Lesser Logic, the Philosophy of Nature, and the Philosophy of Spirit or Mind. This last Science reaches its peak in Absolute Spirit, which comprises Art, Religion, and Philosophy.

These three main Sciences develop what Hegel calls the Idea. This is thought that is also being.[6] In Logic, the Idea is implicit or *in itself.* The Idea here is the pure, timeless form of all things. Nature, the object of the first "real" or concrete Science, is the Idea in its self-externalization or otherness: the Idea in space and time. Here, the Idea is *for itself* or actual. It sacrifices itself to the realm of *Dasein* or being-there. And spirit (the realm of freedom) is the Idea that is *in and for itself* or logically complete. Spirit logically *contains* nature (the moment of self-externalization). It is the reconciliation of the out there and the in here. As spirit, the Idea is at home in its self-otherness.

Hegel originally conceived Phenomenology as the first part of his System [35]. It was to be "the Science of the experience of consciousness" [88].[7] In later years, he seems to have changed his mind about this.[8] But whether or not the 1807 *Phenomenology* is the first part of the System itself, Hegel continued to believe that Science needed an introduction. The *Phenomenology* is that introduction. [9] It is the individual's ladder to the absolute [26]—what I have called Hegel's logic of desire. The difficulty is that the reader is expected to share Hegel's scientific perspective right from the start: he must be a phenomenological observer who can follow dialectical logic.[10] And if, as often happens, the reader is not already familiar with Hegel's logic, then he must learn the motions of the Concept and the dialectical syllogism while grappling with the complex permutations of consciousness.

The last chapter of the *Phenomenology* has three parts. In the first, Hegel describes the "overcoming" of the religious object. This overcoming transforms religion into absolute knowing [788–89]. In the second, he shows how this transformation takes place [790–99]. And in the third, he explains why time is essential to the Concept and to spirit [800–808].

The central drama of the chapter is the transition from religion to philosophy, faith to knowledge. It is important to grasp the radical character of this transition. Absolute knowing is not confined to what goes on inside the philosopher's head. It is the spirit of the new era and world Hegel mentions in his Preface [11–13]. Up to this point in history, religion had been the medium in which a people contemplated the divine spirit of its communal life. That role will now be played by philosophy in the form of Science (Hyppolite, 597). The true "savior" that overcomes all forms of alienation will be, not the Logos or Word that is Christ, but the *logos* that is Concept.[11]

In Chapter 15, I noted that the central problem of modernity is that of reconciling knowledge and life. I posed the question: How can man be happy, or rather non-alienated, after eating the bitter fruit of self-consciousness and asserting himself as an individual? In Greek Eden, man was happy to the extent that he did not inquire into his origins. Custom, not knowledge, was the basis of community and man's relation to the divine. The enlightened, perverse world of culture was the negative of custom. Christian believers rose above this world and found refuge in a Beyond, the hoped-for land of divine insight. Absolute knowing must be regarded in the context of this historical movement from ancient custom to modern culture. It is both the ascent from philosophy to Science and the solution to the existential problem of knowledge and life. With the dawn of absolute knowing, concrete self-knowledge rather than Greek custom or Christian faith becomes the spirit and element of human *Dasein*. Our Here-and-Now, which started out as an object of mere sense-certainty, becomes a *lived* world of knowing.

This does not mean that all our desires are satisfied, or that the world is perfect. It means that we recognize the world's overall reasonableness and meaning, and (as we saw in Chapter 20) *forgive* others and ourselves for entering into the impure realm of self-interested action. Reason was selfhood that wanted to meet itself in the external world [241]. Absolute knowing fulfills this desire. It is the reconciliation of man to his present world, of man's essence to his existence. In the condition of absolute knowing, we experience life as the work of the Concept, which is also our own self-consciousness. We do not cease to suffer, or to find things wrong with the world. But, to use Heidegger's word, we no longer feel "thrown." We are no longer troubled by the thought that our actual world is meaningless and strange: our finitude *makes sense*. Death itself makes sense as a logically necessary part of life.[12] We have no more need of a Beyond.

Overcoming the Object [788–89]

Religion is the self-consciousness of spirit [672]. It is spirit that has retreated from its worldly manifestations in ethicality, culture, and morality in order to worship God as absolute being. The religious community distinguishes between its divine essence (the thought of God) and its actual existence [678]. It posits a separation between worship and the rest of life, Sunday and the other days of the week. Believers live *in* the Here-and-Now but *for* union with God in a future Beyond. In the final chapter of the *Phenomenology*, spirit will cancel these distinctions and fulfill itself in the "daylight of the present" [177].

In making our way through Hegel's final chapter, we must remember that our goal—the completion of philosophy in the form of Science—is possible only if it can be shown that truth is subject as well as substance [17]. In his Preface, Hegel equates these two assertions (that truth is actual only as System, and that substance is essentially subject) [25]. In other words, the Concept, which is the soul of the world, has the same structure as human self-consciousness. I can know the truth because I *am* the truth. Divine truth is alive in my selfhood. In the course of history, various absolutes or versions of God have appeared. But only Christianity has posited the absolute or God as *spirit*, "the most sublime concept and the one that belongs to the modern age and its religion" [25]. As spirit, God (or Mind) humanizes himself or makes himself actual in time and nature. He is at home in his self-externalization or self-otherness [759]. The Christian idea of God as spirit implicitly overcomes the split between subject and object, and thus makes possible philosophy in the form of Science.

Absolute knowing emerges from the dialectical unpacking of the Christian God. This is not immediately evident from the text, where Hegel refers to God simply as "the object." His avoidance of the word God makes sense, since we are approaching the purely conceptual understanding of the divine and the purgation of religious images. The transition from religious to philosophic consciousness consists, we might say, in getting over the need for the word God.[13] Having generated truth as a divine object, spirit must now *recover* from the burden of its religiosity in order to re-experience itself as self-certain and self-knowing.[14] This is precisely why Hegel will take us back into the realm of action. The relation of the self to religion is like that of the Greek sculptor to his statue of a god. Just as the sculptor must become a singer of hymns in order to be one with his artwork, the devout self must take up the "music" of philosophy—the song of the Concept—in order to be one with the divine truth of religious pictures.[15]

The for-us opening paragraph of the chapter compresses an enormous amount of experience (in Hegel's sense) into a brief compass. The central idea is the overcoming or *Überwindung* of objectivity. Christianity is still afflicted by the subject-object opposition of consciousness. Once self-consciousness gets beyond thinking of God as an object separate from itself, it will be fully reconciled to the actual world from which, as religion, it withdraws. There will be, for it, *only one world.*

In his opening sentence, Hegel tells us that religious spirit "has not yet overcome its consciousness as such, or what is the same, its actual self-consciousness is not the object of its consciousness" [788]. The Christian community thinks of God as a separate divine essence. It does not see its actual selfhood in this essence that is its object. In religion, absolute truth has "fallen into" picture-thinking and has taken the form of objectivity [*Gegenständlichkeit* or "standing-against-ness"]. This imaginative form must be canceled. Picture must rise to Concept.[16] Once this happens, the absolute content of religion will have its absolute form (as pure thought or logic); object and Concept will be adequate to each other [84]; and self-consciousness will recognize the divine essence or God as its own act.[17]

The picture-thought of Christianity contains all of spirit's various moments, that is, everything that has happened in the journey of consciousness. The reason is that religion, like philosophy, is the attempt to transcend finite thought and *think the whole.* Self-consciousness must now come to see this journey as its own work.

Overcoming the sacred object must not lapse into previous forms of relating to God [788]. It must not be the skeptical *comic* consciousness, where the divine essence (the Greek picture-gods) vanished into the human self, but rather selfhood that produces its object through self-externalization. This self-externalization, however, must not be negative, as it was for the *unhappy* consciousness. It must be positive, "not only for us or in itself, but for self-consciousness itself." Such positive self-externalization has already occurred in Christianity, where God "empties" himself as a mortal and man sacrifices his will to the divine will.[18] But the believer does not see himself *as* God, or God *as* himself.[19] Though not wretched, he is still alienated.

Christianity believes that man's highest good is the vision of God, that the divine sacrifices itself for man, that individuality requires universal community, and that self-fulfillment comes through self-sacrifice and mutual forgiveness. For Hegel, it is rational to believe all this. But the devout community does not know that what it believes and pictures to itself is rational. Once absolute knowing replaces piety, a new community will emerge, that of philosophic knowers.[20] These devotees of reason will not oppose religion, like their enlightened precursors, but explicate it.[21]

Absolute knowing occurs when the self completely overcomes its alienation from the divine essence. This can happen only when the self grasps divine otherness as *self*-otherness, when it sees that all modes of divine objectivity are in fact modes in which the self objectifies and externalizes itself. The purely logical formulation of what must happen is as follows. Having externalized itself as an object (separated itself from God), the self must *cancel* this self-externalization and return to itself out of otherness. It must negate a negation, alienate an alienation. Then, it will be "with itself [*bei sich*] in *its* otherness as such" and no longer in need of a Beyond. The self will find itself as the substance of all the objective shapes of God that spirit, as consciousness, contains. It will be able to identify the self-externalization of the divine object (God's becoming man) with the self-externalization of *itself.* Self-consciousness will thus become spirit according to Hegel's definition: "the knowing of its own self in its externalization; the essence, which is the movement, of retaining the sameness with itself in its being other [*Anderssein*] [759]."

In being able to recognize otherness as *its* otherness, self-consciousness will be able to see itself in the *movement* in which consciousness "is the totality of its moments" [788]. It will recognize God as "an implicitly spiritual essence [*Wesen*]" that becomes truly spiritual for consciousness when all objects are seen as determinations of the *self.* We must note here that Christianity already has an historical self-understanding: it posits history as the story of God's relation to nature and man. Once the self grasps the objective determinations of God as self-determinations, it will re-write the *mythos* of God's relation to man as the *logos* of humanity's own historical unfolding.

Hegel's review of these determinations conflates three sequences: the stages of consciousness, of religion as a whole, and of manifest religion [789]. His point is to show how the object of religion (divine essence or God) is a self-determination of the knowing self. In one aspect, God is an immediate being, the object of religious *sense-certainty* (both nature-religion and the experience of God as Jesus). In another, he is a thing-like person with universal properties, an object of religious *perception* (both Greek religion and Jesus as a divine individual who, in dying and rising, takes on universal meaning). And in a third aspect, God is a pure essence, a universal self or spirit—the object of religious *understanding* (both manifest religion as a whole and its highest moment of spiritual community). These aspects form a syllogism in which the universal, through determination, becomes particular, and the particular universal. In Christian terms, it is the movement in which God (the universal) becomes man (the particular), and man rises up to God, through the mediation of Jesus as the universal individual.

In these determinations, the self comes to know the divine object *as itself* [789]. As Hegel stresses, this is not the pure knowing of divine essence that we find in the Science of logic. It is not "the pure conceptualizing-grasp

[*Begreifen*] of the object," but rather the knowledge of the movement or *coming-to-be* of the object as a determination of the knowing subject. It is the knowledge, not of the Concept as such but of the *shapes of consciousness*—the knowledge contained in the *Phenomenology of Spirit.* In order to further reveal the process by which the self posits itself as object, Hegel brings together several shapes that pave the way for the historical emergence of the divine object or God.

A Gathering of Shapes [790–94]

The shapes in which the self alienates itself as a thing are phrenology, the enlightened world of utility, and moral action.[22] These correspond, respectively, to thinghood as immediate being (the skull), the thing as related to me, and the thing as embodying my essence as a self (Hyppolite, 593–94). Hegel gathers these shapes to reveal the transition from religion to absolute knowing. He shows how the overcoming of the divine as object is implicit in the positive self-externalizations that have already occurred. Absolute knowing will emerge from the unity of religion and moral action [795–97]. Religion will provide the absolute *content,* action the absolute *form* (i.e. self-consciousness).[23]

Phrenology was the peak (and nadir) of observing reason [790]. It was reason's effort to read spiritual depth in the skull, the organ in which the self is presumed to express itself objectively.[24] Phrenology lays bare, and identifies, spirit's two sides (inner and outer) in their most extreme form: the most intimate secrets of the self and the bluntest bodily thing. Its truth is contained in the infinite judgment: "the being [*Sein*] of the 'I' is a thing [*Ding*]."[25] Taken at face value, this judgment is non-spiritual. But in its *Concept,* it is "the most richly spiritual." Its deepest meaning is the death of God, the final image of Hegel's book. In the philosophically comprehended Golgotha or *Schädelstätte,* the *skull* [*Schädel*] of phrenology finds its spiritual *place* [*Stätte*].[26]

"The being of the 'I' is a thing." But it is no less true that "The thing is 'I'" [791]. In other words, the thing is what it is only in its relation to the self. This logical conversion of phrenology's infinite judgment brings us to the next shape in which the self alienates itself as a thing. This is the Enlightenment world in which absolute truth is *utility* [579–81]. The thing *is* only insofar as it is useful to someone.[27] Through the self-alienation of the modern culture world, self-consciousness has thus produced the thing as its own self. It knows that external things are only a being-for-another (i.e. for man).

But the knowledge of the thing is still incomplete [792]. Pure insight knows the thing as useful or *for* the self, but does not know it *as* the self. It does not see its selfhood and act as the very substance of the thing. This brings us to moral self-consciousness, Hegel's third shape in which the self knows itself as a thing. Here, the self goes beyond utility by positing being as "simply and solely pure willing and knowing." In its retreat into itself, moral self-consciousness lets nature go its own way [see 599]. But in its all-embracing world-picture [*Weltvorstellung*], it also incorporates nature and happiness, and pretends that the ideal of pure Duty is somehow real. This was the hypocrisy of Kant's moral postulates. Conscience overcame this hypocrisy. It abandoned Duty as a non-existent ideal that somehow also exists in an indefinite future. Conscience is its own end. It makes its very knowing real. Knowing is *there* or exists in my pure certainty of myself, my will to power [791]. For this Napoleonic consciousness, the action *is* the knowing, and the knowing action. The object is the self's "pure knowledge of itself."

In these three shapes—phrenology (Reason), utility (Culture), and moral certainty (Spirit)—spirit reconciles itself "with its own consciousness," its awareness of itself as a thing [793]. Conscience, as the identity of inner knowledge and thingly being-there, sums up the whole movement of reconciliation and unifies all the separately appearing moments. It does so in the dialectic of action and forgiveness. Here, the self experiences the three stages of the Concept: before action "simple unity," in action the Concept's *Entzweiung* or splitting, and in forgiveness its "return out of this division." The result, as we saw earlier, is individual selfhood that is also universal: the mutual recognition in which the individual experiences the truth of his self-certain "I = I" or "I AM MYSELF."

Hegel's review shows how the reconciliation of consciousness and self-consciousness, thingly existence and inner thought, has occurred in two separate ways: in religion (through God's grace) and "in consciousness itself as such" [794]. The two must now be combined, since each embodies only one side of complete or absolute reconciliation. In religion, reconciliation is only *in itself* or divinely objective, in morality only *for itself* or humanly subjective. Each side must make up for the lack in the other by giving itself to the other. The objective divine must be infused with the *form* of self-certainty, and moral action must be infused with absolute *content* or truth. Once this mutual infusion occurs, self-consciousness will experience the world in which it actually lives as the home of divine presence, the house of God. It will know divine truth divinely, that is, as Science. This unification of religion and morality "closes the circle of the shapes of spirit" [794].[28]

The Rise of Absolute Knowing [795–99]

The final reconciliation has already occurred implicitly [*an sich*] in the last stage of manifest religion, where picture-thinking "returned" into self-consciousness [795]. The picture-thought of God as an individual man "died" and was "resurrected" as the spirit of the Christian community [781]. The community received the spirit that was shed when Jesus died and absorbed the divine into itself. But spirit still lacked its properly spiritual form: conceptuality. The community *pictured* spirit as an object over and against "the movement of self-consciousness."[29] This spiritually enriched object was God in heaven surrounded by the reconciled community of the faithful.[30]

The required unification must therefore take place within the *non*-religious moment of reconciliation. This is the moment of conscientious action, in which the Napoleonic self posits *itself* as absolute. As the subjective side of reconciliation, conscience "contains both itself and its opposite, and not only implicitly [*an sich*] [as in religion] or in a universal sense, but explicitly [*für sich*] or in a developed and differentiated way" [795]. This development is the dialectic of action.

In attending to the transition from religion to absolute knowing, we must bear in mind what I mentioned earlier: the replacement of the historical reign of religion with the reign of philosophy. Hegel's return to moral action *undoes* Christian piety by making the rational individual once more the active center of his own life and world. Hegel is thus using Christianity to bring about the goal of the Enlightenment: the transformation of all existence and life into the pure Concept, which expresses the self. As a believer, man receives the meaning of his life as a gift. As a knower, he experiences his selfhood as producing and constituting that meaning. The self-absolutizing *movement* of the knowing self replaces the absolute *object* of the devout self.[31]

As we proceed, we must keep in mind the following points. 1) Christianity is absolute truth in objective form (God). 2) This truth is grasped as Concept when it has the form of self. 3) Selfhood is manifest in the self's *act*. That is why we are going back to the realm of action and will. It is here that the self is aware of itself as self-absolutizing. 4) The goal is for the self to experience, in its *moral* drama, the *cognitive* drama in which the self recapitulates the moments of divine self-sacrifice, thus experiencing the divine essence as the structure of its own act. 5) The self will then have appropriated the whole of human experience. It will be conscious of itself as actively generating rather passively receiving truth and meaning (all given-ness will be abolished). It will be conscious of itself, in the act of knowing, as individuality that is also universal. Thinking and object of thought will both belong to one and the same world. And truth will be grasped as subject [17].

The subjective certainty that laid claim to objective truth appeared as a specific shape of consciousness: the *beautiful soul*. Hegel starts here rather than with the acting self because he wants to draw our attention to the self-certainty that most reveals the *pure form* of selfhood, the certainty that is most withdrawn and self-sufficient, and that claims to be absolute or Godlike by virtue of knowledge alone. For the beautiful soul, knowledge is all that is *there.* In its purism and iconoclasm, it expresses "the simple unity of the Concept." As Hegel now reveals, the beautiful soul is "not only the intuition of the divine but the divine's *self-intuition* [*Selbstanschauung*]" [795]. In other words, the beautiful soul is the subjective human experience of the divine *essence* that for manifest religion was a remote divine *object.* Hegel's demonstration that God is already in man or self-consciousness has begun.[32]

As we know, the beautiful soul clings to inwardness and shuns all contact with the outside world. In its pathological, romantic moment, it vanished "into thin air" [658]. But in another aspect of its experience, it went on to *act* [659]. Action, here, is a self-externalization, the making of infinite selfhood into a finite thing: the "betrayal" of pure inwardness. This moment of betrayal is the further development of phrenology, which "reads" the meaning of spirit in a bone. It is also the second, self-divisive moment of the divine object (God) in manifest religion. On the objective side, God parts with his pure essence and abandons himself to nature and death. On the subjective or human side, conscience parts with its purity and acts.

In the end, action gave rise to reconciliation between the Doer and the Judge. On a logical level, this was the reconciliation of worldly being-there and pure knowing. The universal selfhood or community of consciences that emerged from this reconciliation is the *fulfillment* of self-consciousness. It is also the realization of the Concept "in its truth" [795]. The Concept, here, ceases to be abstract and undeveloped. It is not knowledge in the abstract but "*this* knowledge, *this* pure self-consciousness." As a beautiful soul locked up inside my intuition, I am only implicitly self-conscious, since selfhood has mutual recognition as its goal [178]. In the community whose members recognize each other as pure selves, knowledge is no longer trapped inside the individual. It is *there* as the act in which individuals both give and receive forgiveness. In the communal self, knowledge itself is an object. And the Concept is "the self that is for itself" [795].

In his review of conscience, Hegel has shown that moral self-certainty contains the three moments of Christianity's divine object and truth. The beautiful soul is God intuiting himself (the Concept in its pure self-identity). Action is God in his moment of self-externalization or creation (the Concept in its self-difference). And the reconciliation of human selves is God as spirit (the Concept that is self-identical in its self-difference). Consciousness will itself realize all this when the static religious *thought* of God becomes for it the awareness of its own act of *thinking.*

THE MOMENT WE'VE ALL BEEN WAITING FOR

We now reach the movement that produces absolute knowing, the last shape of consciousness and the final "deed" of the individual self.[33] Hegel *names* absolute knowing only after he has deduced it from moral action [798].

For now, it is simply "pure knowing." This is the ability to think like Hegel: logically or dialectically, in terms of pure concepts. Absolute knowing arises when consciousness recognizes the philosopher in the moral Doer (Hegel in Napoleon), when it realizes that the dialectic of acting and willing is also the experience of pure knowing. This realization occurs in the crucial (and extremely difficult) paragraph in which absolute knowing rises to the surface of consciousness [796]. At this point, consciousness realizes that the act in which the philosopher thinks the world conceptually is "imaged" in the willful self-creativity of moral action. We must now enter the movement of the acting self and re-experience it from the perspective of the philosophic knower.

Religion and conscientious action are separate reconciliations that must be reconciled with each other [796]. In religion, the Concept fulfilled itself on the side of *content.* Christianity is absolute truth in the form of picture-thoughts. In action, the Concept appears as pure *form,* that is, pure self-certainty. Since the goal is to give the content of Christian picture-thinking or imagination the form of selfhood, the comprehensive reconciliation must emerge from within the self that acts as a morally self-certain knower.

The acting self "carries out the life of absolute spirit" [796]. That is, action contains the whole journey of spirit in the logical structure of its movement. The acting self is in fact the three-fold Concept realizing itself in the world. It recapitulates the three stages of the Christian God: self-identical Father, the Son who is the Father's other, and the Spirit by which the Son returns to the Father. Action is the Concept that sunders itself from itself and "surrenders its eternal essence" (like God the Father). This self-sundering is implicit in the purity of the Concept, which is "abstraction or negativity itself." In other words, the self-splitting that occurs in action (the split between one's inner selfhood and outer deed) is the same split that occurs when thought "goes outside itself" in order to think what is, the external world of objects. Thought loses itself or dies in these objects, which thought seeks to know. As we shall soon see, this is precisely how thought also finds itself as the truth of those objects.

Hegel distinguishes between the moral thinking of the Doer and the morally disinterested, truth-directed thinking of the philosopher, even as he interweaves them. The former is *negative* (or desirous), the latter *positive* [796]. The Doer embodies thinking as willing. His goal is not to know the truth but to change the world and put his mark on it (like Napoleon), to negate what is there and replace it with something new. Action in this sense is revolutionary. Philosophic "action," the act of thinking, is by contrast not a product of will. It is positive in the sense that it seeks to change, not the content of what is there but only its immediate, sensuous form. The philosopher observes what is there in his sense-experience with conceptual understanding. He strives for knowledge of the truth. In his relation to what is there, he is conservative rather than revolutionary or progressive. The Hegelian philosopher preserves what has been rather than brings about what will be. He is the exact opposite of an ideologist.[34]

In thinking the world, the philosopher pulls the world into and toward himself. He experiences the withdrawal into self or *Insichgehen* that religion called a being-evil [*Bösesein*]. Like the beautiful soul, the philosopher "*does not act* and *is not actual.*" This withdrawal into pure knowing is "the antithesis of the Concept." The morally acting individual yielded to his Napoleonic impulse and found himself opposed to his pure inwardness or knowledge. He had a bad conscience. But the pure disinterested thinker "participates in" and consciously posits antithesis or other-being. Otherness does not take him by surprise.

To the extent that the philosopher is a particular self who turns within, his act of knowing is "for itself" or egotistical and evil: my knowing is *my* knowing. But insofar as the object or "in itself" content of this thinking is universal *knowledge* of what is, rather than mere self-assertion or will to power, pure thinking is good [796]. Philosophic knowing thus overcomes the dialectic in religion between good and evil. It is the act in which self-assertion—our will to power and divinity—*sacrifices itself* for the sake of the thing known. In Christian terms, pure philosophic knowing is the act in which an individual (the philosopher) dies to his pure *form* (self-assertiveness) in order to know a *content* (the absolute or divine truth of the objects of experience). The philosopher, in this sense, is a Napoleon who has been humbled by the love of objective truth, and a Christian who has been made justly proud of himself as a rational being. Philosophy is born when pride and humility, will and devotion, drink in each other's spirit.

At this point of our journey, what was previously only implicit or in itself, consciousness now experiences explicitly or for itself. Consequently, the act of conceptual knowing—qua action of a singular self—does not need absolution, the correction of its exclusive being-for-self, from another (either God or the human community). Unlike moral action, it is self-sublating or, as we may also call it, self-absolving.[35] The pure knowledge of the objects of experience validates or justifies itself because its end is not private self-actualization but knowledge that is concrete and universal or open to everyone. The philosopher is the singular self that loves the universal for its own sake and wants what he knows to be known by all human beings. Philosophic knowing is selfhood that becomes God in the very act of dying to self for the sake of the things known—for the sake of truth.[36]

This knowing is the new spirit that overcomes the one-sidedness of the two previous spirits: morality and religion (formal willing and content-rich believing). Moral self-will and religious self-sacrifice experience what Hegel calls an *Ablassen* or *letting-go*. Each side lets go of the stubborn determinateness that keeps it apart from the other. In the act of pure knowing, the self experiences the reconciliation in which each of these spirits dies [*stirbt*] to its one-sidedness. The moral Doer dies to his will to power, religion "to its non-living self and to its unmoved universality" (its static heaven) [796]. The former achieves a universal *essence* and content (knowledge of the truth), the latter a living *self.* Absolute knowing comes to be *there,* to be existent and manifest, in this final moment when these two already existent shapes transcend their limitations and self-destruct.

All this happens through *action, das Handeln:* "It is only through action [i.e. selfhood at work] that spirit is in such a way that it is there, that is, when it raises its being-there into thought and thereby into an absolute antithesis, and returns out of this antithesis, in and through the antithesis itself" [796]. This is the positive self-externalization Hegel talked about at the beginning of the chapter. Only in philosophic knowing conceived as a lived event (by analogy with moral action) does consciousness experience the being-there of spirit. In pure knowing, which only now becomes an historical event, spirit is *there* in such a way that its self-otherness is explicit and contained within spirit itself. Simply put, when I think the external world conceptually, I am communing with my own selfhood. And my thinking is the actual appearance and manifestation of spirit that is *bei sich* or with itself in its externality.[37]

Hegel now summarizes the previous movement: "Thus, what in religion was *content* or a form for representing an *other,* is here the *self's* own *act* [*Tun*]; the Concept requires the *content* to be the *self's* own *act*" [797]. The self, in thinking, goes outside itself only to find itself as the essence and substance of the external world of things.[38] Truth, at last, is grasped, by consciousness itself, as subject as well as substance [17]. *Our* act has consisted only in gathering separately appearing moments, each of which contains the whole life of spirit, and watching them develop conceptually.[39]

At long last, Hegel names the final shape of spirit: *absolute knowing* [798]. This is spirit that gives the vast range and content of its experience the form of self or Concept. In the act of thinking its objects conceptually, in thinking the logic of the whole, spirit finally "knows itself in the shape of spirit" and transcends the depictions of religion. Picture has become *logos.* In contemplating divine truth, I am also contemplating my act of thinking—my very selfhood. *I* die to my particular self in order to know objects in their universality, and at the same time *they* die as beings separate from my act of thinking. They have my form of selfhood and I have them as my objective content. *What was formerly the work of divine self-sacrifice is now manifested in my actual self-consciousness.* Thanks to man, essence or pure Concept is *there:* it exists. This essence of pure thinking that also exists is *Science.* Science, *Wissenschaft,* is spirit that appears or manifests itself in the element of *Dasein* or being-there. It is inwardness that is present to itself as an object of consciousness.

Self-consciousness, we recall, is "the native kingdom of truth" [167]. The meaning of this assertion is now clear. Science is self-consciousness that has gotten beyond its mere negativity or desire, and experiences itself as the divine, positive essence of the world. It is the "pure being-for-self" of the preceding dialectic of action: the self-affirmation that renounced its willfulness and became the animating soul of religious truth. This being-for-self that now constitutes absolute truth is *both* this particular I and no other, *and* the mediated or universal I [799]. That is, absolute knowing expresses both my unique selfhood and the identity of this selfhood with the universal self of absolute spirit. As a fully rational being, I find my particular self manifested in the universal selfhood of all humanity, in "an achieved community of minds" [69].[40] This community is the *Concept* (the universal form of intelligibility) as the self-differentiating One—the being-at-home of identity within difference.

As Hegel reminded us earlier, absolute knowing is not itself the Science of logic (where the subject-object opposition is absent) but the preparation for logic [789]. It is Science as it appears within *consciousness,* the realm of objects. Absolute knowing is what allows consciousness to see the *Phenomenology of Spirit* as the story of its own self-generated life. It is the self-knowledge in which the self has for its content only itself, its divisions and movement [799]. The self is finally transparent to itself in its self-objectifications. It is only when the self is "with its own self" [*ist bei sich selbst*] in its otherness or objects that the complete range of conscious experience is conceptually grasped [*begriffen*]. As Hegel now sums it up, the true content of this Science of experience is the history and movement of consciousness. This movement is spirit "that traverses its own self and does so *for itself* [or knowingly] as spirit by the fact that it has the 'shape' of the Concept in its objectivity [*Gegenständlichkeit*]." In absolute knowing, the journey of consciousness is *for* consciousness itself.

We get a clearer idea of the problems Hegel claims to be solving in this section if we consider, on the basis of what we have seen above, what absolute knowing is *not.* It is not a comic consciousness that scorns religion and the divine, thus abandoning absolute truth. It is not the Enlightenment, whose pursuit of conceptuality merely dissolves and "sees through" things but does not shed any light on them. It is not Christian faith in any of its forms, although it inherits and preserves the entire content of that faith. It is not a Napoleonic will to power or an effete beautiful soul. It is not Plato and Aristotle, since objective being has been thoroughly imbued with self-consciousness. And it is not Kant's transcendental philosophy, since the self's spontaneity or act of knowing is not limited to the subjective organization of sense data.

The complex path to absolute knowing has encoded within it Hegel's attempt to solve *all* the problems of philosophy at one stroke. The Christian religion is central to this pan-solution because it contains, in picture form, all the reconciliations, self-sacrifices, and paradoxes that point to dialectical overcoming as the absolute truth. Once the Concept's self-sacrificial or "Christian" movement is experienced as truth, "hard" determinations become solvent, opposites flow into each other without ceasing to be opposite, and all the universal rifts are healed.

Science and the Kingdom of Time [800–804]

The final part of Hegel's chapter is about the necessary relation between the Concept and time, that is, between self-knowledge and history. Spirit's self-knowledge takes the form of Science. In its general meaning, Science refers to Hegel's whole System. Here it is, more specifically, spirit's awareness of itself in history: its ability to give a purely conceptual account of itself as the divine *logos* of historical *Dasein* or being-there. As I noted earlier, this is the knowledge contained in the *Phenomenology of Spirit.*

Science is the Concept that is *there.* It "does not appear in time and actuality before spirit has attained to this consciousness about itself" [800]. History is spirit striving to know itself as the substance of all things. It achieves this self-knowledge by assuming various experiential shapes. Through these shapes, spirit objectifies its self-knowledge and makes it concretely present. As Hegel puts it, spirit must equate its self-consciousness with its consciousness [800]. Spirit is like an artist engaged in self-portraiture. It struggles in one work after another until the object that stands before it fully captures its self-knowledge, or rather until spirit fully *occupies* what it has made. Self-knowledge, for Hegel, is not simply discovered. It is produced in time so that it may be discovered. Self-knowledge as something produced rather than simply found is the direct result of the previous part of Hegel's chapter, which established the identity of acting individual self and divine universal truth.

A huge amount of experience was necessary in order to reach this point. At first, truth was in the object rather than the subject: in the This, the thing, and force. But soon it became clear that force was nascent self-consciousness, and that the subject was the truth of all objects. Self-consciousness, the true "force" in the world, was initially violent. Its desire for recognition, the self's first inkling of itself as absolute, led to a fight to the death. All the self-assertiveness that comes on the scene with self-consciousness, from the fight for recognition to the Reign of Terror, is selfhood seeking to make itself absolute. The self does not yet know that its practical-productive will to power is in fact the speculative will to truth as self-knowledge.

THE SELF IN HISTORY

The history of self-consciousness is the saga of alienation. Expelled from Greek Eden (the garden of nature-like custom), individuals are aware of themselves as meaningless atoms of subjectivity. This is the spirit of Rome, the historical epoch in which spirit's consciousness of objects and its self-consciousness are utterly disparate. The Roman individual *feels* the self-differentiating moment of the Concept but can make no sense of it. Lacking experience of a concrete universal self or community, he flees his actual world and seeks freedom as a stoic, a skeptic, or an unhappy consciousness.

With the rise of Christian Europe, history becomes explicitly the history of spirit or God on earth. Hegel's "knowing substance" [801] is "the Christian world of the Empire and the Papacy" (Harris, 2:729). Christianity begins with an "as yet undeveloped in-itself" [801]. This is the rigid objectivity of the medieval Church, which stands over and against the individual as the Christian Rome. The Church is the Concept in its "unmoved simplicity." Inwardness and self are not yet manifest. The "turn to self" comes on the scene with Luther's Reformation. This is the true beginning of modernity. At first, the cognition [*Erkennen*] embodied in Christianity has only a "poor or impoverished object." That is, the unhappy consciousness experiences God as simply not here, and itself as merely destitute. In reformed *faith,* the believer experiences God and the consciousness of God as "richer." He looks with confidence toward the Kingdom of Heaven. But this happy thought of God only seems to reveal the truth. In fact, it is a *concealment,* an act in which the individual buries his selfhood and reason. God is still only a "being without selfhood," and the believer has revealed to him, not divine truth, but only the fallible self-certainty of his *credo* or "I believe."

As we saw in Hegel's chapter on religion, Christianity's triune God (Father, Son, and Holy Spirit) spells out the three moments of the Concept. But for the believing self, these are only "abstract moments of [divine] substance," not moments of the self's own spiritual life and knowledge.[41] The three moments of the Concept are experienced as the self's own movement in the *secular* life of spirit—the spirit of self-actualizing *reason.* Ultimately, reason becomes the Enlightenment, which seeks to bring heaven down to earth. In the course of this whole secular movement, "self-consciousness enriches itself until it has wrested from consciousness the entire [divine] substance and has absorbed into itself the entire building or structure [*Bau*] of the essentialities of this substance" [801]. In other words, human self-consciousness, as reason, appropriates the world and makes itself rather than God the essence of that world. Reason is self-absolutizing.

The appropriation looks like theft. The world belonged to consciousness (the realm of objective authorities and institutions): now it belongs to self-consciousness. But as we saw in the previous dialectic, the secular spirit of self-assertion and the sacred spirit of devotion *give themselves to each other* and are reconciled in the higher, more comprehensive spirit of absolute knowing. The objectivity that the self "steals" from consciousness or objectivity it gives back in an enriched form. Absolute knowing transcends the Enlightenment's merely negative, revolutionary attitude toward what *is* (the world-destroying *desire* of the Terror). The self that knows absolutely—the philosophic self—appropriates the world. But in that same act, it also reproduces the world as the self's objective embodiment or incarnation [801].[42] Subjectivity, which is both individual and universal, constitutes the world and gives it divine objective meaning. It is subject that is also substance, self-certainty that is also truth.

Hegel now observes that from the perspective of "the Concept that knows itself as Concept" (the perspective of pure knowing), the whole comes to be from the movement of its separate moments. Logically, these moments precede the emergent whole. This is the order we readers have followed in our phenomenological journey. For consciousness, however, the whole comes first. That is, the experience of the world comes first. The whole, though not yet comprehended, must be lived in its wholeness before it can be analyzed, before we know what our conceptually grasped moments are moments *of.*

TIME

With this observation, Hegel reaches what is perhaps the most remarkable revelation in the whole *Phenomenology:* the rational essence of *time.* Prior to absolute knowing, time is experienced as the always vanishing Now of indefinite on-goingness. This Now, as we saw in sense-certainty, is the Now that always negates itself and becomes a Then or Has-been. Time slips through our fingers. It seems to flow from an indefinite Way Back When off into an equally indefinite Yet to Be. This is the "bad infinity" Hegel first mentioned in his chapter on reason [238]. Eternity, by contrast, is posited as utterly beyond time and in no way participating in time. It first emerged in the Platonism of the understanding and its "restful kingdom of law" [149].

Absolute knowing unites time and eternity, pure negativity and positive divine essence, motion and rest. Soon Hegel will identify absolute knowing as recollection or *Erinnerung* [808]. Absolute knowing neither loses God and truth in an endless time-sequence nor "blasts off" into a timeless Beyond. Philosophy looks back and sees that time is not an indefinitely long straight line but a self-completing circle. In his role as phenomenologist, the philosopher weaves spirit's past into a whole, or rather *lets* that past appear in language as the whole that it really is. "Time," Hegel says, "is the Concept itself that *is there* or exists, and that presents itself to consciousness as empty intuition; for this reason, spirit necessarily appears in time, and it appears in time just so long as it does not grasp [*erfaßt*] its pure Concept, i.e. does not annul [*tilgt*] time."[43]

Time is the other-being of human *Dasein,* whose logical structure the *Phenomenology of Spirit* seeks to uncover. Spirit is present to itself "in" time so long as it is outside itself, that is, so long as its essence is not present in its existence.[44] This being-outside-itself or other-being is inherent to spirit and to the Concept. Time is not an indifferent receptacle or "river" in which the Concept simply happens to appear.[45] The Concept is "in" time only because time, as actual self-otherness, is logically implicit "in" the Concept. That is why spirit *necessarily* appears in time: why man experiences himself temporally.

Spirit intuits itself in time—or rather, *as* time. It is in immediate contact with itself as *on the way* to its destined end. Time *is* spirit insofar as spirit suffers, or is burdened with, the subject-object opposition—insofar as it endures the hard life of consciousness and other-being.[46] Once absolute knowing arrives, that is, once spirit knows itself as spirit (as essentially self-alienating), time *as historical transition* is canceled or annulled. The Concept is no longer strange to itself in its otherness. It has reached the point at which it is not the self's immediate intuition of itself but a mediated logical movement—a perfectly rational, self-knowing *grasp.* Time as process is necessarily deleted when the Concept gets beyond its step-by-step becoming (its being other than itself) and grasps that becoming as a whole, when, in an atemporal act of knowing, it grasps the logic of its movement.[47] In Spinoza's phrase, time is annulled when it is seen "under the look of eternity."

Intuition, for Hegel, is deficient because it lacks the mediation that dialectical logic alone can supply. As spirit (communal selfhood) unfolds in time, it intuits itself. To this extent, it fails to *know* itself. When the moment of absolute knowing arrives, spirit "sublates its time-form" and enjoys a logical grasp of what was previously only intuited [801]. It is important to recall, in this context especially, that "sublate" means preserve as well as destroy. In absolute knowing, spirit transcends its temporality. But it also *preserves* time by revealing time's purely logical, timeless structure. Hegel makes this point by saying that absolute knowing is "a conceptualized and conceptualizing intuition" [801].

Time "appears as the Fate [*das Schicksal*] and necessity of spirit that is not yet complete within itself." In Hyppolite's formulation, time is "the disquiet [*inquiétude*] of consciousness that has not attained itself, which sees itself as outside itself" (579). Hegel's reference to Fate recalls Greek tragedy. But Fate is no longer the blind necessity that descends on individuals, cities, and peoples from the outside. It is not unaccountable or strange. On the contrary, Fate is inner compulsion that has the logical structure of the self.[48] It is the tension within consciousness that drives consciousness through its appointed Stations of the Cross [77] on toward complete self-knowledge. Spirit, to be sure, learns through suffering. But this suffering is spirit's self-imposed burden and act.[49]

Hegel cites the familiar generality that knowledge must begin with experience [802]. In the present context, this refers to religious, Lutheran experience. Nothing is known to be true "that is not *felt to be true,* not given as an *inwardly revealed* eternal verity, as something sacred that is *believed.*" Time is the Concept that does not yet know itself as Concept. That is why religious experience is temporally prior to philosophy. The object—God as the embodiment of divine wisdom—must be present to consciousness before it can be infused with selfhood and logical movement. Religion must complete itself, run through its course, before truth is grasped as subject or self. Spirit must complete itself as *world*-spirit, as the "belief of the world," before divine truth becomes reflective and is transformed into philosophy as Science. Absolute content necessarily precedes absolute form (conceptuality or logic) because consciousness must precede self-consciousness, just as actual immediate experience must precede knowledge. Before we can think purely, we need something to think about.[50]

Experience is the medium in which spirit is conscious of itself as object [802]. *Spirit is not a being but a process.* It is "the coming-to-be [*Werden*] of what it is in itself [or as substance]; and it is only as this self-reflecting coming-to-be that it is in itself truly spirit." Spirit's movement is its cognition. It is the transformation "of substance into subject, of the object of *consciousness* into an object of *self-consciousness.*" Spirit's reflective movement is "the circle that returns into itself, the circle that presupposes its beginning and reaches it only at the end." Initially, spirit only intuits itself in its wholeness. Spirit must first build a world that is the home and temple of its self-knowledge. This world provides the substantial basis of spirit's reflection into self, its "matter." Again, experience here is *religious* experience. Religion is temporally prior to philosophy because spirit must be felt before it can be conceptually known: it must be conscious of its object before it can be self-conscious, or see itself in its object. Religion builds the substantial social world and belief-system, of which philosophy is the internal movement and self-knowledge.[51]

MODERN PHILOSOPHY AS THE EVOLUTION OF THE TIME-CONCEPT

Hegel now turns to the *movement* in which spirit brings forth "the form of its self-knowledge," that is, truth in the form of self [803]. This labor is spirit's "actual history."

The history of spirit that knows itself as spirit begins with the medieval Christian Church and ends with Hegel's absolute knowing. The religious community of the Holy Roman Empire is absolute spirit at the level of substance (divine authority on earth). The consciousness of this community is raw or brutal [*rohe*]. Its "barbaric" existence (Hegel is no doubt thinking of the Crusades) derives from its spiritual *depth,* which, because undeveloped, makes spirit obstinate and immovable. The Church does not incline to change from the inside but must be forced to change through the Reformation. With Luther, spirit reaches a breaking point. Despairing of overcoming man's alienation from God through external "works" and exercises imposed by the Church, it *turns to itself,* to inner conscience and heart as the first expression of true freedom [803].

But this inward turn is incomplete. The individual feels his absoluteness, the presence of God within him, but does not yet regard himself as the truth and end of the actual world. This is the project of modern science and modern philosophy. The self no longer merely feels: it thinks. In thinking, I make the world my own, my *property* [803]. The first stage is Baconian observation, which embodies the Category, the immediate identity of thought and being [235]. This identity reaches "a purer form" in **Descartes**, who champions reason as "the primal Light." This is truth as *clarity and distinctness.* Through Descartes, the modern spirit of self-certainty expresses itself as the posited but unexplained unity of *thought* and *extension,* or, equivalently, *thought* and *space.*[52] *Dasein,* being-there, at this point means only being-in-space.

The oriental aspect of Descartes' Zoroastrianism, his "worship" of intellectual light, becomes explicit in **Spinoza**, whose God is the single *substance* in which extension and thought are unified. Spirit, however, "recoils in horror" from this abstraction, which suppresses selfhood and individuality. For a truer expression of its essence and freedom, spirit manifests itself in **Leibniz**. Leibniz' metaphysics of the monad preserves the unity of thought and being. But unlike the substance doctrine of Spinoza, it "affirms individuality" by giving all human beings a share in divine substance. We are all "little gods" in what Leibniz calls "the most perfect republic" (*Discourse on Metaphysics* 36).

Spirit reaches self-knowledge through world-historic revolution. In its initial, inert life of substance and external authority, spirit had to be shaken by the Reformation in order to reach a clearer knowledge of itself as self or subject. This upheaval enables Descartes, Spinoza, and Leibniz to bring Luther's inward turn to the level of universal reason—to raise *heart* to *mind.* Spirit must now be shaken once more in order to reach a clearer self-knowledge, this time by the self-alienating culture world and the French Revolution [803]. Before spirit can rationally articulate its deeper self-knowledge, the world must first experience a new burst of self-certainty and freedom.

Culture and the Enlightenment produce the next triad of modern philosophic heroes: **Kant**, **Fichte**, and **Schelling**.[53] This is the reign of German

Idealism, whose crowning moment is Hegel himself (the King of the Moderns). Kant's Copernican Revolution in philosophy, which makes the self the ground of nature, inaugurates the "second wave" of modern thought—the "first wave" having started with Descartes' "I think." Descartes and Kant are the philosophic co-founders of the modern age and Hegel's most important forerunners.

In German idealism, spirit becomes more acutely aware that absolute truth resides in the self or subject, that selfhood is the ground of all being, essence, and value. *Utility* provides the bridge to the emergence of the self as knowingly absolute. The public belief that the world is *for me* paves the way for the French Revolution and its orgy of sheer willing. Through this violent world-experience, the self, at last fully aware of itself as absolutely free or unbounded, can reveal its "inmost depths" in Kant's I = I (the transcendental unity of apperception). This I = I expresses the certainty that all objects of experience are *for* my knowing and are grounded in the self's unshakeable "I AM MYSELF!" The "activism" of self-certainty is, however, only implicit in Kant's formal, static I. Fichte makes the I's activism explicit. He reveals the primordial act of *self-positing*, in which the I makes itself real and affirms its absolute freedom or "I AM MYSELF."[54] The I here posits itself as op-posed by a non-I or object. It posits an "absolute difference" between subject and object, which difference, however, does not affect the I's absolute self-identity [803].[55]

But although Fichte expresses the absolute activism of the self, he, like Kant, ignores the self's dialectical character and treats I = I as a static tautology. Self-identity is a mere equal sign, not the *movement* in which the I differentiates itself from itself in order to be the same as itself [803, 166]. Hegel notes that the self-difference that Fichte unveils within the structure of the I (the internal difference between the I and the non-I) is properly expressed as *time*. Time is the experiential medium in which the self experiences itself as objective and other, the medium in which the self is *for itself.* Hegel observes that the first wave of modernity (as I have called it) asserted "the unity of thinking and extension." It posited *space* as essential and all other properties as accidental.[56] To think was to think something that was there, and things were there insofar as they were extended or in space. But the *self-difference* that is implicit in Fichte's I = I suggests, on the contrary, "the unity of thinking and time" [803].

Schelling is the third shape in the post-revolutionary phase of the self's rational expression. He goes beyond Kant and Fichte for several reasons. One is that philosophy, for Kant and Fichte, is confined to the inner workings of subjectivity. Schelling, by contrast, brings philosophy back to its passion for knowing the *truth.*[57] Another reason is that, in his so-called Identity Philosophy, Schelling posits an absolute that overcomes Fichte's opposition of the self and the non-self. Unfortunately, Schelling's absolute does not preserve opposition but simply obliterates it. The absolute is a tertium quid or "third something" that is neither subject nor object [804]. Schelling therefore cannot explain why thinking has any content. Content, or difference, is either tossed "into the empty abyss of the absolute" or merely "picked up in external fashion from sense-perception." The latter refers to Schelling's philosophy of nature. The former recalls what Hegel wittily said of Schelling's absolute in the Preface: that it was "the night in which all cows are black" [16].

Hegel ends his review of spirit's "actual history" with the two philosophic shapes that frame the dichotomy spirit must overcome. One is the *beautiful soul,* which is God's self-intuition [795]. Its historical archetype is **Hölderlin**, whose theories of identity and difference had a major influence on Hegel.[58] The beautiful soul tried to preserve the purity of its selfhood by "the withdrawing [*Zurückziehen*] of self-consciousness into its pure inwardness" [804]. The other philosophic shape is **Schelling**, whose absolute represents "the submerging [*Versenken*] of self-consciousness into substance" and the suppression of difference.[59] Hölderlin and Schelling both take refuge in an intuition that shuns "the labor of the Concept" or philosophy as *work* [70].[60]

Spirit is neither of these shapes but rather the movement that combines them as its moments. This is the self-alienating movement of the Concept that has been revealed as the rational essence of time. In this movement, the self "makes itself external to itself and sinks itself into its substance [or social world], and also, as subject, has gone out of that substance into itself, making the substance into an object and a content at the same time that it cancels [its] difference from [its] objectivity and content." Spirit is not Descartes' "I think," or Kant's formal I = I, or Fichte's absolute ego, or the pure inner of the beautiful soul, or Schelling's Absolute Indifferent. It is rather the movement of actual, European history—the unfolding experience of humanity as universal selfhood. History reveals the self-otherness and self-alienation that are essential to spirit. It is the realm in which universal selfhood externalizes itself by making various social worlds. These worlds are selfhood that has made itself into substance. In other words, human history reveals divine truth, the eternal logic of the Concept emptied out into time. Time is the self-otherness, the *suffering,* of spirit.

The self at first finds itself completely united with its social substance (the Greek *polis*). This is its temporal experience of the Concept's first, atemporal moment. Then the self distinguishes itself from the social substance in which it is immersed. The I feels its own spontaneity or independence, experiences itself as something on its own. This is the modern alienation embodied in the Concept's second, self-differentiating moment. Its extreme form is the self-withdrawal or *Insichgehen* of the beautiful soul. As Hegel puts it, the self experiences the *rising* [*Aufgehen*] of its own *Dasein* or being-there. In the third stage of its historical self-movement, the self must then *go back down* "into the simple substance [of its social world]." This third moment is that of *absolute knowing*, which Hegel soon calls recollection [808]. Here, the self, having suffered alienation, and having resisted the Siren song of romantic despair (Hölderlin), immerses itself once more in the realm of self-difference. This time, however, it acknowledges self-difference as its own act, the act in which it comes to know itself. Spirit can now sing its own epic and produce its own play. It can present itself to itself as self-fated rather than fated by blind necessity or the gods. Spirit, manifested in Hegel, can write its glorious memoirs and be, at once, Philosophic Poet and Hero. It can see itself in its various historical shapes and in the logical movement that connects these shapes.

The central problem of philosophy, and of humanity, is that of overcoming the dichotomy of self and world, subject and object.[61] Fichte made this perfectly clear in his primordial opposition of the I and the non-I within the structure of the I itself. But in order to solve the problem, in order to heal the rift in man, we must resist the intuitionism of both the beautiful soul and Schelling. Since self-otherness (time) is the realm in which the self is fully itself, the I does not need to shun objectivity and existence and withdraw into itself, as if it had a fear [*Angst*] of being self-external. Nor does it need to overcome dichotomies in an absolute Indifferent that is neither self nor non-self. Genuine selfhood is spirit, which is communal or social. Spirit, in other words, is at home in the realm of temporal self-externalization [759]. Its absolute knowing is the "seeming inactivity [*scheinbaren Untätigkeit*], which only contemplates how the differentiated itself moves in its own self and turns back into its unity" [804].

The Passion According to Hegel [805–8]

With absolute knowing, spirit concludes "the movement of its shaping [*seines Gestaltens*], insofar as this process was burdened with the difference of consciousness, a difference that has been overcome" [805]. This difference is the separation of subject and object [82]. Spirit now grasps itself *as movement.* In so doing, it has "won the pure element of its *Dasein,* the Concept." Spirit now sees past all its previously postulated or pictured Beyonds. It sees that the Beyond is, in truth, not a static otherworldly place but the logical process of self-transcendence, the *beyond-ing* by which spirit dies in one shape in order to rise again in another.[62]

Hegel here continues his critique of Schelling's Absolute Indifferent. The true absolute is not the passive night in which all cows are black but the "anxious" or dialectically tense *night of self-consciousness,* out of which spirit generates its own content. Spirit is like Jesus, that beautiful soul in the garden of Gethsemane, who accepts the cup of suffering—the "Cross" of time, self-loss, and death—in order to fulfill his divine destiny as a divine self. In accepting the cup of suffering, Jesus, as the religious symbol of philosophic truth, is the God who *wills* to be historical and self-other.

Spirit gives itself content through the process of self-alienation: it makes itself an other, that is, an object. This object is its social substance or world. Spirit is not a vague transcendent God that works outside of time but rather the immanent divine force of universal selfhood that constitutes history. Spirit's movement is both free and necessary [805]. It is free because spirit's content or world is generated by spirit itself, necessary because the various worldly shapes that spirit assumes have a logical structure and are logically interrelated. Hegel's main point is that this determinate content or difference is not an *in-itself* that stands over and against consciousness with no necessary grounding in consciousness. It is the result of the self's own "restless process of superseding itself," the negativity that *is* the self. This is the "beyond-ing" I noted above. The self's other is spirit in its necessary moment of self-otherness. Consequently, the various shapes of consciousness that spirit has assumed are all shapes of self, that is, *Concepts.* In having "won the Concept," spirit has acquired the ability to know itself purely, apart from its phenomenal shapes. It has won what Hegel calls the "ether of its life." This is Science, *Wissenschaft,* whose first part is the Science of logic.

In logic, the specific moments of dialectical movement are no longer "shapes of consciousness" but "determinate Concepts," pure thoughts [805]. Instead of beginning with the shape of *sense-certainty,* for example, logic will start with the Concept of *pure being.* Phenomenology studies the difference between knowledge and truth, and the path by which this difference is overcome. Logic embodies the "immediate unity" of knowledge and truth. In logic, thinking and being are the same (idealism in its precise sense). Logic, here, is not the logic of desire but the logic of pure conceptual unfolding and development. Although phenomenology and logic are distinct, they mirror each other: "to each abstract moment of Science [logic] corresponds a shape of appearing spirit as such."[63] Phenomenology and logic are thus *equally rich in content.* The difference is that phenomenology is spirit in the mode of historical being-there and actuality, while logic is spirit in the mode of eternal essence and pure thinking.

We have gone from phenomenology to logic, from spirit's existence to its pure self-knowledge. But absolute knowing is more than the end of spirit's historical movement. It is also that movement's true *beginning:* "Science contains within itself [the] necessity of externalizing the form of the pure Concept" [806]. That is, the Concept contains the necessity of its actual appearance as a shape of consciousness. We have come full circle. In absolute knowing, spirit or universal selfhood "grasps its Concept" and thus is identical with itself in its self-difference. This immediate identity of subject and object is precisely "*sense-consciousness*—the beginning from which we started" [806]. Sense-certainty is the "supreme freedom and assurance" with which the Concept steps forth into the realm of existence or *Dasein.* The Concept freely *releases* itself from the ether of its pure thinking, from its pure form, because it is sure of finding itself in its other.[64]

This self-externalization is, however, still incomplete [807]. In the subject-object opposition that we encounter in phenomenology, the self merely *relates* to an object and so "has not yet won its complete freedom." It does not yet experience itself as having become other to itself *as* this object, and so has not reached its extreme of self-alienation—its *death* as spirit. "To know one's limit," Hegel says, "is to know how to sacrifice oneself." This complete surrender and abandonment to objectivity, which goes beyond mere relation-to-object, is the "free contingent happening" of *nature.*[65] Nature exists as an independent realm apart from our conscious relation to objects. It is spirit's radical other. It is spirit itself in its most extreme alienation from itself. As nature, spirit intuits itself as time and space. Nature is not the result of creation, as it is depicted in the book of Genesis. Creation, philosophically understood, is not a miraculous past event but rather the "eternal externalization of [spirit's] *continuing existence or being-there* and the movement that produces [*herstellt*] the *subject.*" The movement reinstates the subject because natural *Dasein* or being-there is the necessary ground of self-consciousness. Man as self-consciousness exists in nature because nature is selfhood in its extreme self-otherness and self-alienation.

Spirit "dies to self" in nature, its radical other, knowing that, after an initial oblivion or self-forgetting, it will eventually find itself there. This refinding of itself is the "other side" of spirit's coming-to-be or *Werden: history* [808].[66] Nature is spirit's "living immediate becoming." History, however, is "a *conscious* self-*mediating* process—spirit emptied out into time." In other words, although nature is a realm of change, this change is only repetition of the same: in nature the same things happen over and over again.[67] History, by contrast, is genuine change, by which old things become new. It is a change in the human order of things, the emergence of *what it means to be human.* As nature, spirit posits itself as simply alienated from itself. History is the process by which this self-externalization is inverted and overcome. In history, spirit externalizes its self-externalization, alienates its alienation, and comes home to itself. This historical movement is necessary because nature *is* spirit externalized. History makes explicit the self-identity that is implicit in spirit's self-difference as nature.

Hegel now puts forth his image of history as a spiritual *picture gallery* [808]. The colorful shapes of consciousness—the various character types we have met in Hegel's book—emerge successively. To pursue Hegel's theological metaphor, they are all divine self-portraits, scenes from the biography, or rather the autobiography, of God. Each shape or "picture" contains "all the riches of spirit." These shapes are not parts of spirit but, like Leibnizian monads, the *whole* of spirit from a specific point of view. That is why the procession of spirits is slow: because "the self has to penetrate and digest this entire wealth of its [social] substance."

Spirit empties itself in two acts of self-alienation: as nature and as history. But whereas in nature spirit is starkly self-alienated, in history spirit comes home to itself through the inwardizing process of *recollection, Erinnerung.* Platonic recollection is the remembrance of the interconnected whole of eternal Forms (*Meno* 81C).[68] For Hegel, however, recollection is a necessary moment of the temporal, historical process itself. History does not simply advance from one substance-world to the next. Inwardness is involved, a dynamic interplay of inner and outer. Spirit empties itself, makes itself present as a substantial world in space and time. It then abandons this outer world it has built and, in order to comprehend that world, "gives its shape over to inwardizing or recollection." It *extends* itself as a world and then plunges into its own depths.[69]

Hegel's description of this inwardizing process recalls the suffering of Jesus in the garden of Gethsemane.[70] In leaving its daylight social world, spirit "is sunk in the night of its self-consciousness." But in abandoning its outer world, spirit also preserves that world and raises it to a new level. The former world is *sublated* or *aufgehoben.* Whereas the "old world" was merely intuited, the "new world" that now arises embodies spirit's self-knowledge. It is the world born of spirit's alienation and suffering. In recollection or inwardizing—*Er-Innerung,* as Hegel writes the word—spirit does not simply leave its substantial world: it achieves "the higher form" of that world. Thanks to recollection, we now have a true *world of knowing.*[71]

The *Phenomenology* ends with world-history as the home and vessel of spirit. There is only one spirit. But it reveals itself, makes itself concrete, as a succession of spirits. Each age has its distinctive governing spirit. In the order of historical time, each spirit takes over "the empire of the world" from its predecessor [808]. Their goal is "the revelation [*Offenbarung*] of the depth of spirit, and this is *the absolute Concept.*" In this revelation, spirit spreads itself out and opens itself up to the world. It embraces time as spirit's own self-otherness (rather than as incomprehensible Fate). Time is not merely the realm of mortality. It is also the "time of the Concept," the time in which self-knowledge and eternal truth become *real.*

Absolute knowing is spirit that knows itself as spirit. This self-knowledge has been the goal of spirit's whole journey. Spirit knows itself by knowing where, and what, it has been. By spirit, here, we must remember that Hegel does not mean a God who hovers over human existence. Spirit is universal selfhood that is concretely present in human communities. It is the unity of time and eternity, existence and knowledge. In absolute knowing, spirit gives a logical account of its past shapes. It weaves them together into the *logos* of *phainomena* that is the *Phenomenology of Spirit.*

Hegel ends with the twofold meaning of history. In one sense, history is the free emergence of spirit's various shapes. It is the sphere of contingent happening or nature. But insofar as history is philosophically understood, it is "the Science of knowing in the sphere of appearance," or the *Phenomenology.* Both together constitute what Hegel calls *begriffene Geschichte,* "conceptually grasped history." The outer and inner senses of history form "the inwardizing or recollection and the Skull-Place of absolute spirit, the actuality, truth, and certainty of [God's] throne, without which he [God] would be the lifeless Alone."

To bring his philosophic epic to a close, Hegel summons the spirit of poetry. Only, he says, "from the chalice of this realm of spirits / foams forth for Him his infinitude." Hegel takes these lines from the finale of Schiller's poem, "Friendship."[72] A translation of the whole stanza reads as follows:

> Friendless was the great Master of the World,
> He felt a lack, and so he fashioned spirits,
> Blessed mirrors of His blessedness!
> The highest Being found no equal;
> From the chalice of the whole realm of souls
> There foamed forth for Him infinitude.

As Kojève observes in his commentary, Hegel changes the passage in three ways (166–67). First, he substitutes "realm of spirits" for "realm of souls"—not in itself that big a change, since Schiller uses "realm of spirits" [*Geisterreich*] in his first stanza. Second, he substitutes "*this* realm" for "*whole* realm," thus excluding angelic beings and limiting the reference to humans. Third, Hegel adds the possessive "his" to Schiller's "infinity." In "this realm of spirits," history, God sees, not an image of himself but himself. In fact, Hegel makes a fourth change: he prefaces the altered stanza with the word "only": "*Only* [my emphasis] 'from the chalice of this realm of spirits / foams forth for Him his infinity.'" This "only" suggests that the Creator is fully present in his creation: that God is fully present in historical time.

At the conclusion of his early work, *Faith and Knowledge* (1802–3), Hegel announces the need for a "speculative Good Friday in place of the historic Good Friday" (190–91). This is the philosophic, purely conceptual account of the "infinite grief" and suffering embodied in the expression, "God is dead." This saying, which defined the unhappy consciousness, sums up all the alienation of the modern world. It is the experience Pascal captured in his "lost" and "hidden" God. Only by giving a logical account of this profound suffering can man attain true freedom and the resurrection of his spirit. In Christian faith, Good Friday is the day on which God sacrificed himself for man and opened up the gates of eternal life. For Hegel, it is the philosophic *image* for world-history as the saga of man's self-alienation in modern culture. At an even deeper level, it is the image for the philosophic *logos* that discloses the finite and the infinite, man and God, as united in time. Philosophy must "go down" in order genuinely to "go up." It must produce the rational form of loss and death, in order for man to experience his life as truly his own, as the earthly embodiment of his divine self-knowledge.

The speculative Good Friday, because it is conceptual, is the ultimate reconciliation of man and God. It is the revelation that God needs man in order to be fully God. God is revealed as spirit in the dialectical process of history, in which the human-divine spirit or "universal individual" [28] dies in one shape in order to be resurrected in another.

It is significant that Hegel's book ends with the Passion rather than Easter Sunday. The true resurrection of spirit—man in history—is the determinate negation within the historical process itself, not a separate moment in which we ascend to heaven.[73] Spirit triumphs over time and death within, and through, the structure of time itself. This is another way of saying what we have noted before: that the whole labyrinth of the *Phenomenology*, with its endless complexities, is simply the persistent mediation of sense-certainty's Here-and-Now, which has been transfigured into historical being-there, and comprehended in the eternal Now of absolute knowing. The *Phenomenology* is the philosopher's unflinching effort to see, say, and preserve what is there. Joseph Conrad said that his vocation as an artist was "to render the highest kind of justice to the visible universe."[74] This is also the goal of the philosophic Passion According to Hegel.

Hegel and the Image

It is fitting that the *Phenomenology* ends with poetry, especially poetry that sings of the need for universal friendship or reconciliation between human beings, and between man and God. Poets speak of human experience and suffering, which is also the realm of Hegel's book. Poets also have their heroes, whose greatness they sing, and the *Phenomenology* is Hegel's book of heroes. For the most part, these heroes are left unnamed. They are universal types—Shapes of Man—that fill out the great drama of human history. Hegel's book regularly refers to philosophic theories. But it is not principally about them. It is about Man in his various archetypal roles: Proud Warrior, Master or Slave, Sad Lover of an Absent God, Scientist, Seducer, Reformer, Knight, Cynic, Nihilist, Moralist, Beautiful Soul, and, yes, Philosopher. By positing itself in these historical shapes, and the concrete worlds of knowing to which they belong, the human spirit comes to know itself divinely, or rather to *be* the condition of absolute knowing made concretely *there* in the community of rational beings.

The *Phenomenology,* again like poetry, is addressed not exclusively to professional philosophers but to the populace at large, or, to put this more cautiously, to the educated public. As Hegel tells us in his Preface, Science, in spite of its extreme difficulty, is *for everyone* [13]. And the *Phenomenology* is not simply a "possession for all time," to quote Thucydides. It is also a ladder for the individual reader who seeks to be educated with respect to the rich past whose child he is.

Hegel's book, like the works of the poets, is also a tribute to the power of the *image.* In this respect, the philosopher whom Hegel most resembles is Plato. In the final chapter of the *Phenomenology,* we ascend from picture to Concept, image to thought. This ascent is possible only because of the wealth of images that have been stored up in the course of our journey. These images are the soil from which pure thought emerges. Thought needs imagination as well as feeling. Concept needs picture.[75] The Hegelian philosopher does not turn his back on images when he rises above them to do pure logic. He must remember that he needed a phenomenology—the logic of desire—in order to reach the logic of divine fulfillment. Moreover, pure logic is the logic *of* the world that is transcended in pure thought. The philosopher must remember that the Concept is "the simple essence of life, the soul of the world, the universal blood" [162]. Having "gone up" to pure Concept, he must always remember to "come back down" to the human experience that was the beginning, and food, of his philosophizing. Every so often, in other words, the lover of Hegel's *Science of Logic* should re-read the *Phenomenology.*

The final image of Golgotha conjures many thoughts. One is the historical necessity of Christian faith and self-sacrifice for the completion of philosophy—as well as the necessity of overcoming that faith in conceptual knowing. This *Überwindung* is the goal of Hegel's final chapter, and of the entire *Phenomenology of Spirit.* Another thought summoned by the final image is that philosophy can at last incorporate suffering and death into its thought of the eternal [32]. To ignore this suffering and negativity is to ignore both human life and divine truth.

In his Preface, Hegel singled out edification as an obstacle to philosophy [9]: we desire to be uplifted. In its final image, and as a whole, the *Phenomenology* counteracts this anti-philosophic desire. It expresses the warning of Nietzsche's Zarathustra, whose plea captures the spirit of Hegel's *Phenomenology:* "I beseech you, my brothers, *remain faithful to the earth.*"[76]

Are we still yearning for something further in what was said . . . something that's being left out?
PLATO, *Timaeus*

Epilogue

OUR LONG JOURNEY THROUGH HEGEL'S LABYRINTH IS NOW AT AN end. The Minotaur of Difficulty has surely not been slain. But I hope he has become less terrifying.

My goal has been to make the *Phenomenology of Spirit* sufficiently accessible and interesting, so that my readers will continue to study it on their own. A secondary goal was to introduce them to Hegel "in and for himself." If you have had the patience to follow me this far, you are now ready to take on his other major works.

Hegel's masterpiece is the *Science of Logic.* This is the "speculative philosophy" for which the *Phenomenology* supplies a ladder [37]. The *Logic* is a must for anyone who wants to understand Hegel properly. Unfortunately, it is far more difficult than the *Phenomenology.* Readers may want to start with the so-called *Lesser Logic* (Part One of the *Encyclopaedia*). This work is not a rigorous presentation of Hegel's argument. But it does offer a clear overview of the topics of logic and has very helpful remarks in the Additions or *Zusätze.* It is preceded by a highly readable Introduction to the entire *Encyclopaedia.* The *Encyclopaedia* as a whole is not difficult for those who have worked their way through the *Phenomenology.*

Still difficult, but more accessible than either the *Phenomenology* or the two *Logics,* is Hegel's *Elements of the Philosophy of Right.* This is the most deeply philosophic political work of modernity. It contains, among many other things, Hegel's account of the will and his powerful critique of modern liberalism (social contract theory).

Finally, there are lectures on the history of philosophy, the philosophy of history, religion, and fine art. These are the most accessible things Hegel wrote. They reveal Hegel's commitment to grasping and preserving everything that came before him.

English translations of these works, and of other works by Hegel, are listed in my Brief Bibliography.

Why Read Hegel?

Hegel is above all a model of the philosopher as *student.* He immersed himself in the intellectual and cultural tradition he inherited. Only by studying this tradition can we hope to know ourselves. We may reject what Hegel does with the tradition. But we should seek to emulate his painstaking attempt to think it through in all its aspects.

Hegel is a formidable *critic.* Throughout the *Phenomenology,* we have seen him go deeply into a claim to know and awaken the contradictions that sleep there. The philosopher must be a practitioner of non-being or otherness: a dialectician. He must know how to make trouble in the household of apparent stability. This is the lesson young Socrates learns in the *Parmenides.* In that dialogue, Socrates loves the noble "rest" of Form but neglects the risky "motion" of thought (*dianoia*). He seeks intellectual safety in separate Forms and shuns the negative (i.e. contradiction). Parmenides' brilliant dialectical treatment of the One shows Socrates how to conquer his fears by generating opposition and contradiction within one's own beloved theories. Like Plato in his *Parmenides,* Hegel reminds us that the philosopher, if he is to grasp the implications of his own assumptions, and those of others, must follow rather then fear the devious path of the *logos* that steers its way through all things (136 E).

Hegel's logic of inner tensions is especially suited to modernity. The divisive spirit of modernity reaches its peak in the Enlightenment and the self-tearing world of culture. Since this is in large part the world in which we still live, Hegel can be a valuable ally in our effort to grasp the oppositions that define our own times.

Hegel is a keen *observer* of the human drama. His shapes of consciousness remind us that the philosopher must be a student of the human soul. Like the Platonic dialogues, the *Phenomenology* compels us to search for divine truth in the confusing realm of human types that appear all around us. Hegel's shapes are philosophic images that help us to personify, and thus better understand, philosophic positions that came before, and also after, Hegel. They also help us to know ourselves. "Where am I," we must ask, "in Hegel's picture-gallery? Am I the Stoic, the Skeptic, the Unhappy Consciousness, the Knight of Virtue, the Beautiful Soul—or some hybrid composed of several shapes? Am I—could I be—Hegel's absolute knower?"

The most valuable thing we learn from Hegel is the importance of examining what it means *to give an account.* Hegel helps us to see, and to articulate, the profound difficulties in deduction, mathematical formalism, intuitionism, empiricism, positivism, and the various methodologies—both phenomenological and analytic—that emerged in the twentieth century. We may conclude that Hegel is wrong about what it means to give an account, that his dialectical logic is flawed. But if we can say why we think so, based on a serious effort to understand him, we will have gained considerable insight into our own positions.

Hegel's obscurity is sometimes used as an excuse to dismiss him. Thinkers who came after him either used rhetoric to reject him (Kierkegaard), or else appropriated his terminology and what they took to be his method in ways that falsified his teaching (Marx). Few great thinkers have understood Hegel, or cared to: they wanted to get past him. I hope this introduction has persuaded my reader that we cannot hope to get beyond Hegel without going *through* him. We cannot afford to neglect the profound attempt he made to think through all the fundamental problems of philosophy at their deepest level, especially the problem of what it means to think and to be rational beings. A sentence by Stanley Rosen sums up everything I have been saying in praise of Hegel: "To submit oneself to the study of Hegel is . . . to take oneself with great seriousness" (266).

Erōs and *Wissenschaft*

At various points of our journey, I have recalled the goal Hegel states in his Preface: to replace philosophy as the love of knowing, philosophy as *erōs,* with actual knowing. This is Science, *Wissenschaft.* What, then, has happened to the *love* of wisdom under Hegel's tutelage? What does it mean to have *completed* this love? Does it mean that philosophy is no longer possible because no longer historically necessary? Has Hegel perhaps *killed* philosophy in order to complete it?

Hegel completes philosophic desire by re-interpreting it.

This statement raises several points. I touched on some of them earlier in Chapter 7, in the context of life and desire. One is that, in order to complete philosophy, Hegel transforms Platonic *erōs* into *thymos.* By *thymos* here I mean the middle part of the soul in Plato's *Republic* (4.439E ff.), the part that feels anger, and loves honor, competition, and victory. The modern term for this part of the soul is *will.* Even in Romanticism, where love seems to reassert itself, the lover is really in love with his own feeling and his own ego. His love is will or self-affirmation. He is the narcissistic *beautiful soul,* whose *thymos* reveals itself in his stubborn rejection of life and his harsh judgment of the insensitive people around him.

In the *Phenomenology,* the modern preference for *thymos* over *erōs* (one thinks here of Machiavelli and Hobbes) is evident in the fight for recognition, which begins the drama of self-consciousness. Desire, here, as I noted in Chapter 7, is not other-affirming but self-affirming and other-negating. It is not an erotic yearning for the Other (in the case of philosophy, wisdom), but the spirited drive to self-assertion, mastery, and freedom. This drive is expressed in the self's Declaration of Independence, his "I AM MYSELF!" Hegel grounds Science in the movement of self-consciousness. Man *is* truth because he is self-consciousness (Kojève), and because the logical structure of his selfhood is identical with the logical structure of the universal Concept. The Concept, here, is the identity of intelligence and intelligibility. It replaces the Platonic idea of the Good—the power that binds knower and known (*Republic* 6.508E ff.). To know what *is*, is to recognize *oneself* in what *is*—oneself as universal selfhood or spirit.

Rationality, for Hegel, requires the elimination of all "action at a distance." Desire or love, in its classical sense, is the psychic version of such action: it is a response to the enticing Other, that moves without being moved. Aristotle's Mind moves the heavens in this way—*hōs erōmenon*, "as beloved" (*Metaphysics* 12.7). This relation of lover-and-loved seems not to be susceptible to a rational account. Perhaps it can be captured only in a philosophic myth. For Hegel, by contrast, man is his own end, and wisdom is the expression of man's self-affirmation and divinity. It is not so much discovered as *posited.* The human drive to know must be self-solicited. On this condition alone can there be a *logic* of desire, that is, a purely rational account of the *process* by which wisdom is attained.

Strictly speaking, there is no *erōs* for Hegel. Or rather, Hegel interprets the striving of individual philosophers as posited by spirit or the *historical process.* Indeed, he is so devoted to this process that he seems to have forgotten his own individuality. He presents the *Phenomenology*, and his whole System, as the work of spirit in history, apparently forgetting that Science would not have "appeared" unless he, G. W. F. Hegel, had climbed the ladder to the absolute first, made his own "voyage of discovery," and then returned, like Dante, to guide his fellow men (Rosen, 130).

Philosophy can be complete as Science because there is no supersensible Beyond, the objective correlate of *erōs.* If there were, then historical manifestation would not be the arena of actuality and truth. Truth would be atemporal and non-historical. Socratic philosophizing would "go with" the Greek spirit, but would not be its historical product. Greekness would be at most a condition, but not a cause. To be sure, the philosopher, in this view, would respond to his social-political milieu, as every philosopher must. But he would not be confined to or determined by it. This is the *non*-historical view of Plato and Aristotle.

Hegel's critique of the supersensible Beyond goes hand in hand with his rejection of *intellectual intuition*—what Plato called *noēsis.* This is the irreducible "seeing" that guides, checks, and is the goal of philosophic *logos.* Intuition, here, is not the empty intuition of conscience and the beautiful soul. *Noēsis* allows us to "see" what we are talking about. For Plato, philosophers are lovers of sights, that is, *insights* (*Republic* 5.475E). The Forms are the eternal objects of insight and the proper objects of philosophy. They "appear," problematically, in their sensuous counterparts, but are not vanishing moments of a dialectical-temporal process. For Plato, in other words, essence and appearance are not identical, as they are for Hegel. Napoleon was once *there*, and he can now be recollected by Hegel's absolute knowing. But the Form of justice is posited as *there* in a different sense: as always calling forth individual lovers of wisdom to "see" what justice *is*. The Forms, which ordinary language points to and supports, are the eternally approachable objects of non-historical recollection, or *inquiry* [*zētēsis*]. They are hypothesized as *there* in a supersensible Beyond, not to make philosophy actual as Science but to make it eternally *possible*, and to make *insights* possible.

Make no mistake about it: Hegel's critique of the supersensible Beyond is potent, and we should take it very seriously. But that does not mean that it is correct, or that upon careful examination the critique is not shown to have logical problems of its own. Plato, after all, was the first critic of the supersensible world. In the *Parmenides*, he took his own Forms to task, precisely on the grounds of their separateness from the realm of things. As the old but still feisty Eleatic tells young Socrates, the separate Forms are beset by even greater perplexities than the ones he, Parmenides, has just revealed. And yet, he adds, to reject them would be "to destroy the power of dialectic" (135C). Perplexity with respect to the Forms, in other words, does not necessarily imply that the philosopher should abandon them. It may be that genuine philosophizing will always depend on hypotheses that are not completely, if at all, susceptible to a rational account.

Even if the love of wisdom can never be scientific in Hegel's sense, the erotic philosopher is not therefore an unhappy consciousness. Inquiry, for him, is intensely enjoyable, if laborious. There are divine insights, or might be, along the path of discourse, insights that can be deepened with every renewed effort to know. That is why the erotic philosopher is also not a devotee of the *Sache selbst*. He knows better than to make the search more important than the goal (Lessing), and to identify the wisdom he loves with the self-love of sincerity. Nor is the philosopher—let us say, Socrates, as he appears in the *Symposium*—a romantic beautiful soul. He is an earthy fellow who begets children, converses with friends, goes to drinking parties (without getting drunk), and serves his country in battle. He is at home in the city, even if he is also at odds with the city and its "right" opinions.

As I now leave you, my fellow traveler, I would have you consider what is gained in Hegel's effort in the *Phenomenology of Spirit*, and what is lost. Hegel's pantheon preserves the greatness of ancient philosophic heroes and their erotic disposition toward wisdom, but only as a past greatness and a past *erōs* that do not need to be repeated. Socrates, Plato, and Aristotle—not *for Hegel* but *in themselves*—offer a powerful alternative to Hegel's impressive completion of modernity. For them, philosophy is the day-to-day activity of individual human seekers. It is not the public *Wissenschaft* of an age, but an on-going love affair and a way of life—something to be shared with one's philosophic friends. If philosophy is *for us* what it was *for them,* then the study of Hegel is a necessary part of that life.

A BRIEF BIBLIOGRAPHY

The secondary literature on Hegel's *Phenomenology* is huge. The following bibliography is highly selective and is meant for readers who are relatively new to Hegel. A much more extensive bibliography can be found at the end of the two-volume commentary by H. S. Harris, *Hegel's Ladder*.

My list of secondary materials is restricted to commentaries in English on the *Phenomenology* and reference books likely to be helpful to first-time readers.

As I noted in my prologue, the German edition I used for this introduction to the *Phenomenology* is that of Johannes Hoffmeister, Hamburg: Felix Meiner, 1952. Readers who know French should consult the excellent translation by Jean Hyppolite, *Phénoménologie de l'esprit*, 2 volumes, Paris: Aubier, 1941, 1946.

Works by Hegel in English Translation

TRANSLATIONS OF THE *PHENOMENOLOGY*

Hegel's Preface to the Phenomenology of Spirit. Trans. Yirmiyahu Yovel. Princeton: Princeton University Press, 2005.

The Phenomenology of Mind. Trans. J. B. Baillie. 1910. Reprint, New York: Humanities Press, 1977.

Phenomenology of Spirit. Trans. A. V. Miller. Oxford: Clarendon Press, 1977.

Spirit: Chapter Six of Hegel's Phenomenology of Spirit. Ed. Daniel E. Shannon. Trans. Hegel Translation Group. Indianapolis: Hackett, 2001.

Aesthetics: Lectures on Fine Art, 2 vol. Trans. T. M. Knox. Oxford: Clarendon Press, 1975.

The Berlin Phenomenology. Trans. M. J. Petry. Dordrecht and Boston: D. Reidel, 1981.

The Difference Between Fichte's and Schelling's System of Philosophy. Trans. H. S. Harris and Walter Cerf. Albany: SUNY Press, 1977.

Early Theological Writings. Trans. T. M. Knox. Chicago: University of Chicago Press, 1948; Philadelphia: University of Pennsylvania Press, 1971.

Elements of the Philosophy of Right. Ed. Allen W. Wood. Trans. H. B. Nisbet. Cambridge: Cambridge University Press, 1991. [*Elements of the Philosophy of Right* is also known as *The Philosophy of Right.*]

The Encyclopaedia Logic: Part 1 of the Encyclopaedia of Philosophical Sciences. Trans. T. F. Geraets, W. A. Suchting, and H. S. Harris. Indianapolis: Hackett, 1991.

Faith and Knowledge. Trans. W. Cerf and H. S. Harris. Albany: SUNY Press, 1977.

Hegel: The Letters. Trans. Clark Butler and Christine Seiler. Bloomington: Indiana University Press, 1984.

Introduction to the Lectures on the History of Philosophy. Trans. T. M. Knox and A. V. Miller. Oxford: Clarendon Press, 1998 Reprint.

Introduction to The Philosophy of History. Trans. Leo Rauch. Indianapolis: Hackett, 1988.

The Jena System, 1804–5: Logic and Metaphysics. Ed. and trans. John W. Burbridge and George di Giovanni. Kingston and Montreal: McGill-Queen's University Press, 1986.

Lectures on Natural Right and Political Science: The First Philosophy of Right. Trans. J. M. Stewart and P. C. Hodgson. Berkeley: University of California Press, 1995.

Lectures on the History of Philosophy. 3 vol. Trans. E. S. Haldane and Frances H. Simson. Lincoln: University of Nebraska Press, 1995.

Lectures on the Philosophy of Religion. 3 vol. Ed. P. C. Hodgson. Trans. P. C. Hodgson, R. F. Brown, and J. M. Stewart. Berkeley: University of California Press, 1984–87.

Lectures on the Philosophy of World History: Introduction: Reason in History. Trans. H. B. Nisbet. Cambridge: Cambridge University Press, 1975.

Logic: Part One of the Encyclopaedia of the Philosophical Sciences (1830). Trans. William Wallace. 1873. Reprint, with a foreword by J. N. Findlay, Oxford: Clarendon Press, 1975.

Miscellaneous Writings of G. W. F. Hegel. Ed. Jon Stewart. Evanston: Northwestern University Press, 2002.

This volume includes Hegel's *Philosophical Dissertation on the Orbits of the Planets.*

Natural Law. Trans. T. M. Knox. Philadelphia: University of Pennsylvania Press, 1975.

On Art, Religion, and the History of Philosophy: Introductory Lectures. Ed. J. Glenn Gray. Introduction by Tom Rockmore. Indianapolis: Hackett, 1997 (reissue with revisions Harper Torchbook ed. 1970).

The Philosophical Propaedeutic. Ed. M. George and A. Vincent. Trans. A. V. Miller. Oxford: Blackwell, 1986.

The Philosophy of History. Trans. J. Sibree. 1857. Reprint, New York: Dover, 1956.

Philosophy of Mind: Part Three of the Encyclopaedia of the Philosophical Sciences (1830). Trans. William Wallace. Notes trans. A. V. Miller. Oxford: Clarendon Press, 1971.

Philosophy of Nature: Part Two of the Encyclopaedia of the Philosophical Sciences (1830). Trans. A. V. Miller. Oxford: Clarendon Press, 1970.

Philosophy of Nature. 3 vol. Trans. M. J. Petry. London: Allen and Unwin, 1970.

Philosophy of Right. Trans. T. M. Knox. Oxford: Oxford University Press, 1969 (first published 1952).

The Philosophy of Right. Trans. Alan White. Newburyport, Mass.: Focus, 2002.

Philosophy of Subjective Spirit. 3 vol. Trans. M. J. Petry. Dordrecht: D. Reidel, 1978.

Political Writings. Ed. Laurence Dickey and H. B. Nisbet. Trans. H. B. Nisbet. Cambridge: Cambridge University Press, 1999.

Political Writings. Trans. T. M. Knox. Oxford: Clarendon Press, 1964.

Science of Logic. Trans. A. V. Miller. New York: Humanities Press, 1976.

System of Ethical Life and First Philosophy of Spirit. Ed. and trans. H. S. Harris and T. M. Knox. Albany: SUNY Press, 1979.

Three Essays, 1793–1795: The Tübingen Essay, Berne Fragments, The Life of Jesus. Trans. P. Fuss and J. Dobbins. Notre Dame: University of Notre Dame Press, 1984.

Helpful Books on Hegel's *Phenomenology* and Related Topics

Adorno, Theodor. *Hegel: Three Studies.* Trans. S. W. Nicholson. Cambridge: MIT Press, 1993.

The essays are "Aspects of Hegel's Philosophy," "The Experiential Content of Hegel's Philosophy," and "Skoteinos, or How to Read Hegel." This last essay deals with the role and meaning of *clarity* in Hegel and in philosophy in general.

Beiser, Frederick, ed. *The Cambridge Companion to Hegel.* Cambridge: Cambridge University Press, 1993.

This contains Robert Pippin's lucid and insightful article, "You Can't Get There from Here."

Fackenheim, Emil L. *The Religious Dimension in Hegel's Thought.* Boston: Beacon Press, 1970 (first published 1967).

Fackenheim attempts to establish the role of Christianity in Hegel's thought. He also articulates the so-called "Hegelian middle" that steers between the extremes of the *left-wing* Hegelians, who affirmed the actual world, at the expense of a comprehensive rational System, and the *right-wing* Hegelians, who affirmed a rational System, at the expense of the finite, contingent world.

Findlay, John N. *Hegel: A Reexamination.* London: Allen and Unwin, 1958.

This book is useful for its highly readable summary of Hegel's System, as it appears in the *Phenomenology* and the *Encyclopedia.*

Flay, Joseph C. *Hegel's Quest for Certainty.* Albany: SUNY, 1984.

Flay interprets the stages of consciousness in light of reason's various "interests." This book is not for beginners, but it is very worthwhile for its careful analysis of Hegel's argument.

Gadamer, Hans-Georg. *Hegel's Dialectic.* Trans. P. Christopher Smith. New Haven: Yale University Press, 1976.

This contains five highly interesting, very readable essays on Hegel: "Hegel and the Dialectic of the ancient Philosophers," "Hegel's 'Inverted World,'" "Hegel's Dialectic of Self-consciousness," "The Idea of Hegel's Logic," and "Hegel and Heidegger."

Greene, Murray. *Hegel on the Soul: A Speculative Anthropology.* The Hague: Martinus Nijhoff, 1972.

This book is highly recommended for its insightful account of Hegel's conception of life, soul, and consciousness.

Harris, H. S. *Hegel's Development I: Toward the Sunlight (1770–1801),* Oxford: Clarendon Press, 1972. *II: Night Thoughts (1801–1806),* Oxford: Clarendon Press, 1983.

———. *Hegel's Ladder.* 2 vol. Indianapolis: Hackett, 1997.

Both works by Harris are indispensable for any serious study of Hegel. They are a goldmine of information regarding Hegel's development, ideas, and references.

Heidegger, Martin. *Hegel's Phenomenology of Spirit.* Trans. Parvis Emad and Kenneth Maly. Bloomington: Indiana University Press, 1994.

In these lectures from 1930–31, Heidegger reflects insightfully on what phenomenology and Science are for Hegel. He comments on the *Phenomenology* up through the chapter on self-consciousness.

———. "Hegel's Concept of Experience," in *Off the Beaten Track.* Ed. and trans. Julian Young and Kenneth Haynes. Cambridge: Cambridge University Press, 2002.

This is Heidegger's reading of Hegel's Introduction to the *Phenomenology.*

Hyppolite, Jean. *Genesis and Structure of Hegel's Phenomenology of Spirit.* Trans. S. Cherniak and J. Heckman. Evanston: Northwestern University Press, 1974.

Hyppolite strikes a good balance between logical analysis and attention to human experience. His book—first published in French in 1946—is helpful to beginners, and is an exciting read.

Inwood, Michael. *A Hegel Dictionary.* Oxford: Blackwell, 1992.

Inwood's dictionary is generally helpful in clarifying Hegel's terms, and in alerting the reader to what some of these terms mean in ordinary German.

Kedourie, Elie. *Hegel and Marx: Introductory Lectures.* Ed. Sylvia and Helen Kedourie. Oxford: Blackwell, 1995.

In this highly engaging collection of lectures, Kedourie discusses Hegel's relation to Schiller, Lessing, Feuerbach, Marx, and Paul Valéry.

Kojève, Alexandre. *Introduction to the Reading of Hegel.* Trans. J. H. Nichols. New York: Basic Books, 1969.

This is perhaps the most provocative book on Hegel available in English. For Kojève, a committed left-wing Hegelian, Hegel is an atheist who liberated man for happiness in the Here-and Now, and who *succeeded* in bringing philosophy to the level of wisdom. His lectures are full of interesting pronouncements regarding philosophy, wisdom, and time.

Lauer, Quentin. *A Reading of Hegel's Phenomenology of Spirit.* New York: Fordham University Press, 1976; second edition (revised) 1993.

Lauer's book is clearly written, careful in its analyses, and generally helpful to the first-time reader.

Loewenberg, Jacob. *Hegel's Phenomenology: Dialogues on the Life of Mind.* Lasalle, Ill.: Open Court, 1965.

This spirited dialogue between two philosophic friends helps the reader identify possible objections to Hegel's argument and positions.

Löwith, Karl. *From Hegel to Nietzsche.* Trans. David E. Green. New York: Holt, Rinehart, and Winston, 1964.

This scholarly work is essential to an understanding of Hegel's century and the aftermath of his philosophy.

Pinkard, Terry. *Hegel's Phenomenology: The Sociality of Reason.* Cambridge: Cambridge University Press, 1994.

Pinkard does a good job of setting out the large themes and problems in the *Phenomenology.* He pays special attention to the historical social dimension of spirit. As the author indicates, his book is not a commentary but "a kind of Hegelian analysis of Hegel's text itself."

———. *Hegel: A Biography.* Cambridge: Cambridge University Press, 2000.

Pinkard's biography is fascinating, clearly written, and informative. It helps one reach a better understanding of the substance of Hegel's thought.

Pippin, Robert. *Hegel's Idealism: The Satisfactions of Self-Consciousness.* Cambridge: Cambridge University Press, 1989.

This is an excellent analysis of the *Phenomenology* and *Logic* in light of Hegel's Kantian roots. It is definitely for scholars rather than first-time readers.

Rosen, Stanley. *G. W. F. Hegel: An Introduction to the Science of Wisdom.* New Haven: Yale University Press, 1974.

This is the best introduction, in English, to Hegel's thought as a whole. It focuses on the *Science of Logic* and the *Phenomenology.* Rosen champions the centrality of the *Logic* in Hegel's thought. He also discusses Hegel's relation to Plato, Aristotle, and Fichte.

Taylor, Charles. *Hegel.* Cambridge: Cambridge University Press, 1975.

In spite of Taylor's non-Hegelian view that spirit is a transcendent consciousness that "expresses" itself through finite consciousness or man, this highly readable overview of Hegel's System contains many helpful insights and analyses.

Verene, Donald. *Hegel's Recollection: A Study of Images in the Phenomenology of Spirit.* Albany: SUNY Press, 1985.

Verene underscores the poetic, imaginative aspect of the *Phenomenology.* His discussion of the inverted world is especially interesting.

NOTES

The numbers in brackets refer to paragraphs in A. V. Miller's edition of the *Phenomenology.* I have occasionally adjusted Miller's translation to a more faithful rendering of Hegel's German.

Prologue

1. Richard Kroner, intro. to Hegel's *Early Theological Writings,* trans. T. M. Knox (Philadelphia: University of Pennsylvania Press, 1971), 45.

Chapter 1: A World of Knowing

1. The influence of Rousseau is strong here. See Jean Hyppolite, *Genesis and Structure of Hegel's Phenomenology of Spirit,* trans. S. Cherniak and J. Heckman (Evanston: Northwestern University Press, 1974), 11. The following passage from Rousseau's *First Discourse* foreshadows Hegel's task in the *Phenomenology:* "It is a grand and beautiful sight to see man emerge somehow from nothing by his own efforts; to dissipate, by the light of his reason, the shadows in which nature had enveloped him; rise above himself, soar by means of his mind into the heavenly regions; traverse, like the sun, the vast expanse of the universe with giant steps; and, what is even grander and more difficult, return to himself in order to study man and know his nature, his duties, and his end" (*Basic Political Writings,* trans. Donald A. Cress [Indianapolis: Hackett, 1987], 3). Prime examples of the *Bildungsroman* are Goethe's *Wilhelm Meister's Apprenticeship* and Novalis' *Henry von Ofterdingen.*

2. The centrality of freedom in the *Phenomenology* is suggested by the word "absolute" (in German *absolut*), which appears often in Hegel's text. The word derives from the Latin verb *absolvere*—to set free, release from a debt, or relieve of a burden. Absolute knowing is free knowing. It is knowledge that has been liberated from the mere appearance of knowledge [78].

3. Richard Kroner has commented on Hegel's powers of philosophic mimesis: "It was his peculiar gift to be able to project himself into the minds of other people and of other periods, penetrating into the core of alien souls and strange lives, and still remain the man he was" (intro. to *Early Theological Writings,* 9).

4. In *Hegel's Phenomenology of Spirit,* Heidegger offers a useful interpretation of Hegel's title, and an explanation of how the term "phenomenology" here differs from its meaning in Husserl (trans. Parvis Emad and Kenneth Maly [Bloomington and Indianapolis: Indiana University Press, 1994], 23–24, 28–30). The first to use the term "phenomenology" was the German thinker, Johann Heinrich Lambert (1728–77). In a book on truth and error published in 1764 (*New Organon*), Lambert calls phenomenology "the doctrine of illusion [*Schein*]." Hyppolite, summarizing Lambert's teaching, writes: "the presentation of an untruth as untruth is already a movement beyond the error" (*Genesis and Structure,* 14). The other important use of the term occurs in Kant's *Metaphysical Foundations of Natural Science,* where it refers to the treatment of motion and rest "as an appearance of the external senses" (trans. James Ellington [Indianapolis: Bobbs-Merrill, 1970], 15).

5. The word is especially prominent in Johann Gottlieb Fichte's *Science of Knowledge* (trans. Peter Heath and John Lachs [New York, NY: Appleton-Century-Crofts, 1970]). As the translators of this edition observe, Fichte sometimes writes "as if *setzen* and its compounds were the only verbs in the German language" (xiii). This makes sense if we agree with Fichte that the self or "I" is absolute: positing is I-ing.

6. Spinoza's metaphysics exerted a powerful influence over Hegel and his contemporaries. In his *Ethics,* Spinoza identifies will and understanding or intellect (trans. Samuel Shirley [Indianapolis: Hackett, 1992], part II, corollary to proposition 49, p. 96).

7. Hegel will regularly say that a shape of consciousness "comes on the scene." The German word, *auftreten,* means "step" or "tread," but also "appear on stage." This is one of many indicators that Hegel intended to write a philosophic drama or stage-play. The hero is *Geist* or spirit, which appears on the stage of world-history. The "happening" or event is spirit's struggle to know itself by taking on various roles.

8. H. S. Harris observes that the *Phenomenology* fulfilled Hegel's desire to write a "biography of God" (*Hegel's Ladder* [Indianapolis: Hackett, 1997], 1:10). This desire is present in Hegel's early "Life of Jesus" (1795) (in *Three Essays, 1793–1795,* trans. Peter Fuss and John Dobbins [Notre Dame, Ind.: University of Notre Dame Press, 1984]).

9. In his *Lectures on the Philosophy of Religion,* Hegel identifies philosophy as a form of theology. Speaking of the need to reconcile the worldliness of the Enlightenment with the otherworldliness of faith, Hegel writes: "This reconciliation is philosophy. Philosophy is to this extent theology. It presents the reconciliation of God with himself and with nature, showing that nature, otherness, is implicitly divine, and that the raising of itself to reconciliation is on the one hand what finite spirit [the worldliness of the Enlightenment] implicitly is, while on the other hand it arrives at this reconciliation, or brings it forth, in world history" (3 vol., ed. P. C. Hodgson, trans. P. C. Hodgson, R. F. Brown, and J. M. Stewart [Berkeley: University of California Press, 1984–87], 3: 347).

10. "In fact, Aristotle excels Plato in speculative depth, for he was acquainted with the deepest kind of speculation—idealism—and in this upholds the most extreme empirical development" (Hegel, *Lectures on the History of Philosophy,* 3 vol., trans. E. S. Haldane and Frances H. Simson [Lincoln: University of Nebraska Press, 1995], 2:119). I have used the Haldane & Simson translation for all subsequent references to *Lectures on the History of Philosophy.*

11. The first to speak of Mind as the essence of all things was Anaxagoras, whom Hegel mentions in his Preface [55].

12. Aristotle uses the word *athanatidzein,* literally, to be without death (*Nicomachean Ethics* 10.7.1177B31–78A2). Dante makes up a word to convey a similar transcendence. To enter the heavenly realm of intellectual light is "to pass beyond the human," *trasumanar* (*Paradiso* 1.70).

13. As Hegel says in his *Philosophy of History:* "In the Christian religion God has revealed himself—that is, he has given humans to understand what he is; so that he is no longer something concealed or secret. And this possibility of knowing him, thus afforded us, imposes on us the duty to know him" (trans. J. Sibree [New York: Dover, 1956], 15). I have slightly emended the translation.

14. On this point, see Hyppolite, *Genesis and Structure,* 27–50.

15. In the Introduction to the *Philosophy of History,* Hegel reflects on the "abstract determinations" of spirit, *Geist.* The essence of spirit is *freedom.* Spirit is self-contained existence—the whole. Or, as Hegel puts it, it is *Bei-sich-selbst-sein:* "being-with-its-own-self" (17). More concretely, I am free when I do not seek the center of my existence in another but find it in myself: "when I am with [or at home with] my own self" (ibid.). Spirit's freedom is its self-sufficiency and totality. Toward the end of his lectures, Hegel says: "world-history is nothing but the development of the idea of freedom" (456). At an advanced stage of the *Phenomenology,* Hegel will describe the self-sufficiency and totality of spirit in terms of *motion:* spirit is the mover, the moved, and the motion itself [786].

16. These formulations appear in the Preface to Hegel's *Philosophy of Right* (1821) (trans. Alan White [Newburyport, Mass.: Focus, 2002], 9–10).

17. Terry Pinkard, in his excellent biography of Hegel, has a nice formulation of how spirit may be said to wake up to itself: "God is . . . not some 'outside' force or entity directing nature to a certain end; God, as spirit, is already metaphorically asleep in nature, and the divine principle of 'spirit' comes to fruition only as humans appear on the planet and create religions as the modes of social practice in which reflection on their relation to nature, each other, and to the divine principle itself is carried out" (*Hegel: A Biography* [Cambridge: Cambridge University Press, 2000], 580).

18. See Spinoza's *Ethics:* "It is in the nature of reason to perceive things under a [certain] aspect or 'look' of eternity" (*sub quadam specie aeternitatis*) (trans. Shirley, 93).

19. For an illuminating discussion of some of the most important problems of transition in Hegel's *Phenomenology,* see Robert Pippin, "You Can't Get There from Here," in *The Cambridge Companion to Hegel,* ed. Frederick C. Beiser (Cambridge: Cambridge University Press, 1993), 52–85.

20. The phrase is reported by Hegel's student, Karl Ludwig Michelet: "[Hegel] was in the habit of calling this piece, which appeared in 1807, his voyage of discovery, since here the speculative

method, which for him uniquely befitted the history of philosophy, in fact encompassed and traversed the whole sphere of human knowledge" (quoted in Pinkard, *Hegel: A Biography,* 203).

21. Walter Cerf, in his illuminating introduction to Hegel's *Faith and Knowledge* (trans. Walter Cerf and H. S. Harris [Albany: SUNY Press, 1977], xiv).

Chapter 2: What Is Experience?

1. "Thinking as *understanding* stops short at the fixed determinacy and its distinctness vis-à-vis other determinacies" (Hegel, *The Encyclopaedia Logic,* trans. T. F. Geraets, W. A. Suchting, and H. S. Harris [Indianapolis: Hackett, 1991], 125).

2. Throughout my introduction, I have rendered *Begriff* "concept" rather than notion, which appears in the translations of Baillie (1910) and Miller (1977). Notion sounds too close to what is "in our heads," a merely subjective idea, what Hegel calls a *Vorstellung* or representation.

3. Plato was keenly aware of the philosopher's susceptibility to an unreflective acceptance of his own givens. He dramatizes the problem in the *Parmenides,* where young Socrates posits the Forms, only to learn that this hypothesis brings on more serious difficulties than the ones he was seeking to avoid. As the dialogue shows, young Socrates too is limited by picture thinking and the spatial representation of the purely intelligible. At one point, he even generates a "fence of consciousness" between the divine knowing of Forms and the human knowing of their imperfect participants (133B–134E). He cannot, that is, get past understanding or *Verstand.*

4. Hegel discusses mediation, *Vermittlung,* in the Preface [21]. Mediation is the logical relation something has to its own identity. When something is mediated, for Hegel, its identity is taken not as an inert given but as the result of a logical process or becoming. In the Introduction to the *Encyclopaedia Logic,* he gives the following simple account: "For mediation is a beginning, and a having advanced to second, in such a way that this second is only there because one has come to it from something that is other vis-à-vis this second" (36).

5. For Hegel's more extensive discussion of the term "method" in philosophy, see the final chapter of his *Science of Logic* (trans. A. V. Miller [New York: Humanities Press, 1976]). There Hegel stresses that dialectic is not merely the subjective mode of cognition but rather the "soul and substance" of the truth itself (826).

6. The "tragic" formulation of Kant's position, for Hegel, is that the very structures that make experience possible (the pure forms of intuition and the pure concepts of the understanding) prevent us from knowing things as they are in themselves.

7. As Hegel writes in the Introduction to his *Science of Logic*: "The Notion [or Concept] of pure science and its deduction is therefore presupposed in the present work in so far as the *Phenomenology of Spirit* is nothing other than the deduction of it" (49).

8. In Spinoza's famous formula, every determination is negation. I cannot say yes to something without saying no to everything else. Hegel adds to Spinoza's formula its complement: every negation is a determination. Spinoza's dictum appears in his letter to Jarig Jellis (*Works of Spinoza,* trans. R. H. M. Elwes [New York: Dover , 1951], 2:370).

9. On the meanings of "sublation" in Hegel, see Michael Inwood, *A Hegel Dictionary* (Oxford: Blackwell, 1992), 283–85. In the *Science of Logic,* Hegel asserts that German is, in general, especially suited to expressing the fluid or dialectical nature of thinking: "In this respect German has many advantages over other modern languages; some of its words even possess the further peculiarity of having not only different but opposite meanings so that one cannot fail to recognize a speculative spirit of the language in them: it can delight a thinker to come across such words and to find the union of opposites naively shown in the dictionary as one word with opposite meanings, although this result of speculative thinking is nonsensical to the understanding" (32).

10. Hegel got the term *aufheben* from Schiller. See Schiller's *On the Aesthetic Education of Man,* Letter 18. For Schiller, beauty unites the opposites of sensuousness and thought, matter and spirit. In beauty, these opposites "are canceled" [*aufgehoben werden*].

11. For Hegel's discussion of the meaning of the verb "sublate," see *Science of Logic* (106–8). It may seem at first that Hegel's logic, in which opposites become identical, violates the principle of non-contradiction, as formulated by Aristotle in *Metaphysics* 4. That this is not the case is beauti-

fully explained by Eva Brann: "The Aristotelian law is time-qualified but pertains to fixed, identifiable *moments* of time, while Hegelian dialectic is pretemporal but pertains to fluid conceptual *passages*" (*The Ways of Naysaying* [Lanham, Md.: Rowman & Littlefield, 2001], 62, note 11). She concludes: "From this perspective the temporal universe of the Aristotelian Law of Contradiction is not even tangent to the atemporal sphere of Hegelian dialectic, and therefore Hegel's dialectic cannot be said to abrogate Aristotle's law."

12. Miller's translation of this sentence leaves out the word "immediately" (*unmittelbar*).

13. Plato's *Phaedo*, trans. Eva Brann, Peter Kalkavage, and Eric Salem (Newburyport, Mass.: Focus, 1998), 57.

14. For a helpful sorting out of different meanings of the term experience, see Heidegger, *Hegel's Phenomenology of Spirit*, 18–23.

Chapter 3: Of Mere Being

1. Aristotle distinguishes between what is first to us and what is first in itself (for example, in the opening of his *Physics*). Given the circular character of Science for Hegel, this distinction does not apply to the beginning of the *Phenomenology of Spirit*. Science must be circular because an appeal to first principles would reduce Science to natural consciousness (there would be a *given*). Sense-certainty is not a first principle from which conclusions will be derived in the usual sense. Nor is it first to us in Aristotle's sense. This raises the question of how the *Phenomenology* can be a ladder for the individual reader. How can a ladder be a ladder if it, like the Science it takes us to, is circular? How does one "break into" the ladder's own system of knowing? Every reader of Hegel surely feels this difficulty. Plato and Aristotle did not have absolute knowing in Hegel's sense. They could therefore make a genuine beginning, since philosophy for them grows out of the marketplace of ordinary experience and ordinary language: there is no claim to have given a scientific account of beginnings.

2. There are two German words for "thing": *Ding* and *Sache*. The former refers to objects like the individual table, house, or tree. The latter refers to the thing with which I busy myself or take an interest in—what the Greeks called a *pragma*. Throughout this section, Hegel uses the more indefinite word *Sache*. *Ding* will come on the scene with the thing of perception.

3. "Of Mere Being," the title of a poem by Wallace Stevens, seems to echo what Hegel means by "only the being of the thing [*Sache*]." In his poetry, Stevens often contemplates, and seems to desire, the pure perception of things as they are, apart from all human interpretation and meaning. His aesthetic quest for such an experience seems in line with the anti-universal purism of sense-certainty—the most inhuman as well as the most immediate of all cognitive stances.

4. Hegel has several explicit formulations of this thought. The best one is in the *Philosophy of Right:* "Such dialectic [of the concept of right] is then not the external doing of subjective thinking, but is rather the content's very soul organically putting forth its branches and fruit" (36). In his warnings about misunderstanding the title of Hegel's *Phenomenology*, Heidegger observes: "Hegel uses the term *phenomenology exclusively* in reference to spirit or consciousness" (*Hegel's Phenomenology*, 24). In reference to the caricature of Hegel as having a triadic method of Thesis-Antithesis-Synthesis, one editor writes: "To use this jargon in expounding Hegel is almost always an unwitting confession that the expositor has little or no first-hand knowledge of Hegel" (Allen W. Wood, intro. to Hegel's *Elements of the Philosophy of Right*, trans. H. B. Nisbet [Cambridge: Cambridge University Press, 1991], xxxii).

5. We recall what Hegel says in the Preface: "The matter at hand [*die Sache*] is not exhausted in its *end* or *goal* but in its *development;* nor is the result the actual whole but the result together with its coming-to-be [*Werden*]" [3].

6. In the *Lectures on the History of Philosophy*, Hegel acknowledges his debt to Heraclitus: "there is no proposition of Heraclitus that I have not adopted in my Logic" (1:279). Hegel's dialectic is the logical spelling out of Heraclitus' notion that *logos* is the profound, living truth that steers its way through all things. The *logos* is a fire that preserves what it consumes.

7. For a helpful discussion of these terms, see Inwood, *A Hegel Dictionary*, 133–36.

8. When we get to the level of Self-Consciousness, being-for-self will take on the additional meaning of aggressive self-assertion. We hear this meaning in expressions like: "From now on, I'm out *for myself*."

9. It is significant that the journey of consciousness begins at *night*—the time of darkness, fear, and longing. Throughout the *Phenomenology*, night will be associated with the brooding and unhappiness of self-consciousness. Harris insightfully observes that this first reference to night signals Hegel's contribution to the dawning of the "new era" that he talks about in the Preface [11]. The *Phenomenology* is the philosophic "sunburst" that will take us from our centuries-long anxiety to the universal knowledge that exists in "the daylight of the present" [177]. See Harris, *Hegel's Ladder*, 1:215.

10. The true "romantic" appears much later, at the level of *reason*. His archetype is Faust, who, in Goethe's poem, tries to make himself real as a human This through his sexual union with the innocent Gretchen [360 ff.].

11. Sense-certainty is not only a romantic who wants to live in the Now. It is also a *pointillist*. Everything is discrete for it—a This. There are no continuities. And yet there must be continuity if This-ness is to abide. This is what sense-certainty learns through suffering: that immediacy cannot abide, for abiding *is* mediation. It is the going beyond one moment of time in order to exist at another.

12. See Kant's "Refutation of Idealism," where Kant argues: "the consciousness of my existence is simultaneously a direct consciousness of the existence of other things outside me" (*Critique of Pure Reason*, B 276, trans. Werner S. Pluhar [Indianapolis: Hackett, 1996], 290).

13. The dialectic of pointing reminds us of Heisenberg's Indeterminacy Principle, according to which observation changes the event observed.

14. *Odyssey* 4.351 ff.

15. It is clear from this hard-to-follow argument that thinking, for Hegel, does not proceed in a straight line. The "steps" we take after the first positing are rather a *going back*, a re-thinking and re-positing of what was posited at the outset. For Hegel, genuine thinking moves in a circle. That is why it makes our heads spin.

16. In his *Philosophy of Nature*, Hegel formally defines time as "the being [*das Sein*] which, while it *is*, is *not*, and while it is *not, is*" (Part Two of the *Encyclopaedia of the Philosophical Sciences*, trans. A. V. Miller [Oxford: Clarendon Press, 1970], para. 258, p. 34). I have slightly emended the translation.

17. Try the following experiment. Look at a circle, O. Now try to confine your Here to the *inside* of the figure. Can you do this without making the circumference part of your Here? If not, then can you let it be part of your Here without the proscribed region *outside* the figure also slipping into the Here? What is within a spatial boundary can be my Here only if what is *outside* that boundary is also part of the Here. To point to a spatial limit is to have gone beyond that limit.

18. This is perhaps why Leibniz defined space and time as *relations:* "Indeed, *space* is only the order of existing for possibles that exist simultaneously, just as *time* is the order of existing for possibles that exist successively" (Leibniz to de Volder, *Philosophical Essays*, ed. and trans. Roger Ariew and Daniel Garber [Indianapolis: Hackett, 1989], 179).

19. Hegel likes to combine pagan and Christian images. Here, the mysteries of Ceres and Bacchus (the deities presiding over bread and wine) recall the bread and wine in the Christian Mass. Ceres and Bacchus will return when Hegel takes up Greek cult-worship [718].

Chapter 4: The Crisis of Thinghood

1. "[Hegel's] derivation is incorrect: *wahr-* in *wahrnehmen* is not etymologically related to *wahr*, 'true,' but to the English 'aware'" (Inwood, *A Hegel Dictionary*, 146). The false etymology works, nevertheless, as a revealing pun in the present context.

2. See *Science of Logic* (498): "when [spirit] is thought of as soul, it is quite frequently taken as a *thing*."

3. For Hegel's purely logical development of the thing and its properties, see the chapter entitled "Existence" in *Science of Logic*, 484–98. The reader should note how late thinghood appears in the

Logic, as opposed to how early it comes up in the *Phenomenology.* The order of scientific or purely logical development, in other words, does not simply mirror the journey by which consciousness arrives at Science.

4. The passive medium reminds us of Aristotle's prime matter and, in some respects, of Plato's *receptacle,* whose only attribute is its power to receive form (*Timaeus* 50A ff.).

5. The cube of salt as an example of thinghood shows how basic a thing is for perception. We are not in the world of Aristotle, where instances of individual things or "substances" (*ousiai*) are the individual ox, horse, or man, each made the thing it is, made one, and made thinkable by the form or *eidos* that is at work in the thing's material (*hylē*). Rather, we are in the modern world of Descartes, whose example of a thing, *res,* is a piece of wax (*Meditations on First Philosophy, The Philosophical Writings of Descartes,* trans. John Cottingham, Robert Stoothoff, and Dugald Murdoch [Cambridge: Cambridge University Press, 1984], 2:20–23).

6. Hegel presents the dialectical and self-negating structure of this law in the *Science of Logic,* in the section on essence (413–16).

7. The image of radiating recalls the emanation of the One in Plotinus. The One gives rise to Intellect, *Nous,* through a sun-like process of shining forth or *perilampsis* (*Enneads* V, 1, 6) (Loeb Classical Library [1984], 31).

8. The problem of the thing is ultimately the same as the problem of *counting.* When I count, I take separate units or monads and combine them to form a whole. This whole is a *number* as an assemblage of monads. For the centrality of the problem of number and counting in ancient Greek accounts of being, see Jacob Klein, *Greek Mathematical Thought and the Origin of Algebra* (Cambridge: M. I. T. Press, 1968), 46–113. The problem of counting is also central to Kant's important notion of synthetic unity. See *Critique of Pure Reason,* trans. Pluhar, 55–58.

9. In the dialogue *Theaetetus,* we are told that Theaetetus and Socrates have similarly ugly faces (143E).

10. At this point, the thing starts sounding almost like a self-conscious human individual, though we must remember that "for itself" does not necessarily mean "consciously for itself." In his translation of Hegel's *Philosophy of Right,* Alan White offers a persuasive argument for rendering the phrase *für sich* "as itself" rather than "for itself" (264–65), thus avoiding the unintended suggestion of self-consciousness. He bases his argument on Hegel's account of being-for-self in the *Science of Logic,* 156 ff.

11. This is the dialectical origin of the modern distinction between primary and secondary qualities. In Descartes, for example, color (a so-called secondary quality) is merely the result of my sensory apparatus, whereas extension (a primary quality) belongs to the thing itself.

12. A clear statement of Leibniz' principle occurs in *Monadology* 9 (*Philosophical Essays,* ed. Ariew & Garber, 214). In one of his letters to Samuel Clarke, Leibniz calls the identity of indiscernibles and sufficient reason the "great principles" that "change the state of metaphysics" (328).

13. Hegel discusses the hypothesis of different "matters" in both the *Science of Logic* (496–98) and the *Encyclopaedia Logic* (197–99), where the different matters interpenetrate by means of tiny pores. Combining a critique of physical science with a critique of natural consciousness, Hegel writes in the *Science of Logic,* "It is one of the commonest determinations of ordinary thinking that a thing consists of a number of independent matters" (496). The most famous of these hypothetical "matters" was caloric, the matter of heat. Lavoisier calls caloric "that exquisitely elastic fluid which produces [heat]" (*Elements of Chemistry,* trans. Robert Kerr [New York: Dover, 1965], 5).

14. For Hegel's enormously complicated account of reflection as a logical event, see the section entitled "The Doctrine of Essence" in *Science of Logic,* 394–408.

15. In the next two chapters we will explore the deeper implications of a One that posits difference within itself.

16. Perception's interpretation of properties as multiple relations recalls Socrates' discussion of the three fingers in the *Republic* (7.523A ff.). Sense takes a finger as a jumble of opposites: big and little, thick and thin, hard and soft. Intellect in its relational capacity avoids contradiction by distinguishing each member of an opposition as a different aspect of the finger. It *counts* the opposing elements in such a way that "each is one and both are two" (524B–C). Unlike perception in the *Phenomenology,* Socrates' appeal to relational distinctions is for the sake of a higher goal: "summoning

thought," through perplexity, to the investigation of what things like big and little *are,* that is, to dialectical inquiry as the study of being.

17. In Plato's *Sophist,* the stranger from Elea does something similar in his effort to interweave the five greatest classes or kinds: "And we shall assert that this nature [the Other] has indeed run through all of them; for each is other than the others not because of its own nature but because it participates in the look of the Other" (255E, trans. Eva Brann, Peter Kalkavage, and Eric Salem [Newburyport, Mass.: Focus, 1996], 66).

18. "Thanks to this dialectic we proceed from *thing* to *relation,* from the thingism of perception to the relativity of the understanding" (Hyppolite, *Genesis and Structure,* 116).

Chapter 5: The Dynamics of Self-Expression

1. Throughout this chapter, the reader should occasionally compare the meaning of understanding, *Verstand,* as it appears here, with what Hegel says about understanding in his Preface: "the activity of dissolving or separating [*Scheiden*] is the force [*Kraft*] and work of the *understanding,* the most astonishing and greatest, or rather absolute, power [*Macht*]" [32]. In the present chapter, understanding does not know this about itself. It does not know that, rather than having force as its object, it *is* the absolute force.

2. The history of force in physics is long and complex. For a highly readable account that traces the idea from the ancient Greeks to Leibniz and Newton (and beyond), see Max Jammer, *Concepts of Force* (Cambridge: Harvard University Press, 1957).

3. Hegel, *The Jena System, 1804–5: Logic and Metaphysics,* trans. John W. Burbidge and George di Giovanni (Kingston and Montreal: McGill-Queen's University Press, 1986), 54.

4. According to the First Law, a body persists in its state of rest, or its motion in a straight line, unless it is compelled to change by an outside force. According to the Second, a body's change of motion or acceleration is directly proportional to the force impressed on it (in our familiar equation, $F = ma$). And according to the Third, for every action there is always an equal reaction in the opposite direction. This Third Law, the law of *interaction,* is crucial to Hegel's dialectic of force.

5. *The Assayer,* in *Discoveries and Opinions of Galileo,* trans. Stillman Drake (New York: Doubleday Anchor Books, 1957), 237–38.

6. The negative One of perception was not the source of the properties themselves—not their essence. It was only the source of their general determinateness. It merely sorted and distinguished them.

7. Leibniz regularly distinguishes between *phenomena bene fundata* and what he calls monads. For various references, the interested reader may wish to consult the index, under "phenomena," in Leibniz, *Philosophical Essays,* ed. Ariew & Garber.

8. *Ethics* I, proposition 29, scholium 51–52. *Natura naturans* ("nature naturing") refers to what Spinoza calls substance, or that which is its own cause (*causa sui*) (definition 1). *Natura naturata* ("nature that has been natured") refers to what depends on substance: what Spinoza calls attributes and modes.

9. See "A Specimen of Dynamics," where Leibniz distinguishes between "dead force" (for example, gravity) and "living force" (for example, the force at work in collision) (*Philosophical Essays,* ed. Ariew & Garber, 121–22).

10. Life comes on the scene just before self-consciousness or man [168]. It is explicitly an object of study at the stage of Observing Reason [254 ff.]. In the *Science of Logic,* life is more advanced than mechanism and chemism, and is *very* high in Hegel's hierarchy of logical categories. It is the first moment of what Hegel calls the Idea (761–74). The only categories higher than Life are the True, the Good, and the Absolute Idea. The explicit rejection of kind-characters or natural heterogeneity in modern physics can be seen in the use of blank terms like "particle" and "body."

11. For a helpful account of the difference between the ancient non-mathematical physics of Aristotle and the modern mathematical physics of Newton, see Heidegger's *What Is A Thing?* (trans. W. B. Barton Jr. and Vera Deutsch [Chicago: Henry Regnery Company, 1967], 66–95).

12. A very different account of the object of understanding appears in the Additions [*Zusätze*] to the section of the *Encyclopaedia* entitled "Phenomenology" (Hegel, *Philosophy of Mind,* trans. William Wallace, notes trans. A. V. Miller [Oxford: Clarendon Press, 1971]). There, Hegel includes both life and purpose in understanding, although he does not do so in the main body of the text (164). He also makes no mention at all of force but goes straight to appearance and law. In the *Encyclopaedia,* Phenomenology is between Anthropology (which studies the soul) and Psychology. It presupposes the phenomenon of life.

13. For Hegel's purely logical, scientific account of force, see *Science of Logic,* 518–23.

14. In *The Jena System, 1804–5,* Hegel says that force "expresses relationship in truth" (56). He adds: "Force thus expresses relationship itself and the necessity to be within itself even in its being-outside-itself, or to be self-equal" (ibid.).

15. See Plato's *Sophist,* where the Eleatic stranger at one point defines being as power, *dynamis:* the power of acting and being acted upon, more broadly, the power that elements have to partake of each other's natures (247D ff.).

16. Force, as Leibniz understands it, is self-necessitation—essence that necessarily exists or appears. Leibniz, through his science of dynamics, is spelling out what Spinoza meant by substance or God as *causa sui,* the cause of itself: "By that which is self-caused I mean that whose essence involves existence; or that whose nature can be conceived only as existing (*Ethics* I, definition 1). As Harris observes, Spinoza and Leibniz, as representatives of the understanding, in this way posit *contradiction* as the ultimate truth of things (*Hegel's Ladder,* 1:314, note 44). The reason for the contradiction is that God (i.e. nature) as self-caused is a single being that is the unity of opposites (cause and effect). "What they [Spinoza and Leibniz] fail to do," Harris continues, "is to see how the contradiction arises; and consequently, they cannot resolve it." This is another way of saying that they do not think in terms of the self-differentiating Concept.

17. In his account of Plotinus' emanation or radiance theory, Hegel observes that these figurative expressions lack the Concept: "Severance, emanation, effluence or process, emergence, occurrence, are words which in modern times have also had to stand for much, but in fact nothing is expressed by them" (*Lectures on the History of Philosophy,* 2:429).

18. In several places, Hegel defines Spinoza's metaphysics as the archetype of truth as substance. Although Hegel criticizes this view, pointing out that it suppresses self-consciousness or individual subjectivity, he also asserts that Spinoza articulated the proper beginning of the true metaphysics: "thought must begin by placing itself at the standpoint of Spinozism; to be a follower of Spinoza is the essential commencement of all philosophy" (*Lectures on the History of Philosophy,* 3:257).

19. In *The Encyclopaedia Logic,* Hegel responds critically to those who assert that we perceive only the effect of force and that the nature of force itself is unknown: "the whole *determination of the content* of the *force* is just the same as the content-determination of the *utterance* [or expression]; and because of this the explanation of an appearance through a force is an empty tautology" (193).

20. "We can see that, properly, force expresses the whole causality relation within itself, or the cause as one with the effect and in truth actual substance, but [that] the causality relation is sublated. In other words, because cause is inseparable from effect and the distinction is null and void, their unity as force is the actual substance; for only because it posits itself as an actual outside itself [is] the cause outside itself only a possible" (Hegel, *The Jena System,* 49). Heidegger makes much of Hegel's identification of force with the logical category of relation and points out the connection between the concept of force in Hegel and the so-called "dynamic categories" in Kant (*Hegel's Phenomenology of Spirit,* 101–5).

21. Substance, here, refers not to things as such but to the power of emergent properties as "happenings" within the flux of appearance. As Harris observes, "Aristotle employed the concept of 'Substance' [a somewhat misleading translation of his term *ousia*] for *things.* Hegel's concept of 'Substance' is both pre-Socratic and modern, but not Aristotelian" (*Hegel's Ladder,* 1:275).

22. Leibniz uses the term in his "A Specimen of Dynamics" (*Philosophical Essays,* ed. Ariew & Garber, 121). In another context, he defines solicitation as "potential force" and "infinitesimal motion" (Pierre Costabel, *Leibniz and Dynamics,* trans. R. E. W. Maddison [Ithaca: Cornell University Press, 1973], 102). Hegel does not use the term in the same way as Leibniz. For Leibniz, solicitation is the inner, infinitesimal striving or *conatus* of the body itself, force proper. For Hegel, it is the

incitement that comes from *another* body: one force solicits, another is solicited. In other words, Hegel is using the term in the context of dynamic reciprocity.

23. Kant is helpful on this point. In his *Metaphysical Foundations of Natural Science,* he proves what Leibniz before him had argued, that the very extension of matter is the result of a force: "Matter fills a space, not by its mere existence, but by a special moving force" (trans. Ellington, 41). So too, a body is *a* body because of the force of cohesion.

24. The action of force on force strongly echoes the teachings of the Jesuit-physicist, Roger Joseph Boscovich (1711–87). Building on the dynamic theory of Leibniz, Boscovich asserted that force was more primary than matter, and that the impact between two colliding bodies was the result of interacting repulsive forces (action at a distance). No material contact or touching is involved. For a clear account of this theory, see Max Jammer (*Concepts of Force,* 170–87).

25. The idea of force is used extensively by Johann Gottlieb Fichte to explain the phenomena of consciousness and self-consciousness. Just as force requires solicitation by another, so too the self, in order to reflect on itself, requires a shock or impetus [*Anstoß*] from the non-self or external world (*Science of Knowledge,* trans. Heath & Lachs, see index under "check").

26. Leibniz gives a detailed analysis of collision in part two of "A Specimen of Dynamics." One of his main points is that "*what happens in a substance can be understood to happen of that substance's own accord*" (*Philosophical Essays,* ed. Ariew & Garber, 131), more especially that "*every passion of a body is of its own accord,* that is, *arises from an internal force, even if it is on the occasion of something external*" (134).

27. Appearance as the play of force is similar to what goes on in the mysterious receptacle of Plato's *Timaeus,* where the four elements of body keep changing into each other and point beyond themselves to their unchanging archetypes (49C ff.).

Chapter 6: Principles of Motion and the Motion of Principles

1. As Hegel says in the *Science of Logic,* the I or self-consciousness is the pure Concept, the principle of unity within self-differentiation, that "has come into *existence*" [*zum Dasein gekommen ist*] (583).

2. Hegel's extensive account of the syllogism may be found in the *Science of Logic* (664–704). It is one of the most readable, accessible parts of this formidable work.

3. The syllogism was already present in the preceding dialectic of force, where the single force that splits into active and passive is described as a "middle term" [136].

4. Hegel's purely conceptual derivation of the supersensible world from appearance may be found in the *Science of Logic* in the chapter entitled "Appearance" (499–511). In the *Phenomenology,* force comes before law: in the *Logic,* law comes before force.

5. Or, as Hyppolite puts it: "The essence of essence is to manifest itself; manifestation is the manifestation of essence" (*Genesis and Structure,* 125).

6. "First, the very thing we've now named water we see condensing, thereby becoming, so it seems to us, stones and earth; and this same thing again, by melting and dissolving, we see becoming wind and air; and air, having been heated, becoming fire; and conversely, we see fire, having been contracted and quenched, going back once more to the look of air; and air, by coming together and thickening up, going back to become cloud and fog; and when these are compressed still more, we see water flow from them, and from water back to earth and stones—a circle—thus passing on to one another, as it appears, birth" (*Timaeus* 49B–C, trans. Peter Kalkavage [Newburyport, Mass.: Focus, 2001]).

7. In the nature part of the *Encyclopaedia,* Hegel defines time as "that being which, insofar as it *is,* is *not,* and insofar as it is *not, is;* it is *intuited* becoming [*angeschaute Werden*]" (*Philosophy of Nature,* 34).

8. The stabilizing function of the Forms is prominent in the *Timaeus,* where the demiurge gazes at utterly stable being in order to craft a beautiful image within becoming (28A ff.).

9. There are many connections between Hegel and Plato's *Parmenides.* Young Socrates appears in the dialogue as a combination of perception and understanding. He wants separate Forms in order to avoid the otherness and self-difference revealed in Zeno's paradoxes. In other words, he

wants to avoid the inherent negativity of dialectic, and he wants the Forms to function as explanatory devices that dissolve contradiction (128E–130A). Although he posits the Forms as separate from things, he tends to treat them as though they *were* things. Old Parmenides shows him the error of his ways and gives a magnificent display of the logical exercise he must practice if he is to be fully philosophical. It is this display that Hegel, in his Preface to the *Phenomenology,* calls "the greatest artistic achievement of the ancient dialectic" [71].

10. The inverse square law also holds for electrical charges. This is Coulomb's Law, named after its discover, Charles Augustin Coulomb (1736–1806). This makes even stronger Hegel's point that the modern physicist is constantly in search of higher and higher levels of generality. The most explicit and dramatic effort toward the ultimate unity of law was Einstein's uncompleted quest for a "unified field theory," which would cover both gravitational and electromagnetic fields. Max Born, a fellow physicist with Einstein, wrote: "to Einstein is due the merit of having insisted on the importance of the problem, namely, to find all-embracing laws which unify the whole of the physical world" (*Einstein's Theory of Relativity* [New York: Dover, 1965], 372).

11. The German word for actuality is *Wirklichkeit,* which contains the word for work, *Werk.* German is very close to Greek here. Aristotle's term *energeia,* often translated "actuality," is literally "being at work" (*ergon*).

12. Kant attempts to refute Hume's assault on necessary connection in the *Critique of Pure Reason.* He does so by arguing that causality is the irreversible temporal sequence of our perceptions, and that this sequence is the necessary condition for our experience of the world. See Book II, Analytic of Principles, Second Analogy of Experience (trans. Pluhar, 259–76).

13. Hume, *A Treatise of Human Nature* (Oxford: Clarendon Press, 1968), bk. I, pt. 3, sec. 14, p. 165.

14. For a powerful non-Hegelian critique of mathematical physics, see Husserl's *Crisis of European Sciences.* According to Husserl, Galileo and Descartes covered the life-world of ordinary experience with a "garb of ideas" (trans. David Carr [Evanston: Northwestern University Press, 1970], 51), and presented as objectively true what was in fact only a *method.*

15. In the Preface, it is clear that the focus of Hegel's attack is not the form of mathematical account giving but the pretensions of the account-givers. Mathematics must be stripped of its "fine feathers" by a critique of mathematical proofs in physics [46]. In the *Encyclopaedia,* he puts forth a remarkable dialectical proof of the inner (i.e., non-mathematical) necessity at work in Galileo's law of free fall (*Philosophy of Nature,* 57–59). Especially remarkable is Hegel's account of what it means for the time-variable to be *squared.*

16. This clearly resembles the stage at which perception took responsibility for either the One or the Many of the thing.

17. This famous joke appears in Molière's *Imaginary Invalid.* Harris has the following valuable observation: "We laugh with Molière at the 'formalism' that makes it possible for someone to pass himself off as a physician. But there is an important philosophical truth to be learned from the very fact that the imposture is possible" (*Hegel's Ladder,* 1:315, note 19).

18. Hegel, *The Jena System, 1804–5,* 62. Hegel's account of explanation in this early version of his System is much clearer than the one he presents in the *Phenomenology* of 1807. Hans-Georg Gadamer rightly observes that understanding can avoid the tautologies of explanation by appealing to so-called positivism: "the truth of positivism is precisely that it replaces the concept of explanation with that of description" (*Hegel's Dialectic,* trans. P. Christopher Smith [New Haven: Yale University Press, 1976], 57). Hegel shows how the understanding's search for causes necessarily implies this non-causal view of science.

19. Helpful accounts of the inverted world include those by Jean Hyppolite (*Genesis and Structure,* 136–39), Stanley Rosen (*G. W. F. Hegel: An Introduction to the Science of Wisdom* [New Haven: Yale University Press, 1974], 140–50), Hans-Georg Gadamer ("Hegel's 'Inverted World,'" in *Hegel's Dialectic,* 35–53), Joseph C. Flay ("Hegel's 'Inverted World,'" *Review of Metaphysics* 23, no. 4 (June 1970), Murray Greene ("Hegel's Notion of Inversion," *International Journal for Philosophy of Religion* (fall 1970): 161–75), Donald Verene ("The Topsy-turvy World," in *Hegel's Recollection: A Study of Images in the Phenomenology of Spirit* [Albany: SUNY Press, 1985], 39–58), and H. S. Harris (*Hegel's Ladder,* 1:290 ff.).

20. Verene observes that a play by Ludwig Tieck, entitled *The Inverted World* and written in 1799, may have been an inspiring influence on Hegel's account. He develops the possible connections in his book, *Hegel's Recollection* (50–52).

21. Self-consciousness, we shall see, is the actual experience of contradiction or inner tension. With the inverted world of the understanding, consciousness is on the *threshold* of experiencing contradiction. Or rather, it *is* experiencing contradiction but only within its attempt to think the rational objective order of nature.

22. In a sense, this is a compliment to the scientific understanding. The inverted world, as the praxis of understanding, reveals that understanding not only thinks, but also is *ingenious*. Verene characterizes the inverted world as follows: "The topsy-turvy world is ingenuity run wild, ingenuity performed for ingenuity's sake" (*Hegel's Recollection*, 45).

23. "The great joke, Hegel wrote in a personal note, is that things are what they are" (Hyppolite, *Genesis and Structure*, 125).

24. For a helpful treatment of Hegel on the magnet, see Harris, *Hegel's Ladder*, 1:293–94. The magnet plays an important role in Schelling's philosophy. For Schelling, differences in nature follow a three-stage process of evolution: "in magnetic phenomena we see matter still at the first stage of construction, where the two opposing forces are united in one and the same point." Magnetism is thus a function "of matter in general" (*System of Transcendental Idealism, 1800*, trans. Peter Heath [Charlottesville: University Press of Virginia, 1978], 87).

25. Hegel treats crime and punishment extensively in an early work entitled *The Spirit of Christianity*. There he uses the language of inversion explicitly in reference to Macbeth, who in murdering Banquo succeeds only in bringing about his own destruction: "In his arrogance he [Macbeth] has destroyed indeed, but only the friendliness of life; he has perverted life into an enemy" (*Early Theological Writings*, 229).

26. As Hyppolite notes, "In the Sermon on the Mount, Christ repeatedly opposes appearance—'it has been said'—to profound reality—'I say unto you'" (*Genesis and Structure*, 136). The connection between inversion and Christianity supports Gadamer's claim that *Verkehrung*, for Hegel, carries the sense of perversion (*Hegel's Dialectic*, 45 ff.). The teachings of Christianity—especially the teaching that "the first shall be last"—are offensive to our worldly standards. They seem perverse.

27. The superficial view of inversion affects how some view the history of philosophy—as no more than a series of externally conflicting positions on the absolute. Hegel criticizes this view at length in the Introduction to his *Lectures on the History of Philosophy* (1.7 ff.). The critique is deeply related to Hegel's attack on true and false as "wholly separate essences" in the Preface to the *Phenomenology* [39].

28. Overreaching comes up again in Hegel's next chapter as defining self-consciousness [166]. Emil Fackenheim claims that overreaching [*übergreifen*] "is perhaps Hegel's most important term, and the presence of overreaching power in spirit may be called without exaggeration *the* decisive condition of the possibility of the complete philosophic thought" (*The Religious Dimension in Hegel's Thought* [Boston: Beacon Press, 1970], 98).

29. This is how Aristotle defines the infinite [*to apeiron*] in *Physics* 3.6.

30. "Bad infinity" appears in the *Phenomenology* in the chapter on reason [238]. For Hegel's full discussion of this important concept, see *Science of Logic*, 138–43.

31. This retention of self-difference within ultimate self-identity is what distinguishes Hegel's absolute from Schelling's absolute, which Hegel derisively calls "the night in which all cows are black" [16].

Chapter 7: On Life and Desire

1. The simple observation that my experience is *my* experience, and that objects of perception are *my* objects, led Kant to his "transcendental unity of apperception." This formidable term means simply this: that if there is to be universal knowledge of the perceptual world, then there must be a pure, radically self-identical I that provides the *necessary condition* for such knowledge by unifying the manifold data I receive from my senses. As a necessary condition for my sense-experience, this pure self cannot itself be experienced, for then it would be contingent and changeable. It must be, in

Kant's terminology, *a priori.* The transcendental unity of apperception appears for the first time in the *Critique of Pure Reason* in the Transcendental Deduction (A 106). Kant also calls it the "I think" (B 131). Fichte takes Kant's transcendental ego and makes it into what he calls the "absolute self." The shift is not merely a change in terminology. For Kant, the transcendental self is a logical condition for the possibility of experience. For Fichte, it is a *metaphysical* principle by which the self, at the deepest level of its being, actively posits both itself and the world. See *Science of Knowledge,* trans. Heath & Lachs, index entry for "Self, absolute."

2. For an extremely lucid discussion of the structure of the *Phenomenology,* and the problems with that structure, see Robert Pippin's essay, "You Can't Get There from Here," 52–85.

3. As Rosen observes, "the last section does not go *beyond* self-consciousness but considers it as a totality in its attempt to preserve or transform itself into self-knowledge" (140).

4. In an early writing entitled *Fragment of a System* (1800), Hegel, largely under the influence of Schelling's philosophy of life, develops the idea of life as internal opposition (*Early Theological Writings,* 309–19). On the one hand, the living thing is independent and self-identical. On the other, it is "capable of losing its individuality" through its interaction with other living things (310). To live is to be a One in constant danger of death. Life, says Hegel, consists in opposition. It is "the union of union and nonunion" (312).

5. Reason, in its observational mode, will attempt this biological formalism [271 ff.].

6. Unlike Socrates in the *Symposium,* Hegel does not connect procreation with the striving for immortality. The natural end of striving is not an unchanging Beyond but infinite self-expression. To use the language of Leibniz, procreation, for Hegel, is an "unfolding" of the animal monad: it is not for the sake of anything beyond the unfolding itself.

7. In the *Philosophy of Nature,* Hegel says the following: "The animal is intrinsically the most lucid existence in nature, but it is the hardest to comprehend since its nature is the speculative Concept" (358).

8. The quotation is from the first in a trio of prose poems entitled *A B C.* The letters are the first letters of the words with which each piece begins but also no doubt signal the "basics" or "elements" of self-conscious experience. The trio of poems can be found in *Paul Valéry: An Anthology,* selected by James R. Lawler (Princeton: Princeton University Press, Bollingen Series, 1977), 173–78. Valéry was haunted by the mystery, and suffering, of self-consciousness. In his early poem, "The Young Fate," which Elie Kedourie calls "a Hegelian poem," Valéry presents an extended soliloquy on the painful dawning of self-awareness. See Kedourie, *Hegel and Marx: Introductory Lectures,* trans. Sylvia and Helen Kedourie (Oxford: Blackwell, 1995), 105. The theme of Self-Consciousness also pervades Valéry's meditative poem, "The Graveyard by the Sea" ("Le Cimetière Marin").

9. In Plato's *Timaeus,* the rotation of the celestial sphere is an outward sign of the perfect and happy life of the cosmos (34A). The image is used to great effect in Dante's *Paradiso,* where the swiftest motion, that of the celestial sphere, is closest to God's perfect rest.

10. For Hegel, sex and death are intimately connected: "this process of propagation [*Fortpflanzung*] spends itself in the bad infinity. The genus preserves itself only through the destruction of the individuals who, in the process of begetting [*Begattung*], fulfill their vocation and, insofar as they have no higher vocation, in this process go to their death" (*Philosophy of Nature,* 414).

11. The genus or kind [*Gattung*], and its differentiation into species, will become important at the level of reason's observation of nature [291]. For Hegel's systematic, logical account of the Kind, see *Science of Logic* (772–74) and the *Philosophy of Nature* (409 ff.).

12. In the *Philosophy of Nature,* Hegel calls man "the perfect animal": "this highest organism therefore presents us in general with a *universal type,* and it is only in and from this type that we can ascertain and explain the meaning of the undeveloped organism" (357).

13. "According to Hegel, self-consciousness is at first a simple genus for itself; it 'covers' itself as its only instance or object" (Rosen, *G. W. F. Hegel,* 159).

14. For a fascinating discussion of how emergent self-consciousness has its *Gestalt* in Faust, whom Hegel discusses at the level of reason [360–65], see Harris, *Hegel's Ladder,* 1:328–29.

15. Another way to put this is to say that actual knowledge, for Aristotle, is prior to potential knowledge.

16. In *Genesis,* the temptation of Eve presents a complex case of desire for an external object. She eats the forbidden fruit because of what the serpent *persuades her* are its inherent properties.

She sees "that it was good for food, and that it was pleasant to the eyes, and a tree to be desired to make one wise" (3, 6). But her true desire was to be independent—a god. In eating the fruit, she succumbed to the demands of her self-consciousness and natural self-love. The object of her desire was *herself.* In *Paradise Lost,* Milton makes much of Eve's narcissism (see Eve's speech to Adam in Book 4, 440–91).

17. As we saw in Chapter 7, infinity, for Hegel, is not continual unendingness but the logical process by which opposites contain one another and thus form a prospective *whole* or System. Infinity, like the syllogism, is self-enclosing. This radical re-interpretation of infinity is deeply connected with Hegel's overall optimism—his view that desire, philosophy, and world history "have a happy ending" by *producing* rather then gratuitously receiving their end and fulfillment.

18. The phrase is from Descartes' *Discourse on Method* (6).

19. In the Jena *Realphilosophie,* Hegel identifies all desire, including the bestial form, with anxiety, *Angst* ([Hamburg: Felix Meiner, Philosophische Bibliothek, 1967], 157–58).

20. As Harris points out, the self at this stage of immediacy is infantile *but not an infant* (*Hegel's Ladder,* 1:331). It is the adult self that wants whatever it wants, and will cunningly adopt any means to get it. The self as abstract desire is the self of a tyrant. Like the tyrant, he is perpetually unhappy. In the image from Plato's *Republic,* the tyrant—the creature of unphilosophic *erōs*—is always trying to fill the leaky, appetitive part of his soul with things that have no lasting being (9.586A–B). A similar image, in which the pleasure-seeking soul is compared to a leaky jar, appears in the *Gorgias* (493A ff.). Harris ingeniously connects the whole discussion of self-consciousness as desire with the three-part soul in Plato's *Republic* (*Hegel's Ladder,* 1:328 ff.). Hegel takes us from the *appetitive* part, or merely natural desire, to the *spirited* part, which loves honor and victory, in order to point ultimately to the *rational* part, which loves knowledge.

21. The tragic resurrection of the object is especially evident in sexual *erōs.* In Racine's *Phèdre,* Phaedra prays to Aphrodite that the goddess free her from her indecent love for her stepson Hippolytus. As she offers the burnt sacrifice, she finds that her heart is really offering adoration to the beloved himself, "that god I dare not name" (act 1, scene 3). Her prayer is a determinate negation that posits the object in seeking to negate it.

22. See the end of note 20 above on Plato's three-part soul.

23. The language of a self that finds its satisfaction in another self raises the possibility that Hegel is talking about *love.* As we see in the next section, the meeting of two self-consciousnesses will instead be competitive and warlike. For Hegel, Ares rather than Eros presides over self-consciousness. Why did Hegel choose war over love at this point? Why did he not follow the German Romantics, and the praise of love in his own early writings? Hyppolite, quoting Hegel's Preface to the *Phenomenology,* offers a persuasive answer: "Love does not dwell sufficiently on the tragic nature of separation; it lacks 'the seriousness, the torment, the patience, and the labor of the negative'" (*Genesis and Structure,* 164). Another formulation might go something like this: love is too positive, too advanced, to serve as the negativity out of which community arises. It lacks sufficient logical tension. It also embodies the self-sacrifice that can appear only at a much later stage of spiritual development. Perhaps, too, it is not sufficiently universal in that love is love for a single beloved. For Hegel's early views of love, see the fragment entitled "Love" in *Early Theological Writings* (302–8). Later in the *Phenomenology,* at the level of reason, self-consciousness will appear as erotic love. Its archetype will be Faust [360 ff.]. This is the second major appearance of desire or *Begierde* in Hegel's book.

24. This opposition, which recalls the "Now is night" in sense-certainty [95], will reappear at crucial moments in Hegel's book. In the Greek ethical world, it will manifest itself as the difference between the night-like, private realm of family and the dead, and the day-like, public realm of government [455–57].

25. For Hegel's praise, and criticism, of Rousseau's general will, see *Philosophy of Right* (trans. White, 190) and *Lectures on the History of Philosophy,* 3:400–402.

26. Hegel's understanding of community in this highest sense is a combination of Aristotle's "thinking of thinking" and the Christian Trinity of Father, Son, and Holy Spirit. Hegel ends his *Encyclopaedia* by quoting the passage from *Metaphysics* 12.7, in which Aristotle defines divine thinking as the thinking of itself. The most beautiful formulation of the Christian God's communion with himself is that of Dante at the end of his *Paradiso:* "Oh Light Eternal, that alone abidest

in Thyself, alone knowest Thyself, and, known to Thyself and knowing, lovest and smilest on Thyself!" (33.124–26).

Chapter 8: The Violent Self

1. In the *Science of Logic,* Hegel offers some helpful comments on the logical category, being-for-self (157–58). One is: "we say that something is for itself insofar as it cancels or sublates otherness [*Anderssein*]." Another is: "Being-for-self is the polemical, negative attitude toward the limited other." Hegel goes on to say that self-consciousness "is being-for-self as consummated [*vollbracht*] and posited."

2. Hegel's chapter on morality is the only chapter of the *Phenomenology* that generates a tragedy but then dispels it in "divine comedy," that is, a happy ending. The two chapters that follow, Religion and Absolute Knowing, are not further stages of struggle and suffering but elaborations of the spiritual victory that occurred at the end of Morality in the phenomenon of forgiveness and reconciliation. For religion and philosophy, there are no tragedies.

3. The neutral mode of recognition, in which I merely "register" someone's identity, is conveyed by the verb *erkennen,* which is related to Hegel's word *Erkenntnis,* cognition.

4. In the Platonic dialogues, Socrates sometimes utters the jingle, "Each is one, and both are two." See *Republic* 7.524B. For Hegel, human selves do not behave like mathematical monads. The dialectical structure of self-consciousness obliges us to invert the Socratic jingle and say: "Each is two, and both are one."

5. Heidegger discusses "thrownness," *Geworfenheit,* in *Being and Time,* trans. Joan Stambaugh (Albany: SUNY, 1996), 127.

6. Compare Spinoza's definition of "free" in the *Ethics:* "That thing is said to be free which exists solely from the necessity of its own nature, and is determined to action by itself alone" (part I, definition 7).

7. Gadamer has a helpful discussion of how the reciprocity of recognition is at work when two human beings greet each other on the street (*Hegel's Dialectic,* 64).

8. The phenomenon of impact or *Anstoß,* and the concept of force generally, play a central role in Fichte's analysis of consciousness in the *Science of Knowledge* (see chapter 5, note 25 above). But for Fichte the shock comes from the external thing, not another self-consciousness. For Hegel, unlike Fichte, subjectivity is necessarily intersubjectivity. Hegel is closer to ordinary experience: other human beings *are* more shocking to us than mere things.

9. Hegel plays on the words *gegen* [183], against or toward, and *gegenseitig,* mutual or "sided against" [184]. The *gegen* part of *gegenseitig* captures the role that negation plays in mutual recognition.

10. For Hegel's full discussion of being-for-self as a logical category, see *Science of Logic,* 157 ff. There, Hegel says: "*Self-consciousness,* on the other hand [as opposed to consciousness, which is object-oriented], is being-for-self as *consummated* and *posited;* the side of connection with an other, with an external object, is removed" (158). Being-for-self is, as it were, the self-assertiveness or "I AM MYSELF!" of every logical determination.

11. In his *Anthropology from a Pragmatic Point of View,* Kant describes the dawning of self-consciousness in the child who has just begun to use the pronoun "I": "It is noteworthy, however, that the child who already speaks fairly well begins to use the pronoun *I* rather late (perhaps after a year), in the meantime speaking of himself in the third person. . . . A light seems to dawn upon him when he begins speaking in the first person. From that day on he will never again revert to the third person. At first the child merely *felt* himself, now he *thinks* himself" (trans. Victor Lyle Dowdell [Carbondale: Southern Illinois University Press, 1996], 9).

12. This is the classic beginning of the schoolyard or street corner fight for recognition: "You lookin' at *me*?" Offense, like judgment, needs no more than a look.

13. Aggressive egotism is an especially vivid example of the "clenched" immediacy I mentioned in Chapter 4, the immediacy without which there would be no dialectical motion.

14. As Rosen points out, Kojève falls into this trap in claiming that what Hegel is doing in the present chapter is giving an historical, empirical derivation of self-consciousness (*G. W. F. Hegel,* 158–61).

15. Rosen puts this even more forcefully: "This relationship [of master and slave] is a figure intrinsic to human consciousness, and no more a historical 'event' than the transition from the 'state of nature' to a political society in pre-Hegelian political philosophy" (ibid., 155). Nevertheless, Hegel does, like Hobbes, regard the fight for recognition as in some way the temporal origin of civil society. In the Phenomenology part of the *Encyclopaedia,* Hegel writes: "The fight for recognition and the subjugation under a master or lord is the appearance in which there has emerged the communal life [*Zusammenleben*] that is the beginning of states" (*Philosophy of Mind,* trans. Wallace, 173).

16. Rosen makes a valuable observation in this regard: "At every stage of history prior to its completion (assuming that to be possible), each human being is at once master and slave, stoic and skeptic, or the living unity-within-difference of the inversion process which we studied previously with respect to the sensuous and supersensuous realms" (*G. W. F. Hegel,* 155).

17. At a crucial point in the *Critique of Pure Reason,* Kant points to the need for something that will mediate the radical heterogeneity of sensuous intuition and pure concept. This mediator is what he calls a *schematism,* which is the configuration of a logical category—a pure shape of *time* (trans. Pluhar, 209–19). Hegel's shapes of consciousness in the *Phenomenology* are analogous to Kant's schemata. They are shapes or figures of time that mediate the sensuously, historically present and the logically necessary.

18. For Hobbes' description of the state of nature, which is also the condition of civil strife, see *Leviathan,* part 1, ch. 13.

19. Harris suggests that Antigone's brothers, Eteocles and Polyneices, who killed each other in their fight to be lord of Thebes, "are probably Hegel's own paradigm for the struggle to the death" (1:355). This fits nicely with the reciprocity of self-consciousness. Achilles, in his fight with Hektor, is nevertheless a better example of the godlike individual who chooses honor over life. In the *Odyssey,* when Odysseus meets the soul of Achilles in the underworld, Achilles regrets his choice: "O shining Odysseus, never try to console me for dying. I would rather follow the plow as thrall to another man, one with no land allotted to him and not much to live on, than be king over all the perished dead" (*Odyssey* 11.488–91, trans. Richmond Lattimore). Here we see the transition from the fight-to-the-death to the upcoming master-slave relation.

20. In Hobbes' words, man's life in the natural state, "where every man is Enemy to every man," is "solitary, poore, nasty, brutish, and short" (ibid.).

21. In the *Timaeus, thymos* is housed in the chest (70A–B), intellect in the head (44D) and appetite in the belly (70D–E). The *Timaeus* has a special bond with the middle, spirited part of the soul. The whole drama is sparked by Socrates' spirited desire to see the ideal city *prove itself* in the speeches and deeds of war (19B–20C).

22. Later in the *Phenomenology,* person refers to the human individual insofar as he is the bearer of legal rights, especially the right to own property. Hegel calls the person a "sheer empty unit" [480], and the collection of persons is a "soulless community" [477]. In the *Philosophy of Right,* Hegel observes that the term "person" is dialectical and that the person "is thus at once what is high and what could not be lower" (trans. White, 41).

23. "Men without Chests" is the title of the first chapter of Lewis' *The Abolition of Man.*

24. The most famous modern interpretation of the master-slave dialectic is that of Alexandre Kojève (*Introduction to the Reading of Hegel,* trans. J. H. Nichols [New York: Basic Books, 1967], 3–30. Other insightful interpretations are those of Hyppolite (*Genesis and Structure,* 172–77), Rosen (*G. W. F. Hegel,* 154–64), and Gadamer (*Hegel's Dialectic,* 54–74).

25. The reader is strongly encouraged to compare Hegel's account of the master-slave relation with Aristotle's account of slavery, and the *natural slave,* in the *Politics* (1.2.1253B 15 ff.). In an Addition to his *Philosophy of Right,* Hegel offers the following provocative view of slavery: "If one adheres to the aspect of human beings as free in and as themselves, one thereby condemns slavery. But that someone is a slave lies within his own will, just as it lies within the will of a people if the people is subjugated. It is therefore not the case that wrong is done only by those who enslave or who subjugate; in addition, wrong is done by the enslaved and the subjugated themselves. Slavery occurs in the transition from the natural condition of human beings to the truly ethical situation; it occurs in a world where a wrong is still right. At that stage wrong is valid [*gilt das Unrecht*], and thus is necessarily in place" (trans. White, 55).

26. The investment of the self in an object is central to Hegel's understanding of *property* and *ownership.* To own a thing, to call it "mine," is to place my will in it. Ownership is the will's self-objectification. In his *Philosophy of Right,* Hegel says: "The person has as its substantial end the right of putting its will into any and every thing and thereby making it 'mine,' because the thing has no such end within itself and receives its determination and soul from the person's will" (trans. White, 45). The passage makes clear that the institution of slavery is the large-scale reduction of selves to *things.*

27. This is the life we see all around us today. We think that not being a slave means being without fear of any power over and above us, not needing to work in order to improve ourselves, and not needing to serve others. Our freedom is merely the impulse—as many see it, the right—of natural desire. It is the freedom of slaves who do not know that they are slaves.

Chapter 9: Freedom as Thinking

1. *Lectures on the History of Philosophy,* 3:402. The context is Hegel's discussion of Rousseau.

2. For Hegel's fuller account of the Greek stoicism that later became Roman stoicism, see *Lectures on the History of Philosophy,* 2:236–76.

3. On the correct translation of Hegel's sentence, see H. S. Harris, *Hegel's Ladder,* 1:385 and 1:436, note 3. There is a clear connection here between the freedom of the stoic and the assertive "I think" of Descartes. Like Descartes, the stoic is interested in mastery. But unlike Descartes, he does not want to master or even change the world. He masters the world *only* in thought. The stoic masters *himself,* his *inner state* as it relates to the external world. The stoic's thinking enters into things only insofar as they give him an opportunity to preserve his freedom.

4. As Hegel says in his *Lectures on the History of Philosophy,* "In Stoicism, pure Thought develops into a totality" (1:103).

5. *Nicomachean Ethics* 10.7.

6. *Lectures on the Philosophy of Religion,* 3:308.

7. The language of essence, *Wesen,* is significant. Hegel here recalls the same play on the two meanings of *Wesen* (abstract essence and concrete being) that he used to define the master consciousness at the beginning of the section [197].

8. The stoic is the first of several "purists" we will meet along the Way of Despair. His refusal to do the "dirty work" of negation foreshadows the self-destructive *beautiful soul* we meet much later [658].

9. Pyrrhonism figures prominently in Montaigne's *Essays.* There is an especially interesting account of "Pyrrho and other Skeptics" in "An Apology for Raymond Sebond" in *Essays,* trans. Donald M. Frame (Stanford: Stanford University Press, 1965), 371–75. According to Montaigne, "There is nothing in man's invention that has so much verisimilitude and usefulness [as Pyrrhonism]" (375).

10. "Skepticism is an ability to place in antithesis, in any manner whatever, appearances and judgments, and thus—because of the equality of force in the objects and arguments opposed—to come first of all to a suspension of judgment and then to mental tranquility" (Sextus Empiricus, *Selections from the Major Writings on Skepticism, Man, and God,* trans. Sanford G. Etheridge [Indianapolis: Hackett, 1985], 32–33). Sextus also says something that connects his teaching with both the stoic tradition and modern authors like Spinoza and Hobbes: "For the person who entertains the opinion that anything is by nature good or bad is continually disturbed" (41).

11. Plato's *Sophist,* 216B.

Chapter 10: Infinite Yearning and the Rift in Man

1. Kierkegaard, in *Either/Or,* offers a clear definition of Hegel's unhappy consciousness: "The unhappy person is one who has his ideal, the content of his life, the fullness of his consciousness, the essence of his being, in some manner outside of himself. He is always absent, never present to himself" (trans. David and Lillian Swenson [Princeton: Princeton University Press, 1971], 1:220).

2. As Rosen observes, the unhappy consciousness "has pagan, Jewish, and Christian forms, and modern as well as ancient variations" (*G. W. F. Hegel,* 169). He adds that terms like "infinite yearning," "musical thinking," and "the feeling heart" apply to various German Romantics whom Hegel criticizes in other writings. These phrases recall, in particular, Friedrich Heinrich Jacobi, whose Romantic subjectivism Hegel critiques at length in the early work, *Faith and Knowledge,* 97–152). Harris observes in his commentary that Jean Wahl "has made a powerful case for the whole movement of the 'syllogism of Self-Consciousness' in the mind of *Pascal*" (*Hegel's Ladder,* 1:438, note 18). This view finds support in Hegel's own assertion, in *Faith and Knowledge,* that Pascal's reflections on infinity give voice to the "infinite pain" of modern man (190). Harris correctly observes, however, that Pascal is more appropriately placed in the more advanced category of faith, which is "the *reconciled maturity* of the Unhappy Consciousness" (*Hegel's Ladder,* 1:439, note 22).

3. For Hegel's account of the progression from Jewish to Christian consciousness, see *Early Theological Writings,* the discussion of Christianity in the *Philosophy of History,* and the *Lectures on the Philosophy of Religion.* Harris points out that commentators who identify the first phase of the unhappy consciousness with "the Jewish experience" "ignore the necessary and important distinction between Judaism proper and 'the Old Testament'" (1:441, note 33).

4. Hegel, *Lectures on the Philosophy of Religion,* trans. Hodgson, Brown, and Stewart, 3:307–8.

5. Hegel, *The Philosophy of History,* 323.

6. For a summary of these three appearances of Christianity, see Chapter 16, "Interlude."

7. See Pascal's reference to the *deus absconditus* in his *Pensées,* where Pascal speaks of *la presence d'un Dieu qui se cache,* "the presence of a hidden God" (Fragment 449, trans. A. J. Krailsheimer [New York: Penguin Books, 1966], 170). See also Fragment 427 for Pascal's explicit reference to the phrase in *Isaiah* (155). At the end of *Faith and Knowledge* (190), Hegel quotes the fragment in which Pascal says: "Nature is such that it *signifies* everywhere a *lost* God both within and outside man."

8. This tragic condition, as it applies to man's desire to know the highest things, is signaled by Kant in the first sentence of the Preface to the *Critique of Pure Reason:* "Human reason has a peculiar fate in one kind of its cognitions [speculative reason]: it is troubled by questions that it cannot dismiss, because they are posed to it by the nature of reason itself, but that it also cannot answer, because they surpass human reason's every ability" (trans. Pluhar, 5).

9. Hegel, *The Difference Between Fichte's and Schelling's System of Philosophy* (1801), trans. H. S. Harris and Walter Cerf (Albany: SUNY Press, 1977), 89.

10. An analogous formulation occurs in the Preface to the *Phenomenology,* where Hegel speaks of the difference between the ancient and the modern world [33]. Among the ancient Greeks, spirit was in the midst of actualizing itself as a living, intelligent universal. The modern individual, by contrast, "finds the abstract form ready-made or prepared [*vorbereitet*]." Hegel goes on to describe the modern work of spirit as that of "freeing determinate thoughts from their fixity so as to give actuality to the universal, and impart to it spiritual life."

11. Hegel, *Difference,* 91.

12. Kedourie, *Marx and Hegel,* 28. Kedourie's remarks are in the context of what he perceives as a close connection between the poetic idealism of Schiller and the philosophic idealism of Hegel.

13. The terms changeable and unchangeable are also firmly *within* the Christian tradition as epithets, respectively, for man and God. They are especially prominent in St. Augustine. In his *Confessions,* Augustine, lifting an evocative phrase from Plotinus, speaks of his sinful past as exile within a "region of unlikeness." In a more explicit borrowing from Plotinus, he calls God "the One." God, for Augustine, is "the Selfsame," and sinful man is inconstant, dispersed, distracted, and self-other. Plotinus' "region of unlikeness" appears in *Enneads* I, 8, 13. Augustine uses the phrase (in Latin) in *Confessions* 7.10.16. He addresses God as "the One" in Book 11.29.39, and speaks of him as "the Selfsame" in several passages. One of the most poignant references to man as changeable occurs in the same passage in which Augustine addresses God as the One: "But I am distracted amid times, whose order I do not know, and my thoughts, the inmost bowels of my soul, are torn asunder by tumult and change" (*Confessions,* trans. John K. Ryan [New York: Image Books, 1960], 302).

14. This word *Versöhnung* will recur throughout the *Phenomenology.* Its most dramatic occurrence is at the end of the chapter on morality. There, the two antagonistic human selves, in becoming reconciled to each other's and to their own sinfulness, give rise to God manifested as the indwelling spirit of human community, God as "absolute spirit" [670–71].

15. See, for example, Paul's Letter to the Colossians: "For it pleased the Father that in him [the Son] should all fullness dwell; and having made peace through the blood of his cross, by him to reconcile all things unto himself; by him, I say, whether they be things in earth, or things in heaven" (1:19–20).

16. The difference between Plato's philosopher and the unhappy consciousness is the difference between two versions of separateness or *chōrismos.* Plato raises the problem of separateness in several places, notably in the *Parmenides* and the *Symposium.* Separateness is the separateness of the Forms from their experiential counterparts, of the Forms from one another, and of the human from the divine—the mortal from the immortal. In the *Symposium,* we hear that *erōs* is the *daimōn* or spirit, the between-being (*metaxu*), that mediates between gods and men, and overcomes their opposition (202D ff.). This love, however, which is fully revealed in the philosopher, has no component of self-loathing and recognition of sin. *Erōs* is not the same as infinite yearning. It longs to *be* divine, not to be *recognized* and *absolved* by the divine.

17. "The specific destiny of consciousness is concentrated in this ascent, an ascent admirably evoked by the Psalms and the Hebrew prophets" (Hyppolite, *Genesis and Structure,* 200). Hyppolite is referring to Hegel's remark in *The Philosophy of History:* "The state of feeling in question we find expressed most purely and beautifully in the Psalms of David, and in the Prophets; the chief burden of whose utterances is the thirst of the soul after God, its profound sorrow for its transgressions, and the desire for righteousness and holiness" (321).

18. Generally, from the standpoint of Hegel's Lutheranism, Catholic Christianity is defined by unfreedom and an absorption in externals. Luther liberates the Christian from his bondage to externals and makes explicit the inherent *inwardness* of Christianity: "Luther proclaimed the great doctrine that the Host had spiritual value and Christ was received only on the condition of *faith* in him" (*The Philosophy of History,* 377). It is not clear how Hegel resolves the problem that Protestant thought, as Fackenheim observes, "all too often (as in romanticism) dissipates the divine eternal Presence into sheer feeling" (*Religious Dimension,* 216). In its scorn for mere "externals," Protestant inwardness and subjectivity runs the risk of reducing the worship of God to self-worship or spiritual narcissism. Hegel takes up just this problem in the dialectic of the beautiful soul.

19. *Deuteronomy* 6:4.

20. The general problem of knowledge as the suffering of an unhappy consciousness is already present in Kant and Fichte. In the note above, I indicated the "tragic condition" of speculative reason in Kant. In Fichte, the problem is more explicitly that of reconciling the empirical (individual) ego and the absolute (universal) ego. Lacking Hegel's dialectical understanding of splitting, or the self-differentiating One, Fichte has no way to explain how the self-same can become self-other, that is, how opposition can occur *within* the absolute ego. A more careful examination of the connection between Fichte's two egos and the unhappy consciousness is well beyond the scope of this study.

21. My reading here follows Harris' observation that Hegel, in this passage on pure thinking, "means to embrace the ratiocinative method and arguments of the Scholastic philosophers and theologians" (*Hegel's Ladder,* 1:411). Harris does an excellent job of distinguishing the thinking of the medieval unhappy consciousness from the stoic and skeptic on the one hand, and Descartes on the other (1:412–13). We must note two things about the medieval Christian thinker, as Hegel understands him. First, as Harris observes, the theologian's thinking becomes "mute" once he enters into devotion, especially during the Mass (1:411). Second, his thinking, in spite of its apparently conceptual character, is really no more than a formalism, whose static terms never reach the subject matter to which they are applied. For Hegel's critique of Scholastic thinking, see *Lectures on the History of Philosophy,* 3:97 ff.

22. St. Anselm, *Proslogion,* trans. M. J. Charlesworth (Notre Dame, Ind.: University of Notre Dame Press, 1979), 111. The phrase "inaccessible light" is from Paul's *First Letter to Timothy* 6:16.

23. *Proslogion,* 137.

24. Ibid., 139.

25. The word translated "heart," *Gemüth,* is more general than *Herz,* which occurs later in Hegel's phrase "the law of the heart" [367]. In his *Philosophy of History,* Hegel identifies *Gemüth* as the principle of the Germanic peoples (350 ff.). The possible allusion here to Schiller's use of the term (Harris, *Hegel's Ladder,* 1:442, note 39) suggests that, for Hegel, Catholicism is a form of romanticism. Through ritualized feeling, it substitutes the beautiful for the true.

26. The word *Andenken*, "remembrance" (a veiled reference to the celebration of the Mass), is also part of Hegel's play on similar-sounding words (Harris, *Hegel's Ladder*, 1:413–14).

27. Plotinus, for whom contemplation is escape, offers an extreme case of this effort to shed one's individuality. The divine life of intellectual vision is "a deliverance from the things in this place" and a "flight of the alone to the alone" (*Enneads* VI, 11).

28. "Christ appears as a definite and present existence in a sensuous form as the *Host*, consecrated by the Priest" (Hegel, *The Philosophy of History*, 390).

29. For Hegel's discussion of the Crusades, see *The Philosophy of History*, 389–98. The Crusades, for Hegel, represent "the perversion of religion and of the divine Spirit" (394). They are also the beginning of the modern age and the true conception of God: "from them we may date the commencement of self-reliance and spontaneous activity" (393). Through this historical event, "the world attains the consciousness that man must look within himself for the [sensuous] *This* which is of a divine nature: subjectivity is thereby authorized absolutely, and in its own self determines the relation [of all things] to the Divine" (393). (I have emended Sibree's translation of this sentence.) In his famous poem, "Sunday Morning," Wallace Stevens repeats Hegel's point: "The tomb in Palestine / Is not the porch of spirits lingering. / It is the grave of Jesus, where he lay."

30. On Miller's translation of *gebrochne*, "broken," as "incomplete," see Harris, *Hegel's Ladder*, 1:443, note 44).

31. The basis for Hegel's heterodoxy is the opening of the Gospel of John. In the Nicene Creed, Christ, as God's power of creation, is said to be the one through whom "all things were made." But Christ himself was "begotten, not made." John does not draw this distinction between "begotten" and "made." He says; "by him [the *Logos*] all things were made, and without him was not anything made that was made." For a discussion of this point, see the translator's note to Hegel's *Difference*, 171, note 24.

32. Much later in the *Phenomenology*, Hegel will refer to God's act of kenosis or self-emptying [755, 808]. According to this Protestant theological teaching, God does give of his substance. He externalizes or alienates his very godhood in order to become man. He becomes a changeable, mortal consciousness.

33. In his analysis of the Christian unhappy consciousness, Hegel omits reference to the Passion. The unhappy consciousness focuses on its own suffering and seems oblivious to the suffering of God and the whole drama of redemption. In part, this characterization stems from Hegel's Protestant caricature of Catholicism. But the more interesting point is that, true to where consciousness is at this point of its journey, Hegel focuses on the believer's *subjective suffering*, on the necessarily *unhappy* aspect of Christian experience. This unhappiness (an intense form of desire) is the negative energy that propels consciousness to its further development. The Passion appears only at the very end of the *Phenomenology* in the book's closing image [808]. The meaning of this image, as it relates to Hegel's project, will be taken up in our final chapter. Neither here in the unhappy consciousness chapter nor in the final image does Hegel mention the Resurrection. For Hegel, there is no personal immortality. In absolute knowing, we are rationally reconciled to death, which is a necessary part of life. Christ's Resurrection is simply an image for the dialectical resurgence of world spirit.

34. St. Augustine, *Confessions* 10.38.270: "But words coming out of man's mouth and deeds known to men contain a most perilous temptation. This arises from love of praise which, to build up a sort of private superiority, begs for and hoards up marks of approval. Even when this is rebuked within myself, it affords temptation by the very fact that it is rebuked. Often, out of very contempt of glory a man derives an emptier glory. No longer, therefore, does he glory in contempt of vainglory: he does not despise it, in as much as he glories over it" (trans. Ryan, 302). In a similar vein, La Rochefoucauld writes in his *Maxims:* "The refusal of praise is a desire to be praised twice" (Maxim 149). Translations from La Rochefoucauld's *Maxims* are my own.

35. Harris argues that by "animal functions" Hegel means only the excretory functions since eating, drinking, and sex all have something "redeeming" or "high" about them. He notes further that Hegel's lurid description of unhappiness in this passage "points unmistakably to Luther" and to Luther's spiritual struggle with constipation (1:427–28). Although he is not in the medieval time-frame, Luther reveals (on Harris' reading) the depth of degradation to which the medieval Christian is brought—the pathetic result of desire and work.

36. The role of the mediating priest resembles that of *erōs* in Plato's *Symposium*. Quoting his teacher, Diotima, Socrates says that *erōs* is a "great spirit" [*daimōn megas*], who mediates between the mortal and the immortal (202E). This mediating spirit has the power of "interpreting and transporting things in the human realm to the gods and things in the divine realm to humans."

Chapter 11: Idealism

1. Descartes' famous *cogito ergo sum* does not occur in the *Meditations* itself but in the *Objections and Replies* that were appended to that work (Second Set of *Replies, The Philosophic Writings of Descartes,* trans. Cottingham, Stoothoff, and Murdoch, 2:100). Its French version (*je pense, donc je suis*) occurs in the *Discourse on Method,* part 4 (ibid., 1:127). In his *Lectures on the History of Philosophy* (3:229), Hegel repeats what Descartes himself says in the *Replies:* that the "therefore" does not signal a deduction but rather an intuition, and that "the connection between Being and Thought is only immediately posited."

2. In the *Science of Logic,* Hegel identifies idealism with philosophy: "Every philosophy is essentially an idealism or at least has idealism for its principle" (154–55). He goes on to say: "the principles of ancient and modern philosophies, water, or matter, or atoms are thoughts, universals, ideal entities, not things as they immediately present themselves to us, that is, in their sensuous individuality—not even the water of Thales" (155). For Hegel, Aristotle is the ancient paradigm of this idealism: "Aristotle excels Plato in speculative depth, for he was acquainted with the deepest kind of speculation—idealism—and in this upholds the most extreme empirical development" (*Lectures on the History of Philosophy,* 2:119). Aristotle's idealism is most clearly seen in his assertion that the mind, in the act of thinking a thing, becomes that thing, i.e. the thing's *eidos* or intelligible form (*De Anima* 3.8). What Plato and Aristotle lacked in their idealism was the notion of a *system*—the idea that "one principle should be maintained and consistently carried through the particular" (Hegel, *Lectures,* 2:229).

3. Fragment 3 from Parmenides' famous poem about the Way of Truth and the Way of Semblance. A more literal translation reads as follows: "For it is the same thing to be thought and to be." Hegel interprets this fragment, not surprisingly, as a statement of what he calls idealism in the present chapter: "Thought produces itself, and what is produced is a Thought. Thought is thus identical with Being" (*Lectures on the History of Philosophy,* 1:253). He concludes: "Since in this an advance into the region of the ideal is observable, Parmenides began philosophy proper" (254).

4. Kant, *Critique of Pure Reason* (trans. Pluhar, 25). In his footnote, Kant explains that just as Copernicus shifted the perceived motions of the heavens from the heavens themselves to the spectator, so too he, Kant, will shift the order of nature from nature itself to the human thinker.

5. For Kant's laying out of what I have summarized here, see the sections of the *Critique* entitled "Transcendental Aesthetic" and "Transcendental Analytic" (Analytic of Concepts).

6. In his *Lectures on the History of Philosophy,* Hegel says that Kant "remains restricted and confined by his psychological point of view and empirical methods" (3:430–31).

7. From Hegel's viewpoint, the enlivening of Kant's theory of cognition begins with Fichte. In his *Science of Knowledge,* Fichte not only tries to make Kant's edifice of reason more systematic and unified: he also uses the language of desire, striving, and force to describe the very action of the self. In the end, however, Fichte remains trapped in Kant's psychological or empirical view of thought. His theory "is from the very beginning subjective" (Hegel, *Lectures on the History of Philosophy,* 3:481).

8. For Kant's table of categories, see *Critique of Pure Reason,* book I, part II (trans. Pluhar, 132). Kant bases his table of categories on the table of judgments (124). In his introduction to reason, Hegel criticizes Kant for deriving his table of categories from this table: "But to pick up the plurality of categories again in some way or other as a welcome find, taking them, e.g. from various judgments, and complacently accepting them so, is in fact to be regarded as an outrage [*Schmach*] on Science" [235]. Hegel treats Kant's categories thoroughly in the *Science of Logic.*

9. The word category comes from the Greek noun *katēgoria.* The noun is related to the verb *katēgoreuein,* "to accuse." In Aristotle's use of the term, it means "to say one thing of another" or "to predicate." For Aristotle's treatment of the categories, or ways of predication, see his *Categories.*

10. Ironically, rationality as the incarnation of the self will not be complete until religion posits *the* Incarnation. Reason does not know that the Christianity it rejects is the *perfection* of reason. I will discuss this connection between reason and Christianity in Chapter 23.

11. For Kant's discussion of the schema, see *Critique of Pure Reason,* book II, chapter 1 (trans. Pluhar, 209–19).

12. At only one point does reason appeal to a God—fleetingly. This occurs when reason is forced to postulate "another understanding," an Author or Designer of nature, in order to affirm its belief in final causes [258]. This postulate appears in Kant's *Critique of Judgment.* It is a good example of how modern enlightened thinkers *use* God for their worldly purposes [561].

13. In the *De Anima,* Aristotle uses the hand as a metaphor for the mind. He says that just as the hand is a "tool of tools," so mind or intellect is a "form of forms" (3.8). The difference between Aristotle and Hegel on mind-as-hand is that, for Hegel, the Category expresses the individual self's consciousness of itself as absolute.

Chapter 12: Adventures of a Rational Observer

1. In the opening of the chapter on self-consciousness, Hegel presented the dialectic of life. Here, in reason, life is the object of endless natural observation. The earlier account, which was *for us,* was deeper and more revealing of what life really is. The dialectical account or logic of life is to naturalism as Concept in its high sense is to concept in its low sense. The present section of the *Phenomenology* is about observing reason's view of nature, not Hegel's. For Hegel's view, see his *Philosophy of Nature.*

2. The extreme length of the section on observing reason perhaps suggests that Hegel did not quite know what sort of book he was writing, or rather would come to write.

3. The instinct of reason is to be contrasted with the "cunning of reason" [*die List der Vernunft*], which Hegel discusses in his *Philosophy of History* (33). Reason, as self-concretizing spirit, cunningly uses the passions of individual men of action to advance its universal ends, ends that are concealed from these men.

4. All the dichotomies of reason, especially the split between inner thought and outer being, have their origin in Descartes' strict distinction between mind and body (Harris, *Hegel's Ladder,* 1:501). On the one hand, reason is a bold intellectual adventurer. On the other, it gets "cold feet" because it cannot think the conceptual unity of its self-consciousness and its consciousness (mind and body). It has a cognitive "bad conscience." In other words, Descartes' mind-body split necessarily culminates in Kant's posture of *critique.*

5. The skepticism or "bad conscience" of reason reminds us of Hegel's critique of Kant in the Introduction. Since reason has not yet "found itself" in things, it distinguishes between its self-reflection and its awareness of the external world.

6. The role of necessity and concept in organisms is a cornerstone of Schelling's philosophy of nature: "Every organic product carries the reason of its existence in *itself,* for it is a cause and effect of itself. . . . Thus a *concept* lies at the base of every organization, for where there is a necessary relation of the whole to the part and of the part to the whole, there is *concept*" (Schelling, *Ideas for a Philosophy of Nature* [1797, revised 1803], trans. Errol E. Harris and Peter Heath [Cambridge: Cambridge University Press, 1988], 31).

7. "It is as if an experiment were a *sensuous conception* [*conception sensible*], an elaboration of the sensuous which reveals within it the necessity of the concept" (Hyppolite, *Genesis and Structure,* 239). Hegel's reference to "pure conditions" reminds us that every experiment is abstract or ideal: it isolates certain physical variables and ignores others. When Galileo did experiments with free fall and the inclined plane, he abstracted from air resistance and surface friction.

8. The theory of "matters" appeared before: in *perception* [115] and *understanding* [135]. The most famous example is Lavoisier's hypothesis of caloric as the material ground of heat.

9. The theory of a "great influence" of the environment on organisms was championed by the biologist, G. R. Treviranus. See Harris, *Hegel's Ladder,* 1:497. Hegel quotes Treviranus frequently in the *Philosophy of Nature.*

10. In his Preface, Hegel defends Aristotle's notion of finality in nature: "the end is the Immediate, *Restful,* Unmoved, which is self-moving; and so, is *subject*" [22]. Aristotle grasped the unity of being and end. In Hegel's view, he thought in terms of the Concept, even though he lacked the dialectical logic in which the Concept fully manifests itself: "Aristotle's conception of nature is . . . nobler than that of today, for with him the principal point is the determination of end as the inward determinateness of natural things. Thus he comprehended nature as life, i.e., as that which has its end within itself, is unity with itself, which does not pass into another, but, through this principle of activity, determines changes in conformity with its own content, and in this way maintains itself therein" (*Lectures on the History of Philosophy,* 2:157). The *eidos,* for Aristotle, was the formal, efficient, and final cause all in one (*Physics* 2.7). The final cause or "for the sake of which" is not something "added" to the organism by human thought but is at work *in* the organism. Modern science builds its cognitive Rome on a sometimes-vicious critique of Aristotle's concept of nature, *physis.* In his account of modern observing reason, Hegel shows the consequences of modernity's failure to understand the immanent causality it has rejected.

11. This unmediated distinction is the ground of Kant's critique of speculative reason.

12. See note 10 of this chapter, above.

13. God as the Author of Nature is the closest that reason ever gets to positing a Beyond. This God, however, is merely a hypothesis or postulate that makes nature fully rational. Observing reason is afflicted by the split between mind and body, thought and nature, theory and truth. End or purpose is intellectual, nature sensuous. Reason *wants* to unite the two and think of nature in terms of ends. The compromise is Kant's critical philosophy, according to which consciousness thinks of nature *as if* it were end-directed. To complete this thought, it postulates "another intelligence" (God) that thinks these ends directly. Kant develops these ideas in his *Critique of Judgment.*

14. The turn to organic soul or life-force is known as *vitalism.* The vitalist Hegel is thinking of is M. F. X. Bichat (1771–1802). Hegel refers to him in the *Philosophy of Nature.* Bichat was the founder of histology, the study of human tissues. He believed that life itself could not be observed. As Harris points out (*Hegel's Ladder,* 1:547, note 51), Bichat's definition of life as "the ensemble of functions that resist death" is the negative version of Hegel's understanding of the organic end as self-preservation. A more recent argument for vitalism can be found in Hans Driesch, *The Science and Philosophy of the Organism* (1908).

15. Animals are now the primary focus of reason because they exhibit the Concept of organism in its fully developed form [265]. Commenting on the difference between plants and animals, Hegel says: "The plant lets its wood, its bark, die and shed its leaves; but the animal is this negativity itself" (*Philosophy of Nature,* 357). This is the sense in which plants are passive and animals active. For Hegel, a plant merely lets itself die, whereas an animal incites and necessitates its own death (441 ff.). This is the extent to which it is "negativity itself." Animals, as examples of natural individuality, are one step away from what Hegel calls "the perfect animal"—man (357).

16. Hegel discusses these in greater detail in his *Philosophy of Nature.* See para. 353 of that work (p. 357 in Miller's translation). On the historical origin of the triad—sensibility, irritability, and reproduction—see Harris, *Hegel's Ladder,* 1:508. These three powers also appear in Hegel's discussion of life in the *Science of Logic,* 768–69.

17. For a fuller account of the animal body as it expresses itself through these systems, see *Philosophy of Nature* (359 ff.). In that work, Hegel puts forth the following analogy: "In the solar system, sensibility corresponds to the sun, the moments of difference are comet and moon, and reproduction is the planet [Earth]" (358, Addition).

18. Hegel's critique of mathematics, especially its use in physical science, is the direct descendant of Aristotle's similar critique.

19. In his Preface, Hegel uses anatomy and physiology as images for thinking [1–2]. The critique of mathematical biology is, of course, an example of the *formalism* Hegel also criticizes there [15–16, 50–52]. The biological formalism that Hegel attacks in his Preface [51] is the medical theory of John Brown (1735–88).

20. It is worth noting that, from Hegel's viewpoint, Aristotle knew better than to search for mathematical laws in living nature. This is only one of many ways in which Hegel prefers Aristotle's philosophy of nature to that of modern science.

21. "Hegel conceived of 'specific gravity' in strict accordance with its name. It was a *specification* . . . of the primitively undifferentiated force of gravity. In Hegel's interpretation, this makes it analogous to our concept of atoms and molecules. What the number corresponds to in the object . . . is a numerically determinate quantum of energy" (Harris, *Hegel's Ladder,* 1:526). The connection between specific gravity and cohesion apparently comes from Schelling (1:528).

22. The attempt to devise a scale of metals based on specific gravity was the work of Heinrich Steffens, whom Hegel mentions in his *Philosophy of Nature* (see ibid., 1:527). If specific gravity (a number) cannot tell us why gold differs in its nature from iron, then it can hardly account for differences in organic nature. Steffens' theory is, for Hegel, a prime example of formalism in natural science.

23. In the active phase of reason, Faust is undone by precisely this self-transcending aspect of nature. His effort to be "for himself" in the sexual act produces another: a love-child [362–63].

24. Harris puts this beautifully: "Both the genus and the singular organism are everywhere but nowhere; the genus [or life process] being everywhere permanently present but nowhere complete, and the individual everywhere self-completing [ending its life], and in consequence nowhere present" (*Hegel's Ladder,* 1:531).

25. "Because it is sexually divided, the species becomes a web of living connections or what we call a gene-pool" (ibid.).

26. Reason wants nature to be sober and orderly. That is why it likes, and envies, mathematics. But if reason could see nature the way Hegel does, nature in terms of the Concept, it would have a different notion: "Nature is spirit estranged from itself; in nature, spirit lets itself go, a Bacchic god unrestrained and unmindful of itself; in nature, the Concept is concealed" (*Philosophy of Nature,* 14).

27. In the *Philosophy of Nature,* Hegel calls the Earth an "inanimate organism" (293). As the stable ground and fluid medium of living things, it is "only *implicitly* organism" (277).

28. This is the basis of the *double series* to which Hegel refers [290].

29. See his *Creative Evolution* (1907).

30. In the *Science of Logic,* Hegel mounts his masterful account of the formal laws of thought (411–43). Here in the *Phenomenology* he is interested, not in the truth of the laws per se but in their significance for observing reason: that is, for the claim that such laws are, *as inner observation attests,* "the essential principles both of form and of things" [299].

31. This is the de-spiritualization of precisely those phenomena Hegel most associates with spirit.

32. The physiognomy Hegel critiques in this section is that of Johann Kaspar Lavater (1741–1801), whose book *Essays on Physiognomy* was very popular in Hegel's time. The physiognomic impulse is not confined to the 18th century. Who among us does not try to read people's hearts in their looks, motions, and body language? The most entertaining display of this impulse is the myth of Plato's *Timaeus* (to which Hegel refers [326]). Timaeus gives an extensive depiction of how the gods, as techno-ministers of providence, fashion our bodily looks to fit the invisible looks of our souls. The skull, in Plato's witty invention, not only houses the brain and protects the divine circles of thinking that live in the brain. It also expresses and signifies in its spherical shape the divine perfection of thought itself (44D). For Timaeus, we are what we look like.

33. The general problem of the expression of an inner in an outer, we should note, had already appeared at the level of observational biology [262 ff.]. Both physiognomy and phrenology are special cases of this problem.

34. This dualistic approach is characteristic of modern thought. It appears most famously in Descartes' dualism of mind and body. Descartes separates mind and body and then connects them in what is sometimes called *psychophysical parallelism.* Mind and body are "joined" in the sense that to every event or modification in the one there corresponds an event or modification in the other. The human individual remains metaphysically inexplicable. He is the intimate union of the radically heterogeneous. Reason covers up this incoherence in the rule, law, or regularity that governs the correspondence.

35. Hegel distinguishes physiognomy from palmistry. The former reads a human interior in an outward sign. The latter merely connects one exterior with another—the lines in our palm with, say, our future or lifespan [314]. For the physiognomist, the individual's hand and handwriting

reveal his inmost soul, apart from what happens to him. Moreover, they reveal acquired as well as inherited characteristics, what the individual has made himself through "culture or education" (*Bildung*) [316].

36. Goethe's novel, *Elective Affinities* (published two years after Hegel's *Phenomenology*), contains a striking physiognomic moment. The child of the husband and wife combines the facial features, not of its parents but of the two people with whom the parents are each secretly in love (pt. II, ch. 8). It is a double love-child that bears the physical imprint of its parents' erotic *intentions* during their sexual union.

37. The word phrenology derives from the Greek *phrēn,* which means the indwelling mind or spirit. The founder of this "science" was Hegel's contemporary, Franz-Joseph Gall (1758–1828), who called it cranioscopy. The term phrenology was coined by Gall's followers.

38. Hegel presents phrenology as arriving at its position through a process of elimination. He considers organs like liver and heart (with a passing reference to the physiognomy of Plato's *Timaeus*), then the nervous system, then the brain and spinal cord, then the skull and spinal column together, and finally the skull by itself [326–28]. The skull is just what reason wants: an organ that does nothing and signifies nothing (Hamlet's reflection on Yorick notwithstanding) but is "a purely *immediate* being" that reveals the physical impact of psychic energy [333].

39. Hegel returns to phrenology in his final chapter [790]. In claiming to have a scientific account of how spirit or mind manifests itself, phrenology is both a rival and a precursor to Hegel's *Phenomenology of Spirit.* The skull, *der Schädel,* will reappear at the very end of Hegel's book. There, it will achieve its true meaning as the Place of Skulls, *die Schädelstätte,* the Calvary of spirit's historical manifestation [808].

40. Hegel expands on this irony in the *Philosophy of Nature:* "In many animals the organs of excretion and the genitals, the highest and lowest parts in the animal organization, are intimately connected: just as speech and kissing, on the one hand, and eating, drinking and spitting, on the other, are all done with the mouth" (404, Addition).

Chapter 13: The Romance of Reason

1. Hegel does not explain the parallelism between the three phases of consciousness and the three phases of observing reason. A possible account would be the following. Observing reason in its first phase resembles sense-certainty in its attentiveness to the Thises of organic nature. In its second phase, it posits the rational self as a Thing with many properties—properties for which reason finds laws. And in its third phase, it repeats the understanding in positing a distinction between essence (invisible selfhood) and appearance (outward signs).

2. "*Volk* means 'people,' both in the sense of the 'common people,' in contrast to their leaders, and in that of a community united by customs, sentiments and language" (Inwood, *A Hegel Dictionary,* 212). As applied to the world of ancient Greece, the *Volk* refers not to Athenians or Spartans or Thebans but to all the Hellenes. A given *polis* is a specification of the *Volk.* The idea of a *Volk* or nation, and of a *Volksgeist* or "spirit of a people," were popular with the German Romantics. As Inwood points out, the phrase "spirit of the nation" first appeared in Montesquieu's highly influential *Spirit of the Laws,* which Hegel read and admired. Hegel develops his rational version of the *Volk* in the *Philosophy of Right,* where he argues that the *Volk,* which starts out as family, clan, and multitude, does not achieve genuine ethicality until it becomes politically organized as a state (para. 349; see also the supplement to para. 274 in White's edition, 214–16).

3. "Hegel's contemporaries, and Hegel himself, saw Greece as a paradise lost, a moment of spirit's youth. They sought the land of the Greeks, as Goethe wrote in his *Iphigenia,* with the eyes of the soul: 'Das Land der Griechen mit der Seele suchend'" (Hyppolite, *Genesis and Structure,* 337). Terry Pinkard is helpful in establishing Hegel's view of Greek life: "Hegel's concern [in the *Phenomenology*] therefore was not with the historical details of Greek life per se but with whether the idealized Greek life described by many of his contemporaries really could *on its own terms* be counted as a genuine alternative to modern life . . . he was concerned with the way in which these idealized Greeks would have been 'for themselves,' not as they are 'for us'" (*Hegel's Phenomenology: The Sociality of Reason* [Cambridge: Cambridge University Press, 1994], 137).

4. For Hegel's fascinating account of Socrates in relation to Athens and Greek ethicality, see his *Philosophy of History* (269–70), and the much longer account in the *Lectures on the History of Philosophy* (1:430–48).

5. Hegel is referring to Socrates, who defends the *nomoi* or laws in the *Crito.* To live in accord with the laws and customs of one's people is to recognize what Hegel famously announced in the Preface to his *Philosophy of Right:* that only the actual is truly rational (trans. White, 8). Hegel reads the *Republic* as supporting this view: "Plato's *Republic,* which has proverbial status as an empty ideal, in essence grasps nothing other than the nature of Greek ethicality" (ibid.).

6. For Hegel's extensive treatment of the beauty and limits of Greek ethicality, see his *Philosophy of History,* 223–77. Athens falls because it cannot sustain what it itself had generated—the moral inquiry of Socrates, that is, the individual's search for a good that goes beyond custom (269–70). In condemning Socrates to death, Athens condemned itself. Spartan ethicality also falls because of individual self-assertion. But in its case, self-assertion is not moral inquiry but "blank immorality, flat selfishness, greed, corruption" (271).

7. The difference between ethicality and morality will become clearer when we take up morality in Hegel's chapter on spirit [596 ff.]. Broadly stated, ethicality grounds the good in the specific customs of one's concrete community (family, city, church or religious community). Morality grounds the good in universal laws that transcend specific communities—laws that *every* rational being finds within himself. In the *Phenomenology,* morality is higher than ethicality because it is a further development of self-consciousness. In the *Philosophy of Right,* ethicality is higher than morality. It takes the sheer subjectivity and abstractness of morality and makes morality into something real and alive. The difference in the order is due in part to Hegel's later development of his philosophy of the state and in part to the different goals and characters of the two writings.

8. Hegel, *Aesthetics,* trans. T. M. Knox (Oxford: Clarendon Press, 1975), 2:1224. The version of Goethe's story that was known to Hegel was the so-called "Faust-Fragment," published in 1790. Part I of the expanded poem appeared in 1808, a year after the *Phenomenology* was published, and the complete *Faust* in 1832, the year of Goethe's death. For a helpful discussion of Hegel's use of the "Faust-Fragment," see Harris, *Hegel's Ladder,* 2:24–32.

9. Faust here plays the role of Adam. In the biblical story, *Eve* is the figure of infinite desire, self-transcendence, and narcissism. As Harris observes, Goethe clearly wants to invert the Adam-Eve relation in the story of the fall (ibid., 28). Adam becomes the seducer and Eve the willing partner in crime.

10. In Chapter 3, I called sense-certainty a "cognitive romantic." Sense-certainty wanted cognitive satisfaction in the temporal Moment. Now this romanticism becomes explicit.

11. The goal of self-consciousness is mutual recognition. When self-consciousness first came on the scene, it manifested itself as a state of *war.* At the level of reason, or what we might call positive desire, mutual recognition takes the form of romantic *love.*

12. The affair of Faust and Gretchen bears a certain resemblance to that of Paulo and Francesca in *Inferno* V. Like Dante's adulterous lovers, Faust and Gretchen try to make feeling their absolute. They act as though they are the only two beings in the universe.

13. The tempter devil plays no role in Hegel's dialectic of Faustian consciousness (except as a commentator). Mephistopheles is merely the supernatural means by which Faust gets to gratify his desire. In Goethe's complete poem, which Hegel did not know, there is a happy ending: Gretchen and Faust are both saved.

14. Hegel juxtaposes the opening and closing couplets of Mephistopheles' soliloquy. On Hegel's slight alteration of the latter couplet, see Harris (*Hegel's Ladder,* 2:67, note 30). Hegel was fond of Goethe's lines and quotes them elsewhere, notably in the Preface to the *Philosophy of Right* (trans. White, 5).

15. When Dante finally sees Beatrice in the heavenly place that is most her own, she is very far above him. But he *sees* her more clearly than ever: "her image came down to me unmixed with anything in between" (*Paradiso* 31.77–78). He sees *her,* not his unity with her. For Dante, the beloved is not part of the structure of the lover's self-consciousness. Beatrice is not Dante's concretized selfhood. She is herself. This is a fundamental difference between Dante and Hegel. In the final vision, in which Dante "sees" God, he grasps, in a flash, the unity of God and man. But again, this does not mean that Dante has become God, or that God is concretized selfhood.

16. For Hegel's discussion of marriage, and of offspring as the parents' love for each other made real and objective, see *Philosophy of Right*, "Ethicality," trans. White, 132–39.

17. As Harris points out, it is Gretchen, not Faust, who experiences an "alien necessity" (*Hegel's Ladder*, 2:31). Faust *knows* that he is the one who has brought this upon her. At the end, he is a helpless observer who looks upon the tragic consciousness he has generated in the beloved.

18. Again, Harris is very helpful on this point: "It is Gretchen who illustrates the comprehensive inversion and transition" (ibid.).

19. Harris directs our attention, in particular, to the "Profession of Faith of the Savoyard Vicar" in Book 4 of Rousseau's *Emile* (*Hegel's Ladder*, 2:34–35). This crucial part of Rousseau's masterpiece contains much that pertains to Hegel's *Phenomenology*, especially in its discussion of *conscience*.

20. Pascal, *Pensées*, 423/277. The opposition of heart and mind, feeling and thinking, is one of the many dualisms of modernity. The supremacy of sentiment over reason finds its most brutal formulation in Hume, who said that reason "is, and ought only to be the slave of the passions" (*A Treatise of Human*, bk. II, sec. 3, p. 415). Of course, if one starts out by reducing reason to an "inert faculty," as Hume does, and moreover reduces it to our ability to do formal logic, then the superiority of sentiment is a trivial inference—that is, if one also believes, with Rousseau, that the human heart is naturally good.

21. Harris cautions us not to bring in Karl too soon. The teachings of the heart are not limited to violent revolutionaries like Karl: "Most bleeding Hearts are not bomb-throwing nihilists" (*Hegel's Ladder*, 2:73, note 73). Karl and his frenzy are the dialectical *result* of the bleeding heart humanitarian, whose origins are in Rousseau. Nevertheless, Hegel's description of the proponent of the heart fits Karl very well.

22. Hegel discusses *The Robbers* in his *Aesthetics*. There he observes that although Karl is a tragic figure, "it is still only boys who can be seduced by this robber ideal" (1:195).

23. One is reminded of the end of *Beyond Good and Evil*, where Nietzsche, the bad boy of philosophic idealists, expresses sadness that his thoughts, now that they are written down, are already beginning to resemble ordinance-like *truths* (section 296). From Hegel's perspective, this is the sting that the self-admiring *artiste* feels when the personal, in being formulated and publicized, becomes universal. Here we have an excellent example of the absence of spirit in Hegel's sense of the term, that is, the inability to find truth and fulfillment in the dialectical unity of individual and universal, inner and outer, private and public.

24. Early in Schiller's play, Karl denounces the evil of all hearts other than his own. He calls men "false hypocritical crocodiles," whose eyes are water but whose hearts are iron-ore. Karl's misanthropy is provoked when he reads the letter in which his father disowns him and rejects his plea for forgiveness.

25. The actualized law of the heart is a mirror that fails to reflect the face of the rebel humanitarian. From his perspective, the only thing worse than a mirror that distorts one's face is one in which one sees only the faces of other people.

26. This very *Entzweiung* or inner split is dramatized at the beginning of Schiller's play: Karl's father has a prodigal son whom he loves as his own flesh and blood, and at the same time disowns.

27. The most chilling depiction of such a war is the gang of nihilists in Dostoevsky's *Demons*.

28. This conflict is dramatized in Karl's band of thieves, especially in the character of the ambitious Spiegelberg.

29. This is where Karl stands at the end of Schiller's play. Lamenting his insolent past, he hands himself over to the law. The virtuous individual, for Hegel, begins where Karl left off, just as Karl began where Faust left off.

30. This is the opposition between the *idealist* and *realist*. For a fascinating discussion of these two character types, see Schiller's essay, "On Naïve and Sentimental Poetry," in *Essays*, trans. Daniel O. Dahlstrom (New York: Continuum, 1993), 250–60.

31. Harris argues, convincingly, that the Knight of Virtue is *not* Don Quixote (*Hegel's Ladder*, 2:74–75, note 79). Quixote was a man of deeds who physically, and often painfully, engaged the world. Hegel's Knight renders his own action ineffective and is only a man of words [390]. Furthermore, Don Quixote was a lover: he does everything for the sake of his Lady, Dulcinea. The modern Knight is devoted to an abstract ideal. He is not motivated by romantic love, which is a form of self-interest. Harris observes that, insofar as this Knight is an edifying rhetorician, we see a glimpse

of him in Fichte, who preached "high ideals" (*Hegel's Ladder,* 2:62). He also makes the interesting point that a more advanced Knight of Virtue appears in *Robespierre.* As Hegel says in the *Philosophy of History:* "The principle of virtue [*Tugend*] was set up as supreme by Robespierre; and one can say that with this man virtue was a serious matter" (450). Of course, as Hegel goes on to say, it is a virtue whose completely abstract nature makes it inseparable from widespread *death.*

32. See also Daniel E. Shannon, *Spirit: Chapter Six of Hegel's Phenomenology of Spirit* (Indianapolis: Hackett, 2001), 179, note 19. Traces of Hegel's Knight appear in the character of Alceste in Molière's *Misanthrope.* Alceste identifies virtue with sincerity. He is the self-appointed critic of cultured society and all its hypocrisy. He misses the "good old days" when people spoke only what came from their hearts. His friend Philinthe tries to convert him from his idealism by appealing to the Way of the World. He tells Alceste that vices are "united to human nature," and that he would be no more offended "to see a man false, unjust, and self-interested than to see vultures hungry for carnage, monkeys mischievous, and wolves full of fury" (I, 1).

33. Another spokesman for the realist Way of the World is La Rochefoucauld, whose book of maxims focuses on the pervasive influence of amour-propre or self-esteem. Its heading is the following: "Our virtues are most often only vices in disguise."

34. The Knight is not yet at the stage of Kant's moral duty (Harris, *Hegel's Ladder,* 2:73, note 71). He has no way to test the validity of any specific laws but is at the mercy of a completely empty ideal: the good in itself. Law, for him, can only mean universality as the absence of self-interest.

35. Jacob Loewenberg calls the Knight "a reformed reformer" (*Hegel's Phenomenology: Dialogues on The Life of Mind* [La Salle, Ill.: Open Court, 1965], 163). In one sense, this is true: the Knight does not openly oppose the status quo. But that is because the status quo that most needs to be overturned is the human heart. *That* he most definitely wants to reform.

36. Harris calls the *Weltlauf* the "Rat-race" (*Hegel's Ladder,* 2:56), and Quentin Lauer "the course of events" (*A Reading of Hegel's Phenomenology of Spirit* [New York: Fordham University Press, 1976], 160).

37. At one point in the play, the Marquis tries to bring about a change of heart in the worldly Philipp II. He tries to inspire the king to "reestablish the lost nobility of humankind" (act 3, scene 10).

38. This cunning is evident in Schiller's Marquis, who works behind the scenes and attempts to change the world by eliciting the deeds of others (especially Carlos).

39. The Greeks had substantial ethical life, which absorbs individuals into the political whole. But they also celebrated what Hegel calls "beautiful individuality" (*The Philosophy of History,* 238). This individuality is grounded not in self-consciousness or individual being-for-self but in gifts of character. In other words, it is an individuality that depends on a natural *given,* and lacks the infinity of self-consciousness.

40. In Schiller's *Don Carlos,* selfishness includes the romantic love that Carlos feels for the Queen. According to the idealistic vision of the Marquis, this love distracts Carlos from his true vocation: to be a leader of men and the inaugurator of a new, humane age.

41. This faith is not religious faith: reason is humanistic or worldly and rejects a transcendent God. For Hegel's critique of philosophers who espoused belief as intellectual intuition and the highest form of knowledge, see his early *Faith and Knowledge.* The targets of Hegel's attack are Kant, Jacobi, Fichte, and Schleiermacher.

42. His purism reminds us of Kant's moral philosophy, in which moral action must be done *from* duty and not merely *in accordance with* duty. For both Kant and the Knight of Virtue, pleasure and happiness, which belong to the actual world, have nothing to do with "the good in itself." See Kant's *Foundations of the Metaphysics of Morals,* section 1.

43. Something like this happens near the end of *Don Carlos.* The Marquis tells Carlos: "The kingship is your calling. To die for you has been mine." Deeply moved, Carlos exhorts the Marquis to join him in going to the king in order to ask pardon for their sedition, and to explain that it issued from the noble desire for self-sacrifice: "He won't, he can't possibly refuse sublimity [*Erhabenheit*] like this!" Right after this hopeful speech, the Marquis is shot. And at the very end of the play, Philipp hands over his son to the Inquisition. The Way of the World triumphs.

44. In *Don Carlos,* the Queen accuses the noble Marquis of being simply *proud:* "May a thousand hearts break, what is it to you if you may only feed your pride. Oh now—now I can understand you! You only courted admiration" [*Bewunderung*] (act 4, scene 21).

Chapter 14: Rational Animals and the Birth of Spirit

1. See Harris, *Hegel's Ladder,* 2:136, note 6. Civil society is the open field of diverse works and productive self-interest. "The norm is provided by the ordinary skilled artisan, especially in a world organized into guilds" (2:84). In his edition of the *Phenomenology,* Baillie observes that civil society, as the ensemble of gifted self-actualizers, "prepares the way for the constructive interpretation of organized society" ([New York: Humanities Press, 1977 Reprint], 417). This is the condition of ethicality, which we meet at the beginning of Hegel's next chapter.

2. See *Theodicy,* section 147, and *Monadology* 83. Harris points to the centrality of Leibniz' monads for this stage of reason. He aptly refers to this realm of individual self-actualization as "The Monadology of Reason" (*Hegel's Ladder,* 2:82).

3. "Emmanuel Hirsch claims that the phrase [spiritual animal kingdom] may be taken from a passage in Hölderlin's novel, *Hyperion*" (Pinkard, *Hegel's Phenomenology,* 381, note 98). The context is Hyperion's hard-hearted judgment of human nature as having "resolved itself into the multifarious species of the animal kingdom" See *Hyperion,* in Friedrich Hölderlin, *Hyperion and Selected Poems,* ed. Eric L. Santner (New York: Continuum, 1994), 15.

4. Some commentators read the spiritual animal kingdom as a description of *academia.* See, for example, Loewenberg on scholars (*Hegel's Phenomenology,* 170–71). One of the first to apply this interpretation was Hegel's contemporary, H. F. W. Hinrichs, who wrote to Hegel complaining of the academic backbiting at his university. Hegel's response may be found in *Hegel: The Letters,* trans. Clark Butler and Christine Seiler (Bloomington: Indiana University Press, 1984), 501–2. For a critique of this view, see Harris, *Hegel's Ladder,* 2:136, note 6.

5. The realm of talent is like the thing of perception. Talents are indifferent determinations gathered in the grand Also of multi-potency—the talent-pool. Their determinateness is the work of a negative One that keeps talents separated in their gatheredness. Instead of different properties of a Thing, we have, in talent, a *spiritual* medium that is modified in various ways to bring out different "colors."

6. Early in the Preface, Hegel uses the example of natural growth to illustrate determinate negation in both the history of philosophy and the *Phenomenology of Spirit.* His description applies to the gradual actualization of a talent in a particular work: "The bud disappears in the bursting forth of the blossom, and one might say that the former is refuted by the latter, similarly, when the fruit appears, the blossom is shown up in its turn as a false manifestation of the plant, and the fruit now emerges as the truth of it instead. These forms are not just distinguished from one another, they also supplant one another as mutually incompatible" [2].

7. The negativity of action reflects the negativity of *freedom.* In the *Philosophy of Right,* Hegel argues that a truly free will is one that makes decisions, or closes something. It cancels its inherent indeterminateness (para. 12). Freedom is not arbitrariness but self-determination.

8. That the given is only a moment of action highlights the fact that the self-actualizer, unlike Karl and the Knight of Virtue, is not interested in changing the world, that is, improving it. The change his action necessarily implies is simply the byproduct or epiphenomenon of his desire to bring himself out into the open.

9. The paradox reminds us of the stumbling-block Meno uses to argue that learning is impossible (*Meno* 80D–E).

10. There are several inaccuracies in Miller's translation of paragraph 405. His "quality" is really determinateness [*Bestimmtheit*], and "void" is not void [*das Leere*] but space or room [*der Raum*]. The emphasis is not on emptiness but on openness and availability.

11. Talent is universal because it is a potential that becomes specific only in action. It is analogous to the *property* of the thing. Other individuals share my talent, just as other things can share a property. Talent is the human property, the one's-own, that has been enriched by the concept of *force* as self-expression. It is human *energy:* the capacity for work.

12. Goethe, for example, was annoyed that Schubert had set his poems to music. Of course, even someone who recites my poetry in public also appropriates it in order to express *his* selfhood.

13. For Hegel's views on plagiarism and copyright, see *Philosophy of Right,* para. 69 (pp. 62–64 in White's translation).

14. This also happened to Faust, who wanted to make himself special but instead became a generic male.

15. Dancing, singing, playing an instrument, playing tennis—all these are no less static in this sense than poems and statues. They are all actions that become determinate works: this dance, that song, this performance, that game on that particular day.

16. In the opening sentence of the Introduction, Hegel says that the *Sache selbst* or serious business of philosophy is "the actual cognition of what truly is" [73]. In the Preface, he takes us through various attempts to evade the *Sache selbst* [3]. These include edifying discourses, mathematical formalism, and intuitionism.

17. Harris identifies *Lessing* as the "outstanding representative of the *Sache selbst*" (*Hegel's Ladder*, 2:103). He quotes the following passage from one of Lessing's works: "It is not the truth which a man possesses, or that he believes, but the earnest effort which he puts forth to reach the truth, which constitutes the worth of a man" (ibid.). Nietzsche cites this passage in *The Birth of Tragedy* to show that Lessing was "the most honest theoretical man" (section 15).

18. Lauer renders *die Sache selbst* "what really matters." In his footnote on the phrase, he writes: "Perhaps no expression of Hegel's has caused translators—into any language—so much embarrassment as this. Apart from the fact that there is no precise English equivalent for *Sache*, there is no one *meaning* of it in the various contexts in which Hegel uses it" (*A Reading of Hegel's Phenomenology*, 165). For a review of Hegel's uses of *Ding*, *Sache*, and *Sache selbst*, see Inwood, *A Hegel Dictionary*, 288–90.

19. At this stage of reason, there is no *theōria*, no purely theoretical interest or activity. Pure mathematics, for example, inquires into the truth for its own sake about quantity or magnitude. But for me as a self-actualizer, the goal is not the search for objective truth but the manifestation of my ability or talent. I do mathematics because I am good at it. This doing *is* my truth.

20. The "method" consciousness uses here to satisfy itself resembles the sophistry of "directing the intention" (*diriger l'intention*) satirized in Pascal's *Provincial Letters*, letter 7. As Pascal's Jesuit shows, by the proper directing of one's intention, it is possible to escape every sin.

21. The word "poem" comes from the Greek verb *poiein*, to do or make.

22. Honesty, here, resembles self-esteem, as La Rochefoucauld depicts it in his maxims. Self-esteem or self-interest (amour-propre) is the consummate sophist and tyrant, who knows how to take on whatever form suits its purpose—even the form of being *above* self-esteem and self-interest: "Self-interest speaks all sorts of languages, and plays all sorts of roles, even that of being disinterested" (Maxim 39).

23. On the difference between the fight for recognition and the phenomenon of mutual deceit, see note 25 below.

24. The list of possible examples of deception within professionalism is endless. Professional "philosophers" in philosophy departments work just as well as scientists, in some ways even better, since their ostensible claim is to love wisdom for its own sake. In the example I have chosen—the search for the self-consciousness gene—I hoped to recall *phrenology*, which, like molecular biology, tries to explain spiritual phenomena by locating their material basis and site.

25. The battle here is not a fight for honor or recognition, say, the Nobel Prize—at least, not primarily. What is at stake is the sheer *mine-ness* of my projects or professional actions. As a self-actualizer, I become angry with my fellow professionals not because they steal an honor from me but because they are intruding on my techno-space or "turf." Honor, as Aristotle tells us, is the greatest of external goods (*Nicomachean Ethics* 4.3). But the self-actualizer is interested only in what we might call the internal good of self-expression, that is, a good that he gives himself. To the extent that recognition enters at this stage, it does so not as a goal but as a sign that others acknowledge my work as mine.

26. Consider La Rochefoucauld's maxim, "If we had no pride, we would not complain of the pride of others" (Maxim 34). Or even better, "What makes other people's vanity unendurable to us is that it wounds our own" (Maxim 389).

27. Hegel's critique here is directed, not against self-involvement or egotism, but against the *pretense* of pure objectivity. Nothing gets accomplished if we are not personally involved in our projects, if we do not invest ourselves. My projects must be *mine* if they are ever to be *ours*.

28. Hegel had already mentioned ethical substance in his introduction to active reason [349]. Harris gives an extremely helpful account of what Hegel means by the term. In relation to the Greek world, which we enter in the next chapter, ethical substance is not the individual *polis* but the whole ethical world of the Hellenes (*Hegel's Ladder,* 2:112). The *polis* "is not the Ethical Substance, but the ethical thing" (ibid., 12).

29. The abstractness of the moral law at this stage foreshadows the more far-reaching and deeper abstractness of morality in the chapter on spirit [596 ff.].

30. As Harris notes (*Hegel's Ladder,* 2:112), modern ethical substance, as Hegel reveals in his *Philosophy of Right,* has *four* "masses" or regions: the family, modern civil society, the state, and the Church.

31. On Kant's distinction between the hypothetical and the categorical imperative, see *Grounding for the Metaphysics of Morals,* trans. James W. Ellington (Indianapolis: Hackett, 1993), 25 ff. Harris is right to point out that Hegel's account of law-giving reason is *not,* however, a critique of Kant (*Hegel's Ladder,* 2:110–11). There is nothing particularly Kantian about assuming that moral laws are meant to be absolute.

32. For Kant's defense of his claim that our duty to tell the truth is unconditional, see his essay "On A Supposed Right to Lie Because of Philanthropic Concerns" (in *Grounding,* trans. Ellington, 63–67). Hegel's critique of this law in what follows does *not* depend on the usual objection that one must sometimes lie in order to help people or at least protect them from harm.

33. The problem is similar to that raised by the command, "Speak from the heart" or "Be sincere." This presupposes that we *know* our hearts.

34. In the *Grounding,* Kant argues that the commandment to love others refers not to the feeling of love, which comes and goes, but to *duty,* which abides: moral love is practical and not, as Kant calls it, pathological (trans. Ellington, 12). It must be emphasized that, throughout this section, Hegel is not arguing against these laws as such but against their being taken as abstract formulas for action.

35. See *Grounding,* trans. Ellington, section II, 30 ff. In his *Critique of Practical Reason,* Kant stresses the connection between the moral law and the universal *form* of law: "If a rational being is to think of his maxims as practical universal laws, then he can think of them only as principles that contain the determining basis of the will not by their matter but merely by their form" (trans. Pluhar, 40).

36. Kant, *Grounding,* trans. Ellington, 30.

37. It is not clear what it would mean for a maxim to *pass* the consistency test. Is there no contradiction because none exists, or because I have failed to detect it?

38. The situation here reminds us of Heisenberg's so-called Uncertainty Principle (whose correct title is the Indeterminacy Principle), according to which my effort to observe the position of, say, an electron, displaces it from that position.

39. As Harris puts it, the immovable law of the gods is "suprarational," since it transcends the finite reason that appears here, but it is not "supernatural" (*Hegel's Ladder,* 2:131).

40. The difference between Greeks and non-Greeks or barbarians is beautifully illustrated in the conversation in Herodotus between the Spartan defector Demaratus and the Persian King Xerxes. Xerxes cannot comprehend how an army could march into battle on their own, without fear of a Master and a lash at their backs. He cannot, in other words, comprehend how a free people can be a strong people (*Histories* 7.101–5).

41. "Athena, the goddess, is Athens itself, namely, the actual and concrete spirit of the citizens" (Hegel, *Philosophy of History,* 252).

42. Hegel is thinking of the Olympian gods, here, as having the beautiful "fixity of sculpture" (Harris, *Hegel's Ladder,* 2:132).

43. The lines are spoken by Antigone to Creon, who has just accused Antigone of daring to disobey the law by burying her brother Polyneices.

44. Hegel is apparently referring to Fichte, who tried to derive the ethical structure of a community from his own reason or insight (see Harris, *Hegel's Ladder,* 2:111).

45. This example comes up famously in the first book of Plato's *Republic.* The first definition of justice (which Socrates attributes to Cephalus) combines two of Hegel's examples of moral law: truth-telling and respecting other people's property. As Socrates shows, the return of property that

has been left in my keeping is problematic when the property is a weapon and the owner has gone mad (331D ff.). The discussion thus incorporates the underlying assumption of the law that commands me to love my neighbor: that being just aims at another's benefit, not his harm. In response to the problem of returning weapons to a madman, Hegel would no doubt say that I must exercise prudence in returning what might be used for ill. I like Harris' explanation of the ethical way to handle this situation: if a friend lends me his weapons, and he goes mad, I should certainly withhold the weapons. But I should also call other friends and community members to witness that I am doing so in his own best interests, not as a thief (*Hegel's Ladder,* 2:133). This is *not* to say that a conflict of laws and rights does not come up within ethicality, as we see in Hegel's account of Sophocles' *Antigone.*

46. This is an even more insidious use of the *diriger l'intention* that Pascal satirizes in his *Provincial Letters.* See note 20 of this chapter, above.

Chapter 15: Ethical Life

1. For an excellent translation of this entire chapter of the *Phenomenology,* see *Spirit: Chapter Six of Hegel's Phenomenology of Spirit,* ed. Shannon.

2. Ethical life in the *Phenomenology of Spirit* is confined to the ancient Greeks. For Hegel's more comprehensive treatment, see *Philosophy of Right* (trans. White, 125 ff.). A helpful scholarly overview of ethical life in Hegel can be found in Laurence Dickey's general introduction to *Hegel, Political Writings,* trans. H. B. Nisbet (Cambridge: Cambridge University Press, 1999), xviii–xxxiii.

3. In the *Philosophy of History,* Hegel calls the *polis* a "political work of art" (The Greek World, 250–74). The reader should consult this book for Hegel's full account of, and admiration for, the Greeks.

4. Spirit is what Spinoza called *causa sui,* self-caused: "By that which is self-caused I mean that whose essence involves existence; or that whose nature can be conceived only as existing" (*Ethics* I, definition 1). This famous idea in Spinoza is the antecedent to Hegel's formula: "What is rational is actual; and what is actual is rational" (*Philosophy of Right,* Preface). Spirit is self-actualizing reason.

5. In the *Lectures on the History of Philosophy,* Hegel refers explicitly to "the fruit of the tree of the knowledge of good and evil" as the subjective, modern principle that is at odds with Greek ethicality (1:447).

6. Hegel observes in his *Philosophy of History* that the Greeks lacked *conscience.* That is, they did not ground moral goodness in individual self-consciousness as an "inner voice" (253).

7. This is the end of what I called the "great arch" in Chapter 8. It extends from the fight for recognition at the beginning of self-consciousness to the emergence of mutual recognition at the end of morality.

8. For a helpful account of Hegel's interpretation of the *Antigone,* and Greek tragedy in general, see Dennis J. Schmidt, *On Germans and Other Greeks: Tragedy and Ethical Life* (Bloomington: Indiana University Press, 2001), 89–121. Schmidt takes up Hegel's view of Greek tragedy as it appears in the *Phenomenology* and the *Lectures on Fine Art.* Schmidt notes that, in the former work, "Hegel is not offering a reading of the *Antigone;* nonetheless it is abundantly clear that he is interpreting the ethical life of spirit by reading *Antigone* as the preeminent illustration of how this life must unfold" (103).

9. Miller omits the word "masses" from his translation both here and in the preceding paragraph [445]. This makes it hard to see the continuity with Hegel's use of this curious term in the section on legislative reason [420, 421, 437].

10. Divine law in Hegel's chapter does not refer to Greek religion as a whole but is confined to the private religion of the family. Religion as divine manifestation on a grand scale comes on the scene *after* the chapter on spirit.

11. Hegel's account of death as the completion of life reminds us of what Solon tells Croesus in Herodotus: that one should count no man happy until he is dead (*Histories* 1.32).

12. For Hegel's general account of marriage and family, see *Philosophy of Right* (trans. White, 132–46). Here, and elsewhere, Hegel attacks Kant's definition of marriage as a contract.

13. Orestes and Electra in Aeschylus' *Libation Bearers* provide the ancient paradigm for this relation.

14. This is the ground of Hegel's admiration for the character of Antigone: "Antigone is the most beautiful description of femininity; she holds fast to the bond of the family against the law." The sentence (from Hegel's untranslated *Lectures on the Philosophy of Right*) appears in the editor's notes to *Elements of the Philosophy of Right,* ed. Wood, 439. In the *Lectures on the History of Philosophy,* Hegel calls Antigone "that noblest of figures that ever appeared on earth" (1: 441). The context is Athens' condemnation of Socrates.

15. Originally, the gods who watched over a family's food supply (*penus*), the Roman *Di penates* or "gods in the store-cupboard" eventually became the divine guardians of the entire household. The close connection with the Latin word *penitus,* "inner," fits nicely with Hegel's emphasis on the family as the indwelling, "homey" essence of ethical community.

16. Of course, he becomes *purely* her brother only in death. Only then is he a brother who is not *also* a naturally living being and a citizen.

17. As Harris notes, Goethe was repulsed by these lines and could not believe that Sophocles had written them (*Hegel's Ladder,* 2:188). Hegel clearly disagrees: he shows, convincingly, that the lines are perfectly consistent with Antigone's moral stance.

18. Hyppolite (*Genesis and Structure,* 342) refers to a passage from an early writing in which Hegel asserts: "In the course of nature the husband sees flesh of his flesh in the wife, but in ethical life alone [i.e., political activity] does he see the spirit of his spirit in and through the ethical order" (*System of Ethical Life and First Philosophy of Spirit,* ed. and trans. H. S. Harris and T. M. Knox [Albany: SUNY Press, 1979], 143).

19. See especially Hegel's remarks on how the Greek spirit manifests itself in the relation between nature and art (ibid., 238–39).

20. The saying "Character is Fate" is a free translation of Heraclitus' saying, *ēthos anthrōpōi daimōn:* "A human being's character is his guiding spirit" (fragment 119). Fate first came on the scene in Hegel's analysis of Faust [363]. Faust *rejected* ethicality as something inimical to happiness. In the end, Gretchen (the living being in whom Faust sought his reality and truth) experienced ethicality as a brutal, irrational force that shattered the hope for pleasure. At the current level of spirit, Fate is the work of individuals who act as the passionate *agents* of ethicality. Faust and Antigone are tragic in exactly opposite ways.

21. Greek tragedy helps us to appreciate the tragic dimension of the *Phenomenology* as a whole, and of world history. Hyppolite points to what he calls the *pantragedism* that characterized Hegel's youthful understanding of spirit (*Genesis and Structure,* 353). He refers to the essay on natural law (1802–3), in which Hegel calls tragedy "the absolute relation" ("On the Scientific Ways of Treating Natural Law," in *Political Writings,* ed. Dickey, 155). In Hegel's more mature writings, Hyppolite notes, pantragedism gives way to panlogism: Fate becomes the *Begriff* or Concept. Later in the *Phenomenology,* in the chapter on religion, Hegel will give a more general account of Greek tragedy [733–42].

22. Hyppolite observes that Hegel's reading of the *Antigone* is "ingenious rather than convincing" (*Genesis and Structure,* 346). Two things can be said on this point. First, Hegel does not in general attempt to read famous authors in order to be true to their intentions. Second, Sophocles, in the case before us, is merely the conduit for absolute spirit, which "speaks" in the conflict between Antigone and Creon. The work, in other words, is essential: the author inessential. So too, the *Phenomenology,* strictly speaking, is the work of spirit rather than the work of Hegel.

23. In the *Lectures on the History of Philosophy,* Hegel defines the condemnation and death of Socrates as tragic for exactly the same reasons. In the death of Socrates, we have "the universally moral and tragic fate, the tragedy of Athens, the tragedy of Greece. Two opposed rights come into collision, the one destroys the other" (1:446). One is the divine, objective right of the city. The other is the right of "subjective freedom," that is, the individual pursuit of knowledge. It is in this context that Hegel refers to this knowledge as "the fruit of the knowledge of good and evil" (ibid., 447). See note 4 of this chapter, above.

24. Action occurs all the time, of course, in the ethical world. As citizen and family member, I do things and, in doing them, become aware of the two laws that govern my life. Normally, these laws do not conflict, and my "action" is really my active twofold *submersion* in communal life. Action in

this sense is not fully the action of an individual. But now, with Antigone and Creon, action is fully the action of an individual who champions one law over another.

25. In Greek, *kharaktēr* (from the verb, *kharassein,* to make sharp or pointed) refers to the impress on coins or seals—a mark. It also refers to what "marks" a human being as distinctive. In his discussion of character (*Hegel's Ladder,* 2:210–11), Harris draws a helpful distinction between character for Aristotle and character as we see it in Greek tragedy. For Aristotle, character is a disposition [*hexis*] that inclines rather than compels. In tragedy, character compels. It exhibits the ideal case, in which an individual is completely one with the law as he (or she) sees it. Character, here, is one's nature. Character is absent from the previous forms of self-consciousness. The closest approximation was the stoic. But stoic virtue seeks detachment from nature and circumstance. It is not strength of character, revealed in action, but the freedom of thinking or non-action. The ethical agent, by contrast, reveals his being-for-self through *formed* individuality, by being an individual of a certain kind. This formedness or beauty is the source of the ensuing tragedy.

26. Character here is not *simply* identical with sex (ibid., 211). It also includes the character of one's family and one's own innate strength of character and will. Ismene, Antigone's sister, represents family and the place of women within the polis better than Antigone does. She knows her place and, at the very beginning of Sophocles' play, advises her sister to know hers. But this "knowing a woman's place" is precisely what prevents her from acting and thus showing that she is true to the nature and character of her noble father. In representing only the natural place of women in the civic whole, she proves herself incapable of asserting the natural right that women have within that whole.

27. Antigone buries Polyneices *twice.* The second burial seems to indicate that she wants her deed to become public.

28. In Harris' words, they confront each other as *tyrant* and *rebel* (*Hegel's Ladder,* 2:211).

29. The German terms for these pairs of opposites are very similar. Conscious and unconscious are *bewußt* and *unbewußt.* Known and unknown are *gewußt* and *ungewußt.* Both pairs come from the verb *wissen,* to know.

30. Solon, the great Athenian law-giver, firmly believed in "taking sides." In the *Life of Solon,* Plutarch writes: "Among his other laws, there is a very peculiar and surprising one which ordains that he shall be disenfranchised who, in time of faction [*en stasei*], takes neither side" (*Plutarch's Lives,* Loeb Classical Library [1967], 1:457).

31. Shannon suggests that Hegel's interpretation of this passage is influenced by Hölderlin's translation of the *Antigone* (*Spirit: Chapter Six of Hegel's Phenomenology of Spirit,* 24, note 41).

32. Harris makes the following crucial point about how Creon, no less than the brothers who fought, is a creature of nature, even though he defends the city against natural ties: "Creon issued the edict as the 'government' of the City, appointed by the City. But he was a stupid man, and it was a stupid edict. Simple obstinacy and wise flexibility happen just as naturally as passivity [Ismene] and activity [Antigone]" (*Hegel's Ladder,* 2:223).

33. The pyramid, as Harris points out, is the "tribal monarchy" (ibid.).

34. With the rise of Rome, the "living spirits" of Greece degenerate into dead abstract symbols. On the abstract nature of the Roman gods, see Hegel's *Philosophy of History,* 292.

35. Hegel's reference to points [*Punkte*] recalls the root meaning of individual as *in-dividuum,* the un-divided. As Euclid says in his *Elements,* a point is that which has no part.

36. The "low" aspect of personhood recalls what Hegel said in the chapter on self-consciousness: "The individual who has not risked his life may well be recognized as a *person,* but he has not attained the truth of this recognition as an independent self-consciousness" [187].

37. The main source of Hegel's account of Rome is Gibbon's *Decline and Fall of the Roman Empire* (Harris, *Hegel's Ladder,* 2:245, notes 35–39).

38. For Hegel's full account of the Roman world, see his *Philosophy of History,* part 3. Rome, for Hegel, is a spiritual wasteland. But it is also the birthplace of modern history, Christianity, and the rule of law. Here in the *Phenomenology,* Hegel's depiction of Rome is even more negative than his account in the *Philosophy of History.* The reason is that here Rome is not primarily a necessary force within world history but the *legal standing* that generates self-alienation as a new form of self-awareness.

39. For Hegel, this brittleness is evident even in the Roman family. In the *Philosophy of History,* he stresses that Rome is hard and unfeeling. Marriage, in keeping with Roman legalism, is a contract, in which wife and children are the husband's property (286).

40. As Hegel tells us in the *Philosophy of History,* the world-historical function of Rome is that of unification through power: the individuality of persons, families, cities, and even gods must be sacrificed to the claims of a universal justice. With Rome, "the world is sunk in melancholy: its heart is broken, and it is all over with the natural side of Spirit, which has sunk into a feeling of unhappiness" (278). The *Gestalt* for this broken-heartedness is Virgil's Dido, who, in being abandoned by Aeneas, embodies the sacrifice of Love to the universal claims of world dominion and world history.

41. Roman legalism in this sense resembles the legalism of Kant and the empty formalism of I = I, the unity that makes me the owner of my experience. In general, Roman abstraction with respect to law is the origin of all the formalism that pervades modernity.

42. In the *Philosophy of History,* Hegel calls the emperor *monas monadum,* the Monad of Monads (320). We should note here that *monos,* in Greek, means solitary or alone. Daniel E. Shannon observes that Gibbon, who is Hegel's source for the history of the Empire, first uses the title "Lord of the World" to describe Commodus (*Spirit,* 33, note 55).

43. *Antony and Cleopatra,* act 3, scene 13, line 72. The phrase refers to Octavius Caesar.

44. This is a primary meaning of the Latin word *impotens.* Miller (following Baillie) mistranslates Hegel's phrase, *die machtlose Umschließung der Boden ihres Tumultes,* as "the defenceless enclosed arena of their tumult." Shannon gets it right: "the powerless wrapping and the field of their tumult" (*Spirit,* 33). The *Umschließung* or wrapping, here, is the emperor's purple cloak, which anyone who killed the emperor could claim as his prize. As Harris observes, the robe did not confer any constitutional power but simply meant that the army had acknowledged the "winner" as their military chief (*Hegel's Ladder,* 2:237). Needless to say, the robe offered no protection in battle and served only to mark the "winner" for death. Hegel's use of the image thus serves two purposes: it points to the emperor's inability to control the political and military chaos around him, and it is an image for the emperor's unruly soul.

45. For an account of how Hegel's description of the emperor reflects the actual wars that Rome, in her pagan decline, waged against the German tribes, see Harris, *Hegel's Ladder,* 2:236–39. Harris interprets "the wild orgy of mad destruction" as referring to the near incessant war that threatened the empire with anarchy (2:238).

46. Hegel is no doubt thinking here of emperors like Tiberius, Caligula, and Nero. Shannon points out that Hegel's description fits two emperors in particular: Commodus (who was nothing but a rage of appetites) and Antoninus (who renamed himself Elagabalus, after the Syrian sun-god) (*Spirit,* 33–34, note 58). The stoic-emperor Marcus Aurelius seems to be an exception. He is not monstrous, nor is his inner self a storm of passion. Nevertheless, whether he likes it or not, he is, as emperor, the titanic Ego of Rome, the Ego worshiped as a living god.

47. In the *Philosophy of History,* Hegel describes the emperor's self destruction: "Individual subjectivity thus entirely emancipated from control, has no inward life, no prospective nor retrospective emotions, no repentance, no hope, nor fear—not even thought; for all these involve fixed conditions and aims, while here every condition is purely contingent" (315).

48. We think of the distraction and pathological brooding of Tiberius, the madness of Caligula and Nero, the obscenities of Commodus and Antoninus, and the melancholy of the otherwise stoic Marcus Aurelius. As Harris observes (*Hegel's Ladder,* 2:245, note 39), the unhappiness of Marcus is revealed in the following passage from the *Meditations:* "Everything above and below is ever the same, and the result of the same things. How long then?" (Book VI, 46).

Chapter 16: Interlude

1. Plato's line is divided proportionately, or according to *analogia.* Mathematical proportionality is here an image of a non-mathematical or dialectical relation that connects the four powers of the soul. For an insightful account of the divided line, especially in relation to imagination or

image-recognition [*eikasia*], see Jacob Klein, *A Commentary on Plato's Meno* (Chapel Hill: University of North Carolina Press, 1965), 112–25.

2. Absolute knowing corresponds to the moment in Dante's *Purgatory* when, having ascended the mountain of purgation and walked through the fires of lust, and having been reconciled with Beatrice, Dante now stands ready to make his way through the heavens and, eventually, see God. He has grown his wings.

3. The spiral resembles the spiritual journey of Dante's *Paradiso.* In Hell and Purgatory, circles start wide and become progressively narrow. Hell is a funnel, and Purgatory is a mountain. The heavenly paradise, by contrast, is depicted as a series of ever-widening circles. The arrangement suggests that as we approach God, the point from which all goodness flows, we are not only moving higher but also taking in more of the world. To know God is to know the Whole that reveals his Providence.

4. The reader is encouraged to inspect the diagrams Kojève provides in his commentary on Hegel (*Introduction to the Reading of Hegel,* 105). They are meant to illustrate, not the journey of consciousness, but the difference between Hegel's absolute knowing and non-Hegelian positions.

5. In the *Phaedo,* Socrates speaks of refutation as the death of a trusted argument or *logos.* When the argument for the immortality of the soul seems to have been rendered untrustworthy, Socrates rallies his young friends (89A ff.). He enjoins them not to let the *logos* die. He encourages them, in spite of all obstacles, to continue to philosophize. For Socrates, philosophy, in addition to being the practice of being dead, is also a continual rising from the dead, the unending quest for a *logos* that will withstand the most rigorous scrutiny. The Forms themselves must be threatened with "death by refutation" if they are to be ever alive (a task Plato dramatizes in his *Parmenides*). What distinguishes Hegel's revival of *logos* from that of Socrates is determinate negation. Negation, for Hegel, is *itself* the process by which truth asserts and proves itself. Even more dramatically, divine Mind, for Hegel, enters time and suffers. For both these reasons, the Christian image of resurrection is appropriate to Hegel, but not to Plato.

6. In his Letter to the Galatians, St. Paul calls the follower of Christ a *kainē ktisis,* a new creation (6:15).

7. Hegel, *Faith and Knowledge,* 191. Why the Crucifixion rather than the Resurrection, Good Friday rather than Easter Sunday, is the final image will be taken up in our last chapter.

Chapter 17: Culture as Alienation

1. *Bildung* is related to the word *Bild,* which also has a central place in Hegel's book. A *Bild* in German is a visible form. It can be a picture, scene, image, or model. In the last paragraph of the book, Hegel tells us that the *Phenomenology* is a spiritual "picture gallery" [*eine Galerie von Bildern*] that reveals the stages by which spirit comes to be *gebildet,* that is, educated and formed [808].

2. "Culture is essentially concerned with form [*Form*]; the work of culture is the production of the form of universality, which is none other than thought" (Hegel, *Philosophy of History,* 417).

3. The historical era of *Bildung* begins with the conversion of Constantine (Harris, *Hegel's Ladder,* 2:247).

4. Hegel's account of culture takes its cue from what Rousseau called man's *perfectibility* (see *Discourse on the Origin of Inequality,* part 1). In his *Discourse on the Sciences and the Arts,* Rousseau brilliantly exposes the moral corruption and dehumanizing effects of progress. As Rosen observes, "Culture is a substitute for morality" (*G. W. F. Hegel,* 184).

5. Roman atomism lays the foundation for the modern liberalism of Hobbes, Locke, and Rousseau. "'Liberalism' sets up . . . the atomistic principle, that which insists upon the sway of individual wills; maintaining that all government should emanate from their express power, and have their express sanction" (Hegel, *Philosophy of History,* 452). Liberalism, for Hegel, emanates from France and spreads to the rest of Romanic Europe (452–53). It is merely formal or abstract freedom and as such is doomed to failure.

6. Hyppolite translates *Entaüßerung* and *Entfremdung,* respectively, as *aliénation* (alienation) and *extranéation* (estrangement). For a helpful discussion of the difference between the two German terms, see Rosen (*G. W. F. Hegel,* 172–73).

7. Hegel thus lays the foundation for Marx's concept of alienated labor. See the section entitled "Estranged Labor" in Marx's *Economic and Philosophic Manuscripts of 1844*, trans. Martin Milligan (Amherst, New York: Prometheus Books, 1988), 69–84).

8. Rousseau puts this social-political task of denaturing most strongly in his *Emile:* "Good social institutions are those that best know how to denature man, to take his absolute existence from him in order to give him a relative one and transport the I into the common unity, with the result that each individual believes himself no longer one but part of the unity and no longer feels except within the whole" (*Emile or On Education*, trans. Allan Bloom [New York: Basic Books, 1979], 40).

9. Alienation is the work of *infinity.* Infinity, we recall, first appeared at the end of "Force and the Understanding," where it signaled the birth of self-consciousness [161 ff.]. It is the process in which distinctions are simultaneously posited and canceled—the immediate transition into other that we saw in the inverted world. In culture, the inverted world becomes a lived reality. And like that earlier "upside down" world, culture, as Hegel's language constantly reminds us, is the realm of *Verkehrung* or inversion as *perversity.*

10. Homer's underworld is the realm of flitting shades—the loss of substance. It is nothing to yearn for.

11. The *supersensible world*, "the holy of holies" [146], now finds its true meaning within the higher realm of spirit. This Beyond is only abstractly conceived as a buttress for scientific explanation. In its higher truth, the supersensible world responds to a spiritual need, namely, the desire for happiness and the fulfillment of one's selfhood through union with the divine.

12. Insight is the radicalization of Roman skepticism. The Roman skeptic is different from the modern proponent of insight, who is ultimately a nihilist. The former annihilates the world to achieve tranquility through resignation and is not deliberately perverse. The latter seeks to generate perpetual unrest and, as we shall see, wills his perversity.

13. Denis Diderot (1713–84) was the famous author and intellectual who was the chief editor of the *Encyclopédie*, the masterpiece of the Enlightenment. In his novel, *Rameau's Nephew*, Diderot presents a satire of French society in the form of a dialogue, in which a bourgeois "philosopher" recounts his amazing conversation with the titular nephew. The nephew is a "free variation" on the real-life nephew of the famous composer and theorist Jean-Philippe Rameau. The novel remained unpublished in its author's lifetime and first appeared in Goethe's translation (1805). This was the version Hegel knew. For a spirited English translation (with a helpful account of the novel's history), see *Rameau's Nephew/D'Alembert's Dream*, trans. Leonard Tancock (New York: Penguin Books, 1966).

14. Hyppolite puts this nicely: "To cultivate oneself is not to develop harmoniously, as in organic growth, but to oppose oneself and rediscover oneself through a rending and a separation" (*Genesis and Structure*, 385). To be cultured is to be self-analytical.

15. The context for this mordant reflection is the rearing of children. The nephew derides people who, as a result of misguided education, cannot make up their mind about what they are naturally suited for and become "equally inept at good or evil." "A great rogue [or good-for-nothing] is a great rogue," says the nephew, "but he is not a 'type'" (*Rameau's Nephew*, trans. Tancock, 108).

16. The analogy strongly reminds us of the turbulent and unsteady receptacle [*hypodokhē*] of Plato's *Timaeus* (48E ff.). Harris offers a detailed interpretation of what the four elements correspond to in the culture world (*Hegel's Ladder*, 2:263–65).

17. Our current language of value (as in "family values") is a sign of alienation. We speak of values precisely when there is a split between meaning and life, theory and praxis. The Greeks did not have values, nor were they "sincere": they had virtue. Instead of "family values," they had family life in the context of custom.

18. See Rousseau, *Social Contract*, bk. 1, ch. 6.

19. This is the Artificial Man from the introduction to Hobbes' *Leviathan.*

20. In seeking his own gain, the individual "is in this, as in many other cases, led by an invisible hand to promote an end which was no part of his intention" (Adam Smith, *An Inquiry into the Nature and Causes of the Wealth of Nations* [Indianapolis: Liberty Classics, 1981], 1:456). Hegel discusses the cunning of reason [*die List der Vernunft*] in various places. See *Philosophy of History* (33 ff.) and *Encyclopaedia Logic* (284, para. 209 and Addition).

21. Harris argues that the adjective *niederträchtig* should be translated "contemptuous" rather than "base" or "ignoble" (*Hegel's Ladder,* 2:274 and 2:310, note 33). I have retained "base" (Miller's rendering) and rely on the context to make clear that this consciousness *knows* it is base and feels contempt. Similarly, we must note that the nobles are not simply noble [*edel*] but noble-hearted [*edelmütig*]. Both shapes of consciousness, in other words, are defined not by their objective character but by their inner disposition and self-image.

22. In Dostoevsky's *Brothers Karamazov* (pt. 2, ch. 7), the good-hearted Alyosha tries to give a large sum of money to the poor, dishonored father of the boy Ilyusha. At first, the father responds with joy and gratitude. But then the promise of wealth reminds him of his need and humiliation. In a fit of frenzied pride, he tramples the money in the dust. The episode is part of Dostoevsky's larger meditation on the dialectic of pride and humiliation. The father is a good example of how self-contempt is part of the self-image of resentful consciousness.

23. In the Greek *polis,* there is harmony rather than opposition between the in-itself and the for-itself. Because the Greek individual does not experience a split between himself and the whole that defines him, there is no need to negate an underlying egotism in order to affirm the common good. In other words, egotism versus altruism is an example of modern alienation.

24. For Hegel's account of the historical transition from feudalism to monarchy, and the rise of French power in Europe, see *Philosophy of History* (398–404).

25. "The 'haughty vassal' is most likely Prince de Condé, who fought for the crown against the people in the first battles of the Fronde (1649), but then demanded rewards for his service that were finally refused to him by Cardinal Mazarin" (Shannon, *Spirit,* 51, note 93).

26. In the *Philosophy of Right,* Hegel argues that the best regime is constitutional monarchy, and that there can be no true state sovereignty without a monarch and without majesty (trans. White, 218 ff.). This is why, for Hegel, France became a state in the full sense, whereas Germany (like Italy) did not. In an early work entitled *The German Constitution* (1798–1802), Hegel develops his view that Germany "is a state in thought but not in actuality" (*Political Writings,* ed. Dickey, 41).

27. The universality of the pronoun "I" was *resisted,* we recall, at the level of immediate being-for-self. Instead of language and the effort to communicate, there was a fight to the death.

28. In Hegel's description of speech as a life-in-death, we see the close connection for him between *logos* as human discourse and the divine, creative *Logos* that is Christ. The very thing that makes speech seem tragic or at least non-essential, the fact that it *flows,* contains the seed of philosophy in the form of Science, the logical "flow" of the self-mediating Concept.

29. Once we are *both* engaged in language and thus "pass into each other," we become an I that is We and a We that is I. This is the mutual recognition that is the goal and destiny of self-consciousness. It does not occur until the very end of Hegel's account of morality, where the language of reconciliation signals the appearance of God within human community [671].

30. The French monarch, unlike the Roman emperor, is *radiant*—like Louis XIV, the Sun King. He is the personal embodiment and shining forth of the general will. Under the Roman emperor, individuals were slaves. Under a monarch, they are dignified subjects. As Hegel notes in his *Philosophy of History,* monarchy is "the source of real freedom," and "the supremacy implied in monarchy is essentially a power emanating from a political body, and is pledged to the furtherance of that equitable purpose on which the constitution of a state is based" (399).

31. This inversion recalls that of the master-slave relation, where the master gets honor but does no work; and the dishonored slave, through work, "cultures" himself or acquires form [196].

32. "The reign of Louis XV is when the state power loses its honor and respect. The monarch is admired only in name. The real power lies in the ministers of government" (Shannon, *Spirit,* 57, note 106).

33. Hegel, *System of Ethical Life* and *First Philosophy of Spirit,* 171. The reference to "the unmitigated extreme of barbarism" occurs in the former work.

34. In language, this would be expressed by the judgment, "I am a thing" or "The subject is an object." Hegel calls this the "infinite judgment," in which "subject and predicate are utterly indifferent" [520]. This immediate identity of the infinitely unlike is the ground of the self's division into separate selves or personalities.

35. Excellent accounts of the precise ways in which Hegel draws on Diderot's novel may be found in Hyppolite (*Genesis and Structure,* 410–17), Harris (*Hegel's Ladder,* 2:298–305), and Lewis

P. Hinchman (*Hegel's Critique of the Enlightenment* [Tampa and Gainesville: University Presses of Florida, 1984], 115–21).

36. The nephew says at one point: "I am a person who isn't of any consequence. People do what they like with me, in front of me, without standing on ceremony" (*Rameau's Nephew,* trans. Tancock, 46).

37. This self-contradiction exactly describes the young Rameau, about whom the philosopher says: "Nothing is less like him than himself" (ibid., 34).

38. In feeling his selfhood as a unity of opposites, the client experiences the "identity within difference" that characterizes the Concept. He thus represents a significant advance toward spirit's goal of absolute knowing.

39. Hegel's portrait is inspired by the nephew's description of his rich benefactor as a gloomy motionless *idol,* who seems more like a mechanical puppet than a man (*Rameau's Nephew,* trans. Tancock, 71).

40. As Shannon observes: "Rameau first appears in the dialog as one whose clothing is torn, but soon it is made clear that his mind is torn because of his service to Bertin's family" (*Spirit,* 61, note 114).

41. "Is there anybody there with nerve enough to be of your opinion?" the philosopher asks. "What do you mean by anybody?" responds the nephew, "It is the sentiment and opinion of the whole of society" (*Rameau's Nephew,* trans. Tancock, 78).

42. For an insightful discussion of Hegel on "cultural nihilism," see Rosen (*G. W. F. Hegel,* 194 ff.).

43. The dialectic of conscience occurs in Hegel's discussion of morality [632 ff.].

44. In *Candide,* Voltaire satirically attacks both Christianity and Leibniz' "optimism" or belief that this is the "best of possible worlds." For Hegel's praise of Voltaire and his "common sense," see *Faith and Knowledge,* 178.

45. Hegel's difficult last paragraph reminds us that the dialectic of culture has erased both the quantitative and the qualitative distinctions among human beings. All finite, natural and quasi-natural distinctions have been dissolved in the *infinite judgment* that arose with the disrupted consciousness [520]. Now the self has only *itself* as object. This self-beholding is intensely painful to the disrupted nephew, who is enmeshed in the world he despises. But in pure insight, self-awareness becomes the *Begriff* or Concept—the basis for egalitarian enlightenment.

46. From Kant's essay "What Is Enlightenment?" (in *Foundations of the Metaphysics of Morals,* trans. Lewis White Beck [Indianapolis: Bobbs-Merril], 1959). Beck notes that this was "the motto adopted in 1736 by the Society of the Friends of Truth, an important circle in the German Enlightenment" (85).

Chapter 18: From Pure Insight to Pure Terror

1. For the definitive statement of insight's opposition to religious picture thinking, see the Appendix to book one of Spinoza's *Ethics* ("On God"). For Spinoza, the source of prejudice and intolerance is the *imagination* or picture thinking. Reason alone knows the nature of things. Imagination reveals nothing more than the believer's temperament and physical constitution. The Enlightenment rejects natural and divine purpose and, as we shall see, identifies the good with the useful. This rejection too appears in Spinoza's Appendix: "Now all the prejudices which I intend to mention here turn on this one point, the widespread belief among men that all things in Nature are like themselves in acting with an end in view" (*Ethics,* trans. Shirley, 57).

2. Hegel, *Aesthetics,* 2:1110.

3. The interest in making a collection of the nephew's insights reaches its higher stage in the collection and promulgation of *all* human insight and knowledge. This was the goal of the famous *Encyclopaedia,* for which Diderot served as principal editor.

4. The enlightened version of God is the inhuman "substance" of Descartes and Spinoza, who laid the foundation for modern deism.

5. Pure insight's accusation of priests and despots recalls Karl's attack on the Establishment. The difference is that whereas Karl attacked external institutions for being unfeeling crocodiles, insight attacks inward faith for being simple or naïve.

6. The Enlightenment reveals the deep skepticism of modern philosophy, which shows its true colors in its spirit of negativity. Whereas ancient philosophy began in wonder, modern philosophy begins in the will *not to be deceived:* freedom means, above all, being nobody's fool. This will is most clearly at work in Descartes' *Meditations.* Doubt is a method by which the mind identifies and opposes the enemies that would tyrannize over it—including the potentially tyrannical influences of our own nature as bodily beings. Descartes' famous "evil genius" is, from the Enlightenment point of view, a priest-despot writ large. Through the method of doubt, the mind gains access to what Descartes calls "the natural light of reason." The negative, suspicious muse of modernity reaches its peak in Kant's *Critique of Pure Reason.*

7. Again, there is an analogy here with Karl Moor, who is offended that other people's hearts actually "go for" the evil teachings of the Establishment.

8. Hegel here recalls the passage in the Gospel of John in which John compares Jesus, who has taken all sin upon himself, to a "brazen serpent" lifted upon the Cross (3:14–15). John is referring to the passage in Numbers, where Moses constructs a bronze serpent and sets it on a pole. Whoever has been bitten by a serpent and looks upon this bronze image is saved (21:8–9). One implication of Hegel's use of this image is that Enlightenment is fueled by a religious impulse: it pursues reason with the zeal of Faith. Whoever looks upon reason will be saved from "Faith-bite." In the *History of Philosophy,* Hegel observes that French philosophy raised the banner of Reason and changed the meaning of what Constantine saw in the heavens. It said to mankind: "In *this* sign thou shalt conquer" (3:397).

9. It is also a lapse into the *spiritual kingdom of animals,* where conflicting self-interested geniuses "cheat and struggle over the essence of the actual world" [537].

10. As I noted in Chapter 11, Hegel appropriates Kant's term "category" in an effort to transform the latter's transcendental philosophy (or "bad idealism") into a metaphysical claim, to transform category as a mere mode of thought into Category as the real unity of thought and being.

11. Strange as it may seem, the religious community is the unity of self and thing that was the object of *reason's* will and desire.

12. To the question posed by Frederick the Great—"whether it is permissible to delude a people"—Hegel responds with a resounding negative. For him, it is impossible for a religion to be forced on a people. Religion is not imposed but grows naturally from a people's spirit and self-awareness. As Hegel puts it here, "in the knowledge of that essential being in which consciousness has the immediate *certainty of itself* [i.e. religion], the idea of delusion is quite out of the question."

13. The Enlightenment recalls the voice of the Way of the World. It focuses on what it takes to be an impossible, and wrong, intention or motive.

14. Hegel notes in passing that insight itself is not empty but rich—rich, that is, "only in particularity and limitations." In dealing with God, insight exercises prudence: it wisely refrains from letting God sink to the level of ordinary sense-objects. The God without predicates reminds us of Spinoza's undifferentiated Substance. Hegel draws a parallel between Spinoza and French materialism in his *History of Philosophy* (3:382).

15. Reason also regarded the world as its own but made no appeal to a rational theology.

16. That is, religion becomes subservient to politics and to self-interest (the pious *succeed*).

17. Insight "saves" God from the taint of human imagining. In making him useful, it also "saves" him from being self-sacrificial (the Savior God of besotted, anthropocentric Christians). Utility is the enlightened version of transcendence. The irony at work here is that, from the for-us perspective, there is no true rationality without self-differentiation—*self-sacrifice.* The Concept splits itself into extremes and finds its unity in the identity of these extremes. In attacking the Christian Savior God, insight thus attacks the highest form of rationality, here expressed in representational form.

18. Enlightenment rises above faith for precisely the same reason that the self-negating nephew rises above the culture world.

19. A similar "falling back" into body and self-interest occurred for the unhappy consciousness.

20. This distinction is the ground of Spinoza's attack on superstition. To confuse image and concept is to confuse "dumb pictures on a tablet" with ideas as pure acts of the mind that involve affirmation and negation (*Ethics* II, proposition 49, scholium, p. 97).

21. The models for deism and materialism are, respectively, Robinet and von Hollbach (a German living in Paris). Hegel discusses them in the *Lectures on the History of Philosophy,* 3:393–98. Hegel goes on to say in the present context that the terms matter and God fail to capture the true meaning of nature and spirit. Matter fails to convey the sense of nature as a principle of outer organic self-differentiation and development, and God (as the term is used here) fails to convey the inner self-differentiation of true selfhood—God as *spirit.*

22. One of Hegel's most interesting points here is that matter is the listless motion of thought itself [577], the to and fro movement that insight received by "contact" with faith. Matter is not dead. It is the projection of insight's brooding and pacing over a lost spiritual world. Matter is thought that has "fallen" into a state of self-otherness.

23. Hegel mentions in passing that Descartes' metaphysics overcomes the split between deists and the materialists [578]. He does so in his "I think, therefore I am," which Hegel interprets as affirming the identity of *thought* and *thing.* In the *cogito* [I think], according to Hegel, thought grasps itself *and thinghood* as pure: thought is untrammeled by sensing and imagining, and being (as matter or extension) is untrammeled by predicates.

24. Husserl captures this connection between thinking and eating in the *Crisis of European Sciences:* "The subjective part of the world swallows up, so to speak, the whole world and thus itself too" (180). He does not, however, acknowledge the dialectical implications of this insight.

25. For Hegel's more directly historical account of the French Revolution, see *Philosophy of History* (438–57).

26. In the *Philosophy of Right,* Hegel defines the will as "a particular way of thinking, thinking translating itself into existence, as the drive to give itself existence" (trans. White, 18–19).

27. "The principle of [absolute] freedom emerged in Rousseau, and gave to man, who apprehends himself as infinite, this infinite strength" (*Lectures on the History of Philosophy,* 3:402).

28. For Rousseau's account of the general will, see *Social Contract,* bk. I, ch. 6.

29. In a sense, man recovers the *mutual recognition* that was present in ethical Eden (the Greek *polis*). But he does so on modern, enlightened terms. The basis of community is not custom and piety but man's self-consciousness, man qua individual, not man qua Athenian. This universality is codified in the *Declaration of the Rights of Man and Citizen,* adopted in 1789.

30. It is worth noting that Robespierre was himself a deist who tried, unsuccessfully, to establish a civic religion devoted to the Supreme Being.

31. Fury here recalls the avenging Furies of the Greek ethical world. The modern Fury is the dark and all-consuming Self.

32. In the *Philosophy of History,* Hegel sums up the three ideals of the Revolution in one word: Virtue [*Tugend*] (450). Robespierre, for Hegel, was, in a sense, a Knight of Virtue: "The principle of virtue [*Tugend*] was set up as supreme by Robespierre; and one can say that with this man virtue was a serious matter" (ibid.).

33. In his *Philosophy of History,* Hegel notes that under Robespierre's Reign of Terror, as under the Roman emperors, "mere disposition, unaccompanied by any overt act or expression, was made an object of punishment" (426).

34. In the *Philosophy of Right,* Hegel says: "[Freedom as indeterminacy] appears in the active fanaticism of political and of religious life. Here belongs, for example, the time of terror of the French Revolution . . . This time was an agitation, an upheaval, a refusal to tolerate any particular, because what fanaticism wills is a specific abstraction, i.e., the utter absence of articulation: where distinctions develop, fanaticism finds them contrary to its indeterminacy and suspends them. For this reason, in the revolution the people destroyed the institutions it itself had made, because any institution is contrary to the abstract self-consciousness of equality" (trans. White, 21).

35. Ghastly as the Terror was, Hegel regarded it and the whole French Revolution as necessary to spirit's development in history. In a letter to a student, he writes: "Thanks to the bath of her Revolution, the French Nation has freed herself of many institutions which the human spirit had outgrown like the shoes of a child" (*Hegel: The Letters,* 123). Hyppolite makes the following general point: "Although the implications of Hegel's system are conservative, the advance of the dialectic is revolutionary, whatever Hegel's intention may have been" (*Genesis and Structure,* 398).

36. Whereas the French Revolution was a revolution in the actual world, the German Revolution (the Reformation) was a revolution of the inner man—the liberation of his conscience. The former

failed because it was "a Revolution without a Reformation" (Hegel, *Philosophy of History,* 453). It also failed because modern liberalism, "which insists on the sway of individual wills" (452), cannot produce genuine human community. Hegel's hope, which was never fulfilled, was that the German nation would build on the French Revolution, transform its inner Revolution into an outer one.

Chapter 19: Pure Willing and the Moral World-View

1. The reader should compare Hegel's account of morality in the *Phenomenology* with that in the *Philosophy of Right* (trans. White, 88–124). Whereas in the former work morality is higher than ethicality, the order is reversed in the latter. The reason has to do with the close connection in the *Phenomenology* between morality and the claim to absolute knowing.

2. Spirit seems to reverse the order we have seen at earlier stages of experience: it begins with *truth* (ethicality) and ends with *certainty* (morality). But "truth" here refers, not to the dialectical outcome of experience but to spirit's immediate relation to its concrete world. The experiential motion from certainty to truth as dialectical outcome is still present throughout the chapter on spirit. The dialectic of Antigone's world of knowing begins with her absolute *certainty* in one side of the law and ends in the passing away of that world. This passing away is the truth of ethicality [596].

3. On the identity of the moral law with my certainty of myself, see the following passage from Kant: "Two things fill the mind with ever new and increasing admiration, the more frequently and persistently one's meditation deals with them: the starry sky above me and the moral law within me. Neither of them do I need to seek or merely suspect outside my purview, as veiled in obscurities or [as lying] in the extravagant: I see them before me and connect them directly with the consciousness of my existence" (*Critique of Practical Reason,* trans. Pluhar, 203).

4. Nowhere in the *Phenomenology* does Hegel take up Kant's moral teaching as a whole. In the chapter on reason, he revealed the contradiction within law taken as Kant's categorical imperative [429]. Here, in morality, he focuses on the moral postulates. Hegel treats these elements of Kant's moral doctrine as defining different shapes and levels of consciousness, each with its own dialectical life.

5. Kant's distinction between *autonomy* and *heteronomy* is central to morality. I am autonomous when the determining ground of my will is the will itself, and when I act for the sake of pure duty. Heteronomy, by contrast, occurs when I make a given content or authority other than my will (God, for example) the determining ground. Kant discusses this fundamental distinction in various places. The clearest is in the *Grounding for the Metaphysics of Morals.* There, Kant calls autonomy the "Supreme Principle of Morality," and heteronomy the "Source of All Spurious Principles of Morality" (trans. Ellington, 44–45).

6. Kant puts this priority of practical over speculative reason in terms of the *interest* of reason. The theoretical could never serve the practical "because all interest is ultimately practical and even the interest of speculative reason is only conditional and is complete in practical use alone" (*Critique of Practical Reason,* trans. Pluhar, 126). In Fichte's *The Vocation of Man,* the character named Spirit tells Fichte: "Your vocation is not merely to know, but *to act* according to your knowledge" (trans. Peter Preuss [Indianapolis: Hackett, 1987], 67). The moral voice within me is an Ought that demands "a better world" (100).

7. The moralist is different from the stoic, whose freedom is purely negative, a turning away from actuality. The moral individual is obliged to act morally. He experiences the world not as something to flee but as the medium for his moral creativity. The moralist is also different from the Knight of Virtue, whom he in part resembles. Again, the difference has to do with how the individual regards both himself and the external world. The moralist and the Knight both have good intentions or a good will. Both want to make the world a better place. The difference is that, for the Knight, the good is nothing more than the suppression of self-interest. He defends the good by opposing egotism. He lacks the certainty of himself as a moral agent. He does not posit duty as that which commands the person of good intention to make his intention real through action.

8. As Hyppolite observes, Hegel here revises Kant's "vulgar eudaemonism," his definition of happiness as the gratification of bodily desires (*Genesis and Structure,* 476). The Knight of Duty

finds his happiness not in these lower desires but in moral accomplishment, in what Hyppolite calls "the plenitude of realization" (477). For Kant's view of happiness, see *Critique of Practical Reason:* "The principle of one's own happiness [*Glückseligkeit*], however much understanding and reason may be used with this principle, would still comprise no determining bases for the will different from those that are appropriate to our *lower* power of desire" (trans. Pluhar, 37).

9. The unity of morality and nature is the chief goal of Kant's system. This unity or highest good appears in all three *Critiques.*

10. In Euclid's *Elements,* a postulate is an *aitēma,* from the Greek verb *aitein*—to ask or beg. In various places Kant is at pains to distinguish the mathematical from the philosophic use of the term. In the *Critique of Practical Reason,* he says the following: "The postulate of pure practical reason . . . postulates the possibility of an *object* itself (God and the immortality of the soul) from apodeictic *practical* laws, and therefore only on behalf of a practical reason. This certainty of the postulated possibility is thus not at all theoretical, hence also not apodeictic, i.e., a necessity cognized with regard to the object, but is, rather, an assumption necessary, with regard to the subject, for complying with practical reason's objective but practical laws, hence merely a subjective hypothesis" (trans. Pluhar, 17).

11. This otherness or duality is vividly described in Paul's Letter to the Romans: "So then, I of myself serve the law of God with my mind, but with my flesh I serve the law of sin" (7:25).

12. Both ethicality and the Moral World-View are interested in harmony. But whereas the ethical individual experienced harmony in his everyday life, the moral individual, "locked up" inside himself, knows harmony only as a not-yet-experienced ideal.

13. In the moral world-view, in other words, morality is higher than religion, which is there only to serve morality. This is a direct result of the Enlightenment, which finds the idea of God *useful.*

14. As Harris observes (*Hegel's Ladder,* 2:425), this is an explicit reference to Kant's *Religion Within the Boundaries of Mere Reason* (first edition, 1793). In that work, which is devoted to giving a rational account of original sin, Kant writes the following: "For what in our earthly life (and perhaps even in all future times and in all worlds) is always only in mere *becoming* (namely, our being a human being well-pleasing to God) is imputed to us as if we already possessed it here in full. And to this we indeed have no rightful claim (according to the empirical cognition we have of ourselves), so far as we know ourselves (estimate our disposition not directly but only according to our deeds), so that the accuser within us would still be more likely to render a verdict of guilty. It is always therefore only a decree of grace . . ." (trans. Allen Wood and George Di Giovanni [Cambridge: Cambridge University Press, 1998], 91–92).

15. What Hegel is describing here is evident in Kant's references to God. Is God real for Kant, or is he only a thought? Hegel shows, convincingly, that from the moral perspective God is both. He is the being who is necessarily thought of as real.

16. For Fichte's moral philosophy, see *The Vocation of Man* (book 3, "Faith") and the *Science of Knowledge* (part 3, "Foundation of the Knowledge of the Practical"). Fichte plays a central role in Hegel's thought. For Hegel's interpretation of this major philosophical figure, see his early work, *The Difference Between Fichte's and Schelling's System of Philosophy,* the *Lectures on the History of Philosophy* (3:479), and the fascinating account of Fichte as the father of modern irony in the introduction to the *Aesthetics* (1:64–65).

17. For Fichte's identification of the self with *striving* [*Streben*] and *drive* [*Trieb*], see the *Science of Knowledge* (trans. Heath & Lachs, 253 ff.). Fichte sometimes calls this striving *yearning* [*Sehnen*], a word that echoes the infinite yearning of the unhappy consciousness [217].

18. The impetus for this thought is clearly Leibniz, who argued, against Descartes, that force of action rather than mere extension is the substance of things. In this context, we should recall that force for Hegel is incipient self-consciousness and will.

19. Pierre, in Tolstoy's *War and Peace,* is an example of this idealism. In his French captivity, Pierre is morally awakened by the unspoiled self-sufficiency of Platon Karatayev, and discovers true freedom. Tolstoy gives the following account: "Pierre glanced at the sky, at the far-away, twinkling stars. 'And all that is mine, and all that is in me, and all that is I!' thought Pierre. 'And all this they caught and shut up in a shed closed in with boards!' He smiled and went to lie down to sleep beside his companions" (trans. Constance Garnett [New York: Modern Library, 2002], 1161). The reader should compare this passage with the end of Fichte's *Vocation of Man:* "So I live and so I am, and so

I am unchangeable, firm, and complete for all eternity. For this is no being assumed from without. It is my own, my only true and essential being" (trans. Preuss, 123).

20. Harris spells out the complex way in which this higher shape combines Kant and Fichte (*Hegel's Ladder,* 2:428–37). He makes the valuable observation that Fichte's more dogmatic, self-assertive version of morality is necessary if morality is to display its shiftiness (434). As Harris observes, Kant's theoretical skepticism—his "Philosophy of As If"—makes him harder to pin down.

21. Shannon points out that Schiller's version of Kant's moral doctrine plays a crucial role in this part of the dialectic (*Spirit,* 206–9).

22. Kant refers to "an entire nest of dialectical claims" in connection with the cosmological proof for God's existence (*Critique of Pure Reason,* B637, trans. Pluhar, 591). The moral individual's reasoning that takes him from an observed imperfect moral condition to the projection of one that is morally perfect is analogous to the cosmological argument, which reasons from an imperfect world to God as the perfect being (Harris, *Hegel's Ladder,* 2:443). In short, Kantian morality falls victim to the same sophism of which Kant accuses speculative reason.

23. See Kant's *Critique of Pure Reason,* "The Antinomy of Pure Reason" (trans. Pluhar, 454 ff.). The First Antinomy deals with whether the world had a beginning in time; the Second with whether there are material atoms; the Third with whether freedom exists; and the Fourth with whether there is a highest being or God.

24. In the *Philosophy of Right,* Hegel cites a French saying along these same lines: "*Le meilleure tue le bien*" ("The best kills the good") (trans. White, 168).

25. Hegel compares the complexity of the real life situation with the thing of many properties. For a helpful interpretation of this comparison, see Harris, Hegel's Ladder, 2:447–48.

26. "The use of the word 'syncretism' implies that Hegel has in mind the philosophy of W. T. Krug, especially Krug's attempt to blend the 'eternal truths' of religion and morality with the empiricism of Kantian philosophy, while all along denying the transcendental Self. Krug called his synthesis of the pure and the empirical 'transcendental syncretism'" (*Spirit,* ed. Shannon, 133, note 248).

Chapter 20: Conscience and Reconciliation

1. The sentence occurs in Jacobi's *Letters to Fichte* (see *The Main Philosophical Writings and the Novel Allwill* by Friedrich Heinrich Jacobi, trans. George di Giovanni [Montreal: McGill-Queen's University Press, 1994], 516). Hegel quotes it in his early writing *Faith and Knowledge,* 143.

2. "The figure of the 'Beautiful Soul' has its philosophical origin in Shaftesbury; and it was naturalized in German literature by Wieland" (Harris, *Hegel's Ladder,* 2:479). Of course, beautiful inwardness is ultimately traceable to Luther, the father of modern subjectivity in *all* its forms.

3. The translation is that of my friend and colleague, Eric Salem. In his *Aesthetics,* Hegel credits Schiller "for breaking through the Kantian subjectivity and abstraction of thinking and for venturing on an attempt to get beyond this by intellectually grasping the unity and reconciliation as the truth by actualizing them in artistic production" (1:61).

4. Schiller's version of the beautiful soul reminds us of Aristotle's "great-souled man," who lives for the sake of inner beauty—what Aristotle calls *to kalon* (*Nicomachean Ethics* 4.3). But this beauty has an objective ground: ethical virtue. For the conscientious individual, who eventually becomes a beautiful soul, there is no such ground. He is beautiful in his singularity or this-ness, which he experiences as the source of his moral creativity. Beautiful, for him, means *rarefied,* not *virtuous.* In historical terms, there is no way to assimilate Aristotle into a fundamentally *Lutheran* conception of man—that is, without being Hegel.

5. Hegel to Niethammer, *Hegel: The Letters,* 114. Hegel had just finished the *Phenomenology* (except for the Preface) when Napoleon's army marched into Jena. On Monday, October 13, 1806, he watched Napoleon reviewing his troops. In the letter cited above, he writes the following: "It is indeed a wonderful sensation to see such an individual, who, concentrated here at a point, astride a horse, reaches out over the world and masters it."

6. Conviction, in the present context, derives from Jacobi, who wanted to replace reason with intuition and faith, more generally, with pure subjectivity. For Hegel's discussion of Jacobi, see *Faith*

and Knowledge and the account of Jacobi in the *Lectures on the History of Philosophy,* 3:410–23. The German word for conviction, *Überzeugung,* derives from *über,* "over," and *Zeugung,* "witness." Conviction is the witness that trumps all other witnesses.

7. Harris observes that, "my conscientious conviction . . . comes from what we rudely but insightfully call a 'gut-feeling'" (*Hegel's Ladder,* 2:470). "'Conscience,'" he continues, "is a gut-commitment; and it is not Reason that the guts are full of" (ibid.).

8. Hyppolite quotes this letter in his commentary (*Genesis and Structure,* 514–15).

9. As Hyppolite notes, Goethe is highly critical of the beautiful soul, who is sharply contrasted with the heroine Nathalie, for whom thought and feeling must gain outward expression in worldly action. Hyppolite quotes the passage in which Nathalie, no doubt Goethe's spokesman here, says: "The destiny of man is to be active, and every interval between actions should be occupied with learning about these exterior things which subsequently facilitate activity" (ibid., 515).

10. The sentence occurs almost at the end of the beautiful soul's "confession."

11. In the *Philosophy of Right,* Hegel presents conscience in its concrete, substantial form: "True conscience is the disposition to will what is good in and as itself. It therefore has fixed axioms, and these are for it the determinations and duties that are objective as themselves" (trans. White, 108).

12. Hölderlin is a good example of the disdain for determinateness. He praises Empedocles, the subject of his tragic poem, as one who was "a sworn enemy of all one-sided existence and thus . . . dissatisfied . . . even in truly pleasant conditions simply because they are particular conditions" (quoted in *Hyperion and Selected Poems,* ed. Santner, xiv–xv).

13. In this context, we should recall Hegel's caution in the Preface to the effect that philosophy must not seek to be edifying [9], and the harsh assertion: "Beauty hates the understanding for asking of her what she cannot do" [32].

14. To reject determinateness as such is to desire the annihilation of the world. This desire is eloquently expressed in Paul Valéry's poem, "Sketch of a Serpent" ("Ébauche d'un serpent"). Valéry's cultured serpent derides creation as a beautiful lie that hides the primordial Non-being and *vanitas* that is the truth of all things. The universe "is nothing but a fault [*un défaut*] in the purity of Non-being" (stanza 3). And the serpent, himself a finite creation, embodies the vain, unsatisfiable desire for absolute knowing. To be desirous is to be full of nothing. Man's fate, which we witness in the serpent, is to be eternally *possible* or never complete.

15. Novalis, *Henry von Ofterdingen,* trans. Palmer Hilty (New York: Frederick Ungar, 1972), 164–69.

16. As Harris observes (*Hegel's Ladder,* 2:480), the moral genius is not only Novalis but also Schleiermacher's "religious artist," as Hegel calls him (*Faith and Knowledge,* 150). This is the Protestant minister who, Hegel says, mediates between the congregation and God by virtue of his intense feeling and "personal originality" (151).

17. In the *Lectures on the Philosophy of Religion,* Hegel writes: "This [pure subjectivity] is an inward weaving of spirit within itself, which can just as readily assume the form of hypocrisy and extreme vanity as it can peaceful, noble, pious aspirations. This is what is called the pious life of feeling, to which *Pietism* also restricts itself. Pietism acknowledges no objective truth and opposes itself to dogmas and the content of religion, while still preserving an element of mediation, a connection with Christ, but this is a connection that is supposed to remain one of mere feeling and inner sensibility" (3:344).

18. In his fascinating study of Rousseau, Jean Starobinski refers to the "small group of *belles âmes,*" who enjoy reciprocal transparency in their idyllic life at Clarens (*Jean-Jacques Rousseau, Transparency and Obstruction,* trans. Arthur Goldhammer [Chicago: University of Chicago Press, 1988], 85). Starobinski quotes Rousseau's description of this life in the letter of Madame de Wolmar: "Admit at least that the whole charm of the society that reigned among us is in this openness of heart, which makes us share all our feelings and all our thoughts, and makes it so that each person, sensing what he ought to be, shows himself to us as he is" [my translation] (*La nouvelle Héloïse,* part 6, letter 8). Starobinski also has a penetrating comparison of Hegel and Rousseau on the beautiful soul (262–65).

19. Fichte, for Hegel, is the father of this irony (*Aesthetics,* 1:64). Irony was further developed by Novalis, who, according to Hegel, was "one of the nobler spirits who took up this position," and "was driven into a void with no specific interests, into this dread of reality, and was wound down as

it were into a spiritual decline" (1:159–60). In the *Lectures on the History of Philosophy,* Hegel goes through the further developments of Fichtean irony. These include Friedrich Schlegel, Schleiermacher, and Novalis (3:507–12).

20. At the end of the chapter, this community will be truly spiritual—that is, for Hegel, *reconciled to external reality.* Pious feeling will be transformed into full-bodied religion.

21. Faust, too, was an instance of spiritual poverty [363]. The bond that connects his pursuit of sensual love and the beautiful soul is immediacy.

22. Hegel, *Philosophy of History,* 239.

23. Ibid., 253. See also Hegel, *Aesthetics,* 1:278. Hegel's discussion of Orestes is especially interesting. Orestes is pursued by the Furies, but he is not conscience-stricken.

24. In his *Aesthetics,* Hegel calls the beautiful soul who cannot make himself real *morbid,* adding: "For a *truly* beautiful soul acts and is actual" (1:67). This qualification may explain why, in the *Phenomenology,* Hegel speaks of the "so-called" beautiful soul.

25. See Harris, *Hegel's Ladder,* 2:497–98. Loewenberg reminds us that Hegel too can be a merciless judge. His character Hardith remarks that Hegel's "polemic" is "in questionable taste." He says: "The allusion, obviously to Novalis, is too cruel to be condoned." The other character, Meredy, responds: "You are very hard on Hegel. His criticism, though indeed merciless, must not be taken apart from the analysis of which it often, and here in particular, forms an integral part." Nevertheless, Meredy (Loewenberg) concludes: "principally dialectical, [Hegel's] treatment is unfortunately suffused with a polemic unusually venomous" (Loewenberg, *Hegel's Phenomenology: Dialogues,* 287).

26. See Hegel's description of Novalis in the *History of Philosophy:* "This subjectivity does not reach substantiality, it dies away within itself . . . The extravagances of subjectivity constantly pass into madness; if they remain in thought they are whirled round and round in the vortex of reflecting understanding, which is ever negative in reference to itself" (3:510). Hegel's most pointed critique of romantic subjectivity occurs in *Faith and Knowledge* (146–47). The context is his critique of Jacobi. The beautiful souls in Jacobi's two novels, *Woldemar* and *Allwill,* exhibit "subjectivity holding fast to itself." This subjectivity "puts extreme meticulousness, nostalgic egoism and ethical sickliness in the place of ethical freedom." Hegel calls such introspection "inner idolatry" and a "spiritual debauch." He compares it to Dante's Hell, where damnation is "being alone with what is most peculiarly one's own." Hegel seems to be thinking in particular of Francesca, who continues to play the romantic heroine in Hell, and proudly clings to the feeling of *amore* (*Inferno* 5).

27. In an early theological writing, Hegel identified Jesus as a beautiful soul (*The Spirit of Christianity,* in *Early Theological Writings,* 234–37). This is Hegel's "first portrait" of the beautiful soul (Harris, *Hegel's Ladder,* 2:498). The young Hegel also wrote a "Life of Jesus" (1795) that makes Jesus sound like Kant and ends with the Crucifixion. It appears in *Three Essays, 1793–1795.*

28. For Hegel, the beautiful soul, although a fanatic, is not delusional. It responds to an important truth about human existence. This truth is that all action *is* finite, one-sided, self-interested, and therefore sinful. On the "sin" of finitude, see Hyppolite (*Genesis and Structure,* 519).

29. This is the word Aristotle uses in his discussion of tragedy in the *Poetics.* The hero goes from good fortune to bad, "not through any wickedness, but through a great error" [*dia hamartian megalan*] (1453a15–16).

30. The emergence within conscience of this antithesis between individuals echoes the conflict between Antigone and Creon in Ethicality. There, too, a community (the *polis*) was harmonious and unified only at the surface. There, too, action awakened the dormant antithesis.

31. In a short philosophic essay, Hölderlin plays on the words *Urteil,* judgment, and *Teil,* part ("Judgment and Being," in *Essays and Letters on Theory,* trans. Thomas Pfau [Albany: SUNY Press, 1988], 37–38). He defines judgment as the "original parting"—the *ur-teilen*—of the self into subject and object. Judgment is divisive. Here in the *Phenomenology,* where Hegel takes up a similar idea, judgment is the verbal act by which the community "shuns" or *parts with* the worldly individual who is out of step with the community of conscience. At one point, Hegel refers to the judging consciousness as holding to a "divisive thought," *teilenden Gedanken* [670]. Hegel makes the connection between judgment and partitioning explicit in his *Science of Logic:* "The judgment is the self-splitting of the Concept . . . It is thus the original division [*Teilung*] of what is originally one; thus the word *Urteil* refers to what judgment is in and for itself" (625).

32. "Luther's Reformation had succeeded admirably in reforming Christian doctrine by providing a religious sanction for subjective freedom (i.e. freedom of conscience); but it had fallen short of reforming Christian life. Thus, like others before him, Hegel distinguishes between a 'first' and a 'second Reformation'" (*Hegel, Political Writings*, ed. Dickey, xxv). Hegel suggests this need for a second Reformation in a late writing (1830) on the Augsburg Confession (ibid., 186–96).

33. In the *Philosophy of History*, Hegel calls this syndrome Thersitism (32), after Thersites, the ugly troublemaker in the *Iliad* who rails against heroes, and who must be physically beaten by Odysseus for his insubordination.

34. The original saying, which Hegel also quotes and discusses in the *Philosophy of History* (32), was simply, "No man is a hero to his *valet de chambre.*" Hegel added the reason why. This addition was given another twist by Goethe, in his *Elective Affinities*, where the reason is that "a hero can be recognized only by a hero." For a brief summary of the history of the saying, see the editor's note in Hegel's *Elements of the Philosophy of Right*, trans. Nisbet, 424.

35. The moral valet's precursor is the moralist, whose envy caused him to be offended when he saw "good people" faring badly in this world and "bad people" prospering [625].

36. Hegel develops his idea of the world-historic individual in the Introduction to his *Philosophy of History* (29 ff.).

37. The oft-quoted saying attributed to Madame de Staël is apparently a misquotation. What she really said was: *Tout comprendre rend très indulgent* ("To understand all renders one very indulgent"). For the reference, see Harris, *Hegel's Ladder*, 2:517, note 74.

38. In using the integral calculus as his model for historical knowledge, Tolstoy tries to understand "big" events as the result or "sum" of things infinitely small. We are reminded of what Napoleon himself said of the great mathematician Laplace, who worked in Napoleon's government: "A mathematician of the first rank, Laplace . . . carried the spirit of the infinitely small [the calculus] into administration." Tolstoy does the same thing when he enters the realm of history.

39. Harris observes that in his analysis of the "hard heart" Hegel is drawing on Hölderlin's *Hyperion* (*Hegel's Ladder*, 2:480). The effete beautiful soul is hard on others. This is true to life. Sensitive types are often merciless judges. Kierkegaard is an excellent example of the beautiful soul as a hard-hearted judge of people (especially "Christians") who are not pure, like him. Another is Rousseau.

40. This is an explicit reference to the death of Novalis. See note 26 of this chapter, above. Hegel's reference to madness recalls his description of Karl Moor [367–80]. For Hegel, madness seems to be the inevitable fate of those who place the absolute in the heart.

41. Harris presents this whole last phase of moral experience as referring to Jesus and his forgiveness of Peter (*Hegel's Ladder*, 2:504–7).

42. In *Faith and Knowledge*, Hegel connects Protestantism with the "quest for reconciliation in the here and now" (150).

43. Hegel is not saying that all hard hearts eventually soften. Nor is he explaining how a human being is converted from judgment to forgiveness. The dialectic simply explores the next level of experience, at which the Judge, *for whatever reason*, yields to the spirit of forgiveness. Hegel is not giving us a causal account of how people come to forgive each other.

44. Lauer states this well: "Very simply, we might say that since sin is a human and forgiveness a divine prerogative, the forgiveness of sin is a model for the reconciliation of the human and the divine, the finite and the infinite. On a more complex level, however, it is necessary to say that, in Hegel's view, the forgiveness in question here, and the reconciliation, are both human and divine, the divine dimension of the human" (*A Reading of Hegel's Phenomenology*, 229).

45. A similar "letting go" will generate absolute knowing in the final chapter [796].

46. Terry Pinkard puts this in the following way: "The reconciliation is thus between *politics* and *reflection*, between the 'doers' and the 'thinkers' of modern social practice (between the 'Napoleons' and the 'Hegels' of modern life)" (*Hegel's Phenomenology*, 264). It might be more correct, however, to say that Hegel himself is ultimately the synthesis of action and reflection. The reconciliation of thought and action occurs within *thought.* That is why philosophy, or developed rationality, is essential, for Hegel, to healing the rift in man and establishing a fully human community in the Here-and-Now.

47. Hegel's formulation of this point recalls Spinoza's substance doctrine in the *Ethics.* There is only one substance (or "God") for Spinoza. But substance is known to us through two so-called *attributes,* thought and extension. Each expresses the whole of substance from its own point of view, which we may call inner and outer. The Pure Knower and the Impure Doer are the self-conscious versions of thought and extension, respectively.

48. Hegel himself is often judgmental and apparently unforgiving. In the present section, he clearly means to condemn the beautiful soul. He does not do so out of envy. Nevertheless, he judges this soul, and other types in the *Phenomenology,* very harshly. If absolute knowing is the perspective from which all things are seen as either necessary or tolerable, one wonders how Hegel's own harsh judgments of people and their positions fit into this scheme. More broadly, one wonders about the connection between reason and judgment in philosophy. Is the philosopher allowed to condemn, or does genuine rationality preclude all condemnation?

49. "[Heroes] die early, like Alexander; they are murdered, like Caesar; transported to St. Helena, like Napoleon" (*Philosophy of History,* 31). In this same context, Hegel observes that people who need to console themselves for not being heroic use this unhappiness to dismiss heroism. As people nowadays say: "Look where it got him!"

Chapter 21: The Depiction of God

1. In the transition from conscience to religion, "the God within is projected outwards" (Harris, *Hegel's Ladder,* 2:521).

2. The role of religion in Hegel's thought was the source of intense disagreement among his students. The so-called "left" Hegelians, notably Feuerbach and Marx (and later Kojève), concluded that Hegel's philosophy was atheism and that spirit was *only* human: truth was the finite actuality of human existence. The so-called "right" Hegelians put the emphasis on the *divine* aspect of spirit and argued that Hegel was preserving some form of a transcendent God. As Hyppolite puts it, the debate has to do with whether God is absorbed into man, or man into God (*Genesis and Structure,* 543). What Hegel no doubt intended was that each is absorbed into the other: God must be *humanized* in order to be self-conscious, and man *divinized* in order to enjoy absolute self-knowledge. The historically actual and the eternally rational imply rather than exclude each other. In other words, Hegel wants to *preserve* Aristotle's God as the thinking of thinking. In this connection, I repeat the statement by H. S. Harris that I quoted in Chapter 1: "Hegel's God is Aristotle's God only after he has undergone his Incarnation in his human family" (*Hegel's Ladder,* 1:60). For a helpful discussion of the "left" and "right" Hegelian positions, see Fackenheim, *Religious Dimension in Hegel's Thought,* 75–112.

3. Hegel, *Philosophy of History,* 377. At the end of the dialectic of conscience, we had "God appearing in the midst of those who know themselves in the form of pure knowing" [671]. This is the Lutheran Community of the Faithful. But the community at that stage did not regard itself from the standpoint of objective self-expression or "works." In that sense, it was pre-artistic.

4. Hyppolite offers a helpful discussion of why religion must undergo a development (*Genesis and Structure,* 536–39).

5. In the *Phenomenology,* Hegel combines religion and art. In his later, more systematic *Encyclopaedia of the Philosophical Sciences,* he distinguishes them as separate moments of absolute spirit, whose three stages are Art, Revealed or Manifest Religion, and Philosophy.

6. In the *Philosophy of Mind,* Hegel calls Christianity *die geoffenbarte Religion,* manifested or revealed religion (297, para. 564).

7. As Harris observes, Christianity, in Hegel's interpretation, "is *not* identifiable with any traditional form of Christianity at all" (*Hegel's Ladder,* 2:533). The true Christian, the one who understands what his religion really demands of him, is not otherworldly. He sees God in the actual world, and lives the spirit of forgiveness and reconciliation independent of any Church.

8. At the end of the dialectic of the unhappy consciousness, the Church was present. But it was not experienced as an expanded I, or community. In Hegel's Protestant view of Christianity, the medieval Church was over and above the individual, not, as it is for Luther and the Reformation, the devout community itself. Faith, as it appeared in the culture world, was individualistic and seemed

to have no mooring in any actual community at all. It did not know how to live its faith *completely* in the Here-and-Now. In the present context, we must understand by "Church" the community of all mankind, held together by the spirit of reconciliation. See previous note.

9. An iconoclastic religion like Puritanism is therefore a contradiction in terms. It falsifies what religion is.

10. Essence, for Hegel, always involves self-reflection or inwardness. In the *Science of Logic,* Hegel calls essence [*Wesen*] "timelessly past being," that is, being that logically "has been" [*gewesen*] (389).

11. In the Greek ethical world, the transcendence of the individual in death is incomplete: the individual becomes a mere shade. Faith, by contrast, looks ahead to an ultimate unity with God, the "universal essence."

12. Religion is higher than all previous forms of thought in the *Phenomenology* because, like philosophy, it embraces paradoxes or the unity of opposites. Religion is the effort to think the whole. All the previous self-contradictions and hypocrisy that have appeared were the result of hard and fast distinctions—the rejection of reconciliation with an opposite. By positing the truth as infinity (or infinite depth), religion avoids being the victim of infinity, the "force" by which opposites contain each other [160].

13. In the *Lectures on the History of Philosophy,* Hegel describes philosophy as uniting the finite concern of the physical sciences and the infinite concern of religion: "Philosophy demands the unity of these two points of view; it unites the Sunday of life when man in humility renounces himself, and the working-day when he stands up independently, is master of himself and considers his own interests" (1:92).

14. This image of clothing will recur throughout Hegel's chapter.

15. Hegel does not explicitly associate the third stage of religion with reason. But as Harris points out, "[Hegel] knows that logically we are bound to identify 'the unity of consciousness with self-consciousness' as 'Reason'"(*Hegel's Ladder,* 2:546).

16. This view is precisely the one Kojève rejects: "For Hegel, the real object of religious thought is Man himself; every *theology* is necessarily an *anthropology*" (*Introduction to the Reading of Hegel,* 71). In other words, Kojève simply repeats the atheistic view of Feuerbach.

17. Recapitulation occurs throughout the *Phenomenology,* which is a circle of circles. Reason, for example, recapitulated the stages of consciousness and self-consciousness [348].

18. For a more detailed discussion of how religion, as the totality of logical moments, grows, see Harris, *Hegel's Ladder,* 2:534–47.

19. Hegel's sources for pre-Christian religions can be found in the editorial introduction to the *Lectures on the Philosophy of Religion* (trans. Brown, Hodgson, and Stewart, 2:3–12).

20. For a fuller account of Persian religion and culture, see Hegel's *Philosophy of History* (173–94) and *Lectures on the Philosophy of Religion* (2:609–21).

21. This must be distinguished from the pantheism of Spinoza: "The Indian view is a universal pantheism, a pantheism, however, of imagination, not of thought" (*Philosophy of History,* 141).

22. As Hegel observes, the religious form of perception (Indian religion) only *seems* to get beyond the dead abstraction of thinghood that appeared in ordinary perception. Abstraction reappears in the form of the real death that results from the spirit of animal-worship. Harris observes that the Indian religions of Life and Death (or conflict) embody the two aspects of *self-consciousness:* mere life and armed combat (*Hegel's Ladder,* 2:555–56).

23. Hegel describes this constant state of war in the *Philosophy of History,* 165–66.

24. Persia and India exhibit self-consciousness as desire: light and animality are both violent and consuming. In Egyptian work, as in the slave's work, desire is "held in check" [195].

25. A *Werkmeister,* in modern German, is a foreman, one who oversees the work of others. For Hegel, Egyptian spirit oversees itself. It assigns itself project after project, always struggling to make itself clear to itself. In the *Philosophy of History,* Hegel refers to the Egyptian spirit as "a gigantic taskmaster," that seeks, "not splendor, amusement, pleasure or the like," but "self-comprehension" (214). Egyptian spirit is *driven* to produce monumental structures. It practices art without joy.

26. The "incommensurability of the round" is mathematically captured in the ratio of a circle's curved circumference and straight diameter. These lack a common measure of length, or are incommensurable. They do not have to one another the ratio of a whole number to a whole number. The incommensurability is represented by the modern irrational number, π.

27. As I noted in Chapter 5, force, the object of understanding, was vibrant but not alive. Life was the scandal of scientific, mathematical understanding.

28. Hegel describes the statues and identity of Memnon in his *Aesthetics* (1:358, 2:643–57). Memnon, according to Hegel, was worshiped as the "son of dawn." The colossal statues appeared in rows and were used as columns. Unlike Greek statues, they portrayed the human figure in a sort of rigor mortis: "the arms glued to the body, the feet firmly fixed together, numb, stiff, and lifeless" (1:358).

29. Harris observes that Hegel's "black stone" is not, as Miller (following Baillie) suggests, the Black Stone in the Kaaba at Mecca, but rather the material aspect of the statues of Memnon (*Hegel's Ladder,* 2:565 and note 50). Black stone also furnishes the material basis for animal forms in Egyptian art. Hegel refers to these forms in the transition to Greek sculpture [707].

30. The religious obscuring of spirit in *stone* mirrors phrenology's irreligious, scientific obfuscation of spirit in a *bone.*

31. In the *Philosophy of History,* Hegel calls the Sphinx "the symbol of the Egyptian spirit" (199). In the *Aesthetics,* the Sphinx is "the symbol of the symbolic itself" (1:360).

32. "In the *Greek* Thebes we meet the hero [Oedipus] who will purge the animal form of the Theban Sphinx of Egypt" (Harris, *Hegel's Ladder,* 2:566).

Chapter 22: The Greek Phase

1. In the *Philosophy of History,* Hegel is more explicit about the Greeks' relation to nature (234–39). Nature, for the Greeks, is important, not in itself but only as an occasion for inspired human activity and artistic transformations.

2. Ethicality is historically undone in various ways, both noble and base. The noble ways include tragic action (Antigone), art, and philosophy (Socrates). The ignoble ways include self-serving politicians and apolitical professors or sophists. For Hegel's account of the degeneration of Greece, see *Philosophy of History* (265–77).

3. It is worth noting, in this context, that Aeschylus and Sophocles were warrior-citizens, as well as poets. They were not beautiful-souled artistes.

4. Hegel had referred to this sort of mourning over a lost world in his discussion of culture [573].

5. For an excellent discussion of *pathos,* see Hegel's *Aesthetics* (1:232–33). There, Hegel calls *pathos* "an inherently justified power over the heart, an essential content of rationality and freedom of will" (1:232). In his tragic suffering or *pathos,* Oedipus "takes responsibility for what he has done as an individual and does not cut his purely subjective self-consciousness apart from what is objectively the case" (2:1214).

6. "First," here, does not mean first in time. Hegel's account of Greek art in general reveals the inner logic of that art rather than its chronological development.

7. Along with his contemporaries, Hegel believed that the whiteness of Greek statues was deliberate rather than due to weather and the passage of time. He believed that color was used only at an early stage but was then abandoned when Greek sculpture was at its peak (*Aesthetics,* 2:706, and translator's note).

8. In the Oracle, spirit also manifests itself in artful language [711–12]. But this primitive mode of divine expression is not that of "universal self-consciousness." It is not the shared lyricism of an inspired people but only the language of "an alien self-consciousness." The cryptic speech of the Oracle comes through a divinely inspired individual to other individuals. But it does not gather them up into a community or express their common soul. Oracles are therefore not part of the dialectic of abstract art. Their importance lies in tragedy [737].

9. The cult is already implied by the hymn, which is a form of devotion [*Andacht*]. Hegel calls this devotion "the immediate, pure satisfaction of the self by and within itself" [715]. The purpose of devotion is purification. The worshiper, through ritual purification, prepares himself for union with the god. But he is not a Christian unhappy consciousness. He is not "the self that has descended into its depths and knows itself as evil." Impurity is only at the surface, and the devotee makes himself clean by washing his body and putting on white robes. His effort is "a fulfillment only in imagination, not in actuality" [716].

10. In Euripides' *Bacchae,* the prophet Teiresias says that when libations are poured to the gods, Bacchus himself comes to be poured out (line 284).

11. The Earth-Spirit or *Erdgeist* appeared earlier in Hegel's discussion of Faust [360]. In the present context, earthiness is not the turn away from God but rather intimate union with God.

12. This is the same word Hegel used in his Preface when he defined truth as "the bacchanalian frenzy or whirl [*Taumel*] in which no member is not drunk" [47].

13. "Homer is the element in which the Greek world lives, as man lives in the air" (Hegel, *Philosophy of History,* 223).

14. The athlete is not a warrior, as Miller calls him. The German is simply *Fechter,* a fencer or, more broadly, one who fights or contends (Harris, *Hegel's Ladder,* 2:644, note 47).

15. As Hegel notes, this assemblage of nations is not a permanent unity but a temporary alliance [727]. The Greeks unite "only for the purpose of a common action." This common action is the Trojan War, which brought the Greeks together and gave them their first sense of national unity. Afterwards, Homer, through his *Iliad,* represented, in idealized or imaginative form, the self-consciousness of this unity.

16. Homer, for Hegel, is part of an oral tradition: "The *Iliad* [for Hegel] is the product of the communal genius of the Greek people" (Harris, *Hegel's Ladder,* 2:612).

17. We meet such a rhapsode in Plato's *Ion.* The *rhapsōidos* engages in "stitching," *rhaptein.* He strings together songs, *ōidai.*

18. This syllogism will be *inverted* in the dialectical movement from the epic to comedy (Hyppolite, *Genesis and Structure,* 554). In the comedies of Aristophanes, the singer appears as essential rather than as a mere vanishing moment, and the gods are reduced to the level of mere mortals.

19. See Harris, *Hegel's Ladder,* 2:615–16.

20. Harris suggests that Hegel's "mighty self" refers specifically to Odysseus (ibid., 616–17).

21. It is especially comic when the quarrel is domestic—when, for example, Zeus, king of the gods, chases mortal women, and his wife Hera, goddess of marriage, berates him for it.

22. Zeus weeps *tears of blood* (*Iliad* 16.459–460). Hegel describes Fate in terms of a "universal self" that hovers over all individual selves, of gods and men alike. The phrase reminds us of Rome as the first actual world of self [633], and of the emperor, who is a "gigantic self-consciousness" [481]. More generally, what appears to the Greeks to be irrational necessity is really the force of history, which is *rational* happening: divine selfhood that realizes itself in time and human events. Harris argues that the universal self is also the singer, Homer (*Hegel's Ladder,* 2:619). Even if Homer invokes a Muse, the song comes out of Homer's resourcefulness and thought. As the invisible self-conscious source of the poem, Homer "hovers over" the whole figured world that emerges from his selfhood. Homer is a *dark* force because selfhood has not yet come out into the open. It is a void that has not yet been clarified by the Concept. Homer never appears as an individual.

23. Miller mistranslates the first part of Hegel's sentence here. It ought to read as follows: "The content of the world of representation plays [out] its motion, set free for itself [or on its own] in the *middle.*" As Harris observes (*Hegel's Ladder,* 2:645, note 56), Hegel is referring to the famous saying by Horace that Homer's poems begin *in medias res,* "in the middle of things" (*Ars Poetica* 148). The middle term of the epic syllogism is generally "the nation in its heroes" [729]. But the brilliant center around which the *Iliad* turns is not the war at Troy but Achilles and his wrath.

24. It is worth noting that at one significant moment in the *Iliad,* when the embassy comes to persuade Achilles to re-enter the battle, they find the hero playing the lyre and singing of the glory of men (*Iliad* 9.186–91).

25. For Aristotle, tragedy arouses the emotions of fear and pity in order to purge them (*Poetics* 6).

26. As we saw in Hegel's earlier discussion of ethicality, the *polis* works to the extent that it suppresses the conflict at the heart of self-consciousness. Its element is trust, not knowledge.

27. The Furies, in being transformed into the well-disposed Eumenides, are absorbed into the *polis* and honored as gods.

28. The Chorus, the main characters of tragedy, and the audience see selfhood only in the protagonists, not in "the mediating aspect or middle [*die Mitte*] of the movement" [742]. In other words, the Greeks lack a sense of *history* as purposive movement. The divine enters time but in no way guides or shapes it. Movement is only Fate. God is not yet spirit. At the level of manifest religion

or Christianity, tragedy (man's "fall") will be sublated in the historically unfolding relation between man and God.

29. Harris points out that the slipping of the tragic mask applies to the dramas of Euripides. For Euripides, there is no true *pathos*—only one passion after another. Whereas Aeschylus and Sophocles preserve the divine, Euripides uses the gods to reveal human motives (Harris, *Hegel's Ladder*, 2:633). The hero is reduced to an actual (ordinary) self-consciousness. His heroism is only a pretense.

30. Aristophanes represents so-called Old Comedy, which flourished in Athens in the fifth century. In his *Aesthetics*, Hegel lavishes much praise on Aristophanes, who "did not make fun of what was truly moral in the life of the Athenians, or of their genuine philosophy, true religious faith, and serious art" (2:1202).

31. This was already prefigured in the "mighty self" of Homeric heroes, who exerted power over the gods through prayers, offerings, and offensive deeds that got a rise out of the gods.

32. The *Frogs* is the only surviving play by Aristophanes in which an Olympian god appears on stage. Most translations of the *Clouds* omit the brief appearance of Hermes in some manuscripts. Of course, the Clouds, in a sense, are "gods" too.

33. Hegel says that in its serious subject matter comedy becomes "more wanton or mischievous and more bitter" [745]. The wantonness or mischief may refer to family matters and sex. The bitterness perhaps refers to matters relating to Athenian politics and the current war with Sparta.

34. In the *Frogs*, the god Dionysus and his slave descend into the underworld to bring Euripides back from the dead. On their way, they meet a chorus of initiates on their way to celebrate the Eleusinian mysteries (316 ff.).

35. At the end of the play, old Demos is boiled back to his youthful self by the sausage-seller and returns to his senses. He becomes just—the enemy of all flatterers.

36. The Clouds, as natural phenomena, are part of Socrates' replacement of Zeus, in Aristophanes' play, with the new god, Vortex or Whirlwind.

37. In the *Philosophy of History*, Hegel praises Athens for her ability to be cheerful in the face of her corruption and her defeat in the Peloponnesian War: "Amiable and cheerful even in the midst of tragedy is the light-heartedness and nonchalance with which the Athenians accompany their [national] morality to its grave" (270–71). In the plays of Aristophanes, "the people made merry over their own follies" (271).

Chapter 23: Christianity, the Figure of Science

1. Hegel's precedent here is Jacob Boehme, whom Hegel discusses at length in the *Lectures on the History of Philosophy* (3:188–216). Boehme's "profoundest interest," says Hegel, was "the Idea" (193). His "only thought" was that of "perceiving the holy Trinity in everything" (196). But his speculative effort was ultimately a "barbaric" intermingling of sensuous images and abstract concepts, popular religion and philosophy (193). Even so, Hegel admires Boehme for his solidity, depth, and sincerity.

2. In his *Lectures on the Philosophy of Religion*, Hegel calls these moments the three "kingdoms" of God (3:362–73). They are the kingdoms of the Father, of the Son, and of the Spirit.

3. Hegel never mentions Jesus by name. Nor does he ever call manifest religion Christianity. We are reminded that in the account of the unhappy consciousness, God was "the unchangeable consciousness." Hegel generally avoids proper names in the *Phenomenology*. Here, this avoidance is especially important. Jesus represents a logical *moment* in the development of manifest religion. Manifest religion is fulfilled, not in Christ but in the universal spirit that rises up when Christ dies. From this perspective, it is even misleading to call this religion Christianity.

4. The whole purpose of Christianity is to make the spirit of reconciliation actual. Once the perfectly rational character of reconciliation comes on the scene, there is no longer a need for faith. Christianity will have been completely assimilated into active forgiveness and reconciliation in the Here-and-Now. To recall the title of Kant's book on Christianity, religion will be "within the boundaries of reason alone."

5. It is noteworthy that Hegel goes straight from the pagan world to Christianity. "In this way, Hegel detaches Christ from the Jewish tradition, and presents him as a necessary historical conse-

quence instead of as a miraculous discontinuity in human history" (Rosen, *G. W. F. Hegel,* 221). As Harris observes, manifest religion "is not simply a Gospel that came forth from Judaea; it is a gospel about the 'inwardizing' of the Pantheon that the Romans established" (2:657).

6. Hegel used the word light-mindedness to describe ethicality in its pre-artistic existence [701]. Art replaced this levity with "unrestrained joyfulness." With comedy, light-mindedness or levity returns, but it has been rendered self-conscious.

7. Originally, self-consciousness was desire, or the drive to destroy all objectivity [174]. Greek laughter is above desire. It is a more lasting and satisfying way to destroy objectivity—at least, until unhappiness sets in with Rome. Comedy knows that the gods have destroyed themselves: they have become outmoded.

8. Rome was the first "world of self" [633].

9. Hegel's remark about the boring Pax Romana comes from his biographer, Karl Rozenkranz. For the reference, see Harris, *Hegel's Ladder,* 2:245, note 37.

10. The saying, "God is dead," appears in Luther (see Harris, *Hegel's Ladder,* 2:700, note 12). It also appears in a seventeenth-century hymn,which Hegel quotes in his *Lectures on the Philosophy of Religion,* 3:125, note 163.

11. Clearly, Hegel means to conflate the unhappy time just before Christ's birth with the unhappy time when Christ dies and is buried. When Christianity is properly understood, this conflation will make sense. The death of Christ will then be grasped, not as a factual event but as the unhappy moment of spirit's unfolding in world-history.

12. Hegel's description of the loss of Greek-ness recalls a poem by Hölderlin: "But the thrones [of ancient Greece], where are they? Where are the temples, the vessels, / Where, to delight the gods, brim-full with nectar, the songs? / Where, then, where do they shine, the oracles winged for far targets?" ("Bread and Wine," trans. Michael Hamburger, in Hölderlin, *Hyperion and Selected Poems,* ed. Santner, 181–83)

13. For Hegel's general discussion of Gnosticism, see *Lectures on the Philosophy of Religion* 3:196–97. The prime example is Philo of Alexandria (84, 196, 287).

14. Christianity escapes the "bad infinity" of the understanding by positing a God who is the unity of the infinite and the finite. The Christian God embodies infinity as "inner difference" [160]. If God were only infinite, then he would exclude the finite and consequently have the finite over and against him. He would be *limited* by the finite and therefore *be* finite. Hegel spells out this "good" infinity of the Christian God in his *Lectures on the Philosophy of Religion,* 3:263–64.

15. "To all of the theologians coming from a pagan philosophical background—as much as to the Jews, or to a hybrid mind like Paul's—this incarnation of God appeared to be self-humiliating on the most sublime and awe-inspiring scale" (Harris, *Hegel's Ladder,* 2:668).

16. Rosen observes that, for Hegel, "God becomes man in order to become God. This is Hegel's heresy, and the aspect of his doctrine which, like his historicizing of eschatology, has no counterpart in orthodox Christianity" (*G. W. F. Hegel,* 234).

17. Throughout Hegel's account of manifest religion, it helps to remember that reason was the effort to embody one's selfhood, to find oneself in the world. Manifest religion *perfects* reason by lifting this effort into the realm of absolute or divine truth.

18. In the *Lectures on the Philosophy of Religion,* Hegel says: "[the Christian religion is] the unification of the infinite antithesis [between man and God], the one and only genuinely speculative [enjoyment] of the nature of God, or of spirit. This is its content and vision, and it is there for the ordinary, uneducated consciousness" (3:140–41). The religious goal of "seeing God" as he really is paves the way for divine "seeing" or *theōria* in the form of philosophic Science, especially the Science of logic.

19. For Hegel, there is no literal resurrection and ascension into heaven (which belong to Christian picture thinking). Miracles in general play no role in manifest religion: "Faith . . . rests on the witness of the spirit, not on miracles but on absolute truth, on the eternal idea and its content" (ibid., 3:147). Miracles serve not faith but mere edification. If, however, miracles refer to the intervention of spirit in mere nature, the "miraculous" work of spirit is present all the time in the phenomena of *life* (148).

20. As we shall see, even at its highest, most conceptual level, Christianity will retain its bond with picture thinking or imagination [787].

21. In the *Science of Logic,* Hegel calls logic "the exposition of God as he is in his eternal essence before the creation of nature and a finite spirit or mind" (50).

22. As Harris notes, "one can be as 'enlightened' as D'Holbach and Voltaire (or Marx)—holding firmly to the precept 'Ecrasez l'infame' ['Crush the infamous one,' i.e. the Church]—and still agree with what Hegel found in the *Vorstellungen* of Christian faith" (*Hegel's Ladder,* 2:678).

23. In Hegel's account, Eve is superfluous. Here Hegel follows Paul, who regards Adam as the one in whom we all sinned (Romans 5:12).

24. It is generally the case, for Hegel, that abstraction is self-canceling. This is another way of saying that non-being or nothingness is not a static void but a dynamic *push* for self-realization. Spirit is higher than force in this respect because, as I have noted, it contains its own otherness and makes itself real spontaneously. The logic of spirit that is at work here is the philosophic decoding of the *creatio ex nihilo* and of Spinoza's *causa sui.*

25. This is how good and evil were regarded by the Manicheans—as separately existing quasi-physical substances. Augustine sets out to refute this view in his *Confessions.*

26. In his *Lectures on the Philosophy of Religion,* Hegel struggles to convince us that to explain Christianity in philosophic terms is merely "to reconcile reason with religion," to *defend* religion from the shallow attacks of the Enlightenment, that "vanity of understanding" (3:246–47). He tries to persuade us that philosophy negates, not Christian religion itself but only its *form* of cognition: picture thinking. But this negation of form clearly alters the *content* of Christianity, which, on Hegel's terms, would no longer depend on faith in God's grace and in eternal life. Believing Christians of all denominations can rightly say to Hegel: "With friends like you. . . ."

27. This view of Christ as the successor of a fallen first son was central in the thought of Jacob Boehme. In the *Lectures on the History of Philosophy,* Hegel quotes Boehme: "But this Lucifer has fallen and Christ has come in his place" (3:205). See also *Lectures on the Philosophy of Religion,* 3:200, 293.

28. As Hegel goes on to say, the effort to locate the original being that turned to evil is related to the problem of assigning a determinate *number* to God's supposed heavenly "others." How many beings were there in the realm of pure thought or "heaven"? Was it four: God, God's Son (the good other before he became Jesus), the good angels, and the bad angels? And how many angels, whether of the good or bad variety, were there? This effort to count heavenly beings, Hegel says, is "altogether useless" [776]. His critique in the Preface of theological arithmetic is an instance of the general critique of mathematics as lacking the Concept [43–46].

29. The generation of Christ as Savior from Adam's sin recalls the passage in Paul's letter about Adam's being a type [*typos*] of the One who was to come (Romans 5:14).

30. This is another reference to the speculative thought of Jacob Boehme (Hegel, *Lectures on the History of Philosophy,* 3:206).

31. Spirit is said to be "poured forth" in *Acts* 2:17.

32. There is no need for a subsequent, individual resurrection or ascension (which, we recall, belong to picture thinking). The death of God in Christ is the determinate negation of death itself as a natural event. The dialectical transition to God as "resurrected" in the religious community makes clear why, for Hegel, manifest religion (spiritually understood) does not posit the immortality of the individual soul.

33. Spirit is present, not in the *collection* of believers but in their common *work.* Believers, in other words, are "justified" not by faith (which manifest religion has transcended) but by concrete "works" (of forgiveness). Hegel's manifest religion is thus clearly not that of orthodox Lutherans.

34. Christ does not seem to play a significant role at this final stage of the "Church." Harris is right when he says that manifest religion "is not a 'particular' faith; if it is a 'faith' at all, it is one that recognizes itself wherever the forgiving of finitude can be found. Lessing's Nathan [a Jew] is a model of it—and of course, he is *not* a Christian. Salvation 'in the name of Jesus' (or any *other* 'name') belongs to the phase of 'religious perception'" (*Hegel's Ladder,* 2:690).

35. Lauer puts this very well: "God and man are *not* one and the same *being;* they *are* one and the same process" (*A Reading of Hegel's Phenomenology,* 254).

36. The transfiguration refers to the picture thought of Christ's appearing in all his glory in Matthew 17:1–8.

Chapter 24: Speculative Good Friday

1. As we approach the end of our journey, let us recall that the *Phenomenology* has only three main sections: Consciousness (A), Self-Consciousness (B), and an untitled third section (C) that includes Reason (AA), Spirit (BB), Religion (CC) and Absolute Knowing (DD). The division into eight chapters is therefore somewhat misleading.

2. In his *Science of Logic,* Hegel says that the result of the *Phenomenology* is "the *concept* of Science" (48) [my emphasis].

3. The journey of consciousness in the *Phenomenology* parallels the soul's journey in Dante's *Purgatorio,* where the "human spirit" makes itself worthy of ascending to heaven (1.4–6). For Hegel, spirit must come to realize the "sins" of consciousness, or finite thinking, and purge itself of this thinking in order to reach logic, the "heaven" of pure conceptuality. The final purgation is the overcoming of religious images and imagination.

4. The Philosophy of Spirit (or Mind) contains Phenomenology in a revised (and truncated) form. It studies consciousness, which is spirit or mind at the level of appearance (*Philosophy of Spirit,* 153). Phenomenology, here, is not an introduction to Science. In the System, it appears within Subjective Spirit (or Mind), between the Sciences of Anthropology and Psychology.

5. The *Phenomenology* and the *Science of Logic* are Hegel's only two real books. His other writings take the form of articles, essays, lectures, and lecture notes. There were, in fact, three incarnations of Phenomenology: the Jena *Phenomenology* of 1807, the so-called *Berlin Phenomenology* (which Hegel used as the basis of his Berlin lectures), and the *Encyclopaedia* Phenomenology that appears in the Philosophy of Spirit between Anthropology and Psychology. In the latter two versions, the exposition stops with *Reason.* For a discussion of the *Berlin Phenomenology,* see the intro. to *The Berlin Phenomenology,* ed. and trans. M. J. Petry (Dordrecht, Holland: D. Reidel, 1981), xiii–cix.

6. Hegel offers a helpful discussion of the Idea in the Preface and Introduction to his *Philosophy of Right* (1–13). Alan White, in the Glossary to his edition of this work, defines the Idea as "an actualized complex of conceptual determinations" (269). Idea is the Concept at its highest level. The meaning of the Idea is contained in Hegel's oft-quoted saying: "What is rational is actual [*wirklich*]; and what is actual is rational" (8). Hegel's Idea thus finds its antecedent in Aristotle's *eidos,* which is both an object's actuality and its intelligible form.

7. This was Hegel's original title for the book. Hegel changed the title to *The Phenomenology of Spirit* just before the book's publication.

8. For a helpful discussion of Hegel's "change of heart" about the 1807 *Phenomenology* and its problematic relation to the System, in particular the *Logic,* see Rosen (*G. W. F. Hegel,* 123–30). Rosen argues that, in the end, "Hegel came to see the *Phenomenology* as a general introduction to the science of wisdom, even though not a part of the system itself" (124). For an extremely lucid summary of the history of criticism surrounding the *Phenomenology,* see Pippin, "You Can't Get There from Here," 52–85.

9. That Hegel never abandoned the 1807 *Phenomenology* is evident from his preparing a new edition shortly before his death in 1831.

10. This tends to support Rosen's claim that "the *Phenomenology* is not genuinely intelligible without a knowledge of the *Logic*" (*G. W. F. Hegel,* 129). Of course, in my introduction, I have assumed, as have other commentators, that the *Phenomenology* is *sufficiently* intelligible on its own.

11. No doubt many will still long for a Beyond and need religion. Not everyone will be able to think dialectically. Nevertheless, knowledge rather than faith will be the spirit of the "new era." It will *be there* in the prevailing culture for whoever can be, and wishes to be, part of it.

12. Harris offers some extremely helpful comments on the precise meaning of Hegel's absolute perspective on history. He argues that Hegel is *not* expecting us to cease acknowledging evil in the world (*Hegel's Ladder,* 2:738–39). Absolute knowing is not a recipe for happiness. For Harris, it means simply this: "Everything is to be known as *ours;* and how it is to be known is for us to choose" (738). As Hegel insisted in his discussion of the Christian religion, good and evil are *dialectically* identical, which is to say that the distinction between them is preserved [780].

13. Hegel issued a warning about the term God in his Preface. This word, Hegel observes, does not immediately convey a conceptual meaning, like the terms Being and One [66].

14. This is a strong reminder that although Hegel is highly critical of the Enlightenment, he regards himself as its culmination. The Enlightenment, for him, is finite or shallow, and Christianity infinite and deep. But the Enlightenment is on the side of rational comprehension, truth in the form of Concept and self-consciousness.

15. In the Preface, Hegel referred to logical necessity as the *rhythm* of the organic whole [56].

16. Religion, for Hegel, fails to exercise what Socrates, in the *Republic*, calls *eikasia:* image-recognition (6.511D–E). This is the bottom segment of the divided line. It refers, not to the entrancement with images but to the recognition of images *as images. Eikasia* is the power of the soul that allows us to "ascend" the divided line, and, indeed, to grasp the line itself as a philosophic image. For an account of how *eikasia* functions at the level of intelligible objects, see Jacob Klein, *A Commentary on Plato's Meno,* 112–25.

17. The seeing of oneself in God is the final moment of Dante's *Divine Comedy,* although Dante would hardly agree with Hegel's identification of man and God.

18. At several points in the *Phenomenology,* Hegel refers to the theological idea known as *kenōsis* or emptying, from the Greek *kenon,* empty [755, 808]. The German word is *Entaüßerung.* Kenosis refers to the belief that in becoming man in the person of Christ, God emptied himself of (or alienated) all his divine powers and attributes: he becomes thoroughly human. This Protestant idea derives from a passage in St. Paul's Letter to the Philippians: "[Jesus] emptied himself [in Luther's translation, *entaüßerte sich selbst*], taking the form of a servant, being born in the likeness of men" (2:7).

19. It is crucial to distinguish the *reduction* of God to man from Hegel's dialectical *identity* of God and man. Contrary to Feuerbach's teaching that God is nothing more than human nature (*The Essence of Christianity,* 1841), Hegel appears to retain God in a way that is, admittedly, hard to describe. As I noted in Chapter 21, Hyppolite has an excellent discussion of this notorious problem in Hegel's philosophy (*Genesis and Structure,* 541–44).

20. In the *Philosophy of Religion,* Hegel distinguishes three "estates" or *Stände* of the spiritual kingdom: the estate of naïve religion and faith, the estate of understanding, culture and the Enlightenment, and the "community of philosophy" (3:247).

21. In the *Philosophy of Religion,* Hegel draws a fascinating parallel between philosophy and religion. He calls philosophy "an isolated order of priests—a sanctuary . . . untroubled about how it goes with the world, [who need] not mix with it, [and whose work is to preserve] this possession of truth" (3:162). For an extremely lucid discussion of the difference between philosophy and religion, see Hegel's Introduction to *Lectures on the History of Philosophy,* 1:64–92.

22. Harris has an illuminating discussion of why Hegel selects precisely these shapes (*Hegel's Ladder,* 2:716 ff.).

23. The content-form opposition corresponds to two other dichotomies that will also be overcome: truth/certainty and substance/subject.

24. For the phrenologist, the inner spirit or self is an unconscious *artist.* It is psychic activity that works through the nervous system and eventually, through nervous action in the brain, makes its hieroglyphic mark on the skull.

25. Infinite judgments express "the total incompatibility of the subject and the predicate," as in Hegel's example, "The spirit is not an elephant." They also include tautologies like "A lion is a lion." In effect, infinite judgments "are not really judgments at all." The judgment of phrenology, "The 'I' is a thing," expresses the identity of the incompatibles, anti-thingly I and ultra-thingly skull bone. (*Encyclopaedia Logic,* 250–51, para. 173.)

26. If we consider observing reason as a whole from the standpoint of Christianity and its absolute truth, we see that its object is nature as God's extreme other. Observing reason appropriates the realm that must ultimately be reconciled with God, and in which God will sacrifice himself—the realm of being-there and death (Harris, 2:716). Phrenology has a spiritual import of which reason is unaware. It is the seed of the whole modern search for self that begins with Faust's disenchantment with the dead skull of science and ends with divine self-sacrifice.

27. The absoluteness of the useful appears in Rousseau's education of the young Emile: "It is not a question of knowing what is but only of knowing what is useful" (*Emile,* trans. Bloom, 166). The decisive question, as Rousseau calls it (179) is not, "What is it?" but "What is it good for?"

28. We should note here that absolute knowing is not the result of a dialectical *transition* from a previous phase of knowing. It is rather the result of the *merging* of religion and morality.

29. The picture-thought here is the Holy Spirit taking the form of a dove or fire and coming down among the gathered believers. Christianity pictures a mediating divine being (the Paraclete) rather than thinks mediation.

30. The breathtaking beauty with which Dante presents this divine picture in his *Paradiso* might make some of us regret its transformation into dialectical logic. Hegel, of course, sees this as the ascendancy of reason over faith. Still, we must also ask: What, possibly, is *lost* in the move from picture to Concept?

31. The idea of God as act appears in Aristotle, for whom the divine is a pure activity or *energeia:* the "thinking of thinking" (*Metaphysics* 12.9). But this thinking lacks the dialectical movement and *suffering* of self-consciousness. The true nature of thinking cannot "come home" to the thinker without the pre-conceptual experience of self-sacrifice as the highest and deepest truth—without a whole modern *world* that believes in "dying to self" as the prerequisite for divine vision.

32. In the Novalis version of conscience, the individual experiences identity with God. What he does not know is that God, in order to be God, must sacrifice himself by becoming man. The beautiful soul is higher than the Christian by virtue of his self-certainty, but also lower because he has an imperfect understanding of divine self-identity and God's relation to man.

33. The importance of a primordial *act* of the self recalls the subjective idealisms of Kant and Fichte (especially the latter). The transition from religion to philosophy in this last chapter of the *Phenomenology* supersedes Kant's transcendental deduction of the categories in the first *Critique,* where the self's act is limited to processing sense-data, that is, organizing appearances. The transition from religion to philosophy via moral action is Hegel's demonstration of his *absolute* idealism. In this idealism, the self is not a mere subjective organizer of appearances, with no cognitive access to things themselves. On the contrary, its primordial act is the divine work of self-negation that constitutes things as they are.

34. The ideological view has its clearest formulation in Marx: "The philosophers have only *interpreted* the world, in various ways; the point is to *change* it" (last of the *Theses on Feuerbach*).

35. Heidegger is on to something like this when he translates Hegel's *absolutes Wissen* as "absolvent knowing": "We shall be speaking of restless absolute knowledge as *absolvent* (in the sense of absolution). Then we can say that the essence of the absolute is the in-finite absolving, and therein negativity and positivity are at the same time absolute or in-finite" (*Hegel's Phenomenology of Spirit,* 51).

36. In his book on the soul, Aristotle tells us that in the act of pure thinking, the soul becomes what it thinks, that is, the form or *eidos* of an object (*De Anima* 3.5–8). In our current context, Hegel is spelling out the dialectical movement that this ultimate identity necessarily involves. Two steps are necessary. First, Hegel replaces the Aristotelian *psychē* or soul with the self, more precisely, with self-assertive willing. Second, he interprets pure philosophic knowing as the act in which the self dies to self-interest in order to know what is of universal interest—the truth. In other words, Christianity, which posits death to self as having absolute value, implicitly contains an account of the philosopher in relation to knowledge.

37. All other actions, even so-called "good deeds," throw inwardness outside itself into alienation, in need of absolution and return, either from the community of consciences or from God. Thinking alone, in going "outside itself" to engage the world by assimilating the various objects of thinking, never leaves itself.

38. Hegel thus resolves a problem implicit in Aristotle's conception of divine thinking. What does Aristotle's divine mind think? Only its own act, or the whole of all things as well? Hegel's answer is clear. In the act of pure thought, the individual human self becomes universal or divine and grasps itself as the truth and substance of all things.

39. Harris takes Hegel's "particular moments" to refer not to morality and religion but to the three shapes of phrenology, utility, and conscience—which Hegel said he was going to "bring together" [789] (*Hegel's Ladder,* 2:725–26).

40. We are reminded here of two statements by Aristotle. The first is that all human beings by nature desire to know (*Metaphysics* 1.1). The second is that mind or intellect seems to be "the very thing each of us is" (*Nicomachean Ethics* 9.4).

41. The three moments of the Concept first appeared in the three stages of the unhappy consciousness [210].

42. As Hyppolite rightly argues, Hegel maintains the dualism of nature and mind (*Genesis and Structure,* 603): "there is no reason to speak of a causality of logos which would engender nature" (thereby reducing nature to logos). Logos (or Concept) and nature are not two separate substances. But neither is the former the substantial "cause" of the latter as a mere offspring or "effect." Nature is spirit in its mode of self-otherness. Nature must be *really* other if this unity is to be dialectical, just as self-consciousness must be *really* multiple if it is to exist at all. Tension must be preserved. Without the real duality of Concept and nature, Hegel's System, Hyppolite observes (603), "would not know 'the seriousness, the torment, the patience, and the labor of the negative'" [19].

43. The definition of time as "the Concept itself that is *there*" appears in Hegel's Preface [46].

44. Space and time both express nature's self-externality. Time, however, makes this self-externality explicit or for itself (*Philosophy of Nature,* 33–34). Time is "that being which, insofar as it *is,* is *not,* and insofar as it is *not, is:* it is becoming directly *intuited*" (34).

45. A *Zusätze* or additional note in the *Philosophy of Nature* makes this point clear: "Time is not, as it were, a receptacle in which everything is placed as in a flowing stream, which sweeps it away and engulfs it. Time is only this abstraction of destruction. It is because things are finite that they are in time; it is not because they are in time that they perish; on the contrary, things themselves are the temporal" (35–36).

46. The reader should consult Kojève's fascinating discussion of time in his *Introduction to the Reading of Hegel* (130–49). Commenting on time as history, and on the close connection between man and time, Kojève writes: "Without Man, Nature would be *Space,* and *only* Space. Only Man is in Time, and Time does not exist outside of Man; therefore, Man *is* Time, and Time *is* Man—that is, the 'Concept which is there in the [spatial] empirical existence' of Nature (*der Begriff der da ist*)." One must nevertheless be very cautious here: man is *not* time when he is thinking the divine science of Logic. He partakes of the timeless.

47. We may liken this to religion's eternal Now that atemporally embraces and comprehends all of time (Harris, *Hegel's Ladder,* 2:731).

48. Hegel's "Fate" is very close to what Spinoza means by freedom: "That thing is said to be free (*liber*) which exists solely through the necessity of its own nature, and is determined to action by itself alone" (*Ethics* I, def. 7). In Greek tragedy, selfhood is recognized in the individual characters but not in the movement of human events [742]. The Greeks lack a sense of history as temporal development. History, as Hegel understands it, is selfhood that transcends individual selves, even as it works through them.

49. The idea of suffering as act begins with Leibniz. For Leibniz, when two bodies collide, each is the cause of its own passive reaction as well as of its action on the other body. More generally, each "independent substance" contains everything that will ever happen to it (*Discourse on Metaphysics* 8). The monad of Julius Caesar contains not only his crossing the Rubicon but also his assassination in the Senate.

50. Consciousness is first like a vector that points outward toward objects. We become aware of ourselves as selves only by a subsequent reflection, by rebounding from the object.

51. We should recall what Hegel says in his *Difference Between Fichte's and Schelling's System of Philosophy:* that the intellect "erects a building and places it between man and the Absolute" (89). In the Preface to the *Philosophy of Right,* Hegel presents philosophy in a somewhat melancholic light, as the "old age" of an age: "the owl of Minerva begins its flight only with the falling of dusk" (trans. White, 10).

52. Extension is, for Descartes, what is intellectually *luminous* about bodily nature. In the clarity and distinctness of extension, the non-extended mind is at home in its otherness.

53. As usual, Hegel avoids proper names. We must glean the identity of these philosophers from their descriptions. Hegel describes Descartes' philosophy in religious terms. This is a reminder that religion contains the whole of truth in picture form and sums up the whole *Phenomenology.* Bacon, Descartes, Spinoza, and Leibniz seem to belong to the oriental substance-thinking of modernity. Kant, Fichte, and Schelling perhaps recapitulate the for-us or subjective moment of history we find in Greek religion. Hegel would then be, not surprisingly, the Christian moment.

54. Fichte's emphasis on thinking as positing [*Setzen*] spells out the implications of Spinoza's striking statement that will and understanding *are the same* (*Ethics* II, corollary to proposition 49).

55. Fichte's absolute ego, in its infinity, is indifferent to all content. That is why, for Hegel, it is the origin of modern irony (*Aesthetics,* 1:64 ff.).

56. The primacy of space is closely connected to the modern faith in mathematics.

57. "In the philosophy of Schelling the content, the truth, has once more become the matter of chief importance, whereas in the Kantian philosophy the point of interest was more especially stated to be the necessity for investigating subjective knowledge" (*Lectures on the History of Philosophy,* 3:521).

58. For Hölderlin's views on various philosophic topics, including the separation of subject and object, see *Essays and Letters on Theory,* ed. Thomas Pfau.

59. Harris rightly associates the submergence in substance here with Schelling rather than Spinoza (*Hegel's Ladder,* 2:737–38). At this point, we are past a mere substance doctrine and are interested in an absolute that overcomes an acknowledged opposition between the self and the non-self or object.

60. The two final spiritual shapes that are overcome by the conceptualization of Lutheran inwardness happen to be Hegel's two roommates at the Tübingen seminary in the early 1790s. Pinkard writes: "Both Hegel and Hölderlin quickly discovered that Schelling shared their antipathy to the Seminary, and the three became fast friends and shared a room together there. They came to be among the chief catalysts for Hegel's eventual turn towards a career in philosophy" (*Hegel: A Biography,* 21).

61. As I noted in Chapter 10, Hegel regarded dichotomy or "splitting" [*Entzweiung*] as "the source of the *need of philosophy*" (*Difference between Fichte's and Schelling's System of Philosophy,* 89).

62. The supersensible Beyond of the understanding was the first logical step in the direction of the Christian religion. It was the "holy of holies" [146]. My use of beyond-ing here is meant to convey what Hyppolite says so well in his commentary: "The entire phenomenology appears as a heroic effort to reduce 'vertical transcendence' to a 'horizontal transcendence'" (*Genesis and Structure,* 544, note 18).

63. Moments in the *Science of Logic* seem to mirror moments in the *Phenomenology.* Being, for example, mirrors the immediacy of sense-certainty, and the Concept (as I noted in an earlier chapter) mirrors self-consciousness. But Hegel does not mention this mirroring in the *Logic,* and it is not clear whether an exact parallel exists. For a helpful discussion of this point, see Harris, *Hegel's Ladder,* 2:743–44. In the *Phenomenology,* stages of consciousness are claims to absolute or divine knowing. Similarly, the various determinations of being, indeed all the logical determinations that arise, "may be looked upon as definitions of the Absolute, as the *metaphysical definitions of God*" (*Encyclopaedia Logic,* 135).

64. An analogous moment occurs at the end of the *Science of Logic,* where the absolute idea "freely releases itself in its absolute self-assurance and inner poise" (843).

65. Hegel, in this passage, is offering a sketch of his whole System. The System begins with Phenomenology, the philosophic deduction of Science or the Concept. It then proceeds to the Concept in its purity (Logic) and to the two "real" or concrete Sciences: the Philosophy of Nature and the Philosophy of Spirit (or Mind).

66. Recollection implies a previous forgetting. In emptying itself into nature and historical *Dasein* —in creating itself as something really there—spirit loses its self-knowledge. It does not undergo its historical experience knowing where it is going, or why it is going there. Its experience is a genuine suffering, and the biggest part of this suffering is self-ignorance. Time is the medium in which the self recovers from this ignorance and "remembers" what it is. Time *is* the self-externality of the self qua self.

67. One wonders how Hegel would have responded to Darwin's theory, according to which plant and animal forms are not fixed but rather develop, and continue to develop, over time. See the discussion of this point by Harris, *Hegel's Ladder,* 2:536–38.

68. In the *Lectures on the History of Philosophy,* Hegel distinguishes between Plato's recollection (*anamnēsis*), which he takes to be a remembrance of a temporally past idea, and recollection in its true and non-temporal sense. Regarded as a temporal process, recollection "is certainly an unfortunate expression." The "profound meaning" of *Erinnerung* is that of "making oneself inward, going inward" (2:34).

69. The process Hegel is describing is the one we have seen in our journey through the *Phenomenology.* Each successive shape of consciousness was born of the inward turn or reflection of the previous stage. Perception, for example, came about when consciousness, as sense-certainty, was driven back into itself through the experience of its self-contradiction. Now the process that we have called experience is revealed as the process of historical manifestation.

70. Here, we should recall Hegel's reference to Gethsemane at the beginning of Greek art-religion. Greek art is the "night in which substance was betrayed and made itself into subject" [703].

71. Hegel's hyphenation of *Er-Innerung* makes the inwardizing stand out. But it also stresses the *Er,* which means "he." Harris suggests that Hegel's pun is meant to emphasize our role in spirit's recollection (*Hegel's Ladder,* 2:761, note 53). The "he" is potentially every one of Hegel's readers. Every reader, every individual "he," is the concrete individuality in which spirit's recollection may be said to live. This fits with Harris' point (with which I agree) that the *Phenomenology* is not about philosophers but about "Everyman" and his various human embodiments or types (2:752).

72. Hegel quotes the entire stanza in the *Lectures on the History of Philosophy* (1:75). The context is Hegel's attempt to distinguish philosophy from religion.

73. There is a beautiful passage from Hawthorne's novel *The Marble Faun* that captures Hegel's final theological point in the *Phenomenology.* Commenting on Sodoma's painting of Christ bound to a pillar, Hawthorne writes: "Even in this extremity, however, he is still divine. The great and reverent painter has not suffered the Son of God to be merely an object of pity, though depicting him in a state so profoundly pitiful. . . . He is as much, and as visibly, our Redeemer, there bound, there fainting, and bleeding from the scourge, with the cross in view, as if he sat on his throne of glory in the heavens! Sodoma, in this matchless picture, has done more towards reconciling the incongruity of Divine Omnipotence and outraged, suffering Humanity, combined in one person, than the theologians ever did" (ch. 37, "The Emptiness of Picture Galleries").

74. Joseph Conrad, Preface to *The Nigger of the "Narcissus."*

75. The philosopher's need for images is expressed in the fragment probably written by Hegel but sometimes attributed to Hölderlin, *The Oldest System-Program of German Idealism:* "We need a new mythology; however, this mythology must be at the service of the ideas, it must become a mythology of reason. . . . Thus the enlightened and the unenlightened finally have to shake hands; mythology must become philosophical in order to make the people reasonable, and philosophy must turn mythological in order to make the philosophers sensuous" (from Hölderlin, *Essays and Letters on Theory,* 155). Hegel's *Phenomenology* seems to satisfy this need.

76. Nietzsche, *Thus Spoke Zarathustra* I, 3.

INDEX

A

B

D

E

F

G

H

I

J

K

N

O

Q

R

T

U

V

W

Y

Z

PETER KALKAVAGE received his undergraduate and graduate degrees in philosophy from Penn State University.

Since 1977 Kalkavage has taught in the all-required liberal arts program of St. John's College in Annapolis. In 1993 he received, through St. John's, a National Endowment for the Humanities grant that allowed him to study Hegel's *Phenomenology* in depth and to produce the lecture "Hegel's Logic of Desire." He is also director of the St. John's Chorus, which regularly performs great works of sacred choral music.

Together with his colleagues Eva Brann and Eric Salem, he translated Plato's *Sophist* (1996) and *Phaedo* (1998) for Focus Press. The trio is currently working on the *Statesman.* In 2001 Focus brought out his edition of the *Timaeus.* Kalkavage has published three essays on Dante, his most beloved poet: "Dante and Ulysses: A Reading of *Inferno* 26," "Peter of the Vine: The Perversion of Faith in *Inferno* 13," and "Love, Law, and Rhetoric: The Teachings of Francesca in Dante's *Inferno.*"

Most recently, Kalkavage, along with Eric Salem, edited *The Envisioned Life: Essays in Honor of Eva Brann* for Paul Dry Books (2007). He is currently writing a book on music, soul, and being.

www.ingramcontent.com/pod-product-compliance
Lightning Source LLC
Jackson TN
JSHW030255160726
105174JS00002BA/10

* 9 7 8 1 5 8 9 8 8 0 3 7 5 *